CHARLOTTE PERKINS GILMAN

CHARLOTTE PERKINS GILMAN

A Biography

CYNTHIA J. DAVIS

Stanford University Press · Stanford, California

Stanford University Press
Stanford, California

This book has been published with the assistance of the College of Arts and Sciences and the Department of English at the University of South Carolina.

Printed in the United States of America on acid-free, archival-quality paper.

Library of Congress Cataloging-in-Publication Data

Davis, Cynthia J., 1964-
Charlotte Perkins Gilman : a biography / Cynthia J. Davis.
    p. cm.
Includes bibliographical references and index.
ISBN 978-0-8047-3888-0 (cloth : alk. paper) -- ISBN 978-0-8047-3889-7 (pbk. : alk. paper)
1. Gilman, Charlotte Perkins, 1860-1935. 2. Women authors, American--19th century--Biography. 3. Women authors, American--20th century--Biography. 4. Feminists--United States--Biography. I. Title.
PS1744.G57Z66 2010
 818'.409--dc22
 [B]
                                   2009040019

Typeset by Bruce Lundquist in 10/13.5 Adobe Garamond

I dedicate this book to what Charlotte called
"that extended self—a family," my family.

Contents

Illustrations

Introduction
The Living of Charlotte Perkins Gilman

> The little "I" that suffered was but a part of me—
> A fraction slight as a wavelet light on a world-encircling sea.
> I may sorrow for it, as for others; there is pain man should not bear,
> But the joy and the power of Human Life makes that an easy care.
>   "I Am Human," 1904[1]

Charlotte Anna Perkins Stetson Gilman was a woman of several names, many hats, and controversial fame. Initially acclaimed for her gifts as a poet and lecturer, she sealed her reputation by writing a series of books on women's economic dependence, domestic confinement, and desire for public service. The theories that inform these efforts were wrung from her own difficult experiences as a woman, wife, daughter, mother, and worker.

Scholars have struggled over how to refer to someone who in her lifetime went by three different surnames. There is no perfect solution to this problem. "It would have saved trouble had I remained Perkins from the first," she admitted late in life, and it is hard to argue with her.[2] While many have opted to use "Gilman" consistently, I am reluctant to do so because she assumed this name at forty, when some of her most influential publications and many of her most difficult challenges lay behind her. To call her "Stetson" throughout would be equally troubling, since she gladly shed that name when she took her second husband's. Nor does "Perkins" seem appropriate for a woman who made her major public contributions under her married names. I have thus reluctantly settled on the one name she never relinquished, "Charlotte"; although uncomfortably intimate and informal, it at least avoids confusion with relatives or spouses.[3]

Today, Charlotte is remembered primarily for her haunting story "The Yellow Wall-Paper," an anomalous tale that does little to indicate its author's civic-mindedness or her profound aversion to psychological theories of identity—indeed, most of her works explore ways of countering the despair and madness documented in her famous story. She was rediscovered during the "second wave" of feminism partly for this story but largely for her insights into gender politics and issues that remain unresolved decades after her death.

In Charlotte's own day, "The Yellow Wall-Paper" and her other literary works received limited attention compared to her numerous polemical lectures and sociological treatises. A remarkably prolific author, she published in her lifetime nearly 500 poems, several dramas, roughly 675 fictional works, and over 2,000 works of nonfiction. She was widely hailed as the "brains" of the U.S. woman's movement due to her arguments on behalf of women's transformation from excessively feminine to fully human—a transformation whose acceleration she made her life's work. She set her sights on women's domestic, maternal, and wifely duties whenever she believed they unjustly restricted women to the home and hence prevented them from pursuing fulfilling work in the public sphere.

Prominent reform-minded authors held Charlotte in high esteem: William Dean Howells regarded both her profile and her mind as the best of all American women's, Rebecca West declared her "the greatest woman in the world today," and H. G. Wells's first request upon visiting the States was to meet her. At the dawn of the twentieth century, her name routinely appeared on lists of the world's most famous women; the suffrage leader Carrie Chapman Catt, who ranked first on one of these lists, insisted that Charlotte deserved the top spot.[4]

Yet she was and remains a polarizing figure, feted by some, lampooned or lambasted by others. By the time of her death in 1935, none of her numerous works remained in print, and several decades passed before their gradual recovery. In her final years, her once-radical views and her oft-reiterated message of public service had, by her own estimate, come to seem dated.

Most biographical accounts have suggested that, beginning with the triumph of *Women and Economics* (1898), Charlotte's fame remained fairly constant throughout the early decades of the twentieth century and only began slowly to wane after her one-woman journal, the *Forerunner*, ceased publication in 1916. My research suggests instead that she remained a well-known but controversial figure throughout much of her long career. For a period around the turn of the century, she earned mostly positive attention, but for the majority of her years on the public stage she was about as infamous as she was famous. Nor does my research suggest that she ever officially retired. Instead, it seems more true to say that her public finally tired of her, despite her recurrent efforts to reclaim the limelight and to her lasting chagrin. By 1929, Charlotte ruefully informed her only child that she had become a "back number."[5] Since a young girl, she had habitually compared her life to a text, but she had never anticipated her own remaindering.

During her final decade, Charlotte sought to correct persistent misunderstandings of her life and legacy by writing her autobiography, *The Living of Charlotte Perkins Gilman* (1935). An uneven, unreliable, and opaque text, it makes for riveting reading if only because the stuff of her life outstrips in drama and complexity nearly everything she ever wrote. Padding out the facts with retrospective feeling, *The Living* offers a skeletal account of her personal history—her birth in 1860; her parents' separation; her troubled, love-starved childhood; her aspirations to public service; her tempestuous marriage to a young artist; her difficulties mothering her newborn daughter; her nervous breakdown; her divorce and the ensuing scandal over child "abandonment"; her burgeoning career as a lecturer, writer, and reformer; international fame; her happy second marriage; her prodigious work ethic even as her fame waned; her reluctant retirement; her breast cancer diagnosis; her husband's sudden death; and finally, in 1935, at the height of the Great Depression, her own carefully planned suicide (she "preferred chloroform to cancer").[6]

There have been subsequent attempts to flesh out this life story. Ann J. Lane's 1990 biography, *To Herland and Beyond*, provides a thematic overview focusing intensively on Charlotte's relationships. A 1980 effort, Mary A. Hill's well-researched half-life, ends its account in 1896. While neither biography is exhaustive, both have made significant contributions to Gilman scholarship. Yet another important work, Gary Scharnhorst's 1985 literary biography, freed me to concentrate on the life and the literature that best illuminates it.

Additional influential studies include Polly Wynn Allen's monograph on Charlotte's architectural feminism; Larry Ceplair's edition of the nonfiction; Catherine J. Golden's casebook, sourcebook, and co-edited collection; Hill's edition of Charles Walter Stetson's diary and her abridged edition of Charlotte's letters to Houghton Gilman; Carol Farley Kessler's study of Charlotte's utopian feminism; Scharnhorst's invaluable bibliography; and Denise D. Knight's two-volume edition of the diaries, several editions of Charlotte's works, and thorough study of her short fiction. To this date, however, no comprehensive scholarly biography exists despite an exponential expansion of interest in Charlotte's life and works, which shows little sign of slowing.

~

> To do, to strive, to know, and with the knowing,
> To find life's wildest purpose, in our growing.
>
> "The Commonplace," 1898[7]

While visiting Charlotte's grandson, Walter Stetson Chamberlin, in Los Alamos, New Mexico, in the fall of 2001, I spent an exhilarating day in a rented storage room filled to brimming with dusty relics. Box upon box of rare books vied for space with letters, clothing, furniture—including the rocker in which Charlotte whiled away so many of her days—along with various odds and ends. Amid the jumble, I discovered a packing box filled with wooden jigsaw puzzles. Charlotte and her second husband (and first cousin) George Houghton Gilman had spent many a companionable hour in their twilight years bent over such puzzles, including those sent as gifts by her lifelong friend (and her first husband's second wife) Grace Ellery Channing Stetson. My father collects wooden Victory© jigsaw puzzles, so I arranged to purchase a half dozen from Mr. Chamberlin. The only one I have yet to relinquish is missing two pieces, as noted faintly on the side label of the box in what appears to be Charlotte's hand.

This incomplete puzzle provides an apt analogy for my efforts to shape Charlotte's life story. Although I have attempted to assemble all the pieces, there are inevitable gaps. Several pieces have been inadvertently lost, perhaps still lurking under some metaphorical carpet despite my best recovery efforts. Others were intentionally destroyed, including crucial artifacts Charlotte herself discarded for fear that they would prove misleading or, perhaps, too revealing. My version is thus partial, not only for missing these components, but also because it is shaped by my own interests and background. No single, coherent life story exists somewhere waiting to be accessed. There are instead fragments, red herrings, possibilities.

In her autobiography, Charlotte makes her own attempt to impose retrospective form upon her story. The way she tells it, her life took shape prospectively—that is, she claims to have lived her life according to a plot she had carefully scripted. "It is a good and wholesome thing to plan out one's whole life; as one thinks it is likely to be; as one desires it should be; and then act accordingly," she advised elsewhere. "[Y]our future is very largely yours to make." While still a young girl, she charted her future as one of "absolute consecration to coming

service" to humanity, and she posited this "world service" as antithetical to domestic service. (Charlotte often relied on antitheses to make sense of her world;
others on her list included mother/father, femininity/masculinity, home/work,
marriage/career, private/public, and individual/collective.) She then doggedly
pursued the unconventional course she had mapped for herself, despite several
costly detours.[8]

In order for self-making to emerge as a dominant theme in her autobiography, however, Charlotte needed to dwell on certain events and obscure others.
She also had to believe that life lends itself to form rather than being inherently
chaotic. Yet even the ultra-rational Charlotte could never fully grasp the complex
forces that move us, including those that operate behind our back. Charlotte was
the principal actor in her own dramatic story and helped to write its script, but
she could not claim sole authorship, predict the outcome, nor prevent alternate
interpretations.

Her first-person account, moreover, overlooks what one theorist calls "the narrative of the unconscious self" as well as "the third-person stories that problema-
tize these selves."[9] A biographer has more room and more of an inclination to
put all these versions into dialogue without seeking to unify them. Rather than
producing a (singular) "life," I have instead sought to illuminate the multiple and
complex facets of what Charlotte called her "living."

Charlotte preferred the term *living* to *life*. She insisted on this distinction because, she wrote, "[l]ife is a verb, not a noun. Life is living, living is doing. . . ."
Doing is more important than being, and thus what matters is our active role in
the world, not who we are in our most private moments. We only truly begin "living," she argued, when we feel "*well used*"—when, that is, we find and perform
our "right work in the world." Only when we identify and fulfill our special functions in the project of social betterment will we achieve the happiness that ensues
from participating in "the broad clean daylight of orderly social life; a range of
feeling which," she insisted, "covers all humanity in the past, lives in its world-
circling activities in the present, and projects itself with boundless hope, assured
and strong, into its marching future."[10]

Whenever Charlotte experienced this feeling of participating in human history
and human progress, she felt that she was truly living. She believed so strongly in
this distinction that she chose to substitute *The Living* for the conventional biographical term *The Life* in the title of her autobiography. By lingering over the
shifts and contradictions in her story and by resisting the impulse to produce a tidy,
unified narrative, this biography seeks throughout to honor her distinction between
the verb form and the noun, the process and the product, the living and the life.

~

> A man or woman to-day, who has no interest beyond the directly personal, is as out
> of place among real human beings as an ape would be—almost. Human life is not
> personal, it is social . . . not for a greedy little you.
>
> "The Vision and the Program," 1915[11]

Charlotte's challenges to conventional understandings of both *life* and *self* initially
drew me to this project. She may have disdained the person she revealed herself to
be in her private moments, but I continue to find that person fascinating largely
because of this disdain. Reading through her papers for an earlier project sparked
my interest in her construction of identity, a construction familiar to her generation but harder to access from our own post-Freudian, late capitalistic vantage
point. For counter to our own private sense, Charlotte clung to a primarily public
sense of self. Rather than prioritizing some "saturated and free interiority" accessed in isolation and considered co-extensive with identity, she derived her sense
of self—and self-worth—from her perceived role in the larger world.[12]

Indeed, she specifically and fervently rejected the psychoanalytic conceptions
of subjectivity that seem commonsensical to us today, even as she paradoxically
devoted many a diary entry and letter to scrutinizing who she was in her private
moments and why she was so. Deeming Freud's relief map of the self too cavern-
ous and cramped for her capacious tastes, she schematized identity in a way that
inverts our modern cartography: "The difference is great between one's outside
'life,' the things which happen to one, incidents, pains and pleasures, and one's
'living,'" she mused in *The Living*. "Outside, here was a woman undergoing many
hardships and losses, and particularly handicapped by the mental weakness which
shut down on her again, utter prostration and misery. But inside her was a conscious humanity, immensely beyond self; a realization of the practical immortality
of that ceaseless human life of ours, of its prodigious power, its endless growth."[13]
This map of identity turns our present-day notions of inside/outside inside-out.

Charlotte frequently maintained that she lived "mostly outside personality":
she considered personality a "limitation" and associated it primarily with individual, intense, but ultimately insignificant feelings, needs, and desires. She claimed
to be happiest when she was unconscious of her personal wants and foibles, when
she felt that she had "no personality" but was "simply being an active conscious
factor in Life—in the great ceaseless stream. . . ."[14]

She thus advocated holding "personality in abeyance"—by which she meant
checking the inclinations that tempt us to put our selves first—as the surest route
to health, happiness, and progress at both the individual and social level. As socially created beings, she maintained, humans could never be satisfied "trying to

feed a social hunger an ego meal" because, deep down, we really craved a larger slice of the pie than the portion allotted to each individual. She used the terms *personality, individualism,* and *egotism* synonymously to signify the stubborn, primitive urges responsible for all of modern civilization's mistakes. To her mind, an ethical society could be predicated only on the recognition that human life is "collective, common, or it isn't human life at all." She admitted that the personal realm held some value and represented intimate relationships as healthful, sustaining necessities. But she insisted that they paled in comparison to the truly social relations that make us human.[15]

In her own life, Charlotte reduced the ego's portion primarily to rein in what she regarded as her needy, greedy impulses. She considered herself "a wreck on that side of me; the inside; the personal side," so her shrinking and cordoning off of this personal side could be considered a self-protective gesture, shielding herself from further damage and preventing others from gaping at the wreck. With every hard knock, she reminded herself that the world outside ego was a less vulnerable place to reside. Lingering feelings of isolation and insufficiency could be offset by a philosophy that denied the significance of the isolated self. Suicidal wishes evident since at least her early twenties could be counteracted or at least forestalled by a mode of living that allowed her to feel she could, as she put it, "leave off being me."

She thus repeatedly sought the assurances she offered the "Little Cell" in her poem of that name:

> . . . you are but a part!
> This great longing in your soul
> Is the longing of the whole, . . .
> You've been noble, you've been strong;
> Rest a while and come along;
> Let the world take a turn and carry you!

Like her little cell, Charlotte's own longing for "the whole" or for "the world" usually arose from a deep-seated desire to rest her overweary and overburdened self. In her darker moments, she shunned the praise others offered her for living impersonally since her "personal life was so full of reproach and agony." "I *can't* live in my own company," she confessed, "—it's too unpleasant. I *have* to live for others. . . ."[16] Her negative dialectic makes her embrace of human life's social dimensions a necessity, not a virtue.

Public, social, and *human* functioned interchangeably in Charlotte's lexicon as antonyms and antidotes for the private sphere she blamed for her own and other women's woes. For example, she confessed to being a confident and "useful public character" but simultaneously "such a poor dolorous unreliable shaky goodfor-nothing private character!"[17] Ironically, while her treatises protest the separation of public and private spheres—given that separation's potentially devastating effects on women prevented from pursuing public roles—she found this distinction enabling vis-à-vis her own understanding of self. If she could (but she couldn't), she would have located her identity primarily and securely within the public realm she believed made living worthwhile.

Gender provides one explanation for why Charlotte felt she could never exclusively situate her self publicly, repeatedly hindering any easy folding of the self into the world. She worried that, from birth, women of her class had been trained to egotism as opposed to public service, to the extent that even she—for all her anti-individualism—still felt the ego's pull. She identified her "particularly lively woman's body" and her "woman's heart" as palpable and occasionally pleasurable diversions from the "world feeling" that lifted her out and above such limits as time, space, embodiment, and personality.

She saw herself as engaged in a tragic tug-of-war between "The World and The Woman"—and the best she could hope for was an uneasy truce. At times, she felt immersed in the larger world; at other times, she felt imprisoned in her flesh, achingly aware of every bump, bruise, and boundary. Although she strove to present "the little tired lonely woman" as only a small portion of her identity, especially when compared with "the rapidly increasing rest of her," it still remained an integral, ineradicable remnant.[18] For Charlotte, the feminine stood in essentially the same relation to the human as the "I" stood to the "We," making it difficult to disentangle her desire to subsume the self from her desire to shed a gendered identity she often considered a liability.

Charlotte's difficulties transcending the personal only seemed to intensify her enthusiasm for the collective. In *Human Work* (1904), the book she considered her masterpiece, Charlotte outlines the compensatory, oceanic sense of identity she saw as the aim of human existence: "What we call altruism should be called . . . 'omniism': it is a feeling for all of us, and *includes* the ego. It is, if you please, an extension of self-consciousness, a recognition that my self is society, and my 'ego' only a minute fraction of the real me," the remainder being occupied by the larger "We" she idealized but did not consistently experience, lone wolf that she was.[19]

Expanding and contracting, cheerleading for the collective "We" and bemoaning her "little me"—such vacillations set the tempo of Charlotte's adulthood. The story of her life suggests that her desire for a selfless, service-oriented transcendence of personality remained elusive and yielded mixed results. Every time she stumbled over an intense emotion or engrossing personal concern, she criticized herself for failing to measure up to her own standards.

At times, the gap between her aspirations and reality can make her appear a bit delusional. But at other times the tension generated by that gap inspired meaningful work as she imagined the synthesis of self and selflessness she had difficulty living. In these more productive moments, she extracted a general recommendation for social reform from her own self-abnegating insights, arguing that humans would never fulfill their potential until they grasped "that the permanent and holy thing in human life is not personality, but Humanity." Her most influential sociological work thus criticized the competitive individualism of the capitalists and social Darwinists and touted the altruistic service so important to her own equanimity as indispensable to both social progress and human evolution.[20]

Charlotte's selfless ideal, therefore, deserves consideration not simply as a subjective coping mechanism or personal ethos but also as a historically specific philosophy she promulgated alongside other public intellectuals during the age of reform that defined her career. Her dualistic philosophy resonates with thinkers as diverse as the social Darwinist Herbert Spencer—who understood human psychology as a competition between the inherent faculties of "Egoism" and "Altruism"—and the Christian socialist Washington Gladden, who positioned self-love in opposition to benevolence.[21]

Many of the female reformers populating the public sphere in increasing numbers around the century's turn shared Charlotte's faith in the power of association versus the scattershot efforts of individuals. Persuaded by evolutionary narratives, relying on maternal values, and trusting in the benefits of efficiency, they deemed progress inevitable with the help of a little collective elbow grease.

Yet even while she espoused similar ideals, Charlotte remained relatively distant from the contemporaneous movements that might have afforded the opportunities for self-abeyance and world-immersion she craved. For all her contributions to these movements, both theoretical and practical, she expressed qualms about suffrage's narrow focus, socialism's revolutionary politics, progressivism's practical agenda, and feminism's self-absorption. She felt the greatest affinity for two movements: the first, Edward Bellamy's nationalism, which waned before her enthusiasm did; and the second, eugenics, which suited her only late in life, after she had narrowed her definition of collective humanity to include only fully functioning Anglo-Saxons within its circumference.

In certain respects, Charlotte represents a counter-trajectory to the pragmatists who drew on Darwinian and non-Lamarckian theories about evolution to promote pluralism, skepticism, tolerance for diversity, and individualism and in so doing, as the historian Louis Menand has argued, helped Americans to "cope with the conditions of modern life." Although also linked to reform, Charlotte's ideas built instead on the antebellum Beecher tradition, combined Darwinian and Lamarckian insights, and ultimately dead-ended in xenophobia.[22] Charlotte's story is also the story of this counter-trajectory and her vigorous efforts to make and keep it viable.

~

The true scientific spirit is the perfect obliteration of self. . . .
                    "Our Most Valuable Livestock," 1891[23]

In 1899, Charlotte sent her cousin and lover Houghton her poem "Eternal Me," whose title ironically comments on the speaker's desire to shed the personal pronoun:

What an exceeding rest 'twill be
When I can leave off being Me!
To think of it! At last be rid
Of all the things I ever did!

Done with the varying distress
Of retroactive consciousness;
Set free to feel the joy unknown
Of Life and Love beyond my own. . . .

But Heaven! Rest and Power and Peace
Must surely mean the soul's release
From this small labelled entity
This passing limitation—me![24]

A subject who longed to leave her self behind presents a unique challenge to a biographer: the very identity she sought to relinquish I have sought to recover. While Charlotte remained more invested in doing than in being, I have investigated what it meant to *be* a person who believed her self mattered most when she was doing things, even as she increasingly defined "doing" in more abstract and subjective terms.

In this recovery effort, I have often had to read against the grain, but in other moments, I have tried to approach Charlotte on her own terms. Thus, the stronger her sense of a discrete self, the more I explore its contours; the stronger her sense of identification with or alienation from the world, the longer my glance at larger circumstances. Yet even in her early, headstrong years, I have endeavored to place her living in a wider context and to examine the extent to which her notions of identity and purpose meshed with those of her peers.

This comparative approach facilitates a better understanding of her definitions of both self and world as well as the degree to which the two ever merged—goals that are essential to my project. As a methodology, this approach honors her belief system while interrogating its potential idealizations, generalizations, and exclusions. Similarly, my focus on Charlotte's inner life includes a thorough examination of the rationalizations, self-delusions, vanities, inconsistencies, phobias, and prejudices through and by which she (as who does not?) made her own "living" possible.[25]

The bulk of Charlotte's papers are located at Radcliffe's Schlesinger Library, though diverse manuscripts are housed in repositories in some dozen states. Several of the Schlesinger's manuscript collections contain caches of letters and autobiographical documents written by Charlotte, her close friend and "co-mother" Grace, her ex-husband Walter, and her daughter Katharine—many hitherto unplumbed for biographical evidence. The Schlesinger's primary Gilman collection is remarkably extensive: Charlotte saved virtually everything, even jottings and doodles. Page after page of introspective letters and diverse manuscripts provide unprecedented access into who she was and what she wanted, making the writing of her life a tantalizing project for those interested—as I am—in the various ways a self can be fashioned.

Charlotte disdained biographers, especially the "Freud-poisoned" ones, comparing them to hyenas cackling over a carcass. In her hierarchy, to teach and uplift represented a writer's highest tasks, while writing "to dig up the dead to vilify" constituted the basest. Writing this biography has required some digging, and not everything I have uncovered has preserved well. Charlotte held a number of objectionable views and made a number of questionable decisions. As I see it, however, a biographer's task is not "to vilify" but to present a "thick description" of the subject's life and times.[26] By examining Charlotte's "living" in detail and in context, I have attempted to provide both a thorough account of her particular life story and, simultaneously, new insight into the roles available to women vis-à-vis both the public and private spheres at the turn of the last century.

Charlotte Perkins Stetson Gilman was a child of her age, a product of her times even as she helped to shape them. Born roughly a century apart, we have traveled a long way together, and she has proven an engrossing, if occasionally exasperating, companion. While initially captivated by her dynamic, idealistic worldview, over the years I have grown more aware, to paraphrase T. S. Eliot, of the life she lost in living.[27]

Still, she continues to speak meaningfully to pressing issues, including the work–family balance, childrearing, love, loss, marriage, divorce, faith, aging, and life's meaning and purpose, offering solutions that at times belied her private anxieties. Yet even though she could not always reconcile her private and public personas, I have sought throughout this biography to emphasize their profound and complicated relationship.

Acknowledgments

During the decade I have worked on this book, I accumulated numerous debts I am happy to acknowledge here. I completed much of the necessary research thanks to the support of a Fellowship for University Teachers from the National Endowment for the Humanities for the academic year 2000–2001 and a Schlesinger Library Research Grant from the Radcliffe Institute for Advanced Study, Harvard University, for 1999–2000. I also received much-needed support from the University of South Carolina: the English department provided me with a number of able research assistants over the years in addition to awarding me a research grant for the summer of 1999 as well as a research professorship for the spring semester of 2006; the College of Liberal Arts and Sciences provided a research grant for the Summer of 2000; and the University's Women's Studies Department awarded me both the Carol Jones Carlisle Research Award (2001) and the Josephine Abney Award (2006). The department and the college also helped to fund additional pages and illustrations, for which I am grateful.

I am indebted to numerous libraries for supporting my research in their collections. My greatest debt is to the staff, especially Ellen M. Shea, at the Schlesinger Library at the Radcliffe Institute for Advanced Study, Harvard University, for offering such kind and generous help during my numerous visits; Diana Carey deserves my thanks as well for her kind and capable assistance with illustrations. Thanks also to Barbara Grubb at the Bryn Mawr College Library for helping me to procure the cover photo.

I also wish to acknowledge for their curatorial support the librarians at the Bancroft Library at University of California Berkeley; the Barnard College Library; the Brown University Library; the Butler Library at Columbia University; the Colby College Library; the Cornell University Library; the Fruitlands Museum; the Harriet Beecher Stowe Center; the Hingham Public Library; the Horrmann Library at Wagner College; the Houghton Library at Harvard University; the Henry E. Huntington Library; the Manuscript Division of the Library of Congress; the Rhode Island Historical Society; the University of Rochester Library; the Smith College Library; the Vassar College Libraries; the Bailey-Howe Library at the University of Vermont; the Wisconsin Historical Society; and the Women's History Museum and Educational Center.

Versions of portions of several chapters have been published separately: an expanded discussion of Grace and Charlotte's Bristol, Rhode Island, summer appeared as "The Two Mrs. Stetsons and the Romantic Summer," in *Charlotte Perkins Gilman among Her Contemporaries: Literary and Intellectual Contexts*, edited by myself and Denise D. Knight, published by the University of Alabama Press in 2004. My reading of "The Yellow Wall-Paper" resembles the one I advanced in my 2000 Stanford University Press monograph, *Bodily and Narrative Forms: The Influence of Medicine on American Literature, 1845–1905*. A condensed version of Chapter 8 appeared as "Love and Economics: Charlotte Perkins Gilman on 'The Woman Question,'" in a December 2005 Special Issue of *ATQ: 19th C. American Literature and Culture* on "The Woman Question"; some of my points about Charlotte's view and style of mothering also appear in "'Concerning Children': Charlotte Perkins Gilman, Mothering, and Biography," in a 2001 Special Issue of *Victorian Review* on the cultural work of biography. The discussion of "The Woman's Journal" in Chapter 10 began as an entry on the journal for the 2006 Twayne *American Historical Through Literature, 1870–1920*, edited by Gary Scharnhorst and Tom Quirk. Finally, an essay I wrote after finishing the manuscript, which critically assesses Charlotte's legacy and argues that she sentimentalized the public sphere, was accepted for publication by *Arizona Quarterly* in the fall of 2008; some of the evidence I present in that article is culled from the biography.

I could not have written this book without the help of *my* "forerunners," especially Denise D. Knight and Gary Scharnhorst. Denise, whose editions of Charlotte's diaries and late poems greatly simplified my task, also served as my first reader, and her early encouragement proved consistently heartening during the hard slog. Gary's bibliography and literary biography proved indispensable. I am particularly indebted to him for allowing me to tap his expertise and pirate his Gilman materials when I visited New Mexico. He later put everything else aside while on sabbatical to read the entire manuscript.

Seven additional colleagues read this big book in its entirety, and I am grateful to them all for their suggestions and support. Carol Farley Kessler helped me to whip my prose and my thinking about utopias in particular into shape; Catherine J. Golden's painstaking efforts with the manuscript improved it both broadly and specifically; Judith A. Allen's "big picture" assessment helped me to focus on what mattered and what was new, enabling me to sheer pages from a bulky early draft. Charlotte Rich offered a clarifying and encouraging assessment, while Robin Cadwallader read the manuscript with a copy editor's meticulous eye.

The generosity of two of my colleagues in the Department of History at the University of South Carolina, Lawrence B. Glickman and Thomas J. Brown, will be hard to repay; both read the entire manuscript carefully and provided numerous, invaluable insights. I also want to thank Shelley Fisher Fishkin for her warm and helpful response to the preface and Jennifer Lunden for reading the first half of the manuscript with such care and attention.

Also deserving thanks are the many graduate students who have offered essential research assistance over the years: Evelyn Westbrook who helped me to organize my initial notes and make sense of the scope of the project; Todd Richardson for his able research; Eme Crawford, whose cheerfulness and efficiency got me through some difficult patches; Jim Pickard, whose work converting microfilm onto zip drives saved me from motion sickness; Joe Goeke, whose dogged detective work paid off; Stephanie Todd, who helped with permissions; Catherine England, who kept her cool while helping me hunt down missing sources one summer; and Kevin Trumpeter and especially Grace Wetzel for helping me to polish the notes and the bibliography during the final months.

I must also thank Charlotte's nephew, Thomas Perkins, and his wife Jeanne, who met me at the Huntington for lunch, told me stories, and drove me around Pasadena, hunting down Charlotte's addresses. I cannot thank enough Walter, Sally, and Linda Chamberlin, who fed and put up with me for a week during the late summer of 2001 as I sifted through Walter's grandmother's books, paintings, and papers, and who generously granted me permission to make many of these private treasures public.

Finally, I want to thank my family: my in-laws, Allen and Nancy Clapp, who provided me with a wonderful place to stay with each return trip to the

Schlesinger; my parents, Jill and Tanner Davis, who have always taken pride in what I do; my husband, John Reagle, who encouraged me to write the biography in the first place and whose assurances and interest in the project have helped sustain me throughout; and, finally, my three children, two of whom are younger than a project that began while the eldest was still in diapers. Someday, I hope the three of you will read this book and finally understand what your mom was doing at her computer all those long hours.

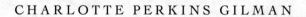

CHARLOTTE PERKINS GILMAN

New England

1   "Beginnings"
            (–1876)

> It takes great strength to train
> To modern service your ancestral brain;
> To lift the weight of the unnumbered years
> Of dead man's habits, methods, and ideas. . . .
>   "Heroism," 1898[1]

In the summer of her fourth year, Charlotte Anna Perkins and her five-year-old brother Thomas eluded their caretakers and snuck into an old graveyard. They wanted to find out if dirt could extinguish fire. The experiment failed, and the flames soon spread beyond their control, consuming the surrounding hillside and leaving the siblings soot-blackened, tear-streaked, and terrified. Charlotte went on to claim this incident as the beginning of her incendiary career. A dedicated conflagrationist to the end, she torched decrepit ideologies, methodologies, and ontologies and fiddled while they burned.[2]

This irreverent self-portrait is hard to reconcile with Charlotte's genealogical pride, however. Her autobiography begins, after all, with references to her distant connection to Queen Victoria as well as to governors, lords, dukes, kings, and conquerors. Charlotte prided herself most of all on her Beecher relations, "that family of world-servants." Her Aunt Isabella's motto, "the world is my country; to do good is my religion," succinctly conveys both the Beecher commitment to reform and the family's belief in its own crucial, historical role, convictions Charlotte inherited as if Lamarck were right and acquired traits *could* be passed down.[3]

At the height of her fame, Charlotte was hailed as the most "emphatic exponent of the Beecher character" and as the epitome of the family's world-reforming, convention-defying missionary zeal. She boasted of her Beecher heritage from every lectern, in every puff piece, and at every opportunity. Her friends helped to advertise the connection: the writer Zona Gale described her as "direct, abrupt, blunt, devastating, as the need arises, and oblivious—as any Beecher ever was." Another writer friend, Martha Bruère, maintained, "[t]he husband of Mrs. Gilman says that she was born saying, ''Tain't so!' And we should be prepared to believe this on account of her heritage—from that famous line of Beechers who each and all undertook to set their country right-about-face."[4]

As a young girl, Charlotte admired the Beechers for modeling the service-oriented life she hoped to lead, a life her more immediate family seemed to want only to thwart. The more she lamented her home life, the more she idealized the Beechers and their contributions, and the more she vowed to take up their mantle and set the problems she confronted as a girl "right-about-face." She boasted of descending from the Beechers, but what she really wanted was to ascend to their seemingly lofty level, the better to transcend the difficulties she experienced closer to home.

~

So proud of our grandsires are we. . . .
                                    Untitled limerick, 1920s[5]

Throughout the long nineteenth century, Beecher was a household name. Charlotte's great-grandfather, Lyman Beecher (1775–1863), was acclaimed in his heyday as the most famous minister in America—that is, until his son Henry outshone him in the 1850s. A revivalist and theologian who preached an alleviated Calvinism, Lyman wedded God's anger to God's love and Christianity to rationality. He boasted of "switching," "scorching," and "stomping" his congregation with his impassioned sermons while simultaneously envisioning his church as a "spiritual hospital," where he preached a "clinical theology" and attended to his parishioners' bodies along with their souls.

As a member of the "New School," Lyman recoiled from the notion that the inheritance of original sin damned infants and other innocents; he also modified the Calvinist doctrine of predestination by arguing for free will in choosing faith and salvation and by maintaining that spiritual redemption derived from the choices people make rather than from some foreordained plan.[6] Charlotte inherited his skills as a polemicist and his emphasis on reason, agency, and the will, as well as his self-definition as a missionary with a message.

Less evidence exists of a family resemblance between Charlotte and her great-grandmothers, if only because these women's stories remain obscured by the impressive shadow their husband cast. Lyman's first wife, Roxana Foote, hailed from a relatively affluent Anglican family. During their courtship, Lyman sought to woo her both to him and to Calvinism. Lyman later declared Roxana his ideal mate, having "sworn inwardly never to marry a weak woman" but to seek instead a wife who combined both sense and "strength to lean upon." Throughout their marriage, Roxana appeared the "calm and self-possessed," submissive and domestic counterweight to Lyman's more passionate model.[7]

A letter Roxana wrote to her sister-in-law hints that she learned her revered Christian submission at bitter cost: she alludes to vexing domestic circumstances and mourns her limited knowledge and her inability to find time to read more than a page or so a week. She also confesses to eagerly devouring information gleaned from conversation and envying other women their greater opportunities to pursue further education in the arts and sciences. Along with her sister Mary, who lived with Roxana and Lyman, Roxana had opened a school to teach young girls English, French, art, needlework, and, for a time, chemistry. The school's success only heightened Roxana's regrets over the gaps in her education. Charlotte shared Roxana's thirst for knowledge and remorse over its lack, which may explain why she insisted that she resembled her great-grandmother as much as her great-grandfather.[8]

In eighteen years of marriage, Roxana bore nine children, one of whom died in infancy, before dying quietly of consumption in 1816, at age forty-one. She told the children gathered around her deathbed that she hoped they would all grow up to become missionaries. A Beecher biographer suggests that guilt over the possibility that overwork had hastened Roxana into her grave prompted the family to make "a legend out of her sensitivity, gentleness and purity, remembering only an angel who had never grown old—perfect mother, ideal woman."

With eight mouths to feed and a flourishing ministry, Lyman determined to remarry. Within a year, he had located his new wife in the lovely and accomplished Harriet Porter. Catharine Beecher described her stepmother as "a model of propriety and good taste." Catharine's younger sister Harriet portrayed her as "so fair, so delicate, so elegant that we were almost afraid to go near her" and joined her siblings in remembering their stepmother as a poor substitute for the saintly Roxana.[9]

Group portrait of Lyman Beecher (center), Henry Ward Beecher, and Harriet Beecher Stowe, ca. 1860. Photo by Brady's National Portrait Gallery. Courtesy of the Schlesinger Library, Radcliffe Institute for Advanced Study, Harvard University.

Harriet Porter Beecher initially welcomed the "great cheerfulness and comfort" of her new circumstances but eventually felt the strain of so many responsibilities. She bore Lyman four additional children: Frederick, Isabella, Thomas, and James; Frederick died in his second year. After Harriet died of consumption in 1835, Lyman married his third and final wife, an efficient widow named Lydia Jackson. While two of his wives were "consumed" in midlife, Lyman survived until his eighty-eighth year, lionized as an American "Cato."[10]

Lyman Beecher's fame was augmented by his role as paterfamilias: Theodore Parker called him "the father of more brains than any other man in America." There did appear to be a Beecher gene for prominence. One Beecher descendent claimed, "Lyman Beecher's children were just as sure as he was, that they were God's agents, commissioned by Him to carry out His will." By all accounts, Lyman was a doting father, kind-hearted and playful when he was not warning his children of the hellfire awaiting them if they failed immediately to repent and convert. He may have considered his dozen offspring "his own personal band of apostles," but most of them eventually rejected their father's stern Calvinism and his pitiless Old Testament God for a more sentimental religion featuring a more parental, loving, and suffering deity who deserved emulation, not fear.[11]

Their greater investment in human conduct as the test of piety also led most of Lyman's offspring to take a sharper interest in worldly concerns. Lyman had desired moral reform to preserve the traditional social order that his reform-minded children sought to dismantle. As the biographer Milton Rugoff observes, "where Lyman was a priest and a prophet, his children were social servants and reformers; where he was intent on saving men's souls and fixing their thoughts on the life to come, his children sought to change men's ways here and now. . . ." In truth, though, his children kept their eyes on both prizes.[12]

Even as they diverged from their father's orthodoxy, each of Lyman's sons became a preacher. One of them, Henry Ward, occupied the country's most influential pulpit, mesmerizing his congregation from his self-designed stage at New York's Plymouth Church and from editorial positions at the *Christian Union* and the *Independent*. With one exception, the Beecher daughters were also illustrious. The first-born, Catharine, devoted herself to education, founding a renowned seminary in Hartford and teaching the readers of her treatises the benefits of domestic economy, fitness, health, and happiness according to largely circumspect and circumscribed middle-class ideals. Harriet Beecher Stowe became an international celebrity with the 1851–1852 serialization of her anti-slavery novel, *Uncle Tom's Cabin*. When published in book form, the novel soon rivaled the Bible in sales and purportedly led Abraham Lincoln to credit its author with "starting this

Portrait of Charlotte's grandmother, Mary Beecher Perkins, ca. 1861. Courtesy of the Schlesinger Library, Radcliffe Institute for Advanced Study, Harvard University.

big war." Isabella Beecher Hooker, the lovely youngest daughter, was a prominent socialite who helped to organize and lead the radical wing of the woman's suffrage movement.

The only child of Lyman Beecher who did not make a public contribution was Mary Foote Beecher, "the anomaly," "the lady," Charlotte's grandmother. Mary apparently enjoyed basking in her siblings' reflected glory. At the end of her life, she observed contentedly, "When I was a young woman I was known as the daughter of Lyman Beecher. In my middle age I was introduced as the sister of Harriet Beecher Stowe and Henry Ward Beecher. Now in my old age I am identified as the mother-in-law of Edward Everett Hale."[13]

To her family, Mary appeared an oasis of calm amid the crosswinds of fame and scandal buffeting the others. Her father faced a heresy trial in 1835 for preaching the doctrine of immediate repentance, which, in affording man free will to repent of his sins, seemed to his accusers to undermine the Calvinist concept of preordination and to challenge God's almightiness. At the height of the Civil War, her brother Charles was tried for heresy on account of his belief in the preexistence of souls; he was convicted, but the verdict was later overturned.

Henry was embroiled in a sordid controversy, accused (with apparent justification) by Theodore Tilton of adultery with Tilton's wife Elizabeth. This national scandal lasted three years and culminated in a skeleton-exposing, ego-bruising trial. The jury voted nine-to-three in Beecher's favor; his enemies believed the vote had been rigged. Isabella entered the fray when she sided against her brother and with the outrageous Victoria Woodhull—the controversial stockbroker, presidential candidate, and journal co-editor who published the allegations against Henry in hopes of claiming him as a fellow apostle of "free-love." Henry subsequently pronounced his half-sister insane.[14]

Harriet's most famous novel outraged southern slaveholders, one of whom sent her a human ear in the mail. Another scandal ensued when she vindicated Lady Byron and in the process published the rumors of Lord Byron's incestuous relationship with his half-sister. In short, the Beechers seemed to cultivate scandal as readily as sanctity.[15]

Mary Foote Beecher Perkins witnessed the turbulence at some remove. She remarked to Isabella, the half-sister she essentially raised and whom, in the wake of the Beecher–Tilton scandal, she disowned, "I could not perform any of my duties if I gave way to my feelings and allowed myself to attend meetings and become as much interested as I easily could." For Mary, domesticity was paramount. Her family considered her the personification of the angel enshrined within domestic ideology, the true spiritual daughter of her sainted mother Roxana.

During the antebellum period, middle-class ideologues revered the "true woman" for her piety, purity, domesticity, and submissiveness.[16] Of course, "true womanhood" remained more of a prescription than a description, but Mary, of all the Beecher siblings, seemed closest to this ideal. Her granddaughter Charlotte would attempt to topple this paragon but not without cost, as the angelic, domestic ideal was used by many (and even, at times, by Charlotte upon herself) as a yardstick to measure a woman's personal failures.

Born in 1805, Mary Beecher initially showed great promise as a student, winning prizes and praise. She helped establish her elder sister Catharine's Hartford Female Seminary and taught there briefly before marrying Hartford lawyer Thomas C. Perkins in 1827. Like her granddaughter, she suffered from poor health and underwent a therapeutic regime resembling the one Charlotte would find so detrimental, for it too proscribed exercise and activity. Throughout her marriage and until the ripe old age of ninety-five, she lived in apparent style in downtown Hartford.[17]

Yet her married life was never as blissful as family members and some scholars have suggested. In a letter describing her forebears, written at a desperate time in her own life, Charlotte claimed her paternal grandmother "hated matrimony. Had 'nervous fevers' . . . and was obliged to leave home at recurring intervals. Could not bear to see her husband at such times." Money also remained a perpetual problem: the Perkins family routinely took in up to a dozen boarders, usually students, to help make ends meet. In 1837, during the financial panic, her husband lost virtually everything to his creditors, including Mary's piano. While Thomas had suffered failure once before, he now had twice as many (four) children to support among his expanding financial obligations. The family weathered this storm, but they endured a rocky ride back to financial stability.[18]

Mary's eldest son and Charlotte's father, Frederic Beecher Perkins, grew up to dabble in assorted careers, desert his first wife and children, and achieve limited renown as a librarian and author before dying in relative obscurity and depleted mental health. About the second son, Charles, little is known. Charlotte referred to him as a "fine lawyer" in his father's law office but scarcely mentions him otherwise.

The two Perkins daughters led variously troubled lives. Charlotte described her Aunt Emily as suffering from "nervous prostration" and her Aunt Katherine as of "infirm mind." Emily Perkins married quite well, to Edward Everett Hale. The great nephew of the Revolutionary War hero Nathan Hale, he was a Unitarian minister (later chaplain of the U.S. Senate), reformer, and prolific author who is perhaps best remembered for his story "The Man Without a Country."

Katherine ("Katy") married William Gilman, a lawyer who during the financial panic of 1877 forged a certificate so that it read $30,000 instead of $3,000, got caught, lost his reputation and business, and went to prison. His wife subsequently suffered a nervous breakdown, from which she recovered only to die two years later in her forty-fifth year. According to Charlotte, she was "out of her mind when she died. . . ." Katy and William were the parents of George Houghton Gilman, called "Houghton," Charlotte's first cousin and second husband. During their courtship, Charlotte told Houghton, "I think my life would have been smoother if I'd grown up with my father's side of the home . . . ," only one of her lifelong idealizations of the Beecher line.[19]

A franker look reveals that most of the Beechers suffered from depression. In Lyman's day, it was known as melancholia or "the hypo," a condition that plagued the Beecher *père* and several of his children. Indeed, Charlotte once declared melancholy "dyed in the wool—the Beecher wool." Both Catharine and Harriet experienced bouts of depression in their twenties and thirties. Harriet's daughter Georgiana underwent S. Weir Mitchell's rest cure in 1876, a decade before her cousin Charlotte would entrust herself to Mitchell's care; in both instances, the cure failed.

Nor were the uncles immune: in 1843, the chronically depressed George Beecher put a gun in his mouth and fired; nearly a half century later, James, the youngest Beecher, copied his older brother's final, fatal act to the letter. Eight years after James's death, shortly after his ex-wife's death, and only five years before his own death, Frederic Beecher Perkins, Charlotte's father, married James's widow Frances. "Frankie" had been Frederic's childhood sweetheart, the woman he had rebounded from in marrying Charlotte's mother Mary; Isabella Beecher Hooker once noticed a disconcerting resemblance between Frankie and Mary.[20]

Isabella herself periodically succumbed to depression and frequently experimented with various alternative cures. These included hydropathy or "the water cure" (a regimen Harriet Beecher Stowe also favored), during which the patient was subjected to wet wrappings, uterine injections, and sitz baths, among other water-related remedies. Isabella believed that marriage—even as a prospect—initiated her malaise: she worried that her siblings' marriages "did not start rightly" and fretted that if her own married life resembled what she had witnessed in her own family, she might never muster the courage "to fulfill an engagement. . . ." Like Charlotte, Isabella prolonged her engagement in a state of vacillation and uncertainty for two years, though unlike Charlotte's, Isabella's first marriage was her only marriage and, apparently, a happy one.[21]

Being a Beecher was not all doom and gloom: the family prided itself on both its optimistic zeal and keen sense of humor. "There is," Isabella observed, "the strangest and most interesting combination in our family of fun and seriousness." The editor Amy Wellington suggested that Charlotte inherited from her Beecher ancestors "the irresistible wit and rapidity of thought and expression—'rapid as light itself' at times, as some one said of her great-aunt, Harriet Beecher Stowe."

Charlotte may also have inherited her great-aunt's penchant for literary didacticism. When Harriet informed George Eliot that "art as an end, not instrument" failed to interest her, she voiced Charlotte's own aesthetic priorities. Charlotte also considered this great-aunt a precedent-setter for being a woman whose writings mattered more to the world than did her children.[22]

By and large, Charlotte's themes were Beecher themes. Like them, she thought deeply about religion, devoting one of her best books to the topic late in her career. Adapting the family tradition of evangelical reform to her own earthly ends, she promoted the repression of baser passions and the project of human betterment. Like Isabella and Henry, she became a prominent suffragist. Like Catharine, she sought to redefine the home and to encourage physical fitness.

But above all, Charlotte's intense identification as a Beecher stemmed from her sense of herself as carrying on the vital intellectual tradition she associated with her forebears. Along with Catharine and Lyman, for instance, she believed the individual less significant than the social whole, saw self-absorption as a chief obstacle to human happiness, and connected salvation to human agency. Charlotte secularized Lyman's desired virtues of self-abnegation and social cohesion, representing these aims as evolutionary rather than strictly spiritual apotheoses. She joined her great-grandfather in defining sin as "in its nature antisocial," though she made that antisociality identical to sin rather than its consequence. She thus shared her Great-Uncle Edward's conviction that altruism constituted the basis of a moral society.[23]

She also joined her Great-Uncle Henry in adopting a "warm, sentimental, organic view of developing human life." Henry derived this notion from Herbert Spencer's "conception of gradual development," which held that nature, society, and the individual would inevitably evolve if left alone. Inspired by Spencer, Henry viewed life as an ever-evolving, ever-improving process whereby "the whole physical creation is organizing itself for a sublime march toward perfectness." Styling himself a "cordial Christian evolutionist," Henry defied his father's puritanical take on man's fallen state and maintained that man had instead risen as a race. In Henry's progressive evolutionary scheme, God served as the force shaping human history and guiding it to its remote and glorious culmination.[24]

The darker side of Henry's evolutionary theology emerges in his social Darwinist take on a class structure he presents as god-given: "God has intended the great to be great and the little to be little . . . ," he wrote. It surfaces as well in his notorious "Cleveland letter," which questions whether blacks possessed the "stamina . . . sobriety, virtue, industry and frugality" to take their place among whites. Henry opposed slavery, inviting the abolitionists Frederick Douglass and Wendell Phillips to speak from his stage when they had been driven away elsewhere. From that same stage, he trampled on chains said to have shackled the recently hanged John Brown; raised money to purchase and liberate "quadroon" girls displayed before the congregation as if at auction; and faced down angry mobs intent on attacking the anti-slavery preacher. But Henry was hard-pressed to recognize blacks as social equals.[25]

His doubts were shared by his sister Harriet, whose famous antislavery novel represents colonization as the logical next step after emancipation. Lyman himself supported the American Colonization Society; he unconsciously possessed, according to a son-in-law, "not a little of the old Connecticut prejudice about blacks." For several years, he held two black girls as indentured servants. In her prejudices, Charlotte was a Beecher as well.[26]

Although Charlotte idealized her Beecher ancestry, she took equal pride in her matrilineage. Late in life, she told her daughter Katharine, a budding genealogist, that "[i]t is through the Perkinses & Pitkins that we go back to all creation!" The Perkinses were one of New England's first families, described by Charlotte as "all born fighters and talkers to a purpose from Protectorate days in Old England to Colonial Battles in the New." Both Charlotte's mother and her father had Perkins blood. Her mother's mother was Clarissa Fitch Perkins, whose father was the cousin of Frederic Perkins's father—making not only Charlotte's parents, Frederic and Mary, but also Charlotte and her own daughter, cousins.[27]

Her mother's father, Henry Westcott, descended from Stukely Westcott, who with Roger Williams helped to settle Rhode Island. A Unitarian and a pacifist, Henry was thirty-six when he married his second wife, the fifteen-year-old Clarissa; three years later, their only surviving child, Mary, was born.

Charlotte remembered her maternal grandfather as "intensely loving and benevolent. Nervous and fretful over his family as he grew old." She recalled her maternal grandmother as a delicate creature who "suffered much" and who was confined to an invalid's bed for most of her life.[28] Each of Charlotte's grandmothers thus represented a prevailing stereotype of middle-class womanhood: her father's mother personified the conventional "true woman" and her mother's mother, the conventional female invalid. Charlotte's career as an iconoclast was fostered by her intimate familiarity with icons.

~

My mixed ancestry has given me here and there a noble streak, but mostly anything but!
Letter to Grace Channing Stetson,
May 26, 1924[29]

Charlotte revered her own ancestry, but she also disdained those who idolize "buried bones." She instructed her lecture audiences to "let sleeping forefathers lie,"
reminding them that, however luminous, "their light is not our light." Her ameliorative agenda entailed improving on the past and focusing on the future, it
meant moving ever onwards and upwards, not backwards or downwards. Hence
she cajoled readers of her one-woman publication, the *Forerunner*, to

> Forgive the Past—and forget it!—don't carry a grudge against
> graveyards.
> Accept the Present—you have to!—and here it is.
> Concentrate on the Future—still yours to make—and get busy![30]

A quasi-fictional, first-person sketch entitled "My Ancestors" encapsulates
Charlotte's views and finesses the seeming contradiction between her personal
pride and her retrospective disdain. Its narrator habitually bragged of an "Old
Family . . . Genealogical Tree, several Coats of Arms, and a Gallery of Portraits"
until being visited one night by a spirit who leads the speaker deeper into the
past. The speaker is ultimately forced to count as kin gibbering ancestors who
appear "[s]horter, hairier, fiercer, more bestial." The spirit chastises the narrator
for shrieking at the sight and insists that the time had come to forgo honoring
ancestors and instead "honor, love and serve the human race."[31]

Ancestor worship could take one only so far. Her Great-Uncle Henry may have
embraced evolution for teaching that mankind would inevitably ascend "from ape
to angel," but Charlotte found she could not discount those original apes.[32] As
a Beecher-Perkins-Pitkin-Westcott, she felt she had cause to boast in a society
where, for all its democratic aims and claims, lineage still mattered. But her debt
to Darwin led her to take a global, evolutionary perspective and remember that
at the root of all genealogies lurked primate progenitors. In the short term, she
may have descended from kings, but in the long term, she, too, had evolved from
beasts. Throughout her life, Charlotte tended to take the longer view.

Haunting personal decisions also lent urgency to her past-rejecting preach-
ings. As she wrote her cousin Houghton in her thirty-eighth year, she had lived all
her life "with—not all gravestones, but some, and some kind of trap-door-stones
that keep things down. When the will-strength, or brain-strength, or whatever it
is that keeps me happy and steady and brave, gives out, up hop all these buried

things, dead and alive."[33] For every instance when she danced publicly through graveyards, there were other, more cloistered moments when she tripped over memories all too shallowly buried.

~

There now follows a long-drawn, triple tragedy, quadruple perhaps, for my father may have suffered too. . . .

The Living of Charlotte Perkins Gilman, 1935[34]

In 1857, the pampered Mary Fitch Westcott married her second cousin, Frederic Beecher Perkins. Mary was twenty-nine, an age considered overripe at the time. Frederic had proposed on the rebound, and the engagement was broken off at one point. The Beecher clan disapproved of the match, although Isabella would eventually conclude that she had been "agreeably disappointed" in Mary, finding her charming, despite her reputation as a flirt and her status as a veritable old maid.[35]

The petted and feted daughter of an indulgent father and an indulged child-bride, Mary had battled consumption in childhood and was thrice expected to die of it, making her all the more precious to her doting parents. She allegedly began entertaining suitors while still playing with dolls, so her late marriage aroused suspicions of a fickle heart. Her one claim to fame appears to have been the introduction of English ivy as an interior decoration in American homes. In her daughter's eyes, she appeared "femininely attractive," "[d]elicate and beautiful, well educated, musical, and what was then termed 'spiritual minded.'"[36] Although raised to be a wife and trained in dependency, she ultimately overcame the blow of her husband's desertion and emerged as a marginally self-supporting woman.

"If unswerving love, tireless service, intense and efficient care, and the concentrated devotion of a lifetime that knew no other purpose make a good mother," Charlotte later reflected, "mine was of the best." Her conditional phrasing connotes her doubts about her mother's qualifications, doubts that intensified with age and experience. In her twenties, Charlotte described her mother as "in every way an exaggerated type of the so called 'feminine' qualities, love of husband home and children being almost manias." She scorned the slavish, sentimental devotion that compelled Mary to preserve even Frederic's hair and nail clippings. (Ironically, Charlotte would also save locks of her ex-husband's hair, although a note accompanying the keepsake indicates she did so for her daughter's sake.) [37]

Prevailing bourgeois gender ideologies might equate selflessness with fulfillment, but Mary's life struck Charlotte as "one of the most painfully thwarted" she had ever witnessed. Indeed, Mary provided Charlotte with an early example of the feminine ideal she would devote her career to toppling. "A home life with

Portrait of Charlotte's father, Frederic Beecher Perkins, ca. 1865. Courtesy of the Schlesinger Library, Radcliffe Institute for Advanced Study, Harvard University.

a dependent mother, a servant-wife," she later wrote in *Women and Economics*, "is not an ennobling influence."[38] In her treatises and in such bitter poems as "The Mother's Charge," Charlotte sought to spare other daughters her own fate.

In her loyalty, sense of duty, hunger for love, and impulsive affectionateness, Charlotte was by her own admission her mother's daughter. But she identified more with her father, even though she disparaged his "fickle fancy" compared to her mother's constancy. Photographic evidence suggests she inherited her father's intense brown eyes and long face but her mother's prominent nose and dimpled chin. Charlotte credited Frederic with her "urge to social service" and her "Beecher wit and gift of words"; she also believed she owed him her "solitary disposition." She judged her father's nature, though "perverted," the nobler of her two parents': "He failed and failed, but he meant the biggest best things."[39]

Charlotte's father Frederic was born in 1828, the eldest child of Mary Beecher Perkins and Thomas Perkins. He attended Yale but left in his second year after he quarreled with faculty and was arrested for fighting with a policeman. He subsequently studied law in his father's office in Hartford and was admitted to the bar in 1852; during this time he also taught school in both New York City and Newark.

Feeling little affinity for the law, Frederic decided to cast his lot fully with the school system—teaching, clerking in the Connecticut Superintendent of Schools' office, and editing the *Connecticut Common School Journal*. Through this last, he developed an appetite for editing and soon made it his profession, serving for a period as an editor of the *New York Tribune*. He then switched hats once more and became a librarian, presiding over the Connecticut Historical Society, a position he held when his daughter was born.

All the while, Frederic continued to dabble in editorial work, often as a result of family connections. He assisted his Uncle Henry Ward Beecher on the *Christian Union*, his Aunt Harriet Beecher Stowe with fact-checking for her 1867 *Men in Our Times*, and his brother-in-law Edward Everett Hale with his *Old and New* magazine. He also wrote fiction, usually under a pseudonym; his best-known and most critically acclaimed work was a collection of stories and sketches called *Devil Puzzlers and Other Studies* (1877). He published a well-received life of Charles Dickens as well as a classified bibliography, "The Best Reading," which became a standard reference book. He was widely praised for his intellect but not particularly well liked: his curt and inflexible manner "made him unpopular with many," one obituary claimed.[40]

For five years in the 1870s, Frederic served as an assistant librarian at the Boston Public Library. In 1880 he became the chief librarian at the San Francisco Public Library. While in San Francisco, he instituted a policy requiring library pages to wear slippers so they could climb ladders silently while retrieving books for patrons. He also removed "dirty books" from the collection and proved particularly tough on "loafers and criminals." He resigned in 1887 after a contretemps in which he was accused—but ultimately vindicated—of rough-handling the "skylarking" son of an influential patron. In 1894, he returned to the East to marry his childhood sweetheart, Frankie Perkins. Failing mental and physical health landed him at the Delaware Water Gap Sanitarium two years later, a broken man; he died in yet another facility in New Jersey in January 1899.[41]

Frederic's peripatetic professional life may have suited his temperament, but it took its toll. The narrator of "The Compensation Office," one of his semi-autobiographical *Devil Puzzler* sketches, offers a caustic assessment of just such a life: "I have . . . given up my noble aspiration to . . . live for the good of others; and have fallen back upon the purpose of evolving my own thoughts. I am only a literary vagabond now. . . . I earn money enough. . . . Yet I am deeply disgusted. I accomplish nothing."

His daughter sought to channel the drift by claiming that Frederic's life was about books: "He read them, he wrote them, he edited them, he criticized them, he . . . classified them." His friend, the author Charles Dudley Warner, maintained that Frederic "had talents of a very high order—a touch of that which is called genius—and it is safe to say that if he had confined his effort to any one pursuit he would have attained great distinction."[42]

Frederic acknowledged a tendency to vacillate between generosity and selfishness. In one *Devil Puzzler* sketch, the youthful narrator gave away all his gingerbread to a pauper, only to react against such benevolent impulses "into an equally unjudging disregard of the wants and needs of others." Charlotte recognized this trait in her father, accusing him of taking "money his family needed to buy some precious book." She summarized his personality as "eccentric," "solitary," "remote," "reserved," "proud," and "[b]rilliant," seeing him in much the same light as he saw himself. In terse and ultimately disdainful physiological terms, she itemized his "[l]arge brain, susceptible nerves, small moral sense."[43]

Frederic viewed himself as a man in whom intellect dominated, but the desire for approbation scarcely made a dent. He could be courageous on behalf of his principles, as when he defended an African American from an angry mob during the New York City race riots in the midst of the Civil War. But he had none of his daughter's enthusiasm for the collective, even in principle. He was a liberal who abhorred organized forms of resistance. He sympathized with the poor, with blacks, and with women who desired an extra-domestic life, but only to an extent.

Frederic presented his views on women's duties as citizens in a speech before Connecticut teachers. He concluded that women who teach do so "to earn a little money before they get married, or to satisfy imperfectly that divine zeal for useful exertion, which, after all, is only to find its perfect gratification in their own homes, in their own families." In his sketch "The Compensation Office," he places the burden of marital success on the young wife and asks, "Have you faithfully endeavored . . . to cherish your husband, and to guide, and attract, and instruct your children; and so to make their home the centre, and yourself its queen and beloved source of their happiness?"[44]

Although Frederic publicly informed women that their place was in the home, he did little to secure such a shelter for the women in his own life. Best suited to a bachelor's life, he instead found himself married to a dependent wife who loved him desperately and whose affection he returned grudgingly. The children resulting from their vexed union received little in the way of unconditional affection but learned a good deal about desperation and grudges.

Charlotte was born in 1860, a year in which the population of the United States doubled from its 1840 level, reaching 31.4 million, of whom some 4 million were foreign-born. That same year, Abraham Lincoln was elected president by 40 percent of the popular vote; Elizabeth Cady Stanton spoke before a joint session of the New York State legislature to urge representatives to support woman suffrage; and Elizabeth Palmer Peabody opened the nation's first English-speaking kindergarten in Boston.

In short, it was an auspicious year for a person of Charlotte's reform inclinations to be born, and her birth would have been all the more auspicious had it occurred a day later. All her life, Charlotte regretted being born late on Tuesday evening, the third of July. "If only I'd been a little slower and made it the glorious Fourth!" she lamented. "This may be called the first misplay in a long game that is full of them."[45] Throughout her seventy-five years, especially in her darker moments, Charlotte would berate herself for having been, since birth, a day early and a dollar short.

~

. . . The crying of a little child at night
In the big dark is crowding loneliness. . . .
"Our Loneliness," 1898[46]

In April 1865, Catharine Beecher was visiting the Perkins family at their temporary residence in Apponaug, Rhode Island. The square white house was built in the shotgun style, with a central hall running from front to back, and with what to youthful eyes looked like a huge backyard. At the time of Catharine's visit, Mary Perkins was in the first trimester of her last pregnancy; Charlotte was nearing her fifth birthday. The visit indelibly inscribed itself in the young girl's memory—less so for her distinguished great-aunt's presence than for the tragedy occurring midmonth. The family learned on the fifteenth of April that President Lincoln had been assassinated the previous evening. The papers delivering the news arrived framed in black, and soon both Apponaug and Providence were draped in mourning colors.

Although Charlotte does not mention her father in her recollections, Frederic shared in the national heartache. Before two years passed, he had compiled a biographically based tribute book to both Lincoln and the artist Francis B. Carpenter, who had painted a famous picture of Lincoln's first reading of the Emancipation Proclamation. The preface describes the author-compiler as an extreme radical dedicated to preserving the Union. Frederic gave a presentation copy to his wife, inscribed "with the respects & compliments & Love of the author."[47]

Frederic wrote this inscription on February 22, 1867. By this date he had been renting separate rooms for some time, insisting that he "'could not be broken of his rest.'" For a time, he boarded with one of his sisters, but he soon found even this arrangement too constraining. He had not cut off all ties with his wife, however, as Mary's 1865 pregnancy attests. Despite medical warnings about the consequences of another pregnancy, Mary delivered the couple's fourth and final child, Julia De Wolfe Perkins, in late January 1866; the baby died that September. According to Charlotte, "[t]he small sister made no impression on me, her visit was too brief."[48]

The circumstances and timing of Frederic's departure remain unclear, but the presence of his children may have hastened it. One of his *Devil Puzzlers* sketches, "My Forenoon with Baby," depicts a hapless bumbler who fails miserably at soothing a screaming infant and concludes, "In the paradisiacal state we should all have merely come into existence, at eighteen for women and twenty for men. . . . A baby is providentially provided as an 'awful example' for the warning of maids and bachelors, as terrific consequences universally follow great follies. It is the delirium tremens of matrimony. If you don't want to have it, let the causes alone."[49] By the time Frederic decided he could do without a family, he already had one.

Charlotte learned to mirror his detachment. "The word Father, in the sense of love, care, one to go to in trouble, means nothing to me," she reflected, "save indeed in advice about books and the care of them—which seems more the librarian than the father." As a child, she wrote her absent father several plaintive, chatty letters. Amid buried pleas that he write her back, since "nobody writes to me but you," she gently chided him for his infrequent correspondence. Frederic brusquely dismissed her pleas and stressed his own preoccupations.[50]

Once, after a long separation, Charlotte visited Frederic at the Boston Public Library and rushed to embrace him, only to be promptly and soundly repulsed for her public display of affection. Charlotte maintained he treated her "as a mere caller" throughout the visit, teaching her a painful lesson in quelling spontaneous emotional outbursts.[51]

In "The Nurse and the Snake," one of Charlotte's juvenile poems from the 1870s, a child inadvertently treads on a snake that then swiftly kills its attacker, prompting the child's nurse to cut off the snake's tail. When the nurse subsequently seeks to make amends, the snake claims that their mutual acts of revenge had not canceled each other out but had demonstrated instead an invaluable truth: "He who does you a wrong, is sure not to love you." The meaning of wrongs done, of love's absence, of vengeance, however futile, count as some of the bitterest lessons Charlotte learned from her father.

Charlotte may have enacted her own revenge in her *roman à clef, Benigna Machiavelli*, which depicts the "hateful" father figure as a relentless, resentful, fault-finding man who enjoys reducing his wife to tears. He also drinks—only enough to be an "offense in private"—which may explain Isabella Beecher Hooker's reference to one of the Perkins sons as an alcoholic.[52]

While intact, the family rarely settled in one place for long. But after Frederic left, Mary and the children wandered of necessity. The narrator of one of Frederic's literary sketches recalls living in at least twenty houses growing up and concludes that he was "cheated in heart by injurious superfluity of houses." The father's fiction became his children's reality. The family moved from house to house, town to town, state to state—totaling some nineteen moves in eighteen years.

Most of these moves occurred back and forth between Connecticut (to Hartford, the hilly, prosperous town where Charlotte was born and where many of Frederic's relatives lived) and Rhode Island (most often to Providence, the booming port city that was home to Mary's bedridden mother and grandmother), with prolonged detours to New York and Massachusetts. On one memorable sojourn at Harriet Beecher Stowe's new, large "wonder house," Oakholm, in Hartford—built with the proceeds from the bestselling *Uncle Tom's Cabin*—Charlotte sat quietly watching her great-aunt paint, sessions she later credited with inspiring her own enduring interest in art.[53]

Charlotte had a literary aunt on her mother's side as well: Caroline Robbins, Mary's half-sister, the child of Henry Westcott's first marriage. At times, Mary and the children stayed with the widowed "Aunt C.," as her niece referred to her, and at other times, particularly after they settled in Providence in 1873, Aunt C. lived with them. During this period, Caroline authored a volume of poems as well as an anti-slavery drama, published in 1876. Yet she apparently wielded little influence on her niece: Charlotte later deemed both her aunt and her mother "unutterably remote."[54]

In a return visit to Hartford in 1868, Mary and her children found themselves "most lovingly entertained" by Frederic's aunts, Charlotte and Anna Perkins, for whom Charlotte had been named. The sisters' sympathy for the broken family remained heartfelt and unwavering even after the divorce. Charlotte and Thomas eventually received legacies of a quarter share each in the aunt's Hartford house—referred to in family conversations and correspondence as "the Hartford Hope." During this Hartford stay, Mary began her sporadic career as a schoolteacher, holding classes for her own and several neighboring children.

Mary thus eked out a "scanty and irregular" living, with some help from her aged father while he still lived and less help from her husband. From an early age, Thomas contributed by keeping a vegetable garden and hunting partridge, rabbits, and squirrels with a shotgun his father had given him. Charlotte recalled many meals consisting of only potatoes in their jackets accompanied by a bowl of hot, salted, and buttered milk, or of cornmeal mush enhanced by molasses, milk, and butter—meals that at the time struck her as "highly appreciated delicacies I now surmise to have been bottom-line necessity."

From March to December 1869, the year her parents permanently separated, Charlotte, Thomas, and Mary stayed in a four-story New York City boarding house run by Ann Swift. The memoirist W. L. Alden recalled the house as "one of the literary centres of New York"; its one-time tenants included Richard Henry Stoddard, Edmund Clarence Stedman, Bayard Taylor, and Frederic Perkins's daughter, Charlotte. Charlotte's most vivid memories involve tormenting the landlady and her poodle Pinky, hiding matches under oilcloths to startle boarders who unwittingly stepped on and ignited them, clogging one boarder's sewing machine with masticated gingerbread, and dousing another boarder's hairbrush with ink. She also remembered a spanking reluctantly meted out by her visiting father at the behest of her mother for one of Charlotte's more audacious pranks: she had spat from the landing onto the unsuspecting landlady's head.[55]

Charlotte was by her own account a precocious child, rhyming at three (her first couplet ran "Here I come, doll in hand, / This is to obey my mother's command") and learning to read, sew, and dress herself by five. Her brother Thomas recalled a "secret consciousness of having to 'step lively' to keep up with my sister mentally." He confessed that this induced "much of the unkind teasing I visited upon her." Thomas gave Charlotte her first haircut when she was three and he, four. With better results, he gave his sister her first diary at age fifteen,

*Charlotte Anna Perkins as a small child, early 1860s. Courtesy of the Schlesinger Library,
Radcliffe Institute for Advanced Study, Harvard University.*

thus enabling her to vent the emotions and explore the imaginings already brimming over inside. As an adult, Charlotte derided the self-absorption of those who wrote only to relieve themselves, but for many decades she made a habit of just such relief, finding in her own case that journaling disencumbered the self rather than immersing her further therein.[56]

Thomas retained an impression of his younger sister as "a dark-haired and dark-eyed, very good-looking girl, demurely sober, with a rather wistful, far-away look, but whose face was unusually expressive of anger, delight, mischief, or other aroused emotion, and whose words and actions were apt to be accordant with and strongly expressive of the emotion aroused." The two siblings were never particularly close: Charlotte complained of Thomas's relentless teasing and resented the privileges he enjoyed as a boy. She later told him that while she wished him well, "'Brother' brings no answering thrill to my heart. Perhaps because we had so little genuine loving intercourse when we were together. Fun we had in plenty, and a large fund of common intelligence; but I can never remember any companionship more [than] beautiful ideas." Nonetheless, the family's continual uprootings meant that the siblings were often forced to rely on each other as playmates.[57]

While replete with parental abandonment, poverty, loneliness, and various deprivations, theirs was no bleakly Dickensian childhood. Thomas possessed fond memories of shared larks, including the times "the two investigators" dug up artichokes and uprooted and peeled all the onions in a heartbroken neighbor's garden. He also recalled their snitching sugar, studying swamp life, making "sweet-pea ladies and trumpet flower men," and consuming "finger-buttered bread" at their Aunt Harriet's house, where they also pursued the less innocent pastime of taunting the "'long, lank, lean, devilish nigger-wench Josephine.'"[58] Charlotte remembered running barefoot in the country, learning to swim in Little River, and episodes of mischief-making, including rolling muddy hoops into ladies' crinolines and squirting water on the heads of passers-by, including the town mayor's.

One of Charlotte's most enduring memories occurred when she was eight years old, during a procession celebrating Grant's election. Charlotte believed she bested the lit candles blazing in most windows by impersonating "a Goddess of Liberty," standing on a table in the doorway in full view of the street, dressed all in white with "a liberty cap" and "a liberty pole . . . and a great flag draped all around" her. She reminisced, "there I stood, Living. One crowded hour of glorious life that was, to a motionless glorified child." She declared it a "soul-expanding experience."[59]

Many of Charlotte's richest recollections of childhood, however, were not of stasis but of motion, of journeys between and among cities by train, steamboat, and hack. In one of her earliest extant autobiographies, Charlotte plots her life story via the timing and place of each successive move.[60] This conflation of identity and geography would fundamentally inform Charlotte's emerging sense of self. She doubtless found the moves discombobulating as a child, and she represents her nomadic childhood pathetically in *The Living*. But moving as she later theorized it became essential to her dynamic understanding of "living": it signified growth, change, and progress and was vastly preferable to the stasis that she took to mean stagnation or death. Charlotte repeatedly endeavored in her theories to make the best of her own bad situations.

All the moves meant that she had little exposure to formal schooling, though she did accumulate some four years total, near the national norm at that time. Education remained a household imperative: Mary not only made time to instruct her children formally, she also made schooling her first budgetary priority, paying tuition before she purchased necessities.

Charlotte spent her last year of formal education as a child at Mrs. Fielden and Miss Chace's Young Ladies' School in Providence, leaving in her fifteenth year. In March 1875, Miss Chace sent home a report card, which, the teacher noted, "you will not expect to be very good, on account of protracted absences." At this same school, Charlotte lost a point on an otherwise perfect assignment for finishing it with flourishes (appending "ye end. Finis" and "three little curly lines under my signature"). She continued to resent this reduction so much that she confronted her teacher about it when they met at one of her lectures some two decades later.[61]

Motivated by their mother's as well as the Beechers' commitment to learning, the two children eagerly attempted to teach themselves what their schools had not covered. Charlotte's daughter Katharine recalled her mother as "an omnivorous reader. . . . [S]he could quote almost all the Bible . . . [a]nd unlimited quantities of poetry," though Charlotte herself claimed she lacked the mental stamina as an adult to read anything for long.

The young Charlotte devoured many books and periodicals published explicitly for children and especially enjoyed the stories published in the new illustrated juvenile magazine *Our Young Folks*. One story by J. T. Trowbridge serialized in that journal's inaugural year deeply impressed her. "Andy's Adventures" taught the five-year-old a lifelong aversion to lying that often inspired her to place truth before tact, harming her relationships with others.[62]

Her childhood library contained many studies of the natural world, but she also read Charles Dickens, George Eliot, Sir Walter Scott, Louisa May Alcott, and Mrs. A. D. T. Whitney. Indeed, although she complained in *The Living* that Mary forbade novel-reading, until at least Charlotte's fourteenth year mother and daughter frequently partook of their shared pleasure in sentimental novels as well as in books of "strong ideas," which Charlotte read aloud with Mary all ears.[63]

Most nights, Mary would feed the children supper and then read from "exciting books" like *Oliver Twist* before putting them to bed "at the stroke of the clock"; Charlotte maintained she never saw eight o'clock until a teenager. Toward her husband, Mary apparently acted "as loving as a spaniel which no ill treatment can alienate." Yet she typically withheld affection from her children, hoping to make them independent and spare them her own lovesick fate. In her autobiography as well as in several thinly fictionalized accounts, Charlotte suggests that Mary compensated for her daytime standoffishness by cuddling her sleeping children. Awakened once by her mother's caresses, the young Charlotte vowed subsequently to stay awake while feigning sleep, "hugging her doll for pure lonesomeness" in the interim, so hungry was she for proof of her mother's love.[64]

Tucked in without the affectionate gestures she craved, Charlotte resorted to "castle-building for sure consolation; dreams of fair days to come, her own continuation of the story she had heard, or those that grew in her own mind; and always herself as she might be, with power free to work her will [and] . . . the whole world about her to be loved and cheered and sent on its way rejoicing." She reworked some of these fantasies during daylight hours into poems, sketches, fables, and even a short novel in fragments populated with romantically named characters like Roderigo, Angelica, and Alphonso. The budding author also experimented with pen names, such as "Capusa" (her own initials plus the nation's).[65]

In her tenth year—shortly after the family settled in the country, about four miles from the town of Rehoboth, Massachusetts, for what would prove a roughly three year stay—Charlotte compiled an ostentatiously ambitious tome entitled the "Literary and Artistic Vurks of the Princess [and 'poetess'] Charlotte." The volume contains her own original writings, drawings, and versions of childhood games, as well as poems and pieces she copied from favorite authors. "Princess Charlotte" was one of her father's terms of endearment, though perhaps he cribbed it from his daughter's self-styling. By the time she reached adulthood, Charlotte's tropes had become decidedly self-deprecating, as when she compared herself to a duck hatched from a hen.[66] In her youth, however, Charlotte bedecked her soul in the "royal robes" and "glittering raiment" she associated with fairy tales and romances.

Many of her ennobling fantasies were conspicuously compensatory. In one elaborate tale, the fairy Elmondine rescues the lonely Princess Araphenia from her boredom and isolation. The fairy urges Araphenia to hasten to the side of her father the king, whose forces were losing a critical battle. The princess dons knightly

garb, equips herself with magical weapons and horses, and routs her father's enemies, saving both king and country. A daughter longing for a father spins a fantasy
about a daughter saving a father and about a father who needs his daughter, not
the reverse. For Charlotte, stories were invariably remedial.

Yet another tale about a magical prince and princess who collect unhappy
children from all over the world and bring them to an island paradise further
testifies to Charlotte's loneliness; it also demonstrates her tendency to use real-life
disappointments as springboards for fantasies that enabled her to "make a world
to suit" her, an ambition she clung to even after she relinquished fantasy.[67]

Sometimes Charlotte needed no fantasy for fulfillment. For instance, she considered her twelfth Christmas, spent in Rehoboth, "the best ever": it featured a
tree, sledding, twelve people, and eighteen and a half presents (she shared one
gift with her brother). Mostly, however, pleasure for the young Charlotte meant
dreaming. She doled out fantasies like treats: "Once a week I would imagine
things a little more impossible than the every day repast. Once a month things
still more unusual and delightful. Once a *year* anything I chose!" Occasionally, she
had nightmares, like the one she recorded set initially in a forest, then in a cavern
containing a pool of blood, then in a Gothic hall lit by torches and populated by
servants and ancient Romans, and ending in an ocean where a sea serpent drowns
the protagonist. A psychoanalyst would doubtless interpret the cavern, bloody
pool, burning torches, and dangerous serpent as signifying the dreamer's discomfort with encroaching puberty.[68]

Looking back on her teens from her twenties, Charlotte maintained that she
indulged "a sea of Poe-like visions" until she willfully suppressed these "wicked"
and "unhealthy" reveries. Charlotte cast her adolescent self as the servant of two
masters—the first named fantasy, the other repression. Alexander Black, a writer
and friend, pondered the pathetic aspects of Charlotte's youth. "As a young girl,"
he wrote, presumably basing his impressions on Charlotte's own recollections,
"there was a bit of weirdness in her blending of conscience and adventure, of
enormous restraint and a plunging mind." Black's imagery suggests Charlotte held
one end of the chain she bound herself with, letting it out only to the point of
self-defined danger, then abruptly jerking it back.[69]

Charlotte cast her demons as internal ones; for example, she claimed of her
indulgent fantasizing, "no one stopped it, till I myself, growing in health and
wisdom, saw the evil, and resolved that I would *think* no longer, but *do*." In other
moments, however, she externalized her adversary in the person of her mother.
Mary readily stepped into the fray. Never trained to be a breadwinner yet forced
to assume the role, she also felt compelled to play both mother and father to her

children. Her despondency and stoic resignation exacerbated her difficulties with her fanciful, headstrong daughter.

Persuaded by a friend whom Charlotte later described as possessing a "pre-Freudian mind," and dreading the potential consequences of allowing her daughter's imaginative world to flourish unchecked, Mary ordered the thirteen-year-old Charlotte to forever cease and desist. Victorian physicians and parents suspected that children's fantasies encouraged sexual indulgence as well as eccentricity and impulsiveness. Doctors recommended a range of repressive tactics to instill traits mothers like Mary valued, including self-control and dutifulness.

On Charlotte, the discipline apparently succeeded only too well. She later claimed that she took her mother's command to mean that she must "close off the main building" of her fantasy-prone mind and subsequently "live in the 'L'." Even though she knew it to be impossible for anyone to determine the degree of her acquiescence, Charlotte believed it her duty to be obedient and so felt compelled to "shut the door" in fantasy's face and "hold it shut."[70]

Fourteen years later, recounting the origins of her nervous exhaustion to a medical specialist, Charlotte lingered over the damage inflicted by this particular battle of wills. "The most serious injury is done in childhood," she later wrote. "Our cruel waste of the nerve force of children is only more pathetic than it is absurd. The mere business of growing up, . . . which should be a process unconscious or full of joy and rich accumulation, is made by our ignorant mishandling a confusing, irritating, exhausting process, often leaving permanent injuries to the machine, as well as waste of power." As she told her doctor in 1887, Mary's insistence that she shut down her imaginative life had caused just such a lasting injury.[71]

If Charlotte did indeed dwell thereafter in the "L"—although her prolific fictional output suggests even this anteroom to be capacious—this early battle of wills may have triggered her bourgeoning antipathy for the ego. Forced to repress her personality at an age when most teens are exploring and expanding its boundaries, Charlotte increasingly sought external validation. She later concluded that she traded the possibility of being a princess for "behaving like one." She traded her marvelous, if "always philanthropic," superpowers for an equally fantastic pursuit of goodness and obedience in the real world—a fantasy she knew her mother would approve.[72]

With so much youthful energy, both suppressed and unleashed, Charlotte had, in a friend's estimate, "reached a kind of incandescence. And she wanted to be a voice." This desire to be a voice surfaced early. At ten, she purportedly began "scheming to improve the world," claiming she had learned from hardship that *doing* was more satisfying than *having*. She recalled singling herself out from her peers during a playground storytelling game by recounting her "plans to capture and punish that social malefactor, Boss Tweed." William Macy Tweed, boss of New York's Tammany Hall, had recently been accused of embezzling millions.

Charlotte's decision to tackle one particularly notorious reprobate demonstrates her precocious and persistent inclination to tilt at windmills. Her plan combines two Beecher traits: do-goodism and a belief in personal invincibility. As she recollected in her autobiography, her first wish when as a child she devised her personal list of "three wishes" was for all her wishes to "be Right! To be Right was the main thing in life." By her own estimate, from the moment she forsook fantasy and dedicated herself to "the humanitarian interest," she rode a metaphorical horse "so tremendously high" and so difficult to mount that she "could not easily get down."[73]

~

Through all these weary worlds in brief;
Who ever sympathized with grief
Or shared my joy—my sole relief?
Myself.

Juvenile poem, ca. 1870–1871[74]

For additional reasons, 1873 was a momentous year in Charlotte's life. A financial panic ushered in an economic depression lasting six years, comprising the period of Charlotte's adolescence. That same year, influenced by well-meaning friends, Mary Perkins resolved to divorce her feckless husband, thinking to set him free to marry another; she had also finally relinquished all hope of Frederic's ever paying the bills.

The historian William L. O'Neill estimates that some 11,000 divorces were granted in America in 1870. By contrast, roughly 167,000 divorces were granted in 1920; the latter number still reflects only 1 percent of the population. The 1870 figure represents 1.5 divorces for every 10,000 marriages. Half of these divorces were obtained by childless couples, making the split of Charlotte's parents all the rarer. Women more typically filed for divorce since they had an easier time securing one. Yet the desire to divorce was commonly viewed as a character defect in a woman, indicating her inability to trade romantic dreams for marital mundanity. At the time, alimony was rarely awarded or paid.[75]

Mary suffered greatly for her decision. She unintentionally alienated Frederic, who expressed his displeasure over the fuss. His horrified relatives subsequently turned their collective backs on "Mary Fred"—an appellation denoting her perceived role as an appendage. Without "Fred," many of the Beechers decided, there would be no Mary. In *Women and Economics*, Charlotte acknowledges the difficulties facing women who seek an independent life: "At present any tendency to withdraw and live one's own life on any plane of separate interest or industry is naturally resented, or at least regretted, by the other members of the family. . . . [T]he home ties bind us with a gentle dragging hold that few can resist. Those who do resist, and who insist upon living their individual lives, find that this costs them loneliness and privation. . . ."[76] Charlotte could have been describing either her mother or herself in this passage.

In 1873 as well, Mary and the children settled in the Providence area. At this time, Providence was considered the second city of New England after Boston. It grew from about 68,000 inhabitants in 1865 to nearly 105,000 by 1875. Enriched by industry, Providence was enhanced by its hilly, tree-lined streets, its situation at the head of Narragansett Bay (known as "the cove," it was eventually filled in by the city's business-minded leaders to build a railroad station), and the green expanse of Roger Williams Park, founded in 1871.[77]

Mary, Thomas, and Charlotte originally moved into the Westcott house on Vernon Street, where Mary nursed first her mother and then her grandmother through their final illnesses. Soon after arriving, Thomas contracted a virulent case of typhoid fever, which Charlotte managed to dodge. With reason, Charlotte felt her brother more susceptible to disease and more damaged by it. Scarlet fever cost him the hearing in one ear, and diphtheria nearly killed him in 1879. He also lost an eye at age nine.[78]

His mother and sister suffered in less tangible ways. Charlotte served as her mother's harshest critic when she was not her closest confidante. As she entered her teens, she shopped and played chess with her mother, and the two often shared a bed. During these harmonious interludes, Charlotte recognized and sympathized with Mary's unwanted burdens and blamed her father for his fiscal and moral irresponsibility.

At other times, however, Charlotte bristled. In her treatise *The Home*, she laments the recurrent bickering found within even the most cheerful domicile: "Sore from too much rubbing, there is a state of chronic irritability in the more sensitive; callous from too much rubbing there is a state of chronic indifference in the more hardy; and indignities are possible, yes, common, in family life which would shock and break the bonds of friendship or of love, and which would be simply inconceivable among polite acquaintances." She especially deplored the home for its tendency "to exaggerate personality" and for being "necessarily a hotbed of personal feeling." Mary's insistence on making everything personal strengthened her daughter's distrust of personal entanglements and her attraction to a philosophy of impersonality. Her mother, she later claimed, had succeeded in raising a daughter whose first impulse was to flee intimacy and to fear relationships.[79]

Charlotte increasingly viewed her relationship with her mother as "utterly uncongenial." From her teens onward, she stopped trying to live up to Mary's exacting standards and resigned herself to putting up with them. The eponymous heroine of her novel *Benigna Machiavelli* endures a parent's "horrid" behavior by reassuring herself: "'This is an Ordeal.' And I'd stand it. I had to stand it, you see, anyway, but by taking it as an Ordeal it became glorious. And not only glorious, but useful. I was astonished to find . . . that a pain isn't such an awful thing if you just take it as if you wanted it." In her own life, Charlotte did more bearing than grinning.

From her adolescence onward, Charlotte saw herself as "always living out of and away from" her mother's home, deciding that her "principal personal ambition as I grew older was some day to be able to be alone."[80] Such resolutions and their familial motivations help to explain Charlotte's eventual tendency to stand aloof even during the heyday of the collective she preached.

From June 1874 through February 1876, the three Perkinses lived in downtown Providence with several Swedenborgian friends of Mary's in a cooperative housekeeping venture. The Swedenborgian church was quite influential in the nineteenth century; its many followers included the author Sarah Orne Jewett and the fathers of both William Dean Howells and Henry James. A key concept for proponents of this mystical sect was *vastation*—the painful, often terrifying, state of the external self's dissolution or death, which in time enabled the emergence of a new, enlightened being, profoundly connected to the infinite. Stripped of its terror, the process of vastation approximates Charlotte's own desired metamorphosis, yet her exposure to the church at this susceptible age failed to convert her.[81]

The cooperative housekeeping movement had been spearheaded by Melusina Fay Peirce, wife of philosopher Charles Sanders Peirce. She published five articles on cooperative housekeeping in the *Atlantic Monthly* between 1868 and 1869, fueling interest and triggering experiments. As Dolores Hayden explains in her history of domestic reform, Peirce encouraged groups of women to form cooperatives in order to perform domestic duties collectively and seek reimbursement from their husbands. Peirce's fellow advocate Mary A. Livermore believed that the movement could simultaneously remedy "the servant problem," the competing demands of child and husband care, the housewife's ever-expanding domestic duties, and, finally, the sheer and repetitive drudgery of most of these tasks. She therefore insisted that "isolated housekeeping must be merged into a co-operative housekeeping."[82]

While appealing in principle, Charlotte found the practical experiment disastrous. She ultimately advocated getting the kitchen out of the house, not more cooks into the kitchen. Accordingly, she condemned "that oft-repeated foredoomed failure called 'cooperative housekeeping.' . . . The inefficiency of a dozen tottering households is not removed by combining them." She found it hard to fathom why anyone would expect families to succeed working together at domestic responsibilities that they failed so miserably to perform while working in isolation.[83]

The putative leader of the cooperative household on Providence's Major Street was a psychic, Lydia Browning White Stevens. Charlotte considered a dramatic stand-off between herself and Mrs. Stevens "one of the major events of a lifetime, making an indelible impression, opening an entire new world of action." As Charlotte recounts in *The Living*, Mary forced her to apologize to Mrs. Stevens for allegedly thinking "harsh things of her" after Charlotte witnessed the lady taking a bunch of grapes from the house's grapevine. (Mrs. Stevens claimed to be privy to Charlotte's thoughts through her psychic abilities.) When Charlotte denied the accusation, Mary presented her with an ultimatum: if she failed to apologize, she must leave her mother's side. Refusing to apologize for what she had not done or, rather, thought, Charlotte rejected both alternatives. Mary slapped her for her defiance, but the experience left Charlotte "with an immense illumination that neither she, nor any one, could *make* me do anything."[84]

From this realization, she dated her metaphorical "birth." In a poem of that name, Charlotte defines her term via the newly autonomous speaker's exultant self-description:

> . . . I live manifold,
> Many-voiced, many-hearted
> Never dead, never weary,
> And oh! never parted!

For Charlotte, then, birth inaugurates the process whereby a soul feels "unhindered" by personal constraints and no longer torn between personal and larger duties. In short, birth enables those newly reborn to begin "living" as she defined it. This memorable act of defiance ultimately facilitated her decision to overturn the "old condition of compelled obedience" and become a "free agent." Her lingering sense of duty elicited her silent vow to obey her mother's rules until she turned twenty-one; "duty and sacrifice have a fascination for me always," she later wrote. Privately, Charlotte thumbed her nose: leaving the cooperative despite "opprobriums" from the Stevenses, she gleefully rejoiced in her diary, "'Fiddle de dee!'"[85]

At fifteen, Charlotte was long on ambition but short on ideas for viable careers. She therefore wrote a breezy letter to her father requesting "a nice long talk" and describing herself and her goals. She professes her desire—one she speculated most girls shared—for "a great many things, and a lamentable *blank* in the direction of a means of livelihood," and she contemplates possible careers in art, literature, medicine, and the stage. Utilizing religious metaphors to describe her quandary, she enumerates her sins and asks at one point, "What Shall I do to be Saved?" (Her equation of salvation and employment would only strengthen over the years.) She also wryly confesses to "intervals of depression" and extreme fluctuations in mood, fueled mainly by her "total inability to *work*," especially for pay. She closes her exuberant epistle by pleading for paternal guidance.[86]

Frederic's response has not survived, but Charlotte judged it to be coldly indifferent. She had vainly sought her father's recognition via their mutual desire for rewarding work. Such experiences taught her to beware the backlash invariably following her emotional displays. Her longing for love endured, but her fear of rejection strengthened.

～

. . . at about fifteen the individual becomes selfconscious, with new power, and is able to govern his or her conduct in varying degree.
>   Autobiography, "an earlier attempt," undated[87]

The fifteen-year-old Charlotte entertained a brief infatuation with an actor playing the Frog Prince at a local theater. Her crush on this "darling" occupies many of the early pages of the diary she began keeping on the first day of 1876, her dedicated journaling suggesting she had begun to see her life as "somehow *remarkable.*"

Looking back, Charlotte identified 1876 as the year she "plunged in and swam" in life's stream; she therefore derided the trivial entries in her first diary for belying "the desperately serious 'living' which was going on." During this year, she later claimed, she consecrated herself to "human service" and formulated the religion that informed all her living, a personal credo of impersonality that governed her ensuing actions and choices. By insisting in retrospect that she entertained such large questions as early as her sixteenth year, Charlotte implicitly manages to assert the originality of her deductions, since they would then have predated her reading of the influential scientists whose views her conclusions recall.[88]

Regardless of when, precisely, she reached it, Charlotte's decision to base her code of conduct on an undergirding religion provides yet another testament to the Beechers' influence on her thought. Her boast that her religion was based on scientific knowledge rather than on the more customary foundations of faith or tradition suggests that she shared her Great-Uncle Henry's investment in reconciling evolution and religion. Evoking both Henry and Herbert Spencer, she held that science could help to justify ethical conduct, promote an organic understanding of society, and illuminate the inevitability of progress. Yet she sided with the Beechers and against Spencer in viewing human intervention as a boon to progress.[89]

To devise her personal religion, Charlotte claimed, she began by asking herself a series of Socratic questions about her own purpose, as well as the purpose of life and the world. Identifying action as the primary life force and observing it to be not only dominant but also good, she named this force "God" and equated it with evolution. She marveled at its capacity to transform protoplasm into personality and personality over time into something larger, more complex, and more truly human. Evolution, as she understood it, was not Darwin's indifferent, amoral force but eminently moral, inherently rational, and invariably benign. She thus reasoned that human beings ought consciously to "carry out the evolution of the human race," since we are the only creatures who can actively assist this vital progress, and through this assistance we would fulfill God's plan for us on earth.

Charlotte drew an analogy between the individual and society, envisioning both as propelled from within by the force that is God. Individuals who desired to help society advance, then, must first achieve "full social consciousness"—that is, consciousness of the fundamentally social nature of human life. They then could set about building "a social body" befitting "the soul of God." The best way to build this better body and to function as part of "The Working Force of the universe"—in other words, the best way for us both to resemble and to please God—would be for each of us to find our "real job, and do it."[90]

Charlotte's ecumenical, humanitarian religion thus defines God as neither a personal deity, nor a spirit, nor a male—suppositions she derided as "our own wretched personal limitations superimposed upon Deity." Her God was thus not, after all, the Beechers' God—an external force "above us, to be worshipped." It was instead a limitless force within us and inherent in the larger world, a boundless, unavoidable, active force we were obligated as human beings to tap into and use. Her God was first and foremost a "Living God," an ever-present, immortal spirit, and her religion was above all else "a general theory of life," a "large idea of how to live." Rather than joining a sect, going to church, or saying prayers, Charlotte believed we could best worship God "all the time—*by doing things*," she remarked. "And by enjoying the lovely world, appreciating it, learning the laws of life and fulfilling them."[91]

Charlotte began to develop this religion between the ages of sixteen and twenty and continued to refine it as an adult, preaching it to others from both lectern and pulpit. She repeatedly assigned it fundamental importance, maintaining that it undergirded her lifelong commitment to rational laws, a benevolent creator, meaningful work, and service on behalf of humanity.[92] In many ways, it represents her declaration of independence, initiated in the year of the nation's centennial. The love, guidance, and sense of belonging she had yearned for futilely in her personal life became the governing principles of her avowedly impersonal religion of public service. Yet by defining work as impersonal service to humanity, she established a potentially treacherous dichotomy wherein all personal matters threatened to undermine her goals and to interfere with her happiness. Her faith in the absolute nature of this antithesis, as much as the personal intrusions themselves, would nearly prove her undoing.

2 "I'm *Not* Domestic and Don't Want to Be"
(1877–1881)

> . . . Lovely young maids with their light limbs leaping
> Arms tossing wide in the grace of young gladness,
> Joy in their movement, joy in their faces.
> > "To Isadora Duncan," undated manuscript[1]

"[I]mpressionable, vacillating, sensitive, uncontrolled, often loafing and lazy": Charlotte used these words in *The Living* to describe her teenaged self, overlooking diary entries from these years that fairly bristle with energy. The mature Charlotte criticized a life lived without apparent purpose; although an ardent disciple of Walt Whitman, she did not celebrate loafing in herself. Of course, she could not have loafed in her mid-teens had she wanted to: during those years, Charlotte routinely complained of being overwhelmed by the time-consuming household chores her mother assigned. She also grumbled about her contributions going unappreciated, and, as she later opined, "[t]here is no deeper longing in the heart of youth than that for appreciation."[2]

Charlotte's resistance to housework took root during her teens, deepened by her bitterness over the double standard. Conceding that domestic duties aplenty could occupy a girl's time, she demanded, "but how if it does not satisfy? How if the girl wants something else to do—something definite, something developing? This is deprecated by the family." She saw herself as just such a girl, at once determined and deprecated. Desiring "definite," "developing" work, she balked at Mary's expectation that she "remain in her mother's sphere until she entered her husband's."[3] The Victorian ideological division between public and private spheres only intensified Charlotte's desire to work as an alternative to the conventionally domestic life Mary had planned for her.

Although not published until 1884, one of Charlotte's most eloquent poems conveys her aversion to the domesticity her mother believed should satisfy her. In her autobiography, Charlotte remarks that "In Duty Bound" provides "an accurate picture of 'home comfort'" during this period, when her respect for her mother's wishes left her straining at the bit. The poem describes a life "hemmed in" and renders as mere drudgery a mantra Charlotte later found inspiring—"Simply to live, and work." Decrying undesired obligations that bind "with the force of natural law," the poem's speaker bemoans her "sense of wasting power," her lost ideals, and the soul-crushing claustrophobia. The chilling, finely crafted final stanza concludes,

> That is the worst. It takes supernatural strength
>   To hold the attitude that brings the pain;
> And there are few indeed but stoop at length
>   To something less than best,
>   To find, in stooping, rest.[4]

Charlotte intended to be among the few still standing. While living in her mother's home, she dutifully resolved to follow the letter of her mother's dictates, but she was silently vowing disobedience to the law.

Yet another of her frequently cited poems, "An Obstacle," describes an encounter with a personified obstacle and ultimately recommends as the most fruitful coping strategy walking "directly through him / As if he was n't there!" This is precisely how, lifelong, Charlotte handled the double standard: she ignored it the better to trample it. In her own life, she refused to accept domestic confinement and took "a fancy to work hard and be very smart" in order to escape. Anticipating the fin-de-siècle anti-modern impulse documented by the historian T. J. Jackson Lears, she longed to flee "the airless parlor of material comfort and moral complacency," longed "to smash the glass and breathe freely—to experience 'real life' in all its intensity."[5] Yet she found herself constrained by her mother and others who insisted that the parlor was the proper place for a young woman of her background to abide.

The life of the mind appealed to her far more than did a conventional domestic life. Like Vivian Lane in her novel *The Crux*, Charlotte desired worthwhile occupation and "could never hypnotize herself with 'fancy work.'" She railed against the presumption that she must obey the parents who showed her little affection and rebuffed her tender gestures. She was expected merely to settle down, which she knew meant settling for less than she was capable of mentally and emotionally: "She felt the crushing cramp and loneliness of a young mind, really stronger than those about her, yet held in dumb subjection." She desired fulfillment on all levels—she "longed for more loving, both to give and take"—but she was constrained by conventional assumptions "that if a woman had a head, she could not have a heart; and as to having a body—it was indelicate to consider such a thing."[6] Like her fictional heroine, the teenaged Charlotte wanted what she did not get and got what she did not want, and she refused to accept that this was simply woman's lot in life.

~

The large love for humanity seldom combines well with successful relations.
Autobiography, "an earlier attempt," undated[7]

Charlotte was perceived as "smart" but "queer" by her peers and often felt out of place even among friends, "like a horse among kittens, a soldier in a millinery shop." Concerned that she was developing a reputation as a spoilsport, she resolved to try to enjoy herself "like other people." She entertained several suitors, but if any of her callers threatened to stay too late, she took the unusual step of excusing herself by ten o'clock.

During this period, she developed close ties with the daughters of some of the leading families in Providence, including Ada Blake and May Diman, each the child of a distinguished professor at Brown University; in the spring of 1881, Charlotte mourned the tragic death of the "utterly charming" May in a horseback-riding accident. Charlotte often summered with her friend Kate Bucklin at Baldhead Cliff in Ogunquit, Maine, where she routinely leapt between two cliffs, a chasm thereafter christened "Charlotte Perkins Leap" and painted with some skill by the leaper herself.[8]

Charlotte also formed a lasting friendship with Carrie Hazard, daughter of one of the "noble families" of Providence. Her fondness for the Hazards and theirs for her (Charlotte, apparently, was a dead ringer for one of the Hazard daughters) led Charlotte to conclude, "There's a deal of kindness in those people, and much common ground between Carrie and me. . . ." Like Charlotte, Carrie pursued a career as a writer, publishing volumes of poetry as well as local Rhode Island history and genealogy. She served as Wellesley College's fifth president at the century's turn and continued to provide emotional and financial support to Charlotte over the years.

Another lifelong Providence friend was Grace Channing, granddaughter of the leading proponent of Unitarianism, William Ellery Channing, the man whose liberal Protestantism Charlotte's great-grandfather Lyman famously opposed.[9] Grace's older sister Mary befriended Charlotte first, but Charlotte and Grace soon forged a bond that would withstand—at times precariously—professional collaboration and rivalry, marriage (consecutively) to the same man, and "co-mothering" the same daughter.

Charlotte did not confine her socializing to Providence. She made frequent trips to Boston, usually visiting her Aunt Emily and Uncle Edward Everett Hale, finding at their home a measure of peace and tranquility that seemed a sharp contrast to her own experience; she only learned later that her Aunt Emily hated housework. Charlotte paid her first visit to the Hales at fifteen and made repeated visits in the ensuing years, often calling upon her father while in town. During these visits, her male cousins and other college boys often served as her escorts. For a while, Arthur Hale, her cousin, seemed smitten, but eventually the "admiring cousin of Harvard days ceased to admire, ceased with such violence and completeness" that he became "cold and rude and it hurt."[10]

Another male cousin, George Houghton Gilman, proved more steadfast; Charlotte passed a few pleasant days with the Gilman family in Connecticut during the fall of 1879. After boating back to Providence—and learning, a few weeks after her return, of her Aunt Katy's sudden death—Charlotte struck up a short-lived correspondence with the younger cousin who in another twenty years would become her second husband.[11]

Charlotte had no need to leave Providence for entertainment. Two popular, private amusement facilities opened in the city in 1878: Park Garden and San Souci Gardens. Each hosted summer theaters. Park Garden featured a pavilion, a pagoda, and a natural amphitheater with a pond where, at a ship-side performance in 1879 of Gilbert and Sullivan's operetta the *H.M.S. Pinafore*, Charlotte first met her most intimate Providence acquaintance, Martha Luther. The smaller San Souci Gardens sponsored concerts and theatricals and was ultimately the more successful venue. The city's largest public park, Roger Williams, eventually spanned 450 acres; it offered numerous crowd-pleasers, including a carousel, a zoo, a museum and planetarium, gardens and greenhouses, ball fields, tennis courts, a boathouse, lakes for boating as well as for the popular craze of rowing (a sport at which Charlotte boasted of her prowess). Winter activities included sledding,

Group portrait with Charlotte standing on the far left and Mary Perkins seated on the far right (both in similar hats and in profile), Oakland Beach, Warwick, RI, August 17, 1875. Photo by G. N. Lombard. Courtesy of the Schlesinger Library, Radcliffe Institute for Advanced Study, Harvard University.

sleigh riding, and skating, which Charlotte enjoyed along with "many fair damsels & noble youths."[12]

These pleasurable outdoor pursuits contrasted sharply with her life indoors. At home, Charlotte felt like a caged bird, or an anchored boat, metaphors she mixes in her treatise on *The Home*: "Our own personal lives . . . are not happy. We are confused—bewildered. Life is complicated, duties conflict, we fly and fall like tethered birds, and our new powers beat against old restrictions like ships in dock, fast moored, yet with all sail set and steam up." Mary was often ill and expected her daughter to help nurse her, even though Charlotte confessed, "I am no sort of good with invalids."

Mary also seemingly capriciously refused Charlotte various outings with friends, both male and female, affirming Charlotte's opinion of her mother as "*absolutely* illogical." She never forgave Mary for preventing her from seeing the celebrated actor Edwin Booth play *Hamlet*. Intervals of domestic tranquility were punctuated by conflicts that left Charlotte despairing, "I must really abolish all desire for comfort or any sort of happiness if I expect to have any peace."[13] Repressing personal needs, represented in her nineteenth year as bitter necessity, eventually became the essential ingredient in her recipe for "living" as she defined it.

Mother and daughter secured nicer quarters in the spring of 1881, leaving their home of five years and moving into a "dear, beautiful little house" on the corner of Manning and Ives: Charlotte slept in a small bedroom on the third floor near the landlady's rooms; her mother's half-sister, Aunt Caroline, took the second floor. Their new residence lacked indoor plumbing—indeed, Charlotte would not have a bathroom until she moved to Oakland, California, in 1891. Yet she loved her garret nook and celebrated the view of the skies from her window; she also rejoiced at having finally fled their former flat, which she referred to as both "the hole below" and "ungraded 'Coonville'," revealing the early emergence of her prejudices.[14]

The improved surroundings wrought only minor improvement in her relationship with Mary, however. Charlotte "bitterly resented the grasping clutching demands for confidence of my devoted mother. She held on. all over / always." A poem she wrote around this time entitled "My Home" expresses her hunger for a "happy home all mine by use and right," where no mother would insist on her right to intrude on a daughter's privacy without at least knocking first.[15]

Thomas was no longer around to act as buffer, having enrolled at the Massachusetts Institute of Technology. When he failed, his sister wondered whether "he would ever amount to anything." With the help of his influential uncle Edward Everett Hale, Thomas set off for Nevada on November 5, 1879, to pursue an engineering career, launching a long and difficult life marked by penury, job loss, three marriages (the second a particularly unhappy one), and alcoholism.[16]

Charlotte continued to pursue her *ad hoc* education and became actively involved in several local venues, including both a lecture club and an essay club she formed with several friends. She may also have attended the popular free public lectures at the newly opened Rhode Island Women's Club, where authors including Elizabeth Stuart Phelps came to speak on literary matters. Charlotte did eventually read several of Phelps's novels, including two that dramatize the conflict between marriage and career for women: *The Story of Avis* and *Dr. Zay*. On different occasions, she heard both her father and her Uncle Edward lecture. She made frequent use of her library card at the newly opened Providence Public Library and also visited both the local Atheneum and the Brown college library.[17]

In her late teens, Charlotte launched a course of moral instruction, attempting to rid herself of what she considered a "flaccidity of will." She undertook a series of "exercises in which small and purely arbitrary decisions were sharply carried out"—for example, she would tell herself that she would "get out of bed at thirteen minutes to seven." After mastering the method, she used it to develop traits she found lacking in herself, including thoughtfulness, tact, and honesty, determining like a young Benjamin Franklin to practice each virtue until it became a habit. She prided herself on having "undertaken to develop better character and succeeded."[18]

By living deliberately, she whipped her formerly flabby character into shape, but the repression and self-policing required for this transformation exacted its own penalties. Ironically, Charlotte voluntarily sought through her program to instill her mother's precept of stoic self-denial. She now resolved to ward off the disappointment generated by her mother's refusing her pleasurable activities by denying herself everything in advance. The aim of her self-improvement program was to "gradually but relentlessly eliminate" all "small personal preferences."

Charlotte's reflections on this program reveal her ambivalence. "There is a distinct pleasure in self-control," she would later claim, "something like that of mastering a horse and riding it." She wondered, however, if her "'numbness' of sensation even to love and joy, [was] not due to [her] rigid training in voluntary numbness toward pain. Where one has spent years in denying a sensation . . . carefully withdrawing all consciousness from the affected part and pursuing other business, it might very naturally affect one's power to feel anything."[19] When it came to emotional repression, Charlotte suspected that she had succeeded only too well.

Frederic remained an influence from afar. With her father's help, she secured her first publication: her poem describing a "modest plant," "To D. G. [Dandelion

Greens]," appeared in the *New England Journal of Education* in 1880. At eighteen, Charlotte wrote her father requesting a list of works designed to widen her education, improve her mind, and aid in her quest to improve humanity. After several curt paragraphs hedging his recommendations, Frederic tentatively suggested, "Grote's Greece and the Mommsen's Rome . . . Hildreth's United States. . . . And for England, Knight's Popular (*not* Pictorial) History."

The preceding year he had provided a more extensive list, including two books by the anthropologist Edward B. Tylor and two by the anthropologist and entomologist Sir John Lubbock, in addition to every issue of *Popular Science Monthly* she could obtain. Along with her father's other recommendations, this monthly journal—established by Edward L. Youmans, Herbert Spencer's most ardent American enthusiast—helped to teach Charlotte the rudiments of her reform Darwinist beliefs. Although she did not read these works uncritically, Charlotte later maintained that her father's suggested course in reading had taught her "the habit of scientific thinking," "the generalizing mind," and the belief that "[h]umanity is one long unbroken line, or tree, with many fallen branches, but still growing upward," all theories undergirding her personal religion. Her interest in the findings of these leading scientists speaks not only to Darwin's influence on her emergent evolutionary thinking but also to her father's.[20]

During the 1860s and 70s, formerly all-male colleges and universities were opening creaky doors to women, and many independent women's colleges were founded. By 1880, some 40,000 women—a figure representing more than a third of the entire student population—had enrolled in institutions of higher learning. Many of Charlotte's associates in the progressive, socialist, and woman's movements graduated from these institutions in an era that combined increased opportunity with residual misogyny. As M. Carey Thomas, president of Bryn Mawr, recalled in a 1906 address to the National American Woman's Suffrage Association (NAWSA), "I was born with a desire to go to college. . . . It seems to me, in looking backwards, as if the world had been born of persons born to prevent me. . . . My own experience was the experience of hundreds of other women."[21]

In Charlotte's case, both her parents, Frederic especially, supported her desire for further schooling. Prevailed upon by both Charlotte and a family friend who recognized the girl's talents, Mary finally relinquished. She pledged not to "badger" her daughter any longer and gave Charlotte her "*full* and *free* consent" to enter the inaugural class at the new Rhode Island School of Design (RISD). The nation's centennial fervor gave birth to a number of institutions, including this Providence art school, established in 1877 by the city's Women's Commission with surplus funds from Philadelphia's Centennial Exhibition.

Since the 1850s, several attempts had been made to open such a school in Rhode Island's capital, but each had been thwarted by lack of funding. Finally, in the wake of the nation's centennial, the local Women's Commission funded and founded the school and appointed twelve trustees, four of whom were women. RISD opened on October 7, 1878, with sixty-one day students and seventy-nine evening students, Charlotte registering as one of the former.[22] She attended RISD through May 1879 and received in early November a testimonial from the head-master affirming her credentials as an art instructor, an occupation already earn-ing Charlotte necessary funds.

Since her mid-teens, Charlotte had tried her hand at several jobs, including teacher, tutor, and, briefly, cashier; she even assisted in a marble works company. She also painted and sold floral stationery, sewed curtains, and remodeled dresses for friends. While talented, Charlotte never intended to pursue an artistic career, discounting art's lasting contribution to the world. But her skills paid some bills. Mary and Charlotte had to count every penny: Charlotte suffered through one winter mostly barefoot because they could not afford to buy her new shoes.[23]

In the fall of 1880, she began a profitable liaison with the Kendall Soap Com-pany via her kissing cousin Robert Brown, who would become the company's bookkeeper. Robert enlisted Charlotte's help in manufacturing small advertising cards for Kendall's laundry product, Soapine. He designed the cards and she drew them, netting "Perkins & Co. Designers" some $370; since the average income in 1880 only slightly exceeded $300 per capita, this was a pretty impressive return for a sideline. Charlotte continued to produce these cards until shortly before her marriage in 1884.[24]

At her father's prompting, she enrolled for three years in the early 1880s in the Society to Encourage Studies at Home (or as Frederic Perkins termed it, the "society-for-directing-the-studies-of-people-ever-so-far-off"). The Society was founded in 1873 by Anna Ticknor in Boston, to promote continued educational opportunities for women of all classes. Over its twenty-four years of operation, more than 10,000 students signed up for its correspondence courses. Charlotte studied ancient history, the ancient Hebrews, and Egypt. In addition to reading assigned works, students were encouraged to take "memory notes" to help im-prove retention. The students met annually at Ticknor's home on Boston's Beacon Hill, where Charlotte once enjoyed hearing the poet and "autocrat of the break-fast table" Oliver Wendell Holmes, Sr., lecture.[25]

Charlotte's sporadic education left her perpetually uneasy in the presence of college alumnae, which helps to explain why she never felt fully at home in many of the social movements typically led by her college-educated and more affluent peers. She sought their recognition of her native intelligence and beamed whenever she received a "real warm friendly *equal* welcome from genuinely learned women." But she also claimed to doubt the long-term benefits of higher education. "Minds are not vats to be filled eternally with more and ever more supplies," she argued. "It is *use,* large free, sufficient use that the mind requires. . . . Our college girls have vast supplies of knowledge; how can they use it in the home?"[26] What good was wasted knowledge? What good was a college education if all a graduate did afterward was cook and clean? Better to *use* one's mind, however educated, than to permit it to gather dust within the stultifying confines of the home.

~

Learn to be sincere; have real feelings and express them honestly.
"Personal Problems," 1909[27]

Charlotte's attempts to improve her mind were matched by her strenuous efforts to train her body. In conjoining the two regimens, she took a page out of *How to Do It* (1871), her Uncle Edward Everett Hale's popular guidebook for the young, culled from essays he had published in *Our Young Folks* and the *Youth's Companion.* Hale used two metaphors to describe his pedagogical understanding of life: "Life is given to us that we may learn how to live. That is what it is for. We are here in a great boarding-school, where we are being trained in the use of our bodies and our minds, so that in another world we may know how to use other bodies and minds with other faculties. Or, if you please, life is a gymnasium." Charlotte concurred and took the latter trope literally as she devoted herself to physical culture. Studying physiology and hygiene, she "adopted 'reform dress,' cold daily sponge bath, open window at night, gymnastics, etc; abjuring corsets, tea, coffee, late hours and all other known evils."[28]

Sometime around her fourteenth year, Charlotte had heard Dr. Mary Studley lecture at her school and vowed subsequently to follow her advice. In her *What Our Girls Ought to Know,* Studley preaches a gospel of temperance, activity, and cleanliness and encourages her readers to take charge of their health and to learn about their bodies so that they could assume the shape and vigor God intended. Equating beauty with both right feeling and health and depicting health as a matter of "*self-control,*" she also urges those of feeble stock to act as "heroines" and refrain from reproducing.[29] Charlotte learned these lessons at an early age and taught them herself at every opportunity.

At eighteen, after several years of applying Dr. Studley's teachings, Charlotte recorded her weight (roughly 120 pounds, though it could drop as low as the low 110s) and height (5 feet 6-1/2 inches with her shoes on), and then proceeded to evaluate her "[l]ooks, not bad. At times handsome. At others decidedly homely. Health, Perfect. Strength amazing. Character——————. Ah! Gradually outgrowing laziness. Possessing great power over my self. *Not* sentimental. Rather sober and bleak as a general thing." In her pursuit of perfect health and impressive strength, she faithfully followed "[f]ive little rules . . . : 'Good air and plenty of it, good exercise and plenty of it, good food and plenty of it, good sleep and plenty of it, good clothing and as little as possible.'"[30]

Charlotte described her regimen to her brother but warned against his concluding that she was "an incipient Aunt Catherine [*sic*] Beecher. . . ." In her 1856 *Physiology and Calisthenics for Schools and Families*, Beecher links morality to health, arguing for the necessity of regenerating mind, soul, *and* body together. Approvingly citing both the Greeks and the Swedes, she scolds Americans for neglecting bodily health and recommends a system of calisthenics designed to revitalize the nation and check its pandemic of feebleness and disease. She outlines a readable "*short, easy,* and *comprehensive course* of physiology and hygiene" designed for both genders and all ages and classes, replete with illustrations, instructions, and a list of purported benefits.[31]

Charlotte never mentions reading her great-aunt's treatise. She considered William Blaikie's 1879 *How to Get Strong and Stay So* (which she purchased the year it appeared) her fitness bible. Blaikie has been identified as the dean of American physical education during the 1880s. His upbeat book assures readers of their power to make themselves physically well or ill and touts the value and blessing of health. He asks his female readers, "Is there any sphere in woman's life where it will not stand her in good stead, and render her far more efficient at whatever she is called on to do—as daughter, sister, wife or mother, teacher or friend? Nor is the benefit limited even to her own lifetime, but her posterity are blessed by it as well."[32] This last point echoes Dr. Studley's concern regarding future generations and likely reinforced Charlotte's own emerging eugenic convictions.

Blaikie encourages women to spend plenty of time outdoors, to educate their bodies, their minds, and their characters, to walk and run with grace, to develop an erect posture, and to pursue a course of vigorous, muscular daily exercises. Approvingly citing a doctor whom Charlotte would come to distrust, Blaikie enumerates the benefits of regular exercise for women and adds, "Dr. [S. Weir] Mitchell says it is the very thing also to quiet the excited nerves and brain." Blaikie devotes the latter third of his book to spelling out specific exercises for all parts of the body, including the hands; his section on "Daily Exercises for Women" encourages them to walk briskly for an hour daily along with occasional 5- to 6-mile walks, run a mile in 7 minutes without touching a heel to the ground, and perform a routine involving 2-pound dumbbells and twenty-five repetitions of five moves. Charlotte's diary entries from this time note the diligence with which she followed Blaikie's regimen.[33]

Blaikie was capitalizing on a physical culture movement emergent in the early 1800s and intensifying as millennial fervor intermingled with xenophobic fears of Anglo-Saxon "race suicide" at the century's turn. Gymnasiums opened across the country, a phenomenon Blaikie acknowledges in his chapter "What a Gymnasium Might Be and Do." In Providence, Dr. J. P. Brooks—the author of the 1880 *Exercise Cure: The Butler Health Lift, What It Is and What It Can Do*—sponsored several local gyms. With Charlotte's encouragement, Brooks started what Charlotte envisioned as "a class in the higher gymnastics for young ladies. Just a few of us, a nice set and a hall with 'facilities' where we could wear abbreviated garments and elevate the massive dumb bell at our leisure." Charlotte recruited her friends until she had enough girls signed on to overcome Brooks's initial resistance. They held their classes in a gym that had opened in 1866 as an arena for the Swedish Movement Cure. Thanks to Charlotte's efforts and the backing of leading Providence families, in 1882 it became known as the "Sanitary Gymnasium for Ladies and Children."[34]

Charlotte had known Brooks since at least 1875, when she took calisthenics classes from him in her last year of secondary education. Her role as class founder and leader garnered her a free gym membership, which she made regular use of until she married. The class routine included running, kicking, jumping, climbing, vaulting, performing handstands, and traversing the traveling rings, the last Charlotte's personal favorite. She was able to cross the five rings and back again four times in a row, a feat she repeated to the astonishment of observers in her sixty-fifth year. Agile older women feature prominently in her fiction, including the pole-vaulting Mother Gordins in "Making a Change." While a sporadic exerciser in her adulthood, in the months before she married a second time, Charlotte resumed her series of evening gymnastics, stripping down to the buff and performing high kicks, toe-touches, leg circles, and other gymnastic feats.[35]

In the spring of 1882, Charlotte had a rather serious accident, falling straddle-legged onto the back of a bevel-edged chair while helping a friend set a clock. Despite some residual injury, a bruise, and "a profusely bleeding cut" located "in the worst place you can imagine," she was back to the gym in a week. For Charlotte, the gym represented a place to exercise and to socialize, a chance for young women of like minds and "higher aspirations" to get to know one another.

It also served as a springboard for her future writing career: Charlotte published her first piece of nonfiction on "The Providence Ladies Gymnasium" in the *Providence Daily Journal.* In this short article, she promotes the gym, describes the facilities, and mentions its seventy-one regular attendees. She also argues for the established benefits of "the laws of health" for both sexes and identifies, as did both Blaikie and Catharine Beecher before her, beauty's foundation in "harmonious physical development."[36] During these years, Charlotte formulated an equation between health and beauty she would apply to both the individual and the social body, for good or for ill.

~

> And bye & bye if we both persist in scorning matrimony, what joy to be, besides perfectly happy ourselves, a burning and a shining light to all our neighbors, a place where all delightful people congregate, a house wherein young and guileless aspirants for literary or various fame shall believe and tremble. Houp la! We'll be happy anyway.
> Letter to Martha Luther, July 4, 1881[37]

By the time she turned twenty-one, Charlotte exulted in glorious health and considered herself "as well as a fish, as busy as a bee, as strong as a horse, as proud as a peacock, as happy as a clam." Satisfied with herself, she was even more satisfied with Martha Luther. Of all her Providence girlfriends, Martha earned her deepest love and learned her deepest secrets. After meeting early in 1879, the two girls quickly became intimate, exchanging confidences, embraces, and vows of mutual affection. They enjoyed writing verse and playing games together—indeed, the two devised Charlotte's beloved "one-word game," wherein each player takes a turn supplying a word as a farcical narrative evolves. Up until her final months of life, even when so riddled with cancer she could barely speak, Charlotte found this pastime amusing and relaxing, a "massage to the brain."[38]

Soon after meeting Martha, Charlotte informed her friend that she had "an intermittently affectionate nature, should love her very much for a time, then apparently stop, and then return with unimpaired affection." Yet her affection for Martha only intensified with each passing day. By October 1879, Charlotte confided to her diary, "I love the pussy." "Pussy" was one of her favorite terms of endearment for Martha; other pet names included "chicken," "kitten," "little girl," and "gay frisker." Her frequent recourse to "baby talk" in her missives to "Marfa" indicates a level of regression, as if she sought from this new friend the love she felt had been denied her as a child. Martha's letters to Charlotte have not survived, but Charlotte's references to their contents suggest Martha returned Charlotte's feelings, only not as intensely.[39]

Charlotte saw her relationship with Martha as a means to withstand the world's and especially Mary's scorn for her independent choices. Once, after being chastised for her ambitions by her mother and two aunts, she told Martha, "I, myself, am as undisturbed as the moon under clouds—I *know* I am right, defy the world, and in all my lofty isolation am conscious of a human love and tenderness always mine while you live."[40] Charlotte believed a future with Martha in it would allow her to reconcile what for many women of her background were the irreconcilable options of love and work.

Martha made Charlotte feel both loved and invincible, a heady combination. By July 1881, Charlotte was openly confessing her passion for Martha, referring to her as "My little girl! Who lives in my heart, and gives me what no one else in the world ever knows I want!" A few weeks later, she marveled, "It seems improbable to me that two souls *could* be so perfectly matched as ours seem now." Elsewhere, she gushed, "O my little love! I'd like to wind all round and round you and let you feel my heart." She gave Martha several poems declaring her feelings, including a Valentine's Day verse professing "I love you much!"[41]

Who was Martha that Charlotte singled her out as a possible life mate? We know she shared Charlotte's literary aspirations, producing her own newspaper while in Providence and later writing textbooks and other educational materials—work that took her abroad to such locations as Manila and Okinawa—as well as short stories, articles, and plays. She married Charles A. Lane in October 1882 and moved with him to Hingham, Massachusetts, where she raised two children, lived most of her life, and died in 1948. Her husband died much earlier, in 1894, of Bright's disease, a kidney disorder that had killed Emily Dickinson eight years previously.[42]

Charlotte's future husband, Charles Walter Stetson, described Martha as a "sweet little body," full of "energy" and "*spunk*." In her own "Memories" and in a perfunctory diary she kept from 1881 to 1886, Martha itemized her personal flaws, including "carelessness," "idleness," an "exacting disposition," and a "selfish disregard of others unless I happen to care for them especially." She subsequently resolved to be more contentedly domestic and, she vowed, to "[k]eep my blues to myself." (Charlotte had direly predicted Martha's marital "blues" and would find them contagious: after one of her sporadic visits to Hingham, she reflected, "I always get blue at Martha's. Hers is a close range life. . . . It smothers me." If Martha's "blues" predated her marriage, then she and Charlotte shared a tendency to brood that may have further cemented their bond.)[43]

Martha was neither the first nor the last woman Charlotte loved. In her youth, Charlotte had developed passionate crushes on other girls, beginning with her schoolmate Etta Taylor and continuing on to Harriet White, the daughter of the psychic Mrs. Stevens from the family's cooperative housekeeping days. In her autobiography, Charlotte identified Martha Luther as "immeasurably the dearest" of these friendships. But she hastened, from the pathologizing perspective of the postwar period, to qualify her affection by insisting, "This was love, but not sex" with "no Freudian taint."

Yet while the relationship was ongoing, she knew the impression her outpourings might create and assumed many would find their intense attachment objectionable. She ended one of her epistles by cautioning Martha, "What horrid stuff these letters would be for the Philistines! Lock 'em up, and some time we'll have a grand cremation." This letter, as Gill Frank has argued, suggests that Charlotte perceived the relationship at the time as both intense and socially aberrant.[44]

Passionate words do not, of course, necessarily indicate passionate deeds. During the 1800s, well up until its last decade, intimate "romantic friendships" between young middle-class women were common, at times cemented in a shared ambition to improve a world they believed men had tarnished. These same-sex relationships, "or smashes" as they were often called, were widely acknowledged and generally indulged, perceived as dress rehearsals for marriage. The prevailing ideology of separate spheres meant that middle-class women typically spent most of their time in the company of other women, developing bonds that could surpass their love of men. These women often slept in the same bed, kissed, petted, and confessed undying love, all with cultural sanction.

During the Victorian era, the historian Carroll Smith-Rosenberg has suggested, the affection these women experienced ranged along a continuum of emotions as opposed to our starkly dichotomous segregation of relationships into either platonic or sexual; nor in this era did sexual orientation automatically confer identity. (Sex was perceived as an activity, something people did; who they did it with had not yet come to define who they were.) In Charlotte's day, women began combining elements of what Martha Vicinus terms "romantic friendship" and "Sapphic sexuality" into "something new—a personal identity based upon a sexualized, or at least recognizably eroticized, relationship with another women." Some of these women acted on their sexual attraction, others sought to channel it into something "higher," but either way, "mutual recognition of passion" took precedence over "physical consummation" when it came to defining the nature of the relationship.[45]

Charlotte and Martha shared a deep emotional bond, but the extent of their physical involvement remains unclear. The two young women enjoyed blissful days together: on May 14, 1881, for instance, Martha and Charlotte passed the morning shopping for bracelets to symbolize their "bond of union." Later that same day, as Charlotte recalled in her diary, "Martha comes surreptitious over

P.M., I let her in unseen, she prowls up to my room, and we spend the afternoon in tranquil bliss." Thanks to Martha, Charlotte felt deeply loved for the first time in her life. In mid-August, she put her feelings in words:

> I think it highly probable (ahem!) that you love me however I squirm, love the steady core around which I so variously revolve, love me and will love me—Why in the name of heaven have we so confounded love with passion that it sounds to our century-tutored ears either wicked or absurd to name it between women? It is no longer friendship between us, it is love.[46]

Here Charlotte distinguishes love from passion, the latter an apparent euphemism for sex. But the bulk of her private papers attest that such distinctions could rarely be so easily drawn.

Charlotte portrays same-sex relationships positively in many of her short stories, including the 1912 "Lost Women," which describes two girls as "just wrapped up in each other, the way girls are, only there seemed to be more to it. To hear either of them tell, it was one of those very special friendships that mean more than anything else on earth—except love. Sometimes I think they are about as good as love—but I don't know." Likewise, in her 1912 story "A Cleared Path," one woman confesses to another that she cares for yet another woman so much "I *think* I'd love her *if she wasn't a woman*," a remark her friend complacently countenances.

In her influential treatise *Women and Economics*, Charlotte puts an evolutionary spin on these intimate female friendships and concludes, "The force which draws friends together is a higher one than that which draws the sexes together,—higher in the sense of belonging to a later race-development. 'Passing the love of women' is no unmeaning phrase."[47] Here, she uses science to normalize same-sex attachments, deeming them evolved rather than degenerate. She simultaneously demonstrates her enduring tendency to idealize and render abstract experiences she understood at the time to be both concrete and complicated.

Martha's love gave Charlotte the strength to pursue a purpose-filled life outside of marriage. She proclaimed to Martha,

> I am really getting glad not to marry. For the mother side of me is strong enough to make an interminable war between plain duties & irrepressible instincts, I should rage as I do now at confinement and steady work, and spend all my force in pushing two way [*sic*] without getting anywhere. I be spiled [*sic*] like my pa most likely.
> Whereas if I let that business alone, and go on in my own way; what I gain in individual strength and development of personal power of character, *myself as a self,* you know, not merely as a woman, or that useful animal a wife and mother, will I think make up, and more than make up in usefulness and effect, for the other happiness that part of me would so enjoy.

Charlotte understood her ideal self as distinct from her prescribed gender role and aimed to divest herself of the feminine trappings restricting the realization of that ideal. In a later formulation for Houghton's edification, Charlotte suggests she waged her parents' struggle internally: " . . . by nature and experience I am unfit for the pure sweet tender joys of personal union—of home life. I knew it when I was a mere girl—recognized the hopeless incongruity of my mother and father in me—and renounced the one to make the other strong."[48] Repudiating her feminine, maternal side, she relegates woman to the domestic sphere—an allocation whose necessary logic she elsewhere disputes.

Charlotte persisted in viewing Martha as her ideal mate even as Martha began to express reservations. "As for you I could spend hours in cuddling if I had you here," Charlotte wrote Martha during the summer of 1881. "I can see all your manifold little dearnesses, and 'I'd be willing to bet five cents, if I was in the habit of betting' that you will make up to me for husband and children and all that I shall miss." The psychologist Erik Erikson has defined adolescence as an effort to forge an identity "by projecting one's diffused ego image on another and by seeing it thus reflected and gradually clarified." Given the friendship's outcome, Charlotte may have too eagerly projected onto Martha her own emerging desire for meaningful work and her increasing antipathy to the idea of marriage. When friends speculated that Charlotte might never marry, she responded, "Peut-être pas," recording the phrase twice in her diary on two separate days, underscoring its significance for her.[49]

By August, Martha had met the man she would eventually marry and so began openly resisting Charlotte's plans, confessing she would find such a life lonely. Fearful that she might lose her "little girl" for good, Charlotte assured Martha that she did not expect her to make her own sacrifices. She fantasized a happy ending for them both (though not for Martha's beau): "You are to marry, of course, you would never be satisfied if you didn't, and after a certain period of unmerited happiness, his, your young man is to drop off, die somehow, and lo! I will be all in all! Now isn't that a charming plan?"[50]

More seriously, she presented the route Martha was forsaking as the nobler path: "I think I may be a help to you, and you are my greatest comfort now and ever, a loving sister soul, who will see the need of my ascending, and always have a nest for me when I come down." Here Charlotte prophesies an eagle's flight for herself, undertaken with the knowledge that a domesticated Martha would offer her a feathered nest upon landing.

In an effort to come to terms with their differences, Charlotte made her identification with putatively masculine desires and ambitions explicit. She instructed Martha, "Understand once and for all that you are my one stay and support,

—my other self, who makes up to me with tenfold sweetness for the barren places in my own uneven nature. If I can return it in any way, in virile force, or anything which I have & you haven't, so much happier I. . . ." A friendship forged through a common desire and purpose Charlotte now recasts as complementary, wherein she represents the "virile force" and Martha the "sweet," fertile womanly counterpart. The signature Charlotte appends to one August 1881 letter foregrounds this distinction: "Yours in a *calm ordinary wellbehaved friendly* (not intimate) *Masculine*! way, Charlotte A. Perkins."[51]

Faced with the possibility of going it alone, Charlotte astutely identifies her challenges: among them, her incompatibility with a mother who nonetheless depended on her, her resistance to a conventional life, her thirst for intellectual stimulation, her Beecher-derived sense of calling, and her resolution to forsake her "half-developed functional womanhood, and take the broad road of individuality apart from sex." She subsequently declared to Martha: "Child you have no idea of how much bigger I feel. *I have decided.* I'm *not* domestic and don't want to be." Her education in conventional femininity had managed to stifle the ambition she now resolved cautiously to revive, "adding all his prisoned force to mine," while simultaneously smothering her feelings.

Charlotte envisioned a war within herself between the heart and the mind, the sex and the individual, the feminine and the masculine, and she determined to assist the conventionally masculine forces to victory. Depicting her heart (filled by Martha) as fundamentally at odds with her head (filled with thoughts of work and purpose), she dealt with Martha's looming defection by vowing to drop "the heart business once and for all, it never was as strong as my head and the sooner I squelch it altogether the more firmly shall I progress."[52] She aspired to free herself from affairs of the heart, the better to break through gendered constraints, the better to fulfill her human potential. In contrast to her Great-Aunt Harriet Beecher Stowe and other sentimentalists, the heart represented for her not a force through which the world could be moved but the very "obstacle" she needed to walk directly through, as if it "was n't there."[53]

Martha's imminent desertion only strengthened Charlotte's investment in work, or so she told Martha:

> I have boiled it all down . . . into the one word *Work*! And "work!" I say when the bent head turns and the tired eyes stray out of the window; "Work"! when my senses fail and the unconscious hand drops the colorfilled brush right on the paper,— "Work!" when I drowsily open my eyes after 6 hours sleep and would give the world for more, and "*Work*!" this minute when I want to talk for hours to my little love, and must go and wash dishes *and* so forth. Good bye chick! I shan't stop even for you if you don't want to go.[54]

Martha did not want to go, and, true to her word, Charlotte did not stop, though she did stumble for a while on her own.

Charlotte's bravado crumbled once Martha confirmed she had indeed—as Charlotte saw it—chosen another over her. Soon after Martha returned to Providence in mid-September, Charlotte called upon her only to be rebuffed. "Pleasant," she confided sarcastically to her diary, "to ring at the door where you've always been greeted with gladness; to be met by the smile that you value all others above—to see that smile flicker and vanish and change into sadness because she was met by *your* presence instead of her love!" Her best counter-tactics had proven futile. Charlotte tearfully resigned herself to the news of the couple's engagement, announced at the beginning of November 1881.[55]

Swinging wildly between utter despair one day and self-proclaimed victory over grief the next, Charlotte turned to other friends for consolation. Sam Simmons and his brother Jim had been frequent visitors at the Perkins home, where they had enjoyed many conversations and games of whist. For a time, Charlotte and Martha had considered the brothers potential beaus. Charlotte now turned to Sam for solace, sending him emotional missives that afforded her the "only outlet for thoughts and feelings which crowd painfully." In one letter, she compares herself to "one who has safely passed through a serious amputation." In yet another letter, she revives this amputation metaphor and suggests that the loss of "the largest happiness" she had ever known has left her with "a great empty place with a small pain in the middle."[56] This time, her metaphor suggests that losing Martha has cost Charlotte her very heart.

A similar image informs a lugubrious poem she wrote about Martha's defection and which she read aloud in early December to the weeping defector:

. . . "My little girl!" *My* little girl! No more,
Never again in all this weary world
Can I with clinging arms & kisses soft
Call you "my little girl!". . .

"Sweetheart!" You *were* my sweetheart. I am none,
To any man, and I had none but you.
O sweet! You filled my life; you gave me all
Of tenderness, consideration, trust,
Confiding love, respect, regard, reproof,
And all the thousand thousand little things
With which love glorifies the hardest life.

Think dearest, while you yet can feel the touch
Of hands that once could soothe your deepest pain;

Think of those days when we could hardly dare
Be seen abroad together lest our eyes
Should speak too loud.** There is no danger now. . . .

Why sweet, I held your heart
In that large empty space where mine was not.
And you? You must have had mine in your hands,
Keeping it warm until another came
To fill the place, and mine was given back. . . . [57]

Here Charlotte plays the faithful lover to the faithless one, reversing the gender roles she previously ascribed to the couple and implicitly declaring it her turn to play the "little girl," her turn to possess a heart while Martha heartlessly turned away.

Martha's loss made as great an impact on Charlotte's development as did the friendship itself. It inspired her to poetry once again when she sought to explain Martha's importance to the man she would subsequently marry:

Do you think it is nothing to lose a friend
    More dear than words can tell; . . .
Do you think it nothing to go straight on
    When a love like that was dead?

Charlotte floundered for a while but managed to "go straight on" by recalling her intent to undertake purposeful work. That winter she began sitting for local artist Sydney Burleigh for his portrait of a "Dutch Girl in Despair"—a theme well-suited to her mood—and planning a Martha-less life that would instead be work-filled.[58]

Surrounded by relatively unsympathetic friends and a family puzzled over the extent of her grief, Charlotte concocted her own cure for "Loneliness and Grief," vowing to live for others as both teacher and guide and "to crush all personal sorrow and drop the whole ground of self-interest forever." She kept this cure tucked in her "looking-glass to see every day and gather strength from."[59] By the end of the year, she had wrestled her grief into a manageable size and, though exhausted, could declare herself "not much hurt by the work & pain of the past two months, & [so] begin to see light again."

Taking stock at the end of the year, Charlotte determined in 1882 to "live and work" in order to alleviate fatigue and heartache, representing here as a solution the very pairing she presented as a weary grind in her poem "In Duty Bound." She described the past year as quiet and difficult, but also, more positively, as a

year of surprising growth. A year internally dedicated to "discoveries and improvements.["] A year in which I knew the sweetness of a perfect friendship, and have lost it forever. A year of marked advance in many ways, and with nothing conspicuous to regret. . . . Most of all I have learned what pain is. Have learned the need of human sympathy by the unfilled want of it. . . . This year I attained my majority—may I never loose [*sic*] it![60]

Decades later, Charlotte recalled her jubilation upon crossing this momentous threshold: "No manumitted slave, no escaped prisoner, ever felt a keener surge of joy and pride, of thrilling new-sensed power. It was like the up-rush of a volcano; the rising of some world-sweeping tide."

At twenty-one, Charlotte looked forward to an increasingly independent and meaningful life. She staged minor autonomous rebellions—staying up all night, sleeping on the floor, leaving the house without informing Mary of her destination—in preparation for the major insurrection she had been planning all along.

Coming home late and alone that winter, she often paused in an adjacent vacant lot to clamber on top of a boulder and "exult in the white glittering silence, deeply commiserating all those timid women who never know the wonder and beauty of being alone at night under the stars."[61] She resolved never to be timid, to be alone but not lonely, to dedicate her life to service. On the inside cover of her 1882 journal, she declared "work" her "watchword" for the year and simultaneously denounced "love and happiness" with an emphatic "NO!" Work would be her surrogate for Martha and for love. Or so she thought until, only ten days later, she met Charles Walter Stetson.

3 "I Am Not the Combining Sort"
(1882–1884)

Love that can wound love, for its higher need;
Love that can leave love though the heart may bleed;
Love that can lose love; family, and friend;
Yet steadfastly live, loving, to the end.
                              "Heroism," 1898[1]

Charlotte's poetic premise that it is heroic to "live, loving" after having lost love required extending love's reach beyond a single cherished person to the larger cherished world. Committing to this extension took time, however. Martha's marriage left her sorely tempted to prove that she, too, could love and be loved by another. Charlotte enjoyed bragging to the new Mrs. Lane of "a man in Providence whom I would not stay away from for an extra minute even to see you! Now doesn't that show some change," she asked Martha, "some advance in my power of loving since I saw you last? I tell you dear there is no question now except one of time and means. Not even to you can I show my heart now, but you know it well from your own. Happy? Happy beyond words. You know, little girl, you know."[2] If she could not have Martha, she could at least claim to have what Martha had.

Problems at home heightened Charlotte's eagerness to find a new one. "The young woman at home finds her growing individuality an increasing disadvantage,"

Charlotte later acknowledged in *The Home*, "and many times makes a too hasty marriage because she is not happy at home. . . ."[3] If she refused to race down the aisle herself, it was because both man and matrimony gave her pause. The status of wife and the prospects of both children and economic dependence made Charlotte especially wary about marrying. For two long years, she agonized over what seemed to her a necessary choice between marriage and career, rarely permitting herself to hope that with Walter the two paths could ever converge.

The injustice of the double standard increased her hesitation. As she remarked in a 1903 essay, "A happy marriage—for a man, means a wife who gives him all he wants from a wife—but involves also a happy working life outside. Let him sit down in his happy marriage and make an exclusive occupation of it for eighteen hours a day, and its happiness would wear thin ere long." Her simmering resentment of this imbalance led her to conclude on the eve of her wedding, "The whole thing seems to me far different from what it is to most women. Instead of being a goal—a duty—a hope, a long expected fate, a bewildering delight; it is a concession, a digression. . . . I look through it, beyond it, over it. . . . It fills my mind much; but plans for teaching and writing, for studying *living* and helping, are most prominent and active."[4] Because she located these fulfilling activities *outside* of marriage, Charlotte believed she could elude the double standard only by eluding the institution itself.

In *What Our Girls Ought to Know*, Charlotte's well-thumbed guidebook, Dr. Mary Studley insists that marriage should be "the ultimate end and aim of every life." Nevertheless, she cautions girls to take the decision to wed extremely seriously, since it could mean the difference between a joyful and a woeful life. Even the "most forlorn 'old maid,'" Studley warns, appears happy next to the girl who had "rushed headlong into the matrimonial flame and been singed for life." Neither hasty nor inconsiderate in deciding to marry, Charlotte would nonetheless find herself thus "singed." She followed Studley's rule for selecting a mate—"*The best, or none!*"—choosing her lover from among "the best." The problem was, the alternative—"none!"—continued to entice.[5]

~

> If I were out and free, if I had my home to live in and my work to lean on, if I knew as I then should just what I was losing, (I *dare* not count the *gains!*) It would be much easier.
> Letter to Charles Walter Stetson,
> February 20, 1883[6]

On Wednesday, January 11, 1882, Charlotte attended Charles Walter Stetson's lecture on etching at the local art club. She found the event "*Rather* a waste of time." She objected to the subject, not the speaker: with their mutual friend Sidney Putnam, she visited Stetson's studio the following day and decided she liked both the artist and his work. She even wrote a poem to accompany his painting *The Suicide's Burial,* essentially providing the lyrics for Stetson's lugubrious melody.

The painter took note of Charlotte's visit in his diary that evening and declared himself charmed:

> She is an original: eccentric because unconventional, and well versed in almost everything, I guess! . . . She has a form like a young Greek & a face also resembling a cameo. She is an athlete—strong, vivacious, with plenty of bounding blood. She is an indefatigable worker—but I shall see some of her. . . . She is moral, intellectual and beautiful!
> She said frankly, "Mr. Stetson, I must know you better!". . . I think that I shall like her much. . . . [7]

Like her much he did. Less than two weeks after meeting Charlotte, he told her, "were you made a man you were not much different from Charles Stetson." (He usually went by "Walter" but probably used "Charles" here to emphasize that the similarities extended to their names.) Walter described Charlotte's life in a diary entry as "very sad and strangely like my own," observing, "She has suffered similar things; thought like things and conquered herself & grown in the same way." Both were ambitious, poor, serious, artistic, idealistic, lonely, and love-starved. As Charlotte saw it, they both were "unflinchingly devoted to work" and lovers "of beauty and poetry and high ideals."[8] Their differences were equally marked, but their initial attraction sprung from a profound sense of mutual recognition.

In the early 1880s, the self-taught Stetson was still struggling to make a name for himself in the art world. He did not attend his first one-man show in November 1881 because he could not afford to buy himself a proper suit of clothes. In many ways, he personified the starving artist: a slight, striking man, standing 5 feet 8 inches, with loosely curling blonde hair and penetrating blue eyes, Walter was thought to resemble the poet Keats. His disposition matched his looks: "What is an artist but a lover?" he once romantically surmised. "And what am I but both?"[9]

Born March 25, 1858, in Tiverton, Four Corners, Rhode Island, Walter was considerably younger than Joshua and Rebecca Steere Stetson's two daughters. Like Charlotte, he led an impoverished and itinerant childhood: his father was a Free Baptist minister who was called from church to church. In addition to preaching, Joshua Stetson manufactured and distributed proprietary medicines originally developed to heal his invalid wife. Walter viewed his father as a "man of

Formal portrait of Charlotte's first husband, Charles Walter Stetson, February 1880. Courtesy of the Schlesinger Library, Radcliffe Institute for Advanced Study, Harvard University.

eminently good parts who accomplished nothing great because of his ideality and fear of hurting someone" and worried that his own epithet might someday read, "Like father, like son."[10]

By the time the Stetsons moved to Providence around 1869, Walter had already demonstrated artistic talent. At sixteen, he had determined to become a painter. Before his eighteenth birthday, he helped to establish the Providence Art Club, and in his nineteenth year, he started selling his own work. It was difficult to make a living as an artist, however, especially in a business-minded town like Providence, and Walter often lacked money for supplies and models. He never could afford formal training.

Nonetheless, Walter had begun to enjoy a modest success and to attract patrons by the time he met Charlotte. The 1882 Art Club lecture on etchings that Charlotte attended also brought Walter to the attention of Mr. Beriah Wall, leading to a substantial commission. A wealthy couple, the George B. Cressons, sat for paintings and supplied him with friends, contacts, and limited funding. Walter's celebrated sense of color earned him a place in the tonalist or symbolist school of his day.[11]

From the first, Charlotte struck Walter as the ideal woman and lover, his own guiding "bright star." He exulted in her superior mind and flawless physique and anatomized her complex character not two weeks after meeting her: "She is a poetess: a philosopher, and no mean one, and more of a mystic than she guesses. A warm, soft, sensuous nature held in check and overcome by a strong will, a sound intellect & a good moral nature."

Charlotte expressed more ambivalence about Walter. She admired his stoic dedication to his art and his genius, and she admired the way he admired her. Yet she saw herself as "pretty evenly balanced, animal & spiritual" and believed Walter appealed primarily to her animal side. Giving in to him, or "giving up," as she put it, "would mean relinquishment of all my plans." A similar ambivalence surfaces in her comments to friends. She informed one, for instance, that Walter had crowned her a "queen among women" even as she simultaneously questioned whether she was cut out "for that class of work(!)" Her exclamation mark interrogates whether the role of exalted wife qualified as the kind of work she considered essential to living.[12]

During the early weeks of their relationship, Charlotte candidly informed Walter, "I am not the combining sort. I *don't* combine, and I don't want to." She meant by this that she preferred to resist the coupling impulse she believed inspired more traditional young women's dreams. Her dedication to public service led her to conclude that married life could never make her happy. She therefore wrote Walter, "I will give and give and give you *of* myself, but never give myself to you or any man," and signed her letter, "Truly I am in appearance a lady, in nature a woman, but first and always Charlotte A. Perkins."

While in this signature Charlotte prioritizes personal identity, earlier passages in the same letter complicate her hierarchy: the self depicted in her closing lines as preeminent and unyielding is elsewhere represented as a threat. She confesses, for example, that whenever she thrills in Walter's affection, she awakens the slumbering giant she calls her "towering selfhood," and she had devoted the interim between losing Martha and meeting Walter to thinking less of self and more of others. She agrees that selflessness is a virtue, but she believes that she can best attain it (the tenets of conventional femininity notwithstanding) in the public, not the private, sphere.[13]

Torn between the desire for a conventional and an exceptional life, Charlotte continued to send Walter conflicting messages:

> . . . I kneel to you!
>
> You are the first man I have met whom I recognize as an equal; and that is saying a good deal for me.
>
> I would call you grandly superior, but that I am fighting just now against a heart-touched woman's passion of abnegation.
>
> You are the first man I ever saw beside whom I felt humble, the first man I ever saw who *I felt could help me to live.*

Charlotte strokes her lover's ego here while surreptitiously asserting her own. She declares her equality while kneeling supplicant before him. It is as if both the "woman" and "Charlotte A. Perkins" were writing this letter, at consecutive moments. Walter took note of this tendency in his diary: "contrasts seem to rule in her nature. She is independent, but she likes to nestle by my side and depend on me. She is at the head of the Gymnasium, yet she can be as soft & gentle as a weakly woman."[14]

At first, Walter found Charlotte's independent stance noble. Recalling the initial days of their relationship some months later, he observed, "I grasped at her with the instincts of a drowning heart, and—was saved for the time. I loved all that I saw pure in her. She was sweet air for my soul's breathing. She was cleanliness to long for. . . . It was a sort of famished man's cry of thankfulness for bread. My faith in woman began to revive, and my belief in the good of the world." Seventeen days after their first meeting, he openly declared his love. That night, Charlotte wrote in her diary, "I have this day been asked the one question in a womans [*sic*] life, and have refused."[15]

But in truth, she only equivocated, massaging Walter's hopes by agreeing that wife-and-motherhood represented a woman's "great work." She conceded that she felt naturally inclined to fulfill her womanly destiny. Yet she countered honestly that she might perform a greater service as a public servant, and she revealed how tantalizing she found this possibility. The day after her refusal, Charlotte wrote Walter a twelve-page letter affirming the rightness of pursuing her "highest use and happiness" through social service while simultaneously rejoicing that he had "grandly crowned" her with his love. Having successfully withstood the trial of his proposal, she welcomed as "Simply Paradise" further opportunities to test the essential question: "Whether I am most a woman or Charlotte A. Perkins." She remained so convinced she could resist womanly temptation that she portrays herself as a stronger, less persuadable Eve, for whom "Paradise"—here, remaining single—would never be lost.[16]

Two days later, she itemized her many, compelling reasons for refusing to marry in a private document whose title, "An Anchor to Windward," suggests the strength of the gusts blowing her in the other direction. Her list included her overarching love of freedom, her longing for a home all her own and for independence, her desire to perform "the thousand and one helpful works which the world needs," and her resistance to being absorbed by what she refers to as "that extended self—a family."[17] As she understood them, marriage and a family posed graver threats to her integrity than did less conventional choices for women.

Still, a strong physical attraction and even stronger societal pressures tempted Charlotte to marry. "All girls ought to," Charlotte later opines in *The Home*, "unless there is something wrong with them." In her 1904 essay "The Refusal to Marry," she discusses women who, "fully convinced of the need for economic independence, trained in specialized labor and loving it, and keenly aware of the difficulties of married life, both mentionable and unmentionable, have cut the knot by simply refusing to marry." She refuses to idealize this type, noting that such women sacrifice large portions of joy, and she expresses relief that the call to forfeit personal for social happiness remained so rare. The right combination of devotion to social service and depletion in "the force of sex," she allows, might permit a few women to "find joy enough in the full freedom of work to counterbalance their loss." But she declares it a shame for any woman to feel that her "duty to the world" *obligated* her to renounce "what, after all, is necessary to that duty—a fully developed, normal personal life."[18]

Even a "superabundantly human" woman, called to service as Charlotte felt herself to be, could find personal and professional happiness if—and this was a big if—she made the "right marriage." In her twenties, however, Charlotte could claim no personal experience of what a right marriage might look like. Her poem "To Choose" reflects her quandary:

> In youth, hot youth of hungry heart
>   Wild longings and uncertain strife,
> We must foresee the course of years
>   Foresee, forestall regret and tears,
> And choose a mate—for life.

How could a young girl with little experience of life or love be expected to make an informed choice? In the early 1880s, Charlotte had yet to be tested as either worker or wife, leaving it, as she put it, "an open question which life I can work best in." If she chose marriage, there would be no going back. By choosing work and giving it a "fair trial," on the other hand, she might attain the best of both worlds, because marriage would merely be postponed rather than repudiated.[19]

One of Charlotte's favorite parables by Olive Schreiner, "Life's Gifts," teaches this very lesson. Forced to choose between freedom and love, the protagonist wisely pursues freedom and reaps both rewards, whereas the other choice would have entailed sacrificing freedom. Before she even read Schreiner, Charlotte had figured out on her own that giving work a try would allow her to discover what marriage might cost her. For the time being, however, she stood at a crossroads, forced to choose "between living and loving," between serving the world and serving one man. Walter strenuously pointed one way, and she found herself irresistibly drawn to the other. Still, with every hesitant step she took in her preferred direction, she was, she told Walter, "crushing my heart under foot."[20]

Charlotte's indecision persisted throughout their prolonged courtship, explaining why Walter's motto was "Endure!" Whole weeks passed when he could confidently declare, "She has given herself up now to love, and finds pure rapture in it." But these passionate stretches were followed by periods when Charlotte announced to Walter, "my life is not for any *one*, or any *few*, but for as many as I can reach. . . . [M]uch as I love you I love *WORK* better, & I cannot make the two compatible. . . . I am meant to be useful & strong, to help many and do my share in the world's work, but not to be loved."[21] Her mother's lack of sympathy, her father's aloofness, Martha's seeming rejection—all had conspired to convince Charlotte she was unworthy of lasting love.

Charlotte feared that her "unreliable vacillating nature" would destroy her lover, and she declared it sinful to encumber him with so capricious a mate. At other times, however, she blamed Walter for refusing to accept her changeability: "You are like one who would take a fair land on the borders of a shifting river, but insists on it remaining ever fixed." As she aged, Charlotte would stop quarreling with her fluctuations and embrace them as reflecting her conflicting needs for intimacy and purpose: "It's the nature of the beast," she told Houghton in 1899. "I don't *tie*."[22]

~

> I fear I am going to be cruelly, bitterly, utterly, disappointed in what I thought to find in you—with you. It is not your fault, dear, I would not have you a bit different; but the disappointment is in myself.
>
> Letter to Charles Walter Stetson,
> February 8, 1882[23]

In addition to prolix letters—sometimes running to thirty pages—and lengthy conversations, the two lovers exchanged poems expressing their feelings and arguing their respective cases. One poem Charlotte wrote in these early months resentfully rejects Walter's contention that she was putting work first due to selfishness. The untitled, undated poem glorifies marriage and motherhood as "woman's highest-noblest-work" and conveys Charlotte's longing for "the touch of a babies' lips / And the sound of a babies voice." It concludes by expressing her desire

> . . . to turn from my journey wild
> And throw myself like a tired child
> Into arms that are waiting for me.

Charlotte's "uncuddled childhood" likely heightened the attractions of the dependent life Walter was offering her.[24]

Walter vented his own feelings in overwrought and highly stylized verse. He habitually relied on the poetic contractions, convoluted syntax, and archaic pronouns that pepper his poem "To Charlotte":

> . . . By the body and shed blood of Christ our Lord!
>   By the passionate form and pure heart of Love!
>   Would I with this poor script now seek to prove
> That of all women thou art most adored.
> Could my red blood at thy dear feet out poured
>   Assurance greater give, then would I move
> To spill't, e'en, tho' thereby the one reward
> I crave, for sure, I should for this life lose.
> But lack is not, for if thou shouldst refuse
>   To quite believe, so shall my every deed—
> (Through whatso e'er of days my life is long)—
>   And Good-work done, slay any doubts that need
>   The slaying, or stay any wounds that bleed,
> With arguments effectually strong.

Playing Christ to Charlotte's Doubting Thomas, Walter exposed his wounds in every line of anguished poetry. In another poem composed after Charlotte had requested a separation, he casts her as the tormentor to his Christ:

> . . . She came to my uplifting, writ the legend "King"
> To put above my head; pierced then my side,
>   Looked once upon me mournfully, withdrew.

Charlotte countered by invoking a compassionate Christ, anticipating the day when Walter would welcome her back from her "self imposed exile with Christlike forgiveness for the pain" she had inflicted on him.[25] She also remained convinced that her commitment to public service was a god-given and god-sanctioned path, one that would best enable her to "reach the soul's most perfect Paradise." Although equally religious in their conclusions, the two lovers differed over the nature of the sacred.

In several of her poems from this period, Charlotte beseeches God (as well as her implicit audience, Walter) to help her do her "highest and my best in life" and questions whether this ideal might also encompass marriage and children. A poem she wrote on April 1, 1883, conveys her sense of division:

> Can I, who suffer from the wild unrest
>   Of two strong natures claiming each its due,
>   And can not tell the greater of the two;
> Who have two spirits ruling in my breast
> Alternately, and know not which is guest
>   And which the owner true. . . . [26]

Charlotte considered her simultaneous desires for womanly love and world service incompatible and so felt compelled to evict one or the other tenant. Yet her refusal to play favorites, she hints, would leave her forever wondering, post-eviction, if she had mistaken "guest" for "owner true."

Diverting his passion into his brooding poems, diary entries, and letters, Walter brought out a corresponding tendency to the purple in Charlotte. Compared to her uninhibited correspondence with Martha, her letters to "Herodotus"—her initial nickname for Walter—seem stiff and uneven, and she left many unfinished and undelivered. More than once, Charlotte told Walter she wished he were a woman; love with Martha had seemed less complicated. For some time, Martha still held first place in her heart: in February 1882, Charlotte introduced Charles Lane to Walter as "the enemy."[27]

Until Martha married, she essentially triangulated Charlotte and Walter's relationship, but Mary Perkins served as another important mediator. Mary initially made a favorable impression on Walter as "very tender and spiritual minded." His feelings had altered by the end of April 1882, however, as Mary began increasingly to frown on the couple's frequent meetings. Mary informed Charlotte that Walter had no right to show her so much attention unless he intended to marry her.

Mother and daughter argued over Walter's status and his visits; Charlotte attempted to reason with Mary, to no avail. "Now Mrs. Perkins is a gentle woman & means well," Walter observed, "but she does make a perfect hell for Charlotte simply because she does not understand her, and does not sympathize with her ideas as far as she does not understand them." Mary told both that she believed the attraction to be lust-based, and she resented Walter's failure to seek her permission "to *love* Charlotte." Charlotte told Walter that her mother suffered from "little fits of a sort of insanity"; Walter had his own suspicions: "She needs a husband; I think that is the main cause of her disorder."[28]

Charlotte asked her father to serve as her "invisible judge" and to evaluate her plan to postpone marriage for several years while she sought meaningful work. Of her two parents, Frederic was more likely to understand her resistance to matrimony. Yet Frederic greeted his daughter's proposal skeptically and imposed his own stricture, insisting that nothing occur in her relations with Walter that the couple would be reluctant for Mary to see.

For a time, Charlotte strove dutifully to follow her father's mandate, forbidding caresses and other intimacies, but Walter doubted the strength of her resolve: "She will be dammed up so long that when she does give up she will be simply deliciously loving," he concluded. He yearned for the day when, he said, "that so wondrous body shall be offered as the supreme expression of that so great soul to *me*." Yet even the ardent Walter occasionally expressed misgivings. For example, he returned home after their first kiss to record in his diary, "But there was not an atom of joy in my heart . . . for I could but feel it was only preparing a bitterer day for me. And why? I know not. I know that she loves me; but I am sure that we shall both suffer more than we have yet."[29]

Still, the physical attraction between them was strong and the temptation great. Walter had a strong sexual drive, and he believed he had found in Charlotte a woman who would match his passion. He attached a note to some poems dated "New Year '83" that referred longingly to their wedding. He expressed his desire for Charlotte—"I want you tonight"—and acknowledged her desire for him: "I saw in you and in myself last night what makes me sure waiting *should* not be for long." Charlotte wrote several poems in subsequent months that linger over Walter's "pretty mouth" and his "smooth white body soft and fair" and that encourage Walter to

Sleep Love! And in my arms forget
The hours of waiting and pain.

Sleep Love! Until you wake again
And find my arms around you yet. . . .[30]

Many of Walter's diary entries dwell on his lust and defend sexual intercourse as sublime union. For instance, he asked Charlotte not to read her newly acquired copy of Walt Whitman's *Leaves of Grass* and justified his request by insisting: "I wanted her to find love and the sexual relations something so holy and lovely that she goes into some hidden place to enjoy its holiness rather than stands in the market places and cries up the odor of its perspiration, the action of its phallus, the hairiness of sweating breasts—and all the Whitman delicacies." Charlotte consented to her lover's moratorium in 1883 but went on to become a Whitman enthusiast. The poet's *Leaves of Grass* was one of two books (Schreiner's *Dreams* was the other) that routinely accompanied her on her travels. She especially appreciated Whitman's visionary grasp of the fundamentally social and organic nature of human living.[31]

Despite his avowed distaste, Walter embraced his ideal and carnal sides in true Whitman fashion. In mid-February 1882 and sporadically throughout the courtship, he contemplated hiring a prostitute in order to alleviate his "overpowering" sexual desires. While also aroused, Charlotte determined to give Walter her love but not her body. Convinced she would succumb if seduced, Walter sought to withstand the temptation for her sake: "My heart, Charlotte, says to you, give way! My mind says, if you have your conviction still of what is right for you cling to your conviction at any cost."

Even at his most compassionate, however, Walter associated her dreams of world service with selfishness and rejoiced whenever she seemed, during tender moments, to be cultivating selflessness. Reversing Walter's formula, Charlotte equated love with self-absorption and work with self-forgetfulness—an equation her experience of love only seemed to confirm.[32]

By May 1882, Charlotte began to wonder whether Walter might, she asked hesitantly, "fill in my life the large place I had hoped the world would fill?" On another occasion, she wondered how Walter felt about her supporting herself. He replied that he preferred to assume the role of provider, especially if they had children, but he voiced no objection to her writing. According to Walter, Charlotte smiled at his response.

Had she known that Walter found the way "she sets herself up as a pattern of industry and adherence to duty . . . just a little amusing," considered her dreams to "live for many instead of for few" "impracticable," and rejoiced in her "broken" spirit as a "strong rich foundation" for their love, her smile might have faded quickly. Why she smiled in the first place remains unclear, given her ambivalence about becoming a mother. Occasionally, she transferred her own dreams onto future offspring: "Our children, dear love," she informed Walter, "will be ambitious to *do*."[33] Yet for Charlotte, children more often represented a threat to her ambitions than their fulfillment.

~

Strong, indeed, is the girl who can decide within herself where duty lies, and follow that decision against the combined forces which hold her back. She must claim the right of every individual soul to its own path in life, its own true line of work and growth.
The Home, 1903[34]

After vacationing separately during the summer of 1882, Charlotte and Walter reunited passionately in Providence. Charlotte suggested that they marry on the sly and set up house, thereby shocking friends and family kept ignorant of the ceremony. She also offered to pose nude for Walter. She did pose fully clothed for him in early September 1882, while he attempted her portrait. Martha accompanied Charlotte to the sittings, acting as Charlotte's "dear little duenna." But the artist—distracted by his lover's "supple throat" and her "heaving breasts' cream white high mounds"—never felt satisfied with his attempts to capture Charlotte's likeness.[35] During these chaperoned sittings, Charlotte flaunted her affection for Walter, hatching romantic plans to move with him to Nova Scotia to write, paint, and raise children.

Financial constraints kept Walter from rushing Charlotte to the altar: he was $800 in debt and could barely support his parents, let alone a wife and children. Although Charlotte readily acquiesced to a delay of two years, she struck Walter as newly malleable, like "dough to the kneader or clay to the potter, to be fashioned as her lover wills." She seemed to him "whitely aflame" with love and "daily more dependent upon me for the bread of her heart's life," he surmised, as well as more childlike, more self-abnegating, and less daring—all positive developments from his perspective.[36]

Charlotte's self-effacement soon became so extreme that she awoke one morning in mid-October 1882 momentarily confused about whether she was herself or Walter. That same month, however, she also made her lover solemnly swear that he would never expect his future wife to demonstrate any facility in cooking or cleaning and never require her, "whatever the emergency, to DUST!" Charlotte's antipathy for housekeeping endured even as her resistance to being appropriated by a man slackened. Walter took pride in his appropriating powers: "I firmly believe, a lover has power in a great degree to make the loved one do as he wills," he declared, marveling at his influence over the once-defiant Charlotte.[37]

The couple's plans for a May 1883 wedding were boosted when Mary Perkins finally relented, preferring a hasty marriage to the illicit sex she believed the greater and, indeed, imminent threat. Charlotte and Walter figured they might live together comfortably on $500 a year. Yet nearly all of Walter's income was already absorbed by his $200 annual studio rent and the $400 he sent his parents each year. Their outlook brightened in February when Mary offered to let the newlyweds stay in the lower half of her tenement while she visited Thomas out west.[38]

Their wedding plans were set aside in mid-March, however, when Charlotte announced she was undergoing another "relapse." She requested a year's separation and simultaneously inquired if Walter would be willing to marry but live separately, with him visiting her "when the erotic tendency was at a maximum." She later idealized this arrangement in her 1911 short story "In Two Houses." Unlike the contented fictional husband, however, Walter was appalled by his intended's unorthodox proposal.[39]

According to Walter, Charlotte's love for him "had gone for a time in that old mysterious way, and left her full of her old self—the longings after a wholly individual life—her old ambition and all that." He blamed the relapse entirely on her self-aggrandizing tendencies: "She had one of those spasms of wanting to make a name for herself in the world by doing good work: wanting to have people know her as Charlotte Perkins, not as the wife of me," he reflected despondently. He began to doubt whether he could ever find enduring happiness with Charlotte; he feared that she was toying with his affections and detested the pleasure she derived from distinguishing herself from other women. Charlotte traced her "irregularity" to her father, but Walter speculated that it "comes from ill-digested reading of philosophical works mixed with her imagination & the tradition of what she ought to inherit from her parents." Disappointed and hurt, he prayed that God would show Charlotte that her destiny could best be fulfilled by hearkening to the woman in her rather than to the siren call of the larger world.[40]

Once again responsive to that call, Charlotte vowed to find her "true height & size in the world." She determined to focus her will and energies "entirely toward right-doing," in an effort, she said, "to add such force as I have to the Power for Good." At the same time, she admitted to her estranged lover that she sensed "a *lack*, a loss, a part of me dropped out," leaving her feeling incomplete and damaged without him. Their separation, in short, vexed her nearly as much as their potential union. She coped with her sorrow by reminding herself: "it makes no difference whether I am happy or not; what I am to do is to fill my place in the world until I die."[41] A declaration that was mostly bravado at this early point in her career would soon enough—after much unforeseen unhappiness—become credo.

Earlier that year, Charlotte had lectured the Sunday school class she took over from Martha about sin and punishment. She sounded like her Great-Grandfather Lyman in her concern with unavoidable judgment and like her Great-Uncle Henry in her emphasis on "right living": "For every wrong thing which you have done in all your lives you must *pay*," she instructed her young charges. "For every wrong thing you ever will you must pay. There is *no* escape, no 'absolution,' and if there is 'forgiveness' it certainly does not mean avoidance of consequences. . . . In order to be happy you *must* do right!"

Would she be doing right in marrying Walter? That, for Charlotte, remained *the* question. Writing her newly married brother Thomas later that spring, she offers her own definition of "right living" as "such living as will most conduce to the progress and happiness of self and all self touches."[42] In her second year of knowing him, Charlotte continued to wonder whether living with Walter would signify progress or a cowardly retreat.

Walter faced the "cruel" choice between love and work as well, although he seemed not to recognize his plight in Charlotte's. For love's sake, he was contemplating abandoning art to pursue a more lucrative career, and he decried the sacrifice:

> The curse and thralldom of loving and having to give up the purest and best efforts of your life to win the favor. It should not be; it is incongruous, unbeautiful, false. . . . Is it not plain that the two combined would produce great work and calm holy poetry. . . . And these things asundered! Things that I have sought to mate so earnestly. Keep art, give up her—Take her, give up art. I prayed & pray to marry the two.

Charlotte had expressed a parallel desire to "marry" work and love, but Walter idealized his struggle as plain and sacred truth while casting hers as a simple choice between selfishness and selflessness. In his poem "In Pain," he disdains what he took to be Charlotte's selfish aims:

> How rife
> Grew wish for fame and work unwed, and strife
> Of alien thought 'gainst loving heart, and e'en
> Those hateful murmurings of distant dead
> Or living ancestors, interpreted
> Be thee clear calls to single life and free?

He thought he knew how to rid Charlotte of her delusions of grandeur: "The bearing of a lusty pair of twins would weed her of her folly," he speculated privately.[43]

Still uncertain whether he was called to be a painter or a poet, Walter submitted his sonnets to the premier literary journal of the day, the *Atlantic Monthly*. When the poems were rejected without explanation, he turned to the poet, art critic, and collector Charles De Kay—who had praised Walter's paintings—for a candid assessment. De Kay's judgment that the poems showed "no promise" came as a crushing blow. It left Walter doubting himself and his abilities, triggering a profound crisis. Only a week before, Walter had prayed for "some great pain or great calamity" to come to one of them (preferably to him) in order to make Charlotte "see love in his nakedness."[44] That moment arrived sooner than he anticipated: on May 22, 1883, Charlotte promised to marry her dejected lover the following year.

Similarly, Vivian Lane, the heroine of *The Crux*, ambivalently accepts her suitor and then ponders the consequences of saying "that irrevocable word" ("yes"): "if this was happiness, it was not as she had imagined it. . . . He had been so madly anxious; he had held her so close; there seemed no other way but to yield to him— in order to get away." In her novel as in her own private musings, Charlotte portrays as doubt-ridden a night conventionally considered the happiest in a woman's life. Charlotte's sense of entrapment can also be inferred from a "lugubrious picture" she painted soon after her engagement entitled *The Woman Against the Wall*, depicting "a wan creature who had traversed a desert and came, worn out, to an insurmountable wall which extended around the earth." Walter admired the "powerful" painting (now lost) but ominously called it "a literal transcript of her mind."[45]

~

> Perhaps it was not meant for me to work as I intended. Perhaps I am not to be of use to others. . . . [L]et me at least learn to be uncomplaining and unselfish. Let me do my work and not fling my pain on others. Let me keep at least this ambition; to be a good and a pleasure to *some* one, to some others, no matter what I feel myself.
>
> Charlotte's diary entry,
> New Year's Eve, 1883–1884[46]

The lingering pull and potential remuneration of work led Charlotte to accept a job that summer as governess for the Jackson family. Charlotte had been friendly with the recently deceased Isabel Jackson; she was hired to supervise Isabel's younger brother Eddie. She soon grew to "heartily dislike" the position, finding the family "highly obnoxious . . . and the boy in especial . . . abhorrent to my every—antenna." By mutual agreement, she left before three months of her committed year had passed.[47]

Charlotte subsequently pursued additional forms of "outwork." She taught a gymnastic class at the Dimans, tutored students, and decorated houses at Christmastime. After reimbursing Mary for room, board, and personal expenditures, her prospects still seemed so encouraging that her impecunious fiancé predicted her earnings would outstrip his that winter.[48]

Charlotte did her best to commit to marriage. She displaced onto the couple hopes she had formerly harbored for herself alone, and thus she prayed that the "One" she and Walter would become—"one love, one power, one will and high endeavor"—would "help the world!" But she was far from happy in her engagement. At one point she proclaimed "the saddest day" of her life the day Walter fell in love with her. Experiencing yet another of her "turns of affectional paralysis," she tried to persuade herself to love again, this time with less "*wanting*" and more "giving," so as to become the selfless, admirable, womanly creature she knew Walter wanted her, and believed her, to be. Without a lover, she hypothesized, she would need to develop these traits for the benefit of humanity; now, at least, they would benefit her future husband.[49]

A round of holiday parties and visits failed to alleviate Charlotte's melancholy. She rang out 1883 on a blue note. As the clock struck midnight, she sat alone, listening to the howling wind, writing in her diary, and musing over a year she considered "[w]eakly begun, ill lived, little regarded." Dejected and listless, she anticipated "a future of failure and suffering. Children sickly and unhappy. Husband miserable because of my distress; and I———!" The prolonged blank following her "I" graphically represents her sense of her self, married, as evacuated.[50]

The following day, Charlotte learned that an acquaintance, Conway Brown, had shot himself. The news prompted Charlotte to remind herself remorsefully, "How needful to live so that in such times there is enough real work to look back upon to preserve one's self-respect!" When she informed Walter of Brown's suicide that evening, she suggested that she might copy him: "If I were *sure* that death changed life for the better, changed personality and relation, I fear that even my sense of duty &c would hardly save you from what you most dread. . . . I have a frail hope that our life together will have enough of joy to keep me sane."[51] These are sentiments infrequently expressed by a bride-to-be just months before her wedding.

Walter's mood, by contrast, grew increasingly buoyant during the early months of the new year. His prospects improved considerably after receiving the commission from Beriah Wall for a series of etchings that eventually netted him $1,200. In early March 1884, Walter mounted a one-man exhibition of 161 of his works, selling five of his paintings the following day and fourteen the following week.[52] These successes quelled his doubts about art as a profession, leaving him confident that he could provide for Charlotte and a family.

As the days wound down to the ceremony, Charlotte continued to record her misery in her diary and charted her attempts to distract herself by thinking of others. She fared better physically than mentally: a new diet was helping her to regain her "old force and vigor." She had returned to the gymnasium after a brief hiatus, and on January 11 she boasted of picking up a girl her own weight and running with her without effort. The short "talk on self conquest" she gave the girls attending her gym class at the Dimans suggests that physical exertion provided one route to forgetting her own personal sorrows.[53]

Writing proved another route. Her achievements reawakened her ambitions and affirmed her sense that her voice might be needed in the world. She learned on January 5 that her sympathetic poem about a prostitute, "One Girl of Many," had been accepted by the *Alpha* and that the paper would welcome future submissions. On January 12 her poem "In Duty Bound" was published in the *Woman's Journal.* Both venues supported woman's rights, reflecting Charlotte's mounting interest in the cause as her wedding date neared. In late February, for example, she began reading John Stuart Mill's *The Subjection of Women.* The book probably did little to quell her premarital jitters, since Mill advocates freedom and equality for women and defines the domestic and public spheres as incompatible.[54]

Charlotte experienced occasional surges of "love and happiness" as shopping, home furnishing, and gift-getting filled her days. But she informed Grace Channing, who approved of Walter, that she was suffering the consequences of her family and friends' "adverse opinions" of her lover, which were causing her to question her choice. Indeed, she added, she could hardly claim that she had chosen Walter since she had no other suitor; she thought of him instead, she said, as "the man of my acceptance," a phrasing that suggests her sense of entrapment and resignation.[55]

Two months before the ceremony, she declared herself "lachrymose," full of "forebodings of future pain," and increasingly "*miserable.*" By now familiar with such lapses, Walter convinced himself "a cure will come with marriage and *home.*" Charlotte, however, feared the cure would prove worse than the disease. She expressed her anguish in a sermon to her Sunday school class only weeks before the wedding: "I think one of the greatest trials of life is *not* to know which of two courses is right and wise."[56]

Charlotte married Walter on May 2, 1884, still uncertain whether marriage constituted the best course for her. The ceremony was held at 6:30 in the evening in the rooms of the Perkins family, with Walter's father presiding. After "a splendid supper" and a rather chilly parting from Mary, the newlyweds walked to their new home, with Charlotte pocketing a yeast cake for good luck. Their "true ceremony" took place later that night, when Walter gave Charlotte a ring inscribed with "Ich liebe Dich" and placed the crown of roses she presented him on her head. Charlotte summarized the evening's close in her diary:

> . . . I install Walter in the parlor & dining room while I retire to the bed chamber and finish it's [*sic*] decoration. The bed looks like a fairy bower with lace, white silk, and flowers. Make my self a crown of white roses. Wash again, and put on a thin drift of white mull fastened with a rosebud and velvet and pearl civeture. My little white velvet slippers and a white snood. Go in to my husband. He meets me joyfully; we promise to be true to each other; and he puts on the ring and the crown. Then he lifts the crown, loosens the snood, unfastens the girdle, and then—and then.
>
> O my God! I thank thee for this heavenly happiness![57]

The couple spent the next day lolling in bed, further tasting that "heavenly happiness," too immersed in each other to notice the storm clouds gathering on the horizon.

4   "A Life with No Beyond!"
(1884–1888)

Are you content, you pretty three-years' wife? . . .
Have you forgotten how you used to long
  In days of ardent girlhood, to be great,
    To help the groaning world, to serve the state,
      To be so wise—so strong? . . .

Have you no dream of life in fuller store?
    Of growing to be more than that you are? . . .
Be not deceived! 'T is not your wifely bond
    That holds you, nor the mother's royal power,
    But selfish, slavish service hour by hour—
      A life with no beyond!

                    "To the Young Wife," 1893[1]

When Charlotte was herself a "three-years' wife," she determined to try to sever the "wifely bond," end its requisite, demeaning "service," and seek a life beyond conventional marriage. She told Houghton Gilman, the man who would become her second husband, that she had married Walter "*without* that knowledge of right doing" and added, "I did not have my own sanction. I did not reason it out and accept it." Overlooking periods of agonized reasoning and interludes of real tenderness and joy, she viewed her years with Walter as a time of stagnation or, worse, regression.

The experience of her first marriage convinced her that loving was not simply the opposite of living but its opponent. Loving, as she experienced it with Walter, immersed her further in herself rather than in the world she longed to improve. Loving thus seemed to her to entail "being"—being a wife, a mother, a woman, an invalid—rather than the "doing" she valued as indispensable to social service. As she learned with Walter and later argued in *Women and Economics*, marriage tends "to magnify the personal and minimize the general in our minds," a skewing that countered her own ambitions. The ultimate failure of her marriage to Walter led her to view love as a snare holding her "back—holding by the heart!—that unescapable grip which it kills to tear loose from."[2] Walter had caught her in that grip, and Charlotte eventually managed to pry herself loose, but not before she despaired of ever reconciling the living she idealized and the loving she still craved.

~

> But—*this* is not what he offered! And it's not what I undertook! . . . "I will make you happy!" they say; and you get married—and after that it's Housework! . . . [W]hat has "love" to do with dust and grease and flies!
>
> *What Diantha Did,* 1910[3]

In the weeks immediately following the ceremony, Charlotte itemized wedding gifts, wrote thank-you notes, experimented with new dishes in an effort to improve her culinary skills, and maintained the three second-floor rooms the couple had rented in a house on a bank overlooking the Seekonk River. In her autobiography, Charlotte represents these first months as idyllic: "We were really very happy together. There was nothing to prevent it but that increasing depression of mine. My diary is full of thankfulness for happiness and prayers for deserving it, full of Walter's constant kindness and helpfulness in the work when I was not well—the not-wellness coming oftener and oftener."

In this recollection, she blames her illness for an unhappiness that had additional sources: on their one-week anniversary, for instance, Charlotte suggested that Walter pay her for her "services; and he much dislikes the idea," she confessed to her diary later that day. "I am grieved at offending him, mutual misery."[4] Recognizing the nonremunerative nature of housework, Charlotte sought to devalue its currency as a wifely duty, lovingly and freely rendered.

Thirty years before Charlotte married, her Great-Aunt Catharine Beecher had pronounced domestic despair a nationwide epidemic and described the

Charlotte in 1884, the year she married Walter. Photo by Hurd. Courtesy of the Schlesinger Library, Radcliffe Institute for Advanced Study, Harvard University.

anguish of its silent sufferers: "How many young hearts have revealed the fact, that what they had been trained to imagine the highest earthly felicity, was but the beginning of care, disappointment, and sorrow, and often led to the extremity of mental and physical suffering." Subsequent studies confirmed Beecher's random sample and indicated that women worked outside the home less from financial exigency than from needing "an outlet for unused energies, gifts, or powers." At the century's end, the "woman question" essentially turned on the divisive issue of woman's proper role or sphere. While Charlotte numbered among those declaring that the house was not the world, others insisted, "A caress is better than a career."[5]

Denied a career, the new Mrs. Stetson tried caresses, only to find herself similarly thwarted. On June 15, 1884, a little over a month into the marriage, she wrote in her diary, "I find myself too—affectionately expressive. I must keep more to myself and be asked—not born with." Ten days later, she again lamented this "outwardly expressive" tendency. Her emotional neediness, nakedly displayed in such moments, overwhelmed Walter; he may also have found her "unwomanly" advances disturbing. Charlotte feared she might be "making [her] mother's mistake" and alienating her husband through her excessive affection.[6] The last thing Charlotte wanted to do was to follow in Mary's footsteps.

In August, Charlotte began experiencing bouts of nausea, exhaustion, and loss of appetite, leading her to confide her pregnancy suspicions to her mother. At first, the couple wondered if she might simply be suffering from a bowel obstruction. Accordingly, Charlotte consulted Dr. Olive Herrick, who performed an internal exam and diagnosed a prolapsed uterus, which the doctor treated by using an unspecified instrument, installing cotton, and prescribing "bitter medesin" or "enematas."[7] These were risky procedures to perform on a newly pregnant patient, although Charlotte never mentions Dr. Herrick's detecting her pregnancy. The prescriptions only aggravated Charlotte's nausea and vomiting. Once the pregnancy was confirmed, the expectant parents delved into obstetrics manuals and pondered baby names, including Sigurd and Sigmund, tributes to Walter's infatuation with German romanticism.

Walter resented those who "said stale things about the shortness of our honeymoon." He insisted that their love, happiness, and satisfaction with each other had only increased since they received the news. In his diary, Walter noted Charlotte's joy when the pregnancy was confirmed: "her face very often since I've lived with her has seemed divine, but that time she felt sure our child had come to her fair well-kept house from the unseen wide world her face was ineffably heavenly."[8]

Yet however "heavenly" Charlotte's visage appeared to her spouse, her own musings as the pregnancy advanced suggest that her mind often dwelt in murkier regions. She had sanguine stretches when she was capable of envisioning a future enriched by numerous blessings, including "A Home and a Baby, Contentment and Rest." Still, her fears of being tied down or held back by marriage were aggravated by the pregnancy, and her recurrent nausea and illness reinforced her impression of marriage as unhealthy.

Charlotte kept busy as a young wife but confessed herself "mortally tired of doing nothing." While a common side effect of pregnancy, fatigue registered for Charlotte as the result of her lifestyle, or the lack of a fulfilling one ("doing nothing"). She equated women's work with enervation and emptiness and lamented "the dreamed of life of great usefulness" that might have been hers had she chosen otherwise. As she concluded ruefully in October, "O dear! That I should come to this!"[9]

Charlotte's despondency deepened at a time when Walter was realizing many of his own dreams. Approximately two weeks after their wedding, the co-owner of a Boston art gallery publicly praised the "richness of color, the splendid vitality of fancy, the poetry of conception that characterizes Mr. Stetson's work." Noyes of the Noyes & Blakeslee Gallery subsequently mounted an exhibit of Walter's works that proved "an unexpected triumph" and generated further positive reviews and robust sales. One reviewer held that Walter's pictures expressed the artist's innate genius and concluded, " . . . the young man went home to Providence after hanging his pictures with prices like $50.00 and $30.00 marked upon them, and in a few days awoke famous, with the great guns of a fervor over his little things booming in the Boston newspapers." Walter made good use of his newfound purchasing power, their new possessions and increased material comfort making Charlotte "so happy that she fairly ached."[10]

Around this time, Walter began assuming domestic duties initially relegated to Charlotte. With some ambivalence, he made meals and did laundry among other attempts to help and please his bride as her pregnancy progressed. "Sometimes when I am very tired myself," he observed in his diary, "it is a burden to do housework & all the things she asks," unwittingly echoing his wife's complaint. Walter encouraged Charlotte to read his journal, and his words persuaded her to resume some of the housework so that he could better devote himself to art.[11]

As the months passed, Charlotte strove to overcome her misgivings and to welcome motherhood. She wrote a poem portraying the baby as a gift from God intended to teach her maternal selflessness:

> Little little child within me, soft and small;
> May the Power which there has laid thee;

Teach me how I best may aid thee;
With a mother's love enclose thee;
Give thee what a mother owes thee—
Give thee all!

Yet a mother's owing "all" to her child exaggerates the sacrifice necessary, and the poem's concluding line—"Her sorrows are forgotten"—simultaneously invokes what is purportedly "forgotten."[12]

Charlotte continued to bide her time as her due date neared—eating, sleeping, cutting diapers, sewing, drawing, sorting baby gifts, writing and reading letters, and listening to Walter read aloud. In her diary, she recorded periods of ill health, her willingness to die could she avoid hurting others, her husband's generous attentions, and her hopes that her child might become the world helper she despaired of becoming herself. As the year turned, she observed, "Ambition sleeps. I make no motion but just live."

Although enervated and constipated, she rallied in mid-January to write "The Sin of Sickness" for Buffalo's *Christian Advocate*. Written while ill herself, the essay maintains that illness could be prevented by acts of will and the force of reason. "It is the simplest, plainest, most unchangeable duty of every one of us," she concludes, "to so live that our bodies shall be always ready for their best work." As if berating herself, she blames the sick for their sickness and labels sinful any action that causes individuals to deviate from either perfect health or their true calling.[13] These sins, then, would include not only sickness but also marriage as she was experiencing it.

The couple hired a woman to help with the housework during the first three weeks of March, after which a nurse, Maria Pease, arrived to assist with the birth. As her due date neared, Charlotte suffered from night sweats and sleeplessness due to "the muscular force and unreasonable activity of the infant." (Her expectations of "reasonable" behavior from an infant hint at ensuing difficulties.)

Two years after the delivery, she recalled her physical labor as "easy . . . enough" but identified mental anguish as her downfall: "Had terrible fits of remorse and depression all through the time, but thought nothing of them as I had had the same in the two years torture called courtship. Began to show 'nervousness' in the months confinement. Had wild and dreadful ideas which I was powerless to check, times of excitement and times of tears."[14] Linking her courtship and her confinement so that both figure as instruments of torture, she refutes the conventional wisdom that a husband and child constitute a married woman's two chief blessings.

At five minutes before nine o'clock on the morning of March 23, 1885, Katharine Beecher Stetson was born, named for both Charlotte's Great-Aunt Catharine

Beecher and her friend Kate Bucklin. In her diary, Charlotte describes her experience in clipped sentences:

> Brief ecstasy. Long pain.
> Then years of joy again.
>
> Motherhood means————————Giving.

But what did "Giving" mean? The question would haunt Charlotte. Walter assumed their troubles had ended with the birth: "The glorious knowledge that my own heart's Love was safe—safe to me yet and that I was the father of a lovely violet-eyed girl was too much and I broke down." But Charlotte, too, would break down soon after the delivery, and "the darkness" that descended would ultimately eclipse her husband's short-lived sense of joyous relief.[15]

~

> In those days a new disease had dawned on the medical horizon. It was called "nervous prostration." No one knew much about it, and there were many who openly scoffed, saying it was only a new name for laziness. To be recognizably ill one must be confined to one's bed, and preferably in pain.
>
> That a heretofore markedly vigorous young woman, with every comfort about her, should collapse in this lamentable manner was inexplicable.
>
> *The Living of Charlotte Perkins Gilman*, 1935[16]

During the first few postpartum weeks, the nurse tended to Katharine's routine needs while the new mother struggled to regain her strength. But after Maria Pease left and Charlotte passed three sleepless weeks alone with the baby, she broke down so rapidly that the couple sent for Mary. Charlotte welcomed her mother's return from a visit to Thomas in Utah with a mixture of relief, guilt, and envy. Mary proved an indulgent grandmother who took "all care of the baby day times," leaving Charlotte feeling alternately thankful and useless; watching her mother dote on her daughter may also have reminded Charlotte of her own underindulged childhood and thus deepened her dejection.[17]

The couple expected Charlotte to recover her spirits quickly after giving birth, but they gravely underestimated the extent of her nervous exhaustion. She spent many hours weeping, overcome by what she perceived as "an oppressive pain that sees no outlet." She had become a mother but did not feel like one. Indeed, she did not feel much of anything at all, not even for her infant daughter, so consumed was she by "that dull, constant pain." Her idleness proved so sharp a contrast to her dreamed-of usefulness that it only magnified her despair. In her 1916 essay "The 'Nervous Breakdown' of Women," Charlotte maintains that the body and the spirit must mesh, and the "creature must be satisfied with itself, it must do what it likes to do, and like to do what it does."[18] As a new wife and mother, Charlotte neither did what she liked nor liked what she did, increasing her misery.

While her symptoms resemble what we would today call postpartum depression, this was not an available diagnosis in Charlotte's day. Nor does the modifier *postpartum,* with its finite connotations, accurately depict the duration of Charlotte's suffering: she experienced depressive episodes prior to her marriage and courtship and would suffer intervals of depression interspersed with manic bouts throughout her life. At the same time, attributing her despair to clinical depression risks overemphasizing its biological dimensions and obscuring its origins in oppressive sexual politics and practices; in fact, Charlotte's postmarital "darkness" had numerous and complex causes.

In the late nineteenth century, various theories emerged to explain nervous disease or "neurasthenia," an umbrella category including within it mood disorders. Nervous men were typically diagnosed with neurasthenia, while nervous women were often also or exclusively diagnosed with hysteria. In addition to nervousness, neurasthenics suffered from neuralgia, feebleness, and headaches, as well as back and groin pain. Most neurasthenics found themselves oppressed by a "morbid self-consciousness" or anguished, relentless introspection, which in Charlotte's case exacerbated her despondency and self-contempt.

Nerve specialists typically linked women's disorders to the draining powers of the reproductive organs. Viewing the body as a closed energy system, medical specialists held that energy expended in one area was necessarily depleted from another. Women's purportedly voracious reproductive organs were thus portrayed as drawing energy from other areas of the body and especially from the mind. Such arguments were deployed to discourage women from pursuing higher education and from overtaxing themselves intellectually.

Charlotte essentially bought into the idea of the scarcity of bodily energy, but she ultimately proposed a different allotment than did most traditional doctors: "The physical energies of the mother—an enormous fund—denied natural expression in bodily exertion, work morbidly in manifold disease," she wrote in *The Home.* She blamed domestic duties in particular for exhausting "social energies" better directed outward and expended in more healthful, "natural" pursuits like "world-service."[19]

George M. Beard's influential 1881 book *American Nervousness* defines neurasthenia as the necessary consequence of American civilization. The prevalence of the disease indicates the nation's cultural superiority and refinement, he argues, especially when compared to "primitive" cultures where nervous disorders seem rare. Yet paradoxically, as late as 1886, doctors interpreted nervousness in American women as a sign that they lagged behind men in terms of evolutionary development.

To a certain extent, Charlotte embraced this view: she regarded her breakdown as a regression, the sorry denouement of her once-ambitious program of self-advancement. But instead of some inherent, womanly nature, she blamed environmental influences and particularly the home's degenerative effect. By "home" Charlotte typically meant the complex of demeaning domestic, maternal, and sexual duties allotted to the traditional middle-class wife. The wife who remains "more closely bound" to the home, she concludes in *The Home*, "breaks down in health with increasing frequency." She adds, "The effect of home life on women seems to be more injurious in proportion to their social development," a rule that, when applied retrospectively to Charlotte's home life with Walter, yields a flattering interpretation of her own intense anguish.[20]

The couple's first wedding anniversary dawned on May 2, 1885, with little cause for jubilation. Walter opened his diary for the first time in months and reflected, "I felt I *must* on this anniversary of our joy say that love has not waned but rather waxed; that she is not worse, but better; that I am not sorry I married, but rather glad." The gentleman may have been protesting too much, for Charlotte's entry that same day reads, "I am tired with long sleeplessness and disappointed at being unable to celebrate the day. So I cry." They had moved to a nicer house on Humboldt near Wayland and hired an efficient German servant, but neither kept a weak and fretful Charlotte from sinking "into a helpless melancholia."[21]

She tried to rally in early August, returning to her diary and expressing a feeble hope that she might be able to "pick up the broken threads again and make out some kind of career after all." But by month's end, she pronounced herself "wellnigh insane." Walter mourned his beloved's reduction to "a nervous invalid requiring the utmost care and tender treatment, lest it should settle itself into an incurable mind disease."[22]

Inevitably, the marriage suffered. Charlotte expressed her dissatisfaction with Walter so vociferously that, he suspected, "she feels hatred for me." Charlotte recorded her feelings of entrapment in an August 1885 diary entry:

> Every morning the same hopeless waking. Every day the same weary drag. To die mere cowardice. Retreat impossible, escape impossible. I let Walter read a letter to Martha in which I tell my grief as strongly as I can. He offers to let me go free, he would do everything in the world for me; but he cannot see how irrevocably bound

I am, for life, for life. No, unless he die and the baby die, or he change or I change there is no way out. Well.

Her drastic fantasy of liberation reflects the extent of her despair, of her belief that loving had ruined living. When newly engaged she had identified herself as "The Woman Against the Wall"; as a new mother, that wall now appeared unscalable.

That same August, Walter observed,

> There have been violent hysterical symptoms, and long periods of taciturnity, melancholy, and utter loss of the desire or power to will. . . . [N]either words nor medicine availed much, for her illness brought back all the thoughts of how strong she was before marriage, how much she wanted to do, the remembrance of "her mission" and a fierce rebellion at the existing state of things. Poor dear wife! Since that subject has taken the form of a monomania—a terrible thing that crushes all joy, all enthusiasm and sweetness out of my life.[23]

Charlotte resented Walter's freedom to work—even though he, too, had a child, a spouse, and a home—and she resented the double standard that made this disparity logical.

In later works, including her one-act play *Three Women*, she sought to prove that only the woman who combines work and love can find the fulfillment that the woman who exclusively works and the woman who exclusively loves each lack. Similarly, in her story "Mrs. Power's Duty," an enlightened character instructs a depressed wife that her problems stemmed not from marriage itself but from the "social treason" of her wifely subservience and dependence, since she belonged not to her husband but "to God—to humanity—to that worship which is service, that service which is worship." Charlotte Perkins had dreamed of precisely such service, of fulfilling her "duties as a member of the world."[24] But Mrs. Stetson believed that she had been reduced to a domestic drudge and not even that, since at this point she was virtually useless around the house.

In a poem she considered "the most brutal bit of satire [she] ever wrote," Charlotte portrays a ridiculously disproportionate "Brood Mare"—her legs and chest weak and her hind quarters ponderously heavy. When a prospective buyer points out the distortion, the seller retorts,

> . . . I never said it was a horse,
> I told you 't was a mare!
> A mare was never meant to race,
> To carry, or to pull;
> She is meant for breeding only, so
> Her place in life is full.[25]

"The Brood Mare" exemplifies the formula Charlotte began to work out during her first marriage and that she would propound in her groundbreaking treatise, *Women and Economics:* the more feminine the creature, the less capable she becomes of representing the species.

Averting his gaze from other probable causes, Walter noticed that his wife's woes worsened with her monthly periods. Charlotte made this connection occasionally as well, tying her moods "to the approach of internal disturbance presently" and—punning on the "x" she made in her diaries when she menstruated—predicting, "I shall be 'cross' pretty soon!" But Walter also blamed her "strange and terrible" tendency to rush "in her mind from all our sweet life to try to get out into the world to rid it at one fell swoop of all evil, pain and the like."[26] Walter had finally realized what Charlotte had told him repeatedly: she preferred world service to domestic service. But his realization came too late.

Mounting debts made their situation even more desperate. Walter had quickly spent the money he received from the Boston show and the now-completed etching commission. After another ultimately unsuccessful stab at publishing his sonnets, he concentrated on painting, producing several works exploring his deteriorating marriage. *In Grief,* painted in 1885, shows a woman who resembles Charlotte (she adopted a similarly dejected pose at least once in his presence), leaning her head on her hand. Another canvas he called *Remorse* depicts a mother and child on a funeral bier beside which a figure kneels in abject sorrow. Although he conceived it shortly after Katharine was born—reliving his fears of Charlotte's death in childbirth—as he painted this ominous picture he was mourning the death of her love for him.[27]

Walter now regretted his marriage, concluding, "I would not marry if I had the chance again, knowing what I do now." He recorded his most bitter entry on September 11, 1885:

> My darling wife thinks now that she shall some day preach—sermons about health,
> morality and the like—from the pulpit on what you will. Ah well, my dearest love,
> if you have anything to say that will help us, and real solution to offer . . . for God's
> sake preach! And may you have power beyond all the preachers of all time! Leave
> me—Leave mother—Leave child—leave all and preach! We need some one to tell us
> what of all these "truths" *is* truth. Go. God help you!—[28]

Charlotte did eventually do as he said, succeeding beyond both Walter's and her own wildest dreams. Charlotte and Walter both considered her goals antithetical to marriage, which meant that to pursue them she had of necessity to leave those she loved or, at least, at this point, those who loved her.

~

In the many-faceted complexity of our modern personalities it is an extremely difficult thing to be completely married.

"The Artist," 1916[29]

In September 1885, Charlotte's doctor advised her to wean Katharine in order to build her own strength. Charlotte promptly began feeding the baby Mellin's Food and ate it herself. An advertisement for the product reveals that it was marketed for infants and invalids and intended to invigorate both. Charlotte responded better to travel, jumping at Grace Channing's invitation to pass the winter in Pasadena, California. Katharine would stay behind, entrusted to Walter and Mary's care for the duration. "Hope dawns," Charlotte proclaimed. "To come back *well!*"[30]

Walter managed to borrow the necessary funds from a friend's mother and considered the cost justified if his wife returned to him and to her old self. Acquaintances apparently questioned Charlotte's decision to leave home for so long when her marriage and child were still quite young; they pitied her spouse, although he rejected their sympathy. As if sensing this first separation would not be the last, Walter sobbed when the train carrying his "amazingly lovable" wife pulled out of sight.[31]

By contrast, Charlotte felt her sorrows lift with every passing mile: "Feeble and hopeless I set forth, armed with tonics and sedatives, to cross the continent," she reflected. "From the moment the wheels began to turn, the train to move, I felt better." Charlotte habitually associated movement with health, especially after months of immobility.

She stopped for a month to visit her brother and his wife Julia in Ogden, Utah, surprising Thomas by showing up on his doorstep unannounced. She traveled next to San Francisco, where she was met by her father, then head librarian at the San Francisco Public Library. The visit was polite but formal; Charlotte claimed Frederic treated her "as would any acquaintance." A week later, in early December 1885, Charlotte journeyed south toward the city she considered a "heaven" on earth.[32]

Pasadena seemed like paradise to numerous East Coast emigrants who had ventured westward in pursuit of health and wealth. The transcontinental railroad to San Francisco had been completed in 1869, the extension to southern California was finished in the fall of 1876, and soon roughly 70,000 passengers arrived on the West Coast each year. Many had been encouraged to relocate as a form of "climatotherapy." For easterners, the West comprised "tall men, brave women, and valorous deeds," and new arrivals hoped that by transplanting themselves to the region they too might soon epitomize western ideals. Going West "also assists in breaking up pernicious habits and customs," one doctor observed, and removes patients "from the extremely injurious influence of emotional, over-sympathetic, and indiscreet relatives and friends."[33] The lift Charlotte experienced as she approached Pasadena stemmed as much from what she was leaving behind as it did from what she was moving toward.

Charlotte believed beautiful Pasadena deserved its fame as "the Gem of the Valley." A local enthusiast dubbed it "the land of the afternoon" and claimed "people lived out of doors," an invigorating *modus vivendi* for the formerly housebound Charlotte. (She once committed to verse her ". . . Joy universal, keen, / Just to be out of doors.") From Pasadena she wrote Martha Luther Lane that "the country about here is as lovely as a dream. There is mountain and valley and plain, beautiful flowers and fruit and foliage."[34]

Situated between the San Gabriel Mountains to the east and the Arroyo Seco to the west, Pasadena in the 1880s encompassed a lush wooded area, where alder, sycamore, oak, and willow intermingled with flowering plants, including clematis and wild grapes, lending the city the feeling of "a ready-made wilderness retreat." Its mild climate proved especially attractive to invalids and retirees. Some said the millennium had already begun in Pasadena, estimating that there were "more sanctified cranks to the acre than in any other town in America."[35]

When Charlotte arrived in Pasadena, it had become a vibrant resort town. Its streets were crowded with pedestrians, lined with businesses, hotels, and mansions, and crisscrossed by trolley and rail lines. The town's premier hotel, the Raymond, under construction during Charlotte's visit, was completed in 1886. Incorporated as a city that same year, Pasadena experienced a boom in the 1880s. A population of 392 in 1880 soared as high as 15,000 in 1887 before dropping to roughly 5,000 by 1890. Charlotte would later wryly conclude of the boom that it "made such a roar / and left us all poorer than we were before!"[36]

The Channing family had settled in Pasadena in the early 1880s. They had left Providence after Grace contracted tuberculosis from a visiting cousin who subsequently died of the disease. William Francis Channing, Grace's father, practiced medicine and invented "the telegraphic fire alarm which he presented to his native Boston and the handle telephone which he gave to Bell." Grace's mother had run a normal school until she contracted typhoid fever and sank into invalidism. Grace herself had established and taught in Providence's first free kindergarten until her own health was jeopardized. Around 1884, the Channings built a large, two-story house on four acres of land near Pasadena's reservoir. Grace thrived in the winterless climate, playing tennis, riding horseback, and writing outdoors.[37]

Charlotte likewise found Pasadena recuperative: "Kind and congenial friends, pleasant society, amusement, out-door sports, the blessed mountains, the long, unbroken sweep of the valley, with snow-peaks at the far eastern end—with such surroundings I recovered so fast, to outward appearance at least, that I was taken for a vigorous young girl," she recalled. She felt restored to hope and love and sent Walter a Valentine's poem in February 1886 professing her reignited passion. She describes the frigid land back East and asserts, "There in that icy land abideth Love—— / Triumphant Still." And she concludes by portraying her flowering, fragrant surroundings and insisting,

> . . . There in that summer land
>   abideth Love——
> Triumphant still.
>
> Love in your heart O husband! Love in mine!
>   Live where we will!
> Love holds us one with power supreme, divine;
>   Triumphant still.

That same February, Walter delivered a lecture, "The Nude in Art" in which he argued passionately against mistaken attempts to "crush out the desire for sexual pleasure" that he believed fostered and complemented the artistic impulse. He asked, "Why not be men and grant the truth, that the desire is right and good? Why not insist that instead of being wicked and to be done in the dark it must be made the joyous attendant of manly love, its deeds to be done in the sunshine among such fair sights, sounds and odors as may be."[38] What was good for art, one senses, would have been very good indeed for the lonesome, lustful artist.

While in Pasadena, Charlotte wrote poetry, painted, and designed costumes for a New Year's Eve masquerade at the Channings. She also collaborated with Grace in writing a play the two performed locally. All the while, she tried to repress her worries that returning to Providence would undo her advances. Her return date had been moved up to take advantage of the low prices offered during a violent railroad strike. As she prepared for the late March trip, she wrote Martha, "I look forward with both joy and dread to see my darlings again; and dread of further illness under family cares. Well. I have chosen."[39]

Her sister-in-law Julia boarded the train in Utah and accompanied Charlotte to Providence to consult Dr. Keller about her own shaky health (later that fall, back in Utah, a pregnant Julia died of heart disease). Charlotte left Pasadena on March 22, 1886, the day before Katharine's first birthday. She arrived home on

March 29 with a cold that swiftly developed into bronchitis. Walter purchased her ticket on borrowed funds although he was "near pecuniary ruin": he owed more than $800 and was reduced at one point to twenty-six cents.[40]

Initially, Walter believed his wife had "regained health and gladness; learned a great deal about the world; [and] got humility in large measure. . . ." Charlotte took the baby for walks and resumed her other responsibilities, but she noted forbiddingly in her diary during her first week home that she was struggling to "get accustomed to life here. It will take some time." By the end of the month, Walter despaired, "she has been growing troubled & very melancholy again, so that now it is pretty hard to see what real good her winter's sojourn did her." When Dr. Keller examined Charlotte and diagnosed nervous prostration, Walter detected his wife's disappointment and suspected that she wanted to hear "that her brain was organically injured." He tried to "endure" and remain patient and loving but feared "months and months of deepest torture."[41]

Charlotte did perk up after Mary Perkins moved out of their rooms and back to her house. Walter observed that Mary "has a very deadly effect on Charlotte. I think Charlotte's spirits rose as soon as she left the house," he surmised. "She is a woman who sucks the life out of one, I scarce know how. . . . Her love is like that of a porcupine. The nearer it gets to you, the more sharply the quills intrude."[42] His wife's own prickly nature may have led him to ponder certain similarities between mother and daughter.

Still, when Charlotte claimed in her autobiography that "within a month" of her return from Pasadena she "was as low as before leaving," she glossed over interludes of relative marital calm. In late November 1886, for instance, Walter rejoiced that in the year since Charlotte left for Pasadena, he now had her "here, in my very arms nightly, in my heart daily, well, happy, hopeful, good, true, loving beyond anything she ever was before." Charlotte, likewise, sustained the positive note, emphasizing her growth and her increasing contentment over the waning months of the year. She worried that her "self abandoning enthusiasm and fierce determination in the cause of right" had weakened. But she felt that she had "become a person more in harmony with my surroundings," she remarked, "and yet have not lost a keen interest in the world's work."[43]

Charlotte's increasing satisfaction in her marriage and her recovering spirits can be partly attributed to her improving career prospects. Upon returning from Pasadena, Charlotte had stepped up her commitment to reading, writing, and remunerative work. She offered private art lessons and made notepaper and dinner cards to sell to friends. She received her first check for a literary effort when she published her poem "On the Pawtuxet." Her attempts to sell the play she and

Grace had co-authored met with initial success after she interested the celebrated actor William Gillette in the manuscript, but nothing came of it.

Charlotte learned in August 1886 that her poem "The Answer" had earned her a year's subscription to the *Woman's Journal.* The acceptance letter came with a request for additional work. Walter considered the poem "the best she has done," even though its third stanza bitterly indicts marriage as lethal slavery:

> A maid was asked in marriage. Wise as fair,
> She gave her answer with deep thought and prayer,
>
> Expecting, in the holy name of wife,
> Great work, great pain, and greater joy, in life.
>
> She found such work as brainless slaves might do,
> By day and night, long labor, never through;
>
> Such pain—no language can her pain reveal;
> It had no limit but her power to feel;
>
> Such joy—life left in her sad soul's employ
> Neither the hope nor memory of joy.
>
> Helpless she died, with one despairing cry,—
> "I thought it good; how could I tell the lie?"
>
> And answered Nature, merciful and stern,
> "I teach by killing; let the others learn."[44]

The verse itself fulfills nature's didactic intent in aspiring to teach others to avoid the maid's mistake. Charlotte used her own unhappiness as inspiration and profited by it, not for the last time in her writing career.

In September 1885, Charlotte had published an essay in the feminist journal the *Alpha*, arguing, "Young women would take more interest in the affairs of the world if they knew the chance of happy marriage might depend on such knowledge." Her own outside interests, however, typically heightened marital tensions. As Charlotte began more actively to publish, Walter expressed his wish that "she'd strive more for beauty in poetry than for didactics, for when she does let herself forget to preach she writes very very tender & lovely things." As both a writer and a spouse, he preferred Charlotte "tender & lovely" to polemical. He may also have resented his wife's success at publishing poems, given his own failures.[45]

After returning from Pasadena, Charlotte had visited Walter's studio at the Fleur de Lys building he helped to design and criticized his paintings both aesthetically and morally, inspiring him to smash and burn one offending canvas. That October, she had objected to the "loudmouthed contempt of women's

rights" expressed by her cousin and Soapine collaborator Robert Brown. Charlotte's outspoken criticism of two men she had formerly considered allies testifies
to her mounting sense of gender antagonism. She published an allegory in the
December 1886 issue of the *Alpha* called "A Transparency," predicting the coming
of "deadly warfare" between the sexes, with no foreseeable denouement.[46] Both in
her personal life and vis-à-vis the larger world, Charlotte was girding herself for
this battle.

The day after rebuking Brown, Charlotte wrote an essay endorsing dress reform for the *Woman's Journal* that includes a meditation on the long-established
link between pain and femininity: "Physical suffering has been so long considered
an integral part of woman's nature, and is still so generally borne," she reasoned,
that any additional suffering is widely perceived as only a trivial matter of degree.
Charlotte rejected such sadistic formulations, however, and asserted that women
should endure pain only if "it is proved her duty."

Never convinced of "her duty" to be either a wife or a housewife (the conjoined sources of her current pain), Charlotte cast about her for palliatives. Having resolved to read more books on women, she borrowed from the library Elizabeth Barrett Browning's *Aurora Leigh*, a narrative poem detailing the struggles of
a woman married to her art. She also withdrew Margaret Fuller's *Woman in the
Nineteenth Century*, which enforced lessons she had learned at her first woman's
suffrage convention in the fall of 1886. Walter tried to read his wife's pro-women
books, several of which he procured for her, but he privately confessed to finding
her absorption in women's causes wearisome. He worried about the effects of her
reading program and requested a two-week moratorium. Charlotte consented,
but her zeal withstood the ban.[47]

Charlotte's publications in the early months of the new year convey her
mounting dissatisfaction with women's lot. In early January 1887, she wrote the
editor of the *Woman's Journal* to support a woman's right to work even if financially comfortable and concluded that "by all means let every woman work who
will work, and learn the power and pleasure of earning money for herself." Another letter published in the *Woman's Journal* in March chronicles the "reality of
woman's needless suffering," the restiveness of young and old wives, and the logical reasons a woman might wish she had been "born a man."[48]

As spring approached, Charlotte started to "feel dolorous" again and to complain of Katharine's disagreeableness. A record of Katharine's life that Charlotte
had been keeping sporadically notes her daughter's beauty, intelligence, and
"angelic disposition" but also records temper tantrums that had increased in frequency since her return from California. Once, after Katharine burned her fingers

on the stove, Charlotte observed, "I am glad it is done. Now she knows what fire does, and will learn to mind." The existence of this record indicates Charlotte's attempts to grow closer to her daughter and to emulate traditional mothers in focusing intensely on their children's lives. But her clinical approach tended to inhibit maternal empathy, and at times she blamed her child for her misery: "A good week since I've had full sleep, K's *doings* of course."[49]

The couple's financial crisis aggravated Charlotte's sense of antagonism. The loving Valentine Walter gave Charlotte failed to prevent them from quarreling over money the following day, with Charlotte telling Walter he must earn or she would and complaining later, "he don't work." Shortly thereafter, she accepted an offer from Alice Stone Blackwell (Lucy Stone and Henry Blackwell's daughter and the co-editor of the *Woman's Journal*) to launch a woman's column in a new labor-oriented Providence weekly.

The *People* had been established in 1885 as a mouthpiece of the Knights of Labor to champion such working-class causes as trade unionism. Charlotte would eventually write many poems empathizing with the working poor and indicting greedy capitalists; she objected most strenuously to the fate of women and children "driven to lives of shame to keep from starving." But she remained more attentive to issues of gender than to those of class or race, and her sympathy for the laboring classes was often fueled by her resentment over women being denied gainful employment.[50]

One of her *People* columns, published just before she left home for medical treatment in Philadelphia, ponders themes she later expounds in *Women and Economics* while also revealing her middle-class perspective. She declares male complaints about women's obsession with the "fashionable and frivolous" justified; she, too, censures her sex for focusing on attracting men instead of developing "the homely virtues of industry and economy." Yet she reminds men that marriage is a woman's "means of livelihood" and, supposedly, "her one chance of home and happiness"; she reminds women, "But you are not to expect it, not to look forward to it, not to make the least step toward it," words she reiterates almost verbatim in her 1898 treatise.

The catch-22 that girls must marry for a living but simultaneously refrain from actively pursuing marriage infuriated Charlotte as much in 1887 as it did a decade later. Her *People* column proposes an end to the inanity by encouraging young women to "learn a trade or profession as well as boys and have an individual independent life of their own. . . . Marriage would then be free and noble, a matter of love and choice alone. . . ."[51] The column reads like one long lament over her own now bitterly regretted choices.

By late February, Charlotte was crying over her incompatibility with Walter. She commiserated with a visitor she identified as "'another victim'" who entered marriage naively and who routinely endured her husband's "using his 'marital rights' at her vital expense." This idea that a wife owed her sexual services to her husband in exchange for her economic dependence on him would form one cornerstone of Charlotte's critique, elaborated in works like *Women and Economics*, of traditional marriages as primitive and immoral.

Visiting Martha in Hingham, she contracted a cold—"the worst of [her] life"—and subsequently passed it on to Katharine, leaving both wretched. The responsibility of nursing her sick child while ill herself led Charlotte to break down in "helpless tears." She felt increasingly trapped in Providence and her marriage; she also felt "desperately out of place among a lot of young mothers," who appeared as content with motherhood as with lives uncomplicated by ambition.[52] She spent many of the late winter days crying and napping, but slept poorly.

On March 20, 1887, Charlotte suspected she was approaching "the edge of insanity again." Walter's friend Dr. Knight—who was attending Charlotte—found her "simply hypochondriacal," but concerned friends and family agreed she needed help. A gift of $100 from Mrs. Diman, the mother of her deceased friend May, and additional funds from Mrs. Cresson, Walter's sponsor, bought Charlotte a stay at S. Weir Mitchell's sanitarium.

While conceding the treatment's necessity, Walter attributed Charlotte's melancholy to "the result of a mistake as to one's strength and the truth of life! Charlotte, dear girl, strove for self culture, and carried it mentally, physically for five years or more to a perilous extreme. But the end came with Katharine. At last, after making herself and me miserable for four or more years, she has found her real strength, which is weakness." He concluded, "no one is to be blamed unless it be the grandparents of Charlotte," indicting the Beecher zeal for service.

Charlotte, however, placed the blame squarely on Walter's shoulders. Before she left Providence, she wrote an entry in her journal, remarkable for its boldfaced condemnation of her husband:

> I am very sick with nervous prostration, and I think with some brain disease as well. No one can ever know what I have suffered in these last five years. Pain pain pain, till my mind has given way.

> O blind and cruel! Can *Love* hurt like this?

> You found me—you remember what.

> I leave you—O remember what, and learn to doubt your judgement before it seeks to mould another life as it has mine.

I asked you a few days only before our marriage if you would take the responsibility entirely on yourself. You said yes. Bear it then.[53]

Shortly thereafter she departed for Philadelphia. She did not open her diary again until 1890, the year she and Walter irrevocably separated.

~

For many years I suffered from a severe and continuous nervous breakdown tending to melancholia—and beyond. During about the third year of this trouble I went, in devout faith and some faint stir of hope, to a noted specialist in nervous diseases, the best known in the country. This wise man put me to bed and applied the rest cure. . . .
"Why I Wrote 'The Yellow Wallpaper'?" 1913[54]

Before leaving Providence for Mitchell's Philadelphia sanitarium, Charlotte wrote a detailed letter to the doctor. She wanted to relate her symptoms while still of marginally sound mind, "fearing," she admitted, "that I shall soon be unable to remember even this much." The letter provides an etiology of her illness and a pathology of her grandparents, her parents, and herself. Rosily portraying her health during childhood and adolescence, she emphasizes her commitment to "physiology and hygiene" and explains her "theory of self culture." Against the evidence of her own prenuptial diaries, where she complained more than sixty times of fatigue, she contends that until marrying Walter she "was never tired, did not know what the word meant." She could "do anything," she insisted, "and never know I had a body. As for nerves I denied their existence."

Proceeding to her "mental history," she emphasizes the powers of her imagination, its compensatory as well as debilitating effects, and her ultimate resolution to forsake thinking for doing. She speculates that her current nervous depression originated in her earlier efforts to make "mind and body . . . strong and willing servants," subject to "constant self supervision and restraint." This subjugating regimen produced lasting consequences aggravated by her current breakdown: "There is more physical prostration than ever before," she notes of her most recent relapse. "And there are mental symptoms which alarm me seriously."

If self-imposed discipline jeopardized her physical and mental well-being, then her marital experiences proved utterly devastating, or so she informed Mitchell:

Before marriage I had a very cheerful disposition, notably so; I said *I could not imagine the combination of circumstance that would make me unhappy.* Since then I have scarce known a happy moment. There have been changes of course, but no real joy. Do not lay this to circumstances. My husband is devotion itself, my child well and good, I have a lovely home, and a perfect maidservant, there is no outside trouble but poverty, and that I always had and don't mind. Neither is their [*sic*] an inside trouble, of a physical nature. I have been examined twice since the child's birth by a competent physician, and there is nothing wrong.

Neglecting to mention her youthful, melancholic episodes, Charlotte mourns the loss of her once vital self and gestures despairingly toward her aspirations to world service. She enumerates her talents as an artist, writer, poet, philosopher, teacher, reader, and thinker and maintains, "I can do some good work for the world if I live. I cannot bear to die or go insane or linger on this wretched invalid existence, and be a weight on this poor world which has so many now. I want to *work*, to help people, to do good. . . . Surely it is worth while to save a good worker, one who asks little and longs to give much!" She begs Mitchell to make her fit for her larger purpose, or at the least to prevent her from utterly succumbing to the incoherence her final sentences evince: "could go on 'scribbling' now indefinitely," she signs off, "—but the letters don't come right."[55]

If Charlotte was hoping for a sympathetic audience, she chose the wrong recipient. Dr. Mitchell had encountered such patients before. According to Charlotte in *The Living*, he dismissed her letter as proof of "self-conceit." He also revealed "a prejudice against the Beechers," having already treated Harriet Beecher Stowe's daughter Georgiana. He made a point of deriding Charlotte's aspirations: during one consultation, she mentioned an article she was in the process of drafting called "The Inutility of Sporadic Reform," a title (and intent) Mitchell swiftly deflated by suggesting it be renamed "The Uselessness of Spotty Work."[56]

In the postbellum period, Mitchell was considered the nation's foremost specialist in nervous diseases. He also had literary ambitions and, indeed, wrote more literary works than medical treatises. His income from his various ventures (his private practice and consultancies especially) approached $70,000 per annum at a time when the low four figures approximated the norm. A reformed neurasthenic himself, Mitchell's work on neurasthenia evolved from his part-time employment as an army doctor, where he treated numerous patients wounded in the nerves.[57] Soon after the war, he and two associates were chosen to run a hospital specializing in nervous disorders.

Mitchell first elaborated his famous "rest cure" in a paper delivered in 1873. "*Rest* means with me a good deal more than merely saying 'Go to bed and stay there,'" he explained; "It means absence of all possible use of brain and body." In his book *Fat and Blood*, he describes his treatment plan as strictly regimented, ranging in length for serious cases from six weeks to two months, and consisting of a series of restrictions:

> I do not permit the patient to sit up, or to sew or write or read, or to use the hands in any active way except to clean the teeth. . . . I arrange to have the bowels and

water passed while lying down, and the patient is lifted on to a lounge for an hour in the morning and again at bedtime, and then lifted back again into the newly-made bed.

Rich and fatty foods, extreme seclusion, enforced rest, and other essential components of the cure were intended to taste like "a rather bitter medicine," leaving his patients grateful when they finally received his permission to resume their former activities.[58] The doctor also prohibited his patients from dwelling on and voluntarily discussing their pains, thereby thwarting their apparent desire for an audience.

Mitchell's innovative rest cure was adopted in at least four other countries and hailed as a major breakthrough by the newcomer Sigmund Freud. Something of a nineteenth-century doctor to the stars, Mitchell counted among his patients the Hull House reformer Jane Addams, the poet Walt Whitman, the novelists Owen Wister and Rebecca Harding Davis, and the daughter of novelist William Dean Howells, Winnifred ("Winnie"). Mitchell failed to cure some patients, including Charlotte and Winnie Howells, but Rebecca Harding Davis warmly recommended the doctor to her friend Annie Fields: "I owe much to him—life—and what is better than life."[59]

Mitchell held some enlightened views on women, especially where physical activity was concerned, and he possessed a number of warm and admiring female friends. Generally, however, he concurred with his medical colleagues who cautioned that steady brain use would cripple women's health. Mitchell feared higher education would undermine "womanly usefulness," ultimately restricting female graduates to "the shawl and the sofa." Since most of his patients were women, Mitchell came to associate the sex with sickness. He suspected that menstruation and childbirth left women more thin-blooded than men and hence more susceptible to disease.[60]

Mitchell believed his patients could control their symptoms just as they could control their temper, and he instituted lessons in self-control once he saw physical improvements. As he described his method with female invalids, "Above all, you teach her the priceless lesson for a woman of the value of moods, of the ease with which she can get herself into a state of dangerous tension, of the necessity of learning not how to bear a thing, but how to approach the idea of bearing it in a state of calm."[61] Mitchell thus concentrated on teaching his female patients to retain the placid attitude of restfulness even after rest itself had been forsaken for more conventionally feminine activities.

Mitchell diagnosed Charlotte with "only hysteria," not "dementia." He typically evinced less sympathy for his hysterical patients, and he derided those who combined neurasthenic symptoms "with a bewildering list of hysterical phenomena. These are the 'bed cases'," he said, "the broken-down and exhausted women, the pests of many households, who constitute the despair of physicians, and who furnish those annoying examples of despotic selfishness . . . and in unconscious or half-conscious self-indulgence destroy the comfort of every one about them."[62] Given his peremptory references to her letter, her relatives, and her ambitions, the doctor may have placed his latest patient in this troublesome category.

Since Mitchell forbade his patients to write, Charlotte dictated a letter to her husband after the initial consultation. Upon reading the letter, Walter noted that Mitchell "seems to think her case very serious, and says that separation from home for at least a year is very desirable. . . . He says that she cannot live at home—that is the long and short of it, has a most unfortunate temperament with a graft of hysterical disorder of the mind." The doctor recommended at least a month's stay at his sanitarium, to which Charlotte acquiesced.

In her letter, she beseeches Walter to divorce her and find another woman to make him happy. Walter's sponsor, Mrs. Cresson, had accompanied Charlotte to the consultation and wrote the distraught husband "that Dr. Mitchell said that Charlotte was doubtless really insane at times . . ." and that he suspected her condition to be both chronic and incurable. These two alarming letters left Walter prostrate with "a long pent up grief." He doubted he could afford Charlotte more of the "freedom she wants" within their marriage, since already "she has had a bed to herself, has been free of the cares of the house and for the most part of the baby," and so he feared the worst.[63] The cure he had hoped might save his marriage seemed instead to be facilitating its dissolution.

Indeed, Charlotte may have considered Mitchell a potential ally in her efforts to pursue her reform ambitions unchecked. The historian Elizabeth Lunbeck has argued that hysterics often actively sought out their diagnoses in an attempt to resist normalization as well as conventional heterosexuality. Seeking an excuse to leave her marriage and to pursue her long-held goals, Charlotte listened intently when the doctor told her what she wanted to hear but disregarded what displeased her.

Although her symptoms and family history of depression indicated a genetic component, her illness did help her to slip the ties that bind. The symptoms of hysteria so closely approximated the ideals of femininity, historians have suggested, that hysterical patients could be seen as embracing them with a vengeance. Becoming so fragile and emotional that they could no longer care for house and family, they may have been using conventionally feminine behaviors to their advantage, seeking power through the limited means available to them. Put simply, hysteria could be useful to hysterics, releasing them from unwanted tasks and constricting roles, which may help to explain the prevalence of the disease. Hysteria was useful to Charlotte, at least, providing both impetus and convenient explanation for the failure of her marriage.[64]

While staying at Mitchell's sanitarium, Charlotte seemed to enjoy the treatment and the simultaneous respite from her responsibilities. Passivity proved an essential component of the rest cure, and in subsequent years Charlotte frequently relied on rest as a form of therapy. Ideally, she prided herself on being a "doer"; indeed, she argued, "What we need is not 'rest'—the cessation of action—but more power and better engines."[65] In practice, however, the often frail and exhausted Charlotte found rest indispensable to her hoped-for recovery.

Indeed, in a rare acknowledgment of the effectiveness of rest as cure, albeit with the genders reversed, Charlotte conceded in a 1911 *Forerunner* essay that activities were "not tiring or painful until unnaturally prolonged. Take any healthy man and put him to bed. Let a trained nurse wash him, shave him, feed him, and brush his teeth. . . . Keep him continuously in this position of a helpless recipient, and see if he would not exchange all the passive pleasure of the universe for the active pleasure of sawing wood!"[66]

Mitchell would have endorsed Charlotte's contention that enforced passivity teaches the value of activity, but his notion of appropriate activity differed drastically from hers. The goal of the rest cure—reorienting female patients to domestic, wifely, and maternal duties—directly countered Charlotte's own goals. In fact, Charlotte believed that the duties Mitchell saw as signifying restored health had actually caused her disease.

Prevented from writing while undergoing Mitchell's treatment, Charlotte offers her unfiltered perspective in only a handful of texts. These include a brief sketch of rest-cure life, a retrospective autobiographical description, and a harrowing fictional account. In the sketch, published in the *Woman's Journal* in 1904, Charlotte notes,

> One of the amusing things in a rest-cure is the way the nurses congregate in the invalids' bedchambers and chatter like merry magpies. Your own friends you may not see—nor books nor papers; the doctor's calls are short and quiet; no outside influence is allowed to break the charmed silence of the sick room; but these merry nurses, full of health and spirits, flit in and out as freely and converse as fluently as though the rest-cure was an afternoon tea.

Charlotte confirms the rest cure's "amusing" aspects in *The Living*, where she objects less to the rest cure administered at the sanitarium than to the post-cure prescriptions. She says she improved almost immediately under Mitchell's care, "as always when away from home." But the "agreeable" cure had a devastating aftermath, which she attributed to Mitchell's insistence that she subsequently confine herself to the home, devote herself to her child, and "never touch pen, brush or pencil as long as you live." As Charlotte succinctly explained, "I went home, followed those directions rigidly for months, and came perilously near to losing my mind." She thus suggests that it was the prescribed, enforced, and prolonged rest *at home* that exacerbated her neurotic tendencies until she "came so near the border line of utter mental ruin that [she] could see over."[67]

Charlotte's difficulties with domesticity emerged prior to her marriage: her parents' separation along with the family's multiple moves and various housing experiments did little to endear her to the home as found. As a wife, she cemented her equation between domesticity and disease but appended aggravating factors including a sexually demanding spouse and a physically and emotionally demanding child. It is little wonder, then, that she concluded that she "was well while away and sick while at home." In a letter he wrote Mitchell while Charlotte was undergoing treatment, Grace Channing's father similarly blamed "home frictions" for Charlotte's "nervous symptoms." Identifying the home as both the symbol and the cause of her suffering, Charlotte believed that the remedy lay in fleeing its duties along with its confines.

Even Mitchell doubted his cure's permanent success: for some patients the effects might be "lasting," but, he cautioned, "It is a plan never to be used where exercise, outdoor life, tonics, or change have not been thoroughly tested. . . . I never use it if I can do without it."[68] He evidently felt Charlotte needed his traditional cure, but she preferred and, ultimately, pursued the preliminary options he lists as preferable.

In 1890, having repudiated Mitchell's prescriptions and ended her marriage, Charlotte wrote her most famous story "in two days, with the thermometer at one hundred and three." "The Yellow Wall-Paper" is narrated by an unnamed, nervous new mother undergoing a modified rest cure in an ancestral mansion she and her doctor-husband have rented for the summer. Over his wife's objections, the husband chooses the "atrocious" nursery on the uppermost floor as the couple's bedroom; the room is equipped with barred windows, a bed nailed to the floor, rings hanging from the walls, and a peeling, lurid yellow wallpaper, displaying "one of those sprawling flamboyant patterns, committing every artistic sin." Charlotte, whose experience as an artist had taught her "a little of the principles of design," may have been familiar with theories emerging in the 1880s that connected garish designs to nervous irritation, sleeplessness, and other symptoms enhancing the paper's "ghastly and nightmare effect upon the brain." The external "nightmare" of the story's wallpaper triggers a parallel internal one, evident in the narrator's mental deterioration.

Prevented from reading and writing (though she records her thoughts on the sly in her diary, providing the first-person narrative we read), the narrator increasingly scrutinizes the wallpaper for meaning. She describes its pattern as "suicidal," with a recurrent image that "lolls like a broken neck, and two bulbous eyes stare at you upside down"—signifying her own suffocation as a woman, wife, and mother. Initially, she angrily expresses her objections and even attempts to change rooms, but gradually she identifies with the woman she detects "skulking about" in the paper's subpattern, "like a woman stooping down, and creeping about behind the pattern." The narrator, too, soon creeps about, acting out her identification with the wallpaper pattern while devolving from an upright rational woman to a crawling irrational child or, to use her husband's pet name for her, "little girl." Some literary critics interpret this outcome as a victory, with the narrator achieving a higher form of power through madness. But if so, her empowerment comes at considerable cost.

In the end, on the day the family is preparing to leave the rented house, the narrator locks herself in the room and peels off every last scrap of paper. She no longer seeks to liberate the wallpaper woman but instead to ensure her immobilization: she has a rope at the ready should her doppelgänger attempt to escape. Embracing the confinement she initially resisted, the narrator schizophrenically identifies with the woman in the paper, whose voice she takes on in the final lines. When he discovers his wife crawling about the room, her doctor-husband faints dead away, forcing the narrator "to creep over him" as she continues her circumnavigations. The husband's fainting slyly challenges assumptions that women are the more hysterical sex, while the well-worn "smooch" around the lower portion of the paper that "just fits" the creeping narrator's shoulder suggests this is an old story, with the narrator representing "every woman" under patriarchy, or at least every woman of leisure.[69]

Charlotte acknowledges the story's autobiographical parallels in *The Living*. She calls "The Yellow Wall-Paper" "a description of a case of nervous breakdown beginning something as mine did, and treated as Dr. S. Weir Mitchell treated me with what I considered the inevitable result, progressive insanity." Indeed, the narrator's furtive journaling echoes Charlotte's self-description, in her lengthy letter to Mitchell, as "all alone in the house or I couldn't write this"; the fragmented sentences at her letter's close—"I'm running down like a clock—could go on 'scribbling' now indefinitely—but the letters don't come right"—also evoke the narrator's semantic deterioration in the final pages. Writing in her own diary, Charlotte describes her depression in terms resembling the narrator's, noting, "I have long been ill; weak, nerveless, forced to be idle and let things drift."[70]

Likewise, when Walter speculates that "there must be something very morbid in her brain or she could not have said the irrelevant and wild things she did the other night," he calls to mind the narrator's husband. Though not a doctor, nor consistently condescending, nor utterly averse to housework, Walter did espouse conventional understandings of woman's role. The narrator's husband would have applauded Walter's conviction that "anything that takes woman away from the beautifying and sanctifying of home and the bearing of children must be sin."[71]

Yet while the story derives from Charlotte's experiences, reducing "The Yellow Wall-Paper" to autobiography risks neglecting its literary qualities—its inventiveness and aesthetic complexity. Charlotte cautions against a strictly autobiographical reading in her explanatory essay "Why I Wrote 'The Yellow Wallpaper'?" She reminds readers that the story contains "embellishments and additions, to carry out the ideal (I never had hallucinations or objections to my mural decorations)." Rather than merely reflecting her experience of nervous breakdown, the story symbolically conveys her feelings of entrapment and derangement while dealing loosely with the facts.

Many scholars continue to regard this story as her most important work and her most complex literary achievement. Charlotte herself, however, discounted the story's aesthetic value in favor of its didactic message. When it appeared in 1892, reviewers considered the story well-crafted, "powerful and original" but also "horrible"; one critic suggested that husbands should keep the story out of young wives' hands.[72] But Charlotte specifically intended it to reach young wives; she called the story "pure propaganda" designed to save women "from being driven crazy." Indeed, she identifies "The Yellow Wall-Paper" in her autobiography as "no more 'literature' than my other stuff, being definitely written 'with a purpose.'" That purpose, she claimed, was to "reach Dr. S. Weir Mitchell, and convince him of the error of his ways." She subsequently sent Mitchell a copy of the story but never heard back from him. She claims she later learned indirectly that the doctor changed his treatment after reading the tale, but no proof of Mitchell's alterations exists.[73]

Charlotte harbored no ill feelings, applauding Mitchell's 1902 essay on the prevalence of everyday heroism. Mitchell's findings, she argued, proved that the world *was* tilting toward the altruism she celebrates in a social philosophy Mitchell himself, ironically, took to indicate his patient's self-aggrandizement.[74]

~

What time or room for that sweet friendliness and association which is the foundation and fruit of love, have your ordinary married pair? He leaves the home all day
in order that he may maintain it. She toils in it all day in order that she may maintain it. . . . In the ordinary home no person has peace and privacy. It is a laborious
establishment, based on the lowest side of our nature, and requiring the sacrifice of
one or more women's lives to feed its fires.

"A New Basis for the Servant Question," 1894[75]

Charlotte returned from Mitchell's sanitarium on June 1, 1887. Walter surprised
his wife by meeting her boat en route. The couple soon retired to their state room
and passed what Walter described as "a long delightful night" together. They
stopped in Providence briefly before heading to the shore for two weeks. At first
Walter found Charlotte "very much better," but by the end of the month she
had sunk into "melancholia again, with talk of pistols & chloroform." Charlotte
believed she had hit bottom: "The mental agony grew so unbearable that I would
sit blankly moving my head from side to side—to get out from under the pain,"
she recalled. "Not physical pain . . . just mental torment, and so heavy in its
nightmare gloom that it seemed real enough to dodge." At her lowest point, she
added, "I made a rag baby, hung it on a doorknob and played with it. I would
crawl into remote closets and under beds—to hide from the grinding pressure of
that profound distress. . . ."[76] In her darkest moments, Charlotte became the child
she could not mother.

In *The Living*, Charlotte portrays these months as a period of unstinting
misery. Yet in his diary, Walter describes days and weeks when Charlotte felt well
enough to play whist, take vacations, and make social calls. He dwells on loving
interludes throughout the fall and records a pregnancy scare. Speculating that at
times "the actor side of her made her play a part, saturating her real nature with
unnatural misery," he did his best to offer distractions and kept their calendar full
in the belief that his wife needed "more than anything else a little periodical self-
forgetful dissipation."[77] Charlotte may have agreed that she needed to forget the
self, but she would have objected to dissipation as the means to that end.

In 1888, a year supposedly consumed by nervous exhaustion and mental incapacity, Charlotte published her first book, *Art Gems for the Home and Fireside*.
The roughly hundred-page illustrated volume covers forty-nine artists, each work
accompanied by commentary written by the book's author, "Mrs. Charles Walter
Stetson," a formality Charlotte may have adopted to capitalize on her husband's
better renown in the art world. Charlotte never mentions this book in any autobiographical reflection—perhaps because she published it at a time when she had

Charlotte in spring, 1887. In describing the photo, Charlotte stated, "This is what my breakdown did to me." Photo by Hurd. Courtesy of the Schlesinger Library, Radcliffe Institute for Advanced Study, Harvard University.

abandoned her journal, perhaps because she considered the book a compilation rather than an original work, or perhaps because this proof of productivity complicated her claims to debilitating illness.[78]

In August 1887, Charlotte had concocted a plan to save herself and Walter as well. She began trying to sell her share of her aunts' Hartford property, hoping with the $2,000 in proceeds to fund her trip to Pasadena and "a happy life." She encouraged Walter to move to Europe the following May, "keep a mistress," and pursue his artistic career there, "under the influence of the masterpieces." Perhaps, when both were stronger, she speculated, they might reunite in Pasadena and "live joyfully ever after."

Her sexually and emotionally frustrated husband found her plan tempting. After three years of turmoil and misery, Walter now resigned himself to Charlotte's preferences: "I love her dearly, truly, always. But I know she is unhappy, that what I give her is insufficient for her, that all my love to her ambition is as the dried husks of corn to the hungry who craves the fatted calf." He acknowledged that he could never meet her needs and admitted that he might also initially feel relieved at the separation. But he predicted that any relief would soon be outstripped by feelings of anguished longing. Her desire to leave him had already reduced him, in his own estimate, to "a sorry wreck."[79]

By late fall, Charlotte had "decided to cast off Dr. Mitchell bodily" and pursue her own agenda. This decision combined with "the great lift" of her "Western plan" led Charlotte to exclaim, "O I *am* so much better!" Her improvement also partly stemmed from her decision to stop trying to conform to Walter's expectations. As soon as she left Walter out of her "calculations" and made "no attempt to fulfill my wifely duties toward him," she informed Grace, "why straitway his various excellencies become visible again and he becomes a loved companion instead of a nightmare husband."[80] Charlotte's first marriage taught her the benefits of swapping introspection and specificity for a broader, more general perspective, even if the strain of an unraveling relationship made such a perspective hard to sustain at times.

In the new year, Charlotte increasingly clung to Pasadena as if to a raft rescuing her from her wreck of a marriage. Walter complained that his wife, who prided herself on her reasonable mind, was hatching desperate and improbable plans to get a house built for her in Pasadena "and says that it will kill her if they are not carried out."

The couple's initial separation occurred as soon as Grace Channing arrived from the West Coast. On June 7, 1888, the two friends, Katharine, and a nursemaid decamped for a "fine old-fashioned" house they had rented in nearby Bristol through September 1. Charlotte later credited Grace with saving what was left of her that summer and with reanimating her will to live. She believed her friend had rescued her from a "living death," helped her to stand on "staggering feet," and enabled her "to get to work again," situating Grace as midwife to her own emergent work ethic.[81]

Ensconced each morning in a pleasant nook by the shore, Charlotte and Grace revised the play they had drafted and performed together in Pasadena two years before, hoping it would become "the only great Comedy of the age." Charlotte boasted of writing a script that would take "the world by storm" and predicted that the two authors would become "the leading dramatists of the age! We will create a new school! We will combine the most literal realism with the highest art, and cover both with the loftiest morality!!!" Grace was equally immodest, maintaining that their brilliant collaboration would cause such "great luminaries" as William Dean Howells and Henry James to "shake in their shoes."[82]

Copyrighted in 1889, the playscript of *Noblesse Oblige* has since disappeared. Nearly a decade later, Charlotte published a poem in the *American Fabian* also entitled "Noblesse Oblige," which argues that people advantaged by birth, training, and talents owe the world their service; perhaps the play of the same name made a similar point. In a letter to her mother, Grace identified two central tenets of *Noblesse Oblige*: the "sin" of keeping "an engagement if you find you've made a mistake!" and "the divine right of true lovers." Art thus may have borrowed from life: these imperatives crossed purposes in the Stetson marriage, with Walter asserting his divine right and Charlotte ruing her mistake.[83]

As Charlotte's professional aspirations soared, her investment in her marriage dipped. Roughly two weeks into her Bristol stay, she blithely informed Walter, "I'm not homesick a bit, don't think of missing you and am getting well so fast. . . . I haven't felt *unhappy* once since I left. The fogs and mists are rolling away; I begin to feel alive and self-respecting. Oh the difference! You are very dear to me my love; but there is no disguising the fact that my health and work lie not with you but away from you." The lonely artist nonetheless made frequent, uninvited visits to the seashore, provoking his estranged wife into frequent attacks of "hysterics." In matters of love, Walter proved tenacious: even after their permanent separation, he insisted that his love for Charlotte would last "probably forever."[84]

Grace laid most of the blame for the marital breakup at Charlotte's door. She wrote her mother with veiled reference to her friend that "things are hard to us chiefly because we dwell upon them until they lose their due proportion and seem bigger than anything else in the sunrise. If you have other interests to distract and soothe you, the worse part of trouble seems to drop away." She acknowledged that Walter could be a drain on Charlotte and revealed that she had begun to see why this might be so. Yet she expressed more pity for the "delightful and exasperating" Walter and declared him "very loveable." Walter in turn considered Grace elegant, level-headed, and kindhearted, but for some time he thought of her strictly as his wife's companion and, at best, as her well-meaning surrogate.[85]

Acting as intermediary, Grace kept Walter from Charlotte while trying to persuade him to accept a separation. The Stetsons "just *prey* upon one another," she confided to her mother. "He makes Charlotte absolutely sick—she gets so exhausted and depressed. . . . And he grows as bitter and cynical in five minutes with her. But they are both charming, lovable, gifted people!" Grace repeatedly reassured her worried parent that she was standing up under the strain, but by the end of July she longed for a reprieve. She managed to derive some comic relief one night from an ill-timed visit by a pale and lovelorn Walter: the look on Charlotte's face forced Grace to flee to the privacy of her room before she burst out laughing.[86]

Laughter's medicinal effect may explain the friends' decision to write a farcical comedy amid the serious drama of marital breakdown. Even Charlotte thought a comedy an odd way to launch her public career. The genre sold, however, and both playwrights were financially strapped. "My dear girl," Charlotte assured Grace before the two embarked on their cooperative venture, "a good play is a paying thing. . . ." An impecunious childhood had taught Charlotte the power of the purse, and she clutched hers firmly to her side for the rest of her days.

Grace repeatedly informed her mother that "it was a matter of life and death with Charlotte" to have the play succeed, further proving that Charlotte used these stress-filled months to formulate her equation between human work, health, and salvation. Charlotte expected great things of this play on all fronts: "Our names shall be long in the land," she told Grace as they plotted their summer's work: "Dr. Mitchell be ————!"[87]

As summer became fall, Charlotte finalized her plans to move to Pasadena. Rowland Hazard, the father of her friend Carrie, generously agreed to purchase her share of the Hartford property, allowing Charlotte to pay off her debts and offset the costs associated with the move. Charlotte's success in securing a buyer prompted Walter's sally, "She has always had capital luck with the exception of when she married me."[88]

On October 8, 1888, Charlotte and Katharine boarded a train bound for the West Coast, accompanied by a friend of the family who had agreed to watch Katharine in exchange for her fare. The threesome was joined down the line at Niagara by Grace. Walter intended to follow shortly, vowing in the interim to "be strong & *work* to go to her."

Before departing, Grace alerted her family to the fact that Charlotte had embarked on the journey with only ten dollars in her purse; she had depleted her small reserve paying off debts and covering travel expenses. "She feels sure—and I quite so—that she can make plenty of money in a little time . . . ," Grace reassured her parents; "I do believe C. will have *no* difficulty—once started, and I guess we can 'see her through' here!" With the determination of the desperate, Charlotte refused to let her lack of resources faze her. Instead, she was banking everything on the possibility that a "west cure" and meaningful work would restore her once and for all to "hope and health and joy." [89]

California

5   "Begin New"
            (1888–1891)

> I followed Love to his intensest centre,
>> And lost him utterly when fastened there;
> I let him go and ceased my selfish seeking,
>> Turning my heart to all earth's voices speaking,
>> And found him everywhere.
>>>>>>> "Finding," 1895[1]

Charlotte hoped California would offer her the "[c]omfort and beauty and free-
dom and peace" one of her poems identifies as the state's promise to its residents.
Almost immediately after she arrived in Pasadena, she felt her spirits lift: "We are
all wearing summer clothes, and spend a good part of our time on the piazza.
Katharine luxuriates in it all and grows visibly," she informed her mother-in-law.
". . . I get up at half past six and fly about at my work as briskly as you please. . . .
There seems to be a good market for my work here, of all kinds. . . . We'll get on
swimmingly I know."[2]

    But if she swam, it was through rough currents. Charlotte thought going west
meant leaving behind a troubled marriage and heading toward a fulfilling career.
She thought right, but this journey took her longer and cost her more than she

anticipated. As a recent transplant, she expected to embark on "the new life which that great country can so well let grow at last," but the growth she experienced in the state was accompanied by sharp pains. In the past, she could blame her mother and husband for obstructing her goals; now she could blame only herself, or Katharine. Still, each new obstacle only strengthened her resolve

> To keep my health!
> To do my work!
> To live!
> To see to it I grow and gain and give!
> Never to look behind me for an hour!
> To wait in weakness, and to walk in power;
> But always fronting onward to the light,
> Always and always facing toward the right.
> Robbed, starved, defeated, fallen, wide astray—
> On, with what strength I have!
> Back to the way![3]

Part prayer, part manifesto, and a large part bravado, Charlotte's poetic resolution testifies to her optimism and determination during her first shaky years out on her own.

~

> Now with the best of good behavior on all sides persons who were in unison . . . will grow in different directions or in different proportions. . . . Also, the work of either may lie in such direction as to separate. This brings pain.
> "Pain," 1892[4]

In her desperation to flee Providence for Pasadena, Charlotte had contemplated living in a tent pitched on the Channing grounds. To everyone's relief, Dr. Channing managed to find her a "little wood-and-paper four-room house" nearby, which she rented from a Mr. Swain for ten dollars a month.[5] Charlotte moved into the house in late October 1888: "I arrived Wednesday, hired the house Thursday, selected papers Friday, had it papered & whitewashed Saturday, and moved in Monday," she wrote her mother-in-law of her first hectic week. "Since then it has been a famous piece of work to settle." For eleven dollars, she had a kitchen made out of her nine large packing cases, so that the house now contained five rooms in addition to a tiny cellar measuring 6 by 8 feet.

The ramshackle cottage was improved by its overgrown gardens: ivy, roses, periwinkle, and passion flower encroached on the house in a lush tangle of blooms. Katharine later reminisced about these "golden" Pasadena years: "I remember only sunshine and warmth and beauty—no cold, no rain, no fog, just loveliness everywhere." Charlotte and Katharine shared the only bedroom in the little house, "sleeping close to a south window shaded with white Lady Banksia roses," Charlotte recalled, "and with my condition for the only drawback, were very happy together."[6]

The reality of Pasadena, however, never measured up to Charlotte's expectations. Miss Murphy, the dressmaker she had brought from Providence to act as a "mother's helper," demonstrated her ineptitude on the train and became an "incubus" on the household in Pasadena until she was finally persuaded to leave. Charlotte then briefly took in another boarder—"another spinster, from the east"—a minister's daughter addicted to "Conversation along 'Addisonian' and 'Johnsonian' lines"; Charlotte preferred her to the incubus, but not by much.

Even the outdoor living she relished for its "calm sublimity of contour, richness of color . . . and the steady peace of its climate" was marred by the ever-present flies conveniently omitted from promotional brochures. Charlotte's persistent melancholy forced her to devote hours to convalescing; she relied on an assortment of remedies, including a newfound stimulant, cocaine (her small bottle lasted ten years). Her accounts of her postpartum experiences notwithstanding, she also often found rest curative: her little plasterless house grew hot by noon, so she passed many daylight hours seeking "nerve-rest" on the piazza. "Long, long hours in a hammock under the roses," she remembered. "Occasional times when I could write. I felt like a drowned thing, drifting along under water and sometimes bobbing to the surface."[7] Her recurrent use of swimming, drifting, bobbing, and drowning imagery suggests her difficulties staying afloat even in the land of sunshine.

For a time, she clung to her marriage as a buoy. She and Walter wrote each other every day, and her "delightful letters" convinced her ever-hopeful husband that Charlotte "loves me now as I have wished," he exulted. "She is busy very busy and says that she never had the home feeling so strong in her life. . . . Oh I love her, I love her!" Walter resolved to go to her as soon as he could afford to travel.

In December 1888, he auctioned off roughly a hundred watercolors and oils to fund his trip west. Grace Channing had encouraged him by promising commissions and patrons; Walter was easily persuaded he "had a 'call' to Pasadena. As if it were the next step forward." He set out mid-month and arrived by Christmas, moving into the little house with his wife and child. He found the climate exhilarating and Charlotte and Katharine "blossoming." He immediately hung out his shingle, setting up a studio in an unused room in the Channing house and relying on Charlotte, Grace, and Katharine as models when needed. But the local economy was sputtering, and he attracted only a handful of paying clients.[8]

The more Charlotte immersed herself in her new life, meanwhile, the more she tired of her old one: "I have lived and learned a great deal in these long dreary years of illness and melancholy," she told Martha. "Now I am busy and full of interests old and new." She filled her days with reading, writing, teaching art, and learning French, not to mention housework. She had begun writing for local journals, including the *Pacific Review* and the *Pacific Monthly*; she also planned, but never started, a new illustrated monthly to be called the *Californian*, with contributions from Grace and Dr. Channing and illustrations and sonnets from Walter. In addition, she offered a successful literature class to a dozen local women at the rate of five dollars for ten lessons. Absorbed in her work and plans, she declared that she was "feeling pretty well along now, and consequently hopeful."[9]

During her Pasadena years, Charlotte established a work routine that would become her lifelong practice. She typically wrote with her writing pad on her lap for three hours in the morning until noon; after lunch she napped briefly. In Pasadena, she did most of her writing in one of the two rocking chairs on the cottage verandah. "You have no idea how many methods of sitting in a rocking chair there are," Charlotte informed her cousin Marian Whitney; "That is if you are a limber jointed dress-reform enthusiast like me." She devoted the afternoons to visiting, talking, and reading. Occasionally, she returned to work in the evenings; on good days, she wrote until around eleven at night, breaking only for meager meals and Katharine's bedtime. Typically, however, she restricted her efforts to the mornings, since when she tried to do more, "I fizzle out," she confessed, "and have to intersperse days of gloomy idleness."[10] For work to be remedial, she had to mete it out in measured doses.

Worried that his wife might be overextending herself, Walter offered diversions, including a horse and buggy ride to the mountains and a trip to Los Angeles so that "the girls" could assess the theatrical competition. Charlotte and Grace both wrote and acted in plays in Pasadena. Once while on stage, Charlotte accidentally ignited a curtain but managed to extinguish the fire and make the incident seem like part of the script. The accident occurred at the Pasadena Opera House, which Charlotte had been hired to decorate, beating out Walter for the commission.[11]

Charlotte's dramatic aspirations occasionally inspired dreams of heading back "east—in a blaze of glory." She showed little tolerance for others' efforts in this vein, mocking a script Martha Luther Lane had asked her to assess:

Did the man wed the girl?
Yes the man wed the girl.

The same man.
The same girl.
The same old tale.

Charlotte's own variations on this tired formula differed only in degree. In Grace and Charlotte's second co-written play, *A Pretty Idiot*, the heroine hides her intellect and plays dumb in order to teach an arrogant suitor a hard lesson in feminine ideals. After her dishonesty backfires, she discards her insipid persona and falls willingly into the arms of the supportive cousin who loves her and accepts her career. *A Pretty Idiot* initially recalls the repressive script of the Stetson marriage before swerving toward a happy ending that Charlotte would herself discover in her second marriage. Walter may still have hoped his marriage would survive, but this playscript suggests that Charlotte was already plotting a different outcome.[12]

In March 1889, Charlotte informed Martha of the pleasure the transplanted group was deriving from their "hegira" and added, "Walter is very happy here, but has done little pecuniarily so far. Still we think the prospect is good, and he is painting steadily. He and Grace are great friends, which gives me sincere delight." The growing intimacy between Walter and Grace freed Charlotte to pursue her own ends. Ignored by his preoccupied wife, Walter increasingly relied on Grace for companionship. He nursed Grace through an illness that fall, and the two took several outings together, with Grace's mother acting as chaperone. He also began painting a sensual, symbolic portrait of Grace bedecked in a vine of passion flowers, many just beginning to bud. The finished portrait satisfied Walter: "it is what she is to me," he observed.[13]

Charlotte helped to foster the romance by thwarting Walter's lingering hopes of a reunion. As late as May, she still considered following her husband abroad, but by autumn such plans had been laid permanently to rest. In their divorce proceedings, Walter identified July 1889 as the last time he and Charlotte slept together. That same July, he observed:

There is almost always somebody here. Everybody seems to like to come, and Charlotte has a very long list of disciples among the young women. They simply adore her. Not only the young women but the older ones also. It is astonishing how much she has changed for the better in every way. She never was so well or so calm. She is doing lots of good work and making no end of friends without any effort. The worst of it all is that she scarcely has a moment altogether her own.[14]

Walter now believed Charlotte would "make a name for herself that nobody will be ashamed of," but he also marveled when "for a wonder" they "spent the evening at home *alone*." Charlotte similarly linked her new work and friends to her improving health but voiced no accompanying lament over the effect on her marriage. Indeed, she declared she had not felt so well since 1884—since, that is, before she married.[15]

At the end of October, Walter bluntly informed his mother that Charlotte and Katharine would not be returning with him. Walter still loved Charlotte, but Charlotte had concluded his love was simply—as she titled one of her poems— "Too Much":

> . . . some have Love's full cup as he doth give it—
> Have it and drink of it, and, ah—outlive it!
> Full fed by Love's delights, o'erwearied, sated,
> They die, not hungry—only suffocated.

A similar sense of suffocation made Charlotte eager to move on.

Her own dissolution worried her far more than her marriage's. Her devastating "weakness of brain" continued to make working and living a challenge, she informed Martha that fall, and her meager gains in health and spirits while in Pasadena remained precarious. She still hoped for a recovery but never expected to experience again the joy Martha had once inspired. Try as she might to forget her dismal married years, she bore their mark in her lingering depression and its debilitating effects on her productivity.[16]

Love affairs had consumed most of Charlotte's twenties, and the two most all-consuming of these had nearly broken her heart and health. As her thirties loomed, she sought fulfillment in the serious business of living and working. In an early 1891 *Pacific Monthly* piece, she challenges the common assumption that ". . . a woman's fling seems to end at about thirty. After that they are treasures at home, of course, but don't seem to have much individual life and ambition." By contrast, Charlotte at thirty had rejected domesticity to pursue her ambitions unchecked.

Soon after turning thirty, she conceded that she had "[m]ade a wrong marriage—lots of people do. Am heavily damaged, but not dead. May live a long time. It is intellectually conceivable that I may recover strength enough to do some part of my work. I will assume this to be true, and act on it." She recommended to Martha a course she intended to pursue herself, encouraging her friend to derive contentment primarily from becoming "an integral part of our present social world."[17]

Charlotte considered divorce a necessary evil comparable to surgery: "No one elects for his own pleasure to be anæsthetized and cut up; but a surgical operation is often better than dying of what ails you." Walter proved the more reluctant patient. He knew his marriage was over, and he promised his parents he would head home as soon as possible; yet he lingered on in Pasadena into the new year, in part cultivating his relationship with Grace, in part grasping at straws.

He finally left abruptly in January 1890 after receiving a telegram belatedly summoning him to his dying mother's bedside. Charlotte considered his departure the moment of "definite open separation." She kept up the pretense that she was amicably married, if only to preserve her standing in the community. When

Walter's portrait of Charlotte, 1891. Courtesy of Walter Stetson Chamberlin.

speculation mounted as to the "whereabouts of Mr. Stetson," a local paper reported that career demands and climate preferences kept them on opposite coasts but "[t]heir family affairs are altogether harmonious."[18]

Walter continued to write Charlotte "daily, bravely, affectionately, lonesomely." He painted a portrait of Charlotte in 1891 that he dedicated to his estranged wife "in memoriam." He told Grace's mother that the "exquisite torture" Charlotte had caused him could do nothing to taint memories of their intimate years "so infinitely lovely that I am sure they could never be surpassed—not alone in matters of love; I do not mean that, but in matters of character, in her judgments of people; in her intimate personal life," he observed. "She is a very strange, very perplexing, a very trying, and withal a very lovely and loveable woman; and I think it not a little thing that I who have suffered most because of her can say it so heartily."

Charlotte, for her part, felt nothing but numb. Relaying the news of Mrs. Stetson's death to Martha, she conjured up an image of the "sad joyless old woman dying without one glimpse of her last born and best loved; and he not even seeing his mother's face! And no wife to comfort him." She would have offered cold comfort, since she considered herself beyond grieving. "I haven't any heart but a scar," she told Martha, "and I get nothing out of it by patient application but pathetic and agonized squirms. So I will hide the thing away again. . . . I don't venture to *feel* much, about anything. Now I guess I will shut the door of my heart again; and hang on it: '*Positively* no admittance except on Business!'" Charlotte had relied on similar imagery after Martha's defection, as her repeated "agains" attest. The failure of her marriage further persuaded her she would rather work than feel, or rather feel only while working.[19]

~

It matters little about me,
If so I be
Able to make the effort
   of one soul
Help on the whole.

Only not too much *pain*!
Oh not again!
That anguish of dead years
   Terrors and tears!

                    Poem inserted in diary, "Dec. 31st, 1891. Near 12"[20]

Charlotte knew she produced some of her best work between 1890 and 1894. She also knew her emotional and mental turmoil left her more of a "wreck" when she left California than when she arrived. Convinced that work led to fulfillment, Charlotte had difficulty making sense of her bouts of emotional and physical wretchedness during this particularly prolific period. She complained periodically of a "ghastly below-zero weariness" and referred to especially bleak stretches as "drowned time."

She was diagnosed with uterine retroversion and congestion, which she traced back to "those years of prostrate weeping—supine mostly"; she also blamed "the worry and housework" associated with her move to Pasadena, which she suspected had "pulled on those heavy things and upset 'em." She later claimed that over the course of her life she spent far more time helplessly suffering than she ever did energetically achieving her goals, yet because she had successfully managed to compartmentalize her private woes and public successes, others doubted her enduring "wretchedness" whenever she complained of it.[21]

What her acquaintances *could* see were a string of attention-getting successes. Prior to 1890, her total publications numbered some thirty items. In 1890 and 1891 combined, she published roughly thirty pieces of nonfiction, thirteen works of fiction, two dramas and dialogues, and twenty-two poems. In a single month in 1890, she boasted of having "some thirty or forty things out," circulating at various venues.[22]

Charlotte had picked an auspicious place and year for such an outpouring. As a locus for literary apprenticeships, California promised much: Mark Twain and Bret Harte numbered among those who wrote their first stories in the state. Charlotte's residence coincided with a statewide literary renaissance, especially in southern California—a region referred to by locals as "the Mediterranean of America" or "the American Italy." While the West boasted only 5 percent of the country's population and only 4 percent of its adult women, it housed 15 percent of the nation's female authors. Most of the writers who came to prominence during this boom were transplants: one resident defined a California writer as "one who was born in California—or else one who was reborn in California," and Charlotte counted among the latter.[23]

A number of these writers, Charlotte included, participated in the various reform movements sweeping the nation and the state during the nineties. Turn-of-the-century California served as a microcosm of the social conditions and issues that motivated progressives nationwide. Despite or because of five years of grueling economic depression, reformers resolved to transform country and state so that both might achieve their edenic promise.

Two political causes in particular offered Charlotte a platform for her talents during her California years: the woman's and the nationalist movements. After

Colorado passed a woman suffrage referendum in 1893, expectations soared that its neighbors would soon follow suit, and the campaign in California intensified. Charlotte vigorously dedicated herself to the broader cause of women's rights while a resident of the state. Her involvement in the cause had begun while she was living on the opposite coast: in 1887, for example, she had campaigned in Providence for a woman suffrage amendment only to see it defeated at the polls roughly a month before she left for Mitchell's sanitarium.

In California, she identified her chief concern as the "woman question." She supported suffrage, advocated economic independence, and drew upon her own difficult experiences as she worked to attain broader improvements in women's lives. For example, she declared marriage a disaster-in-the-making: "to-day the whole internal lives of man and woman are opposed. They work from different motives, by different means, toward different purposes. . . . And yet these two beings are expected to live together as equals, to understand, to sympathize, to love."[24] When expectations fell short of reality, what were women who had put all their eggs in the marital basket to do?

Rather than promising a happy ending, Charlotte portrayed the battle of the sexes as incessant and escalating. In 1890, she produced a five-act mini-drama for *Kate Field's Washington* encapsulating *The Ceaseless Struggle of Sex*. The male and female protagonists begin each brief seven-line act by greeting each other amicably, only to devolve into a fight before each short act's close. The final act diverges from this reiterated framework by inserting for the first time the adverb "awfully!" after the consistent "they fight" refrain, thus thwarting any hope of progress. The unhappy ending intentionally shatters the rose-colored glasses Charlotte believed most women donned to view both men and marriage. Like her generic female dramatic protagonist, she had become a fighter, not a lover.[25]

For all her dedication to women's issues, Charlotte's first taste of fame came from the nationalist movement. With countless other converts, she learned the principles of nationalism from its founder, Edward Bellamy, via his bestselling utopian novel, *Looking Backward: 2000–1887* (1888). The novel's protagonist, Julian West, awakens from a drug-induced sleep, over a century long, to find himself in the year 2000 and in a society virtually unrecognizable as his own. In this new nation, which had evolved from a formerly debased state into a flawless social system, citizens work in the "industrial army" for one employer, the nation. The workers range in age from twenty-one to forty-five; retirement at forty-five leaves retirees ample time to pursue additional interests. Female workers could also take extended maternal leave. Private industry having been abolished, duty to country and humanity motivates workers instead of personal profit, and the nation runs smoothly and benevolently on the principle of cooperation; the individualism and competition endemic to capitalism have vanished.

Looking Backward became an overnight sensation. One of some forty utopian socialist novels published around the time of the millennium, it proved by far the most popular. More than a million copies had sold by the time it reached its tenth anniversary, and a thousand copies of the novel were sold each day at the height of the "Bellamy craze." Prominent writers sang Bellamy's praises: no less a cynic than Mark Twain called the book "the latest and best of all Bibles." The reclusive Bellamy was thrust reluctantly into the limelight.[26]

A primer in socialism for many of its readers, *Looking Backward* was greeted as a compromised utopia by skeptics. For instance, the anarchistic socialist William Morris—who would write an influential anti-Bellamy utopia, *News from Nowhere* (1890)—criticized its "unhistoric" and "unartistic" vision. Bellamy's middle-class biases and stubborn idealism disappointed even sympathetic readers, including Laurence Gronlund, the author of another influential utopian text, *Cooperative Commonwealth* (1884), from which many of Bellamy's ideas were derived. Gron-lund espoused the nationalist cause but praised *Looking Backward* with faint dam-nation. He deemed Bellamy's work a typical expression of dissatisfaction from the "intellectual classes" (that is, the "million Americans who are not workers") with their increasingly materialistic and commercial society. Fellow reformer Henry George also regretted its idealism, referring to the novel as "a castle in the air with clouds for its foundation."[27]

Bellamy agreed that the novel offered a vision but not a radical blueprint: "There was no thought of contriving a house which practical men might live in," he insisted, employing George's same metaphor, "but merely of hanging in mid-air, far out of reach of the sordid and material world of the present, a cloud palace for an ideal humanity." He had intended simply to sketch an ideal of social happiness via cohesion and solidarity rather than pinpoint the steps necessary to attain his goals. By the time his book had spawned a movement, Bellamy publicly identified nationalism as "essentially gradual and progressive rather than abrupt or violent," and he confessed his inability to "stomach" the "word socialist."[28] Although he would become an increasingly radical and vocal proponent of socialism and popular democracy in coming years, his bestseller's more conservative views enthralled most readers.

"Nationalism" derived its name from the nationalization of industry promoted in the novel. Its mesh with the larger turn-of-the-century social gospel move-ment—whose disciples asked themselves the question "What would Jesus do?" and sought literally to follow "in his steps"—induced Bellamy to call nationalism "nothing more than Christianity applied to industrial organization." At the same time, *Looking Backward* also appealed to scientists and capitalized on the evolutionary spirit of the times. Bellamy maintained that there is "nothing in the National plan which does not already exist as a germ or vigorous shoot in the present order, and this is so simply because Nationalism is evolution." The movement collected converts of all persuasions, so much so that its mouthpiece, the *Nationalist*, "could carry an article defining Nationalism as true conservatism . . . and another calling for the immediate destruction of the bourgeois state."[29] A movement this loosely defined could appear all things to all people, helping to explain its phenomenal popularity.

The first nationalist club formed in Boston in 1888. Its founding members included the reigning "Dean" of American literature, William Dean Howells; the suffrage leader Mary Livermore; the abolitionist, author, and mentor to Emily Dickinson, Thomas Wentworth Higginson; the author, reformer, and eventual surrogate mother to Charlotte, Helen Campbell; and the author, reformer, and uncle to Charlotte, Edward Everett Hale. Some 162 clubs soon sprang up nationwide, a surprisingly successful propagation given Bellamy's boast that "there never was, perhaps, a reform movement that got along with less management than that of the Nationalists. There never has been any central organization and little if any mutual organization of the clubs."[30]

Roughly one-third of the nationalist clubs, the most in the nation, formed in California, and most of the members in that state (true elsewhere as well) were from the middle class. One local observer noted the movement's "strength . . . among the middle classes. For the most part they are people connected with literature and the professions." In California, members were also mostly women, more so than in the movement's point of origin, Boston. Middle-class women may have joined out of sympathy with the nationalist ethos, which emphasized traditionally feminine values such as association, cooperation, mutual love, and interdependence and rejected putatively masculine traits like individualism and acquisitiveness. Bellamy explicitly pitched his movement to women, asserting that nationalism "is particularly and emphatically the cause of women." Organized in May 1889, the active Los Angeles chapter published its own paper and hosted lecturers, including Edward Everett Hale and his niece, Charlotte.[31]

Charlotte explained the nationalist fervor in California by describing the state as "particularly addicted to swift enthusiasms," an addiction she shared. As one of Charlotte's sympathizers remarked in an 1891 sketch, "it is the fear of her friends that she may voluntarily renounce the brilliant literary career now opening before her, and devote her talents to the cause of Nationalism, of which she is an ardent supporter with both pen and voice, believing its doctrines with the faith of a disciple, and advancing them with the ardor of the enthusiast."

Her Uncle Hale initially solicited her manuscripts and encouraged her involvement, but Charlotte quickly asserted herself. She lectured frequently on nationalist topics, and many of these lectures were covered in nationalist papers. After delivering her first "warmly received" nationalist lecture, solicited by a stranger on a bus, she was soon speaking every other Sunday in the greater Los Angeles area. "It was pleasant work," she recalled. "I had plenty to say and the Beecher faculty for saying it." Harriet ("Hattie") Howe, a friend and fan who attended a nationalist lecture Charlotte gave in Los Angeles, affirmed Charlotte's powerful effect on audiences: "a slender woman, seeming on the platform even smaller than she really was, with—Eyes! Such eyes, magnetic, far reaching, deep seeing, nothing could be hid from such eyes, and a Voice, clear, compelling, yet conversational, easily reaching to the farthest end of the hall, entirely devoid of effort."[32] Her nationalist lectures finally allowed Charlotte to realize her childhood dream of becoming "a Voice."

The broad ideals of nationalism appealed to Charlotte, as did its fundamental tenet "that everyone owes the world a reasonable service." She found especially attractive the movement's gradual, noncombative take on evolution and its organic conception of society—within which each individual functioned as merely a cell in the larger social structure. These seemed to her essential truths that jibed with her personal philosophy while simultaneously providing solutions to endemic social problems.

Bellamy's pro-woman rhetoric helped to cement her attachment. His new nation afforded women meaningful work outside the home and eliminated housework inside it (Bellamy advocated public kitchens and laundries); he also appointed working mothers to important positions out of respect for their contributions. Women in his utopia were valued primarily for their consumerism, but they were no longer economically dependent upon their husbands; both men and women depended on the state for their livelihood, leaving them relatively autonomous in their personal relations. Charlotte undoubtedly applauded Bellamy's emphasis on women's economic independence, and she shared his conviction that eliminating women's need to marry for money would result in better marriages, superior offspring, and "race purification."[33]

Many of Bellamy's seemingly radical views on women, however, originated from conventional, even conservative positions. Although women in *Looking Backward* are revered as workers, their hours are limited, and men ultimately "permitted them" to work. Bellamy also insisted on distinct differences between the sexes. Lecturing on woman's rights, he enumerated the problems stemming from women's increased presence in the workplace, arguing that "women are not so strong as men, nor can they, except in a few special lines, do so much work. . . . There is the rub. That is the natural, insuperable difficulty in the way of any plan which proposes that women shall depend upon earning their way to equality with men by the market value of their labor." According to Bellamy, staking woman's claim for equal rights on her economic potential would be profoundly mistaken. He preferred to base her case instead on her status as the race's "burden bearer": "Her weakness is a title, more sacred than his strength, to all the fruits of the human heritage."[34]

What Bellamy deemed a weakness, Charlotte proclaimed a strength, arguing that woman's greatest power stemmed from her role as mother of the race. Charlotte paid more attention to the position of women and the care of children than did Bellamy. Both viewed women as domestic drudges, but Bellamy's solution idealistically erased housework's necessity, whereas Charlotte proposed more efficient alternatives. Neither questioned the logic that made housework "women's work," however.

Charlotte conceded that *Looking Backward* may not be "literature" and instead described the novel as "the supreme triumph of truth over inadequate form." She insisted, however, that "it has far more importance in other ways." Defending Bellamy's "forecasting book" from her friend Martha's criticisms, she countered, "I grant that Bellamy has no style. I wonder if John the Baptist had? Is it possible that you see nothing in that book but its poor execution?"[35]

Charlotte's prophet analogy suggests that Bellamy also served her as a spiritual mentor. Bellamy's religious principles resonated with the theosophists—who preached "the entire renunciation of one's personality." They also echoed certain precepts of Comtean positivism, which Bellamy defined as the individual's "obvious duty to forget the self in service" to humanity. Yet the evolution of Bellamy's religion predates his dalliance with either school.[36]

In 1874, he outlined his fundamental beliefs in a manuscript entitled "The Religion of Solidarity." He begins by identifying a human instinct to lose oneself in the infinite and unite with the larger cosmos. He then argues that mankind would benefit immensely from suppressing the self and merging with this greater, organic collective. Without this merger, he argues, we will remain individuals in the most atomized sense, doomed to discontentment, restlessness, and a "homesickness" "for a vaster mansion than the personality affords."

Bellamy identifies various avenues to this solidarity, including sex and mysticism, but he ultimately champions purposeful endeavor. Once we understand the self as dual, comprising both personal and impersonal aspects, and once we recognize the former as finite, ephemeral, selfish, insignificant, and imprisoning, and the latter as infinite, abiding, great, and true, we can then work consciously toward incarnating this eternal, impersonal identity. To Bellamy, solidarity and personality are antagonistic forces: one's sense of self as unique or separate must be abandoned in order to achieve solidarity and to lead a moral life. Bellamy thus stipulates,

> in losing our personal identity, we should become conscious of our other, our universal identity, the identity of a universal solidarity—not losable in the universe, for it fills it. . . . The individuality is of so little importance, of such trifling scope, that it should matter little to us what renunciations of its things we make, what inequalities, what deprivations in its experiences we endure. We should hold our lives loosely, and not with the convulsive grip of one who counts personal life his all.

Bellamy's emphasis on the communal over the individual and the impersonal over the personal, along with his recommended indifference to personal insult, injury, and deprivation, were convictions Charlotte shared. Bellamy later claimed that this early piece contained the "germ" of all his subsequent thinking, and Charlotte—whose teenaged religion made her all the more responsive to his message—not only caught the bug but sought to infect others.[37]

Nationalism afforded Charlotte a congenial set of precepts at the very moment she was seeking to launch her career as a public servant, and her embrace of these precepts outlasted the movement itself. With the suspension of its magazine in 1894, the nationalist movement folded, a victim of the 1893 financial panic, Bellamy's growing disillusionment with populism, and his followers' attraction to other, newer causes. Of all the movements Charlotte restlessly aligned herself with, nationalism suited her best. At least, she never evinced toward nationalism the impatience and fault-finding she demonstrated vis-à-vis other causes, and she continued to espouse nationalist principles decades after the movement's demise. The historian Mary Beard, who knew Charlotte late in life, attributed her friend's career as a reformer to the "idealistic socialism" embodied in Bellamy's novel.[38]

Around the time she converted to nationalism, Charlotte also read Patrick Geddes and J. Arthur Thompson's influential *Evolution of Sex*. This book shaped her thinking in myriad ways but doubtless strengthened her investment in altruism. The book explores metabolic differences between the sexes, but the two scientists also speculate about evolution's moral and theological thrust and argue that "it is possible to interpret the ideals of ethical progress, through love and sociality, co-operation and sacrifice, not as mere utopias contradicted by experience, but as the highest expressions of the central evolutionary process of the natural world."[39]

Whether cloaked in the guise of science or religion, such observations helped persuade Charlotte of the rightness of her path. She was right to embrace cooperation and solidarity, right to firmly repudiate individualism, right to seek meaning through public service, and wrong to dwell on personal disappointments. The most advanced and celebrated theorists of her day corroborated her deepest personal convictions, emboldening her to make them public.

~

As woman grows into broader and freer life, all mankind will grow with her, and we shall find public spirit and catholic altruism take the place of our callous indifference to matters of general good and exalted self-sacrifice on the home altar.

"Ought a Woman to Earn Her Living?"
August 1891[40]

Lecturing remained Charlotte's principal livelihood during her California years. She supported herself and her small daughter on the proceeds, with some supplemental funds from writing and teaching along with loans from concerned friends.

By all accounts Charlotte was a gifted public speaker, for which she thanked her Beecher blood. She delivered talks in large halls and in crowded parlors, before audiences made up exclusively of women as well as audiences in which the men and women were evenly mixed. In 1891, she began preaching sermons in churches, an activity she preferred to lecturing: she felt that her inherited affinities meant that all her work ought to be considered "preaching." Besides, she wryly observed, "In church people think they have to believe what they hear." Whether from the pulpit or the lectern, she preached a humanistic gospel with "God" her shorthand for the force of progress. When shocked conservatives asked her if she was espousing a "personal God," she rejected the adjective "personal" as too insultingly limited for so pervasive a "Central Force."[41]

In the early 1890s, Charlotte first abandoned her notes and began speaking extemporaneously. This decision enabled her to deliver lectures that struck listeners as "an off-hand talk—a confidential chat with serious-minded people, evidently considered by the lecturer to be her intellectual equals." She soon learned to deal with audiences according to her worldview, refusing to "look at them at all—as persons. . . . I talk to 'It'," she said, by which she meant a generalized, collective humanity. She simultaneously encouraged her listeners to become that collective. She thus instructed one audience that the 2,000-year-old "hope of a better Hereafter" could only be supplanted by the more important "hope of a better Here" once each person finally forsook this "paltry round of self-interest" and began living in "the life of all."[42]

On rare nights, Charlotte confessed to being "not as great as I should have been—as wise, as calm, as patient, as loving. Let my irritation show," she reflected after one less than impressive performance. "Such paltry people! Such feeble minds! Such ignorance!" Once, a crowded house greeted a talk on a beloved theme, "The Ethics of Woman's Work," with palpable antagonism. Charlotte condemned "the wrongness of private housework" in the speech. Anticipating the 1908 Brandeis brief, she reeled off a list of detriments, including "frequent heavy lifting, its long hours, its nerve exhausting variation and repetitions, its constant having of the hands in water, its endless stepping and standing"—all aspects of routine housework Charlotte resisted in whatever place she called home. Her denigration of "women's work" combined with her labeling "all our mothers woman servants" raised hackles.[43]

Yet overall, she experienced far more hits than misses as a lecturer. One listener described her as a "delicious and wholly contradictory jumble of exceedingly clever femininity, whom it is a pleasure to watch and a delight to hear." Particularly successful was her series of three lectures on "The Human Paradox": the first on "An Old Baby" (man), the second on "A Married Child" (woman), and the third on "Heaven Underfoot" (her solution to these paradoxes, which lay in "The making right of the women of this world"). "Her object was to persuade women to think for themselves instead of accepting what they were told to think," one admirer insisted, but Charlotte also enjoyed telling other women what to think. In a series of "Twelve Lectures to Ladies," for example, she confidently propounded solutions to women's problems in terms that render these lectures working drafts for her later treatises.[44]

Charlotte knew how to use props effectively: a memorable talk on dress reform included charts depicting the effects of habitual corset-wearing on a horse; she elsewhere displayed a statue of the *Venus de Milo* or a dressmaker's dummy to illustrate similar points. Audiences came away impressed by her unique mix of pungent paragraphs, humorous anecdotes, and dramatic recitation. She frequently read aloud from Olive Schreiner's allegorical *Dreams*, which she declared a fount of "vital truth, aspiration, reality for the whole human race." If, as often happened, she was asked by an enthusiast to recite her own verse, she "dropped her head like a bashful school girl, and in a clear, distinct, pleasant voice began. When a point was to be made, she lifted her head, and flashed in a witticism upon her audience. Every feature helped to express her meaning."[45]

Nothing unsettled her, not even a pesky fly she once swallowed before calmly proceeding with her talk. One reporter described her manner as "bright and taking. She has a happy knack of clothing conventional ideas in new phrases, as well as uttering original thoughts . . . frequently interrupted by uproarious bursts of applause." Hattie Howe called each lecture "an EVENT." She claimed, "I sat enthralled. I knew at once that I had met the greatest personality that I had ever seen, or likely ever would see." Charlotte thus emerged as a public "personality" at the same time as she privately strengthened her investment in holding "personality in abeyance."[46]

~

> Help me to work! To really do the things I have in mind. To write—write—write. . . . [P]our in—pour in—give me more and more of the great stream of life. Let me feel it and give it out in all the ways I know. This means health and power and all good. Help me O God!
>
> Diary entry, 1894[47]

Charlotte's lectures brought her local prominence, but her poems made her the talk of the nation, or at least of the nationalists. Her most famous poem, the satirical "Similar Cases," was published in the April 1890 *Nationalist* and led to Bellamy's proclaiming her the "poet of Nationalism." An 1891 essay on the literary development of California singles out "Similar Cases" as a "brilliant satire," identifies Charlotte as a rising star, and asserts that "any member of that sex which claims humor as its special prerogative" (i.e., men) would have been proud to claim authorship. Charlotte found the praise of two prominent nationalists especially gratifying: her Uncle Hale congratulated her on the poem's "perfection" and her mounting fame; the influential author and editor William Dean Howells wrote her that he had read the satire with "unfading joy" because it was "so good in a good cause."[48]

"Similar Cases" mocks conservatives who had mocked reformers for idealistically subscribing to the malleability of human nature. The poem relies on evolution to prove that nature changes: the Eohippus realizes his dreams of becoming a horse; the "Anthropoidal ape" evolves into his ideal Man; "Neolithic man" boasts that "in course of time, / We shall be civilized!" and, despite the derision of his "Neolithic neighbors," gets the last laugh. The concluding thrust identifies as the true Neanderthals those who still cling to their outmoded beliefs in the fixity of human nature.

Charlotte dedicated "Similar Cases" to the economist General Francis Walker, a Bellamy opponent who had reviewed *Looking Backward* hostilely. The poem follows a simple, quotable aa–bb rhyme scheme and was quoted "from one end of the land to the other." It was reprinted in numerous venues, set to music, lengthened with additional stanzas by other reformers, freely plagiarized, and beloved by a diverse array of public figures, including President Woodrow Wilson and the sociologist Lester Frank Ward, who called it "the most telling answer that has ever been made" to their conservative opponents.[49]

Seeking to bolster her reputation as a poet and writer in the wake of her success, Charlotte dashed off several new poems similarly debunking conservative views. She also composed a handful of verse celebrating "Little Flutters of California Beauty" and compiled a group of poems originally written for Katharine's entertainment into a book of children's verse entitled *Mer-Songs*, launching her futile quest to see the volume published in her lifetime. She wrote fiction as well, producing at the height of her nationalist fervor several sketches, a ghost story, and her acclaimed "The Yellow Wall-Paper," which took two days to write but two years to publish.[50] Charlotte may have elsewhere struggled to keep her private and public life separate, but both *Mer-Songs* and "The Yellow Wall-Paper" reveal that she felt little compunction about mining private moments for compelling, publishable material.

Charlotte produced her first collection of poems in the fall of 1893, a small 120-page volume entitled *In This Our World*, containing seventy-five poems and measuring roughly 6 by 5 inches. The collection was published by two Oakland socialists; the costs of production were covered by subscriptions totaling roughly seventy-five dollars. Some 1,500 copies of this softcover first edition saw print, priced at a quarter a piece. Charlotte designed the desert-themed soft cover, inspired by Schreiner's sketch "Three Dreams in a Desert."[51]

As the book was going to press, Hattie Howe remonstrated with Charlotte and her printers for their ignorance: when the latter sent the proofs with the flyleaf title page on the lefthand side, Charlotte reacted to the error with a shrug. After yet another friend insisted the book would be ridiculed, Charlotte finally requested a correction. Charlotte marketed *In This Our World* herself, circulating copies among friends and asking them to place the book in local bookstores. She blithely told one friend that the volume represented her "first birth . . . and a fine promising child it seems to the fond mother."[52]

In This Our World was divided into three sections— "The World," "Woman," and "Our Human Kind" (in later editions, "The March")—that illustrated Charlotte's central concerns. The volume expanded over the course of four subsequent editions, each larger than the last. Charlotte took her beloved Whitman as her model not only in the sequential editions but also in a number of the poems, including "Desire" and "Immortality," which rely heavily on grass imagery. Horace Traubel, Whitman's friend and literary executor, warmly reviewed the first edition, although he did caution that substance triumphed over style.[53]

While accomplished in a variety of poetic forms and capable of crafting beautiful verse, by the 1890s Charlotte had become an increasingly didactic poet for whom message rightly trumped craft. In 1890, the same year "Similar Cases" appeared, she published two critical essays in the *Pacific Monthly*. In them she dissociated true literature from popular literature, disdained marketing techniques such as lurid covers and enticing titles, derided love stories in favor of nobler, collective ideals, and defended writing for a purpose as opposed to writing for a profit. She elsewhere delighted in learning that her poems were "useful to, and used in many a pulpit." When her friend the poet Edwin Markham refused to call her verse poetry, she replied, "Granted, but please tell me what it is." Several years later, Charlotte identified their nature to a reporter, calling *In This Our World* "a tool box. It was written to drive nails with."[54]

Henry Austin, a reviewer for the *Bookman*, concurred that the poems were polemical, but he also read certain poems intended to be pedagogical as autobiographical: "To listen too seriously to Mrs. Stetson's raging dithyrambs about the washtub and her denunciations of the 'Holy Stove' might make one believe that she had often been obliged to rise betimes and light the fire, while her liege lord was smoking that *ne plus ultra* of Bohemianism, a cigar before breakfast," he observed caustically. Charlotte doubtless preferred Austin's acknowledgment of Whitman's influence, as in his references to "the 'ultra-barbaric yawp' of this California Apostle of the New Woman" and to her willingness to "'loaf and invite her soul.'"[55]

The praise of famous men proved even more effusive: William Dean Howells informed Charlotte of the pleasure he and others were deriving from her wise and witty book, declaring, "You are not only the prophetess of the new religion . . . but you speak with a tongue like a two edged sword. I rejoice in your gift fearfully, and wonder how much more you will do with it." Edward Bellamy confessed his intent to "pirate" some of her poems for his nationalist journal. He credited her verse with expressing "faith in and aspiration toward the larger life which seems to be opening to women."

She received an especially enthusiastic reception after a British edition was published in 1894: The London *Daily Chronicle* praised *In This Our World* as a "volume of vigorous verse by an American woman, breathing the spirit of humanitarian progress of the warm western type." Such tributes, combined with warm reviews "by certain discerning papers," led Charlotte to conclude the volume was "going off splendidly," bringing "small returns in cash but much in reputation."[56]

As the years passed, except when editing journals, Charlotte devoted less time to poetry and more to prose, even though she claimed to find verse "as easy as

prose." When she did write poetry, she wrote fewer private poems. "Personal emotions are rare and elusive in all of Charlotte Gilman's poetry," her friend Amy Wellington observed: "Never was poet less given to the luxury of self-expression." Yet
Wellington based her judgment on Charlotte's published poems, which tended to
advance her cardinal themes of public service, social reform, and women's progress; those she never published—her love poems, specifically—were deeply personal, often heartfelt testaments to joy, pain, and loss.[57]

Her papers contain few if any private poems written after 1893, the year the
first edition of *In This Our World* appeared and her latest relationship ended badly.
She did write a handful of verse for her second husband Houghton—fairly perfunctory expressions of satisfaction and happiness that lack the introspection and
anguish of her earlier private verse. Charlotte may have felt less passion for Houghton than she did for her previous lovers, but she also may have learned by the time
she remarried how to suppress her personality, at least when it came to poetry.

~

> If it be that I may not have—as indeed I never have had, personal happiness; or rather
> happiness in personal relation; it follows that I must ensure as far as may be, happiness
> in general relation.
>
> "Thoughts & Figgerings," 1894[58]

At a party honoring Susan B. Anthony on her seventy-first birthday, Charlotte
praised the first generation of suffrage leaders for sacrificing so much on behalf of a cherished cause: "They had to triumph over their woman hearts and
woman bodies and become human beings. . . . Do you think this is a light
thing? It is a terrible thing. Their heads knew they were right and they went
ahead, but there were times when their hearts ached for the common woman's
need of praise and petting."

Charlotte's maternal responsibilities brought the activists' dilemma home.
She delighted in her "ecstatic and aesthetic child" and laughed indulgently when
Katharine "reassuringly" informed her, "I love you better than I love a stick!" But
her parenting responsibilities weighed on her, and she could no longer turn to her
husband or best friend for help.[59]

Although her father Frederic lived nearby, he saw Charlotte infrequently and
met his granddaughter for the first time when she was almost seven. Charlotte
had located a school in the parlor of a kind neighbor, which kept Katharine occupied while she worked, but instruction ended each day before her workday did.
Friends, neighbors, and admirers helped to care for Katharine while Charlotte lectured, but she could not rely on such a makeshift solution permanently. Katharine

increasingly resented being farmed out: she once "howled awfully" for her mother after a particularly difficult and lengthy separation.[60]

Charlotte's California acquaintances apparently considered her parenting methods of "suggestion" and "reasonable appeal" outlandish: "Discipline and obedience were still the ideal then," she later remarked. "My ideas looked to them not only wrong in principle but impracticable." Her willingness to dress Katharine in boy's clothing, for instance, led other mothers to accuse her of neglecting her child.[61] During the Pasadena years, however, Charlotte worried more about neglecting her duty to a larger world. Her poem "Baby Love" conveys her difficulties as a parent as well as her emergent priorities:

> . . . Mother Life was sitting there,
> Hard at work and full of care,
> Set of mouth and sad of eye.
> Baby Love came prancing by.
>
> Baby Love was very proud,
> Very lively, very loud;
> Mother Life arose in wrath,
> Set an arm across his path.
>
> Baby Love wept loud and long,
> But his mother's arm was strong.
> Mother had to work, she said.
> Baby Love was put to bed.[62]

In this poem as in life, work preempts child, a justifiable preemption according to Charlotte's social philosophy, which placed "the interests of the one" beneath "the interests of the many." Mother love must be used, she argued: it is not an end in itself, and it loses precious value when squandered too narrowly. A woman who broadens her preoccupations so as to prioritize the welfare of humanity over both self and child will bring a more vital and uplifting love back home to "her dear ones."[63]

Charlotte believed that, "like all passions," maternal passion required "conscientious and rational restraint." This belief informed her efforts to treat the often subjective and irrational parent–child relationship scientifically: her first attempts to publish a scientific method of childrearing appeared in the early 1890s. She considered her dispassionate model an improvement on "primitive" maternal impulses, and she defined an evolved mother as one who allowed her intellect to govern her parenting decisions while simultaneously enlarging her heart so that it would feel fulfilled only when every living child was "more than mothered."[64]

In her own life, however, mothering as Charlotte experienced it often felt closer to smothering. In her treatise on *The Home*, she portrayed the mother as a "poor invaded soul" who "finds even the bathroom door no bar to hammering little hands. . . . So chased and trodden is she that the very idea of privacy is lost to her mind." She loved her daughter, but at times Katharine may have reminded her of her mother, invading her most private spaces and interfering with her public plans.

Charlotte's mounting commitments led her to doubt whether Katharine's best interests were being served under her care. As early as December 1890—four years before she divorced Walter and he married Grace—Charlotte inquired whether the couple might "take Kate." She explained to Grace, "when I can at last stagger out into the open and stretch glad hands abroad and not strike any wall—well then in a year or two I shall be glad to have the little girl who loves me again."[65]

Grace had left town in the fall of 1890, heading east to reconnoiter with Walter before traveling to Florence with a friend. Charlotte missed Grace but defiantly claimed that accumulated losses in the personal realm only made it easier for her to seek compensation in "world's work." If Charlotte resented anything, it was the prospect of losing the friend with whom she had once formed an "inseparable" relationship to her own estranged husband. "Do you know I think I suffer more in giving you up than in Walter—for you were all joy to me," she confessed to Grace. ". . . It is awful to be a man inside and not able to marry the woman you love. When Martha married it cracked my heart a good deal—your loss will finish it. . . . I think of you with a great howlin' selfish heartache. *I* want you—*I* love you—*I* need you *myself*!"

Her intense attachment to women led Charlotte to identify as "a man inside," even while displaying the kind of emotional intensity conventionally associated with women. She had formerly wished Walter were a woman, and now she wished she were a man, regretting in both instances that the deeper bonds she longed to form with women were denied her.[66] At once ardent and achingly lonely, Charlotte repeatedly turned to women like Martha and Grace and asked more of them than either proved willing or able to give.

Charlotte's loneliness was exacerbated by her social inhibitions and her sense that "[a]s a rule people weary me, irritate me, enrage me, or cause me to writhe in sympathy." She speculated that she kept too much to home and, employing yet another of her swimming metaphors, promised that "presently, when I am richer and famouser and so on, I mean to have a species of bathing suit made, put on a life preserver, and plunge in."

The opportunity to take that plunge arrived sooner than she expected. In the spring of 1891, she traveled to San Francisco to speak to the first meeting of the Pacific Coast Women's Press Association (PCWPA). Founded in 1890, the PCWPA brought together women journalists, writers, and artists from the western side of the Rocky Mountains to encourage collegiality and collaboration among women writers and to help promote their careers. A San Francisco paper ran a favorable profile of Charlotte during her visit, and she made many new friends and contacts. On May 12, she met a local reporter, Adeline ("Delle") Knapp; nine days later, Charlotte declared her love. After a month, Charlotte sought unsuccessfully to inaugurate divorce proceedings, a step no amount of prodding from Walter and Grace had hitherto compelled her to take.[67]

Charlotte, who never did anything by halves, soon devoted herself to the woman she called "my girl." She believed she had found in Delle someone who might make her happy as both a lover and a worker. Although she initially felt "very lonesome for Delight" (her pet name for Delle) when the two were apart, she consoled herself by doing the "work I love like play— / And by and by you come and stay—Dear heart! Sweet heart!" She poured all her hopes for the relationship into another poem she wrote about Delle:

> To me at last! When I had bowed my head
> In patience to all pain—buried my dead—
>   Forgotten hope, accepted the long night
>   With only stars for guide—far, cold, and bright—
> Content to work and love, uncomforted.
>
> Then, in an hour, a brightness came and spread
> And all the dark sky flushed with rose and red
>   And gold-lit flowers laughed out—so came the light
>   To me at last!
>
> No more the empty loneliness, the fight
> To live above all loss, for Truth and Right,
>   No more the pale cold heart that ached and bled—
>   O happy heart! So warm and kissed and fed!
> I thank thee, God, for sending this delight
>   To me at last![68]

As this poem suggests, Charlotte was initially as intoxicated with Delle as she had been with Martha. The intimacy between Charlotte and Delle is better documented, however. In August 1891 and several times subsequently, Charlotte tracked Delle's menstrual cycle in her journals along with her own. The two women regularly shared not only a room but a bed Charlotte described in a private poem as "blessed."

In her autobiography, Charlotte protests strongly that what she felt for Martha was "love, but not sex"; she makes no similar protest therein about her feelings for Delle. Delle is also the only person referred to in *The Living* pseudonymously: Charlotte calls her "Dora." Charlotte later confessed to her future husband Houghton her "really passionate love" for Delle and maintains that she loved her "that way." Long after the relationship ended, Charlotte feared that her letters to Delle would resurface (they have not) and prompt newspapers to broadcast "Mrs. Stetson's Love Affair with a Woman."[69]

Charlotte liked shocking Houghton with her confidences, playing the experienced woman of the world to his younger, more naive straight man. But in this instance her confession may not have shocked: according to a contemporary survey of some 22,000 female college graduates and club members, homosexual activity "seemed especially common . . . among women in the social-service group" to which both Charlotte and Delle belonged. Although she loved many people, both women and men, over the course of her long life, Charlotte's most unambivalently passionate and enduring relationships up to this point had been with women. A large portion of her life's work actually affirms the strength and closeness of female bonds, which she extolled in her treatises and in short stories including "Turned," "Mrs. Beazley's Deeds," "Encouraging Miss Miller," and "A Growing Heart," as well as in her utopian novel *Herland.*[70]

In *The Living,* Charlotte describes "Dora" as "the friend with whom I had sincerely hoped to live continually. She certainly did love me, at first anyway." Delle also apparently loved Katharine and frequently took the child horseback riding, outings Katharine recalled fondly, including the time she was bucked and nearly lost an eye. Charlotte's friends concurred that Delle was good to Katharine and most also felt she was good for Charlotte. Even Walter approved: based on a photograph and Charlotte's glowing accolades, he deemed Miss Knapp "a very practical and good person" possessing "a very clean, refined and *strong* face, with a great amount of patient sweetness."[71]

Only Grace objected. By 1891, her feelings for Charlotte had cooled considerably. Convinced that Charlotte was dragging her heels on the divorce, Grace chastised her for doing so in letters that made Charlotte "sad." Upon learning that Delle—whom she refused to like—considered Charlotte a genius, Grace complained,

> I *never* expect anything from [Charlotte's] future which her past has not foreshadowed. . . . Miss Knapp is wrong about C's *genius!* Genius rides over obstacles [*sic*], talent goes under—that is so *every* time— . . . It is just as *pathetic* to see talent crushed but thank God, it isnt the loss to the world the other would be if it *could* be crushed.

> If Charlotte does housework all her life it is because Charlotte lacks just that degree of power which *is* genius—but I hope her talents wont be spent in the kitchen.[72]

At least Grace still sympathized with her old friend enough to acknowledge that Charlotte's skills were better directed outside the home.

The woman who did think Charlotte a genius was born in Buffalo, New York, in the same year as Charlotte (1860). The brunette, bespectacled Knapp was working as a reporter for the *San Francisco Call* when she met Charlotte. Like Charlotte, Delle participated in various volunteer organizations in the Bay Area, including the Pacific Coast Women's Press Association, Oakland's revitalized Nationalist Club, and, later, the state's Woman's Congress. An avid equestrian and outdoor enthusiast, she lived for several years in a cabin she built herself and celebrated in one of her nature books "the beautiful things that the spring and summer bring."[73]

Delle apparently ran her own newspaper for several years in California and may also have run a girl's school. A friend and admirer, the author Edwin Markham, considered her to be "one of the most earnest women and one of the brightest writers in the West." Charlotte described Delle as "most generously kind with money"; in 1900, seven years after their relationship ended, Charlotte identified her largest debt as the $775 she still owed Delle.[74]

In the early 1890s, Delle traveled to Hawaii for the *Call* to cover the Hawaiian revolution, apparently the first woman "ever sent to represent a great daily newspaper in such a crisis." She subsequently journeyed to the Far East, writing accounts of her travels in Yokohama and Manila. She also authored several adventure books for boys. For a few years in the early 1900s, she edited *Household Magazine* in New York, while Charlotte also resided in the city. When she died in 1909, Delle had returned—as Charlotte would also return before dying—to California.[75]

The two women shared enthusiasms and prejudices that doubtless reinforced their bond. Anti-Chinese sentiment was strong in California; attempts to regulate the burgeoning population had led to the passage of legislation restricting and deporting Asian immigrants, including the 1892 Geary Act, upheld by the U.S. Supreme Court in 1893. Delle vocally opposed Asian immigration and may have helped to cultivate Charlotte's xenophobia.[76]

On one key issue, however, the two women ultimately took opposing sides. Initially, both supported women's rights and seemed equally and especially passionate on behalf of working women's rights. The *San Francisco Call* once ran a column (which may have been authored by the paper's staff reporter Delle, or perhaps by its occasional contributor Charlotte) identifying economic dependence rather than disenfranchisement as the primary cause of women's subjugation: "So long as they depend on men for their bread and butter they will be under the orders of men, and it will not help them except indirectly to obtain suffrage," the argument ran.[77]

By the end of the decade, Delle's relative indifference to suffrage had developed into outright opposition. As an "Anti," she drafted "An Open Letter to Mrs. Carrie Chapman Catt" questioning whether women needed the ballot and arguing for "the quiet conservation of the inner things of the home and of society which are permanently in women's hands." She wrote this letter just a year after Charlotte published her most compelling case for women's domestic liberation, *Women and Economics.*

Ten years later, when both were living in New York and while Charlotte was campaigning on behalf of woman's suffrage, Delle provided anti-suffrage testimony before the state legislature, responding negatively to the question, "Do Working Women Need the Ballot?" By this point, Delle's views had departed so drastically from Charlotte's that she could argue that women worked only from necessity and not from preference, thereby directly contradicting Charlotte's understanding of work's fulfilling potential. Delle also maintained that women inherently failed at cooperating whereas Charlotte celebrated this tendency as women's noblest inclination. When in her pro-suffrage writings Charlotte labeled anti-suffragists "traitors," she may have had Delle in mind.[78]

In the heady, early days of the relationship, however, neither woman could have predicted their paths diverging so sharply. For two years, Charlotte tried to make a life with Delle, hoping to have found at last a companion who would fully support her professional ambitions. At the outset, Charlotte delighted in "the new relation" and in having "some one to love me, and whom I love." At the same time, rendered wary by past experience, she tempered her delight with a disquisition on larger duties: "First as always to live higher daily, to be loving, tender, thoughtful, courteous, wise, dignified, true, gracious."[79] Should she once again be disappointed personally in love, she could always fall back on the safety net she had fashioned out of more diffuse, all-encompassing emotions.

6 "The Duty Farthest"
(1891–1895)

Finding myself unfit to serve my own,
I left them, sadly, and went forth alone
    Unto the world where all things wait to do—
    The harvest ripe—the laborers but few.
I studied long to find the wisest way,
Proved every step, worked on day after day
    In those great common tasks that need us all
    But where one's own part is so brief and small
That no one counts the labor one has spent
Yet I could see good grow and was content
    Ah me! I sighed, for home served lovingly.
    And lo! The whole round world was home to me.
                        "The Duty Farthest," 1894[1]

In late July 1891, Charlotte wrote a spoof entitled "An Extinct Angel." Looking backward from a utopian future, the narrator contemplates the peculiarities of a long-extinct species of earthbound angels. These beings acted as a "'universal solvent' to all the jarring irreconcilable elements of human life" and were so numerous in their heyday that they could be found in nearly every family. Even when beaten by their masters, they were expected to keep their cool and their angelic smiles and to emanate sweetness and light. They were also to perform the most menial domestic chores without jeopardizing their seraphic qualities. Paradoxically, their saintly virtues were deemed inherent, but their owners perpetually monitored their behavior and punished those who fell from grace. To ensure their docility, the angels were kept ill-informed, but eventually, through intermarriage and interaction with human males, they learned enough to self-destruct. The tone of the piece suggests that we should celebrate their loss.[2]

"An Extinct Angel" confronts that icon of femininity, "The Angel in the House," first exalted in the 1850s by the Victorian poet Coventry Patmore and effectively slain in the 1930s by the modernist writer Virginia Woolf. In the 1890s, Charlotte enjoyed poking fun at this icon, but killing her would prove surprisingly difficult. At the time, Charlotte assumed her days as a self-sacrificing, domestic drudge were behind her, and that other women would soon willingly throw off the yoke as well. Lecturing on "Our Domestic Duties" that same year, Charlotte again employed a distant perspective to expose present-day inconsistencies, pondering these duties "as if we had never heard of them before—as if we were visitors from another planet—saw half the world waiting on the other half and wondered why they did it. . . ."[3] By wondering aloud herself, Charlotte hoped to hasten the dawning of a more enlightened future. Yet for every step she tried to take in its direction, countervailing forces pushed her at least two steps back.

During these years, Charlotte found herself unexpectedly hindered by domestic circumstances. Residual expectations of domestic sacrifice haunted her, and in attempting to live up to them privately, she wound up closer to her past than to the liberated future envisioned in her public pronouncements. Her personal troubles led her to push her self-abnegating philosophy to a new extreme: "What we call Self-Personality (the personal inclination)," she theorized, "—is the echoing fading force of the Great Life in its Material Limitations. The fresh life force must come direct, . . . not through inherited inclinations. Therefore to hold personality in abeyance and act *direct* from God is to help evolution."[4] She resolved to eschew residual and unhelpful personal needs and desires, confident that as personality became less of a force, progress would become more of one.

Charlotte's motives for abating personality were both positive (she sought to dedicate herself more fully to reform) and negative (she hoped to avoid any more devastating romantic entanglements). She felt certain that "our exaggerated ego-consciousness" operates detrimentally to inhibit the growth of social consciousness. As she saw it, lifting humanity an inch beat lifting "the individual a mile." A series of stumbles in her own personal life further persuaded her that a self-centered life was not just misguided but immoral. Disappointed over having once again found love only to have it fall "to ashes" in her hands, she vowed to cease her "selfish seeking" and derive joy from "the world's glad love so gladly given."[5] She intended to forsake not love but lovers—or rather, she meant henceforth to love the world exclusively.

This decision to detach herself from individuals and attach herself to the larger world shaped Charlotte's evolving definitions of both living and loving. In fact, these formerly incompatible concepts melded around this time: by making the world the beneficiary of both, loving became living's helpmate and no longer its antagonist. For this to work, however, Charlotte needed to commit to loving the world above all else, including her own family—although she believed that by loving the world, she would better all its inhabitants.

Charlotte's poem "Mother to Child" documents her shift from a particular definition of love to an abstract, global one. The poem's mother, seeking to spare her cherished child from pain, ultimately concludes, "Thou art one with the world—though I love thee the best; / And to save thee from pain I must save all the rest— / Well—with God's help I'll do it!"[6] Taking the long view, Charlotte defined a mother as a woman who cared for all children, not just her own, although she felt certain that her own child would ultimately profit from this definition.

To the extent that a woman was a woman, Charlotte believed, she was made for motherhood, but to the extent that she was a human being, she had broader obligations. By sending her daughter away, she became freer to serve society; while the separation pained her, she alleviated that pain by discounting it as merely personal. As it turned out, her attempt to hold her anguish "in abeyance" only exacerbated the backlash triggered by her seemingly hardhearted decision and consequently impeded rather than facilitated her world-serving ambitions. Although she emerged from the ordeal still persuaded by her trickle-down theory of love, she had managed to persuade few others.

~

> Arrange for a noble and successful life and work for it: then, if you fail, you have accomplished something,—you have tried.
> "Living from Day to Day," January 1, 1891[7]

Charlotte and Delle soon came to resent the more than 300 miles dividing them. Visits and letters no longer sufficed; they wanted to live together permanently. Delle had offered to support Charlotte for a year so that she could devote herself exclusively to writing; Charlotte demurred, but the offer seemed to bode well for her personal and professional prospects. Before moving north, Charlotte again explored the possibility of transferring Katharine to Walter, but the logistics proved too difficult. So in September 1891, mother and daughter said goodbye to the little cottage in Pasadena and—escorted on the trip by Grace's mother, sister, and a maid—relocated to Oakland.

They arrived in the city in the midst of a population explosion, the total inhabitants doubling that decade and again the next. Oakland's city limits expanded to accommodate the boom, transforming former vacant lots and countryside into streets lined with houses, stores, and factories, though by the end of the century the city still possessed neither a public park nor a playground.[8]

Charlotte doubtless hoped that her already promising career would continue to flourish once she moved north. A Pasadena paper intimated as much in a flattering send-off: "Pasadenians may well regret the departure of so brilliant and shining a light from her literary and social sircles [*sic*], and will sensibly miss the strong and uplifting influence of so gifted and noble a woman." Katharine's gloomier recollections of the move more accurately evoke its outcome: to the young girl, it was a matter of leaving behind "the land of sunshine" for a place whose days were "mostly gray—foggy, cold, rainy."[9] The barometer measuring Charlotte's emotional and professional health plummeted soon after moving to Oakland, and she would forever recall her years in the Bay Area as the hardest in a life that was rarely easy.

While the southern California papers proclaimed the emergence of a "California Literary Genius," the northern papers evinced more skepticism. No columnist proved more skeptical than Ambrose Bierce, the cynical "Prattle" columnist for William Randolph Hearst's *San Francisco Examiner*. Hearst was a millionaire's son who had been expelled from Harvard for sending his professors gift-wrapped chamber pots with their pictures pasted inside. He had subsequently taken over the floundering *Examiner* and transformed it into a force to be reckoned with regionally. Among Hearst's smarter moves was hiring "Bitter Bierce," an idiosyncratic, misanthropic writer of considerable talent. Bierce's penchant for adorning his desk with skulls intimates his skill at using the pen as executioner. He especially enjoyed deriding women, whom he identified as the true "prattlers" and whose silence he believed you could only secure "with a meat ax." A younger Bierce had written a series of sympathetic articles on "Female Suffrage," but after being hired as a satirist by the "most satiric journal in a city delighting in satire," he soon earned his reputation as both a "woman-hater" and a "poet-baiter."[10]

As both a woman and a poet, Charlotte proved an irresistible target. Bierce did praise "Similar Cases"—perusing Charlotte's collection of poems "for something to poke fun at," he was surprised to find a "delightful satire" he could admire. But

Trestle Glen Ferrotype Gallery
OAKLAND, CAL.

Group portrait including Charlotte sitting with Katharine close on her left and possibly Adeline Knapp standing on her left; Hattie Howe may be standing over Charlotte's right shoulder, ca. 1892. Courtesy of the Schlesinger Library, Radcliffe Institute for Advanced Study, Harvard University more often he enjoyed using "Colonel Stetson" for target practice. The very week she moved to Oakland, he was referring to her poetry as "something to remember on one's deathbed—something to remember and forgive."[11] Bierce's mocking reception offered Charlotte a bitter taste of things to come.

In relocating to Oakland, Charlotte had increased both her opportunities and her responsibilities. She had moved not only to be near Delle but also to find better medical care for her ailing mother. Suffering from as yet undiagnosed terminal breast cancer, Mary had been living with Thomas in Utah until he found that he could no longer keep her and wrote his sister that it was now her turn. Charlotte borrowed money to finance Mary's trip to Oakland. For several months, they all stayed at a pleasant boarding house: Charlotte shared a "lovely room" with Delle while her mother shared another with Katharine.[12]

In late February 1892, Charlotte took over the management of another boarding house located at 1258 Webster Street in Oakland. Adding half a dozen boarders to the burden of caring for her invalid mother and dependent child would have broken most women, her boarder Hattie Howe maintained. But Charlotte "cheerfully assumed" all her responsibilities out of necessity: "according to her religion and her psychology, this had to be done, and, consequently, it could and would be done."

Although men and married couples intermittently lodged there, the female boarders and their assorted illnesses dominate recollections of the establishment. Even Katharine succumbed to the sickening atmosphere, contracting a series of childhood illnesses and further exhausting her mother. Initially, Mary stayed with Charlotte's doctors and fellow nationalists, the Lanes, and did not move into the boarding house until early April 1892. Of the nine residents living with her in the house, eight required board as well, prompting a harried Charlotte to conclude, "I can't have mother yet!"[13]

Hattie Howe began rooming there in September 1892, helping to alleviate Charlotte's burdens and lighten the atmosphere. "We all love her and wear her out with many services," Charlotte noted on the day Howe arrived. Hattie recalled answering the door, conducting errands, and performing other needed tasks, including keeping Mary company in the afternoon while Charlotte napped. Katharine, however, remembered the new boarder as an additional burden and "a very nervous person" and confessed, "I adored popping out from behind doors and making her jump, and when I spilled sugar on the kitchen floor she hated the feel of it underfoot."[14]

Charlotte endeavored to keep the atmosphere on Webster Street lively. The poet Ina Coolbrith lived across the street, and the boarding house soon became a minor center of intellectual life in Oakland, with Coolbrith, her friend and protégé the colorful author Joaquin Miller, the poet Edwin Markham, and the socialist Eugene Hough among those drawn to Webster Street for dinner and conversation. Hough seemed particularly enamored of Charlotte, paying regular calls, lending a ready ear, and escorting her about town.

Her final Christmas at the house, Charlotte invited her father to preside over an impromptu party she threw for a waiflike cohort of seventeen friends and boarders, replete with a tree, candy canes, and fifteen-cent gag gifts, each accompanied by a stanza of humorous verse. The festivities illustrate Charlotte's inventiveness even in desperate times, and her abiding love of fun and games, even as desperate measures.[15]

While admiring the "gay and gallant courage" Charlotte brought to every task and problem, Howe recalled, "We all certainly knew that she was grievously overburdened and under great strain, but the dissimulation she must have used to conceal from her sympathetic household her true condition is now proved to have been no less than heroic." Charlotte occasionally emphasized her heroism to outsiders; she told her cousin Marian Whitney, "At times I don't do as well as a person of my 'parts' might be expected to, but at other times to do anything at all becomes so heroic that the consciousness thereof almost offsets the misery within." Privately, however, Charlotte groused about "doing with painful industry what others scorn to do with ease" and complained of "household irritation amounting to agony." She became so miserable at one point that her doctor feared she would break down under the strain of what Charlotte called "our present family arrangements."[16]

Incessant bickering, mounting bills, onerous household responsibilities: all combined to strengthen Charlotte's equation of domesticity, drudgery, and despair. Whatever comfort Charlotte derived from having those closest to her together under one roof was offset by difficulties ensuing from the mix of conflicting personalities with their conflicting needs and demands. The boarding house experiment refuted her premise that living with others would be easier and more enjoyable if those others were women.

With domestic difficulties continuing to drag her down even after she fled her marriage, she produced her darkest gothic story, "The Giant Wisteria," which turns on an ancient tale of a young woman desperate to escape her home only to be buried—along with that symbol of creativity, a child—deep within it. The gothic's implicit critique of domestic ideology (its homes are no havens) allowed Charlotte to express feelings of rebellion against, and claustrophobia within, even the unconventional dwelling she now called home. Around this time she also wrote "Through This," a story that, like "The Yellow Wall-Paper," explores in chilling detail a married woman's domestic enslavement.[17] Depicting the distracting, stultifying effects of routine household chores on a potential artist, "Through This" conveys Charlotte's own difficulties juggling her responsibilities on Webster Street while simultaneously pursuing her career.

Faring better than her distracted fictional protagonist, Charlotte managed to get a lot of writing done. "Nothing could extinguish her creative powers," Hattie Howe marveled. Charlotte acknowledged at the time that the "creative instinct" was "rising" and saw this as "promising well for work when the strain is off." Although the strain was more often on, she had pledged to do her best for Mary, Katharine, and Delle and calculated that to do so she must earn at least twenty dollars weekly. Accordingly, she taught classes, continued to lecture, and tried her hand at reporting. She churned out articles, skits, lectures, and poems at an astonishing clip during her first year in the city and generally sustained this pace throughout her Oakland years. During January 1893 alone, for instance, she managed to produce roughly nine articles, three poems, and three lectures, for which she received a total of forty dollars. "Fair work for an overworked invalid," she observed wryly.[18]

Charlotte also became increasingly involved in the burgeoning women's club movement while living in Oakland. Jane C. ("Jennie June") Croly, a contemporary historian of the movement, described these clubs as symptomatic of the movement toward popular education that had swept the country "like a tidal wave." Croly believed the movement wonderfully illustrated the appeal of associated effort and argued, "It is in the association that the individual discovers his personality, which he contributes for the good of the whole."

This notion of deriving an identity from association helps to explain Charlotte's enthusiasm for the club movement: she believed it represented the prevailing spirit of the times, which she generously defined as the mass awakening to the collective nature of social life. She applauded the club movement for drawing women out of their private homes and personal interests and into the public sphere on behalf of the common good. The club movement, in short, exemplified the movement out of the self and into the world she had already embraced wholeheartedly.[19]

Charlotte recognized the social and educational benefits of these clubs, but for her they served primarily as vehicles for reform and career advancement: both in California and elsewhere, she derived a reliable income from club talks. While residing in the Bay Area, Charlotte joined dozens of clubs, including the Nationalist Club, the Working Women's Club, the Century Club, the Ebell Society, the Economic Club, the Parents Association, the Woman's Alliance, and the State

Council of Women. A number of these would soon be organized through the General Federation of Women's Clubs—an offshoot of women's activism at the 1893 Chicago World's Fair, an event Charlotte missed due to her mother's failing health, although she was appointed to the Advisory Council of the "Woman's Branch" of the Congress held at the fair. While absent from the Congress, Charlotte shared the organizers' conviction that women needed to forsake narrow personal concerns in order to become world citizens and full participants in the spirit of association "that now moves the world."[20] While in Oakland, however, personal matters kept intruding to keep Charlotte from moving with that spirit herself.

~

> . . . the reason people do not understand me is because I speak of and to the mass— they know only the individual.
>
> Diary entry, March 1, 1893[21]

In December 1892, Walter petitioned the Providence courts for divorce on the grounds of Charlotte's desertion. Two letters that Charlotte purportedly sent her estranged husband over the summer of 1891 were submitted as exhibits and published subsequently in the papers. Charlotte may have consciously written these letters as evidence; they were, as one reporter noted upon reading them, "of a vigorous business turn and refrained from any endearing terms." Both are filled with details and names only Charlotte or someone close to her would know, and the tone, diction, and themes bear her recognizable stamp. For example, the letter dated 16 June 1891 protests,

> Do not deceive yourself dear. My life is too precious to me to waste any more of it like those seven years we spent together. Not wasted in some ways I grant[—]full of deep experience and that pain that means growth. But you well know how it unfitted me for any work and how since you have left I have done good work and lots of it—have made a reputation in one year. The difference is too great. Work I must, and when I live with you I can't. Therefore I shall never live with you again as a wife. I know it is hard for you but I can't help it—you must take the hard truth and make the best of it.

Although the letter makes her feelings abundantly clear, Walter explained in his deposition that he contacted Charlotte again, "asking her to be more explicit." Charlotte responded by stating her position in no uncertain terms:

> No I will not live with you again, not even in the same house. I know too well what that would amount to. Not as your wife in any case. How can you ask me again when you *know*! . . . And for my work—that is my life and I shall pursue it as long as I live, whether you consent or not[,] approve or not. I had my work to do before ever I knew you, you know. I am sorry very sorry to put these things so plainly, but you

would have it. I hope you will not ever need to ask again. We two *must* part—and there is an end to it.[22]

This blunt instrument did the trick; Walter now doubted only whether the courts would echo Charlotte's verdict.

After filing his suit, Walter spent anxious months fretting about its outcome. Acting on legal advice and with Charlotte's consent, Walter planned to emphasize in his testimony Charlotte's literary ambitions, her multiple publications, and the praise she had garnered from famous critics like Howells. He also planned to accentuate her commitment to radical reforms including nationalism, along with "various other true things clearly calculated to prejudice the judge who is a good deal of a fogy."

His aim was "simply to show that she is a woman of unusual mind & character and that when she says she won't she *won't*, especially when she says she won't be my wife. I can't see how it could be better," he concluded nervously. He worried that others would join him in perceiving his suit as "a gigantic lie": not only did he have to hide his serious relationship with Grace, he also had to pretend that he was the one who wanted the divorce and that he wanted it for specious reasons.[23]

Walter had cause to worry, but not for the reasons he expected. As it turned out, his grounds were not exposed as lies but sensationalized as home truths. When the case was tried on a Saturday morning in December, the press was barred from the courtroom, which left a *Boston Globe* reporter "so fired that he faked the most devilish testimony in his power—and insult alike to Charlotte, my attorney, and me," Walter indignantly informed Grace's mother. "That has travelled all over the country, a monumental lie." He lamented the sensation generated by the distorted coverage and despaired of ever winning the case now; he confessed to feeling "sick," especially because "little could be done."[24]

Charlotte, likewise, rued the press attention, which caused her name to become "a football for all the papers on the coast." A meddlesome acquaintance even sent clippings to her ailing mother, darkening Mary's final weeks. Walter did his best to put out the fire, publicly objecting to the disdainful coverage "of a woman of so much genius and sincerity of purpose."[25] But his kind words went unheeded when there were more injurious ones to report.

The papers portrayed the Stetson divorce as an object lesson in the negative consequences of a married woman's literary and reform pursuits. The *Examiner* immediately seized on the story, maintaining that Walter had accused Charlotte

> . . . of not wearing corsets or even waistbelts, . . . of running after fads and fancies in social and dress reform—all to the exclusion of sewing buttons on his shirts and making wifely remarks about his respiration upon his return from "the lodge." He said she followed gymnastics until she became very muscular. G. [*sic*] Walt is not a muscular

man, and somewhat undersized, so his complaint seemed to hint that his wife was rather head of the household before she picked up her dress reform duds, her Bellamy writings and her muscular development and put off for California. . . . [T]he divorce has caused no end of talk and the peculiar allegations have set the tea tables a titter.[26]

The scandal mongering prompted Charlotte to attempt to set the record straight, offering "plaintive denials" she later regretted as "foolish." As Charlotte instructed the reporter who sought her out, she and her estranged husband were mature adults who had made a responsible decision to end an unhappy marriage; they still got along famously, and, besides, their affairs were their own business. When the reporter asked, "Did following your profession interfere with your wifely duties?" Charlotte responded,

> I have been sick most of the time during my married life and I preferred to abandon it. . . . I read the papers this morning with fear and trembling, but when I had finished I laughed. . . . [Walter] never based it upon the ground that I eschewed boot heels or favored dress reforms. . . . All there is to it is I wanted to devote myself to my profession and earn my own bread and butter and I could not do it in double harness. . . . It would be better if there were more difficulty in people getting married and not so much fuss made about it when they wanted to get out of the married state.[27]

The next day she and Walter were back in the papers, under headlines that blared "His Wife's Plans for Bettering the Universe Annoy Him." The *Examiner* ran an alleged interview with Walter, quoting him as saying,

> She thought it her duty to sacrifice the domestic and conjugal relations for what she felt she was called to do in the cause of women's rights, dress reform and nationalism.
>   In order to sustain marriage relations she frequently declared that she would have to stay home more than she wanted to. . . . She often declared that domestic duties took too much strength which should be given to something more important. . . . She often expressed a desire to discontinue our relations, and would have done so long ago could she have reconciled what she for several years regarded as her duty to me with her duty to the work she wished to do.

Though its reliability is moot, the interview does have the ring of both Stetsons. Walter and Charlotte apparently believed that talking to the press would clarify their respective positions and substitute fact for innuendo, but in the end all they accomplished was to stir up debate and sell papers.

After she left the Bay Area, Charlotte boycotted the Hearst empire. She vowed to provide neither interviews nor manuscripts to any source affiliated with Hearst, a vow that came at considerable cost to her career given Hearst's dominance in print journalism. For Charlotte, the *Examiner* exemplified the irresponsible journalism she condemned as "corrupt, sensational and venal"; its gleefully unprincipled coverage of the divorce explains the vehemence with which she denounced the press for its propensity to "lie—and lie—and again . . . lie! Liars!"[28]

Why did the Stetson case grip both coasts? Divorce had become both more common and more accepted, with free divorce supported by thinkers as diverse and influential as Elizabeth Cady Stanton and Herbert Spencer. An 1889 Bureau of Labor report tracking divorces revealed that between 1870 and 1880 the rate grew one and a half times as fast as the population, so that by 1886 the annual number of divorces had topped 25,000.

As the divorce rate increased, however, so did attention to causes and concern over consequences. Venerable magazines ran features analyzing the upswing: the *North American Review* published a series on divorce, impaneling thinkers from the left, right, and center to assess whether it was wrong and whether women should be blamed. *Cosmopolitan* weighed in on what it deemed "The Divorce Germ," and *The Nation* analyzed "The Statistics of Divorce," identifying causes that included societal unrest, greater mobility, and litigiousness, as well as "the greater independence of women resulting from their enlarged legal rights and greater opportunities for self-support."[29]

While many faulted woman's righters, suffragists themselves were divided. The more radical wing favored easier divorce, but most agreed that the divorce rate was rising not because women took their vows lightly but because economic opportunities for women had increased enough to enable the fortunate "to dissolve intolerable unions." Ironically, given her opposition to individualism, Charlotte was taking a step in divorcing that divorce opponents denounced as indicative of "the latter-day cult of individualism; the worship of the brazen calf of Self."[30] The ongoing debates over individualism versus mutualism and over the effects of women's activism on the institution of marriage helped to fuel the incendiary coverage of the Stetson divorce.

The hullabaloo generated by what one paper called the "matrimonial misadventure of Mrs. Charlotte Perkins Stetson and her worthy, or unworthy, spouse" proved something of a nine day's wonder. Not content with airing facts and falsehoods about the divorce itself, reporters petitioned prominent citizens—including authors, dress reformers, nationalists, and other civic leaders—for their views on whether literary, reform-minded women could happily marry. "Neither Bellamy nor Nationalists generally have espoused loosening of marriage ties," one nationalist spokesperson hastened to assure newspaper readers.

Most of the women and a few of the men interviewed on the subject, however, sympathized with Charlotte and spoke of her warmly. While she might have felt like a "football," Charlotte managed to emerge from the melee relatively unscathed, with several new friends to her credit. The next time she became embroiled in a widely covered scandal, however, she would not be so lucky.[31]

With no new developments in the case and all angles exhausted, the *Examiner* wound down its coverage on Christmas day, with Bierce crowing over the scandal: "If Mr. Charlotte Perkins Stetson had sincerely desired not to cast reproach upon his wife . . . he would have based his suit for separation upon the quality of her writing," he quipped, insisting that most judges would consider any of her poems sufficient grounds for divorce. "Apart from her work in literature, she is said to be a very good man," Bierce concluded, thereby reinforcing his earlier insinuation that Charlotte wore the pants in this family.[32]

Another *Examiner* piece that ran this same day refers sympathetically to Walter as "an ordinary man of common sense" who wisely abdicated when his wife decided "to give herself to the welfare of the whole world" rather than to his welfare. The writer speculates,

> There are not many women, fortunately for humanity, who agree with Mrs. Stetson that any "work," literary, philanthropic or political, is higher than that of being a good wife and mother. And as Mrs. Stetson is really a woman of ability it must be assumed that on determining upon such a choice either all her reasons have not been made public (which is probable), or she is wanting in those powerful instincts which render the love of husband and children necessary to woman's happiness.[33]

Ironically, while Charlotte had devoted her career to proving work *as* important, fulfilling, and necessary as marriage and motherhood, her divorce was being used to teach the opposite lesson. While Charlotte was preaching that marriage and career could be combined, the papers were citing her as an example of the disastrous results of that combination. Once again, Charlotte's private life was interfering with her public agenda, enhancing her distrust of the private realm as the locus of fulfillment.

～

> O God of Goodness! Purity! and Truth!
> Help me to hold the standard, of my high-idealed youth!
> Help me back to the patience, to the constant self control,
> To the earnestness of purpose and the singleness of soul.
> To the labor and love for others, with justice still in view,
> And the courage to bear what I had to bear and do what I had to do!
> "Thoughts & Figgerings," 1894[34]

During these Oakland years, Charlotte earned a reputation as a powerful advocate for the working class. She "rejoiced" that "the people" considered her their spokesperson on account of her labor lectures, including the one that garnered her a prize from the Alameda Trade Union. Her involvement in socialist circles led her to support the local strike against the Southern Pacific railroad—one of hundreds of national strikes waged in sympathy for the Pullman workers. She also penned a number of sympathetic poems such as "The Poor Ye Have Always with You." Published in the *New Nation* in 1892, it concludes by contradicting the titular adage: "Let man today / Rise up and put this human shame away—Let us have poor no more!"[35]

Charlotte remained preoccupied with socioeconomic issues during the early 1890s, a time when she herself frequently faced "The Wolf at the Door" (the title of another of her poems). At Christmastime in 1892, for instance, Charlotte found it hard to deny a rumor that she was destitute. She managed to scrape by through a combination of her own efforts and financial assistance from her parents, continuing up until the time of Mary's death in the spring of 1893.[36] Charlotte's own poverty invigorated her efforts to stamp it out across the board.

Managing the boarding house on Webster Street yielded little in the way of comfort, financially or emotionally. Charlotte had difficulty securing permanent help: each woman hired left for different reasons only days later. Juggling work and motherhood also continued to prove challenging. Charlotte had found a local school for her daughter and could now trust her to play outside in the yard alone, but Katharine was still fairly young (nearly seven) and fairly demanding. The two enjoyed "lovely" times together, but mothering often left Charlotte feeling "utterly used up by the worry and exertion."[37]

Katharine's memories of this age do not center around her mother: "Probably I was not often left alone but I do remember making lunches of ginger nuts and other lunches of oranges, and playing in the Southern Pacific railway yards. . . . We climbed on top of freight cars . . . and crawled under them. As I felt pretty daring I am quite sure I was conscious of the fact that my mother would not have approved of the railroad yards as a playground."

Late in her life, Katharine would bitterly declare, "in me you do not see my mother's training—you must always remember that even in my earliest years others were watching over me and caring for me while she lay in a hammock recovering from 'nervous prostration.'" Though ill herself, Mary Perkins often lent a hand: "When I came home from school," Katharine recalled, "my grandmother would be waiting on the side porch and we played parchesi, halma, and gobang [*sic*]. She always had bright red cinnamon drops to offer me."[38]

Soon Mary was too sick to help out. In those days, little could be done to treat cancer, little was available in the way of pain relief, and what there was Mary

Charlotte and her daughter Katharine outdoors, ca. 1897. Photo by Mary Beecher. Courtesy of the Schlesinger Library, Radcliffe Institute for Advanced Study, Harvard University.

refused. She had essentially come not to live but to die with Charlotte, with as much dignity as she could muster but with more suffering than anyone anticipated. Charlotte bore most of the responsibility for her mother's care, deeming it a trial that "must be borne." As a reformer, Charlotte protested the presumption that mothers could use the years devoted to childrearing to assert "a continuous hold" on their adult daughters: "The child does not owe the parent," she argued. "Parental duty is not a loan."

Her resentment of this assumption did not prevent her from taking personal responsibility for her own mother, however. Charlotte acknowledged that she was motivated in part by others' good opinion. "Mother sinks wavering downward, like a tin plate in dark water; sinks and yet fights every step of the way," Charlotte informed Grace. "She has no opiate—demanding pain, but suffers much." Charlotte then added, "Her being here has served me well—made me seem a live human creature to the others, and so made my words better weighed."[39] It was in Charlotte's interest to be selfless, a pattern that extended beyond her private relationships to her role as a public servant.

Determined to see her mother through to the end, Charlotte had not realized how prolonged that end would be. In May 1892, Mary seemed on the verge of death; yet she lingered on another ten anguished months. Her mother's painful experience of dying taught Charlotte an important lesson: "If this should come to me, in future years, I will not go through with it," she told Hattie Howe. "It is needless." Walter pitied his estranged wife: "Just now she is having a particularly bad time. Her mother is dying with cancer. Her last letter said she could not probably live the month out. Charlotte often thought she had very little love for her mother. She finds she has much."[40]

The headache of nursing her mother and the heartache of watching her die damaged Charlotte's fragile constitution and the household's fragile bonhomie. Charlotte's doctor suggested it was better to "break down honestly now than be bolstered up and break more extensively later." By year's end, Charlotte was diagnosed with scrofula, or tuberculosis in the lymph glands, especially those in the neck.[41]

Adding to her woes, Charlotte's beloved "delight" no longer seemed so delightful. For nearly a year, the relationship had prospered, but by the fall of 1892 Delle had worn out her welcome (though she, too, lingered on longer than desired). In December, Charlotte confided to her diary her ". . . anxiety, grief, and shame for many many failures. My last love proves even as others. Out of it all I ought surely to learn final detachment from all personal concerns," she insisted, concluding "there is only to go on."[42] Her public and publishing successes notwithstanding, she associated the year with "failure," suggesting love's importance to her inner calculus.

Delle had prompted Charlotte's decision to run the boarding house; Charlotte considered her "service" in "making a home" for Delle a fair return for Delle's generosity with money. But as the year turned, Charlotte wanted nothing more than to evict her principal tenant. Looking back, Charlotte claimed,

> The kindest thing I can say of her character is that she had had an abscess at the base of the brain, and perhaps it had affected her moral sense. . . . [S]he was malevolent. She lied so freely as to contradict herself in the course of a conversation, apparently not knowing it. She drank. . . . She swore freely, at me as well as others. She lifted her hand to strike me in one of her tempers, but that was a small matter. What did matter was the subtle spreading of slanders about me. . . . At any rate that solace ended not only in pain but in shame—that I should have been so gullible, so ignorant, as to love her dearly.

Once again, apparently, loving someone too much had brought Charlotte only pain and shame, making her even more wary of ever again joining her life to another and even more resolute in her pursuit of "the perfect obliteration of self."[43]

Charlotte's contention that Delle spread slanders finds some corroboration in Hattie Howe's account of the Webster Street years, which mentions a time when a chilly atmosphere descended upon the formerly friendly residents. Charlotte investigated and discovered that one of the boarders had been breeding dissent by telling different residents catty things others had allegedly said of them. Charlotte proposed a remedy wherein the aggrieved party would confront the alleged source of the alleged affront, removing its sting by exposing its speciousness. Charlotte's solution worked so well that only the troublemaker wound up feeling dissatisfied.[44] Hattie's and Charlotte's combined reflections seem to implicate Delle as the troublemaker.

Charlotte also accused Delle of stealing her work, her voice. She claimed Delle used her as a source: "She was a clever writer, and later I learned that she was one of those literary vampires who fasten themselves on one author or another with ardent devotion, and for the time being write like them." Evidence of this literary vampirism surfaces in Knapp's 1894 publication "One Thousand Dollars a Day." The thematic focus on utopian solutions to economic disparities calls Charlotte to mind, while the heavily allegorical style resembles that of a writer both women admired: Olive Schreiner.[45]

Several decades later, two years after Adeline Knapp died, Charlotte named a reprehensible character in her novel *The Crux* Adele—an ultra-feminine parasite who enjoys toying with both men's and women's affections to ruinous effect.

Charlotte typically invented names for her fictional characters; her decision to call this creature Adele suggests a lingering desire to avenge herself on the real-life namesake.

Charlotte's fraught relationships with her mother and with her lover both came to an end in 1893. In mid-January of that year, Charlotte recorded the receipt of Mary's burial robe. As spring approached, Mary was "very low now—going fast." Towards the end, Charlotte sat at her mother's deathbed each night, writing away the hours. On March 6, she described her mother's last moments:

> Mother sinking all day. The laudanum ceases to take effect by nightfall and her cough grows worse. Dr. Kellogg in about 7.30 can find no pulse. Orders chloroform to quiet the cough. I go out with Hattie & get it. Give it to her till after 11. Every time she rouses it is only to cough terribly. Try to rest a little then but am soon up again.
>
> She passed away at 2.10, very quietly. The nurse and I wash and dress her and clear up the room—all done before 5. Then we try to eat—try to sleep. I don't succeed.[46]

The brief final sentence provides the only sign of emotional disturbance in an otherwise impassive account. Either Charlotte had gotten better at keeping her feelings to herself, or she had come closer to her goal of detaching herself from personal concerns.

Charlotte arranged the cremation, an unorthodox choice, and sent the box of ashes back to Providence so Mary could be interred next to her mother. She also contacted her father. Frederic came to Oakland the afternoon of Mary's death, yet, despite the quick trip across the bay and Mary's constant window-side vigil, he had never managed to bid his ex-wife farewell—a lapse Charlotte cited as one source of her own "implacable temper."[47]

Not long after Mary died, Delle finally left. The relationship had been tense for some time, but Charlotte still preferred her lover to "the empty loneliness, the fight / To live above all loss." When Delle returned from Hawaii on April 5, 1893, Charlotte pronounced herself "absurdly glad" to see her. Peace reigned for a time: the two worked amicably together on behalf of various causes, and Delle chipped in around the house, procuring coffee, fixing supper, and bathing Katharine. Yet soon the two were embroiled in public fights and "fusses." Delle began to keep company with a Mr. Wetmore and even at one point attempted to secure him a room in the boarding house. Delle's attendance at the house became increasingly sporadic, and she alternated between intruding on Charlotte with "her affection" and withholding it altogether. Both women were sick and tired, with Delle "in a wretched condition of health" and Charlotte experiencing bouts of "increasing weariness and irritability" that left her feeling "*very* low in all ways—mentally morally & physically."[48]

By mid-May, the two had agreed to part. That same month, Delle wrote a note confessing that she had "left for Mrs. Stetson's good. My ill temper and unreasonable conduct having rendered it impossible for her longer to endure it," she said. Charlotte wearily acknowledged Delle's departure and claimed she had repeatedly asked her to leave ever since the preceding August. When Delle finally moved out in mid-July 1893, Charlotte declared her former lover's behavior "such as to gradually alienate my affection and turn it to indifference. It is a great relief to have her go." She still owed Delle a considerable sum, and Delle's attempts to call in her debts only added to her worries.[49]

"Difficulties are nothing," Charlotte wrote in her diary in February 1893. "The power to live rightly is outside of these difficulties." She delivered a sermon on "Pain" around this time that counseled her fellow sufferers to discover what they were being punished for and to find in the source what they "are wanted to do—and then *do it*." Charlotte felt that she was being punished primarily for loving too much—for loving at all. She resolved to alleviate her pain by doing the work she believed she ought to do and had been called to do. "When a person is doing noble work for a noble purpose, the soul flows into the work, constantly raises work and worker, you grow by what you do . . . ," she told another audience; "Until every one of us women has some part in the work that is for mankind we cannot be great. And it is our special duty to be great, each one of us—in order to help the world."[50] Charlotte took her own advice, intensifying her dedication to global causes even as she privately acknowledged local failures.

Occasionally, Charlotte publicly acknowledged her personal limitations. Lecturing on the human body in a talk on "How Our Surroundings Affect Us," she confessed that neither her dedication to "right living" nor her rigorous physical and mental training regimens had managed to offset her considerable defects, and she concluded, "you need fear no superiority, no self assertion, from a weak and permanently injured organism."[51] She was a savvy enough lecturer to use self-deprecation to rhetorical advantage, but she meant what she said. By this point, her sense of personal injury was so great that she believed asserting the self would only worsen the hurt.

Charlotte honed her pursuit of self-abnegation in 1893 by drafting "A Simple Personal Position":

Here am I.

I am part of something alive—I can feel it push and pull, suffer, enjoy. It is visibly my "duty" i.e. relation, to fulfill my functional part in It's life—this gives the satisfaction known as "a clean conscience." Beyond that my pain or pleasure are not mine but part of It's and can not be helped. Visibly I increase my pleasure by increasing It's—and decrease pain similarly.

I can it is true receive much pain and pleasure through direct personal, even physical relations; . . . As part of it, I have none! . . . The quickest way to ensure my personal happiness then is to ensure It's? Yes. And I can very well see that that cannot be done in a long time. Well? Then can I not be sure of personal happiness! Well— were you—was anybody—ever? But some get it. Certainly, and in no visible connection with their own efforts; all history shows this. Can I command *no* happiness by my own efforts? Yes, the above mentioned "clear conscience". Is this much? It is a great happiness, being in reality the consciousness of social health.[52]

Identifying the self as a part of an impersonal whole, Charlotte identified this larger "It" as the only reliable source of happiness, a narrow definition that ultimately boiled down to the cold porridge of a "clean conscience." The more she improved the world, the more she would improve her spirits, and vice versa. Her proposition allowed her to surrender responsibility for her personal pleasure as well as her pain—these she owed to the world or to chance (happy people were merely lucky). She even disavows the notion of having personal and private affairs, a reassuring deduction given the profound disappointment she had derived from them.

Motivated by her doubts about personal happiness, her "Simple, Personal Position" suggests an impersonal "It" can subsume the "I" that had repeatedly caused her such intense personal sorrow. Loving and losing Delle—as with Martha and even Walter—encouraged Charlotte to embrace an all-encompassing world as more trustworthy. She resolved to rely exclusively on living to bring her joy from here on out. She did not suspect that, over the next two years, this commitment to living over loving would nearly break her heart.

～

How best can I serve thee, my child! My child!
Flesh of my flesh and dear heart of my heart!
Once though wast within me—I held thee—I fed thee—
By the force of my loving and longing I led thee—
   Now we are apart!
                   "Mother to Child," 1893[53]

On the last day of May 1893, Charlotte produced an invigorating self-assessment. She first accurately predicted that she had roughly forty years left to live, and then proceeded to enumerate her goals, chief among them ". . . the utmost attainable advance of the race. Means of accomplishment—the perception and transmission

Charlotte and Grace, ca. 1900. Courtesy of the Schlesinger Library, Radcliffe Institute for Advanced Study, Harvard University.

of truth, applicable truth. Most immediate necessity: the maintenance of self and child. . . ."

Charlotte tried over the next two years to straddle the gap between "the race" on one side and the "self and child" on the other. More often than not, however, she inclined toward the race, distancing herself from both self and child as a result. Ultimately, she decided that the "immediate necessity" of maintaining her child was keeping her from achieving her "utmost" goal, forcing her to make hard choices and accept the consequences. "Waste," a poem she published in January 1894, cautions, "Ye may not pass the near to love the far, / Ye may not love the near and stop at that."[54] Charlotte believed she was following this rule, but others found her priorities appallingly skewed.

In June 1893, the papers reported that Walter's divorce suit had been denied due to insufficient grounds. The judge apparently suspected that the couple had colluded to secure the divorce and so refused to grant them one. The onus now rested on Charlotte and the California courts. Charlotte looked into whether she could obtain a divorce without perjuring herself, but after being told she would not prevail, she quit trying, with Walter and Grace's blessing. Walter insisted to Grace's mother that Charlotte was "not made of the stuff of a liar," he wrote, "and I never knew her in all the ten or eleven years I've been intimate with her to say anything which approached an untruth."[55]

Charlotte did finally pursue and receive a divorce shortly after Grace Channing paid a visit to the Bay Area in February 1894. The visit helped to repair the friendship between the two women; Charlotte felt an "awful hole" when Grace departed two weeks later. Before a month had passed, Charlotte filed suit based on Walter's desertion and subsequent "failure to provide." In truth, Charlotte would have refused Walter's money even if he had offered it; she considered alimony "the meanest money that is taken—by women." Worse even than marrying for money or staying married for money, she ranked taking money from one's ex "when no longer delivering the goods————!"[56] To secure a divorce, Charlotte took the rare step of bending the truth to suit her needs.

In *The Living*, Charlotte reflects, "This time, I having the divorce, there was no uproar in the papers about it, no articles on 'Should Artistic Men Marry?' no noise at all." But here as well she stretches the truth. The day she filed her suit, the ever-vigilant *Examiner* announced Charlotte's desire to "Abdicate" from her "Cook-Stove Throne." Two days later, the paper ran a headline announcing, "There Was Another Woman. She Gives Him to Another." A garbled story followed depicting the love triangle among Grace, Walter, and Charlotte, with Charlotte portrayed as the mastermind who bowed out of the marriage after first sensing and then blessing Grace and Walter's hitherto unacknowledged mutual feelings. Describing the affair as "a very pretty little drama," the story casts Grace as the heroine, praising her as "one of the few successful literary women who yet retain the native grace and gentleness of manner that man holds so dear in the opposite sex and that makes its possessor the favorite of both sexes." The paper insults Charlotte implicitly here and explicitly elsewhere for lacking "the deftness of touch and charm of expression in her work that makes that of Miss Channing so agreeable."[57] The irony of a scandal sheet like the *Examiner* extolling such virtues as "grace and gentleness," charm, and a soft touch likely did not escape Charlotte's notice.

The Stetson divorce was granted on April 18, 1894 by the Superior Court of Alameda County and verified by the county clerk three days later. Charlotte expressed relief at having finally amended the "mistake of an untenable marriage"; the most she felt for Walter was "a sort of big hovering motherly lovingness . . . that sort of large world-embracing affection which," she told Grace, "I always had and which he never yet understood or wanted." She could finally assuage her lingering guilt over having caused Walter unhappiness now that she had facilitated his union with the devoted Grace. The threesome's continued friendship and mutual respect, however, exasperated "pure-minded San Franciscans," whose prurient desires for enmity and melodrama were disagreeably disappointed, or so Charlotte bitterly reflected.[58]

Even more incomprehensible to Charlotte's neighbors than the amicable love triangle was her decision—roughly a month after the divorce was granted and a month prior to Walter's remarriage—to "give up my home, send Kate to her father, and begin new; being now a free woman, legally and actually," she declared at the time. Katharine had recently turned nine, Charlotte's age when her own parents had legally separated. Partly from concern over Katharine also growing up in a fatherless home, partly from anxieties about mothering left over from own distressing experiences as a daughter, partly from personal need, and partly from a conviction that the professional opportunities awaiting her across the bay were located in "a place unsuitable for a child," Charlotte borrowed money and arranged for Frederic to take Katharine with him as he returned to the East by train.

In early May, Charlotte dressed her daughter in her nicest outfit and took her to the Oakland station, where Frederic awaited them. Katharine boarded the train and then rushed to the window to wave goodbye to her mother. Charlotte waved back and threw kisses until her golden-haired "darling" disappeared from sight. Katharine was "all I had," she recalled defensively, and there "were years, years, when I could never see a mother and child together without crying."[59]

Still, Charlotte felt then and continued to feel that she had made the right decision. Her story "An Unnatural Mother" (drafted in June 1893) defends her logic and defines her global concept of mothering. The story centers on a young woman who dashes past her own baby to alert the town to a coming flood, sacrificing her own life for her neighbors' sake (her child miraculously escapes drowning). In the flood's aftermath, the town gossips gather to discuss the protagonist's "unnatural" priorities, chastising the dead mother for putting her only child's life at risk for the sake of the community. "[N]o mother that was a mother would desert her own child for anything on earth!" one sneers; another sniffs, "that woman never seemed to have the first spark of maternal feeling to the end! She seemed just as fond of the other young ones after she had her own as she was before, and that's against nature."[60] Only an empathetic outsider and one defiant daughter recognize the mother's heroic altruism.

Those closest to Charlotte were similarly hard-pressed to view her decision as altruistic. Walter prepared for Katharine's arrival with both dread and longing. His anxiety was aggravated by Katharine's arriving earlier than he had hoped. In April, he had expressly told Katharine, in a letter he knew Charlotte would read, that she must not come to him until after the summer. Much as he would enjoy her company, he would be too busy until fall to care for her properly. He promised to send for her as soon as he could ensure that she would not be lonely in the presence of her loving but distracted father. Yet Katharine did come, only a month later; Frederic's return to the East Coast proved too opportune. Once Charlotte settled on a course, she rarely wavered, regardless of the inconvenience to others. Grace identified her friend's "forgetfulness of people" as her besetting sin, and Charlotte contritely concurred.[61]

For Charlotte, the long-term benefits outweighed all difficulties. The combination of East Coast schooling and the tender devotion of a father and a stepmother "fully as good" as her biological mother seemed, to her mind, vastly preferable to life with a single, hardworking, and hard-pressed mother. She defended her decision if not her timing in a June letter to a concerned cousin. Walter missed his daughter and had a right to see her, and Katharine needed more than just her mother's care: "(You know I don't believe in the 'divine right of mothers.') . . . ," she remarked. "[M]y health and general work and progress will be better for a years [sic] vacation from the constant care of a child. . . . It hurts awfully, and does yet—but what of that? It's a good thing all round, for her, for him, for me."[62]

Charlotte claimed in her autobiography that she was the only one who suffered. And she did suffer: thinking about Katharine hurt so much that "to keep open and thrillingly responsive to *the thought of her* would be, to my temperament, death. Or a mind unhinged," she confessed at one point during their separation; "I cannot bear any more leaks and losses and pains." But Katharine also suffered. As a grown woman, she wrote several incomplete accounts of the transfer, criticizing her mother for, as she put it, "shipping me East to my Father because it was 'his turn,'" without a thought as to how Walter might manage to care for her at a time when he was sleeping in his studio and boarding at the local art club.

Katharine claimed she felt unwelcome during the long railroad journey, stuck in a car with her grandfather and another old man. She also resented that her early arrival meant Grace had to take time off from her job as editor of the *Youth's Companion* in order to retrieve Katharine from the New York train station. Grace subsequently brought the girl back to her small Boston apartment, where she gave Katharine her bed and took the sofa for herself.

In an unpublished memoir, Katharine fretted that she had fatally interfered with Grace's bourgeoning career as a writer and editor. Interviewed by the biographer Mary A. Hill late in her long life, Katharine revealed her abiding resentment and feelings of rejection. She accused Charlotte of seizing "the opportunity to get her freedom by shipping me East. . . . [T]his was the way Grace's married life began, with me dumped on her." She described her mother as "too absorbed in expressing *herself,* making a career for herself, or in her causes" to be a good mother.[63] From her daughter's perspective, Charlotte's idea of selflessness—her primary devotion to larger causes—looked a lot like self-absorption.

By all accounts, Katharine flourished under Walter and Grace's care. Charlotte's relief was palpable. In 1895, Grace and Katharine relocated to Channing's Pasadena home, and Charlotte twice visited them there. Before one of these trips, she experienced "an enormous longing to see my baby," she weepily informed Grace. She was rewarded when their "threeply daughter!" proved herself to be "all the motherliest mother could desire." The "hollow feeling" overwhelming Charlotte at the end of the visit dissipated after a spate of proofreading and was forgotten in the warm greeting of "a whilom disciple" on the train. By this point, Charlotte had mastered repression, using a method recommended by her fictional alter ego, Benigna Machiavelli: whenever a painful thought "popped up into my consciousness," she remarked, "down it went quick—and I stood on the lid. In time I quite got rid of it. Almost everybody has some things they would rather not think of. Very well—don't, then. Self-control, active and passive—that is the first essential."[64]

According to Hattie Howe, Charlotte's "drastic training in self-control" helped her to withstand what Charlotte herself called "the foulest misrepresentation and abuse I have ever known." An unpublished biographical sketch suggests the extent of the backlash: "there travelled over the country with every variety of addition the statement that this woman, Charlotte Perkins Stetson, who had forsaken her child and forgotten all obligations of motherhood and wifehood, was disgracing all womankind by public speech on their meaning." She had some nerve, her critics harrumphed, thinking she could teach mothers how to mother after setting so poor an example herself.

Charlotte suspected that the slander was concocted "in the brain of one of the best known and least believed of the many women yellow journalists," probably Winifred Black (pseudonymously "Annie Laurie"). Black was a reporter for the *San Francisco Examiner* whom Charlotte vituperates in her autobiography; she was also a favorite of Hearst's who went on to write a nasty review of *Women and Economics.*[65]

Charlotte's supporters included the writer Mary Austin, who declared herself "for her, and for the freedom from convention that left her the right to care for her child in what seemed the best way to her." Charles Lummis also "sprung valiantly" to Charlotte's defense. Formerly of the *Los Angeles Times*, Lummis now edited the newly launched *Land of Sunshine* magazine, which featured Austin, Charlotte, Grace, and other western intellectuals on its pages. Lummis took advantage of his editorial platform to denounce Charlotte's detractors:

> It has a good deal interested me to observe the effect of Charlotte Perkins Stetson on the average intelligence. Symptomatically the rabies . . . is marked by slaver, gnashing of teeth, bristling of hair and a blind desire to bite. I have observed excellent people— who make good bread, keep their feet off the table . . . —go rabid at the bare sight or sound of her name. . . . [I]t seems to me fit to remark that Mrs. Stetson is a good woman in spite of her intellect. . . . She is not even an Unnatural Mother, as I have heard her called by many good ladies whose children are hired out to be instructed by strangers five days a week. I cannot even find her dangerously subversive. . . . The vital thing about her is that she has the wherewithal to think, and uses it. . . . [I]t will be just as well for us to pardon the lady for having brains; and to wait with some hope to see what she will do with them.[66]

Charlotte followed Lummis's lead, defending herself against charges of unnatural motherhood by deriding the maternal practices of her critics. She also reflected that she had merely been ahead of her time and maintained that the outcry was "Natural enough. . . . The threshers with flails stoned the first threshing-machines in England, remember."[67]

Charlotte ultimately used the scandal as grist for her mill, helping her to refine her ideas about reforming the institution of motherhood. Her promotion of global mothering and trained childrearing drew upon the social homemaking movement prevalent at the turn of the century, in which women were encouraged to mother the world. But from 1894 on, her agenda was also inevitably informed by her personal choices and lingering guilt over them.

Having learned caution from her ordeal, she sought to assure readers who doubted her credentials: her 1903 treatise *The Home*, for instance, begins by stating "in good set terms that the author does NOT advocate 'separating the child from the mother.' . . ." At the same time, she insisted that a mother "will love her child, as well, perhaps better, when she is not in hourly contact with it, when she goes from its life to her own life, and back from her own life to its life, with ever new delight and power." She told her readers what she likely told herself: when it came to mothering, quality mattered more than quantity. Henceforth, she would base her claims to maternal expertise not on daily interactions with a child but on her philosophy of parenting, one of her numerous shifts from the concrete to the abstract.[68]

In a 1914 lecture on the "Wider Motherhood," Charlotte offered an example of "one model mother who couldn't stand the annoyance of having around her children less than 10 years old." The woman therefore asked her sister, who lived next door, to raise her children in her stead. She made a point of visiting them regularly, bringing presents and maintaining pleasant relations with them until each turned ten, after which "she took them home and mothered them herself. As a result," Charlotte concluded, ". . . there grew up between them a warm and abiding love that might otherwise have been destroyed by grinding friction."[69] In endorsing this iconoclastic model, Charlotte conveys her regrets about her own limited options as a parent as well as the peculiarities of her notion of exemplary parenting.

Echoing Edward Bellamy, Charlotte identified the traits elicited by mothering as the foundation of social service. Now that her child had left her side, she could more readily transfer the tender, nurturing, and protective feelings she associated with maternal nature to the larger, needy world. With Katharine gone, Walter and Grace married, and even her father newly wed to his childhood sweetheart, Charlotte viewed her remaining years as a blank slate on which she could write her own story.[70]

She thought of her life as unfolding in "chapters" and believed herself to be near "the close of the third"; the first had ended at fifteen and the second at twenty-one years of age. The first two chapters had been devoted to self-development and the third to interpersonal relations. This next, open-ended chapter she dedicated to public service. Resolving to "Waste no sorrow on the days that lie behind you, / Waste no fear upon the days that rise before, / Waste no time in fierce complaining that the world is thus and so . . . ," Charlotte committed herself to her social agenda. While today the phrase "work and sleep" connotes the daily grind, around this time Charlotte wrote a poem of that name positing both terms as antidotes for grief, regret, and pain:

Work! It is the password when we waken,
Work! It is the watchword which we keep.
Work! Till day is done and light is taken—
Then you shall sleep!

Think not! for thinking brings but sorrow!
Feel not! for feeling is but pain!
Hope not! for you shall find tomorrow
Today again.

And O remember not! No grieving
Will ever bring again the better day! . . .

Looking over her papers as she prepared to write her autobiography, Charlotte dated this poem as "'94, perhaps," basing her guess on the memorable difficulties of that year.[71]

~

To really admit the pain I do not dare. I am honestly convinced that a full-felt pain would kill or craze me—I haven't brain strength to stand it. But to be prepared with a full line of defences, ready to hustle the new agony into oblivion before I had looked it square in the eye. . . . To consistently withdraw my consciousness from that whole field of thought and feeling; to consistently apply that field of consciousness to other and different fields; to work it hard in those lines and put it promptly to sleep with some set thought in view—as the hapless baby with the empty rubber nipple—that is what I am fixing for.

Letter to George Houghton Gilman,
May 16, 1898[72]

In the weeks after Katharine's departure, Charlotte believed that "in, way in," she had grown wiser and gentler if not stronger. She was certainly no richer. More than once she found herself hunting desperately and unsuccessfully for money. Her empty pockets and clearer path heightened her interest in remunerative work.[73]

Charlotte continued to offer readings, courses, and lectures on social questions, but she devoted most of her time to the Pacific Coast Women's Press Association (PCWPA). She had been elected president of the organization in September 1893, having served as its vice president the preceding year; her success at writing and editing the association's paper, the *Bulletin*, also led to her appointment as its managing editor. She promptly renamed it the *Impress* and fruitlessly devoted her remaining months in California—and her remaining funds and energies—to making the paper a success.[74]

As Press Association President, Charlotte organized two consecutive, annual Woman's Congresses modeled after the successful 1893 Woman's Congress at the Chicago World's Fair. The California congresses sought to convene successful, professional women from across the West Coast to share ideas and strategies. As the first congress grew, so, too, did the enthusiasm of its planners, who volunteered their prodigious efforts. Susan B. Anthony and Anna Howard Shaw, both leaders in the woman's suffrage movement, were invited to serve as keynote speakers. Dozens of women traveled to California for the congress; some, such as Charlotte's friend, colleague, and "adopted mother" Helen Campbell, decided to stay.[75]

The first congress was held in San Francisco's Golden Gate Hall from April 30 through May 5, 1894. It drew part of its crowd from the touring Columbian Exposition—known locally as the California Midwinter International Exposition and colloquially as the Midwinter's Fair. Charlotte reported on the congress for the *Impress*, rejoicing in the intense interest and fellow feeling on display. Women "came early, they stayed late, they invited their friends, they brought their lunches and secreted themselves between sessions to keep good seats. They sat patiently under the papers they could not hear, and applauded vigorously during the ones that were audible," she wrote. She concluded that the attendees "took away new thoughts on new subjects, facts and figures of startling value, and the great uplift and inspiration of the foremost feeling of the age." The success of the event, which Hattie Howe chalked up entirely to Charlotte, resulted in plans for a second congress the following year.[76]

Charlotte's duties as Press Association president were light, however, compared to her duties as editor of its paper. At the May 1894 business meeting, Charlotte had presented several motions pertaining to the *Impress*, which she claimed she wanted to take over herself and expand into "a high-class weekly of twice the size," managed by herself and Mrs. Campbell; she promised the Press Association its own page for three years free of charge. She also proposed to rent an apartment in San Francisco, situating the press headquarters and the *Impress* offices in the parlors. Both motions prevailed. In June 1894, shortly after Katharine left, Charlotte obtained and furnished half of a small house on Powell Street in San Francisco.[77]

Charlotte shared this house with Helen Stuart Campbell and Paul Tyner, her co-workers at the *Impress*. A home economist, anti-poverty advocate, and prolific author, Campbell was especially beloved for her children's books, including the *Ainslee Stories* Charlotte had enjoyed as a young girl. Both women were divorcées, writers, lecturers, reformers, and nationalists who focused on women's economic issues; Campbell authored several books on "women wage earners," whom she identified as virtual "prisoners of poverty."

Prior to moving to San Francisco, Campbell had trained in domestic science under Richard Ely at the University of Wisconsin; she also had helped to organize the National Household Economics Association, inspired by the Women's Congress at the Chicago World's Fair. Campbell considered Charlotte a woman of great potential; anyone who looked at Charlotte's "eager, restless figure," she felt, would know "that while the erratic might, yea would, happen, that unselfish zeal for the right, unceasing battle with wrong, would be the overmastering facts of the life."[78]

In turn, Charlotte considered Campbell, some twenty years her senior, her "real mother 'after the spirit'" and a "world of comfort." At least initially, she described Tyner—a journalist and writer whom Campbell regarded as an adopted son—as a pleasant companion. Campbell took her younger Powell Street roommates under her wing, caring for them and feeding them despite "real illness and awful discouragement and intense personal suffering which I did not dream of then," Charlotte recollected. Her selfless generosity inspired Charlotte to identify Campbell as "the bravest creature—and the lovingest and forgivingest I ever knew."[79]

With such promising and prominent collaborators, Charlotte assumed the *Impress* would succeed. She hoped to make the paper a more comprehensive review under her management. The new *Impress* would promote no particular reform but "all truly progressive measures." It would keep "all the best things in the current life of the world" in view and the women of the West Coast informed via a paper they could truly call their own. The *Impress* would also exemplify "a purer press," setting a high bar for truth-telling and ethical conduct and putting the public good before political or personal gain.[80] In short, the paper would provide a steady income, a larger forum, and a counter-example to the scurrilous *Examiner*—an ambitious agenda for a sixteen-page weekly upstart.

In September 1894, Charlotte presided in triumph over the PCWPA's annual convention and came away with a large basket of beautiful flowers for her efforts. That same September, Charlotte, Campbell, Tyner, and several friends (including her divorce lawyer) formed a joint stock company to finance the *Impress*, with Charlotte listed as company president. At the Press Association's business meeting that month, Charlotte reassured her audience of her good intentions regarding the paper. But she also ominously confessed to "absolute ignorance, inexperience of and temperamental incapacity for—business" when it came to running the paper thus far.[81]

The revamped, weekly *Impress* first appeared on October 6, selling for ten cents a copy. Advertised as a "Journal for Men and Women," the paper contained news, commentary, articles, and editorials on pressing issues, with advice on necessary reforms and praise for accomplished ones. The more polemical contributions were balanced by works of fiction, poetry (one of Grace's poems appeared prominently in the first issue), and humor.

Key features included "What We Are Doing"—a front-page commentary on world, national, and local events; "Everyday Ethical Problems"—an advice column; and "Who Wrote It?"—a series of stories written by Charlotte and modeled on the style of famous authors, including Nathaniel Hawthorne, Edgar Allan Poe, Henry James, Mark Twain, Charles Dickens, Olive Schreiner, Louisa May Alcott, George Eliot, and Mary Wilkins (Freeman). The first reader to identify her model was promised (but never given) a book by that author. These stories displayed Charlotte's considerable literary talents: they allowed her to demonstrate skills rivaling those of established authors while retaining "her own idiomatic voice." Charlotte later called these sketches "the only 'literary work' I ever did; and I think some of it is good." Still, they remained ancillary to the more ambitious reform agenda of the *Impress*.[82]

Campbell headed a section entitled "The Art of Living," featuring the latest in domestic science and offering "Model Menus" for various meals (a typical breakfast menu might contain "Baked Apples, Cerealline with Cream, Broiled Smelts, Creamed Potatoes, Delicate Muffins, Graham Bread, Coffee"). Tyner wrote pieces on spirituality, politics, and the theater. He also served as the paper's manager after the Press Association's manager resigned.

Charlotte actually handled most of the business matters herself—"an arduous task," she soon realized, consuming too much of her time and bringing in scant funds. She had embarked on the venture hoping that it might prove profitable for the Press Association, the state, other women, and perhaps even herself. But as the weeks passed, she began "to feel very greatly appalled" at her responsibilities on behalf of the weekly.[83]

Roughly two months in, Charlotte—too preoccupied to record regular journal entries—hastily jotted down her "Thoughts & Figgerings": "*Now*—Health better able to work some everyday—nothing to hinder building up. I have a Home, a Mother [Campbell], a Brother [Tyner], am loved and cared for, life sort of settled it would appear. . . ." Her immediate responsibilities she could handle. Indeed, she assured Grace shortly thereafter, "I work more regularly now than I ever did, and very enjoyable—the story work in especial is doing me much good. But," she also confided, "I work too hard, and am too much worried and driven to make any gain except in the training itself."[84]

Charlotte's worries were justified; the *Impress* failed to impress many readers. Several reviews praised Charlotte's editorship: "The bright and radical personality of Charlotte Perkins Stetson finds expression in *The Impress*," the *San Francisco Wave* observed, while the *San Francisco Star* assured readers that her association with the paper "should be sufficient alone to ensure its favorable reception."[85] But in the end, the reverse proved true. Charlotte suspected Delle—who had recently resigned from the Press Association—of anonymously sending her a corrected copy of the *Impress* at a time when typographical errors were the least of her concerns. Her most difficult task, Charlotte knew, was "to suppress my rampant personality and make the paper speak simply for the Association." Many in the association concurred, believing Charlotte's imprint on the *Impress* had damaged the paper beyond repair.[86]

The experiment lasted twenty weeks before it failed. As Hattie Howe complained, "Mrs. Stetson was greatly misunderstood, misjudged, and mistreated in San Francisco." The demise of the *Impress* taught Charlotte her standing in the city. When Helen Campbell tried to ascertain why so promising a paper had received so little support, she was warned, "Nothing that Mrs. Stetson does can succeed here" and "You risk your own reputation in joining her." The paper might be incisive and engaging, a woman doctor conceded, but "no self-respecting woman could have it on her table." The doctor apparently particularly objected to Charlotte's publishing Grace's poems therein, thereby flaunting the divorce, remarriage, and friendship in readers' faces. Imagine the doctor's shock had she known that Walter designed the section headers and cover during the final two months of the *Impress*.[87]

Local reporters noted the "Trouble in Their Press Association" and the "lack of harmony" over "Mrs. Stetson's paper." She may have had the goodwill of the association at the outset of her venture, but by the end of the paper's run virtually nothing she did pleased her fellow members. Predictably, Bierce cackled over the demise of the *Impress* in a mock lamentation published in his own successful paper:

> There is weeping in the office, there is wailing in the ways,
> In the market and the workshop is unutterable woe;
> For the woman-paper, *Impress*, hasn't lived out half its days,
> And the Colonels all are sad to see it go.
>
> The Stetson sits disconsolate upon the dusty press . . .
> Ah, indeed, there's some dejection and exceeding dire distress
> In Utopia. There's rapture at Podunk![88]

Charlotte, in turn, wrote her own poem lashing out at her critics and comparing herself to a pearl cast before swine. Published in the *San Francisco Star* in 1895,

"The Pig and the Pearl" features a pig who relishes refuse, gobbling down every-thing unpleasant, but foolishly turns up its snout at an attractive and valuable pearl in its sty. After jettisoning the pearl, the pig is reprimanded by a passing "Philosopher":

> . . . "From even a Pig's point of view
> The Pearl was worth millions to you.
> Be a Pig—and a fool—(you must be them)
> But try to know Pearls when you see them!"

Convinced she possessed immeasurable value to her adopted city, but equally certain that, despite their obsession with wealth, San Franciscans would never recognize her true worth, Charlotte resolved to go where she would be better ap-preciated.[89] "An Unnatural Mother" functioned as an additional parting shot. The story first appeared in the final issue of the *Impress*, which folded without fanfare in February 1895.

Charlotte's hopes for a recovery during her child-free year had been dashed, and her reputation in the state lay in tatters. Her few remaining friends were so concerned that one, Caroline Severance, wrote Isabella Beecher Hooker, alerting the family to Charlotte's incapacity for work and pleading with them to take her in. Her aunt forwarded the letter to Edward Everett Hale, who forwarded it to Frederic Perkins, who forwarded it to Walter, who forwarded it to Charlotte, who kept it forever as a memento of these difficult days.[90]

Before leaving town, Charlotte served as associate director of the Second Woman's Congress. Some 2,500 people, mostly women, attended the event dur-ing the third week in May 1895. The papers reported sessions so packed that the crowds spilled over into the aisles and halls.[91] Charlotte's several extemporaneous talks at the congress were greeted "good humoredly, even humorously." But the press detected dissension in the ranks and highlighted Charlotte's irritation with her listeners. Twice in a single story, for example, the *Examiner* claimed that Char-lotte reproached her audience for neither responding to nor asking questions. "You can always go to church to hear sermons," she scolded.

Delle's paper, the *San Francisco Call*, opted to run a drawing of Katharine along-side its coverage of a speech in which Charlotte insisted that the "the most im-portant business on earth is this of child-raising," as if to remind readers that the speaker had not followed her own advice.[92] Katharine's absence had become a pal-pable presence, haunting her mother's every public appearance and assertion, leav-ing her feeling "[a]ntagonized at every turn." Although Charlotte's eyes were trained resolutely on the future, her past kept getting ahead of her and blocking her view.

As her California years drew to a close, Charlotte wrote Grace, "Always—always—would I rather want something and not have it, than have something and not want it. . . . But there is a little thing inside that hops about and hollers sometimes—a hungry little thing, protesting loudly that it doesn't have its share of home. Then I call it an idiot—blank blank, and ask it to remember how it behaved when it *had!*"[93] Associating emotional neediness and the desire to belong somewhere with a fundamentally flawed core self—which, though diminished, still made itself heard despite her best repressive efforts—Charlotte sought to scold this still-vocal remnant into submissive silence. She reminded herself that, domesticated, she behaved badly, whereas liberated, she could make the world her home. Such reminders, however, never sufficiently managed to muzzle that "hungry little thing" hollering inside.

At Large

"A Woman-at-Large"
                        (1895–1897)

. . . The world was full of music clear and high!
   The world was full of light! The world was free!
And I? Awake at last, in joy untold,
Saw Love and Duty broad as life unrolled—
Wide as the earth—unbounded as the sky—
   Home was the World—the World was Home to me!
                        "Two Callings," 1903[1]

In an *Impress* column written shortly before the magazine failed, Charlotte introduced her readers to "A Woman-at-Large," a type she declared "most essential to the workings of advanced civilization, yet utterly unprovided for in the
way of emolument or recognition . . . cut off from the ceaselessly demanding
duties of private life, . . . left free to ooze silently from house to house and offici-
ate wherever an extra woman was needed." For the next half decade, Charlotte
assumed this identity, traveling from town to town as she sought to promote her
desired reforms and escape the demands of private life.

As a "Woman-at-Large" herself, she recognized the importance of this func-
tionary even if others did not: "this wandering life of mine has increased the

natural breadth of vision and constantly added to its power," she later observed. "Never having had a settled home, but always feeling perfectly at home anywhere, in this country or others, I have been better able to judge dispassionately and to take a more long-range view of human affairs than is natural to more stationary people."[2] Her detachment from place afforded her a detached perspective she considered well worth the trade-off.

Charlotte frequently used the phrase "at large" to describe her peripatetic lifestyle. For five years—from the time she left California "a repeated, cumulative failure" until the time she settled in New York City a newlywed—she identified her address (even in visitors' books) as "At Large." For a half decade, she wandered across the country from east to west and north to south, traveling "from California to Maine, from Michigan to Texas, from Georgia to Oregon, twice to England," never stopping anywhere for long. She spent most of her time on the train, with, as she put it, "no address in my little book to which to send 'the remains' in case of accident." Asked whether she felt "at sea," she typically responded, "I do. Like a sea-gull at sea." Asked where she lived now, she invariably replied, "Here."[3]

When other reformers expressed a similar desire "to make the whole world homelike," they generally meant that they considered domesticity a virtue and hoped to extend it to the public sphere via a variety of practical reforms. Progressives, for instance, advanced many causes on behalf of the home they perceived as in jeopardy. They fought their battles "waving the flag of domesticity," an enemy flag from Charlotte's vantage point.

Comfortable neither in conventional homes nor with conventional domesticity, Charlotte never experienced a sense of belonging even within the progressive community that otherwise seemed so good a fit. She had specific as well as generic reasons for her discomfort: most progressives applied themselves to devising efficient solutions to practical problems, whereas Charlotte increasingly preferred to offer broad theories others could then translate into practice. Her failures in California had probably intensified both her wariness of concrete interventions and her attraction to primarily intellectual labor.

More generally, as Charlotte once observed, stopping too long in any place or with any community stirred up ghosts and left her feeling paralyzed and depleted. The more temporary her perch, on the other hand, the easier she found it to soar like a gull above the jetsam of her past. Her sense of herself as a "big bird without legs" led her to believe that "as long as I could fly it was all right—; but when I attempted to sit down it was painful and awkward. Nothing but complete prostration brings me down, and then it is a painful spectacle."[4] During these years,

Charlotte flew by traveling, and prostration both explained and ensued from her attempts to land anywhere for long.

Charlotte considered "a wandering life" her "best safeguard" against the recriminations that overtook her whenever she stopped to rest. She had moments of self-pity: "When the suffering was extreme I would look at my self as if it were a little creature in my hand, and stroke it softly, saying, 'You poor little thing! You do have a hard time, don't you.'" But as a rule during these wander years Charlotte enjoyed averting her gaze from the self to the world around her: "What I saw in the world was not its foolish, unnecessary troubles but its splendid possibilities; as a competent promoter sees in some tottering business the success he can make of it." The fulfilling, potentially profitable business of improving society distracted her from her personal troubles, which she could diminish by telling herself that, for all her shortcomings, she still possessed the solution to "the local and temporary misery" plaguing the world.[5]

Charlotte's fictional alter ego Benigna Machiavelli praises the relaxing and broadening effects of travel: "the best fun was my own journey alone. . . . So much of my life was *inside*, so many of the things I did I had to keep to myself, and behaving *just so* to all the people about me was still so much of an effort that it was just magnificent to be At Large. It *rested me*—miles of me." Like Benigna, Charlotte felt most at rest when she was in motion. The more miles she traveled, the more "miles" she grew. Living "at large" may thus have broadened her sense of her own boundaries even more than it did her sense of the world's.

Riding the lecture circuit suited her and brought her closer to dependable happiness than anything she had experienced in her private life: "Pleasanter work I would not ask, nor more suited to my powers—and limitations!" She told Grace in 1896: "The travel of it is delightful to me; the meeting of nice people everywhere. . . . I'm getting to have a sense of homelikeness all over broad America, which will grow mightily as the years pass. To be a living voice and go far and wide with one's best loved truths—it is a great joy."[6]

Charlotte embraced motion for a host of reasons. She was moving toward a goal—moving, as she believed the world did, toward progress. She was also moving away from her past personal and professional failures, from the "Things you wish you had not known" or done that haunted her "[w]hen the house is very still and dark, / And you are alone." Continual movement also enabled her to dodge the hard work of building and maintaining relationships.

While at large, she believed she epitomized "that perpetual motion engine a Reformer." Yet in a more subdued moment she conceded that a better comparison might be to a "much transplanted tree" requiring "very slow work" before it could "take root." When, for the first time in two years, she met someone who made her want to put down "rootlets," the process was checked by her momentum and by "the ingrained terror" that gripped her whenever she felt "fast to anything."[7] Charlotte's volitional homelessness—her desire to make "the world" her home—made it increasingly difficult for her to settle in any one place, for any one person.

~

... Spread selfconsciousness
Into concern for others—
Leave one'self an open door,
A free unconscious channel
For the deep rushing flood
Of Life to pour through
To make sure in one's own
life of what one teaches others! ...
To tell and tell forever
Humanitie's great secret—
That each one *is all the
rest*. ...

Diary entry, 1899[8]

As Charlotte prepared to leave California, she was plagued by debt as well as by the fear that she would never regain the strength required to hold a steady job. Her *Impress* co-workers had already gone East, and she intended to follow as soon as she raised the necessary funds.[9] The moment she decided to travel, her spirits began to soar. "I grow and grow and grow, and Oh!—Life is so good, so great, so real and sweet and joyous!" she exulted to Grace. "I am happier now, freer, stronger, braver, wiser, *gladder*, than in twelve long years. Open sea is before me—the great wide see [*sic*], storms and calms and dangers of the deep no doubt, but no more danger of the shallows."[10] Relying on yet another swimming metaphor, Charlotte suggests that the shallow and dangerous waters she had tread in California had only intensified her longing for the deeper, unfamiliar currents she spied on the horizon.

Her father and his new wife had invited Charlotte to live with them in Connecticut. An even more attractive offer came at the end of June that left her feeling a "great big swelling happiness that makes me love the people and the hills in the same way and very copiously," she said. Helen Campbell, now in Chicago, sent word that Jane Addams (whom Charlotte had met when the settlement movement leader visited the West Coast in 1894) considered Charlotte "her one bright spot in San Francisco" and wanted her to make Hull House her base for at least three months.[11]

Charlotte admired Addams for her serene strength and her involvement in one "of the great humanitarian movements of today." From afar, settlement work seemed to Charlotte to epitomize her altruistic philosophy: "It is the modern phase of the same spirit of interhuman love on which our civilization rests," she observed in an 1894 *Impress* column, "and it is a perfectly normal growth of the extension of consciousness which marks the progress of the race."[12] Charlotte's failures on both coasts left her eager to give the Midwest a try.

She had timed her exit for July 1895, but as late as the Sunday before her planned Tuesday departure, she still could not fund the trip. At the last minute, a steadfast friend, Sarah B. Cooper, appeared with a half-price ticket granted to missionaries (a not inapt classification for its designated passenger). On Monday night, a stranger whom Charlotte approached after a lecture lent her twenty-five dollars. Thus equipped, and with most of her worldly goods either given or stored away, Charlotte boarded her train and began her travels.[13]

In the context of her larger career, Charlotte published relatively little during her wander years. Like her beloved Whitman, however, she was "simmering, simmering, simmering" and about to come "to a boil." Her lack of productivity failed to faze her, she told Grace, since she believed she had done a lot of growing in the interim. She also took comfort from the fact that the poems, lectures, and thoughts that mattered most to her and others had always arrived "in wild untraceable ways, sort of mid-sea currents," she mused in 1898, "While I was afloat and hoped for no harbor."[14]

Much of her growth was in new directions. During her years "at large," her sociological ambitions surpassed her literary ones. The emerging discipline of sociology remained so inchoate in the 1890s that aspirants with widely divergent foci and credentials could readily anoint themselves social scientists. Charlotte included herself among the self-anointed, marveling at her status while wryly conferring it: "How on earth did I get to be a sociologist and the equal of learned men! I never studied it as they have. Some are born learned I guess."

Charlotte's attraction to sociology as an emergent discipline was in keeping with her well-established anti-individualism. From a sociological perspective, as from an economic one, she could address women's issues as she was already inclined to address them: collectively. Sociology also helped her to define her particular contribution to the world. She understood sociology in the same way she understood philosophy: both complemented reform. Reformers needed sociology to learn how to make better people, and sociologists needed reformers to put their theories to practical use. "We need to have the moral enthusiasm and the practical working power of the Reformer directed by the far-seeing wisdom of the Sociologist," she argued.[15] Although Charlotte remained committed to numerous reforms, including woman's rights and socialism, her most valuable contributions to these causes were increasingly sociological rather than practical as she defined the distinction.

Chicago came to be associated with sociology thanks largely to the prestigious faculty at the University of Chicago (established in 1892). Headed by Albion Small, the founder of the *American Journal of Sociology*, the sociology department included Thorstein Veblen, the theorist of the leisure class, and John Dewey, the innovative educator and one of the fathers of American pragmatism. The department's reputation may have helped to attract an aspiring sociologist like Charlotte to Chicago, but her ostensible goal was to join the "community of women reformers" located at Hull House in the heart of a rapidly growing city.

Chicago's population had more than doubled during the 1880s to over 1 million by 1890, making it the nation's "Second City" after New York. Growth continued in the wake of the 1893 Centennial Exposition, so that by the mid-nineties, the city had essentially erased all traces of its prairie town origins. Substandard housing was hastily constructed to accommodate new arrivals, leaving some 35,000 people forced to live within a single square mile surrounding the stinking stockyards. Along with its railroads, department stores, and foundries, Chicago was known for its meatpacking industry, made infamous early in the next century by Upton Sinclair through his exposé *The Jungle* (which mentions Charlotte approvingly).[16]

With overcrowded tenements and lax public health efforts, death rates were high: one estimate from the 1880s held that half of the city's children died before reaching their fifth birthday. The Haymarket Riot, nearing its tenth anniversary when Charlotte arrived, was brought back to public awareness in 1893 when the state's progressive governor, John Peter Altgeld, pardoned the three surviving anarchists. The Pullman Company strike, just one of several clashes between labor and management that would unsettle the city, had commenced only a year prior to Charlotte's arrival. By the mid-nineties, Chicago was widely perceived as given over to immigrants and corrupt politicians.[17] In short, the city seemed ripe for the sort of reforms upon which settlement houses prided themselves.

The settlement movement began in England in the early 1880s, inspired by a romantic longing to counter the materialism associated with the city and appeal to the "humanistic and spiritual values" of the preindustrial era. Beginning with London's Toynbee Hall (1884)—the original settlement and the model for all the rest—settlements were designed to serve as lush cultural oases amid desolate urban slums. Religious concerns were also paramount: many settlement workers were Christian humanists who sought to extend the virtues of "universal equality, brotherhood, and the right to spiritual and material fulfillment" to the less fortunate.[18]

Jane Addams had visited Toynbee Hall in 1888 and had resolved subsequently "to do something concrete to promote social justice in America." In September 1889, Addams and her fellow Rockford College graduate, Ellen Gates Starr, opened what soon became the nation's most famous settlement in an old mansion on Chicago's West Side, situated between a saloon on one side and an undertaker on the other. By 1891, there were six U.S. settlements, Hull House included. That number grew to seventy-four by 1897 and to over 400 by 1910; more than three-quarters of these were headed by women. In the United States as in England, the movement's leaders were young, educated idealists answering the "call to a new kind of social service."[19]

The settlement movement was an offspring of the progressive movement also emergent in the 1890s; it, too, emphasized reform in the hands of a "responsible elite," that is, middle-class intellectuals who sought to bridge the gap between the wealthy and the poor and to check the excesses of each while simultaneously bringing the two extremes more closely in line with bourgeois standards. Settlement house workers typically possessed an optimistic faith in reform, in social responsibility, and, at least initially, in moral rather than material transformation.[20]

On average, settlement workers were twenty-five years old and highly educated: 80 percent had a college degree and 50 percent had pursued graduate work, likely contributing to the unease the largely self-taught, thirty-five-year-old Charlotte experienced during her abbreviated Hull House stay. She did share a similar background with the majority of workers who came "from old-stock American families." Many hailed from attractive residential neighborhoods in northeastern or midwestern cities, children of parents who were often teachers or ministers.[21] Settlement workers were also typically single: although Hull House and other settlements offered housing for married couples, the poor pay and conditions attracted few to the work. The average settlement worker stayed at a house for roughly three years.

When Charlotte moved into Hull House in 1895, the settlement was home to approximately fifty residents, of whom roughly thirty were women.[22] The British socialist Beatrice Webb visited Hull House in 1898 and observed, "the residents consist, in the main, of strong-minded energetic women, bustling about their various enterprises and professions, interspersed with earnest-faced self-subordinating and mild-mannered men who slide from room to room apologetically." By the mid-nineties, those rooms were numerous: the settlement's residential and social buildings eventually numbered some dozen, expanding beyond a city block.[23]

The added space aimed to accommodate the nearly 2,000 people who flowed through Hull House's doors each week, seeking hot lunches; childcare or kindergarten instruction; classes in a variety of subjects, including cooking, sewing, pottery, metalwork, wood carving, millinery, home economics, and English; exercise in its gymnasium or on the city's first public playground; and entertainment via sponsored concerts, lectures, and amateur theater productions.[24]

At night, Hull House workers gathered around the dinner table to discuss the day and plan the next one; Addams often read aloud from her correspondence. The food may have been undistinguished, but the guests were not: university faculty frequently dined there alongside such visitors as the sociologist Lester Ward; the authors H. G. Wells, George Herron, and Hamlin Garland; and the Christian mayor of Toledo, Samuel "Golden Rule" Jones. The conversation and company were so stimulating that the journalist and reformer Henry Demarest Lloyd called Hull House "the best club in Chicago."[25]

The "social spirit" animating these evenings "turned decisively toward social reform" by day. Hull House workers pooled their considerable energies and talents to wage often successful campaigns against local injustices. With varying degrees of enthusiasm, settlement residents supported local textile workers' strikes, protested Eugene Debs's imprisonment during the Pullman strike, and deplored derelict sanitation practices, fighting the city's corrupt political machine to ensure regular garbage collection. The socialist and activist Florence Kelley—a resident from December 1891—spearheaded a campaign for child labor laws and sought to close the sweatshops making life a living hell for many of Chicago's poorer children.[26]

Several years previously, Kelley had been greeted at the settlement door by Addams herself, "holding on her left arm a singularly unattractive, fat, pudgy baby" and additionally hampered "by a super-energetic kindergarten child, left by its mother while she went to a sweatshop for a bundle of cloaks to be finished." The ubiquity of children at Hull House doubtless haunted Charlotte, their perpetual presence acting like Banquo's ghost to reanimate unwanted memories. Like Charlotte, Kelley was newly divorced, but unlike Charlotte, Kelley had kept her children with her and, with Addams's help, had arranged for their board at Henry Demarest Lloyd's comfortable home in the affluent suburb of Winnetka.

Charlotte could have used a Hull House in California; she would have welcomed the assistance settlements offered to women juggling childrearing and career, women like Kelley and scores of other working mothers who used Hull House as a school or daycare. "There is a crèche or day nursery where women who have to work out by the day can leave their babies and feel safe about it," Charlotte explained to Katharine in one of her weekly letters. "They pay five cents."[27]

Charlotte arrived at the settlement when she no longer required such resources but faced daily reminders of what she had missed. Thoughts of Katharine tormented Charlotte during her Hull House stay. "I said to myself the other night—'now why not think about her—just think of her beauty and sweetness and all the lovely things you can remember of her,'" she confided to Grace. "And I opened the door a little and looked in. As well pluck at an amputation! It began to bleed and ached and I hasted [*sic*] and shut it again." The many children at the settlement may have kept that door from closing as firmly as she wished and may help to explain why she lasted less than three months at Hull House when she had planned to remain a year.[28]

At first, Charlotte expected great things: "To me as a resident the place and work are good," she told Grace soon after moving in. "It is meat and drink to me to be among people who *care*, who are in any way living for humanity. It is the kind of house I am most at home in, and I slip into general usefulness very easily." An 1889 article on Hull House advertising its attractions to female workers stressed the opportunity to "beget a broader philanthropy and a tenderer sympathy, and leave less time and inclination for introspection, for selfish ambition, or for real or fancied invalidism"—all results Charlotte would have found appealing. Living at Hull House did help to put her troubles into perspective: "Among so many poor," she reflected, "why should I worry over my own poverty?"[29]

The settlement was justly famous for welcoming women "at large" and offering them food, shelter, and community. It also fostered relationships among women and provided a nonjudgmental space for them to flourish. Addams herself was involved in a longstanding, committed relationship with Mary Rozet Smith. The historian Rosalind Rosenberg maintains that Hull House "provided both a sanctuary and a purpose for many women—a sanctuary from the 'family claim' that so many of them found suffocating, and a purpose that satisfied their desire for independence and accomplishment without undermining their sense of womanhood." In short, Hull House served as a sort of "halfway house" between the stifling, tediously familiar domestic realm and the strange and intimidating world of politics whose barriers to women had only recently begun to crumble.[30]

Charlotte believed her sojourn at Hull House had helped to counterbalance the detrimental effects of her "California, newspaper-made reputation." She remained forever grateful to her fellow residents for providing companionship and kindness when she felt like "a species of refuge from cruel San Francisco." She praised "Saint Jane" especially for her capacity to steady "'on even keel' through all the stress of this mixed living."[31]

This reference to the "mixed living" at Hull House may help to elucidate Charlotte's mounting dissatisfaction with the settlement. Although her prejudices had not by this point become settled convictions, the mix of ethnicities and classes at Hull House seemed to her an unfortunate microcosm of the larger multiethnic city. In 1890, nearly three quarters of Chicago's population identified their parents as foreign, creating what the historian Andrew Feffer has deemed a "disharmonious crazy quilt of ethnicity." Charlotte saw nothing beautiful in this quilt. She felt alienated and exhausted by the pressing throngs at Hull House: "Such a flux of disconnected people," she remarked on a return visit in 1900; "Such a noisome neighborhood. . . . [I]t tires me very much." Two years earlier, she referred to settlement beneficiaries as "a vortex of nations" and struggled while stopping at Hull House to avoid being sucked up into its midst.[32]

"Wonderful Miss Addams" was Charlotte's exact contemporary: both were born in 1860 and died in 1935. They both had been treated in the 1880s by S. Weir Mitchell, and both had resolved in the aftermath to stop resting and to busy themselves helping others. The two women also shared a similar social philosophy and viewed settlements as but one "expression of the wakening social consciousness." Like Charlotte, Addams eagerly anticipated the eclipse of the individualistic Gilded Age by the dawning age of association. Like Charlotte as well, Addams built her career on what one Hull House resident called "a recognition of a sociological fact that we are, none of us, mere atoms independent and apart from each other. . . ."[33]

Addams recognized that settlements arose from an "objective necessity": the need to feed, shelter, teach, and elevate the urban poor. But, she argued, they also satisfied a "subjective necessity," by which she meant that they benefitted the settlement workers themselves, most of whom were privileged idealists "seeking an outlet for that sentiment of universal brotherhood which the best spirit of our times is forcing from an emotion into a motive." Charlotte, however, increasingly preferred the subjective necessity to the objective one.[34]

The hands-on work required at Hull House had taught Addams that "high ideals" were in themselves insufficient, but for Charlotte, increasingly, they sufficed. Wary of the progressives' vaunted efficiency, she noted "how dangerously what people call 'practical' things absorb the energies." In 1895, Charlotte mocked this "ravenous eagerness to 'do something practical,'" only to criticize settlements in 1913 for not doing nearly enough: "The Settlement furnishes an infinitesimal fraction of the necessities of growth to an infinitesimal fraction of the poor. . . . 'A fragment of sponge-cake in a bucket of ink,' Sinclair called it, didn't he?"[35] For Charlotte, the settlements could not win for trying: first she damned them for too much doing and then later damned them again for doing too little.

Charlotte's aversion for practical efforts reflects her evolving understanding of her public role. Unable to vote or hold office, Charlotte increasingly sought other means of making an impact, ultimately settling upon the life of a public intellectual. By the late 1890s, she had come to view herself as not a reformer but "at bottom . . . really a *thinker*, a kind of social philosopher." She later clarified her distinction in *The Living*:

> I worked for various reforms, as Socrates went to war when Athens needed his services, but we do not remember him as a soldier. My business was to find out what ailed society, and how most easily and naturally to improve it. . . . As I had planned the programs for those Congresses of Women, I planned programs for the world, seeing clearly the gradual steps by which we might advance to an assured health, a growing happiness. If they did not see it, would not do it, that was not my fault; my job, my one preëminent work, was to "see" and to "say," and I did it.[36]

This fine-tuning of her concept of service reflects her recognition of her increasing status as a theorist; it also reflects her desire to avoid both responsibility for outcomes and potentially messy entanglements. The historian John Higham has observed that the period proved more congenial to "administrative energy and functional thought" than to "the speculative thinker with interests remote from the facts of contemporary life." Charlotte essentially straddled this line: she became an increasingly speculative thinker, but her most insightful and influential thoughts concerned the most troublesome "facts of contemporary life."[37]

Explaining the function of settlements to Katharine, Charlotte underscored their differences from her own preferred methods. These houses, she observed, were designed less to teach than "to give the poor people a large beautiful place to meet in and do things for themselves." Charlotte's reverence for "teaching," her objections to practical endeavors, and her mounting distaste for immigrants and the indigent likely hastened her departure, although in another letter to Katharine she offered a more mundane explanation: she left Hull House in October, she told her daughter, because she did not enjoy sharing a room with women who kept the windows closed and burned their lamps until midnight.[38]

There are additional reasons why such a potentially fruitful incubator for Charlotte's ideas proved so stifling. Charlotte never managed "to feel at all near" or close to Addams (whose initial impression of Charlotte was apparently "very mixed"). Charlotte was also temperamentally a loner who required a lot of elbow room and never enjoyed "mixing." Her remoteness cost her both professionally and personally: one of her more observant friends identified her as "a watchtower person rather than a contact person. . . . The hill view excited her. Down in the village she was frustrated by personal frictions." Charlotte acknowledged that she lacked "the personal touch" and lamented her inability "to draw and hold people close." Never "aggressively sociable," she spoke of a "gate" she used to close off upsetting emotions that, she acknowledged, had the unfortunate consequence of making others think her cold and unfeeling.[39]

Her friend Alexander Black put a positive spin on her standoffishness: "It is as if to *see* socialization one must be aloof. . . . [T]he all-of-us vision is hard to acquire in contact with the crowd." Indeed, Charlotte prided herself on her willingness to trade the interpersonal intimacy women conventionally valued most dearly for a "thrilling" nearness to the faceless audiences she managed repeatedly to "touch" with her message. The further away others stood, the closer she felt to them. At Hull House, however, the spirit of collaboration prevailed. Charlotte complained of the impossibility of solitude at Hull House, since "it seems to be considered in some way selfish" to keep to one's room; "you must sit around down stairs, on call as it were."

Charlotte may also have left Hull House sooner than planned because she felt unappreciated and underutilized there. She told Grace, "it is for my souls good to be for the first time in my life a small fish in a large pond—well stocked with bigger ones," by which she meant not that these women were more important or successful than her, but that they "make no bones" of her.[40]

At least one San Francisco paper, in noting her departure from the city, had claimed that Charlotte would become Addams's "first assistant" at Hull House, a considerable exaggeration of Charlotte's actual status. By 1895, Addams had drawn about her a tight inner circle resistant to newcomers. New residents had to submit to an application process that included a probationary period and ended with established residents voting each applicant up or down for a permanent stay. Charlotte never mentions a vetting process, but she does suggest she remained peripheral to the activity at Hull House from the beginning: her course of lectures at the settlement was, she believed, "ill attended and rather over the heads of the audience. . . ."[41]

As Charlotte explained to Katharine, "each resident has some kind of a club or class or department to attend to. I am supposed mostly to hold my self free for lecturing, to all kinds of clubs etc. Then I help about in the house, wait on the door, see visitors, and 'tote': That is what they call it when there are visitors who want to see the whole place and we residents take them about—tote them." She insisted that she "rejoiced" in toting, but it was not the fulfilling work she had envisioned for herself in Chicago.

Even John Dewey, a regular visitor at the settlement and a supportive member of the board, recognized the difficulties of getting anything accomplished amid the Hull House hullabaloo: "I sh'd think the irritation of hearing the doorbell ring, & never doing one thing without being interrupted to tend to half a dozen others would drive them crazy." While an unconventional one, Hull House was still a house, and many settlement workers had adopted this line of work because it seemed a safe extension of traditionally feminine duties.[42] Charlotte, by contrast, was too familiar with domesticity's detrimental effects not to be extremely wary even inside homes whose doors stood wide on principle.

~

> It is to me most wonderful—most beautiful—most awe-inspiring and yet tender—to see how my life unrolls now step by step along the lines I trod so in the dark those black San Francisco years. Because of my much blamed labors there do all these things roll out before me now.
>
> Letter to Grace Channing Stetson,
> June 8, 1896[43]

By mid-October 1895, Charlotte was "visiting around." Hull House continued to serve as her base while "at large," a place where she could receive mail and sleep whenever she passed through the city on lecture tours. Before leaving, she had been asked to head another settlement on Chicago's North Side in an area called "Little Hell." She recommended Helen Campbell instead, however, pleading her own unreliable health.

She did agree to move into the Unity Settlement with Campbell, where they were soon joined by two Harvard graduates with sociological aspirations, Hervey White and George Virtue. Charlotte later collaborated with White on a play; for Virtue she developed strong but apparently unrequited feelings. She likely had him in mind when she claimed that she had been "very honestly in love, with a good man" whose inability to return her affection "was a grief of course, a big pain," she admitted, "but I met it calmly; and buckled down to a sort of game of solitaire—proposing to love him as long as I chose."[44]

Charlotte liked the new neighborhood better than Halsted Park; it seemed to her less crowded, less filthy, and less poor. She felt her work at Unity held promise: the settlement sponsored several thriving clubs for boys and girls and, she told a friend, "I find I get on well with the young folks, and hope to put in a very useful winter. It is splendid work for me; work of a kind I never did before, and therefore new education."

She experienced a lift in health and spirits that fall, which she attributed to her capacity to withstand "physical hardships" better than she could tolerate personal enmity: "I do mind being hated," she told a friend in November. "I'd rather live in these slums in this atmosphere of social friendliness and appreciation than to have all California's glorious climate and Century club women going to my doctor to say I wasn't fit to be in her house!" She also claimed to find work more satisfying in Chicago than in California: "All October has been brimful of work and the pleasure that comes of work which seems to be wanted." She had recently delivered sixteen talks in one month, including one at Hull House and several in local clubs, private homes, and elsewhere in the greater Chicago area.[45]

In her autobiography, Charlotte claims she cared little for payment so long as she covered her expenses. When friends asked if she would be paid, she confessed she did not know and did not consider it her business to know: her business was simply to preach. "Complete absence of personal desires, and absolute confidence that I should be taken care of," she insisted of her years on the road, "made lack of money a matter of laughable indifference."

Yet additional evidence belies her nonchalance and reveals money to be a constant preoccupation. She was sending as much as she could to California, "the first beginning of relief from my pile of debt," she remarked. "O it feels so good! So very good!" She begged a California friend to inform her creditors of her good intentions and promised to clear all her debts in five years even if it meant she would be left penniless herself.[46]

On New Year's Day 1896, Charlotte reflected on her progress in the Midwest and planned her next steps:

> For the personal life I need————————————much. Believing what I do I should have a steady calm and peace-disbursing power. I should stand for good will, sweetness, cheerfulness, and *peace*—like a great angel. My personality still stands in my way somewhat. I must not forget to apply to myself the truths I preach to others—
>
> Knowing—seeing—feeling as I do my conduct should be nobler. I must learn to hold more steadily my currents of great joy, and incorporate them. This I have long seen and not yet done.[47]

Remaining calm amid life's tumult, suppressing the stubborn impediment of her personality, practicing what she preached, calibrating her moods: these challenging personal goals must have made her professional objectives—improving her speaking, writing, and organizing skills—appear relatively easy.

She had received a major professional boost in the waning months of 1895 when Susan B. Anthony wrote (via Jane Addams) to invite Charlotte to attend the National American Woman Suffrage Association (NAWSA) convention in Washington DC, scheduled for late January 1896. Anthony wanted Charlotte to participate in the conference and to testify before the fifteen-member Judiciary Committee of the House of Representatives. The suffrage leader had met Charlotte at the California congresses and guessed that her appearance in DC would "be of great personal advantage to her in the way of introducing her and her wonderful powers as a speaker."[48]

Yet another flattering letter had arrived in December from the pioneering American sociologist Lester Frank Ward, then employed as a government geologist and paleontologist in the nation's capital. Ward asked Charlotte for a copy of *In This Our World*, and Charlotte responded by telling Ward that his using her poems as evidence made her feel "like the stone in David's sling—supposing said stone to had [*sic*] a grudge against the giant!—and chuckling as it sped."[49] Ward provided an additional incentive for Charlotte to attend the suffrage convention; the two planned to meet during her week-long stay in DC.

The self-educated Ward is frequently credited with fathering the discipline of sociology in the United States. Ward criticized the biological determinism of the social Darwinists as "a gospel of inaction" and instead emphasized "telic" (i.e., intelligent, social, voluntary, purposeful) evolutionary processes. Reform Darwinists like Ward felt discomfited by the laissez-faire policy recommendations of social Darwinism but inspired by Spencer's faith in the inevitability of progress. Their teleological interpretation of Darwin's natural observations led them to an organic understanding of human life that foregrounded its capacity for growth and transformation. With other reform Darwinists, Ward believed that the brutal laws of nature were countermanded by the powers of human intellect and agency along with the enlightening effects of culture. Taken together, these positive forces could enable the ultimate realization of an equitable and altruistic society even within industrial capitalism.[50]

Most American disciples of Darwin were neo-Lamarckians, including Ward. He learned from Lamarck the profound influence of environment, the power of individual adaptation and intervention, and the possibility of passing acquired characteristics down through generations, views Ward considered fully compatible with Darwinism. Ward's liberal theories were embraced by the progressive Chicago school of sociology; they proved especially attractive to reformers, who with Charlotte welcomed his "*dynamic* sense" of life, his idea "that humanity is a *process*."[51]

Charlotte's knowledge of evolution came largely secondhand; instead of reading Darwin, she read Ward, Geddes, and Bellamy, each of whom reinforced the teachings of the scientists her father had long ago recommended and confirmed the fundamental tenets of her personal religion. Guided by these influences, Charlotte insisted that evolution entailed growth, not struggle, or rather she held that the true struggle was for race preservation, not for self-preservation. With these men, she viewed growth as inevitable and human progress as both cumulative and continuous.[52] Or as she phrased it, there is an ever-present "force called Evolution that is always pushing, pushing, upward and onward, through a world of changing conditions. You can count on it. It is always there. It is 'the will to live,' and behind that is 'the will to improve.'" She diverged from Spencer and joined Ward in emphasizing the human responsibility to use this fundamental will to accelerate the progress of the race.

To explain why women had not kept step with men on the evolutionary path, Charlotte looked to culture—particularly, "the rudimentary conditions of our domestic economy . . . the absurd and irrational organization of household life."[53] Women were not yet men's equals because they were expected to be feminine instead of the humans they were first and foremost.

Charlotte's views on women and evolution were reinforced by Ward's "Gynæcocentric Theory of Life," which she celebrated as "the most important contribution to the 'woman question' ever made." As its etymology suggests, gynæcocentrism posits a female origin of the species and relegates the male to a secondary role based on his reproductive utility. For Ward, "[w]oman is the unchanging trunk of the great genealogic tree; while man, with all his vaunted superiority, is but a branch, a grafted scion, as it were, whose acquired qualities die with the individual, while those of woman are handed on to futurity." At the cellular level, where life began, parthenogenesis is practiced by a single, fertile organism; Ward considered this organism for all intents and purposes maternal, and he therefore speculated that life must be "originally and essentially female." While no activist, Ward drew on his cellular model to argue that "it must be from the steady advance of woman rather than from the uncertain fluctuations of man that the sure and solid progress of the future is to come."[54]

In the 1890s, the notion of the "feminine origins of human society" had legs, thanks in part to O. T. Mason's influential 1894 *Woman's Share in Primitive Culture*. Both Jane Addams and Helen Campbell praised the book, and Charlotte later acknowledged its importance to her work. Mason held that the life of early man could not be told without the efforts and genius of early woman across all categories of industry. Even before either Ward or Mason published his theory, Elizabeth Cady Stanton had propounded the existence of an original "Matriarchate," convinced that "savage women had been free and independent and the originator of civilization."[55]

Ward first presented his gynæcocentric theory in a lecture before a group of suffragists that included Stanton; he subsequently published an expanded version as an 1888 essay for the *Forum*. His original audience understandably rejoiced in his deductions, since they seemed to prove woman's preeminence at a moment when even her equality was doubted. Ward's influence on the suffrage cause led conservatives to identify Darwin as modern feminism's "originator" and Ward as its "prophet."[56]

Charlotte read Ward's *Forum* essay for the first time on the opening day of the 1896 NAWSA convention, while the treasurer was delivering her report. She derived "intense satisfaction" from Ward's thesis, immediately realizing its potential to "change our whole thought as to women." Gynæcocentric theory lent scientific credence to many of Charlotte's deepest convictions. It emboldened her to declare to doubters, "You'll have to swallow it. The female *is* the race type; the male *is* her assistant. It's established beyond a peradventure."[57]

Yet the two thinkers differed significantly, and the influence worked both ways. For instance, Charlotte maintained that she had drawn similar conclusions years before she ever met or read Ward and cited poems like "The Brood Mare" as proof. Reflecting her perpetual optimism and intellectual competitiveness, Charlotte expanded upon Ward's concept of the female origin of human life. She argued that woman was not only the original progenitor of the species but also more advanced than man when it came to modifying the sex. In short, she believed women were improving more rapidly *qua* women than men were *qua* men, a more radical and polemical claim than Ward was prepared to make.[58]

From the moment Ward visited Charlotte in her room at the Arno Hotel on her first day in the nation's capital, he was "most warmly kind." He attended her talks, took her to supper, escorted her to and from her hotel, and spoke with her at length. He also threw an evening reception in her honor, "full of distinguished scientific people" who "knew my work and valued it," Charlotte rejoiced. "This means the beginning of an assured place among the best kind of people as an original thinker—and is a great joy to my heart," she told a friend. The burgeoning sociologist and closet autodidact delighted to find herself hailed as both an innovator and an equal by scientists: she was especially tickled to learn that her host, this "botanist, geologist, sociologist, of great reputation," had "admired my work for years," she said.[59]

The NAWSA convention proved an exhilarating experience for Charlotte. Nellie Bly covered the event for the *New York World* and singled Charlotte out for having "a long name, a large vocabulary, a good voice, an attractive smile and magnificent thinking faculties." But Bly simultaneously lumped Charlotte together with other suffragists for being "daft on dress reform," since she appeared, from her wide waist and narrow skirts, to have discarded both corset and petticoats. The *Woman's Journal* offered unqualified praise, describing Charlotte as "even more interesting than her writings. She is still a young woman, tall, lithe and graceful, with fine dark eyes, and spirit and originality flashing from her at every turn like light from a diamond."[60]

During the week-long convention, Charlotte delivered speeches "of wonderful power which thrilled the audience" even though she had developed the mumps, contracted at the Unity Settlement. The disease did not keep her from testifying before the House Judiciary Committee, where she informed the members that restrictions on women's participation in the public sphere were inhibiting their development. Because suffrage would immerse women in the larger world, women needed it, and it did not matter whether they "know enough to want it."

Elizabeth Cady Stanton appealed to the committee's baser prejudices, reminding the congressmen that "a multitude of coarse, ignorant beings, designated in our constitutions as male citizens—many of them fresh from the steerage of incoming steamers" could vote, while "intelligent, moral, highly cultivated women, whose ancestors for generations have fought the battles of liberty and have made this country all it is to-day" were denied the suffrage.[61]

Stanton provoked additional controversy at the 1896 conference. She had recently published her *Woman's Bible*, which criticized misogynous scriptural passages and praised the few flattering ones. She sought to supplant the biblical "myth" of our origins—which blames woman for man's fall and thus endorses women's subordination—with Darwin's theory, so that "we can exonerate the snake, emancipate the woman, and reconstruct a more rational religion for the nineteenth century. . . ."

The book incensed conservative delegates, who swiftly introduced what came to be known as the "Bible Resolution": "This association is non-sectarian, being composed of persons of all shades of religious opinion, and has no official connection with the so-called 'Woman's Bible' or any theological publication." A vigorous debate ensued. Charlotte attempted unsuccessfully to broker a compromise by proposing that the resolution end with the word *opinion*. Charlotte sided with Stanton partly because she shared Stanton's abhorrence of misogyny, her evolutionary views, and, to a degree, her prejudices; partly because she knew how it felt to be met with outrage and ostracism; and partly because Stanton and Anthony were both "very kind and wise as well as brave and strong," she informed Grace. The resolution passed, however, with fifty-three in favor, forty-one opposed.[62]

This setback notwithstanding, Charlotte left Washington trailing clouds of glory. She believed that "the trip has been of immense personal advantage to me and more to the Truths I love to speak," she exuberantly concluded. She felt that she had considerably advanced her career and finally put the ignominious California years behind her. "Now here is the difference between east and west," she wrote

Grace immediately upon her return, "California was afraid of me on account of my 'views,' took no account of my work, and damned me because of my personal misfortunes." In the East, by contrast, she had an excellent reputation, was considered "farseeing and wise," and her personal history was either overlooked or indulged.

Her success at the convention, Charlotte felt, indicated that she now possessed "sufficient skill in the art to attract." She concluded that she had left behind her "a divided wake—half hating and half loving," which, given her checkered history, counted as success in her books. She predicted that the convention would lead to increased lecturing opportunities, especially in states where she had hitherto been unknown, and sure enough, in the first seven months of 1896, she delivered fifty-seven talks and sermons.[63]

Yet after the lift of the convention and travel, Charlotte's return to Chicago that spring brought with it "a return of the intense nervous weakness and depression," she observed at the time, "enough to make me feel that I can not live so for any length of time." Confined to one place, Charlotte felt claustrophobic: "Things are a little thick," she confided to her diary. "I am too close to people. My own work gets no attention." Charlotte knew herself well enough by now to realize that she never prospered when people proved more pressing than work.

She soon grew so fractious and forlorn that the good-natured Helen Campbell finally threw up her hands and sent her to the Doctors McCracken, married physicians who took Charlotte into their comfortable house on Chicago's South Side and offered her the bed in which their young daughter also slept. According to Charlotte, they "well knew what it meant to me to have a child in my arms again, a little girl child, about the age of mine when I had her in Pasadena." Motherhood still contributed to her depression, although now it was Katharine's absence that plagued her.

In her novel *Mag-Marjorie*, the eponymous heroine longs for the child she relinquished for the sake of her career: "Hers was a hunger unknown to most mothers; a stored, accumulated hunger . . . ," the story reads. "The self-reproach which she bore always within gave a desperate bitterness to her longing." Like her heroine, Charlotte could review the facts and convince herself that she had done right, but rational justifications did little to mend a "defenceless heart" or a guilty conscience. Beneath all her public efforts pulsed "her throbbing motherhood," indelibly staining her every action "like a crimson wound."[64]

This latest bout of melancholia left Charlotte's "mind a heavy dark grey." When "Mr. Doctor" tried to induce her to count her blessings, she informed him,

> Doctor, I am thirty-six, nearly. I have no father—to speak of, I have lost my mother, my brother is unable to help me, I have lost my husband, I have lost my child—

temporarily at least, I have no trade or profession, no "job" and could not hold one if offered; I have no money and am in debt; you know the state of my health,—what do you advise me to think about?[65]

In this dismal summary, Charlotte downplays her own responsibility for the losses she lists. Of course, given the depression that ensued whenever she did blame herself for her past, accepting full responsibility at this low moment may well have proven unbearable.

~

I'd like to get into the lift and swing of my world feeling again. I am never really at peace without it. A sense of easy room and fluent usefulness—that I am here where I belong—in the world and not cramped for space; and an utter absence of time feeling too—no age, no personality, simply being an active conscious factor in Life—in the great ceaseless stream immortal, eternal, that is working out God's will on the glad earth. Then I breathe easily and feel as one does swimming on ocean swells.

Letter to George Houghton Gilman,
September 14, 1898[66]

Charlotte's doctors had advised her to give up settlement work, so she decided to leave Little Hell as soon as she finished helping Campbell organize the Chicago Household Economic Society. "Health comes at once as I take the field again," she wrote Grace from the road. "I shall always have to keep moving I fancy."

Typically, the destination affords more pleasure than the journey, but for Charlotte traveling contributed to an "astonishing revival in health and spirits." She visited every state but four over the course of her career and concluded, "many friends are apparently more conducive to my welfare than one home . . ." She intentionally planned her journeys around her menstrual cycle, frequently modifying departure dates "in view of various hygienic considerations," endeavoring to stay put during her period and start off with clean clothes. But just as often she allowed impulse to dictate when she should move on.[67]

Charlotte did most of her traveling by train, a mode of transportation that offered constant diversions, as Vivian Lane's experience in *The Crux* attests: "The spreading beauty of the land was to her a new stimulus; she watched by the hour the endless panorama fly past her window; its countless shades of green, the brown and red soil, the fleeting dashes of color where wild flowers gathered thickly." When not gazing out the window or writing, she entertained herself by perusing other faces in the car. Each stop brought new people, new possibilities.[68]

Only rarely did Charlotte acknowledge the costs of being "unutterably homeless . . . in the world. *Homeless on principle.* . . ." The practical inconveniences were

Charlotte in front of a train, ca. 1900, during her "at large" years. Courtesy of the Schlesinger Library, Radcliffe Institute for Advanced Study, Harvard University.

legion: impersonal hotel rooms, outrageous prices for food on the trains, over-crowded cars and seats, "being hustled and sat upon by fellow-travelers . . . being poked in the back by fumbling fingers when you are going as fast as the crowd will let you . . . the loud, incessant talking of persons in the seat just behind or just before you. . . ." She complained as well of the countless luncheons, receptions, or teas to attend post-lecture, when all she really craved was rest.[69]

At times, her incessant travel took a psychic toll. It exacerbated her chronic "exhaustion of wilted nerves" and left her in a depression so debilitating she found even basic functions difficult, "as if trying to rise and walk under a prostrate circus tent, or wade in glue. It brings a heavy darkness," she observed, "every idea presenting itself as a misfortune; an irritable unease which finds no rest, and an incapacity of decision which is fairly laughable." Her sense of herself as not "all there" was exaggerated when she was at large and not even sure where "there" was.

Moreover, no amount of warm hospitality nor of genuine human kindness could assuage the loneliness she experienced on the road even at the best of times. In such moments, she longed for "a place to 'let go' in,'" which she claimed she had never had. She was only half jesting when she suggested in 1897, "I'd like to be adopted for a year by vigorous prosperous persons, who wouldn't feel my weight at all—and just vegetate awhile!"[70] Convinced that living meant moving, she never became immune to the attractions of vegetating.

Mid-April 1896 found Charlotte staying at the New York City boarding house run by her father's new wife, Frances "Frankie" Johnson Beecher Perkins. Charlotte described her stepmother as "a dear little lady" and delighted in their mutual affection. She had also gained two stepsisters: "sweet little blond damsels, twins, very like, and looking sixteen though twenty two." Within two years she would attempt to "drop all connection" with these new relations, but for the time being the discovery of a ready-made, agreeable family improved her spirits. She described her recovery as "thin," however: "I have no strength to spare," she observed.[71]

Charlotte was a creature of the coasts; she felt landlocked if she tarried in the Midwest too long. Restored to the East that spring, she was content to "trot about and visit, loafing and working by turns." From New York, she returned to Providence as a last-minute lecture replacement, her first visit to that city since she fled it eight years previously. Expecting a chilly reception, she was instead so warmly welcomed that she "went about all day on the broad grin."[72]

In June 1896, she headed west, speaking to audiences so taken with "the worth and beauty of character of this noble woman" that she wanted to "exclaim with Whitman, 'O I am wonderful'—'I did not know I contained so much goodness!'" Yet despite friends' pleas for help with both the Third Woman's Congress and a closely contested state suffrage campaign, she turned around before reaching California.[73]

Soon thereafter, she set her sights on more distant shores. With a hundred dollars in her pocket, she sailed for England in early July 1896 in order to attend the International Socialist Workers' and Trade Union Congress; she did not return to the States until the end of November. She had anticipated a beneficial, restful voyage, but the steamer *Mongolia* turned out to be a glorified "cattle-boat," whose "bovine passengers grew steadily more perceptible as days passed. . . ."

Mocking the customary promises of peace and quiet, fine food, and invigorating sea air, Charlotte decried sea voyages for the dampness, "the rank squalor of the steerage," the unfamiliar and unappealing food, the inevitable sea sickness (worse for her on the return trip), the rooms without views, and the passengers treading on the deck above while those below vainly sought sleep on a "padded shelf."[74]

Disembarking with alacrity in London on July 21, Charlotte found herself already familiar to her fellow attendees thanks to the British publication of *In This Our World*. She participated in the convention as a delegate for the Alameda County Federation of Trades—the California trade union that had awarded her a medal for a labor lecture in the early 1890s. She originally intended to wear a socialist badge, but she objected to the Marxist views printed on the membership card and refused to sign it.

With other socialists of her background and inclinations, Charlotte distrusted Marx and preferred to rely on the intellectual labors of a native-born intelligentsia that included herself. She acknowledged that many "working Socialists" considered her "merely a 'kid glove Socialist,'" but she refused to let it bother her. For the most part, she sought her desired economic transformations within the capitalist system even while criticizing that system for its intrinsically patriarchal attitudes and practices.[75]

Charlotte's socialism combined her own insights with the teachings of Bellamy, Ward, and Christ. She saw in Christ's example socialism operating at its purest, holiest level, and she interpreted the Lord's Prayer, with its reiterated second-person pronoun, as a testament to the power of collective action and "the very spirit of socialism—the sinking of personal interest in common interest." Socialism thus represented to her the antithesis of the individualism she abhorred. Indeed, the goals of socialism as she understood them resembled her living while "at large": "The wildest dreams of socialism are only what I live in," she maintained in 1899, "—to move freely among the people—to be loved and cared for everywhere—to ask for nothing and get much—that has been my life" during these wander years.[76]

Charlotte passed most of her time in England in the company of socialists. She spoke at a Hyde Park peace demonstration alongside the German socialist August Bebel and the dramatist George Bernard Shaw during a "*drenching* rain," boasting, "I was the last speaker on the last platform to stay it out." After the London congress ended, Charlotte joined Shaw and other Fabian socialists gathered at Beatrice and Sidney Webb's country home.[77]

Throughout her stay, Charlotte socialized with the British Fabians, a diverse, optimistic bunch with affinities to Bellamy's nationalists and the Christian socialists. The Fabians believed social change could best be achieved through gradual evolution rather than violent revolution. They preferred to "permeate" existing parties and organizations in order to disseminate their democratizing message, which led one contemporary to compare them to "the cuckoo, laying their statistical eggs in other people's nests and expecting to see them hatch into enlightened public opinion and progressive legislation." Their preference for creed over party and education over politics appealed to the iconoclast and the generalist in Charlotte. With the Fabians, she denigrated individualism and championed an organic notion of community, and she shared Shaw's conviction that "the true joy in life" lay in "being used for a purpose recognized by yourself as a mighty one."[78]

Charlotte became an honorary member of the British Fabian Society while abroad. Upon her return to New York, she was hailed by the American Fabians as a powerful ally whose wit and gift for satire they hoped to harness. The American branch (founded by the Reverend William Dwight Porter Bliss) was even more eclectic than its British counterpart. Throughout 1897, Charlotte helped edit the *American Fabian* alongside Edward Bellamy and Henry Demarest Lloyd, regularly publishing poems, essays, and "classes" on socialism in the short-lived journal.[79]

Charlotte spent her remaining months overseas touring and lecturing around England and Scotland. She visited the poet and artist William Morris shortly before his death and spent several enjoyable days with the English naturalist Alfred Russel Wallace, who chaired a series of lectures he had arranged for her. "I felt so small," she observed, "to stand up and lecture before that great man!"

As it turned out, Charlotte often felt small during her British sojourn. According to her logic, her first trip abroad should have produced a corresponding enlarging effect. Yet throughout her four-month stay, she felt the lingering effects of her last depressive episode. She rued her "interminable handicap" for making living such "heavy sledding."[80]

In September, Charlotte wrote Charles Lummis to inform him of her whereabouts and her recent successes: "my fame waxeth," she declared, "and I begin to feel quite a considerable Person." She nevertheless sought his advice about whether she might now return to California to preach, write, and lounge in a hammock: "I've been six years getting over a seven year's illness and it don't work as fast as I'd like to see it," she admitted. "Disease—Failure of the Head! My sprightly muse does not hop about as I like to see her—she does but flop convulsively now and then—without spirit enough to do up her hair." As soon as she could pay off her debts, Charlotte and her languishing muse planned to convalesce in "a house in Pasadena!"—a dream she would not realize for another forty years.[81]

~

I wonder why it is that it is so impossible for me to feel loveable and deserving. I don't see that most women feel this way. . . .

Letter to George Houghton Gilman,
May 29, 1900[82]

Charlotte sailed home aboard the *Furnessia* on November 19, 1896, and arrived in New York on November 30. She promptly secured a tiny room in her stepmother's boarding house for seven dollars a week. She returned just weeks after the presidential election in which McKinley soundly trounced Bryan, an outcome seen by many as a negative verdict on communitarian ideals: "the countercrusade for community had failed. . . . The golden day of the utopians was over." Within the next three years, Edward Bellamy, Henry George, and Laurence Gronlund would all die and, with them, many utopian dreams. Charlotte remained a dedicated idealist, but her struggle grew even tougher in the wake of these losses, as she acknowledged in a monosyllabic poem:

> It is not so hard to stand
> And fight on the broad free land,
> But to climb in the wind and night,
> And fight, and climb—and fight—![83]

Charlotte found herself at loose ends back in the States; she had planned her future up to England and no further. She spent New Year's Eve alone "as usual," sitting in her fourth-floor room at the back of the house recording her thoughts while others danced downstairs: "Life lies strangely quiet now. All the wants are gone, and all the pains. . . . [I]t is a question of bearing ahead steadily—a long breath—a thirty years wind. . . . Health and work—it all comes back to that. . . . That's all I see now." Her "That's all I see" might be read two ways, indicating either the intensity of her focus or the emptiness of her prospects.

If she could only get well, Charlotte felt sure she could make a significant contribution to social progress.[84] But it was a hard and lonely row she was hoeing. As she told Grace early in the new year,

> I do not quite know why I should sit here holding Katharine's letter to my heart and sobbing. . . . I have felt so unutterably far away and out of touch with all that is mine on earth . . . just pure selfish longing. . . . I ache a thousand ways at once.
>
> This won't do. I can't afford to ache. Dear, I think if you could see how patiently I try to carry my patched and cracked and leaky vessel of life—how I pray endlessly for strength to do my work!—only that—how I use what strength I have, when I have any, to hold this attitude and do the things which to me seem right, how I have truly and fully accepted the *not having*—O well, there!

She depicts work as fulfilling here only in so far as it keeps her from sinking beneath the waves of loneliness and longing that were buffeting the precarious vessel she called her self.

Yet she may have accentuated her difficulties to Grace so that her "co-mother" would not begrudge Charlotte her freedom. For that same day, she wrote a cheerier letter to her cousin Marian Whitney, claiming to find "life increasingly delicious and entertaining." She did admit that she would have to expend a lot of energy "mending" herself given the damage the past few years had inflicted. But she conjured up a bright future nonetheless. As for money, she had let "the wolf . . . *in* long ago—he don't bite." As for work, she observed, "I expect to traverse all America as the years pass, poking it up in all its peaceful corners. How heartily I shall be disliked—and also adored. Such I find is the lot of lecturing on reform lines."[85]

The balance tipped toward dislike in Rochester, New York. Charlotte visited the city on a lecture tour that took her through Chicago to Des Moines for the Woman's Suffrage Convention, out to Omaha, then back circuitously through Michigan and Washington, DC (where she "shook hands with Mr. Cleveland—a warm soft kind hand") before returning to New York near the end of February 1897.[86]

The reporter for the *Rochester Democrat* who covered her visit claimed to be "charmed" by Charlotte's gifts as both a speaker and a poet and by her common-sensical ideas but concluded,

> Yet, with all her ability, her brilliancy, her magnetism, it cannot be said that this woman's life is a success, even in the chosen field of lecturer. She has no permanent home, no domestic ties, and many of her ventures have been financial failures. Some have said this is because of her unevenly balanced genius, others think she is too erratic and that her ideas are not in harmony with the times, that we have not yet reached a sufficient state of development to assimilate them.

The piece then ends on a speculative note:

> . . . one is tempted to ask if the life she leads wandering from pillar to post, with no abiding place, and trying to teach a world, that sees no need of many of her projects for its betterment, but turns an ungrateful back upon her, after having been amused and entertained for perchance an hour or more by her brilliancy, originality, and magnetism, for the fire of her genius and earnestness always finds her willing hearers, is ample compensation for the loss of nearer ties.[87]

Charlotte saved the article but may not have suffered its sting. For on March 8, 1897, six days prior to its publication, she had taken a fortuitous step that would ultimately land her the "nearer ties" the reporter assumed she had sacrificed forever. That day, she called at the Wall Street law offices of her cousin Houghton Gilman. She found him busily scribbling at his desk. When she interrupted to ask if he knew who she was, he looked up and identified her immediately, despite the nearly two decades that had passed since their last encounter. "This was the beginning of a delightful renewal of earlier friendship, still continuing," Charlotte modestly recalled.[88] Just when she had grown accustomed to her solitary wanderings, this renewed relationship led her to hope that being perpetually at large might not also automatically entail being perpetually at sea.

8   "Living and Loving"
(1897–1900)

... In a strange life—widespread—thin—,
Full of great lights, and fresh with strong cold winds—
With knowledge that the world is coming good,
And this—for me—is the one way to go;
But broken also with deep shuddering gulfs
And robbed to nakedness—in such a life,
Sudden, a little glade of level grass,
Elm trees and robins, lilacs, and a swing—
Old times—old faces—things I used to know,
And things I knew not—, lovers—friends—a home— ...

"Thoughts & Figgerings," April 5, 1897[1]

Alone in Chicago on New Year's Day 1898, Charlotte offered a local reporter a summary of her philosophy. "Go through life like an earth-worm," she advised, "devouring it as you work through it. Don't duck and dodge and try to avoid it." She tried to live by these words as the decade and century wound down, biting off as much as she could chew, working through her experiences, facing up to her foes, and facing down her fears. Yet unlike her model earthworm, Charlotte did more soaring than inching.

She spent her remaining years "at large" almost entirely on the road, propelled by the success of *Women and Economics*. She traveled around and across the nation on two lengthy lecture tours and returned to London, where her fame had preceded her even though her book had not. In late 1899, she returned to California, where old wounds reopened and some finally healed.

Charlotte was at the height of her fame and in love, but this meant she was once again juggling work and love, work and motherhood, a stunt made even trickier now that all three balls were in the air. By the end of this period, she had managed to catch all three—she had Houghton, she had Katharine, and she had meaningful work. To use her own metaphor, she had finally left the desert and entered a terrain irrigated by love and fertilized by a rich compound of emotional, sexual, and professional fulfillment.[2]

The last several years of the nineteenth century comprised a period of rare convergence for Charlotte, since during them she derived simultaneous fulfillment from both her personal and her professional life. For even as her relationship with her cousin blossomed, so, too, did the seeds of her idea for a book on women's economic dependence—seeds that had been planted in the essays she wrote while living in Providence and nourished during her California years.[3]

Published to great acclaim in 1898, *Women and Economics* boldly pronounced economic independence to be the answer to the "woman question." So persuasive did her readers find her calls for progressive changes in sexual relations that Charlotte was hailed as the brains of the woman's movement and *Women and Economics* as "the outstanding book on Feminism" and as "the book of the age." Suffrage leader Carrie Chapman Catt praised *Women and Economics* as an "immortal" book; she credited it with "utterly revolutionizing the attitude of mind in the entire country, indeed of other countries, as to woman's place."[4]

Most remarkable of all from a biographical standpoint is Charlotte's daring proposal of an economic solution to women's existential and marital problems. For while composing the book, she had yet to confirm its central claim that combining marriage and career would allow couples "at last to meet on a plane of pure and perfect love." Her failed marriage to Walter had taught her that a wife could not work without cost to her marriage. Her relationship with Houghton had not yet persuaded her that a working woman could marry without cost to her work. She was contemplating a second marriage around the time of the publication of *Women and Economics*, but she considered it "a big risk," "an experiment" in combining love and work that might prove unsuccessful—"if I can't," she told Houghton, "I can't!"[5] Yet despite her personal history, she confidently asserts throughout *Women and Economics* that this combination would benefit marriage.

For Charlotte, woman remained a question—and life a challenge—because female identity continued to be wrapped up in the roles of wife, mother, and homemaker and because the process of disentanglement could prove so difficult. Charlotte's own experiences of living and loving had taught her that what women wanted was not "love as all of life . . . but love as part of life."[6] As both a lover and a worker, she struggled to ascertain just how big that part should be. She feared that if she gave love too much room, it might nudge aside other priorities, but if she closed the door in its face, loneliness would prevail.

While writing *Women and Economics*, Charlotte was attempting to figure out both in theory and in practice how to reconcile love and work. The book's daring promotion of her most vexing personal problem as a solution reflects Charlotte's fundamental idealism, her hope that by making her aspirations public she might hasten their transformation into done deeds. During these final years "at large," her simultaneous personal and professional successes fueled that hope and increasingly persuaded her that "living and loving," formerly antagonistic, might in the right balance amount to "very much the same thing."[7]

~

> . . . I said to myself, a few years back, when the universe was very large and my path very very long and dark and cold—lying alone at night and fighting various devils, with a whimpering lost child loneliness uppermost—I said all at once— "Perhaps———I do not know but perhaps—even yet—all that I want is waiting for me! A little farther on—very near maybe—the most wonderful happiness may be mine. I do not know. I do not know that it is *not* so, anyway—and if such were to be mine, how foolish to be so miserable now. Maybe God is saving it for me some where."———————————And he was.
>
> Letter to George Houghton Gilman,
> September 19, 1898[8]

Two days after Charlotte visited her cousin's law offices, Houghton returned the call at her stepmother's boarding house on West 32nd Street. Her stepsister May recalled, "She was so lovely & the papers were saying unkind things about her— she used to come into my bed so often & actually cry over her lonesomeness and the world not understanding her—it was in my room mostly that Houghton wooed her." Houghton also visited Charlotte in her own little room up four flights of stairs. For over a month during that 1897 spring the cousins had a *"Delightful time"* dining, sightseeing, and theatergoing together.[9]

Joining Houghton in the audience one evening for one of Charlotte's lectures was the editor and author William Dean Howells, who introduced himself to Charlotte and promised to call shortly. Both that night and afterward, Howells praised Charlotte's accomplishments, maintaining that she had "enriched the literary center of New York by the addition of a talent in sociological satire which would be extraordinary even if it were not altogether unrivaled among us." Mentoring emerging talents was one of Howells's specialties. He treated Charlotte in his characteristically generous fashion, declaring hers "the best brains *and* the best profile of any woman in America. . . ."[10]

Howells had praised "Similar Cases" and helped to get "The Yellow Wall-Paper" published. He now "reached out a strong kind hand" and encouraged Charlotte to put together a new edition of *In This Our World.* Charlotte never cared much for Howells's brand of realism because of its "small artistic value" and his reticence about his "real purpose—a biting moralism." But earning Howells's approval again pleased her because she knew of "no higher authority in this country."[11] In the 1890s, Howells served as the reigning lion of the New York literary establishment and his interest in Charlotte's career augured well for its future. Having Houghton there to witness the great man's attentions only sweetened her pleasure.

Exulting in her widening social circle, "congenial work," and "rising reputation," Charlotte exclaimed to Houghton from the road that spring:

> Life is so *good!* So big and bright and healthy, and it moves so fast! A great splendid play, and we all have front seats, and the curtain rises and rises eternally. . . . And such acting! Such plots and counterplots! Such adorable and interesting and abominable characters! And the heavenly scenery and general magnificence of setting! And it's free! And my own particular time to view it is not half done yet! . . . O life is fine!———As for me I feel so good I just want to hug somebody, and sit and hug myself—literally—for lack of a better.

She was feeling so well and so strong that she boasted of her ability to carry a 150-pound man and of feeling as sprightly as she had at twenty-three. "And if strength holds," she speculated, "it now remains to be seen what I can do."[12]

Her recovery can largely be laid at Houghton's door. A poem Charlotte wrote shortly after becoming reacquainted with her cousin (the epigraph of this chapter) suggests that Houghton stood for what she missed, in the dual sense of that word. His kind eyes recalled his "mother's look," she told him that first spring, which "carries me back to that impression of heavenly tenderness—a very passion of mother love." As a surrogate mother, Houghton filled a spot in Charlotte vacated by his own deceased mother and never satisfactorily occupied by her own.

Houghton made her feel "warm and cosy and safe—like sitting on the doorstep in the sun and eating bread and milk and huckleberries—a purring kind of feeling." For the first time in a long time, she began to dream of "the dear sweet joy of home and love" and to envision these two conjoined entities as sources of something other than sorrow. With Houghton on the horizon, she told him, her "poor wild floating soul begins—just faintly and questioningly begins—to dream of happy human life in personal relation" and to imagine a marriage that might truly offer "both love and freedom."[13]

Seven years Charlotte's junior, George Houghton Gilman was the son of William Gilman and Frederic's sister, Katharine Beecher Perkins Gilman. Born and raised in Norwich, Connecticut, he entered Columbia University at sixteen. After graduating, he received his law degree in 1892 from the New York Law School. He subsequently continued his law studies at Johns Hopkins, where his Uncle Daniel Coit Gilman was president. A Greek and Latin scholar who "read Calculus for fun," Houghton had once served as a physics instructor at Columbia; he remained a lover of opera and orchestra, a game player equipped with a "perfect 'poker face,'" and a crack marksman for New York's Seventh Regiment.

When Charlotte visited his Wall Street offices, he was working as a patent lawyer, a mediocre one by his own admission. As a child, Houghton had weathered his father's forgery conviction, his mother's breakdown and early death, as well as his only sister's death just weeks before his mother's. Charlotte empathized with "[t]he growing boy, realizing more and more what life had given him of loss and heavy handicaps; and simply setting himself to bear and do in spite of all—even because of all." She recognized, in his forbearance her own methodology.[14]

"[T]he people people marry / Are the queerest folks of all," Charlotte observed in 1899, speaking from experience. Houghton was family, a fellow Beecher; he was also kind and undemanding and he loved her, "the real whole inner woman, who has longed so long for such a love."[15] Still, the predilections of the man who would become her second husband might make them appear an odd couple, as she acknowledged repeatedly: "I don't think you are perfect. . . . You are not a 'progressive thinker' to any degree. You are conservative and conventional"; "you fall short of my ideal through your peaceful conservatism. You are content with life as it is, and fail to see the great new duties of today." She considered his individualism "a tremendous bar . . . to have so utterly opposed a basis for our whole views of life." (When she tried to explain to him the "Social Organism"—the organic understanding of society so vital to her philosophy—she despaired, "He don't get it.") Elsewhere, she told him, "you haven't much of the imaginative faculty that enables one to reach far out and see what another person means"; "You are not . . . literary. You do not run to expression in words—written or spoken. I do." Especially in her early letters, Charlotte devoted a lot of energy to defining Houghton as her opposite, but in between the lines of this effort pulsed her keen awareness of how strongly opposites attract.[16]

Charlotte's first cousin and second husband, George Houghton Gilman, ca. 1912. Courtesy of the Schlesinger Library, Radcliffe Institute for Advanced Study, Harvard University.

Physically as well as ideologically, Houghton diverged from her preconceived notions of an ideal mate. Although both her husbands were short and slight, Charlotte voiced her preference for "rawboned lathy domineering big men" to Houghton. She confessed, "I still get kind of mad at you sometimes because you are so unconscionably *un*like anything I ever expected to love and marry—but there you are!" In her taste in men as in other areas of her life, Charlotte's self-conception differed from her experience.

A diminutive, plain, "supernaturally nice," and self-effacing man, Houghton at times left Charlotte wishing he "were somehow Bigger." She wanted a man who could sweep her "right off the ground and say 'Little Girl! Little Girl! Stop thinking. It is all right. You are mine and I've got you and I'll never let you go— never. . . . Rest on me.' Thats what I want," she remarked. "And I lean farther and farther toward you—and you kind of *give*—it don't seem as if it would *bear*, really."[17] After years of struggling to support herself, Charlotte longed to depend on someone else and worried that, with the pliable Houghton as her prop, she might topple over.

Nearly twenty years earlier, Charlotte had visited the Gilmans in Connecticut and singled out twelve-year-old Houghton as a friend she held "so dear." For a while, the two swapped letters, family anecdotes, rhymes, poems, and drawings. After a lapse of four years, Charlotte renewed the correspondence by sending her younger cousin a poem on his birthday and signing herself, "Your aunt Charlotte." As she revived their relationship over the spring of 1897, Charlotte continued to underscore her role as cousin, aunt, "old nuisance . . . tagging unavoidable elderly relative"—anything but lover.[18]

She wrote Houghton several poems emphasizing their blood relation, including a ballade that enumerated the demerits of parents, siblings, then spouses only to conclude, "An agreeable Cousin's the best of all!" She struggled to devise the right term for herself: "I only wish I was your grandma or great aunt or—I have it! An invalid sister that you simply *had* to have around all the time!!!"[19] Her insistence on these titles, and her evident dissatisfaction with their aptness, suggests that she was seeking to maintain a distance she was simultaneously tempted to breach.

The cousins would keep the uncousinly aspects of their relationship a secret from most friends and family right up until the eve of their wedding. They anticipated objections not only to the blood relation and age difference but also to Charlotte's divorce, career, and views. In a lengthy letter to Grace that spring, Charlotte never mentions Houghton but dwells instead on her hopes for a productive year of writing and her joy in the prospect. Proving her literary ambitions had simply been sleeping, she set to work on a number of essays, poems, and an unfinished novel.

In April, she received confirmation of her status as a public intellectual when the Kansas State Agricultural College offered her a chaired position at an annual salary of $1,400. The position would have helped to clear her debts and establish her credentials among the scholars and college graduates whose favor she curried. But she turned the offer down and recommended Helen Campbell instead. She was loath to risk her health, and she refused to waste time better spent either writing (she described herself as "simply bursting out into literature") or visiting with Houghton: "it would take a good deal," she told him, "to make me willing to lose next winter in New York."[20]

Charlotte wrote these words in May 1897 while she was away from the city and her cousin on a four-month lecture tour throughout the Midwest and West— one of many trips she would take before the couple married in 1900. Indeed, she spent the majority of their courtship on the road. Her prolonged absences might have slowed the momentum of the relationship had Charlotte not compensated by writing lengthy, near daily letters to her "Excellent Cousin." Many were composed aboard trains, written on her lap with ink from a bottle placed inside her adjacent open bag. Descriptions of her days and work were interspersed with meditations on her feelings for him and her speculations as to his feelings for her. The spontaneous nature of this correspondence made Charlotte look forward to her "Houghton habit" as "just play time—ease."[21]

The frolicsome, flirtatious prose in these early letters recalls her youthful correspondence with Martha, a comparison Charlotte herself made repeatedly. The content of these letters also rings familiar: just as she had done with Martha and Charles Lane, Charlotte positioned herself as a rival to Houghton's future spouse. She thus wished him "the very *charmingest* of wives" while predicting that this creature "won't *quite* love" her. Elsewhere she conjured up that "fair spectre of the future who," she feared, "will someday loom so large a factor in any question of how much I can have of you!"[22]

As the summer months passed, Charlotte became increasingly convinced that she wanted to have much of Houghton. By July she was writing him, "I wish I were the girl—I do, I do, I do." Pursued by Walter, Charlotte assumed the role of pursuer with Houghton, or as she lamented in a despondent moment, "I took the man's part on myself and wooed you first." She frankly declared her growing fondness for her cousin and confessed, "I don't like it. It makes me unreasonable. It makes me feel—where I don't want to feel, and think, where I don't want to think. It sort of wakes me up where I'm dead, or where, if I'm not dead, I ought to be. Now I can't afford to be fond of anybody in that sort of way—man woman or child. I can't afford to want things." She worried she was coming on too strong: "It's as if you offered your hand to help me down from something, and I fell all over you." A sketch accompanying another letter renders a similar idea artistically, showing Houghton drowning in "Sea P. Stetson."[23]

Acknowledging that "we all have to leak somewhere," she declared it Houghton's "hapless fate to stand on the leaky side" of her. Houghton did his best to stay afloat. He matched Charlotte virtually letter for letter and sought to make himself otherwise useful. He visited her stepmother as well as her ailing father and attended to various long-distance requests. But she valued him most as a confidante and therapist: "all summer," she informed him, "I have sort of carried you around with me and talked to you most of the time." When acquaintances admired her "invulnerable self-belief and self-reliance," she admitted to Houghton that it was a necessary pose; she was actually promiscuously lonesome. At heart, she thought herself "small potatoes. . . . Being so many times marked n. g. [no good] it has sort of struck in!"[24]

By August, Charlotte pined for their reunion. She greeted potential suitors with indifference: "When any of 'em propose to fill a New York winter in a boarding house with warmth and light and color and comfort—with sunshine and sweet air and good talk and friendliness—why, I'll think of it." Her brief stopover in New York City, however, was consumed by Katharine, who was about to embark on a ten-month tour of Europe with Walter and Grace.

Seeing her "people" again while simultaneously masking her feelings for Houghton left Charlotte feeling "very mixed up and tired." All summer, she had anticipated her return to New York as an opportunity to plumb her relationship with Houghton. Instead, during the first several days, she saw him only when he escorted mother and daughter on outings. Katharine was waiting for Charlotte when she arrived back in New York ("Rules or no rules, she fled past the gatemen and came flying down the platform to meet me"). She also slept with her mother in the cramped back parlor of Frankie Perkins's boardinghouse. As a result, the cousins had virtually no time alone together.[25] Charlotte's delight in seeing her daughter again was tempered by her frustration at having to sanitize her interactions with her cousin, a pattern that repeated itself with heightened intensity the following summer.

Katharine only postponed the blossoming of the cousins' "rich wonderful man-and-woman love," however. On this or her subsequent stay in the city, while sitting together on the couch one evening, Charlotte, warmed by Houghton's "pleasant comradeship . . . large usefulness and wide help," turned to him and said, "this is better than marriage . . . or than 'Love.'" As she recalled it to his memory, "you turned your face and looked at me out of those lovely eyes of yours, and said, 'Suppose you had all this and love too—that is what marriage should be!'"[26] It is certainly what *she* thought marriage should be, what she had long preached it *ought* to be, the kind of marriage she was about to devote a book to praising. But it was not the kind of marriage she had ever dreamed might be hers.

~

> I feel—did you ever row on the open ocean? A row boat on the big rollers . . . and withal the tremendous elation of that very power beneath—the vast rise and swell that carries you—that is the way I feel now, carried on by the life that claims me. It was blind creeping and feeling for so long—so long! . . . And now I can see. . . .
>
> Letter to George Houghton Gilman,
> March 10, 1899[27]

Shortly before her return to New York City, Charlotte had been struck by a new sociological insight that afforded her a clearer vision of her remaining summer's work. She first developed the theory informing her most famous treatise, she later claimed, while sitting on the banks of the Arroyo in Pasadena, talking to a friend. By early 1893, she was already organizing lectures and papers around one of the book's main themes: "The essential indecency of the dependence of one sex upon the other for a living is in itself sexual immorality."

On the last day of August 1897, she began her initial, 356-page draft of the book her publishers would name *Women and Economics*. It was composed in five separate houses and completed over the course of thirty-nine days, only seventeen of these devoted to writing. (Charlotte typically produced her best work in the shortest time—"The Yellow Wall-Paper" provides another example of this rule.) She twice revised the manuscript, more than doubling its length, before submitting the final version to the publishing firm of Small, Maynard on January 17, 1898. On her best day, Charlotte wrote some 4,000 words and then "ran, just raced along the country road, for sheer triumph," rejoicing in good work well and easily done.[28]

Behind *Women and Economics* was an "enormous idea": human females were the only animals who depended on their male counterparts for food and shelter— or as Charlotte put it, humans were "the only animal species in which the sex-relation is also an economic relation." In heterosexual human relations, that is, wives provided domestic, sexual, and maternal services in exchange for having their economic needs met by their husbands. She coined a term for this anomaly, calling it "the sexuo-economic relation," and located it at the root of all of women's subsequent problems. As a result of this relation, the species had overemphasized distinctions between the sexes and the subjection of one sex to the other and thereby inhibited both individual and racial progress.[29]

Women had lagged behind men, Charlotte argued, because they had, for natural and beneficial reasons during a primitive stage, allowed their mates to support them while they tended to children. This arrangement had soon and unnaturally evolved into simultaneous service to the adult male and to the home. Unlike the continually evolving men they served, who eventually got to do "their share in the world's work in the largest newest, highest ways," women were thus perpetually relegated to "the smallest, oldest, lowest ways." In other words, to use her terminology, men got to perform uplifting "human work," while women got stuck with degrading "sex work," further widening the developmental gap between the sexes.

This anachronistic distribution of labor had persisted in modern times, exacerbating women's weakness and enhancing their already excessive femininity. The "sexuo-economic relation" had thus deprived women not only of their essential human right to work but also of their essential humanity, thereby thwarting evolution's plan. The process would only reverse itself once these economically dependent women learned to stand on their own two feet. And once they did, both they and the men also imbalanced by current inequities would finally fulfill their human potential, to the world's great benefit.

Women and Economics has been hailed as the first book-length work by a woman to "explicate the economic role of 'nonworking' women." Charlotte joined a chorus of authors arguing for middle-class women's emancipation from the domestic realm, but she built her startling and original case for emancipation partly on these women's "miserable failure" at domesticity. Even as late as the 1890s, women's alleged moral superiority and inherent domestic talents (often cited by reactionaries to justify their confinement to the private sphere) were invoked by reformers to explain why they needed to enter the public sphere—that is, to clean the world's house.[30] In *Women and Economics*, Charlotte makes the opposite argument: only when women improved themselves by participating in the larger world could they safely be trusted to rule the roost.

Published in May 1898, *Women and Economics* earned Charlotte so much attention that she confessed to feeling "like the hen that hatched an ostrich." The book eventually appeared in seven English editions and many foreign ones. Its international audience pleased the author greatly, but a particularly sweet moment came closer to home, when she learned that Walter had read the book and praised it.[31]

The applause for the book drowned out the few grumbles about inconsistencies and generalizations. Many reviewers praised its accessible and engaging style. The *Boston Evening Transcript*, for instance, found it remarkable "to take up a book on economics and find it racy and entertaining reading." A successful novel might make a writer famous overnight but, the *Minneapolis Journal* noted, rarely did a sociological treatise "bring any one, and particularly a woman, into the full blaze of a popular conquest. . . ." One reviewer avowed, "No woman, whatever her position or the conditions surrounding her, can read the book and not feel that the whole argument applies to herself and her concerns almost like a personal appeal."[32]

Charlotte's friends joined in the celebration: Charles Lummis hailed *Women and Economics* as a "most extraordinary book, a book which will never be dropped out of the reckoning so long as its problem is a problem. . . ." Jane Addams, who had been impressed when the two women discussed Charlotte's theories the previous summer, pronounced the published book "a Masterpiece"; Florence Kelley declared it "the first real, substantial contribution made by a woman to the science of economics."[33]

The wide and positive influence of *Women and Economics* may explain why women's club members, surveyed by the U.S. Department of Labor in 1899, now insisted that economic issues explained "nearly all their problems." Its impact motivated the editor of the *Cosmopolitan* to stage an "intellectual duel" between Charlotte and the conservative commentator, Harry Thurston Peck, or "Mediæval Professor Peck" as the *Woman's Journal* dubbed him.[34]

Peck had fired the initial salvo when he reviewed Charlotte's poetry for the *Bookman*, complimenting her with his backhand: "She stands head and shoulders above any of the other minor poets of her sex. In fact, did we not know the author's name, we should have selected many of the poems collected in this volume as having been written by a man." Charlotte found Peck's trademark misogyny asinine. She rejoiced, "Mine enemy is delivered into mine hand—and I'm to have a hundred dollars for slaying him!" Her well-known 1892 poem "A Conservative" had caricatured a Peckish creature for "madly climbing back / Into his chrysalis" rather than appreciating the transformation already wrought. In 1899, she eagerly deflated in prose what she had already successfully mocked in verse.[35]

Charlotte was not always afforded opportunities to rebut misreadings, however. She was especially concerned about the "excessive individualism of woman which a misinterpretation of her book might arouse." Intended to promote a "wide and loving mutualism," *Women and Economics* was instead ironically embraced by many as a primer in individualism that encouraged women to pursue their own interests, including earning a living, regardless of others' welfare.

Ironically as well, Charlotte had written the book to shift women's attention away from the personal, but the renown it brought her only increased her own self-consciousness. Catapulted to celebrity status, Charlotte forged an "engrossing" personality around denying personality: what made her uniquely *her*, what made her a famous person and a fascinating study even to herself, was her message and method of selflessness.[36]

~

> ... much of my living has been done on a basis of self-made and self-held hypothesis. By "flights of imagination" I instantaneously construct, destroy and reconstruct a groundwork on which to act—*and act on it*—have done so always. . . .
>
> Letter to George Houghton Gilman,
> April 3, 1900[37]

Charlotte admitted that she had gathered the facts "all over" and that there were other writers who, she conceded, "would have been my authorities *if I'd read 'em*." Nevertheless, she insisted on the originality of *Women and Economics*. She acknowledged only two sources when the sociologist E. A. Ross asked her: Geddes and Thompson's *Evolution of Sex* and Lester Ward's 1888 "Our Better Halves" (*Women and Economics* is dedicated to Ward).

This pairing influenced other writers in the 1890s. The University of Chicago-trained sociologist William Isaac Thomas, for instance, drew on both Ward's gynæcocentrism and Geddes's "theory of sexual metabolism" for his *American Journal of Sociology* essay "On a Difference in the Metabolism of the Sexes." Published in July 1897, the article corroborated theories similar to those undergirding Charlotte's treatise, first conceived that same month. Whether she read Thomas's article remains unclear.[38]

When Charlotte lived in Chicago, she had mingled with many University of Chicago sociologists, including Thomas's mentor Albion Small. She did not meet Thorstein Veblen at the time, but she did read several of his essays on women's economic dependence before writing *Women and Economics*. Veblen's influential *The Theory of the Leisure Class* postdates her book by a year.[39]

Charlotte did meet the German socialist August Bebel when the two shared a platform at the socialist convention in London over the summer of 1896. Like *Women and Economics*, Bebel's *Women and Socialism* protests woman's bondage, argues for women's emancipation, and concludes that "the progress of humanity could be measured by women's condition." Bebel's text preceded Charlotte's by nearly a decade. She had it in mind as she formulated her ideas, but she acknowledged the debt only to minimize it, insisting that she had special insights into women's subjugation that Bebel lacked, "though he goes a long way."[40]

Some of Charlotte's favorite thinkers also commented on women's status in ways that may have influenced her central arguments. Edward Bellamy, for example, insisted that women's equality would remain "a farce" until women stopped depending "upon the personal favor of men" for their livelihoods. He and Charlotte also both intimated that married women essentially prostituted themselves in accepting "loveless marriage bonds. . . ." Likewise, Elizabeth Cady Stanton had repeatedly argued that men's efforts to shape women according to certain ideals had forced women to respond in ways that frequently "developed the very characteristics both in him and herself that most needed repression."[41] Charlotte dined with Stanton occasionally when in New York, and the two may have discussed at table their similar perspectives on women's past and present.

While working on the first draft of the manuscript, Charlotte asked Houghton to buy her a cheap copy of Olive Schreiner's *Dreams* (her nicer copies remained in Chicago and California); she wanted to re-read some of the sketches. Charlotte's celebration in *Women and Economics* of marriages that combine "love and freedom" takes a page—or a phrase—from *Dreams*. Indeed, throughout her book, Charlotte dresses up many of Schreiner's dreams of women's economic independence in sociological garb.[42] Commenting in 1899 on a paper Schreiner wrote addressing "the woman question," Charlotte remarked, "I don't see that after all she is saying more than I do. But she says it splendidly and it 'carries' far and wide. Let the good work go on!" A friend later told Charlotte that Schreiner knew and admired *Women and Economics*—"thinks it *the* book."[43]

In 1896, Helen Campbell, Charlotte's surrogate mother, published her *Household Economics*. Campbell dedicated the book to Charlotte, "whose deep interest has at various points taken the form of cooperation." She cites both Charlotte and Ward favorably as she promotes a scientific approach to housework and traces the "world's misery" to "the home we love so well and understand so ill." Charlotte visited Campbell while drafting *Women and Economics* and discussed the manuscript with her friend, whom she considered "a good professional 'judge.'" Charlotte was pleased to learn that Campbell thought the new book was proceeding "splendidly."[44]

With respected scientists, revered predecessors, favorite authors, and intimate friends all proclaiming women's former glories and present-day subjugation, Charlotte inhaled many of the ideas expressed in *Women and Economics* with the very air she breathed. Yet she continued to shrug off influences and insist that she had never seen the subject "touched on" before. When Houghton tried to pin her down, she stressed that it was what she *thought* and not what she read that was important. She consistently maintained that her "reading on social economics is the vaguest and most general."[45]

Charlotte did acknowledge Houghton's influence, if privately. While formulating her theories, she feared her cousin would underestimate their value and dismiss her as "another crackbrained enthusiast." Whatever his private opinion, Houghton loyally served as Charlotte's sounding board, first reader, and editor. As Charlotte revised the manuscript, the couple spent many evenings together going over the latest draft and correcting errors. When she had trouble drafting the preface, Houghton offered some suggestions that enabled her to write it "before and after lunch."[46]

Houghton affected the book in less tangible ways as well. While working on the final revision, Charlotte informed him, "you are in it all, under it all, with me continually." During the heady days of the book's success, she assured him, "I had to wait till I was 37 and had begun to love you before I ever thought of the economic side of that theory—in its clear fulfillment that is." Punning on the title's abbreviation (*W. E.*), Charlotte observed, "Why—our book is 'we', isn't it! Of course. No wonder it is so successful. I'll call the next one 'us.'"

Houghton's impact suggests that *Women and Economics* deserves to be read both as a polemic on the necessity of combining love and work and as a register the author's hopes of sustaining that combination throughout her eventual marriage. Her marriage to Walter had taught her first-hand what was wrong with the "sexuo-economic relation," and she drew on those hard lessons to develop her critique in *Women and Economics*. At its best, her relationship with Houghton was teaching her how to set that "relation" aright, and the solutions she offered in her book reflect her new insights. Or as Charlotte optimistically exclaimed to Houghton, "O dearest Heart! To think and work together! If we can do *that* all else will take care of itself."[47]

~

... Life is the great duty. I do not believe in martyrdom and renunciation. Unless women can live and work and still be wives and mothers there's no use trying.
Letter to George Houghton Gilman,
March 6, 1899[48]

Although *Women and Economics* maps life as capacious enough for both marriage and career, Charlotte's letters to Houghton document greater friction. These private letters help elucidate the complexities of Charlotte's theories and provide counterpoints to her book's most positive points. In *Women and Economics*, she criticizes the conventional expectation that women of her class ought to make their living by loving. Her letters reveal, as the book does not, that no simple remedy existed for this jumble and that the solution she proposes in her book—

combining living and loving without equating them—could prove the most troublesome task of all.

In Women and Economics, Charlotte tried to convince women that they could love humanity as well as one man. In private, its author tried to convince herself that she could love one man as well as the world. Charlotte felt certain that, if forced, she would choose her work over Houghton: "This is life, my life," she reminded him,

> rich and sweet with the response of hungry hearts everywhere, full of stimulus and comfort and glorious enthusiasm and deep peace. In it I feel that "flushing of the mains"—that full current of swinging throbbing life for which I have always hungered—for which we all hunger in some degree I think. To fully be—and know that life is well spent—full spent—spent in the right direction.

At times she wondered how she dared to "undertake a personal relation" when she was "so increasingly demanded by the world. . . ." But at other times her priorities appalled her: "All that piled up ancestral womanheartedness cries out Treason!"

As in the past, Charlotte struggled to maintain an even keel with the man she contemplated marrying. She alternated between "flopping down" on her lover and "turning away" from him, careening from the hot to "the cold end of the swing." At her most doubt-ridden, Charlotte believed she was "just as irrational and hysterical" with Houghton as she had been with Walter.[49]

Her problem this time, as she saw it, was neither her lover nor her ambitions but her inability to resolve the "tragic" conflict between "The World and the Woman!" At times she felt like an "incarnate Zeitgeist—invincible—superior to pain." But at others she experienced her "particularly lively woman's body" and "woman's heart" as collaborators conspiring to "bring me slowly home and hold me there," she admitted. Dizzily reeling from "Zeitgeist" to woman and back caused trouble enough, but most vexing were her attempts to embody these culturally incompatible entities simultaneously.[50]

In her more womanly moments, Charlotte identified Houghton as her protector and savior. Although seven years his senior and far more ambitious, she told him only half in jest that she needed "what every woman needs, a man to take care of her." While she might appear self-sufficient in public, in private she wanted only to "cuddle down and clutch [Houghton] remorselessly." She might "soar off" at some later point, but in her hours of need, she envisioned herself as "a sleepy Newfoundland puppy in [his] overcoat pocket!" Her "cuddly puppy" imagery complicates her theory that economically independent women would shed their feelings of subservience and their various forms of dependence in order to meet men as equals. But as she told Houghton, "you don't half realize how I need you.

My notions of not being 'supported' are exclusively economic you see—and by no means let you out of far harder tasks. . . . O it does feel so good to be carried!"[51]

In *Women and Economics,* Charlotte insists that fulfilling world work will eliminate women's "intense self-consciousness," their "sensitiveness beyond all need," and their demand for "measureless personal attention and devotion." Yet, in her love letters, she documents the persistence of these tendencies and suggests that they might even be intensified by the pressures of earning a living. Houghton's loving attention made her feel "like a child, tucked up and 'put to bed' with all due nursery formalities—the right doll on the pillow—'a drink o' water'—everything," she observed. "The sense of wide reeling empty darkness changes to a feeling of closeness and warmth and support." She attributed these feelings to "'the eternal feminine' after all."[52] So even while revising the work that boldly insists on independence for women in order to further develop their human traits and minimize their gendered ones, she was drafting private documents testifying to a residual feminine dependence that in her private missives, at least, does not automatically figure as a negative.

~

O my lover!—my Husband! . . . I am simply *in* you and can't get out . . . and all the time to be happy because I was with you and—O my darling—that blessed time when you were asleep—really sound asleep—and all the time we were so truly one!
Letter to George Houghton Gilman,
August 30, 1898[53]

Shortly before her book was published, Charlotte proposed that the couple separate, at least physically, for two years. She wanted to grant Houghton a reprieve from "the insistent pressure of my intense personality," she said, while she simultaneously secured her place in the world. To survive the separation, she relied on her old remedy, repression. She buried Houghton "way down deep in my heart, till its time to open the door and look," she told him; "If you come out—well. If you have really gone—then I shall be glad I buried you."[54]

Talk of burial grew alarmingly literal when war dominated the news that spring. Popular support for Cuba's resistance to Spanish control—combined with national convictions of Manifest Destiny, the lure of economic opportunity, and sensational press coverage of alleged Spanish infractions—impelled Congress to declare war on Spain in April 1898. Secretary of State John Hay called it a "splendid little war," but others saw nothing splendid about it: the collective outrage of men like Howells, Mark Twain, William James, Grover Cleveland, Samuel Gompers, and Andrew Carnegie—and women like Jane Addams—led to the formation of the Anti-Imperialist League in the war's aftermath.

In May, Charlotte weighed in. She argued in the pages of the *American Fabian* that "under a Socialist regime in a later age neither the horrors of Spain's war with Cuba, nor the horrors of our war with Spain could come to pass." Her position was complex, however, for she also saw war as a potential "Socializer"; even with "all its black record of pain, loss and terror," she believed it could represent "a step in progress, and an essential one."[55] Other public figures also hedged their bets. Many in the progressive community threw their support behind the war, Charlotte's co-workers at the *American Fabian* among them, deeming Cuba's freedom from corrupt Spain essential to the benighted country's progress.

Persuaded by this view, Charlotte still hesitated, maintaining, "I see no earthly reason why a man should go—at present—unless he wants to." Or so she told Houghton in a moment of panic. Alarming news stories suggesting that Houghton's volunteer regiment was slated for the front lines led Charlotte to identify herself as "a woman all right—just like the rest of 'em. Isn't any fun either."

Despite her aversion to the emergent cult of aggressive masculinity, Charlotte managed to wring some comfort from its anti-modern martial ideology, which glorified war as masculinity's forge. She dreaded Houghton's loss, but if he survived, she thought war would "be a splendid thing" for him. "It will—so to speak—coarsen you a little—not in any lowering sense—but against a too intense refinement," she predicted; "You will be the broader bigger man for it."[56]

The papers erred; the Seventh Regiment never even left New York. Charlotte's palpable relief did not affect her travel plans. When most road weary, she longed, she claimed, to "spread myself in closets and bureau drawers!" But such lapses were usually temporary. No lover could make a "homebody" out of Charlotte. She was, after all, "a world critter—absolutely no personal relation can cover my life," she told Houghton. She beseeched him to "give up a certain ideal of home" and "to work out such plan of living as shall leave me free to move as move I must," she declared. Movement was now as indispensable to her idea of successful loving as it was to her idea of successful living. For this relationship to work, Charlotte believed, she needed to feel free to leave it at the drop of a dime. Like an undetected bigamist, she rejoiced in her two lovers, in having "the world to go out to and [Houghton] to come back to."[57]

The more her work beckoned, the more Charlotte envisioned herself as divided—a conventionally masculine "world-worker" outside the home and a more recognizably feminine creature who stayed for a while inside it. She teased him about their unconventional roles: "Can you not see that a man's first duty is to his wife and that this womanish desire to have a business of your own is interfering with our best happiness—threatens the destruction of the home?!?!" Their "paradox," as she saw it, meant Houghton typically took "the woman's part" and she, the man's—the exception, duly noted, being their most intimate moments. If others mocked Houghton for having a wife who wore the trousers, she would be sure to "take 'em right off," she quipped, "when I got home!"[58]

In her final decades, Charlotte earned a reputation for prudishness that has lingered to this day. As early as 1890, after fleeing a failed marriage with an amorous husband, she became involved in a local Social Purity Society. She most likely embraced this movement for a host of reasons, including her zeal to follow in the Beecher's footsteps (earlier in the century, her grandfather Lyman had founded the Connecticut Society for the Suppression of Vice and Promotion of Good Morals), her desire to forge a niche for herself, and her determination to free other women from "the revolting condition of dependence upon the man with whom they hold the relation of marriage."[59]

In her sixties, she vociferously protested the "wild excitement over sex" and proposed the study of natural laws as a sobering antidote. Chastity and monogamy were not ludicrous, outdated values, she argued, but biological facts "practiced widely among both birds and beasts, who are neither 'Puritan' nor 'Mid-Victorian.'" Instead of sexual indulgence, Charlotte yearned during the 1920s for an "equal standard of chastity" for both men and women. She proposed a standard set in her own youth, one that required men to come up to women's level for a change. She believed that men's sexual dominance and aggressiveness needed to be checked, not indulged, if "the sexuo-economic relation" was ever to be corrected and if men and women ever wanted to experience true freedom, mutual fulfillment, and individual and collective growth.

She nevertheless refused to condemn the younger generation's sexual curiosity, just as she refused to endorse the "foolish ideals of celibacy, of self-denial, or of 'sublimated sex.'" In moderation and within sanctioned relationships, she acknowledged, "sex is as good as any other natural force." But she deplored its "unnatural over-development and misuse." Charlotte's objections to sexuality are comparable to her objections to femininity: both were fine in measured doses, disastrous when overdosed. Indeed, she used the same term, "over-sexed," to signify both "excessive indulgence" and excessive femininity.[60]

Charlotte was not over-sexed herself, in either sense, but neither was she a stranger to sexual pleasure. Her relationship with Houghton alone provided "convincing proof," she told him, "that I was more woman than most . . . sometimes I feel like 'a heathen goddess come again'—a wonderful struggling mixed feeling, half shame, half pride, of being—to most people's knowledge a stern cold thinker, a calm pleasant friend of men, dearly loved by women, the favorite of children—a widow—a celibate, a solitary—and inside—Ashteroth!" However she might appear in public, inside and in private she felt as sensual and fertile as an ancient goddess. The misleading nature of their appearances made her laugh: Houghton—innocuous and inconspicuous—and Charlotte—a "cold queer rebellious unnatural sex-failure." Behind closed doors, however, the two enjoyed being "wicked" and "naughty" together.[61]

When Charlotte was on the road (i.e., most of the time), the couple kept the flame burning through ribald jokes and risqué wordplay. Houghton, for instance, made "audacious jests" about their "private Press Association" and punned on the words "'honor' and 'off her.'" As the months passed, Charlotte increasingly sought to assuage her lover's "hungry feeling" by behaving "as calmly and 'sisterfully'" as she could. She claimed she hungered neither for his body nor for sex, though she enjoyed both. She also warned him against reading her admittedly "tempestuous" letters reductively: "When I want you so desperately it is not just—that, which I want," she explained. "It is *you.*"

The couple had been sexually intimate since at least 1898, the year Charlotte wrote Houghton ecstatically of "that blessed time" when he slept soundly and the two remained "so truly one!" By 1899, however, the first flush had faded enough for Charlotte to inform her lover proudly, as if she had evolved along salutary lines, that she was "not afraid any more" of her natural sexual inclinations: "a full personal affection," she told him, "has closed the gate of passion."[62] If this represented her final word—and Charlotte was rarely definitive in matters of love—then with Houghton as with her larger living, a diffuse feeling eventually replaced more specific and personal ones.

~

> You see it has been like some tremendous surgical operation—to me. Old wounds torn open—fractures that had joined wrong broken again—and no chance from my natural temptation to break loose and run away to hide and heal over. You just held me. I couldn't get away. . . . [Y]ou never gave an inch. . . . [Y]ou didn't do a thing but just *hold.* And now I don't scream and struggle any more. You fit. The operation is a success.
>
> Letter to George Houghton Gilman,
> October 28, 1899[63]

The months after the publication of *Women and Economics* should have been delightful ones for Charlotte. Her book continued to receive warm praise, and Houghton continued to prove "the great joy of my life," she said. To top it off, she got to reunite that summer with the thirteen-year-old daughter whose absence made her "ache a thousand ways at once," in a rustic vacation spot on Long Island.[64]

Instead, Charlotte sank into a depression so cumbersome she feared it made her "too heavy" a burden, even for her "solid" lover. The future's promise did little to shake the sensations of regret and shame engendered by her past. Contra to one of her favorite sayings (also the title of one of her short stories), she was finding that circumstances do not alter cases: if she felt this badly with all she had going for her, her depression must be a "permanent condition. Chronic & mean, liable to come at any time."[65] She was convinced that her "innards" were "tipping and slipping this way and that the whole time, with disastrous results." She especially pitied her "poor brain," which, she said, had "indigestion most of the time." Perhaps her doctors were right and menopause would eventually bring some relief.[66]

Against her better judgment, Charlotte had agreed to marry Houghton in 1900. She continued to grumble that he could do better, ruing the unbridgeable distance between her present "hopelessly crippled" persona and the woman she once was, the lover she might have been, the wife she believed Houghton fully deserved but would now never know. Loving Houghton thus only deepened her melancholy rather than alleviating it. She brooded over her "wretched limitations" and her failed efforts to "drop *me* altogether." Identifying Houghton as "her whole personal life" meant that she *had* a personal life, something in a lonelier state she had sought to deny and on most days preferred to do without.[67]

At times, she swore that her commitment to social service would always overrule any wayward impulse toward the "magnificent self immolation of the truly loving woman." At other moments, she felt bowled over by the intensity of her need for Houghton, leading her to worry that, like her mother and also like herself as a young bride, she would alienate her lover with her emotional intensity.[68]

Afraid to make any more of Mary's mistakes, Charlotte reconsidered her fitful desire to have a child with Houghton. She acknowledged the odds against it at her age and enumerated the "consolations," chief among them the ability to devote herself exclusively to her lover. For the time being, at least, Charlotte opted to keep children at a distance. She preferred to relate even to Katharine on paper:

> . . . why I have a simply magnificent opportunity to earn her heart—almost her soul—and influence her mind to an unlimited degree. Through my strongest or one of my strongest arts—literature! What might be the ill effect of nervous personality, she is saved; and the best of me I can give her—give her in such wise that she can have it on hand permanently and yet not be fretted by it . . . in letters I can be a mother. It's beautiful. It's a sort of courtship and guardianship combined.

As her planned summer reunion with her daughter neared, however, Charlotte began to long "for a *conscious active* motherhood." She felt she had never before experienced this with Katharine, since she had never been able to dodge a "queer night-mare-y state" during their previous interactions.[69] When it came to mothering, Charlotte experienced yet another gap between her dreams and reality, as the summer's failed experiment would prove.

Charlotte had visited Cold Spring Harbor with Houghton earlier that spring to inquire about boarding for the summer. She paid in advance for two rooms, which likely enhanced her feelings of entrapment during her stay, as did her enmity toward her landlady. Yet when she arrived in mid-June 1898, her initially favorable impression only strengthened. She found both place and daughter pleasing and anticipated "a beautiful summer." She quickly resumed her place in Katharine's affections and at first reveled in her company. They developed a bedtime ritual where Charlotte pretended to eat Katharine "up inch by inch as she comes out of her clothes, and she, the lovely laughing thing, squirming and screaming like a mad thing, in peals of happy laughter. Last night she fairly bubbled over," she reported to Houghton. "Said I was such a nice mama! And that she did feel so happy. Perhaps I wasn't pleased!"[70]

Soon, however, Charlotte's emotional skies darkened to match the weather: it rained for nearly two months straight. Her attempts to cling to future happiness proved futile: ". . . it all breaks up and flies," she told Houghton. "I *fall through it* somehow, clutching wildly as I pass; and it is all turmoil again." She never blamed Katharine directly, but the added responsibility contributed to what Charlotte called "the same old smothering sense of something wrong." Even the joys of mothering could trigger remorse: "When I get those little glimpses of what a mother's happiness should be—and think how miserably little I have had of it— . . . it just adds a few more layers to the gloom." By the end of August, she wrote off an entire week in her diary with the words, "All bad days and nothing in 'em."[71]

The already convoluted relationship among Charlotte, her daughter, and her larger goals was only further complicated by her love for Houghton. For all her joy in the reunion, she found that Katharine's constant presence hurt her in "queer ways." She pined for the lover who, by contrast, had only ever offered her "joy and comfort and strength." She longed for a life that would someday include the "two live people that belong to me," she said, but that day had not yet dawned. Charlotte was neither ready nor yet able to combine the roles of lover and mother. Houghton simply took precedence: "You are more to me, personally, than all the rest of the world beside. As far as personal happiness goes you are more to me than my child—far more."[72]

Charlotte's desire for her lover interfered with and tainted her reunion with her estranged child. "It feels so funny!" she informed Houghton. "It is so long since I had the blessed child in my arms. And when I had her before I had not had my lover's kiss to mark me his. It almost seems as if the child were trespassing! Isn't that absurd." Katharine shared her days and nights and seized every opportunity to "cuddle and hug and frolic." She reassured Charlotte that she was loved, but Charlotte wanted Houghton most of all. When she was feeling better, she found she could "enjoy Kate more," but she never felt well enough long enough to enjoy her consistently.[73]

In early September, Charlotte sent Katharine off with Grace and Walter as they returned to California. In the several weeks she spent alone at Cold Springs, Charlotte justified her decision by telling herself she could not yet handle full-time motherhood while her health and finances remained so unstable. Her decision only deepened the widening rift between Charlotte and Grace. The Stetsons felt Charlotte had shirked her duty in not relieving them of Katharine's care, and they sent Charlotte several curt letters expressing their sentiments. These letters did not devastate her as they might have previously, shielded as she now was by her grow-ing estrangement from the couple, her increasing fame, and Houghton's love.

Charlotte apologized for springing Katharine on the couple earlier than planned. She acknowledged all Grace had done, and attempted once again to explain her reasons. The two women also sparred over *Women and Economics*, which Grace found unjustly biased against mothering as an occupation. Char-lotte conceded the importance of motherhood but ardently defended women's right to work outside the home. She insisted that the fulfilling human work she advocated would benefit both mother and child. Heedless of how Grace might take her words, she declared, "I believe that children will have a better chance of life, love, and growth at the hands of the kind of mother developed under conditions of economic independence."[74] No abstract debate, their argument was informed by the two women's conflicting personal choices regarding career and Katharine.

Although their friendship endured, Grace privately griped about Charlotte's tactlessness as well as her dubious skills as wife and mother. She bitterly resented Charlotte's apparently carefree existence and her newfound fame: after all, Grace's years as Katharine's "other mother" and Walter's second wife required her to put her own career essentially on hold. Grace believed that Charlotte lived a life "without duty," not recognizing or perhaps not crediting Charlotte's alternative definition of the word.

Grace's resentment of these priorities permeates a short story she published in *Harper's Monthly* in March 1907. "The Children of the Barren" indicts a travelling married couple for leaving their two eldest children with an unmarried relative for six years, precisely the length of time Charlotte initially transferred primary care of Katharine to Walter and Grace. The children's Aunt Anne comes to care for them like a true mother would and, it is suggested, far better than their actual self-absorbed mother does. The story vindicates the surrogate mother: the grown children go to her first and credit her with their successes in life, much as Katharine would ultimately do with Grace. In the end, the surrogate mother is recognized—although not by the brittle and thoughtless "real mother"—as having "saved the children."[75]

Charlotte felt she owed her first duty to "the good of the world." This priority might cause suffering, she admitted, but it ultimately brought fulfillment, whereas when she focused on "some personal goal," she invariably faltered and failed. Her continued renegotiations of the relationship between self and world are encapsulated in her 1898 "Up and Down." The poem starts by describing the self's journey away from its "little beast" of a body and from the places and people it holds dear, out "[i]nto the world above":

> Out where the soul can spread
>   Into the lives of many— . . .
> Feeling and working as one; . . .
>   To a day when the full-born soul,
> World-circling, conscious, whole,
>   Shall taste the world's full worth— . . .

Unusual for Charlotte, the poem does not end with this "world-circling" epiphany but instead returns the soul back

> Down, down, down! Back and in and home!
>
> . . . Here at the end we come
>   To the first gift that was given,
>   The little beast we live in!
>
> Rest and be happy, soul!
> . . . This, too, you may nobly love—
> . . . Feeling that even here,
> Life is as true, as near,
>   As one with the will of God,
>   As sky or sea, or sod—
> Or aught of the world that is.

Charlotte later described this poem as "quite the highest and farthest I ever reached." She may have been crediting her skillful reconciliation of both the ups and downs, both world feelings and personal feelings, without assigning either precedence. Rarely elsewhere did she compare the satisfaction she derived from a sense of living manifold, immersed in the world and extended beyond the self, to the joys of living in the flesh, a container she describes in this poem positively for once as both a "home" and a "gift."[76]

~

I was made to feel that my individual failure was no great matter, but that my social duty was; that the whole of my dirty past was as nothing to all our splendid future; that whatever I had done was merely to be forgotten, the sooner the better, and that all life was open before me—all human life: endless, beautiful, profoundly interesting—the game was on, and I was in it.

Moving the Mountain, 1911[77]

In September 1898, Charlotte sat down and "airily composed a year's life." She planned a profitable lecture tour that had her returning to New York in May 1899 and situating herself for the subsequent summer months "within Sunday distance" of Houghton. She intended to make the most of her "last lap . . . as a single woman."[78]

By mid-November 1898, Charlotte was staying at the Chicago home of one of her beloved "mothers," Mrs. Dow. While there, she made an unsuccessful attempt to write a successful play with Hervey White, her former Little Hell housemate. Her dramatic aspirations had been reignited earlier in the year when the British stage actress Annie Russell asked to see *A Pretty Idiot* and contemplated starring in an original play by Charlotte. Charlotte hoped the profits would underwrite her larger plans. But by the new year she had forsaken the script without "a shadow of disappointment in having it miscarry"; she preferred her first staged play to be "a better one!"[79]

In early January 1899, while still in Chicago, Charlotte learned of her father's death, too late to attend the funeral; Houghton went in her stead. She had expected the news: Frederic had been confined to a sanitarium in 1897 due to what was then called "[s]oftening of the brain." "Well," she wrote Houghton from Chicago, "That's one of the shut doors of my life that never can be opened. . . . What a sad dark life the poor man led." After returning East, Frederic had struggled to find work, deepening his depression and sense of isolation. Her similarly underemployed, despondent, and alcoholic brother seemed to be taking after their father. She had been spared, she told Houghton, "thanks to loving the world and you."[80]

Charlotte mourned the loss of her father's mind more than the man: "It is not right that a brilliant intellect should be allowed to sink to idiocy, and die slowly, hideously." Watching her parents suffer prolonged illnesses strengthened Charlotte's commitment to euthanasia when her own time came. In the aftermath of her father's death and, the following year, the death of her ninety-five-year-old paternal grandmother, Mary Beecher Perkins, Charlotte relied increasingly on Houghton as "all the family I have," she said.[81]

Charlotte's winter peregrinations took her from Chicago to the Ruskin Colony, a socialist cooperative in Ruskin, Tennessee. She joined a bustling community of nearly 200 residents situated some 50 miles west of Nashville. The cooperative was incorporated by J. A. Wayland, the editor of the *Coming Nation*, and modeled after Bellamy's fictional utopia. New members of the colony were required to espouse socialism and pass a test confirming their qualifications, after which existing members voted on their admission. In return, they were guaranteed a fair share, a plot of land, a home thereon, and freedom from "want or the fear of want."

Charlotte applauded the theory but disdained the practice. She found the people "mostly inferior and queer," the rats large and intrusive (she later wrote a poem about them), and the weather so frigid that one day during her stay the temperature plummeted to twelve below. Her visit left her even more convinced "of the hopelessness of colony life—of any attempt to establish little separate organisms within one great inescapable social organism." She imagined for Houghton's sake "the anguish of my Socialist admirers when I marry a man from Wall St.! You know it is Sodom and Gomorrah to them," she chuckled.[82]

Charlotte continued to earn national and international acclaim for her trifecta: currently circulating were three formidable works, *Women and Economics* as well as new editions of both *In This Our World* and "The Yellow Wall-Paper," each representative of a different genre. As she swung through the South, from Alabama through Georgia to North Carolina, she drew huge crowds. In Atlanta, she addressed a room so packed that people fainted, went out for air, and then came back for more. One of her southern fans proclaimed, ". . . to think that a niece of Harriet Beecher Stowe should come down here and make us all love her!"

She frequently stayed with the Royall family in Goldsboro, North Carolina, where the local paper proclaimed it "a benediction to find such master minds in the watchtowers of thought studiously studying the trend of peoples and speaking with ripe wisdom to the necessities of the hour for the right guidance of the world." Charlotte loved the South, spoke of the region warmly, and contemplated living there. She had none of a native New Yorker's affinity for the city—she returned there mostly because of Houghton, lecturing her way up the coast and back to him that April.[83]

The couple passed a cozy week together before Charlotte sailed for England on May 4. She built a trip of several months around the Quinquennial Congress of the International Council of Women, held in London from June 26 to July 5,

1899. Charlotte had missed the first two councils. During the founding meeting in Washington, DC, in 1888, she had been too busy extricating herself from her first marriage and depression. During the subsequent council held concomitantly with the Chicago World's Fair in 1893, she had been too busy nursing her dying mother and depression. The third time proved the charm, however, although depression accompanied her even there.

Houghton had helped her to locate a freighter that charged only fifty-five dollars for the crossing. The sum bought her an inside room for four persons: herself and three "German Jewesses." Charlotte suffered from seasickness for several days en route. She stayed in bed on a restricted diet of hot water, whiskey, oranges, and nibbles of cracker. She recovered her appetite, but not her spirits, before landing.[84]

She later described the congress as "an important part of the world-wide stir and getting-together of women" that characterized the nineteenth century. The councils were intended, first, to unite women across nations; second, to allow them to communicate about pressing issues; and third, to foster "the application of the Golden Rule to society, custom, and law all the world over." Many of Charlotte's compatriots, including Susan B. Anthony and Anna Howard Shaw, numbered among the roughly 3,000 women in attendance.

The London council turned out to be one long and lavish party, as might be expected of an event hosted by the Countess of Aberdeen. "Great houses were opened, invitations poured in, royalty itself was polite," Charlotte recalled. "Brilliant receptions and gay garden parties," "delightful luncheons and teas," and additional entertainments rounded out the days. The opening reception was held at the Duchess of Sutherland's Stafford House, known for being "the finest private house in London." Charlotte was even more impressed with its "Lady . . . so big, so progressive and intelligent, so nobly beautiful," she called her.[85]

On July 4, Charlotte attended the closing reception, hosted by the Countess of Aberdeen. The reception followed a day of events at Gunnersbury Park, including performances by acrobats, jugglers, a female equestrian, and the American Champion Bicycle Polo team. Earlier in the week, a couple of lucky delegates had been introduced to Queen Victoria at Windsor Castle. This attention from "the highest quarters" led one of the attendees, Alice Stone Blackwell, to insist that women's causes could no longer be dismissed. "It marks a long step in advance from the days when Miss Anthony was pelted," Blackwell observed, "and Lucretia Mott was hooted by mobs, and Lucy Stone was played upon with cold water through a hose in the middle of her lecture."[86]

At least fifty-seven sessions were offered during the council. Charlotte participated as a freelance delegate in panels on women in industrial life, women in education, and women in the professions, where she delivered her only formal lecture on "Equal Pay for Equal Work." She possessed the courage of convictions she did not always recognize as divisive. During one panel, for instance, she implored mothers to use trained experts during their children's first four or five formative years. She believed her points well received, but by another account they "appalled her English hearers. . . ."[87]

When Charlotte told a London reporter, "I am an Anglo-Saxon before everything. I want to get to know them all and hear them all talk," she little suspected that the desire was not necessarily mutual. Her "Anglo-Saxon" boast, moreover, suggests she held to a narrower version of sisterhood than did the council itself, which aimed to abolish "discrimination not only on grounds of sex, but also on grounds of race, class and creed."[88] As when she noted the ethnicity of her cabin-mates, her genealogical boast suggests her vision of the world was contracting even as her experience of it was widening (though still fairly homogeneous) and even as other reformers, in principle at least, embraced a broader view.

Reporting on the council for the reform magazine the *Arena*, Charlotte declared it "a great week—a week of stir and bustle and weariness, a week of accumulated impressions to last a lifetime." Other attendees, however, carped about the feminist slant of the council; the incessant platitudes; the brevity and inaudibility of the talks; the lack of any criticism, correction, or coherence; and the "collective fanaticism" and "mediocrity" on display. One reporter concluded dismissively: "The effect of the congress upon public opinion here is nil."

Charlotte's speeches were singled out in the pages of the *Nineteenth Century* as vivid examples of the kinds of "sentences wholly meaningless" heard at the congress. The writer ridiculed Charlotte's views on domesticity and economic independence, reducing them to a "naked gospel," which preached

> that unless you are performing "work" in this world for which you receive an adequate market wage, you are a disgrace to mankind and ought to be in a lunatic asylum. . . . [Y]ou may be the centre of sweetness and light and tender love; . . . unseen by the world yet not unwanted or valueless . . . and yet, according to the doctrine of Mrs. Charlotte Perkins Stetson, you are not fit to live.[89]

While Charlotte's theories may have ruffled some feathers, more often they helped to feather her bed. The British edition of *Women and Economics* had yet to be issued when she arrived in London, a delay that "spoiled all my fine plans for making an impression in England," she complained to Houghton. "I have neither lectured nor written as I should have if they had been here, out, reviewed and discussed." But news of her success had already spread across the Atlantic and may have prompted a more favorable reception than she would have garnered had her contentious book been widely available. Hearsay led the *London Chronicle*, for instance, to hail *Women and Economics* as "the most successful book, discounting novels, published in America last autumn." Indeed, as the author of a reputed success, Charlotte came to feel like "quite a lion" in London.[90]

Her publishers assured her that whatever she wrote now would turn a profit. She knew this was as good as it gets: "I've got to the place I wanted. I can write what I please and say what I please and the world is ready to listen." Nevertheless, she could only flounder "helplessly among my own affairs—doing no work at all," she moaned to Houghton. "It is shameful—shameful." Her depression weighed on her like London's famous fog: "So dark and thick and nightmarish. That clogging weight on every movement. Mire, deep mire, and a gloomy twilight, and everything moving vaguely about so that there's not top or bottom or sideways or distance."[91]

She attended meetings and festivities dutifully, enshrouded by her "usual dreary twilight." A nasty cold united with digestive disorders to further aggravate her "beggarly homeless bottomless longing" for her "husband" and his "dear arms—my house, my resting place" (she elsewhere referred to them as her "sanitarium"). When a bundle of backlogged letters arrived from Houghton several weeks into her stay, she flung herself down in a bed of daisies and buttercups and wept for sheer loneliness.[92]

Houghton arrived in London in mid-July 1899 according to plan, accompanied by his Aunt Louisa. The couple's decision to keep their love affair a secret, however, meant that they scarcely saw each other, a situation Charlotte found "maddening." They sailed for home at approximately the same time but did not even return on the same boat. Charlotte managed to endure the crossing by dosing herself repeatedly with a popular remedy for seasickness.

She arrived back in New York on September 11 with one dollar to her name. By the end of the week, she had received a check for $125 from *Ainslee's*, the most she had received for an article up to that point. After paying some debts and doing some shopping, she tucked her remaining cash in a little buttoned pocket she had sewn on her petticoat (she would later write a story praising pockets for women).

Her spirits somewhat recovered, Charlotte prepared for the cross-country lecture tour that would take her away from Houghton until their wedding day. She planned to spend the winter in California writing her book on work. Her publishers had offered her $500 down, 15 percent on the first 5,000 copies, and 18 percent subsequently.[93]

Charlotte's financial outlook appeared even rosier that fall after the famous lecture impresario James B. Pond expressed his "ardent" desire to manage her. Pond's famous clients included Mark Twain and Henry Ward Beecher. His first client, Ann Eliza Young, was the Mormon leader Brigham Young's nineteenth wife; her riveting talks on her husband's "harem" drew crowds and, thanks to Pond's adept management, earned her $20,000. In the spring of 1899, Pond met Brigham Young's second daughter with his twenty-second wife, Susa Young Gates, who informed him of the harm Ann Eliza's talks had done to the Mormon faith.[94]

Though her fame was now such that she no longer needed introduction, Charlotte may have come to Pond's attention via Gates. The two women had crossed paths at the London council's opening reception, when Gates was "friendless and in charge of a group of Mormon women" equally friendless at the congress. Charlotte took the women in hand, introducing them to their three noble hostesses: the Duchess of Sutherland, her sister the Countess of Warwick, and the Countess of Aberdeen, whose name Charlotte forgot—to everyone's chagrin—even though she ran the show. Gates forever appreciated Charlotte's "gallant friendship," especially after Gates had been "hissed at" by Lady Alston at the conference, and especially at a time when Charlotte was "the cynosure of all eyes, the star of every day's program, and the friend of the mighty." Gates thought Charlotte the "greatest living woman," period.[95]

Before leaving New York City in September 1899, Charlotte met with Pond and was assigned an agent to manage her affairs; a month later, she fired this agent for mishandling bookings. The demerits of the new manager she hired while stopping briefly at Hull House, however, left her longing for "the judicious tyranny of Pond."[96]

As Charlotte worked her way across the country, she called on old friends in the Boston area, stumped for "Golden Rule" Jones in his mayoral race in Toledo, and delighted reporters (and embarrassed herself) by performing gymnastic "convolutions" and bragging "like a school boy." Her feats of pliability included lifting a cup of coffee from the floor to her lips with her toes. "What won't Mrs. Charlotte Perkins Stetson do next, pray tell?" reporters asked.[97]

In Denver, she visited her beloved Helen Campbell, who was experiencing a difficult patch due to her involvement with a man many considered a "crank." Charlotte began scheming to relocate Campbell to New York, to live either with her and Houghton or in a "co-flat." Campbell might help them all feel at home while Charlotte was in town and take care of Houghton and Katharine in her absence.[98] Although Campbell did eventually stay with the Gilmans occasionally, she never moved in permanently.

At nearly every stop on her westward trek, various papers took note of Charlotte's "Sudden Fame" (though reports of its suddenness were exaggerated). They celebrated her magnetism, vivacity, optimism, brilliance, charm, and "forceful individuality." One fan even compared her to the "reincarnation of" Christ. However insecure and mercurial Charlotte seemed in private, in public she impressed strangers as "a healthy, happy, vigorous woman who has a purpose in life which she means to attain as nearly as possible."[99]

Fulfilling work was hers, Houghton was hers, and Katharine would be hers if she had anything to say about it. "Great plot," Charlotte alerted Houghton, "the Traitorous and Seductive Mother—secretly wooing her Child! 'Alienating her affections.' My natural bent of plotting villainy can come out strong." She believed she would "make a much calmer and wiser mother now" that her life was "so much more established—justified . . . ," and now that she no longer had to fret over her career's "arrest and criminal delay." She felt so confident in her maternal powers that she even contemplated adopting Basil, Thomas's "sweet-souled" son from his first marriage, whom she met on a stopover in Utah. But when her brother eventually accepted full responsibility, Charlotte expressed her relief at having at least "one load off [her] mind and heart—and future pocket!"[100]

As she neared San Francisco, Charlotte felt as if a "current" had been switched back on in her "poor, wheezing defective machine." She arrived in the city in early December 1899, her first visit since her humiliating departure in 1895. All her passion for the coast soon returned. "The rest and pleasure of it are balm and strength to me at once," she told Houghton contentedly. "I can feel the poetry coming."[101]

First, though, she attended to prosaic tasks, paying off debts in San Francisco and Oakland in a veritable "financial picnic"—twenty-five dollars here, seventy dollars there, and so on. She fully repaid the $140 she had borrowed from her Oakland landlady, and she made a start on her outstanding debt to her old flame Delle. When the "picnic" was over, she still owed over $2,000.[102]

The local papers announced Charlotte's return to the state and to her "many friends and admirers." Those friends included the sociologist E. A. Ross and his wife; Charlotte enjoyed her visit with the couple in Palo Alto, building on a friendship cemented in London earlier that summer.[103] Charles Lummis also welcomed Charlotte with, he declared, "your unblushing honors thick upon you."

Other Californians, however, felt Charlotte had ample cause to blush. Her efforts to avoid "any unnecessary personal friction" in the state proved futile: even her erstwhile defender Harriet Howe cowered before Charlotte's "very unrelenting enemies" and expressed exasperation over Charlotte's prior "indiscretions."[104]

In late December, 1899, Charlotte left the frying pan of the Bay Area for the fire of Pasadena. Her suddenly tall daughter escorted her from Los Angeles, dressed in a sombrero and suit of gold-brown denim. Grace and a "disagreeable

Grace (on the right) and Augusta ("Gussie") Senter, dressed identically. Gussie was Grace's close friend, Katharine's "third mother," and the woman who slapped Charlotte for being an "unnatural mother." Courtesy of the Schlesinger Library, Radcliffe Institute for Advanced Study, Harvard University.

looking" Walter met the pair at the local train station. Charlotte stayed that winter at a boarding house called Las Casitas Villa, situated in the foothills above town. Katharine recalled visiting her mother and "enjoying the tramps and climbs, playing on the donkeys." Charlotte remembered watching Katharine, lovely in all white, ride her "wheel" (or bicycle) during the Tournament of Roses parade through Pasadena on New Year's Day.[105]

A few days earlier, on Christmas Day, Charlotte had called on formerly friendly neighbors only to be "violently slapped in the face" by Augusta Senter, Grace's bosom friend. In a disconsolate moment past midnight, she informed Houghton of her humiliation: "I went in such open good will—so full of pleasure to be back here—and forgot the way folks think of me in California." Her old doubts resurfaced instantly: what did her burgeoning reputation and all the "popular admiration" matter, she asked, if these stemmed only from superficial knowledge of who she was? How much more telling to be "*known*" and disliked! Accustomed to adulation lately, she was shocked and hurt to be confronted once again with "the 'unnatural mother' racket—same old thing."[106]

The literal slap she received on Christmas Day was repeated figuratively in her interactions with the Stetsons. Charlotte initially felt pleased with the "easy and unaffected" relations she enjoyed with the pair. But she soon detected "a deep bitterness of feeling" regarding her "'free' life" the past five years and her "selfish unloading of Katharine upon them." "They feel that I have shirked a duty as long as it was inconvenient and now wish to assume a pleasure," she explained to Houghton. Grace and Walter brusquely informed Charlotte that they did not want her to regain custody of Katharine.[107]

The Stetsons apparently feared that Charlotte's political agenda would supplant their cultural ideals: they were steeping Katharine in European art and culture. Charlotte conceded that her daughter "need not be a 'reformer'" but vowed she would do everything in her power to make Katharine "an American." Now fourteen, Katharine had a mind of her own. From one perspective she was "overweighted with parents," but from another, three parents afforded her more opportunities to play favorites. Charlotte had by this point fallen out of favor, and Katharine did not care to live in New York when Europe beckoned.[108]

Charlotte brought all her powers of persuasion to bear on the skeptical couple. She eventually managed to soften their opinion of her life and to address some of their grievances. Grace and Walter's dire financial straits—the Channing house had entered foreclosure, and the Stetsons themselves were deeply in debt—eased their decision in Charlotte's favor. So did Charlotte's announcement of her pending nuptials to so stable a man as Houghton.[109]

Her "Great Plot" accomplished, Charlotte told Houghton that she could no longer spare him a thousand words out of her daily 3,000-word maximum. She calculated that her letters were costing her roughly twenty to thirty dollars a day, and at that rate, she joked, "I can't afford *not* to marry you!" As it turned out, *Women and Economics* earned Charlotte widespread acclaim but little money. Her publishers had helped to boost her expectations. When the firm projected sales for the fall of 1898 reaching into the 20,000s, Charlotte did some calculating and tentatively projected that she might expect as much as several thousand dollars by early the next year.

She was right to question her projections. She never understood how such a popular book could produce such "very meager returns." Nearly two years after publication, her royalties amounted to $100.84. By the end of April 1900, she had severed relations with the struggling firm. In the interim, she asked Houghton to lend her $100 to get her out of "a hole" (a California friend ultimately made her the loan). She resolved concomitantly "to write all manner of stuff—hand over fist."[110]

Her new book project remained her top priority. Charlotte began writing the first draft of *Human Work* on February 1, 1900. She worked outdoors, sitting beneath the mellow sky, breathing the "sweet high air," and basking in the "blessed sun," with a bulldog perched on one side and a little Skye terrier on the other, listening to the call of the wood doves echo throughout the forested canyons. She later fictionalized the therapeutic effects of a similar mountain retreat in her short story "Dr. Clair's Place."

A reporter who had interviewed Charlotte in Denver had noted that her next book would be called "'Work,' unless she very suddenly changes her mind and writes something else."[111] Despite intermittent attempts throughout the spring and summer, she failed to make progress on her manuscript; two additional books would intervene before *Human Work* saw print.

Charlotte left California on April 15, 1900 in order to reach the Midwest in time for her June wedding. She and Houghton had inadvertently chosen Walter and Grace's wedding date as their own; Walter magnanimously conceded that he saw "no reason [Charlotte's] happiness should not begin on the same day with theirs!" As she recrossed the country, Charlotte gladly shared her happy news with her friends and followers. During the years of secrecy, she had hated that her "life—as it appears—gives no foundation for my views," she said. Now, she eagerly informed her admirers that she "was really a woman, with a heart as well as a head."[112]

With less than two months to go, the couple decided the time had come to tell their "folks" of their plans. Thomas assured Charlotte he did not blame her for succumbing to "the Perkins matrimonial habit," by which he presumably meant their parents' cousin-marrying precedent. Houghton's relations, however, could blame her, and most did. A few polite if not overly effusive congratulations were mixed in with the cautionary notes. But, as Charlotte had predicted, a number of Houghton's relatives feared he was throwing himself away and confessed their disappointment in the match.

Many who responded teetered on the fine line between heartfelt admonition and outright offense. One cousin asked for time "to get used to the idea" and warned, "this is no ordinary marriage, you will have the eyes of many upon you." Another "truly devoted cousin" who promised to reserve her opinions cautioned, "It is a fine chance for Mrs. Stetson to prove herself a true woman and demonstrate her worthiness to be your wife—no doubt when we come to know her we shall have the same confidence in her that you have." A truer woman (less "clever and aspiring") might have inspired more confidence. Houghton's Aunt Emily pulled no punches, declaring the marriage "both unwise and wrong" and imploring her nephew to "*Stop! Consider!*"[113]

Although anticipated, the chilly reaction reanimated Charlotte's old doubts. It is only "with the utmost difficulty that I refrain from casting myself at the feet of your relatives and beating my breast, with tears," she told Houghton despairingly, "so conscious am I of my demerits." She dealt with her doubts by reminding herself that loving Houghton enabled her to serve the world that much more generously. She later provided a public rejoinder to disapproving types in her *Forerunner* story "Her Housekeeper." A persistent suitor in the story reminds his reluctant beloved that her previous marriage had taught her "what to choose and what to avoid" and that the odds favored a successful match the second time around.[114]

By the time she reached the Midwest, Charlotte had decided to improve her own chances by seeking medical advice. "The Yellow Wall-Paper" has garnered Charlotte a reputation as a harsh critic of the profession, but throughout her life she frequently sought out conventional doctors (both men and women), enjoyed their company, and trusted their diagnoses implicitly.

In May, Charlotte consulted two Chicago doctors about possible "contingencies" (the couple's code word for children) and the risks of degeneracy. Both doctors strongly cautioned her against having children with her first cousin. They gave the couple "a rare one chance in twenty of our having an exceptionally fine child—a genius," she informed Houghton afterward, "and all the rest toward degeneracy of some sort." The doctors listed numerous objections: "Two highly developed brains—the Beecher blood—the close cousinship—my previous mental condition—all very bad."[115] The advice she received in her own case likely strengthened her faith in eugenics as beneficial for society as a whole.

Charlotte spent her last months as a Stetson lecturing in the greater Chicago area and preparing for the wedding. The original plan to marry at Mrs. Dow's large house was revisited when Houghton learned that Illinois law forbade cousins to marry. The couple soon settled on Detroit for expediency's sake. The premarital jitters Charlotte experienced with Walter were nowhere evident by the time she took her second trip down the aisle: "You are everything that I am not and the good things that I try to be—you help me up—and you are a steady base to rest on when I can't climb any more . . . ," she told Houghton just days before the ceremony. "To your pure and noble manhood I come humbly, gladly, fully, bringing all that I have and am—willing to be taken as I am. . . ."[116]

On June 11, 1900 in the presence of a few well-wishers, bride and groom met at the Detroit home of the Corbetts and were married at 7:30 p.m. Charlotte had arrived in the city at six o'clock that same night, Houghton earlier that morning, so both still wore their traveling suits. An Episcopal minister had refused to perform the ceremony because of Charlotte's divorce, but the local Unitarian minister, in whose church Charlotte had preached on previous visits, proved more obliging. The couple had briefly considered a local Presbyterian minister, but Charlotte feared he might ask her "to obey or something dreadful." The short ceremony was followed by a "very nice little dinner," after which the newlyweds retired to a local hotel.[117]

Why did Charlotte become a Gilman when she had earned her fame as Charlotte Perkins Stetson? She generally opposed the custom of women changing their surname, calling it "a nuisance we are now happily outgrowing." In her own case, she took Houghton's name because she was glad to surrender Walter's. She also resented her publisher's request that she remain a Stetson the better to sell books; living on the margin all her life had failed to weaken her disdain for purely mercenary motives.[118]

Charlotte's efforts to prevent the wedding from turning into an exhibition were no match for the national press's efforts to create a buzz. The *Boston Sunday Herald* used the remarriage as an opportunity to rehash the Stetson divorce and, like a long-stale game of telephone, repeated and distorted many of the errors and innuendos originally purveyed in the more irresponsible coverage at the time. The biases of the *Herald*'s source surface in the moral drawn: "And this is what we may all be coming to, if this so-called 'advancement' of women goes on."[119]

Bay Area papers particularly enjoyed spreading the news. The *San Francisco Chronicle* pronounced Charlotte's friends shocked and unprepared "for the present apparent apostasy to her own creed" given her "aggressive attitude against men" and her depiction of "marriage as a cruel yoke weighing women to the earth." Her old nemesis the *Examiner* trumpeted the "unexpected" tidings of "Mrs. Perkins-Stetson-Houghton-Gilman's" hypocritical act. The paper rehashed old scandals and reminded readers that "this brilliant woman had proclaimed from the house-tops her eternal hostility to the conjugal relation in the present unregenerate condition of society."[120]

As Charlotte saw it, however, her marriage to Houghton represented "the happy ending" to her story. By the time she married again, Charlotte's understanding of the institution had altered so drastically that she could envision marriage as the very site of transformation rather than its bar:

> They will say—"There now! See this woman! She was an erratic girl—her first marriage sobered and steadied her. Then when she tried to live alone she got into dreadful trouble. Some desultory struggles but no real achievements. Now as soon as she falls properly in love everything begins to come right. She gets publishers, writes a successful book (with his help) and grows perceptibly sweeter and wiser. After her second marriage—with the background of a Happy Home and a Kind Husband, she becomes really a decent member of society. Ah! It takes a man to manage a woman. . . . [H]e has really made that woman over!"
>
> That's what they'll say, and so will the biographers. And they are quite right. It is the blessed peace of knowing I am loved that has made me better. . . .

Charlotte wanted other couples to consider them a model. She pictured their new home as a beautiful, comfortable place, "with a sense of open country beyond," she remarked. "Not that heavy-lidded finality which so oppresses me in most of 'em."[121] In short, she may have previously fled marriage and the home, but she now desired both at their finest. And she planned to devote the rest of her life to proving the hypothesis of her famous book: that a woman really "could love and work too."

New York

9 "A Cleared Path"
(1900–1904)

Human work is a thing you do
For someone else outside of you;
Not for parent, wife, or son—
Human work is for everyone.

Human work is the special trade
For which your body and brain were made
What you can do and love the best—
Done for you for all the rest.

Human work goes on its way,
Not for praise, and not for pay.
Pay must come and men be fed,
But work goes on or the world is dead.

"Human Work," 1911[1]

Charlotte welcomed the century's turn for its overt reminder to wipe the slate clean and start anew. She encouraged others to join her in living in the present, for "[i]t is always Now, and never in our long history was there a Now so live, so stirring, so luminous with hope and invincible in power half-felt. . . ."

Charlotte's hopes for that "Now," for herself and for the larger world, were sizable. She envisioned the twentieth century as the "woman's century"—an epoch defined by woman's advances as well as her ability to "remain feminine always in her progress"—and she positioned herself as a pacesetter.

Personally, she anticipated pleasant years occupied by writing, short lecture trips, and the joys "of a growing social and family life." Life, as she saw it now, was "really such a simple thing," she commented. "Just to do one's work—if one can! And to bear what happens—with fortitude or gratitude as it may deserve."[2]

By 1900, Charlotte no longer wrote Houghton anguished, lengthy, near-daily letters; by 1904, she had swapped her introspective diary for perfunctory engagement books. Without these often revelatory personal documents, experiences like the ones that helped to make her first four decades so dramatic are not as readily accessible, and her life after 1900 can appear somewhat uneventful in comparison. Charlotte herself seemed to view it this way: she devoted 277 pages of her autobiography to her first forty years and only fifty-seven pages to the remainder. At least one recent biographical sketch follows her lead. It summarizes Charlotte's life and accomplishments up to 1900, concluding with her marriage to Houghton, and then appends a single sentence describing her breast cancer and 1935 suicide.[3]

But thirty-five years intervened between her marriage and death, and they represent more than a postscript to her living. During these years, she was remarkably productive, periodically troubled, and increasingly disaffected. During these years as well, she came close to deriving a satisfying identity from public life, only to find the public increasingly disinterested in her concepts of self and service. The more she felt herself at odds with the larger world, the more she used the podium and pen to castigate others for the breach, and the more fervently she began to search for a new way of defining her place in the world, settling in the end on terms of opposition rather than unity.

Charlotte still believed she had many good years left to her as of 1900. *She* knew her story had not ended with her marriage; she also knew contented brides like herself could "not sit hour after hour and contemplate the fact that you are married—however pleasing that fact may be." Marriage was not "*life*," nor was it work as she defined it. She felt more confident than ever about balancing personal and professional duties now that she had a husband who unconditionally supported her career. In the first four years of her marriage, Charlotte lived happily with Houghton while producing a book apiece on three topics near to her heart: children, home, and work. The fame of *Women and Economics* had made her the "much-talked-about Mrs. Stetson," and these subsequent books were designed to keep the talkers talking about the new Mrs. Gilman.[4]

Charlotte's main task, as she saw it, was to continue preaching her "reasonable practical illimitable philosophy." By encouraging service to others, she would offer fresh hope, valid answers, and a clear vision of the "direct connection between each life and our life." "Come now!" she enjoined herself. "This is what women have got to learn to do, if my new world is to come true! It may be part of my work to accomplish just this thing! To do world's work and live large and glad in it; to love and wed and be great mothers too—this is before the women of the world; and I must at least try at it." If her efforts proved successful, she surmised that she would be "placed" at forty-five and could then anticipate another twenty years of productive work.

But if she *was* established in her career as a public intellectual at forty-five, it was in a relatively precarious way. By the time she published the book she considered her masterpiece, *Human Work* (1904), the widespread attention she had enjoyed for the past half decade was already beginning to diminish. As early as 1900, she worried, "I may not be as famous as I think," at a time when she was about as famous as she was ever going to get.[5]

Even at the height of her fame, moreover, Charlotte did not achieve the correlative fortune, to her puzzlement. She had no desire for great wealth, but she did presume that doing work one loved would inevitably result in financial comfort, and yet her optimistic income projections never matched her actual, meager earnings.

Additionally and unusually, during these years, Charlotte found the things themselves easier than their abstractions. That is, she derived more satisfaction from her actual work, home, and child than she ever did from her books on these topics. Her satisfying personal life had enabled her to dedicate herself more fully and freely to "world work," but the world she considered her employer seemed less and less inclined to appreciate her efforts. This four-year period, however, represents a hiatus: not a calm before the storm but the reverse—a period of bustle and applause before the unwelcome lull that left Charlotte not so much adrift (she stayed doggedly on course) as paddling against the current.

～

> Because God, manifesting himself in Society, calls for ever fuller and more perfect
> forms of expression; therefore I, as part of Society and part of God owe my whole
> service to the Social development.
>
> Comment inscribed on inside cover of
> 1900 diary[6]

Charlotte and Houghton's wedding journey took them through Toronto and Montreal, across Lake Champlain, and then back to Cold Spring Harbor, where the couple had secured rooms for three months starting July 1. Katharine joined them at the end of their first month, and thereafter Houghton commuted from the city on weekends. This time, Katharine slept in the room Houghton had occupied two summers previously, with the newlyweds united behind a locked door.

In between boating, bathing, gazing into her new husband's eyes, and melancholy bouts, recurring even in these otherwise contented days, Charlotte read the latest draft of *Human Work* aloud to Houghton—an unprecedented honeymoon activity, but, she shrugged, she was "a queer species of bride anyway." Her lectures and articles might be solo ventures, but she insisted that her books could not be written without her husband. This particular book, however, refused to be written to her satisfaction even with Houghton's help. She put the manuscript aside and turned to a shorter work—one she described as a slight collection of essays.[7] Begun in early July and completed on 25 August, *Concerning Children* occupied her remaining summer days.

In 1873, Isabella Beecher Hooker had argued that "[o]ne generation of instructed mothers would do more for the renovation of the race than all other human agencies combined. . . ." Yet whatever her sympathies for her grandniece's project, even the radical Isabella considered Charlotte crippled by her maternal history in a world that "will not pardon peculiarities." Charlotte thus had little reason to expect a favorable reception of her critique of conventional mothering practices.[8]

Still, she persisted in viewing the topic of "woman, as mother" as her "special line of study," probably because she had been forced to defend her own parenting choices so often that she considered herself an expert on the topic. Before setting pen to paper, she claimed to sense all the "mothers waiting for me to explain things to them—asking for it," she told Houghton. She further justified her task with thoughts of "the children by the millions that words of mine might really help to a fairer juster homelife. . . ." Her encounters with noisy and recalcitrant children while on the road had made her increasingly "hot to write my book about children," she said, and she trusted in her capacity to shine the light of reason on this most emotional of topics.[9]

Charlotte dedicated her book to the child she had supposedly abandoned, the daughter who had recently returned to her side and who, she maintained in the book's dedication, had "taught me much of what is written here." Her notoriety as an "unnatural mother," her difficulties as an actual mother, and her observations of other mothers combined to inform her polemic on the one topic her critics assumed she had the least right to discuss. Yet nowhere other than in this dedication does Charlotte reveal her personal investment in the project. The tone of the book remains detached throughout, as if to divert attempts to read it autobiographically and avert the sorts of personal attacks generated by her "unnatural" mothering.

Readers familiar with her story, however, would recognize the author's stake in its sociological arguments. She vilifies maternal sacrifice, for instance, sketching grim outcomes including feelings of inadequacy, exhaustion, and the possibility of breakdown or even death. She sanctioned her own rejection of this sacrificial mode of parenting via a logic similar to the one she offers readers: "a too self-sacrificing mother tends to develope [*sic*] a selfish, short-sighted, low-grade personality in the growing life she seeks to benefit, where her honest maintenance of her own individual rights would have had a very healthy effect."[10] Her own experiences may remain submerged in *Concerning Children*, but Charlotte had returned in this treatise to preaching what she had already practiced.

Only once before, while lecturing in Maine in 1897, did Charlotte feel she had satisfactorily answered the charge that she had "given up [her] child." *Concerning Children* provided yet another opportunity. Her chapter on "Mothers: Natural, Unnatural" reads like a defense attorney's summation. "Natural" becomes the derogatory term in Charlotte's rendering. She uses it to signify mere biological parenting, the breeding and suckling of the young, a selfish, exclusive, and often irritable absorption in one's own brood. "Unnatural," by contrast, describes heroic mothers who solve society's problems. An "unnatural mother," as Charlotte redefined her, is trained in theories of childrearing and in her chosen profession, trained to recognize that a child benefits most not from an irascible, amateur domestic but from a mother who finds fulfillment in human work and who trusts professionals to care for her child while she pursues her calling.

According to Charlotte, what was needed was not fewer "unnatural mothers" but a nation of them. Only then would all children's interests come first. And only then—in the book's eerily silent vision of a parental utopia—would a child's cry become "the rarest sound on earth."[11] As with her later fictional utopias, this nonfictional polemic endeavors to make not just the future but the past (her own past, at least) perfect.

A timely book, *Concerning Children* was fueled by the progressive movement's twin engines of rationality and efficiency. Children and children's rights became paramount social policy issues during the progressive era. Kindergartens—a word considered "synonymous with progress"—began to spring up across the nation, informed by the enlightened teachings of Maria Montessori and Friedrich Froebel. The period was also marked by increased concern over children of the poor and "dangerous classes," by accelerated efforts to regulate child labor, and by a widespread recognition of the child as an individual who lacked rights and needed them.[12]

Given the general interest in the subject of children and the intense interest in this particular author's handling of that subject, *Concerning Children* sold fairly well, though not as well as Charlotte had hoped. Late in life, she recalled discovering how "touchingly useful" readers had found it: "mothers have told me with tears in their eyes how it has helped them. . . ."

The book's frank appraisal of existing practices did not touch everyone, however. The book received many positive reviews, but even her friends conceded that she "handles the problems of lives without gloves" therein. Her adversaries removed their own gloves in response. Taking her more radical observations out of context, they sought to dismiss her "as a person who wishes to unsex women, abolish home-life, and who holds altogether absurd and impossible views upon things in general."

Was she trying to separate babies from their mothers? Was she encouraging mothers to hand their babes over to the care of the state? Yes, Charlotte calmly replied. In *Concerning Children*, she calls for the creation of "baby-gardens," an idealized version of daycare. If we reap what we sow when it comes to children, where better to produce a bumper crop than in an environment tended by nurturing professionals? It would at least improve on the scattershot methods of hapless, untrained mothers in isolated homes.

Like many middle-class women in the reform community, Charlotte felt that the world itself needed mothering, which talented women would be freed up to administer once they could entrust their children to trained childrearing experts.[13] Like them as well, she viewed the state as a benevolent force and professionalism as a readily attainable goal and so idealized the stuff of more conventional mothers' nightmares.

~

> We move—we must move—are we not alive?
> "Moving," 1912[14]

"Theorizing about families—and advising improvement in them," one of Charlotte's friends insisted, "doesn't imply alienation from those that are ours—in fact it is the love of one's own that leads to wanting all folks to have all the love there is." Charlotte sought to prove the truth of these words as she, Houghton, and Katharine took up residence together in New York City during the fall of 1900.

Newly married, settled in one city for the first time in five years, reunited with her daughter for the first time in six years, with work that "opens and opens" before her, Charlotte greeted her future optimistically. She believed she had finally put her past behind her: "Life back of me looks so cloudy and mixed and difficult—fogs and blizzards and slow cold—long deserts, and very high mountains. Also holes—ugh! I'm never going to look back," she exclaimed. "I am happy and content," Charlotte noted in her diary as 1900 ended. "Houghton—Katharine—Home."[15]

Over the next several years, Charlotte uncorked her "bottled up motherliness." She sought with Katharine to combine a "wise firmness" with tender loving care. Houghton pitched in as well. He helped his stepdaughter (and first cousin once removed) with her homework and escorted her on outings, including a Yale–Columbia football game, a Yankees baseball game, and a performance of the *Mikado* at the Metropolitan Opera House. Katharine found these cultural excursions with her stepfather baffling, but she did enjoy watching him drill with the Seventh Regiment. Both Charlotte and Houghton endeavored "to make city life attractive" to Katharine and to offset her European education with a healthy dose of American literature and culture.[16] Whether due to Katharine's increased maturity or Charlotte's newfound emotional security or both, mother and daughter seemed to enjoy their nearly three years together.

Domestic harmony never obstructed Charlotte's view of the horizon, however, where she spied "[s]uch clear wide lovely work! Such endless work! Such good work." She embarked on a six-week midwestern lecture trip in early November 1900, leaving Helen Campbell and Houghton in charge. She returned in time to celebrate Christmas with her family and to shower Katharine with fifty-seven presents. None came from Santa Claus, a myth Charlotte heartily disapproved of as a shameful substitute for the "beautiful fact" of the Christ story.

While illustrative of her impulsive, erratic parenting style, such excess was unusual for the characteristically frugal Charlotte. It may not have indicated guilt, however: "We are not to blame for not doing what we cannot," she wrote at this time in a piece on "uneasy consciences" for the *Saturday Evening Post.* "There is no great difficulty in doing what we can." Charlotte also doted on her new husband this same Christmas. She concocted a handmade tree out of a heavy pasteboard spiral and spruce twigs—one for each of his years—and attached a present to each branch, among them gumdrops and a parlor ball.[17]

Charlotte and Houghton remained in New York City for the next twenty-two years. Manhattan boasted over 1,000 acres of parks by the 1900s, most attached to the affluent upper East and West Side residential neighborhoods within which the Gilmans confined their housing search; the couple resembled most New Yorkers in renting at each of their four different addresses in the city.

Even in her housing choices, Charlotte was motivated by a desire to stand apart, or as she put it, to "see out of the crowd," as with each move they relocated farther uptown.[18]

Charlotte's late-summer apartment hunting in 1900 secured them a pleasant top-floor flat in a building named the Avondale, located on the corner of 76th Street and Amsterdam Avenue. Telegraph poles and wires obscured the view, and the stone-paved avenue below raised a racket, but the apartment otherwise satisfied. Two of the seven south-facing rooms in the narrow flat had grated fireplaces, and most had light on three sides. The seven sunny, spacious rooms rented for forty dollars a month.

The apartment was equipped with a kitchen, and the Avondale boasted a commercial kitchen. But the Gilmans secured their board for five dollars a week from Mrs. Barthelmess, who lived down the block. Mrs. Barthelmess was a dark-haired woman with "a deep frown between the eyes which made her look cross"; she had a similarly dark son Richard ("Dick") who grew up to become a star of silent films. Charlotte had promised Houghton she would "blossom into rampant domesticity" once married, but she had only been teasing. During her second marriage, she assiduously avoided the domestic duties that had debilitated her during her first. To ensure a happy ending this go-round, she had persuaded Houghton to agree ahead of time both to keep separate bedrooms and to board out.[19]

Plenty of space, privacy, and comfort, with virtually no kitchen duties to boot: what more could Charlotte have asked? Her own satisfactory experiences as a tenant led her to extol the beautiful efficiency of a city block. She predicted the passing of the home and the abandonment of the kitchen in "Great American Cities" like New York.[20]

On a typical day, the threesome took breakfast at a window-side table in their Columbus Avenue boarding house. Afterward, Houghton rode the nearby "L" to his Wall Street office, Katharine walked to a private school on West 87th run by the Misses Murphy and Gaylord, and Charlotte returned home to work at her big desk. Three hours of writing usually yielded 3,000 words or an average-length article; only rarely did she revise. At one o'clock, she and Katharine lunched together. In the evening, after meeting Houghton's train, they all convened at the boarding house for dinner. Charlotte typically devoted her afternoons to visiting, reading, and napping.

Charlotte's abiding enthusiasm for work may be attributed in part to her abbreviated, flexible schedule. When she celebrated work, she tacitly imposed time restrictions; one of her utopian novels sets the ideal workday at only two hours long. Her curtailed hours did have a negative effect on her income: she closed out the year 1900 with only five dollars and twenty cents in her account.[21]

Charlotte had once publicly asserted that a married woman might easily earn and live comfortably on $1,000 a year. She figured she herself could readily bring in this sum through her continued successes as an author and lecturer. Her income would thus have surpassed Houghton's modest $600. Houghton's salary was above-average for the day but only half of a lawyer's $1,200 average and far less than what a typical Wall Street lawyer made. Houghton never earned a sustainable income; he relied on family money as a cushion.

When Houghton objected to the idea of Charlotte becoming the breadwinner, she dismissed his "mountainous old prejudice." She assured Houghton that since she expected him to care for her in all the ways a wife was usually expected to care for a husband, he should consider her income partial compensation for services rendered. Of course, she deplored this formula when the genders were reversed. Regardless, she never consistently earned enough in her own marriage to implement her unconventional plan.[22]

~

Really, I think that, although some*what* damaged I am a really very advanced "specimen of humanity"—that I belong some way ahead in social development.

Letter to George Houghton Gilman, 1898[23]

Charlotte had arrived in New York City at a fortunate moment, since the pendulum had begun to swing toward reform. In 1900, the Republican legislature investigated the city in an effort to rout corruption; an anti-prostitution campaign this same year aimed to expunge "the social evil," expose "the betrayal of girls on the East Side," and close "many evil resorts." The following year saw the election of a reform mayor, former Columbia University President Seth Low, who in his single term focused on such progressive measures as kindergartens, parks, schools, and playgrounds.

Additionally, in 1903, *McClure's* magazine headed in a "new direction" with its hard-hitting exposés. The bellwether January issue contained investigative articles by Ida Tarbell, Lincoln Steffens, and Ray Stannard Baker. The issue was fronted by a fiery editorial from McClure himself, placing the responsibility to uphold the law when our leaders stumbled squarely on the public's collective shoulders. Borrowing from John Bunyan, Teddy Roosevelt identified *McClure's* stable of dirt-focused journalists as "muckrakers."[24]

During this same January 1903, Charlotte entered into negotiations with McClure. The firm published her next two books—*The Home* that same year and (more reluctantly, after expressing doubts about its quality and salability) *Human Work* the next. Her reform tendencies help to explain McClure's interest in her work, but it would be a stretch to call Charlotte a "muckraker." She preferred envisioning better tomorrows to merely exposing contemporary flaws, and she preferred remaining above the fray to delving into specific evidence of corruption. In short, she disdained the muck.[25]

Not all of New York's journalistic and political trends were progressive, as William Randolph Hearst's rise to prominence in the city attests. Many of Charlotte's diatribes against "Newspaper Sins" from this period should be read with the resurrection of this ghost from her past in mind. In 1895, the same year Charlotte fled the city, Hearst left San Francisco as well, moving to New York to run the *Morning Journal* and, the following year, the *Evening Journal*. Hearst helped to pioneer the "yellow journalism" that emerged in the late 1890s, typified by its lurid print (flamboyantly colorful yellow, red, and green ink rather than the traditional, staid black) and "scare" headlines.[26] His infamous circulation war with his former mentor and employer, Joseph Pulitzer, led each to attempt to out-sensationalize the other's headlines, scoop the other's stories, and steal the other's star reporters (Hearst's thefts included Stephen Crane and Julian Hawthorne).

Hearst's ambitions extended beyond the press: in 1902, he ran as a Democrat and was elected to his first of two terms in Congress. Hearst proved less successful in his bids for president in 1904 (he came in second in the balloting for the Democratic nomination) and for New York governor in 1906. Hearst also lost New York City mayoral races in both 1905 and 1909.[27]

In early April 1901, Hearst published an editorial criticizing President McKinley that included the line, "If bad institutions and bad men can be got rid of only by killing, then the killing must be done." An established critic of the Republican president, Hearst denied authorship of the editorial and stopped the presses, but not before early issues hit the streets. After McKinley's assassination that September by Leon Czolgosz, some believed Hearst had blood on his hands. Charlotte waited with the nation as McKinley lingered on for six anguished days, only to succumb to gangrene in those pre-penicillin days. McKinley's death led to the inauguration of his considerably more progressive vice president, Theodore Roosevelt, and, subsequently, to Roosevelt's landslide victory in 1904.[28]

McKinley's assassination by a native-born anarchist with a foreign-sounding name prompted Congress to pass a general immigration act making an opinions test a prerequisite for immigration. That same year, the American Breeders Association was formed to promote eugenics. Borrowing from Charlotte's sociologist friend E. A. Ross, President Roosevelt sounded the alarm from his bully pulpit over "race suicide." He indicted the "criminal" decline in childbearing rates among Anglo-Saxons compared to the accelerating rate within the immigrant population.[29]

At the time, Charlotte found the distinction between "American stock" and "foreign stock" "amusing," "as if none were Americans save those whose foreign stock came over in a certain century, charter members, as it were—all later additions inferior!" During the first decade of the twentieth century, Charlotte argued that our national blend of "every kind of people . . . is what makes us the splendid world people we are, this blended blood is America."

She did concede the evolutionary logic governing anti-immigrant sentiment: "The lower the grade, the more children; the higher the grade, the less children. A complex personal development, such as accompanies high civilization, means a lower birth-rate." But she refused to share the president's alarm because she knew a solution "better than eugenics": elevating humanity and eliminating poverty and ignorance. These efforts would result in "the swarming masses of inferior people" in good time being replaced by "a lesser number of superior people." Making motherhood more attractive to women of "the American race" by instituting her pet reforms, she added, would help to even out the balance.[30] Toward the end of her more than twenty-year sojourn in the city, however, Charlotte would be hard-pressed to imagine a solution she liked "better than eugenics."

The rapid influx of immigrants into major urban centers like New York fed the xenophobic fears of former residents like Roosevelt and increasingly reluctant ones like Charlotte. Many of Charlotte's fellow reformers viewed the city's ethnic diversity as more threat than promise. They feared that foreign reactionaries and "the vicious" would vote to defeat their pet causes. They were especially concerned about the fate of woman suffrage in the hands of voting immigrants. In the words of two suffragists, New York contained

> as many Irish as the city of Dublin, as many Germans as the city of Munich, as many Italians as the city of Florence, as many Russians as Riga, as many Austro-Hungarians as Prague, as many Norwegians as Christiana, and the sum total constituted a larger population than that of all the thirteen colonies when they arose in revolution against their mother country.

By the time Charlotte left the city, she hotly resented this diversity. During her early years in New York, however, she remained upbeat and removed from petty squabbles, and she concentrated primarily on using podium, pen, and her "far-focused mind" to unify and advance her pet causes.[31]

~

> My gracious I *ought* to get well if human happiness is worth anything. The sense of living an active *recognized* world-helper is very very good.
>
>   Letter to George Houghton Gilman,
>   October 7, 1899[32]

By 1901, Charlotte had two treatises under her belt and the two people dearest to her under the same roof. But she did not have her health, which "showed no real improvement" despite her happiness. Those close to her also suffered: Mother Campbell had begun to show marked signs of dementia, though she lingered on until 1918, and Katharine contracted one illness after another. Charlotte's own recurrent depression caused her reluctantly to relinquish her hope that her husband's loving presence would enable her "[p]atent collapsible brain cells," capable at times of "great expansion," to "build up their weary little walls and stay open."

Since she had already made a name for herself by the time she married Houghton, she could not blame her spouse, as she had Walter, for ruining her life or inducing her depression. In these emotionally sated days, she could no longer pinpoint "that field of the brain used in personal relation" as the culprit that "weakens the whole mass." She was thus forced to abandon her dream of a "permanent recovery" once personal happiness was hers. She continued to view herself as hobbled by "the various disabilities which make life something of a tightrope to my eager feet," she sighed.[33] During these happily married years, illness supplanted loneliness and lovelessness as the main reason she questioned the value of a private self.

Charlotte joined other privileged New Yorkers in fleeing the city during the sweltering summer months. She made regular visits to a variety of mountain retreats. These included Summer Brook Farm, a camp upstate in the Adirondacks owned by the editor and author Prestonia Mann, Horace Mann's daughter, which she ran with her new husband, the British Fabian John Martin. The couple welcomed Charlotte to their camp at the turn of the century and socialized with both Gilmans during the twenties. But their commitment to a more radical socialism and their disdain for suffrage led them to sharply criticize Charlotte in their 1916 book *Feminism: Its Fallacies and Follies* for her naïve and elitist arguments on behalf of women's economic independence.[34]

Since 1895, Mann's "home built of logs with the bark on" had served as a gathering place for likeminded progressives and especially for Mann's *American Fabian* associates. Charlotte first visited the camp in 1897 and took an immediate liking to its owner. Charlotte described her as "my age, tremendously well educated—college and everything else, rich (comparatively) and a nice girl," she told Houghton.

Mann asked "people who interested her" to come to the camp and expected them to pay three dollars for food, tend to their own rooms, "and share in the community work." Residents at the farm, addressed as brother or sister plus their first names, chipped in for several hours of daily manual labor, although the outdoor work tended to devolve onto the men and the domestic chores primarily onto the women.

Katharine, who joined her mother at the farm for several weeks during the summer of 1901, recalled the large living room whose long window and window seat provided spectacular views of the mountains, the "great sunken fireplace on

Group portrait of Charlotte (hand on her chin), Katharine (on Charlotte's immediate right), and others sitting on the steps of a log cabin at Prestonia Mann Martin's Summer Brook Farm in Hurricane, New York, ca. 1902. Courtesy of the Schlesinger Library, Radcliffe Institute for Advanced Study, Harvard University.

the steps of which people could sit as in an amphitheater," and the guesthouse, referred to as the chalet. At the edge of a ravine, from whence could be seen "fleecy clouds," stood a covered porch. It housed "a long table with splint seated shaker chairs where backs stopped in the small of ones back and did not encourage lounging." At lunchtime, guests convened at this table, waiting politely for Mann to finish reading from edifying material, including the *Republic*, the Bible, and *Looking Backward* before sampling the bread, milk, and cottage cheese sprinkled with raisins and nutmeg that made for a typical midday repast. Katharine balked, but Charlotte usually had a "*fine*" time there, luxuriating in the "[s]plendid air. Lots of genuine exercise and some useful work, and a lot of people to play with!"[35]

Back in New York that fall, however, Charlotte slumped. *Success* magazine asked several prominent women around this time what they would do over again if they could. Charlotte identified as "injudicious" a "too lavish expenditure of nerve force" during childhood; her youthful efforts to discipline her will had resulted in painful years of "feverish struggle" as opposed to the "lifetime's strong and steady work" that might have been hers had she been more frugal.[36]

Charlotte's hopes of a recovery revived after Dr. Mary Putnam Jacobi took an interest in her case. A brilliant physician and the eldest of publisher George Palmer Putnam's eleven children, Jacobi put Charlotte through a course of mild electric shock therapy and prescribed "phospho-glycerates in wine" with good effect. She also encouraged Charlotte to undertake relatively simple intellectual tasks to "set that inert brain to work," starting with building blocks and working up to complex intellectual treatises.

To a degree, Jacobi's approach to mood and nerve disorders resembled S. Weir Mitchell's: the Philadelphia doctor had praised Jacobi's work on hysteria, and both doctors traced women's diseases to menstrual disorders. But their differences were more pronounced. Jacobi generally did not prohibit her patients from working: indeed, she encouraged Charlotte to "sail right in." The doctor did recommend a modified schedule, however, with "interruptions to employment every two or three hours." Also unlike Mitchell, Jacobi welcomed a case history from this particular patient, one Charlotte cast this time not in epistolary form but as a chart "with parallel lines showing normal, one super and several sub, down to melancholia . . . with a few peaks and many deep valleys, the average generally below normal."[37]

Charlotte responded favorably to the "amiable" doctor's methods and manner and believed she was finally improving. Jacobi's own failing health likely put an end to the treatment. By the time she attended Charlotte, Jacobi had already developed the meningeal tumor that would kill her in 1906.

The two women were involved in many of the same causes, including suffrage. Each promoted the salutary benefits of developing one's sense of "insignificance in the vast scheme of the universe and a capacity for self-denial." Yet, for Jacobi, health and happiness entailed the "successful adaption to the conditions of existence." For Charlotte, those conditions were by no means set in stone: they *had* to be changed for health and happiness to be attained. As a reform Darwinist, she also believed social forces as well as individual lives could be *"steered"* according to specified ideals.[38]

By the summer of 1903, Charlotte boasted of feeling better than she had in twenty years and of being able to read for sustained periods without cost. As early as January 1902, Charlotte felt fit enough to don sneakers and organize a seven-member women's basketball team, Katharine included, at Barnard College's gymnasium. Invented in 1891, basketball vied with other athletic activities drawing converts during this "strenuous age," including tennis, golf, camping, and bicycling.

The national craze for bicycling as a recreational activity led to the sale of some 10 million bicycles by 1900. Charlotte experimented with cycling but never developed Houghton's enthusiasm. She felt sure it affected her health adversely: a doctor had endorsed her suspicion that straddling a bicycle seat could prove debilitating. Advocates viewed the new contraption as a symbol of mobility, a "vehicle of the healthful happiness," and even, in moderation, a potential cure for neurasthenia. But for Charlotte the bicycle remained a "confounded thing, acting in some occult manner on a ferociously 'sympathetic' nervous system," leaving her "unstrung—low spirited—weak—and this for many days."[39]

Mother and daughter's sporting days abruptly ended in late February 1903 when Katharine was diagnosed first with pneumonia, then with pleurisy, then with scarlet fever. A nurse had to be hired, the family had to be quarantined, their belongings had to be sterilized, and their boarding-out days had to be terminated. Charlotte helped to nurse her daughter through these illnesses. She also resumed kitchen duties, "very contentedly" by her own account, despite her misgivings about the wastefulness of home cooking. As Katharine recovered, the two passed the time by collaborating on several farcical romances.[40]

Confined to bed for three months, Katharine arose a year older (now seventeen) and a good deal thinner. She spent the summer convalescing in the Catskills and Adirondacks. In the fall, she sailed to Italy to join Grace and Walter. With her new sewing machine, Charlotte made Katharine her first long skirts, and Katharine pinned her hair up in order to appear as mature as possible while traveling alone.[41] Although Katharine would live with her mother again, by their next reunion she had turned eighteen, and Charlotte's active parenting days lay behind her.

Whether Charlotte and Houghton ever tried to have a child together, despite doctors' warnings, remains unclear. Charlotte later recalled menopause as a "blow." She confided to Katharine in the 1930s that she had hoped "with all [her] heart for a baby with Houghton." If her recollection is accurate, her inability to conceive represents a rare source of disappointment in her second marriage.

Charlotte had found genuine happiness with Houghton. The "bird-without-legs" had finally "lit." Her frequent travels meant Houghton stayed behind to manage without her (for which the Stetsons pitied him greatly). But when she returned home she could count on Houghton to provide her with "a resting place to do my work," she said. The couple enjoyed an easy companionship and passed their time together writing poems, playing word games, assembling puzzles, and even playing hide-and-seek. They also continued to collaborate on her books. Charlotte derived "great happiness" when Houghton saw the point of her critique in *Human Work*; she had returned to the manuscript and completed a new draft by the end of 1902, though two years would pass before it saw print.[42]

For Thanksgiving that year, Charlotte wrote Houghton a fond and grateful poem:

> I am so thankful, Heart of Mine!
> So thankful through and through
> For Life and Light and Comfort Sweet
> Enough to wear, enough to eat,
> And growing power to DO!
> I am thankful, Heart of Mine
> For peace and power and Work, divine,
> But most of all, for you—
> Most thankful, Sweet, for You![43]

As she had hoped, Charlotte's second marriage ultimately affirmed her argument in *Women and Economics* that pursuing work and love simultaneously made for a contented wife. If the second time proved the charm, the credit may partly belong to the absence of young children and arduous maternal responsibilities. But it may also belong to the intervening years Charlotte spent pursuing and, to a degree, expending the simultaneous and often contradictory passions for work and for intimacy that had ruled and finally ruined her relationship with Walter.

~

Help educate children. Help develope [*sic*] women. Help the world. Help God. Am here to do it. Have no right not to do it.

"God," "Thoughts & Figgerings," 1905[44]

Charlotte began and ended 1902 by talking to clubs and kept up her steady lecturing in between. During the winter of 1902–03, the press extensively covered her New York Civitas Club lecture series on the home, motherhood, and woman's duty, "which besides deep interest & conviction brought a storm of criticism, ridicule, caricature and consternation, reporters flocking and the conservatives shaking in their respectable shoes, yet compelled to smile," or so said a sympathetic chronicler.[45]

Impervious to the "storm," Charlotte continued to dispense "dispassionate," "scientific" advice. For instance, she instructed her female listeners to "[t]ry to think and not feel. Put your hearts in your pockets for a while. Women are too apt to take a personal view of things."[46] Having stumbled over her own heart and trampled on other's feelings more than once, Charlotte had personal reasons for advocating impersonality.

She never became so impersonal as to be wooden, however. Attempts to bring a subject to life on the page are complicated by that page's one-dimensionality. With a subject as charismatic and vivacious as Charlotte was by nearly all accounts, the difficulties mount. Reporters covering her lectures acknowledged this problem: "It is too bad," one wrote, "that the charm and magnetism of Mrs. Gilman's personality cannot pervade the newspaper reports of her lectures, as they do the assembly room when she is speaking."

Charlotte was variously praised for her wit, her sarcasm, her "outspoken conviction as to her own interestingness," her absolute fearlessness, her rapidity of thought and her logical mind, her sense of humor, and her "quick sympathy." And she was consistently praised for her spontaneity and ingenuity: working from a list of subjects she could discuss at a moment's notice, she never delivered the same talk twice but invariably delivered "such scintillating 'thinks!'"[47]

In addition to lecturing and writing books, Charlotte continued to write regularly for prominent venues, including the *Saturday Evening Post*, *Harper's Bazaar*, and *Success*. One *Success* reader wrote the editor protesting Charlotte's contributions, since she was teaching readers a thing or two, and "there is nothing so painful to the human mind as the pain of a new idea. The average American has no use—none—for a sensible woman."

During the years that followed the publication of *Women and Economics*,

Charlotte, by her own estimate, went "Over the Top" in terms of fame. We do not have to take just her word for it. At an 1899 dinner for the fiery orator William Jennings Bryan, the guest of honor insisted on giving Charlotte his seat. In 1901, a popular education series offering reading courses in art, sociology, and literature—and already featuring such distinguished contributors as Senator Henry Cabot Lodge, Mrs. Humphrey Ward, William Dean Howells, Edward Everett Hale, and Grover Cleveland—sought to add Charlotte's name to its roster of writers. That same year, she learned that one of her lesser-known poems, "My Child," was now beloved in translation in some 20,000 Danish homes. And in her own country in 1904, the educator and writer Curtis Hidden Page included her on his list of the "greater American poets," even though, she wrote him, "I hardly call myself a poet at all."[48]

A prophet to some, impractical to others, "perfectly horrid" to a good many, Charlotte was sure to provoke a "Hotbed of Discussion" and to "Stagger Critics" with her radical views on women, babies, and the home. She considered this last topic her "Womanest" and expounded on the home in her lectures, in a series of articles for *Success*, and in a book-length study on "its work and influence." She described her 1903 treatise *The Home* as "the most heretical—and the most amusing—of anything" she had written. A "good and worthy woman" deemed the views expressed therein "blasphemous," and Charlotte gleefully agreed.[49]

As Charlotte well knew, the home stood for many as the last bastion of civilization, both sacrosanct and inviolable:

> Oh! The Home is utterly perfect!
>   And all its works within.
> To say a word about it—
> To criticise or doubt it—
> To seek to mend or move it—
> To venture to improve it—
>   Is *the* unpardonable sin!

When Charlotte first conceived of *The Home* five years previously, she had anticipated "hurling every idol from its shrine." In the book itself, she presents the hallowed home as both a throwback and a prison, whose walls were already crumbling thanks to evolution's improving effects on its inhabitants. While some women might still desire to stay at home out of maternal instinct, Charlotte punned that we have "to use something more than instinct" or we will become "ex-tinct!"[50]

The book debunks nearly all the myths associated with the home, from its so-called privacy to its so-called sanctity to its so-called economy to its so-called femininity. A home life is no substitute for a public life, Charlotte insisted, but such had been woman's lot, and the costs both to her and her family had been great. She scoffed at the Victorian ideologues who had romanticized the private sphere and women's destined, saintly role therein. But she nevertheless occasionally used the same dulcet tones to sentimentalize the public realm and women's potentially meaningful work therein.

To those who continued to defend the home as a "cradle of virtues," Charlotte rejoined, "we are in a stage of social development where we need virtues beyond the cradle size." For all her idol smashing (one review compared *The Home* to "a surgical operation on the popular mind"), Charlotte preferred a more nurturing metaphor: she compared her renovations to pruning a "most precious tree" into a more pleasing shape.[51]

As with many of her other works, *The Home* revisits themes developed in prior incarnations and adds a few new twists. Like her two previous treatises, *The Home* is also deeply informed by personal experiences. Charlotte's struggles as a young woman and wife to escape the "ancient coop" equipped her to itemize its snares in each chapter. Her pledge "to stand against [her] own sex instincts and life habits" and to resist the entanglement of "home duties" gets translated into the general recommendation *The Home* offers every woman. Her upbringing by a mother who personified the most "passionately domestic of home-worshipping housewives" lends increased urgency to her ambitions to dismantle the domestic shrine and encourage women to make the public sphere their home.[52]

In advocating domestic reform, Charlotte was joining a rising chorus. In 1900, for example, the Massachusetts Bureau of Labor Statistics had endorsed outsourcing mundane housework as more cost effective. Charlotte took the lead on such issues, as reviewers acknowledged. The *Los Angeles Express* deemed her "the best advocate on her side of the question in America." The Boston *Transcript* praised her "trenchant pen" even as its reviewer sniped that the "dear but stupid average woman" would undoubtedly find her views "abhorrent."[53]

Such misogyny surfaces in other responses to *The Home*. Indeed, the book engendered a minor critical backlash, including *ad hominem* attacks upon its author. The *New York Times* found "something cold and shivery about Mrs. Gilman's vision of a home." A critic for the *Los Angeles Herald* accused her of bossiness and shuddered to think of her "in his home . . . trying to make home happy according to the rules laid down in the book." Comparable insinuations appeared in even otherwise positive assessments.[54]

One reviewer went so far as to ask, "What kind of homes and what kind of mothers and fathers can it have been the author's misfortune to have known?"

Charlotte's third treatise sold well and received generally positive comment. But it prompted several critics to ask the author if the home—whether her ideal or her actual one—was where her heart was.[55]

~

> You see my business is *living*. To grow and develop and learn all I can. To *Be* as great and good as possible. . . . People have said I wasted power in different kinds of work. I do not. I do what comes to my hand, and am the larger and wiser for each new experience.
>
> Letter to George Houghton Gilman,
> February 3, 1898[56]

Women's economic dependence, disastrous childrearing practices, stultifying domestic conditions: Charlotte went "a-gunning" for all these social ills during this period. While emanating from practical concerns, her conclusions were often judged vague and unconvincing by critics who found her better at critique than at concocting useful solutions. At least her 1901 and 1903 treatises had addressed issues conventionally associated with women's sphere: the home and children. Women who based their public careers on so-called women's issues typically fared better than those who ventured outside conventional boundaries.

Ever-defiant, Charlotte visited even more abstract and putatively masculine terrain in her next book. At the core of *Human Work* lay her critique of prevalent economic theories and her attempt to introduce a new line of thought, in the idealistic belief that correcting people's erroneous ideas about work would motivate them to change their behavior. We do not work to gratify individual desires, she argued against prevailing logic, but to tap into our collective humanity: work "is something you do for others while others do something for you. It is practical, profitable altruism." Since our humanity emerged in our "common effort for the common good," work only mattered when everyone profited, in every sense of the word. Work as she understood it was no mere economic activity but a spiritual and social necessity. It was both an essential right and an essential duty.[57]

Charlotte first ruminated on the nature of work in her teens, when she adapted the Puritan notion of salvation through work to her own more optimistic and earthbound ends. She had learned from her guide Dr. Studley that "[w]ork is the best of tonics and the best of beautifiers." And she had devised a work cure to relieve her own melancholia. Like the doctors she praises as "world workers" in her 1911 novel *The Crux*, her own prodigious labors were strongly motivated by a desire to sublimate personal sorrow, although Charlotte rarely gave this motive conscious precedence.

She suspected that her childhood labors had "crippled" her for life, but her work ethic remained strong, though she avoided and critiqued the mind-numbing, routine manual tasks that comprised the daily experience of the majority of American workers. Even on the verge of nervous breakdown, she believed she could "do some good work for the world if I live," she told Weir Mitchell. She hoped that this work would prove uplifting both for her and for society more broadly.

Once she began to support herself in California, Charlotte devoted several early lectures to the importance of what she even then called "human work." She meant by this term work that aided both human evolution and social progress. She did not identify work as "the only thing in life," but she did believe it conferred humanity—"Man must work to be fully human," she had concluded as early as 1895, "and so must woman."[58]

For Charlotte, the "humanness" of truly "human work" (as opposed to the daily grind) entailed the "joyous, natural expression of abundant force along preferred lines of exercise." Viewing society as an organism, Charlotte depicted work as its heart and soul: "The social organism lives in the fulfilment of its organic functions, that fulfilment is work." The healthiest social organisms function best when every cell (or individual) works freely. Individual organisms function best when, instead of overtaxing personal energy reserves, they tap into and express social energy—the clear and sole route to "exhaustless joy."[59] In Charlotte's own case, at least, some of her happiest moments, her most transcendent experiences, and her strongest feelings of connection had come to her while working.

Human Work provides the most extensive, if not the clearest or most cogent, expression of Charlotte's organic social philosophy. The book clarifies her distinction between the "I" and the "We," the former individual and mortal, the latter social and immortal. "We together constitute another 'I,' which is Human Life . . . that common, mutual social life," she maintains. People routinely misidentify as "human nature" what actually represents only primitive "ego-nature," she argues, for the true nature of humanity is fundamentally "social." When we are just our self alone, according to her definition, we are not human but animal or primitive; when we are social, we are not ourselves alone but fully human, part of humanity's great flow.[60]

Charlotte finds her ideal worker in the ideal mother, whose labor is patient and steady and fundamentally "anti-selfish." "It is more agonizing and more ridiculous for a woman not to work than for a man, because of her initial sex-tendency and her historic habits," she concludes.[61] For Charlotte, maternity thus figures not as a marker of woman's feminine difference but instead as the proof of woman's fundamental humanness.

The final passages of *Human Work* build to a rapturous climax as Charlotte writes her personal manifesto large. Linking human happiness to human work, she enjoins readers

> To feel the world's life, unbroken in its steady pour, from the inchoate nebulae, through age on age of changing orders, into the spreading growth of an organised democracy. . . . To feel the extending light of common consciousness as Society comes alive!—the tingling "I" that reaches wider and wider in every age, that is sweeping through the world to-day like an electric current, that lifts and lights and enlarges the human soul in kindling majesty: To feel the power! The endless power! . . . And so feeling, to Do:
>
> To Do, as only Human beings can; not in the paltry processes of the individual . . . but in the fascinating complexity and rhythmic splendour of the march of social activities; to take part in that huge, thrilling, organic life in which the individual thrives unconscious . . . that is Happiness.[62]

The resemblance between this rhapsodic conclusion and some of Charlotte's most earnest "Thoughts & Figgerings" suggests that in this book, at least, the boundary between her public and private life was fully porous.

Human Work, Charlotte later conceded, was "the greatest book I have ever done, and the poorest" in quality. Her investment in the project surfaces in her repeated attempts at revision. Three of the books she later serialized in her journal the *Forerunner* revise *Human Work*, and she attempted yet another rewrite in her final years.[63] Most of her revisions were stylistic; she rarely reworked her theories beyond her initial formulations, believing them impervious to time. For instance, she continued to propound theories of work she had essentially developed during her nationalist period, even as the economy grew in size and complexity.

Charlotte remorsefully acknowledged that her theme was large, her powers inadequate, her presentation unsatisfactory. Reviewers concurred. They also objected to the overall premise of *Human Work*; they desired more specifics and found her arguments suggestive but ultimately unconvincing. Her friend Charles Lummis praised her irreverence but lamented her "continual tendency . . . toward overstatement," which, he warned, often left her verging "dangerously upon absurdity."[64]

There were additional problems. The scientists whose theories Charlotte continued to cite approvingly as "of measureless importance to the world"—namely, Lamarck and Ward—had been challenged by new genetic research. Lamarck's theory of the inheritance of acquired traits, accepted by both Spencer and Ward, had been widely discredited by August Weismann with the help of Mendel's rediscovered genetic laws. Ward's gynæcocentric theory had never been scientifically proven. Charlotte remained defiantly loyal to these theorists even as all her "biological friends" scoffed.[65]

Human Work expresses Charlotte's dismay over capitalist greed and the increasing gap between the rich and the poor. But her unabashed encomiums to work led some readers to accuse her of class bias. For instance, Walter Lippmann responded to her theories by wryly observing that working-class women rarely extol "the pleasure of earning your own living."

Faced with mixed reviews, Charlotte welcomed a respite from "big books" and determined in the interim "to let out the little things that flock so thickly." She devoted the next several years to this "flock," waiting five years before she published another book and self-publishing the next several.[66]

Despite its flaws, *Human Work* represented Charlotte's most ardent annunciation of her personal philosophy, her strongest case for rejecting what she called the "Ego Concept" and for embracing the "Social Passion," and her most explicit equation of living with doing and doing with "all virtue, joy, and growth." What did it mean to her to have her most important book greeted with relative indifference and dismissed as either a "mirage" or as "monstrous altruism"?[67]

Two years previously, during a stopover in Chicago, Charlotte had been asked by a reporter if too public a life might drain a woman of all her charm. She had dismissed the question at the time, but the prospect would come back to haunt her as the charm of her own works and ideas perceptibly faded. In her own life, Charlotte had derived her greatest happiness in the public sphere as a public self, but her critics disdained the publicity she cherished as too glaring a light to live in steadily.[68]

In *Human Work*, Charlotte depicts the best world servants "as driven from within, by the rising flood of social energy. . . ." These servants continued to work lifelong, without recompense and heedless of opposition. They often died unrecognized, rewarded only by their sense that they remained true to their fundamental human duty: elevating society according to each servant's specialized function. "In spite of their neglect, abuse, and injury," she concludes, "they are not to be pitied; for on the one hand, they had the enormous joy of serving humanity; and on the other . . . they had the intense functional satisfaction of doing the work they were made for."[69] These words presciently illuminate Charlotte's personal response to waning fame. In her remaining years, she repeatedly tapped into this internal "rising flood" for the assurance she had been wont to derive, at the height of her fame, from outside herself.

Around this time, Charlotte shifted her emphasis from succeeding to trying. "It is what the women of the world are *trying* to do that counts. The direction of their efforts, the improvement of their methods—these are the important facts; and the fact that their efforts may be mistaken and their methods imperfect is but the natural condition of life."[70] Over the coming years, Charlotte would invoke this standard not only to motivate other women but also to excuse her own missteps.

10   "Readjustment"
(1904–1909)

> . . . In blessed truth we cannot really stray:
>   Whatever comes is Life; and the strong soul
>   Finds in its living a continued goal—
> All makes for growing—growing is the way.
> "Missing the Way," 1904[1]

Charlotte offered her 1904 New Year's resolutions in poetic form for public consumption:

> As human creatures in a human world,
>   What should we pray?
> To be more human for each others' sake,
> To make ourselves more human, and help make
>   The world that way. . . .

Her poem "For the New Year" was published in the *Woman's Journal*, kicking off her year-long stint as an associate editor for the weekly paper. In addition to the poem, Charlotte produced several short essays for her inaugural issue. One reminded readers that each new year brought a chance for "a new life, a new heaven, and a new earth." "Now is always new," she promised, so leave the past behind "and begin as fresh as if you were just born, but born grown up."

Charlotte had followed her own advice by starting this new venture, modeling for her readers the fresh start she simultaneously preached. But in another column in this same issue, she hedges her bets and cautions, "We should not expect too much, even of the New Year."[2] She had cause to remember this admonition when her trial run as editor of her own department for the journal ended disappointingly with the year.

The *Woman's Journal* had hoped to boost sales, and Charlotte had hoped to enlarge her own audience as well as the suffrage cause she supported but considered too myopic in its focus and too prosaic in its goals. Charlotte viewed suffrage as both important and useful. Granting women the vote would help to end their subservience and their treatment as "mere ornaments"; she predicted that it would also enable men and women to "talk sense" to each other at last. These improvements were indispensable to Charlotte's broader goals of gender equality, race development, and world peace.[3]

Still, with Edward Bellamy, she did not afford suffrage "much importance as an end in itself." She told her *Woman's Journal* readers that its individualistic strain (one vote, one ballot) troubled her, as did its pedestrian aims. For years, she had considered woman suffrage "such a foregone conclusion that I can't get all excited over it," she said. She saw it as a "vitally essential" step toward a larger goal: ". . . Woman Suffrage pure and simple . . . never did interest me," she wrote. "I can only fire up on that subject when I apply it to other things in life." Her list of "other things" included her gospel of "help and service in all human progress," a gospel she had numerous national and international opportunities to preach thanks to her prominence in the suffrage movement as a campaigner and theorist.[4]

During this five-year period, Charlotte's ambivalent relationship with suffrage strengthened. In 1905, several months after her tenure at the *Woman's Journal* ended, she wrote in her diary, "To help [Suffrage] is a clear duty. To oppose it is to stand ridiculous and wrong to future history." She campaigned for suffrage locally, nationally, and internationally: indeed, the sheer quantity of her appearances and writings on behalf of the cause might suggest a more ardent commitment than her ambivalent comments suggest she ever felt. In truth, she wanted suffrage for women, but she also wanted so much more.

The movement was in the midst of a period known as the "doldrums": between 1896 and 1910, no new suffrage legislation passed in any state. Dwindling turnout even for such crowd-pleasers as Susan B. Anthony led Charlotte to worry in 1904 that people grew "indifferent to what they hear often." If indifference to an oft-reiterated message constituted one potential barrier to suffrage's success, then another, as Charlotte saw it, was an accelerating cultural tendency to put self-interest before the common good. "Most people are too rapt in contemplation of their personal interests," she complained that same year, "to have much mind space left for matters of such colossal importance as freedom and justice for half the world." Neither one of these obstacles, as it turned out, tabled the suffrage cause, which swept to victory in 1920. By that point, however, these two obstacles had become Charlotte's own.[5]

~

> Our public duty is most simple and clear—to do our best work for the service of the world. And our personal sin—the one sin against humanity—is to let the miserable puny outgrown Ego—our exaggerated sense of personality—divert us from that service.
>
> "Private Morality vs. Public Immorality," 1910[6]

An anonymous 1904 biographical sketch depicts Charlotte in her forty-fourth year, her youthful glow faded, her face lined and worn but her expression still animated. She is described as securely "anchored" in her New York flat, with her life "rounding out" and her dreams "taking shape before her eyes."

Praise for Charlotte's honesty, earnestness, and ingenuity is tempered by ambivalent comments about her appearance and strong personality: "To a somewhat masculine presence there is added also the touch of Western *gaucherie* in her manner, which is somewhat removed from the culture of the East. With her rather eerie features and her trick of anticipating her own points by a little sound between a laugh and a chuckle, Mrs Gilman might be apt to repel some rather than attract."

By this point in Charlotte's twenty-plus year career, we are told, "the long battle is well over, full peace, devoted affection and care the atmosphere about her, and clearer vision for all her problems is more and more certain. Health has never returned in its early fulness, but shielded at every turn full readjustment becomes more and more a certainty."[7]

For all its rose-colored hues, the sketch offers in "readjustment" an apt term for this period in Charlotte's life: between 1904 and 1909, Charlotte was often forced to readjust her optimistic outlook in order to cope with discouraging outcomes. This process of readjustment began with her lackluster year at the *Woman's Journal.*

The *Woman's Journal* functioned as the official organ of the American Woman Suffrage Association, the Boston-based branch of the woman's movement. In 1872,

Lucy Stone began editing the journal with her husband and fellow reformer Henry Blackwell (like Charlotte, Stone had married a man seven years her junior). Their only child, daughter Alice Stone Blackwell, began contributing to the journal as a teenager and eventually joined her parents at the helm. Alice graduated Phi Beta Kappa from Boston University and lived to see ninety-three; she never married, devoting herself to women's causes generally and the *Woman's Journal* specifically. Father and daughter became co-editors after Stone died of stomach cancer in 1893; Stone used her last breath to whisper to her daughter, "Make the world better!" Charlotte admired the family for "serving society with all their hearts."[8]

As its masthead stipulated, the *Woman's Journal* was "a weekly newspaper, published every Saturday in Boston and Chicago, devoted to the interests of woman, to her educational, industrial, legal and political equality, and especially to her right of suffrage." While not the journal's only concern, suffrage remained its principal focus: whenever the cause was advanced anywhere nationally, the *Woman's Journal* ran a picture of a dove holding an olive branch, a toned-down alternative to the political parties' crowing roosters.

Never self-supporting, the *Woman's Journal* was nonetheless deemed indispensable to the movement. Carrie Chapman Catt later summarized the journal's contributions to the suffrage victory: "There can be no overestimating the value to the suffrage cause of the *Woman's Journal* in its long and vivid career. . . . [I]t has been history-maker and history-recorder for the suffrage cause. The suffrage success of to-day is not conceivable without the *Woman's Journal's* part in it." In her own magazine in 1912, Charlotte called the paper "the only Voice of the Woman's Movement in this country, if not the world" and a "noble paper of which America has every reason to be proud. . . ."[9]

Charlotte's relationship with the *Woman's Journal* began thirty years previously, when her poem "In Duty Bound" appeared on its pages. In late December 1903, the journal announced Charlotte's new "Vital Issues" department as an experiment designed to test Charlotte's proposition that "the woman's movement is larger than the suffrage movement and includes it; and that the very cause to which this paper is devoted will be most advanced by a more inclusive treatment." Throughout 1904, readers could count on "52 installments of original work by C. P. G.—poems and all." Ultimately, Charlotte aimed to make the journal and others like it obsolete: "When women are as human as men there need be no women's papers . . . ," she wrote in her January 1904 debut.[10]

Charlotte followed established policy in working for the journal gratis; she assumed she would share in the profits once the paper began to generate them. Echoing her optimism, the editors predicted that Charlotte's new department would be popular with readers. But they overlooked the relatively conservative nature of the majority of suffragists and the foreboding precedent of other women who had tried to broaden the movement, such as Elizabeth Cady Stanton with her controversial *Woman's Bible.* By March, Charlotte's opinions on how best to achieve "Human Betterment" and her criticisms of conventional domesticity and femininity had readers grumbling. In response, the journal began running a disclaimer that declared "Mrs. Gilman . . . solely responsible for what appears in this department." On several occasions, Alice intervened to smooth feathers ruffled by her guest editor. For example, Alice wrote an editorial in support of readers who accused Charlotte of belittling housekeeping; the editor also defended cooking against Charlotte's deprecations, declaring it an essential human skill.[11]

At the end of the year, Alice bid "Vital Issues" a gracious adieu. The department, she observed, had sustained the interest of those who agreed and disagreed with its contents. She intimated that the latter group was sizable and occasionally included herself. The problem, as she saw it, lay in Charlotte's tendency to state her side forcibly without acknowledging other perspectives, thereby alienating her audience.[12]

Yet additional evidence suggests that Charlotte longed to please her readers and desired their esteem. In "This 'Craving for Notoriety,'" one of her final essays for the journal, Charlotte challenged those who reduced a woman's public life to self-aggrandizement. She insisted instead that "[t]o be *known,* felt, recognized, with love and honor, is humanity's sweetest gratification; to be despised and condemned is our bitterest, most crushing pain." Recognition, she maintained, was both the "natural reward" for service and its incentive. So long as we dedicate ourselves to social and not personal service, so long as we work not just "for self, or a few extra selves, alone" but for "the whole," our cravings for notoriety could never be craven. "Fame is public recognition," she declared, "it is a social condition, rightly desired by a human being, a member of society; and women are human beings—by nature." When we accuse a woman of "craving notoriety," we risk squelching her "splendid impulse toward world service and world power."[13]

The following week, Charlotte's penultimate one at the journal, Alice offered a frank rebuttal in which she argued, "Mrs. Gilman seems to be mixing up two things—the wish to render the widest possible service, and the wish to be widely known and admired."[14] She was right, but then in true Beecher fashion, Charlotte had never understood these wishes to be discrete. Indeed, over the years, the more it began to appear as if neither wish would ever again be granted to her satisfaction, the more she desired their concurrent fulfillment.

~

> . . . it seems to me that one must be blind and deaf not to thrill with excitement at
> the gathering rush of this swiftest of human changes.
> "Is the Woman's Movement Slow?" 1904[15]

Lucy Stone was one of the first suffrage movement founders to, in Charlotte's words, "die in the harness." The next decade witnessed the passing of, among others, Elizabeth Cady Stanton (1902), Susan B. Anthony (1906), and Charlotte's Great-Aunt Isabella Beecher Hooker (1906). The battle for suffrage had entered its sixth decade, and none of its original proponents would live to see it won.

In the new century, a younger generation of more militant and organizationally savvy activists emerged, and they typically opted for arguments based upon "expediency" rather than "justice."[16] Charlotte straddled these two generations uneasily, conflicted about when to hold to absolutes and when to make necessary compromises in order to get the job done. In the suffrage movement, in short, she saw her own tactical dilemmas writ large.

As it aged, the woman's movement had grown more respectable, "no longer considered the province of eccentrics and crackpots." The strength of a movement can often be measured by the strength of the opposition, and even during the doldrums, the anti-suffragists maintained an aggressive attack. Charlotte enjoyed spoofing the "Antis," comparing them to flies on cartwheels who pompously believed the wheel of progress could be turned back; she predicted they would instead be crushed under its inevitable forward-moving momentum.

She once drafted her reticent husband into participating along with her in a lively forum where the twenty-five scheduled speakers each used their allotted five minutes to rebut an "Anti" plank. Charlotte refuted the idea that suffrage would make women more masculine, insisting instead that it would only help make them more fully human. Houghton deployed statistics to prove that suffrage would not increase divorce.[17]

Such innovative forums were the brainchildren of a younger and more creative generation of suffragists. Soon after Harriot Stanton Blatch returned to the United States from England in 1902, she expressed her dissatisfaction with the movement her recently deceased mother Elizabeth Cady Stanton had helped to launch. Compared to the more militant and creative suffrage campaign she had participated in while in Britain, the suffrage movement was "completely in a rut in New York State at the opening of the twentieth century," Blatch declared. "It bored its adherents and repelled its opponents." She joined Charlotte in believing that the cause needed to broaden its appeal.

In 1907, Blatch appointed Charlotte as an executive officer of her newly formed Equality League of Self-Supporting Women (later called the Women's Political Union or WPU). The new organization was designed to unite clubwomen and their working-class sisters behind woman's rights. The WPU orchestrated petition drives and trolley car campaigns. They staged suffrage rallies at Cooper Union and open-air protest meetings throughout the city (the jacket photograph depicts Charlotte speaking at one of the latter venues).[18]

In her speeches at suffrage forums, Charlotte typically mocked the "Antis," dismissed the notion that men already took care of women's interests at the polls, and argued that political citizenship would help women in their quest for advancement. In addition to participating in local events, she crisscrossed the country stumping for the cause. She once passed nine long hours in a car packed with suffragists and stuck in the muck somewhere between Madison and Portage, Wisconsin. She journeyed as far as Seattle aboard the "suffrage special" along with other delegates traveling by train to a convention in Washington State.

In 1908, she attended the Seneca Falls conference commemorating the sixtieth anniversary of the founding suffrage event. A few weeks later, she traveled to Poughkeepsie, where she lectured Vassar students gathered in a local cemetery. The president of the college had prohibited a campus meeting, although this did not prevent the press from reporting, "Suffragists Invade Vassar. How Rude!" The macabre setting did little to dampen the students' enthusiasm. Some forty young women perched amid the headstones to hear their prophet speak. "At that time no one was more popular at Vassar than Charlotte Perkins Gilman," Blatch recalled. "Her *Women and Economics* was . . . the Bible of the student body."[19] Even as Charlotte helped to advance the suffrage cause, the cause helped her to voice her message and sustain her popularity during the campaign's final decades.

~

What can we do to promote the development of the backward race so that it may become an advantageous element in the community?
"A Suggestion on the Negro Problem," 1908[20]

Charlotte's reputation both within and outside the movement fluctuated during this half decade. Her complicated stance on racial and ethnic issues, which shifted with her audience and over time, provides one measure of her mesh with her contemporaries. Over the course of their eighty-plus-year struggle, numerous suffragists had routinely mustered class and racial privilege in their efforts to battle gender discrimination. In the early days, the passage of the Fifteenth Amendment infuriated those who believed educated women should obtain the franchise before black men and who appealed to base prejudice to shame Congress into immediately granting women the vote.[21]

African Americans were never the only nor, at the turn of the century, even the primary antagonists. Many suffragists directed their ire at "illiterates," immigrants, and various ethnic groups permitted to vote while elite white women were still denied. This argument proved so persuasive in rallying support that suffrage conventions routinely displayed "a woman flanked by a ferocious Indian, a convict, a maniac and an idiot, representing the voteless citizens of the United States."

Few suffragists joined Elizabeth Cady Stanton in arguing for the disenfranchisement of illiterate and immigrant men. But many shared her resentment of the "ignorant classes" for their perceived role in helping to table important suffrage referendums. Jane Addams, Florence Kelley, and Lillian Wald numbered among those who protested that immigrants deserved fairer treatment as human beings and potential suffrage supporters.[22] But the largely middle-class suffrage movement commonly sought to advance its cause on the backs of minorities with only infrequent acknowledgement of how many of these minorities were themselves women.

Charlotte was not immune to the movement's prejudices. She could listen attentively to "Mrs. Fred Douglass" and spend the night at her home; she could be cited approvingly by W. E. B. Du Bois and defended by Anna Julia Cooper, but she could also refer to African Americans privately as "coons."[23] To convey women's primitive status vis-à-vis men, she often invoked ethnic stereotypes—including "squaw," "slave," and "harem women." She used these stereotypes as both points of comparison (to symbolize white women's debasement, which presumed these racial others' debasement) and points of contrast (white women in her analogies were destined to evolve above and beyond her stereotypes).

Charlotte had long argued that the men and women presently opposed in the battle of the sexes ought instead to work together to advance civilization and "the race," a term that for her usually meant "the human race." As the years passed, her notions of both "civilization" and "race" became less abstractly human and more concretely Anglo-Saxon, and her images of the men and women involved grew uniformly fairer and more European in feature.[24]

But Charlotte could also view both ethnic and gender relations through the lens of class. Because she believed in the possibility of social mobility, she often blamed existing differences on culture rather than nature. Thus rather than branding an entire ethnic group inherently "uncivilizable," she made class- and culture-based distinctions among individuals. For example, she contrasted a dark-skinned East Indian man "of education, breeding, and refinement, and an illiterate cotton-picker."

Additionally, at a time when polygenesists were seeking to classify different ethnicities as biologically different and inherently unequal species, she tended to view ethnic and racial differences historically, blaming inequities on social policies and practices, including the "enormously costly national mistake" of slavery and the myriad ways in which "we"—by which she meant Anglo-Americans—"cheated," dominated, and decimated marginal groups.[25]

Charlotte's conflicted views on race and ethnicity influenced her arguments on behalf of suffrage. She had moments where she appeared enlightened alongside her fellow activists. At the 1903 national convention, for instance, Charlotte was the only delegate to object from the floor to an educational qualification for suffrage, and she was one of only five who rose to oppose it during an informal vote. Her motives were mixed, however, and her rationale convoluted: as she told the other delegates, granting "illiterates" immediate suffrage would invoke "dread" in the literate classes, forcing them to work swiftly to educate this new voting bloc. She thus opposed educational restrictions in order to encourage assimilation and ultimately "improve the human stock."[26]

The 1903 convention was held in New Orleans, a city that housed the nation's largest slave market before the Civil War, located in a state that offered women fewer rights relative to other states. The proposed educational qualification catered to southern delegates in a region and period defined by Jim Crow and the Klan.

Nevertheless, many northern leaders volunteered to make their support of such restrictions public. After the convention ended, a New Orleans paper criticized the NAWSA for being pro-equality, and Anthony, Catt, and Anna Howard Shaw responded in a letter that denied the relevance of the race question to woman's suffrage. They also claimed that the educational qualification illustrated their support of states' rights.

A month after the New Orleans suffrage convention, the U.S. Supreme Court (which had instituted the "separate but equal" doctrine via its 1896 *Plessy v. Ferguson* decision) upheld Alabama's constitutional education clause, thereby disenfranchising the state's African Americans; neighboring states swiftly followed suit.[27] In passing their resolution, the suffragists proved they had their fingers on the pulse of a segregated nation. In opposing it, Charlotte had tried to institute more drastic revitalizing measures.

A lonely dissenter in 1903, Charlotte more often spoke to and for the mainstream in years to come. At the 1905 suffrage convention, for example, she protested former President Cleveland's recently published attack on women's clubs and causes. She especially objected to his insistence that "the hand that rocks the cradle is the hand that rules the world." She cited Indian, Chinese, and Arab women as exceptions to Cleveland's paean and as proof that today's women were throwbacks to the "20th century B.C." Her examples indicate, however, that she considered some contemporary women more primitive than others.[28] As a speaker, Charlotte was celebrated for her ability to illustrate abstract points vividly the better to stir her listeners' imaginations, but many of her most vivid illustrations took white supremacy for granted.

Charlotte may have switched tropes when speaking to sociologists, but on one occasion, at least, her conclusions proved equally troubling. She first articulated her controversial "A Suggestion on the Negro Problem" in a 1906 lecture in Chicago and later developed it into a 1908 essay for the *American Journal of Sociology*. Her suggestion involved segregating blacks who were lagging in the race for progress into their own army, "drafted under compulsion from the ranks of the uneducated blacks and forced to labor for the development of the country" until they were elevated sufficiently to keep pace with their white counterparts.[29]

As with many of her ideas, her proposal bears the traces of her influences. Her military model may have been derived from Edward Bellamy, who routinely praised military life as invigorating (the workers in *Looking Backward* belong to an "industrial army"). In his 1897 *Equality*, Bellamy wrote, "The population of recent slaves was in need of some sort of industrial regimen, at once firm and benevolent, administered under conditions which should meanwhile tend to educate, refine, and elevate its members." He considered white workers, as did Charlotte, more evolved and thus less in need of "military discipline." Indeed, many of the whites who moved in nationalist, Fabian, and socialist circles considered blacks "biologically and socially retarded."[30]

Charlotte's friend, the sociologist and nativist E. A. Ross, also likely shaped her "Suggestion." Ross's concept of "social control" lauded militarism and other means of promoting group welfare through the "technique of coercion." Charlotte's solution also resonates with safety measures promoted at the time by many in the progressive community. Numerous progressives came to view segregation as a relatively innocuous means of forestalling the violence they feared as a result of the races mixing too closely. The vaunted progressive term *association*, as the historian Michael McGerr has argued, usually signified bridging class, rather than racial, divides. The progressive journalist Ray Stannard Baker admitted as much in 1909: "The plain fact is, most of us in the north do not believe in any real democracy as between white and colored men."[31]

Charlotte's solution appears moderate when compared to the proposals of white supremacists. The unapologetically racist novels of Thomas Dixon, for instance, lionized the Ku Klux Klan and inspired both epic motion pictures and horrific race riots. Indeed, as the century turned, paternalistic proposals like Charlotte's were increasingly greeted skeptically as too idealistic and impractical.

Frederick L. Hoffman's influential *Race Traits and Tendencies of the American Negro* (1896) held that African Americans were destined for extinction "unless somehow made to face the struggle for existence unaided by paternalism. . . ." Was it best to continue to raise the hopes of "Negroes" and sustain their dependence on the white race, doubters asked, or would leaving them to their own devices finally force them to cultivate self-reliance? Hoffman's disciples relied on statistical evidence that seemed to reveal a widening gap between blacks and whites. They attributed that gap not to racist policies and practices but to benevolent yet purportedly harmful interventions. They therefore advocated a new policy of "racial laissez faire."[32]

Dixon and Hoffman were Charlotte's rough contemporaries. But so, too, were Jane Addams, John Dewey, William Dean Howells, Florence Kelley, Lincoln Steffens, and William English Walling—all progressives who protested racial injustice and joined the call for a National Negro Conference that laid the groundwork for the National Association for the Advancement of Colored People, founded in early 1909.

In 1908, the same year that Charlotte published her "Suggestion," Wallace published an exposé denouncing a bloody race riot in Illinois. That same year as well, Ray Stannard Baker published a three-part series in *Cosmopolitan*, "following the color line" and exposing the intolerance that had fueled race riots like the Atlanta tragedy two years previously.[33] In short, many reform-minded people, a number of them Charlotte's friends or acquaintances, offered solutions to racial tensions that did not assume from the first, as she had, that "the Negro" was the problem.

Charlotte elsewhere opposed lynching and Jim Crow and thus could seem less intolerant than many of her contemporaries during a period known to history as the country's "racial nadir." She insisted that she meant her suggestion to encourage "enlistment, not enslavement," but few believed her. The *Literary Digest* quoted her argument with apparent distaste: "This, of course, is the *corvée*, or system of enforced labor, which in its worst forms has been the disgrace of countries like Egypt." Even Walter Stetson, after noting the utter impracticality of his ex-wife's solution, added wryly, "As the slaves were freed, there can by no possible chance be a right to force them again into slavery."[34]

Ironically, the crimes for which Charlotte indicts the "Negro" are the very ones she had long associated with women, but her solutions differ noticeably. For example, she concludes of the "Negro," "He is here; we can't get rid of him; it is all our fault; he does not suit us as he is; what can we do to improve him?"[35] Change the gender of the third-person singular pronoun and her sentence resembles sentiments expressed in her woman-centered treatises. But whereas to improve (white) women she advocated their immediate and full integration into society, to improve "Negroes" she argued for their temporary segregation. Charlotte prided herself on her logical mind, but in this instance prejudice blinded her to her own illogic.

~

> Contentment is the death of Hope . . . Why be contented with bad things when you can have better.
>
> "Hope," 1911[36]

An increasingly volatile figure in the States, Charlotte often experienced a welcome reprieve while abroad. Nearly everywhere she traveled in Europe, she exulted in her international reputation and in the admiration of her fans. On behalf of women's rights, Charlotte crossed the Atlantic several times during the first decades of the twentieth century.

In 1904, she was expressly invited to attend the International Congress of Women Quinquennial in Berlin as a "speaker-at-large": the organizers informed her that they wanted her "more than any one else but Miss Anthony." Charlotte made the crossing on a steamer filled with "all the sisters!" The ship provided no Sunday church services, so the American delegates decided—over the captain's objections—to organize several impromptu sermons. Dreadfully seasick, Charlotte dragged herself from her bed and "made a capital speech." Her fellow passenger Carrie Chapman Catt remembered that effort "as an evidence of tremendous will" and true "grit" and "told the story often."[37]

The 1904 council was kicked off with a reception at the imposing Bremen Parkhaus in Berlin. The Americans were treated to delicious fare and drinks "of a strictly 'temperance' nature," meeting the approval of the teetotaling Charlotte. On the last day of May, delegates crammed into hot, crowded lecture halls filled to overflowing with representatives from nearly twenty countries, more than double the number attending the London Quinquennial five years previously. Charlotte valued these councils for their ability to draw women together from around the globe, proving women's capacity for collective action.[38]

She also enjoyed the personal attention. Lester Ward had warned her that Germany was "intensely androcentric and only half civilized," but Charlotte found her hosts charming (her anti-German bias dates from World War I). While in Berlin, she "had an army of delightful admirers about her all the time," following her from hall to hall. Years later, Charlotte fondly recalled her cordial reception in the capital city and the large crowds filled with her fans.[39]

Charlotte received a standing ovation for her one formal speech at the conference. She spoke at the final meeting on June 18, one of only two featured speakers on the roster that night. Her topic was Ward's gynæcocentrism, which she still considered "the greatest single contribution to the world's thought since Evolution," and which she aimed to make "the recognized basis of a new advance in the movement of women."

The turnout for the speech was so large that Charlotte had to repeat it in a second hall for the overflow crowd. Apparently, the response was as divided as the audience, "half of the women declaring that they would never hand their children over to be cared for by professional trainers and feed their husbands on victuals from a cooperative cookery, while they used their time to aid 'the larger work of the world,'" Ida Harper reported. Meanwhile, "the other half insist[ed] that women in all ages had given too much time, strength, and talent to the nursery and kitchen, and that was why they had fallen behind in all great achievements."[40] For all her rhetoric of global unity, Charlotte could prove to be a divisive figure, both at home and abroad.

Charlotte returned to Europe the following February for a whirlwind lecture tour arranged the previous year. Her itinerary took her through England, Holland, Germany, Austria, and Hungary. According to the London press, the sensation caused by her views on the woman question during her previous two visits had been "reverberating like the uneasy echoes of distant thunder ever since." The storm clouds continued to rumble during her third visit to the city. In one speech, she told her "amazed" listeners what she had argued elsewhere: men were actually the fairer sex. Women were "too short from the waist downward" and waddled when they walked or ran due to years of wearing heavy skirts. The three men in attendance, perhaps fearful of being eyeballed as exemplary beauties, beat a hasty exit out a side door.[41]

Charlotte impressed most audiences favorably during this tour. One interviewer described her as possessing "the straight, lithe figure and quick eloquence of a Portia, and in her bright eyes and nervous, finely chiselled face you can see she is clever, practical, managing, not a sleepy person who groans under the difficulties of domestic life, but a vigorous and capable housewife who has wrestled with its problems, and sees new and better solutions than have yet been realized." Charlotte loathed the term "housewife"—since when does a house need a wife, she quipped. But she would otherwise have found this description, as she did the tour itself, deeply satisfying.[42]

The VIP treatment heightened Charlotte's enjoyment of international travel. She singled out the 1904 Berlin council particularly for the veneration demonstrated to "World Mothers." "It is the great, loving heart, the clear head, the noble devotion to public service of the women of her country which meets the recognition it deserves," she observed in her reflections on the congress. She departed the event feeling "naturally somewhat elated by international admiration."

Charlotte left behind "the incessant whirl and rush in Berlin" for a different kind of whirlwind in Rome, with Katharine playing tourguide to her "exhausted" mother. The two then sailed for the States, where Katharine stayed the summer. If Charlotte expected her "charming daughter" to sustain the admiration she had enjoyed abroad, she was setting herself up for disappointment.[43]

~

> There is God. It is Power. It is upwardness. It is Always Pushing. One has but to "Line Up." Conditions hinder.
>
> "Thoughts & Figgerings," October 9, 1905[44]

The nearly twenty-year-old Katharine now viewed her mother cynically. As she wrote her best friend Anna Waller, "Mama [Katharine had been taught to refer to her parents as 'Mama' and 'Papa,' with the accent on the second syllable] does not mind being considered an invalid and rather likes it in fact." She added, "I only wish she would not be illogical and inconsistent at times." In yet another 1905 letter to Anna, she remarked, "Mama . . . seems full of business and is hoping to get more money than she probably will. This one gets used to in Mama. I don't know anyone who is as young as she is. She builts [*sic*] Castles upon Castles. I may built Castles but I always know they are in Spain. I don't take out any mortgages on them."[45]

Katharine soon got to experience living in one such "castle." In 1906, after six years at the Avondale (the longest residence of Charlotte's life thus far) the Gilmans with "joyous courage" signed a three-year lease on a large, comfortable house with a bay window on West 82nd. The house was so big and, for the time, so expensive that they took in boarders and hired two servants—an Irish cook who roomed in the basement and a Scandinavian waitress who roomed on the top floor near Katharine. Ideally, Charlotte hoped to solve the "servant problem"—"the bread and butter of women's magazines between the Civil War and World War I"—by replacing private homes with "large, humanly-conducted common homes." But in the interim she was glad for the help. One whole floor they let to a tenant, and the extra rooms plus board they offered to several local teachers and writers.[46]

Providing room and board remained a fairly common practice during the early part of the century, more common than one might expect among the better-off. It enabled families to fill empty rooms and cover expenses, and it also allowed two out of every ten women to stay home while still contributing to the family income.

In several of her fictional works, Charlotte portrays women happily running successful boarding houses, but she did not count herself among them. Her failed Oakland experiment still haunted her. Shortly before marrying Houghton, she had told him that additional money in her pocket checked her tendency to "prate gloomily of a boarding house." Her experience running the New York house only heightened her antipathy for the practice; she later titled one of her most light-hearted sketches "Without Bo(a)rders."[47] The couple hastily abandoned the West 82nd Street experiment as soon as their lease expired.

While living at the boarding house in 1908, Katharine sent frequent letters to Walter in Italy complaining of her mother's behavior and seeking her father's guidance. Walter responded bitterly to one such letter. He counseled patience whenever Charlotte grew nervous, despondent, or hysterical. He advised Katharine to

> bring a little real commonsense to your mother—That wont last long, but for the time being she will appreciate it, and may have even more respect for you. . . . She is now just what she was I judge, after you were born. And I can sense that the best way to deal with her is to tell her frankly—that she—well,—wears on you—though you can put it more gracefully than that— . . . She will demand your acknowledgment of her superior genius, which you can give. Then you can say, very quietly, what you *wrote* us, about her destroying all beauty of live [*sic*] by her manner and that you dread to invite people to the house on account of her manner—or manners at table and otherwise—like throwing potatoes, etc—lest the guest may get a false impression of *her*, which they are sure to do. . . . Then if I were you I should attack her *point blank* about her leaving Mr. Gilman. . . . She always did the same with me. She never considered me in the least. If she wanted to go anywhere she went. . . . But she has no right ever to make you feel that you must look after Mr. Gilman. . . . I am sure Mr. Gilman . . . would hate to know that you had given up your own life to make good your mother's deficiencies. . . .

For so long, Walter had pulled his punches. Now, however, he appeared to delight in taking jabs at his ex-wife, bonding with his daughter by commiserating with her over Charlotte's inadequacies. Charlotte's ways were not the Stetsons' decorous ways; across the broad spectrum of illness, manners, genius, and spousal deference, they could count on her to behave both predictably and offensively. She could not recall the potato-throwing incident, but Katharine cited this letter years later as evidence of what she perceived to be her father's "heavier" suffering: "Mama was always just and fair when she saw things," Katharine noted, "but she got absorbed in 'causes' and did not have the kind of imagination that enabled her to know how others felt and thought."[48] According to her daughter, Charlotte's immersion in various movements left her tone deaf interpersonally.

Walter's letter also hints at an unevenness in the Gilman marriage that even Charlotte acknowledged. Taking stock in October 1905, Charlotte listed among her liabilities her "Diseased nervous system" and "sticky habits" as well as "Houghtons [*sic*] heavenly goodness." She feared the latter might "weaken" her, either because she might take advantage of him or because he might divert her from her larger purpose by providing too tempting a port in the storm.

In 1907, Charlotte instructed a Boston suffrage audience that "you cannot love people unless you do something for them." This enthusiastic preacher of service to others felt herself in her second marriage to be more served than servant. Houghton's amenable self-effacement before his stronger-willed wife and his willing accommodation to her career and needs sometimes troubled her conscience. A "true marriage," according to a definition Charlotte offered in 1908, requires desire, gratitude, sympathy, admiration, but above all else "[d]evotion: the selfless service that asks nothing and gives all."[49] In her marriage to Houghton, Charlotte worried that she took more than she gave. Although the same might be said of her relationship with Walter, no evidence suggests that the difference bothered her then. Her sweet-natured second husband, however, occasionally—if inadvertently—made her feel as if she was taking advantage.

In his letter to Katharine, Walter suggests that Charlotte's health fared as poorly in the 1900s as it had when she had broken down in their marriage, and Charlotte elsewhere conceded the point. "For all my happiness at home and various glories abroad," Charlotte observed of this period, "I remained . . . more sick than well; that is, there was more time spent in dull distress of mind and dreary helplessness than in my natural cheerful activity." After returning from Europe, she spent the winter of 1905 a "good for nothing invalid." She wondered at the time if she would ever again find the "power to go out laughing and do one's daily work." Her depression made it harder to remember that she was "only a department" of the larger universe and that the "Big Feeling is not I but It."[50]

For years, Charlotte had vainly sought a sustained self-forgetfulness and a sustaining merger with the universe. Try as she might, her practice of living did not measure up to her theory of it. Her reform Darwinism had taught her that humans were creatures of reason and will. As Theodore Dreiser, another author indebted to Darwin, surmised around this time, evolution was "ever in action" and "the ideal is a light that cannot fail." Once that light shone steadfast, Dreiser continued, all human action would be reasonable and willful, and "man will no longer vary."[51] To the extent that she varied now, Charlotte assumed she was not fully evolved, not fully—as she defined the word—*human*. She attributed this failure not to some flaw in her philosophy but to the weakened force of her will.

Her faith in that will and in evolution, coupled with her idealism, led her to posit transcending the self and merging with the world as a sustainable apotheosis. It simultaneously blinded her to the contingent, shifting nature of identity as it is lived, to the ways in which we fluctuate—often involuntarily—between immersion in the self and in other matters. By clinging to an absolute understanding of identity, and by viewing her ideals as a realizable *modus vivendi*, she could only blame herself whenever she vacillated for failing to measure up to her self-imposed standards.

~

When you're climbing mountain ranges
It takes strength and it takes time;
Ups and downs do not deceive you,—
You just climb!

"Climbing," 1911[52]

In the first decade of the 1900s, illnesses like Charlotte's were frequently anatomized in popular magazines including *Good Housekeeping* and the *Ladies' Home Journal*. These articles fostered a belief in a pandemic of nervousness, infecting even the culture itself. Concomitantly, however, psychologists were declaring the concept of "brain fatigue" a myth, an "'emotional affair,' a feeling, and not a true 'incapacity.'"[53]

These conflicting messages may have heightened Charlotte's anxieties over her illness. She occasionally indulged in self-pity, but more often she reminded herself that "[w]e can not individually be made happy, because we are not only an individual but a social form of life." No matter how ill she became, Charlotte continued to anticipate a future when a woman's body, maybe not her own but others, might cease to prove a liability. That future, she predicted, would materialize in a few generations once women had been "reared on absolute equality with men, and with all human work open to them."[54]

The year Charlotte made this prediction, she wrote her first utopian romance. Three installments of "A Woman's Utopia" were serialized in 1907 in the newly launched *Times Magazine*. In his education, interests, and conservative leanings, Morgan Street, the narrator, favors Houghton Gilman. Similarly, Hope Cartwright, the "sort of cousin" and reform zealot he falls for, resembles Charlotte.

After Hope rejects Morgan's marriage proposal because he questions her social ideals, he gives her $20 million to make the world a better place. The dejected suitor, meanwhile, spends the intervening two decades traveling incommunicado. Upon his return, he visits Hope in her "charming apartment" on Riverside Drive, and together they tour "a happier country"—not perfect, but an "[i]mmense improvement" on the past.

In her introduction to the story, Charlotte insists, "There is an instinctive demand for happiness in the human heart which has been so far most ignorantly misunderstood . . . the longing is in us, the instinct, the demand for heaven, not after death, but here. . . ." Projecting her own demands for happiness onto the nation, she provides an abbreviated blueprint of how to get there from here, since the magazine failed before the serial could run its course.[55]

Charlotte was brought up short on a number of other occasions around this time. In her hometown, she was dogged by an often hostile press intent on mocking her most cherished ideas. The *New York Evening Sun* parodied her cities full of chophouses and apartments empty of babies, while the *New York Times* waged its own war upon Charlotte's "warfare . . . against private life." She remained equally controversial on the West Coast, where a San Francisco paper remarked, "The mere mention of her name is enough to make sparks fly among the argumentatively disposed."[56]

Charlotte displayed her own argumentative disposition in several public debates near the end of the decade. The *Independent*, for example, asked her to critique the home in an issue so charged readers were warned to handle it "with rubber gloves." This proved to be one of several debates during this period where Charlotte's views failed to gain a sympathetic audience. "If all women got rid of their husbands as soon as they gave a day's dissatisfaction," observed a writer for *Harper's* about this particular showdown, "and handed over babies to public asylums while they mothered the race (exactly how this is done is difficult to picture), we should be apt to have a rather chaotic time of it." Her critics accused her of neglecting the small picture for the big one, of being what one of her friends described as "more a telescope person than a microscope person."[57]

Another and more bruising public defeat came early in 1909 at the hands of the current president of NAWSA, the formidable Reverend Anna Howard Shaw. The debate revealed a central fissure within the suffrage cause and reanimated issues that curtailed Charlotte's tenure at the *Woman's Journal*. The two women sparred at New York's Carnegie Lyceum over whether wives were supported by their husbands. Charlotte had debated this topic once before in a 1902 face-off for *Success* magazine.

Portrait of Charlotte, ca. 1910. Photo by Lena Connell. Courtesy of the Schlesinger Library, Radcliffe Institute for Advanced Study, Harvard University.

She took the affirmative once again in 1909 and argued that housework does not make a woman self-supporting but only husband-supporting. It reduced a wife to what she colorfully described as "man's horse." Shaw countered that marriage was a productive partnership: husbands may bring home the bacon, but their wives fried it up as nourishment for the family in addition to providing other essential services, including saving the incomes their spouses might otherwise squander. Although several of her remarks received warm applause, Charlotte did not in the end persuade her mostly female audience, many of whom were working women. The audience voted resoundingly in favor of Shaw's position and thus repudiated the thesis Charlotte had expounded at length in *Women and Economics* and elsewhere.[58]

Several years earlier, Charlotte had counseled Lester Ward—whose star was fading faster than her own—to derive solace from savoring "the Himalayan heights . . . the glorious view—the light—the clear stimulating air; and best of all, the sure knowledge that the big joy is for us all—and will be reached by all. That is the real happiness. It does not matter if only a few of us know you are there." Her metaphor suggests that those who provide keen sociological insights into the laws of progress and the organic nature of society reach heights so high that they might only be discerned by the farsighted. Her imagery says as much about her hopes for her own legacy as it does about her opinion of Ward's.[59]

In the years to come, Charlotte would cling to that symbolic mountaintop in order to justify both a career trajectory and a philosophy premised upon perpetual ascent. Her emphasis on usefulness even helped her to take the half-century mark in stride. In her essay "The Woman of Fifty," she maintains that on average (granting that most women married between twenty and twenty-five and had their children early), a healthy woman of fifty should have "at least twenty years of usefulness remaining" to her. With the children grown and the burden of housework lightened, "the woman of fifty" could count on "fourteen hours when one is up and dressed and must do something." Discounting generously for responsibilities and entertainment still left at least six hours: "a good time to sit through." Charlotte advises these women to fill their spare hours with useful activity. Rather than mourning "the woman that was," the woman of fifty might then become "an active, happy, useful, growing woman that is."[60]

The woman of forty-eight who wrote this piece resolved to make the roughly twenty-five years she predicted she had left "count for more than all before." She meant "count" in both senses of the word. On one hand, she ran the numbers and figured out how much she needed to write in order to earn her desired $2,250 annual income (her current rate was three dollars a page). On the other hand, she desired her potentially "well paying" work also to be "Big work—tremendous powers. Lifters."

When it looked as if the mainstream press would deliver on neither front, she launched her one-woman magazine, the *Forerunner*. In some respects, the magazine resembled another of those "castles in the air" Katharine derided. Charlotte, however, claimed to "thoroughly approve" of her castles; after all, as a perennial dreamer, she had "lived in such all [her] life."[61] She would discover during the *Forerunner* years, however, that living in them was one thing, and making a living out of them another thing entirely.

11 "The Forerunner"
(1909–1916)

. . . those who can see through the future ahead,
   See great truths over things that are small,
See the ages unborn, not the days that are dead,
   These are they who give help to us all.
                                        "There Are Those Who Can See,"
                                        undated poem[1]

Nearly three years after her debate with Anna Howard Shaw, Charlotte once again replied affirmatively to the question, "Does a Man Support His Wife?" This time, however, she took no chances. She restated her position in the September 1911 issue of the *Forerunner*, ostensibly responding to a British suffragist who had recently argued along Shaw's lines. Nowhere does the *Forerunner* piece mention Charlotte's 1909 encounter with Shaw or her defeat at Shaw's hands. Nor in 1911 does Charlotte bother to do more than gesture toward her British opponent's views.[2] Writing, editing, and publishing her own magazine afforded her the first and last word on all matters, an attractive perk.

By choosing to title her magazine the *Forerunner*, Charlotte positioned both it and, by implication, herself on the cutting edge. She wanted the *Forerunner* to operate as a beacon illuminating present-day flaws the better to light the way to a spotless future. If the several utopian works published in its pages enact her "longing to create compensatory feminist utopias as a means to solve the perceived problems of degenerate modernity," then the magazine itself might also be said to serve this compensatory function. For the *Forerunner* allowed Charlotte to devise alternatives to—and, for herself, a refuge from—the disappointing, degraded public and publishing realms she still believed she could change.[3]

Charlotte's efforts on behalf of the journal were both prodigious and heroic. Zona Gale called the *Forerunner* Charlotte's "greatest single achievement," and others have concurred. But establishing her own magazine was also a cautious move, allowing her to fire her salvos with relative impunity. During the *Forerunner* years, Charlotte could state her opinions without fear of editors accusing her of bias or overstatement, as her friend Alice Stone Blackwell had done during Charlotte's previous attempt at regular journal work.

"Real argument is a very pretty game," Charlotte remarked in 1915, "to be enjoyed by both participants." But the game she was playing in the *Forerunner* more closely resembled a favorite pastime: solitaire. Charlotte's simultaneous attraction to solitaire and self-publishing during her fifties underscores her affinity for solo ventures. Since her early days as a self-proclaimed world worker, she had identified the ability to collaborate as the "great secret of all human improvement."[4] Her *Forerunner* experiment offers additional proof, however, that collaboration remained for her an appealing and inspiring societal ideal more than it did an established personal practice or preference.

When controversy swirled around her during the magazine's seven-plus-year run, she neither directly engaged nor backed down. Instead, she took cover behind the safer difference of the *Forerunner*'s pages. Her retreat backfired, however, when it positioned her and her magazine out of view.

In 1910, Charlotte used the pages of the *Forerunner* to bitterly indict the journal editors who rejected her work as too "controversial." Why, she asked, did these editors refuse to acknowledge that there were two sides to every controversy? If, for instance, an article supporting euthanasia was too controversial to publish, would not the same be true of a story depicting a slow and painful death? If only they would stop labeling one side (that is, Charlotte's side) as controversial and start recognizing that "controversy" meant a two-sided "discussion"![5] She had a point, but she never apparently acknowledged, given the one-sidedness of the *Forerunner*, that she had joined the editors at their own game.

Charlotte playing solitaire during the Forerunner years, ca. 1915. Photo by Pearl-Grace Loehr. Courtesy of the Schlesinger Library, Radcliffe Institute for Advanced Study, Harvard University.

~

I can't grind out work since my spring broke. I can only do what interests me.
Letter to George Houghton Gilman,
April 2, 1899[6]

Charlotte first contemplated publishing her own works and her own magazine in 1905. Around this time, she and Houghton formed a publishing company they called "Charlton," conjoining her first syllable with his last.[7] The *Forerunner* was launched in November 1909. Charlotte may have borrowed its name from a flattering 1904 biographical sketch of her entitled "A Forerunner and a Prophet," suggesting, if so, the degree of her identification with the new venture.

Beginning in March 1909, Charlotte devoted most of her energies and, she told a friend, "every cent I can rake and scrape . . . to the New Baby!" In the months before its launch, she sent bundles of circulars to friends and asked them to help her spread the word and build her subscription list. She informed one of these friends that her new journal would be "thin; but meaty." "In these vegetarian days that is no longer a recommendation," she added. "I should say perhaps 'nutty'—only that has another interpretation!"[8] Charlotte retained her sense of humor under pressure, though her joke reveals a sensitivity to potential wisecracks about her new magazine and her efforts on its behalf. The *Impress*, at least, had been a joint venture: this time around, the responsibility for the journal's success or failure rested on her shoulders alone.

Closer to deadline, Charlotte grew more testy. "I hope," Walter wrote Katharine, that Charlotte "will not 'go to smash' under the strain of the Forerunner and moving. I fancy that Mr. Gilman's hay fever prevented him from being helpful as he otherwise would have been." Houghton did what he could when he could. He lent his office address to both the journal and the press and his financial aid whenever possible. Katharine also chipped in and designed the cover. Ironically, given Katharine's own upbringing, it depicts an intact family: a kneeling man and woman support a child standing on a globe balanced between them.

In nearly every other respect, however, the *Forerunner* was a one-woman show, written and edited, Charlotte affirmed, "entirely by myself." She came to think of the *Forerunner* as less a magazine than "'Gilman's Works,' published serially."[9] It was an unprecedented achievement, a journal for which one person served as the "editor, critic, poet, short story writer, novelist," columnist, publisher, and promoter. Her fans considered the *Forerunner* "a *tour de force* . . . a monthly record of one brilliant woman's specialized survey of the passing scene." One admiring reader even joked, "what makes you so lazy? *Why don't you set the type?*"[10]

The *Forerunner* was printed on "ten-by-seven pages." It varied in length for its first fifteen months from twenty-six to thirty-four pages until Charlotte eventually settled on a twenty-eight-page standard. According to Charlotte's calculations, each issue contained "seven hundred and fifty words to a page," which "made some twenty-one thousand to the issue." Based on words alone, she figured, this "equaled four books a year, books of thirty-six thousand words." Each of its seven volumes contained one serialized novel and one serialized treatise, the exception being its second volume, which featured two novels and no treatise. Each issue also included works of fiction, articles, "poems, verses, allegories, humor and non-sense, with book reviews and comment on current events."[11]

In order to meet her quota, Charlotte had to write rapidly. She rarely revised, and her adherence to self-imposed length limitations meant that she often sacrificed aesthetic concerns. Not all of her material was original to the journal: especially while on the road, she recycled pieces she had published in the *Woman's Journal*, the *Impress*, and elsewhere.

Charlotte later explained her decision to self-publish by complaining that editors and publishers no longer wanted her work. "[A]s time passed," she recalled, "there was less and less market for what I had to say, more and more of my stuff was declined. Think I must and write I must, the manuscripts accumulated far faster than I could sell them, some of the best, almost all. . . ." She believed her commitment to important yet unpopular truths had limited her audience. At times she portrayed herself as a martyr to market pressures and debased tastes, this even though many of her *Forerunner* works attempted to capitalize on popular genres, including the western and the utopian novel. She blamed "business" for standing in her way and worked out a solution privately beforehand: "If I could publish and edit myself—and preach," she speculated in 1908, "I should be doing all I could for the rest of my life and have a perfectly clear conscience."[12]

Charlotte exaggerated when she claimed that editors and publishers refused to publish her work. Wearing his editorial hat, Theodore Dreiser had attempted to steer her toward more conventional themes. But even after she scorned his advice, Dreiser continued to solicit her work for the *Delineator*—albeit at a rate she found insulting. Her enduring visibility "in the public eye" led journals as popular as *Appleton's, Booklovers, Broadway,* and *Pictorial Review* to request contributions even after she had started her own magazine.[13]

In her inaugural issue, Charlotte surmised, "there are enough persons interested in my ideas to justify the undertaking." Yet the press greeted her new venture with some skepticism. The *Daily Palo Alto Times* ran a lukewarm editorial warning that "[l]iterary fecundity is sometimes in inverse ratio to true worth. . . ." The

Lounger tied the value of the *Forerunner* to the pleasure her writing would bring readers, implying that its audience might be smaller than anticipated.[14]

So many new little magazines were already in circulation that the *Forerunner's* launch prompted one writer to moan, "one more monthly, may heaven forefend us!" The *Forerunner* proved to be a relatively small fish in the big school of reform-minded monthlies. The list of more successful and popular journals included the *Masses* and the *Liberator.* The former in particular made waves through its "irreverent and unconventional content": the pro-suffrage *Masses* championed prostitution and hedonism and mocked religion and marriage. The editors of the *Masses* also demonstrated a knack for hiring emergent talents, including Sherwood Anderson, Amy Lowell, and Carl Sandberg.

Closer in form and content to the *Forerunner* were two magazines also edited by women: the radical Emma Goldman's more widely-circulated *Mother Earth,* similarly priced at ten cents an issue or one dollar a year, and Josephine Conger-Kaneko's shorter-lived *Socialist Woman* (later the *Progressive Women* and later still the *Coming Nation*), which folded in 1913.[15]

In one of her *Forerunner* commentaries, Charlotte praised little magazines as long-distance runners trudging along in an unending race. "Part of the real literature of this age," she observed, "is to be found in the little 'one-man magazines' put out, generally, by those who must write and who do not find a market; or who have more to say than they can find a medium for. Small voices these, falling for the most part on deaf ears, but keeping on like a relay race . . ." In titling the commentary "So Much Written, So Little Remembered," she hints at her own anxieties over whether her prolixity might inversely affect her legacy. "Her compulsion to write," Patricia Meyer Spacks has argued, "outstripped any conceivable market for what she produced." Charlotte did seem at times to value the process of work even more than the product.[16]

In launching the *Forerunner,* Charlotte had "banked on . . . my really wide reputation, and the advertising possibilities of continued lecturing, and the low price," she said. With subscriptions at a dollar a piece, she netted an annual revenue of less than $1,500, roughly half the cost of production. She attempted to make up the difference by writing for other venues—the proceeds all going "to feed the Forerunner"—and by "speechifying to beat the band!" At least initially, she also tried advertising. She wrote her own copy and recommended only products she knew, used, and liked.[17] But she soon abandoned these testimonials: they secured funds only for the products, not their promoter.

Ultimately, Charlotte declared the best advertisement a satisfied customer. She was particularly proud of her international audience, made up of readers from "as far afield as India and Australia." Reluctant subscribers could purchase individual issues at national and international suffrage and socialist venues. They might also pick up copies as close as Brentano's in New York City or as far away as J. W. Kettlewell's in Sydney, Australia.[18]

Charlotte may have written, edited, published, and, in one supporter's words, "invented" the *Forerunner*, but from the outset she needed her readers' help to sell it. She tested various incentives to drum up revenues, ranging from premiums and rising commissions to a three-month cut rate "trial subscription." Would readers consider giving a subscription as a Christmas gift? Or organizing a Gilman Circle centered around the magazine? How about purchasing the *Forerunner* calendar, each page enriched by a pearl of Charlotte's wisdom?[19] She also periodically ran promotional columns featuring snippets of letters from satisfied readers, who considered a year of "the 'Gilmanian'" "a bargain" at the price.[20]

In deciding to publish the *Forerunner*, Charlotte had traded greater circulation for a writer's dream: utter control over both medium and message. From a business perspective, however, the venture came closer to nightmare. Ultimately, her decision to self-publish isolated her from readers of more "standard magazines." Ironically, then, her bold attempt to reach a wider audience had the opposite effect. She did recruit some new followers, including one Gilmanite who gushed, "Mrs. Gilman is the High Priestess of my religion, though I didn't know it had a High Priestess, or that it was a religion, until I began reading The Forerunner a year ago." But even the converted to whom Charlotte preached fretted about her marginality: "It does seem a crime though, that you should confine your writings to your one magazine of comparatively small circulation," an anxious reader counseled, "Of course to the subscribers it is a jewel, and it means so much to have your writings together, but your voice should reach as many as possible. . . . I feel desperate when I think about it. You need to reach those who are *not* already educated and won over, as your subscribers are likely to be, else they would not be reading The Forerunner."[21] In the end, the *Forerunner* experiment proved this reader's worst fear: Charlotte's grasp exceeded her "reach."

~

> We need not remain as we are. We ought not to remain as we are. Improvement is
> nature's first law.
>
>   "Educated Bodies," 1904[22]

Charlotte's strenuous efforts to increase subscription rates slackened after the first few years. The *Forerunner*'s audience remained small, but she preferred to call it discriminating. "This is not a 'Popular Magazine,'" she announced. "It does not try to be." But it does please its "comparatively few" readers "immensely."[23]

From the outset, the *Forerunner* was designed to buck popular journalistic trends. On the inside cover page of the first issue, Charlotte ran a poem contrasting her new journal with its competitors:

The news-stands bloom with magazines,
   They flame, they blaze indeed;
So bright the cover-colors glow,
So clear the startling stories show,
So vivid their pictorial scenes,
   That he who runs may read.

Then This: It strives in prose and verse,
   Thought, fancy, fact and fun
To tell the things we ought to know,
To point the way we ought to go,
So audibly to bless and curse,
   That he who reads may run.[24]

There was the fast-paced-but-in-place treading of the modern press and the modern world, and then there was the determined, directed striding of her brave new magazine toward a brave new world.

Charlotte identified the "purpose" of the *Forerunner* in the first issue: "to stimulate thought, to arouse hope, courage, and impatience; to offer practical suggestions and solutions, to voice the strong assurance of better living, here, now, in our own hands to make." She intended the journal to address "people, principles, and the questions of every-day life." She explicitly did *not* intend the *Forerunner* to be a woman's magazine and was particularly eager to distinguish it from conventional women's magazines, which she derided as "housekeepers' manuals"; ideally, hers would appeal to a general, reform-minded audience.[25]

The *Forerunner* reads in many ways like an expanded version of Charlotte's "Vital Issues" department for the *Woman's Journal.* In both, she sought to entice readers with "the Near Sure Perfectly Possible Improvement of Life." In the *Forerunner*'s first issue, Charlotte defined "the three governing laws of life" as "To Be, To Re-be, To Be Better" and declared the last the "most imperative of the Life Force's demands."[26] Improvement certainly remained the "most imperative" of the *Forerunner*'s demands, revisited with minor variations in virtually every issue.

While never as consistent an imperative, thematic coherence was occasionally achieved between or within issues. Thus the first volume included a series of articles on "fill-in-the-blank Mindedness" (e.g., kitchen-mindedness, parlor-mindedness, and nursery-mindedness). The February 1911 issue featured poems, articles, and stories devoted to rejecting the past and embracing the future; the subsequent issue focused on the vote. The December 1914 issue took up the threat of world war and—as if to suggest that the times were too serious for fiction— omitted the usual opening story.

During the summer of 1913, Charlotte embarked on her last trip to Europe, lecturing in England, Germany, and Scandinavia en route to the International Congress of Women in Budapest. The Hungarian feminist movement was, according to one of its leaders, fundamentally indebted to Charlotte's and Ward's theories; it also embraced Charlotte's efforts to broaden the movement beyond an exclusive focus on suffrage. The organizers had pleaded with Charlotte to attend: "we [cannot] imagine our victory without having you on the Congress," the invitation read. "Your name, your personality, your work are so wellknown in Hungary and are taken for so valuable, that your absence would cool all the interest people show towards the Congress."[27]

The turbulent voyage proved the trip's only unpleasantness; everywhere Charlotte went in Budapest she was greeted as an "an immense favorite." The strangeness of the city but the familiarity of the people led her to muse that "people were just people—living in the same age, awake to the same ideals, working for the same ends. . . ." The sameness she witnessed about her may have influenced the June *Forerunner.* Charlotte assembled it while in Budapest and described it as "a sort of Motherhood Number": indeed, she worried it was "rather over weighted, as the reader perhaps wearily perceives, with treatment of that theme." She anxiously assured any first-time readers that issues were generally more diverse.[28]

Some readers found it "such a pleasure to read a homogenous magazine," but others viewed that homogeneity as a fatal flaw. The author Mary Austin publicly declared herself bored: "The worst of it was that she wrote it all herself—articles, stories, reviews, poems—and she couldn't write. . . . Everything she wrote was in the same key. . . . I had to drop her magazine with its terrible sameness, its narrow scope. . . . Time went on and left her standing at the old corner, crying the same wares." Charlotte acknowledged that her writings might seem repetitive when compared to one another, but she argued in her own defense that they appeared unique and innovative when juxtaposed with what everyone else was churning out.[29]

Loyal subscribers to the *Forerunner*, however, compared apples to apples each month. Charlotte apparently believed that, to paraphrase Flannery O'Connor, to the hard of hearing one had to shout. "I would not, if I were in your place, crowd out any auditors," Charles Lummis cautioned. ". . . The wise make themselves listened to, as so much per." But Charlotte rarely prioritized appeasing listeners, as yet another friend, Alexander Black, acknowledged: she "was always more absorbed in her ideas than in herself or her readers. This sort of absorption could neither be embarrassed nor thwarted, as she spoke or as she wrote."[30]

Austin and Charlotte once discussed their aesthetic differences. Charlotte conceded Austin's virtuosity and renounced "any pretension to literature" on her part. She nonetheless maintained that she had a distinct style. Austin emphatically objected to Charlotte's using the word *style* to describe her efforts but added, "I do think, however, that if you gave your mind to it, you could write." Charlotte found the whole conversation so amusing that she later parodied Austin's style and proved in the process that she could indeed "write" as Austin would define it.

On another occasion, Austin blamed Charlotte's "misappreciation and . . . neglect" on her "neglect of form" and on a style that reflected "Mrs. Gilman's mind, thin, vivid, and swift as a lightening streak, rather than the carefully finished instrument of communication." Charlotte copied these published comments verbatim in her diary, the only time she bothered to devote an entire entry to someone else's words.

Other New York friends joined Austin in mourning Charlotte's early writings for their "real artistic virtuosity" and their deep sense of beauty, sacrificed, they believed, on the altar of "the scientific spirit." Alexander Black felt "Mary Austin was reflecting the general feeling of Mrs. Gilman's writing friends when she expostulated her for written carelessness." He agreed with Austin that when Charlotte made art, she made not a thing but a case. In short, her more literary friends accused her of trading aesthetics for homiletics.[31]

Charlotte readily admitted that she differed from those who admired technique over purpose. Her early reading of Elizabeth Barrett Browning's *Aurora Leigh* had taught her that "Art's a Service." She penned her most conventionally literary works in the early 1890s, but even then she promised that if she ever wrote novels, "the purpose will be bigger than the novel." At the century's turn, she publicly declared her allegiance to a utilitarian view of literature: "I can't stop to bother with characters. . . . I'm so interested in my own theories that I can't consider theirs. What absorbs me is not the careful analysis and disentangling of individual character, but the deductions from broad fields of observation and experience, of characters in mass. 'Not the individual but the race.'"[32]

This preference for generality over specificity and for sociology over psychology surfaces repeatedly in the *Forerunner*. Charlotte's summary of its purpose explicitly denies that the magazine had any literary pretensions: "The subject matter, for the most part, is not to be regarded as 'literature,' but as an attempt to set forth certain views of life which seemed to the author of real importance to human welfare." In writing her own magazine, Charlotte strove to resemble the model artist in her *Forerunner* parable, "The World and the Three Artists." This artist satisfies a tired, hungry, and ugly world on all three counts by discounting aesthetics and commerce in favor of citizenship and service.[33]

Invested in imagining both a better world and a better world literature, Charlotte considered herself more forward-thinking than the so-called Modernists who emerged on the art scene during the *Forerunner*'s run. New York City experienced a "little Renaissance" during the teens, prompted by artists and writers "motivated by the ideas and spirit of iconoclasm, modernism, and nationalism."

The Armory Show, which heralded modernism's arrival in America, had drawn some 300,000 people over the course of its four-week New York City run in February 1913. Charlotte commented on the show in the *Forerunner* with palpable distaste. Superseding her scorn for modern art's "morasses of weird technique" was its "peculiar offense of unasked 'self-expression.' . . . [A]ll too many [artists] seem to consider art as the X-ray to the surgeon—a means of personal revelation, of a most desirable intimacy," she protested.[34]

With T. S. Eliot, Charlotte sought "a continual extinction of personality." Her interpretation of that goal differed markedly from Eliot's modernist, aesthetic notion of depersonalization, however. Her distrust of personal revelation was amplified around artists, since ideally they were "most exquisitely specialised to the social service. Their work, of all men's, is least valuable to themselves, most valuable to others."

While also fueled by the movement's associations with decadence, misogyny, and homosexuality, her contempt for modernism was deeply informed by her loathing for navel-gazing. She regretted "that the Great Service of Art should be so profaned by these morbid little ones, suffering from an inflamed egotism, from elephantiasis of the soul. . . . This ache for self-expression is by no means the natural overflow of a creative spirit, but the unnatural irritation of a disease."[35] She herself had become an artist to move people beyond ego, and now modernists seemed to want people to believe that there was no better or even other place to reside. Because to her mind self-expression represented a more primitive developmental stage, Charlotte considered her functional aesthetics more truly modern than the modernists'.

Charlotte simultaneously disdained both the trend toward tales of "blood and thunder" and the school of literary naturalism. She declared the latter a "Jack-Kipling school" responsible for "the renaissance of primevalism," "masculism," and brute force in modern fiction. In 1897, the novelist James Lane Allen had led a chorus decrying the effeminate tendencies of modern literature and calling for a new, more virile direction. Charlotte believed the pendulum had swung too far in response. She lamented the "injury to life" inflicted by "Masculine Literature" via its narrow focus and its fascination with primitivism. She routinely condemned any work that glorified the male brutality she associated with women's subjugation. And she insisted that stories of "Love and War" alone did not truly represent life's breadth and essence: "Life is discovered to be longer, wider, deeper, richer, than these monotonous players of one tune would have us believe."[36] The mixed responses to her *Forerunner* experiment proved, however, that monotony is in the ear of the auditor.

~

There came to me Vision—the sight
Of the world made right;
. . . But around me the people strayed
In the desolate waste they made.
And many who heard indeed,
Had forgot, yes, forgot with speed.
And there stirred that urging pain—
"You must say it again——
     And again . . . ."
          "Say It Again," 1914[37]

Charlotte lodged her complaints against "Masculine Literature" in her first serialized *Forerunner* treatise. *Our Androcentric Culture, or the Man-Made World* was Charlotte's book on "men as males," just as *Women and Economics* was her book on "women as females." Charlotte borrowed both *androcentric* and its antonym *gynæcocentric* from Lester Ward. Of her six nonfiction *Forerunner* works, this was the only one she published independently (title and subtitle were wisely flipped in the 1911 edition), and the only one that attracted wide notice. The book drew praise for its "originality of thought, audacity of conception, logical arrangement of facts, and a foundation in the theories which, however hotly disputed, nevertheless are scientific." The *New York Times*, never one to gush over Charlotte's achievements, declared it not only "the first book of its kind ever written" but also "the best that Mrs. Gilman has published."[38]

Forget about Eve, Charlotte demanded therein: men, not women, bore the blame for the world's problems. They had devised the familial, educational, religious, industrial, and political institutions, the customs, sartorial and literary standards, pastimes, and punishments to suit themselves, and they had made a mess of it. In this man-made world, men "fought and made love" and women "were things to be fought for and made love to." War and destruction (masculine traits) thwarted production (a feminine one) and hindered human growth.[39] "Mankind" has meant "men-kind" to our detriment, Charlotte argued, and only when it meant "humankind" would society evolve beyond "despotism" toward the "Human World" her last chapter envisions.[40] Although she had made these points before, by turning her microscope on men for a change, her observations achieved a freshness and vivacity reviewers had missed in her last treatise, *Human Work*.

One commentator noticed that Charlotte's *Forerunner* nonfiction and fiction served complementary functions: with each treatise she "ruthlessly upsets all our pet conceits," and with each novel she aimed to portray "social organization as it ought to be." In truth, the line between them is even fuzzier: both mix social criticism and polemical projection.

Charlotte once joked that her novels proved she was no novelist, but to dismiss them so lightly she had to be employing the modernist or formalist aesthetic standards she elsewhere scorned. Her novels are not inferior to these standards, they are challenges to them. She deftly maneuvers across a broad array of generic forms and literary modes in an attempt to convey her message and, as Janet Beer has argued, "to estrange her audience from the usual subjects and style of fiction in order to make them think anew about the culture in which they lived. . . ."[41]

This project of estrangement is a goal shared by all of her *Forerunner* novels. Each adopts *Moving the Mountain*'s ostensible philanthropic agenda, summarized in a promotional blurb Charlotte wrote for the 1911 novel: "Those who believe this world is a good place, easily made better, and who wish to know how to help it, will enjoy reading this book. Those who do not so believe and wish may not enjoy it so much, but it will do them good."[42] As this description suggests, she ultimately cared more about her works doing good than being good.

Several of the reform novels she serialized in the *Forerunner* recommend "short-distance" improvements—those that could be instituted immediately. Her first *Forerunner* novel, *What Diantha Did,* demonstrates how a woman might overcome penury, parental objections, and male grousing in order to build a thriving business: Diantha performs "a great work for humanity" by professionalizing housework, removing the kitchens from her clients' homes, and rendering them thereby odorless, flyless, and virtually effortless. The 1912 *Mag-Marjorie* suggests that even the most ill-used young girl can transform herself via diligence and the right mentor into a successful and satisfied professional. The following year's *Won Over* locates meaningful work outside the home for its representative lonely, middle-aged female protagonist. And the 1914 *Benigna Machiavelli*—whose "good villain" first appeared in the *Forerunner* as early as 1910—enthusiastically models meddling in other women's affairs to their great benefit. These fictional interventions dramatize Charlotte's desire, expressed in the dedication of *What Diantha Did*, to help "The Housewife" achieve "a happier life, a larger income, better health, and full success in living. . . ."[43]

For Charlotte, "success in living" still entailed the dissolution of the "I" into the "We," or the self into the world. But during this period, she put tighter restrictions on the kind of self and the kind of world required in order for tomorrow to improve on today. Charlotte's brave new world increasingly had only certain creatures in it, and they were largely created in her own mold. Since her utopian novels forced her to make her characteristic abstractions at least semi-concrete, these works vividly illustrate the limits of her idealism.

In his examination of Charlotte's utopian writings, the literary critic Christopher Wilson accuses Charlotte of desiring a world without desire, a world that was all "herd" and "no shepherd," a world where, to quote Nietzsche, "[e]verybody wants the same, everybody is the same." Charlotte would have objected to a logic that equates personal desires with identity, but she did consider an egoless world a far, far better place. Still, Charlotte sought to jettison more than the ego during these years. She became increasingly convinced that eugenics could rid the world of "undesirables" and hence accelerate the improvement of the species.[44]

Charlotte had always taken a complicated stance in the age-old debate between nature and nurture. Neither natural nor cultural attributes were in her books immutable: her "evolutionary paradigm," one critic has observed, ". . . suggested that all aspect of the human condition—including its biological constitution—were open to change." One of her *Forerunner* poems, "The Rabbit, the Rhinoceros & I," illustrates this point by contrasting the two environmentally-determined, eponymous animals with a human being who ". . . can always change the slate / And make the things that make you good and bad." Prior to the teens, Charlotte typically depicted nature as the repository of both our necessary biological functions and the excesses and distortions developed within a patriarchal culture. Increasingly, however, she blamed present imperfections and discrepancies on a mixture of individual agency, parental responsibility, cultural forces, and genetic defects. And she attributed any future perfection to the unveiling of a true, unencumbered, god-given human nature.[45]

Culture thus no longer figured as a potentially civilizing force so much as a differentiating and usually debasing one, whereas nature, when it did not render certain people defective, made us who we are essentially—that is, human. Charlotte's retreat from ameliorative theories of cultural construction may reflect Ward's waning influence, which could have caused her to rethink his emphasis on education and other potentially improving cultural forces. Her retreat definitely hastened the more sharply she distinguished among ethnic groups who currently inhabited the same urban spaces yet, to her eyes, seemed so irreducible in their alterity.

In her younger days, Charlotte had afforded greater significance to the human will: indeed, she frequently read her lecture audiences a poem by Ella Wheeler Wilcox called "Will," which praised it as a force stronger than "destiny." But the more she embraced eugenics, the more the will seemed to drop out of her equations. As she aged, she came to believe that, for some people or peoples, there was neither will nor way.

By emphasizing the collective, Charlotte risked discounting individual agency; by talking about "the race," or increasingly "races," she tended to stereotype, overlooking the variety within the mass. This generalizing tendency affected both her professional and her personal life and was regretted by Charlotte's friends. Alexander Black attributed her social awkwardness to this broad emphasis on "humanity," which led her to falter "before the units. She had much of Emerson's feeling in liking Man better than men." Throughout the teens, Charlotte's faith in eugenics increasingly led her to like some "men" better than others.[46]

Charlotte still viewed eugenics skeptically when she first launched the *Forerunner*. In the May 1910 issue, she criticized what proponents were promoting as "the science of the improvement of the human race by better breeding." She also expressed her discomfort with the social Darwinists and eugenicists who countenanced the "ruthless slaughter of the unfit." "Positive eugenics," or improving existing populations via education and other reforms, still made more sense to her than the "negative eugenics" that entailed weeding and breeding out "inferior" stock.

In 1909, Charlotte published a piece in the *Independent* entitled "Race Improvement." In it she blames poverty and illiteracy on a society that ignores altruistic impulses and builds more slums than "exquisite garden cities." She also reprimands those who deride the "ruined stock" of impoverished slum dwellers, reminding them that "'us' includes them. . . . Humanity is *one*, a living tissue."[47] To use her own metaphor, none of us could be clean if others remained dirty.

During the *Forerunner* years, however, Charlotte gradually abandoned her emphasis on interconnectedness and began to differentiate between "us" and "them." She thus dissociated not only from those she classified as "others" but, when necessary, from the organic social philosophy that had sustained her for so long. As she insisted in the journal's final volume,

> Human life is sacred, far too sacred to be allowed to fall into hideous degeneracy. If we had a proper regard for human life we should take instant measures to check the supply of feeble-minded and defective persons, and further measures to prevent the

reproduction of such unfortunates. . . . Human life is sacred *while it is going on.* It is not merely a matter of filling the world with people—any kind of people; or of keeping alive every wretched little monstrosity. . . . [48]

In the remaining decades of her life, Charlotte swapped her sometimes vaguely defined project of uplifting humanity for an investment in specifying the kinds of humans she considered worthy, or unworthy, of uplift. "Quality, not quantity" became her mantra as debates about immigration and breeding swirled around her.

This apparent about-face has several explanations. To begin with, Charlotte eagerly embraced any theory embossed with a "scientific" stamp. Alexander Black once referred to her as "obstinately biological," and eugenics offered Charlotte a tidy biological explanation of existing discrepancies. Eugenics enthusiasts spanned the political spectrum, but they were united by their embrace of evolution and by "a faith that science, particularly genetics, held the key to improving the race of man" and to solving incontrovertibly "life's inherent mysteries."[49]

The first decade of the new century witnessed the rediscovery of Mendel's studies in genetics and the dissemination of Sir Francis Galton's views on eugenics and heredity. Genes and breeding provided long-sought, exonerating explanations for poverty and hardship. Significantly, eugenics took hold just as reformers began to grow weary. The British Fabians numbered among the converts: H. G. Wells, for instance, espoused negative eugenics, arguing, "It is in the sterilisation of failures, and not in the selection of successes for breeding, that the possibility of an improvement of the human stock lies."[50]

In the United States, the eugenics movement dates from the early 1900s. In 1907, Indiana passed laws permitting the involuntary sterilization of the inmates of mental institutions; other states soon copied the "Indiana idea." In 1910, the Eugenics Record Office opened at Long Island's Cold Spring Harbor (a place Charlotte knew well). Harvard, Columbia, Cornell, Brown, Wisconsin, and Northwestern soon counted among the colleges offering courses in the "new science." The threat of war in Europe and a period of economic depression in the States, with as many as 300,000 unemployed in New York alone, combined to give alarmists a sense of imminent danger and to feed the fires of nativism—also known as "100 percent Americanism" and "anti-hyphenism." The early teens saw the publication of a number of influential xenophobic books, including Josiah Strong's *Our Country* (a 1911 reissue), Max Nordau's *Regeneration* (1912), Frank Julian Warne's *The Immigrant Invasion* (1913), E. A. Ross's *The Old World in the New* (1914), and Madison Grant's *The Passing of the Great Race* (1916).[51]

In the run-up to the First World War, popular magazines ran more essays on eugenics "than on the major progressive issues of slum and tenement reform." In

October 1915, the *Literary Digest* declared "the hyphenate issue . . . the most vital one of the day." The trends toward eugenics and nativism prompted numerous states to host conferences on "Race Betterment," pass sterilization laws, and approve anti-immigration measures. By the mid-teens, the historian Mark Haller has observed, "eugenics had many of the characteristics of a fad: joked about in newspapers, lectured about before women's clubs, introduced into the college curriculum, and supported by the inevitable lunatic fringe."[52]

But supporters only seem "lunatic" from our post-Holocaust perspective. At the time, proponents of eugenics included eminent members of society, among them leading scientists at Stanford, the University of Chicago, and Harvard. Alexander Graham Bell was a vocal proponent, as was E. A. Ross. Lonely dissenters included Lester Ward; the stalwart activists Jane Addams, Lillian Wald, and Florence Kelley; and the cultural anthropologist Franz Boas. The eugenics tent was broad enough to encompass diverse causes associated with the burgeoning school of public health, including anti-prostitution campaigns, "sex education, sanitation, prenatal culture, prevention of venereal diseases, and pure milk for babies," all of which Charlotte endorsed. City dwellers like Charlotte numbered among the most ardent supporters. Many felt overwhelmed by close encounters with the "great slums, in which were massed the diseased, the deficient, and the demented. . . ."[53]

The feminists and activists who, to varying degrees, espoused eugenics included Margaret Sanger, Emma Goldman, Olive Schreiner, and of course Charlotte herself. They shared the belief that life would be better if the population was smaller and, as they defined the term, healthier. While essentially conservative, eugenics came to have "the air of a 'reform,'" emerging as it did during an era of progressive reform. The historian Richard Hofstadter has maintained that the eugenics movement shared with other reform movements an "acceptance of the principles of state action toward a common end and spoke in terms of the collective destiny of the group rather than of individual success."

This sense of society as "a collective whole rather than a congeries of individual atoms" formed the basis of Charlotte's organic philosophy. In her 1914 essay, "What May We Expect from Eugenics?" she argues for society's fundamental right "to arrest its own decay" and claims such a right was challenged only by her anathema: "extreme individualists."[54]

Eugenics, therefore, was never so foreign to Charlotte's worldview after all. It helped her to hone her sense of what and who might best enable the collective to grow and thrive. Like other converts, she saw eugenics as "a new ethic and a new religion." It promised the swifter attainment of her long-sought dream: a healthy, happy, human world—a veritable heaven on earth. She found two of the central tenets of eugenics particularly appealing: first, "[w]e are beginning faintly to realize that The Race is the thing—not merely one passing generation," and second, "[o]ur Past we cannot help. Our Present slips from us in the making. Only the Future can be molded." Both were abiding and heartfelt convictions, culled from personal experience and frequently propounded from the lectern.[55] In short, eugenics fused so nicely with her personal religion, her scientific faith, her anti-individualism, and her futuristic orientation that it would have been more surprising if she had resisted its logic.

Charlotte explicitly advertised her 1911 *Forerunner* novel, *The Crux*, as "a novel along eugenic lines." In *The Crux*, she locates racial regeneration on the frontier. The story revolves around women from the East who "go west" to start life anew amid the surplus of single men in the territories. Read today as a vexed commentary on racial purification through marriage and as a polemical woman's western promoting the reestablishment of white supremacy on the frontier, *The Crux* reveals the extent to which Charlotte's utopian longings deepened with her growing alienation from a city and a country she considered too heterogeneous for its own good.

While she herself had gone west in the 1890s to escape both marriage and domesticity, in *The Crux* she advises women to go there to marry and make their homes on the range. The West depicted in her novel offers not only "enough men to choose from" but also ample opportunities, in a region that demonstrated early support for women's rights, to institute needed social reforms and make better marriages. Charlotte's view of cities on the East Coast as teeming with immigrants may also have led her to romanticize western states like Colorado for their wide-open spaces and relative whiteness. Indeed, by the time she wrote *The Crux*, homogeneity was becoming for Charlotte both a formal and a cultural mandate.[56]

Yet despite Charlotte's identification of the West as an oasis of purity, health, and happiness, the novel focuses on the prevalence of disease there, especially venereal disease. The violence perpetrated in Charlotte's western revolves not around men and gunfights but around men and sex. In *The Man-Made World*, she complains, "If a man gives his wife arsenic, he is held criminally responsible; if he shoots his child or maims him with an axe. Wherein is a man less guilty who knowingly transmits disease to a trusting wife, who causes blindness and deformity and idiocy in his children, whose lightest offense is to bring sterility and merciful death?"[57] The crux of *The Crux* was Charlotte's outrage over the knowing transmission of venereal disease to unknowing women.

Although nearly every cause Charlotte adopted so fervently had a personal stake, no conclusive biographical evidence exists to indicate that she ever contracted venereal disease. There are, however, some intriguing grounds for conjecture: In *The Crux*, she identifies venereal disease as causing the suffering routinely attributed to "any or all of those diseases 'peculiar to women' as we used to call them!" She also scoffs at the men who earned pity because they "'were so good to their invalid wives!'" Of course, Charlotte had been one such invalid herself, married to a passionate husband who at least contemplated sleeping with prostitutes.

Charlotte's concern with venereal disease dates to the dissolution of her first marriage. Around that time, she read Ibsen's play *Ghosts* aloud to Hattie Howe; the same year (1893), Sarah Grand published the bestselling *The Heavenly Twins*, a book Charlotte owned. Both works make venereal disease a central theme.[58]

The sterility often caused by venereal disease may shed light on Charlotte's inability to conceive a child in her second marriage, or another child in her first marriage, despite Walter's insistence on conjugal rights. Grace, Walter's second wife, also experienced several miscarriages and never brought a pregnancy to term. But speculation only takes us so far. More evidence exists to suggest that Charlotte objected to venereal disease as a symbol of masculinity run amok.

If Charlotte did escape, she was lucky. She estimates in *The Crux* that three quarters of all American men were infected with syphilis or gonorrhea or both. She borrowed her statistics from Prince Morrow, a crusading New York urologist and organizer of the social purity movement who claimed "that 75 per cent of all adult males had or had had gonorrhea, and from 18 to 20 percent syphilis."[59]

The *Forerunner* years paralleled an increasing "international and wartime concern" with the spread of disease and its deleterious effects on "the American 'stock.'" Charlotte frequently applauded in the *Forerunner* any book, magazine, or organization that shared her outrage and her agenda. She even praised the *Ladies' Home Journal*—an overtly "woman's magazine" she otherwise disparaged—for performing the "great public service" of informing women about the threat of venereal disease. Publicizing this threat was one goal of the social purity movement Charlotte supported. The movement, which peaked between 1905 and 1917, fostered campaigns at state and local levels to eradicate "the red menace" of venereal disease and other "social evils" including prostitution.[60]

Designed to provide "the PROPER SEX-GUIDANCE OF YOUNG PEOPLE," *The Crux* represents Charlotte's literary contribution to the social purity movement. The novel's self-designated guidance counselor is Dr. Jane Bellair, who had been rendered sterile as a young woman after marrying a man with gonorrhea. Her candor with her patients serves as a sharp rebuke to prevailing medical practices. The venereal disease epidemic alarmed Charlotte, but the hypocritical collusion between infected men and their doctors infuriated her.

Known as the "medical secret," physicians and male patients, pleading female modesty and patient confidentiality, refused to inform unsuspecting women of their lovers' afflictions.

Charlotte dramatizes this "secret" in *The Crux* via the character of the taciturn male doctor, but she inflicts no deadly consequences like those enacted in her powerful short story "The Vintage." Instead, Dr. Bellair finds a fellow truthteller in the novel's sprightly grandmother, who advises her granddaughter Vivian to help "religiously rid the world of all these 'undesirable citizens' . . . [b]y not marrying them."[61] In *The Crux*, at least, the diseased degenerates eugenics would eradicate are found within, not outside, the white population.

In each of the *Forerunner*'s three explicitly utopian novels, eugenics expedites the journey from here to utopia. These imaginary lands improve on "Ourland" through policies designed to keep immigrants out and "defectives and degenerates," "criminals and perverts" from reproducing. Charlotte called her first *Forerunner* effort, the 1911 *Moving the Mountain*, a "Baby Utopia." One reviewer elaborated and called it "a short-distance utopia. . . . [A] little one that can grow" to fruition in a few decades.

Resembling her aborted 1907 "A Woman's Utopia," *Moving the Mountain* also takes place in the near-future and also features a conservative American who leaves the country and then reappears after several decades. This time that man is named John Robertson, and his excuse is a fall from a Tibetan precipice and subsequent memory loss. Robertson returns in the 1940s to a city and a country transformed when "women woke up . . . saw their duty and they did it." His sister Nellie, a doctor and coeducational college president, proudly introduces her brother to the changes the newly awakened women have wrought. Their concerted efforts have eliminated poverty, pollution, kitchens, flies, pets, hunting, and war (the latter alone freeing up 70 percent of the national budget). They also managed to shorten the workday to a compulsory two hours. Essentially, by arousing social consciousness and eradicating a "belated Individualism," the mountain was moved.[62]

Collective health takes precedence in this improved world, so individual lives could be discarded if doing so served the greater good. When John asks his sister Nellie where all the "wretched, degenerate creatures" have disappeared to," she responds soberly that they were dealt with "very thoroughly": the "hopeless degenerates" were "promptly and mercifully removed," the curables were cured, and the incurables-through-no-fault-of-their-own were placed in asylums until they died. The new nation also practiced positive eugenics and adopted as policy a promise not to "make that kind of people any more." With the *New York Times* calling the novel's picture of a future Manhattan "alluring" and "suggestive," *Moving the*

Mountain apparently tapped into fantasies about urban life and urban transformation in a city whose population was now roughly 40 percent foreign-born.[63]

Charlotte serialized her most widely read utopian novel in the 1915 *Forerunner*. The plot of *Herland* resembles Tennyson's "Princess," which Charlotte read in 1881. It also calls to mind Gilbert and Sullivan's *Princess Ida* (Charlotte had recently tried her hand at comic operetta and had vainly searched for a Sullivan to her Gilbert). Yet *Herland* is an original work bearing what one reader referred to as Charlotte's unmistakable "think marks."[64]

"Herland" is the name three male scientists give to a secluded and strange "Woman Land" they "discover" in the heart of a dark continent, having learned of its existence on a previous expedition. The explorers expect the women to conform to stereotypes and are surprised by how femininity is construed in a world without men: it resembles the humanity Charlotte believed would define us when the traditional sexual division of labor no longer does:

> We had expected a dull submissive monotony, and found a daring social inventiveness far beyond our own, and a mechanical and scientific development fully equal to ours.
>
> We had expected pettiness and found a social consciousness besides which our nations looked like quarreling children—feeble-minded ones at that.
>
> We had expected jealousy, and found a broad sisterly affection, a fair-minded intelligence, to which we could produce no parallel.
>
> We had expected hysteria, and found a standard of health and vigor, a calmness of temper, to which the habit of profanity, for instance, was impossible to explain—we tried it.

Two thousand years previously, this race of Aryans had endured a bloody war followed by a disastrous volcanic explosion, which decimated the population and isolated the survivors from the rest of the world. Two revolts followed: the first a slave rebellion that resulted in the wholesale slaughter of masters, old women, and mothers; the second a counter-revolt against the slaves by the surviving virgins. With all the men gone, the young women soberly prepared to face their own extinction. Instead, they were saved by the miracle of parthenogenesis (both Ward and Geddes get a nod here). The survivors ultimately created the matriarchal culture that dumbfounds the three Americans.[65]

Bent on easy conquest, the explorers find themselves instead imprisoned by creatures they had assumed would fawn and simper. Soon, only the macho Terry (part Ambrose Bierce, part August Weismann) resents his captivity in this land without "Love, Combat, or Danger." Each man is assigned a teacher, and each pursues a lover; the Herlanders are open to heterosexual procreation, even if they lack the "faintest idea of love—sex-love, that is."[66] All three Americans marry their lovers, but when Terry attempts to "master" his new wife by raping her, he is swiftly expelled; his bride wants him killed.

Before his expulsion, Terry is threatened with perpetual imprisonment and anesthesia unless he promises to keep the country's location a secret—a warning that typifies the Herlanders' cool response to "undesirables." When its population began to exceed sustainability, the Herlanders had implemented a form of "negative eugenics": if they could willfully conceive, then they could willfully decide "not to 'make' any more people." The occasional rotten egg was strongly persuaded to forgo parthenogenesis for the sake of upholding the overall quality of the stock.[67]

The following year's *With Her in Ourland* picks up where the prequel left off. Accompanied by her spouse, the sociologist-narrator Van, Ellador journeys through Ourland, a "bisexual" world she assumes will compare favorably to her unisexual one. Her exposure to war (the novel is set in 1916), rampant poverty, disease, and suffering soon leaves her reeling and longing for Herland. Van sheepishly concurs that his land is both inequitable and individualistic.

After touring Europe and Asia, Ellador arrives on American soil, expecting to confirm the country's reputation as "the Crown of the World!" Instead, she recoils from the press of immigrants, the dilution of the nation's superior stock, the overcrowded, polluted cities, the depleted soil, the shameful politics, and the equally shameful gap between rich and poor. Ellador is so appalled by the country's "*unmotherliness*" that she vows she will "die childless" if she and Van stay in Ourland; for a Herlander of her evident quality, this amounts to sacrilege.[68] Ellador concludes that hers is a separate, superior race and ours a population bordering on savagery. Although she insists that the ills plaguing Ourland could be cured if only we would "*think in terms of community,*" Ellador refuses in the end to belong to any community but Herland's.[69]

A younger Charlotte might have scripted a different ending than the couple's flight back to that hypothetical land. After all, utopias are premised upon the possibility of improving the present world. But by this point in her career, Charlotte considered many of Ourland's problems endemic and intractable. In short, by 1916, she no longer believed the mountain could be moved.

～

Pain and loss and want have not stood between me and my work. Joy does not either.
Letter to George Houghton Gilman,
February 5, 1899[70]

In the *Forerunner*'s initial volume, Charlotte launched an advice column entitled "Personal Problems." By the eighth issue, she used the forum to ask readers why they were not submitting questions. She then quickly segued to her own most pressing "personal problem"—that is, her problem with the personal: "What has always been a problem to me is how people can be alive and take so little interest in the performance." Life, death, love, happiness, world events: all await us, and "here are we—making button holes in the back parlor—breaking our heads in a sham fight in the back yard! Question: Why don't people wake up and LIVE! World-size?"

Readers took her rhetorical question seriously and sent in responses. One asked Charlotte to explain how people were supposed to "live world-size" when so many were focused on mere personal survival. Charlotte replied that personality is a distraction from and a fraction of social consciousness. When we dwell on purely personal problems, we ensconce ourselves in our "own little circle of pain" rather than placing it in the context of "the general pain." Devoting our energies to alleviating this wider suffering, she argued, would help us to recognize the insignificance of personal anguish and consequently to trade suffering for joy everlasting.[71]

Yet the *Forerunner*'s concerted efforts to transport readers beyond the personal rarely brought its founder either that transcendence or its ensuing joy. Ironically, Charlotte had assumed she would finally be "free" at fifty. When still a girl she had chosen fifty as the best possible age, for by then "people will respect my opinions if they are ever going to, and I shall not be too old to work," she predicted.[72] She had looked forward to her fifties as a blissful, productive period—a utopian decade, we might say—but the reality never measured up to her ideal. At fifty, she had respect, but it was often grudging, and she had work, but it was often more than she could handle.

In the months before launching the *Forerunner*, Charlotte dreamed that the enterprise would fund the good life. She hoped the proceeds from her new venture would enable her to buy a house in the country where she would find "peace and health" and to travel around the world with Houghton; she intended to own a "Big popular place in N. Y. also." In short, the success of the *Forerunner* would enable her to "rest, travel, grow strong, and do what further work opens to the best of my powers," she optimistically projected. At the least, she wanted her "Two Rooms and a Bath," the minimum space she believed each individual required. For all her insistence on the fundamentally social nature of human identity, she did admit that "[t]he human individual needs privacy."[73]

Yet the magazine intended to compensate her for life's disappointments and to end them for others in general often wound up costing her more pleasure than she received. For the *Forerunner*'s sake, she forsook a vacation in the mountains that first summer and with it the opportunity to "swim in the maple syrup, row up and down mountains, sleep in the blueberries and pick gallons of tents and cabins this year—alas!"

She did manage to sneak in some play amid all her work. During the summer of 1915, for instance, she visited Katharine at the MacDowell Colony in Peterborough, where she taught the artists in residence "to write sestinas—and play games." That winter, mother and daughter joined the legions of fans who attended Isadora Duncan's performances. The "motherly" dancer inspired Charlotte to both poetry and prose and Katharine to paint a frieze of dancers on a wall in her mother's apartment.[74]

By and large, however, the *Forerunner* years were lean and mean. That first winter, Charlotte passed "a sulky xmas. No money, overworked, 'didn't do a thing. . . .'" Her health continued to plague her, and dental problems in particular left her "limp." In 1913, she was diagnosed with an abscess in the jaw; she hoped its treatment would help her to get "well at last," she told Katharine. She apparently also felt socially isolated: twice she resolved in her diary to socialize more, to "See more of people—have friends in once a week and go out once or twice."[75]

After the lease on the boarding house expired in 1909, the Gilmans had hastened to "the heart of their desire": a top-floor apartment on Riverside Drive, between 94th and 95th, near Riverside Park. The lovely views from her "river windows" inspired Charlotte to write a series of fourteen poems; the vivid imagery, effective use of consonance, and regular rhythm and rhyme in the one she called "Good Cheer" prove that she could still write formally complex poetry when so inclined:

> Going gaily down the stream;
> Flagged with forward-flying steam,
>   Brisk and red the tug-boats run,
> Twinkling blue the river's flow,
> Bank and border crisp with snow,
>   All ablaze with morning sun.

For a short time, the Gilmans tried taking in boarders here as well, but they stopped altogether in 1911, since the experiment netted them only an extra "10.00 a week!"[76]

Charlotte's brother Thomas visited the Gilmans during their three years on Riverside Drive. For a while in the early teens, the couple counted both Grace and Katharine as neighbors (they could visit over the roofs of their adjoining buildings). Walter, long deaf and in failing health, had died in Rome in July 1911 from

Charlotte's brother, Thomas Adie Perkins, ca. 1912. Courtesy of the Schlesinger Library, Radcliffe Institute for Advanced Study, Harvard University.

complications associated with intestinal surgery. Grace and Katharine were at his side, and they scattered his ashes in the Mediterranean as they sailed back to the States to help organize a memorial exhibition.

Upon hearing the news, Charlotte wrote sympathetic notes encouraging the two women to stay with her and Houghton on their return. She praised Walter for having accomplished "Great Work" and Grace for having found great love. Grace agreed: she still pitied Charlotte "from the depths of my soul," she told a friend, for having forsaken the "earthly paradise" of Walter's love.[77] Though restored to a physical proximity, the two friends remained divided over their respective notions of "earthly paradise."

Two perennial complaints of urban apartment dwellers—lack of closet space and an abundance of rats and other "traveling pets"—drove the Gilmans from Riverside Drive when their three-year lease expired. They made their last move within the city in 1912, to a top-floor front apartment in a walk-up on West 136th Street, where they stayed for ten years.[78]

Under the strain of running the *Forerunner*, financial pressures mounted. The couple kept no "evening hours" during the winter of 1914 as Houghton was working nights. Charlotte's resolutions for that year included getting well and earning $3,000 through lectures and writing. Their financial outlook did not improve until the following year, when Charlotte received a nearly $3,000 legacy for some shares of stock she held in the Adie Brown Land Company.[79]

As is true of her larger career, throughout the *Forerunner* years Charlotte had to rely on lecturing for needed income. In January 1910, she complained to a friend about having to assemble the next issue of the journal aboard a chilly train bound for Fargo, North Dakota, where she would lecture as part of her futile campaign to make the magazine self-supporting. Charlotte annually renewed the effort, even though she found "these lecture-and-write-just-the-same trips . . . wearing."

Charlotte soon realized that her dreams of a California retirement would have to be postponed. She had her "sulky" bouts but generally remained optimistic: "there's a lot of work to do yet," she told a friend in 1911, "and I love it!"[80] Over the seven years and two months she devoted to the magazine, she only published roughly twenty pieces in other venues, so the *Forerunner*, the lecture circuit, and her husband remained her primary revenue sources.

Charlotte could still draw crowds, though not unqualified raves. Praise she received as "intellectually the superior of all the women leaders in this country" was countered by complaints that her enthusiasm masked neither her ignorance nor her "most conspicuous" limitations. On the road, Charlotte garnered largely favorable press. Miles Franklin, the Australian author of *My Brilliant Career*, heard

Charlotte lecture in the States and maintained that her idol was "just as great on the platform as in her writings and just as lovely personally and privately as on the platform. She is so brilliant, so lucid, so humorous in a high, clean way that I think it takes a trained audience to take in the whole banquet once [*sic*]." Franklin's cautionary note was sounded elsewhere: an Oregon paper described Charlotte as "Young in thought and Spirit" for a woman of her years and as "heroically forming an unpopular philosophy and presenting it with the illumination of genius."[81]

In New York, the reviews were more mixed and that unpopularity more pronounced. "In terms of public recognition," the historian Larry Ceplair estimates, "the years 1912–14 probably were the apex of Charlotte's career." The post-*Women and Economics* period seems the higher peak, but 1914 did bring her a lot of regional attention, primarily on account of her participation in a series of well-publicized "feminist" gatherings. In the 1910s, the term *feminism* emerged to connote a broader and more modern understanding of gender relations and gender identity. Charlotte initially adopted the term uncritically; she often used it interchangeably with the relatively dated expressions, like *woman's rights* and *woman suffrage*, which the coiners of this neologism had hoped to replace.[82]

In February 1914, Charlotte participated in one of two "feminist mass meetings" at Cooper Union, where she spoke for ten minutes on "The Right to Specialize in Home Industries." She generated even more buzz for two consecutive lecture series offered at the Hotel Astor later that spring: the first on "The Larger Feminism," the second on what the *Times* referred to as "the, till now, larger, 'masculism.'" The audience for each lecture in the series ranged in size from fifty to over 200. The eight lectures brought her a good deal of publicity but only a measly $244 after her manager took his cut.[83]

The playwright George Middleton, one of the few men in attendance, liked what he heard: "Slim and erect, with a narrow face and sparkling eyes, she spoke incisively, without notes, never hesitating for a word. She presented her facts in chiseled phrase but, like all feminists I knew, with devastating humor. . . . She herself was a mistress of sarcasm, amusing juxtaposition, peppered with ridicule and irony." Others were less amused. One irate *Times* reader ranted, "Men will not much longer listen patiently to brutal attacks on the home by the absurdly so-called 'feminists,' whose aim is to eliminate femininity, or what men chiefly adore in this world."

Clara Savage—an editor, writer, and future war correspondent who at the time served as the press chair of the National American Woman Suffrage Association— attended the entire series "as everyone else is doing" and recorded her mounting distaste in her diary. Charlotte, she wrote, had "a lovely face but a harsh voice and I didn't like her especially." The "masculism" series made Clara Savage particularly "*furious.* I dislike her manner and her voice so much," she fumed. "She may have facts but that's about all she reveals to her audience and the conclusions she draws from them——!!" Charlotte's last lecture provoked Savage to sarcasm: "Sore throat, curse and C P G! It made a merry morning."[84]

George Middleton claimed that this was "almost the first time any serious publicity had been given" to Charlotte. The *New York Times* providing most of the coverage. By reporting on her lectures, the paper helped to air her views before a larger audience, but it filtered them through its conservative lens. In an earlier incarnation, the *Times* was "an 'anti' paper" openly hostile to woman's causes. It declared suffrage "repugnant to instincts that strike their roots deep in the order of nature. It runs counter to human reason, it flouts the teachings of experience and the admonitions of common sense." And right in its own backyard lived the woman many still considered the "Most Famous of 'Feminists.'"[85]

The target proved too tempting. The *Times* ridiculed Charlotte, for instance, for inferring that our female progenitors must have been "slow women," since the swiftest women would have outpaced their male pursuers. The *Times* gleefully elaborated on her premise: each fast woman must then have preferred escape and freedom to settling down, preferred to "broil her own bear meat [and] . . . catch her own bear, to seize the Hyrcan tiger by the tail and beat his brains out against a tree trunk, to skin the armed rhinoceros with a flint hatchet" rather than submit to conventional domestic arrangements.[86]

The *Times* did not confine its derision to this particular lecture series. When Charlotte advocated women's haircuts or "bobs," the paper accused her of sounding the "End of Romance." When Henrietta Rodman, one of Charlotte's disciples and the founder of the Feminist Alliance, planned to build a feminist apartment house inspired by Charlotte's municipal reform and baby garden ideas, the *Times* published a column deriding the structure (never built) as an example of feminists' "monstrous egotism." For Charlotte, this may have been the unkindest cut of all.[87]

Charlotte actively participated in public protest meetings against the press and fulminated in the *Forerunner* over its manipulation of public opinion for private ends. But her retreat to the *Forerunner* had left the field open for her adversaries, who were as eager to air their grievances in the mainstream press as the press appeared eager to publish them. For example, M.I.T. biologist William T. Sedgwick warned that if feminists did not stop their nonsense, men would rise up and lock women back in the homes where they belonged. Sedgwick's alarm was echoed by Dr. Dudley Allen Sargent, who deplored the increasing comparability of male and female bodily types, which he blamed on women doing men's work. Out-trumpeting them all was Sir Almroth Wright, who declared the suffragists ungrateful wretches "who want to have everything for nothing" instead of recognizing how beholden they were to "the virile and imperial race" for their well-being.[88]

A distinctly feminine voice joined the doomsayers when the muckraker Ida Tarbell published her series on "The American Woman" in the *American Magazine*. Tarbell agreed with Charlotte that the modern woman was obsessed with "self-discussion," but the two differed drastically over the solution. Tarbell defended the traditional woman's course against the misguided few who "struggled and suffered to gain for her what they believed to be her rights"; she identified homemaking as "nature's plan" for women and dismissed Charlotte's contention that extra-domestic work was essential to life. Charlotte, in turn, accused Tarbell of reiterating the "standard reactionary views about women" espoused by those "who have always feared that if women did anything whatever outside of child-rearing and housework they would be unsexing themselves."[89]

Charlotte took all these conservatives to task in the *Forerunner* and, when given the chance, elsewhere. She accused them of a reactionary form of moral housekeeping that left them "trying to sweep back the tide with a broom." But one sign that this tide was turning against her came when even the friendly editor of the *Progressive Woman*, Josephine Conger-Kaneko, backed Tarbell and upheld women's "part in the upbuilding of civilization"—a part that, both women claimed, Charlotte denigrated.[90]

Increasingly in the teens, Charlotte found herself attacked from the left as well as the right. During the *Forerunner* years, Charlotte faced a steady barrage from followers of Ellen Key, who since the early 1900s had identified herself as Charlotte's "strong antithesis." As William English Walling observed at the time, "Of the leaders of present-day opinion on woman and related subjects, marriage, love, sex, and the home, the most influential with the general public are undoubtedly Ellen Key and Charlotte Perkins Gilman."[91] He might have added that to follow Key was to reject Gilman, and vice versa.

A Swedish teacher and reformer, Key lectured and published regularly on women, motherhood, and the misuse of woman's power. Her essays appeared in the *Atlantic Monthly*, *Harper's Monthly*, and other journals whose circulations vastly outstripped the *Forerunner*'s, although the digest *Current Opinion* routinely summarized both sides of the debate.

Like Charlotte, Key embraced evolution and eugenics, but any likeness essentially ends there. Charlotte emphasized similarities between men and women, while Key stressed women's uniqueness and men's fundamental difference. Charlotte desired woman's emancipation as a human being, while Key sought her emancipation as a sexual being. Charlotte prioritized woman's economic independence and her public role, while Key disparaged her quest for happiness and independence in male-dominated spheres and promoted woman's right to be a mother and a lover, "regardless of church or state" (indeed, she expected the state to fully subsidize mothers of young children).

Charlotte extolled work's emancipatory powers, but Key held that woman's public work was "socially pernicious, racially wasteful, and soul-withering." Indeed, Key criticized the historic women's movement for setting up male models and male standards of success and fulfillment. Finally, Charlotte sought to liberate women from the suffocating home and to establish professional daycares, while Key (herself childless) identified motherhood as the optimal road to personal and social fulfillment and sought reforms that would support mothers within individual homes.[92]

Key apparently accepted the notion of a woman's body as a closed energy system: she believed maternal functions expended amounts of physical and psychic energy so vast that a mother's intellect was necessarily depleted. She thus concluded that women were incapable of ever attaining the public significance of men. Yet she used this conservative theory for radical ends. She endeavored in her writings to unite women's sexual and maternal identities, which were usually represented as dichotomous. She also sought to eradicate marriage, the traditional family, and all patriarchal structures suppressing women's feminine nature and maternal destiny.[93]

At first, Charlotte underestimated her opponent. She made sense of their differences by publicly identifying herself as a "Human Feminist" and Key as a "Female Feminist," merely two branches of the same stream. She regularly reviewed Key's works in the *Forerunner*, beginning with her largely favorable review of Key's *The Century of the Child*, which she proclaimed "one of the most important books of this Twentieth Century." She believed they agreed more than they disagreed, especially since both declared "the child . . . the most important personage." She did, however, criticize Key for assuming that the biological parent could supply a child's every need and for dwelling on individual motherhood rather than encouraging the practice of "social parentage."

Key's subsequent book, *Love and Marriage*, also earned Charlotte's praise for its power, its premise that "there should be no marriage without love," and its support of "free divorce." But again, Charlotte strenuously objected to Key's insistence that children be raised primarily by their biological mothers.[94]

Initially, Charlotte had been puzzled to learn that Key considered their work antithetical, "as I found myself in full agreement with so much, so very much, of her teaching," she confessed. Only after reading Key's 1913 *The Woman's Move-ment*—which sharply criticizes Charlotte's allegedly "amaternal theory"—did she fully grasp their fundamental differences. Key, she now realized, was committed to "the development of personality, of individuality" in modern women. She seemed "to miss entirely the attitude of social service" so essential to her message of reform. Even her initial praise of Key's noble work had been offset by her concern that its "great limitation" was "its exaltation of the individual at the expense of Society."

Key, in turn, scolded feminists like Charlotte for making "Individualism, and the assertion of self . . . degrading words, with a sinful significance." Key was not an unfettered individualist: she believed that every woman's freedom was limited by the rights of her potential child. But she did sanction and promote the tendency toward "individualisation" over the countervailing tendency toward the "imper-sonal" that she associated with thinkers like Charlotte.[95]

Defending her social service ethos against this mounting tide of individualism, Charlotte concluded in 1913, "If Ellen Key—with the whole world behind her—is right, then I am absolutely and utterly, foolishly and mischievously, wrong." The problem was, more people found Key to be right. One feminist recalled that even though suffragists regarded Key's views as "anathema" and Key herself as a "tremendous radical," "everybody who used to read Charlotte Perkins Gilman was now reading" Key.

Key was hailed as the author of the new "Talmud of Sexual Morality" and as the first flapper (both H. L. Mencken and Fannie Hurst connected her to that twenties icon). Key cited Nietzsche approvingly, and she dedicated *The Renais-sance of Motherhood* to sexologist Havelock Ellis, who wrote introductions to her books. Although a decade older than Charlotte, Key seemed to provide a refresh-ing antidote to the old school whose banner Charlotte still proudly waved.[96]

By the teens, the "human work" Charlotte revered, "the once-sacred assump-tion that work was the primary locus for meaningful human action," had come under challenge in a culture increasingly attracted to leisure, pleasure, and what Herbert Croly in 1909 called "the promise of American life." A backlash ensued against working women even from liberals like Walter Lippmann, who consid-ered "the presence of women in the labor market . . . an evil to be combatted by every means at our command." Lippmann endorsed Key's contention that women should channel their productive energies back into the home.[97]

Key, Ellis, Lippmann, and others served as torchbearers leading the way from a progressive emphasis on public service to the pursuit of the self and pleasure that would for many—even in the face of successful progressive measures like the en-actment of protective labor legislation—come to define the postwar era. In 1913,

Charlotte identified the "Ego-Concept" as the premier threat to "Our Human-ness," which she persisted in locating "not in us, but between us, among us." For Charlotte, Key's ascendancy proved the Old World's corrupting influence on the New, rendering this school's claims to novelty ironic.

Bidding her *Forerunner* readers a bittersweet farewell in 1916, Charlotte lashed out at Key and her disciples for "their reversion to primitive promiscuity." From her perspective, their vaunted "New Morality" resembled nothing so much as the "the old immorality."[98] Yet by 1916, this "New Morality" had begun to make her own morality—the one she had devoted every word and page of the *Forerunner* to elucidating—appear comparatively antiquated.

~

> In the world as at present arranged our normal human desires are largely unsatisfied;
> and being unsatisfied, dominate our thoughts.
> "Giving," 1911[99]

The *Forerunner* folded without ever paying its way. Charlotte blamed the maga-zine's failure on her poor business sense and her inability to drum up subscribers. She also blamed the critics, who generally failed to consider "this literary *tour de force* by an established author as worth mentioning." (Its uniqueness alone, she believed, deserved greater notice.) Finally, she blamed her own heresies: "There were some who were with me on one point and some on two, but when it came to five or more distinct heresies, to a magazine which even ridiculed Fashion, and held blazing before its readers a heaven on earth which they did not in the least want—it narrowed the subscription list."[100]

Charlotte addressed her "Real Readers" in the final issue of the *Forerunner*. She assured them she did not mind having "paid . . . for the privilege of writing it, for the satisfaction of doing more work in seven years than I should have been able in any other way. It is a satisfaction," she concluded. She thanked the paper's cordial supporters, "those from some of whom most kind and appreciative letters have formed the sufficient income from an otherwise somewhat expensive piece of work." The recognition of these "real readers," she acknowledged ruefully, had served as her most reliable form of "income" throughout the journal's run.[101]

In a final "Announcement To All My Readers and Friends," Charlotte de-clared that she was stopping production, first, because the seven years of inces-sant productivity had "relieved the pressure of what I had to say," she explained. Second, she acknowledged that "seven years is ample time to show that there are not enough people who want the magazine to support it, and it is sociologically incorrect to maintain an insufficiently desired publication." Third, she conceded that she could no longer afford to keep up the work gratis: "it is an expensive method of living."

She claimed to be neither sorry to have started the journal nor sorry to have to stop, and she thanked her loyal supporters for standing by her. "When weary or not well, when the steady task of turning out twenty-one thousand words each month for all these years seemed a little heavy," she concluded, "then I had but to read over some of my 'Letters from Subscribers,' and go on with renewed vigor, with grateful joy."[102]

To those who regretted her wasting seven years on this specialized forum when she could have presented her vital message "through the medium of established publications," she countered that "[t]he larger the subscription list, the more 'average' [a magazine] becomes. The average reader does not care for the sort of stuff carried in The Forerunner. Neither does the big advertiser approve of such far-reaching social iconoclasm," she observed caustically. She also acknowledged that the way she pitched her reform message may have limited her readership: she conceded that she may have been "too specific for the 'average reader' and not specific enough for the reform devotee . . . ," leaving everyone, including herself, dissatisfied with the outcome.[103]

Charlotte received scores of letters mourning the *Forerunner*'s demise. Half a world away, Australians lamented "The End of a Great Paper" but predicted its editor would keep "marching on." Initially, Charlotte planned to spin off several books—including a volume of short stories and collections of essays—from her *Forerunner* publications; she also hoped to see a library edition of the *Forerunner* itself.[104] But she would publish only one more book in her lifetime, and that an original work. Even her autobiography postdated her.

In the penultimate issue of the *Forerunner*, Charlotte reflected, "suffering remains to most of us, and is to be borne by looking outside of and beyond it." What suffering remained to her she attributed not to her usual culprit, the insistent ego, but to the social consciousness she had elsewhere credited as the source of human happiness. In order to explain her own lingering pain, that is, she determined that "[p]eople with the most social consciousness suffered most, as long as social processes were not healthy"; therefore, social conditions had to improve before someone like herself could experience lasting joy.[105]

But what if social conditions did not improve? What if things seemed instead to be falling apart all around her? During her last two decades, Charlotte increasingly responded to suffering by indulging a longing to get—literally—"outside of and beyond it." Where transcendence no longer worked, in other words, flight might.

12   "Begin Again"
(1916–1922)

> Begin again. The law is clear . . .
> Each new day blossoms from the bier
> Of night forgotten. Have no fear—
>   Let us, who are the world, be bold,
>   Take hope once more, take heart, take hold
> Rise now with the risen year—
>   Begin again.
>
>   "Begin Again," 1913[1]

During her remaining years as a New Yorker, Charlotte prided herself on her ability to resist the currents that seemed to be sweeping up her more willing neighbors. She obstinately positioned herself as the leader of the "monogamous" school of feminism in an era and a city where bohemianism, free love, and the Freudian frenzy led one magazine to declare it "Sex O'Clock in America." And she continued to associate the "beast in man" with devolution at a time when primitivism was all the rage. Her former adversary Harry Thurston Peck may have credited her with mothering the "New Women" and the "Bachelor Girls," but many members of this cohort considered their foremother decidedly straitlaced.[2]

Charlotte knew how members of her generation were viewed, and she resented it. "There is a splendid stir and push among our youth, what is called a 'revolt,' against pretty much everything that was before good, excellent, necessary," she wrote; "but what have they to propose instead? So far there has not been put forth by all this revolted youth any social improvement that I have heard of."[3] During these years, she increasingly positioned herself as a truth-teller amid naysayers.

During the teens, many progressives found cause to hope "that the age of sheer individualism is past and the age of social responsibility has arrived." By 1920, however, the reverse seemed truer. When even the nation's president sought "not nostrums, but normalcy," it could only spell "a bad day for idealists," as one reformer acknowledged. Similarly, Jane Addams noticed a kind of "political and social sag" in the wake of the First World War and the defeat of various progressive measures.[4]

The postwar period has borne various monikers—among them, the Roaring Twenties; the Era of Fords, Flappers, and Fanatics; the Era of Alcohol and Al Capone; the Decade of the Dollar; the Period of the Psyche; and the Time of Tremendous Trifles—any one of which seemed designed to make Charlotte cringe. By war's end, the country had begun its "marked retreat from politics and public values toward the private and personal sphere," thus reversing Charlotte's desired trajectory.[5]

"The most genuine comfort I know, for the folks who are not doing all, or as they wanted to," Charlotte counseled Grace Channing's discouraged brother, "is what I call *The Chessman Attitude.* That is to place ones interest in The Game, and if it is going well, one doesn't mind so much what one is on—or even if off the table!" The engrossing process of playing "The Game" of living, in other words, should always take precedence over any setbacks. She offered similar advice to the activists whose causes she supported but whose antagonism irritated her. In a frequently reprinted poem, she reminded her fellow socialists and suffragists:

"Your work is all the same:
  Work together or work apart,
  Work, each of you, with all your heart—
Just get into the game![6]

Charlotte, however, not only often frowned on others' ideas of fun but also switched sides in the games she still wanted to "get into": she joined social clubs only to leave them in disgust; helped to organize the peace movement and yet eventually supported America's involvement in the war; celebrated the suffrage victory but lamented its aftermath; wrote a daily newspaper column despite her antipathy for the press; and continued to preach eugenicist doctrines while allowing "[t]he best and most valuable people on earth have almost always been 'unfit.' . . ."[7]

Criticized for her predictability in the past, she became unpredictable in unsettling ways. Her unwavering convictions wavered or at least narrowed. She continued to discount the "I" but no longer felt as inclined to celebrate the "We." Progress no longer seemed inevitable, the human race no longer seemed unifiable, service meant something far less global than it had when she first launched her career as a public servant.

Charlotte's faith in evolution had persuaded her that time brings complexity. As we age, both as a race and as individuals, we become "more complex—and we must continue to become so." Her commitment to teleology convinced her that each passing year brought us closer to a "larger living." She admitted that age did not guarantee wisdom and that there could be "no fool like an old fool," but she had never counted herself among the foolish.[8] Yet by all measures, including her own original yardstick, her concept of living had shrunk over time. Living may still have been a verb, but her notion of doing contracted, and her agenda became less bold. No longer convinced she could change the world, she changed herself, retreating along with the nation from the promise of collective action into more personal preoccupations.

~

> Here is planned a New Life. Emergence, Achievement, Triumph. All that I have meant to do, done, and more. It means Joy, Peace, Health, and wide helpfulness to others. It would fairly guarantee the accomplishment of further work.
> "Thoughts & Figgerings," 1920[9]

Charlotte reflected on her accomplishments a few weeks after turning fifty-seven. She figured that she had already "paid [her] board" by writing the equivalent of "thirty books worth keeping."[10] She was not yet ready to rest on her laurels, however, nor could she. Without her own journal, she no longer had a guaranteed forum for her work. In 1917, she published just one article in a popular magazine; in 1918 she published two, only one in a journal of wide circulation. She deserved a break after the tremendous outpouring of the *Forerunner* years, but she was not necessarily seeking one. Although her opportunities increased by 1919, Charlotte could never again rely on magazine writing as a regular source of income.

Before the last issue of the *Forerunner* appeared, Charlotte had set off on the lecture circuit, and she routinely made such trips during her remaining years on the East Coast. She had raised her fee to $100 per lecture, but she often waived or reduced it for the good of a cause. In addition to single engagements, she also devised a series of "Gilman weeks"—six consecutive lectures on a theme, available to any interested locale. She believed these weeks "tremendously effective" and promoted them as the "best work I've ever done."[11]

Still, her lecture opportunities had dwindled by the late teens, and she blamed World War I for the fall-off. She offered several lecture series on the war and considered the few bookings she did get "better than nothing." She claimed that all the attention to "war work and war cost" had reduced her income from lecturing by as much as 80 percent and had "practically obliterated" her finances.

Charlotte tried to make the most of the fraction of lectures still coming her way. She continued to devise new topics, often ripped from the headlines. She shrewdly marketed herself in an attempt to demonstrate that her topics and person fit within the mainstream of American thought and values. She had based her refusal to grant interviews on a desire to be judged entirely on her work, yet in promotional materials she sought to filter her message through others' positive remarks on her appearance and demeanor. Asked to assemble some publicity materials for a 1920 lecture in Syracuse, for instance, she produced a string of blurbs playing up her physical charms and grace (the word "gentle" appears in nearly all excerpts) and playing down her reputation as a "radical heaven stormer." She quoted glowing reviews that noted her "engaging smile and general charm of manner," her "perfectly delightful" gestures, and her ability to be at once "gentle, persuasive, feminine" *and* "lucid and logical." Even the review that made the most of her international fame made almost as much of her unthreatening appearance: "Personally she is just a little grey woman, with a voice like laughing music, and a smile which included all humanity," it read.[12] The bigger the "smile" and the smaller her person, the less threatening she might appear to potential audiences.

The *New York Times* rarely raved, but the *New York Evening Mail* deemed Charlotte "the ablest woman in the United States," and the *New York Tribune* listed her among the four living women it considered "'born for the universe' who have fulfilled their callings" (Jane Addams, M. Carey Thomas, and Edith Wharton rounded out the list). Such tributes, however, came at greater intervals after the war.

Charlotte recognized her waning appeal to popular tastes. She counted among her failures from this era her work for "one of the smaller Chautauquas," a kind of public university conducted via lectures in rural areas. For six weeks, she traveled through small towns "in rather backward regions," attempting to interest her listeners in the world according to Gilman. By her own reckoning, she failed to win over her audience of fidgeting children, enamored couples, tired housewives, and glum farmers and miners, especially when compared to the "Revue" ("a group of girls who danced and sang and otherwise pleased the audience") accompanying the tour. Even Charlotte liked these girls better than she thought she would. The performers appeared equally fond of the woman they called "Good Old Scout," a nickname that expresses the younger generation's perception of Charlotte as aged, nonthreatening, and perhaps slightly ridiculous.[13]

In 1919, Charlotte jumped at the chance to write a daily column for the *New York Tribune* syndicate. For over a year, she churned out a series of at times biting critiques mixed with "pleasant platitudes" she hoped would please syndicate readers. The money appealed to her most: for the first and only time in her life, she received a regular "pay-envelope." When her employer worried that she would not be able to "keep it up," she cited the *Forerunner* as evidence of her stamina. As it turned out, her readers tired first. Charlotte regretted the failed experiment: "alas!" she reflected in *The Living*, "though I tried my best to reach and hold the popular taste, I couldn't do it."[14]

"There are fewer people every year who care anything about what used to be perhaps the greatest name in America (outside of politics!): Beecher," a reporter

Charlotte writing at her desk, ca. 1919. Courtesy of the Schlesinger Library, Radcliffe Institute for Advanced Study, Harvard University.

observed in 1920. A few of Charlotte's loyal friends sought to reverse this trend by publishing tributes to "The Woman Who Saw It First" as well as to her Beecher-inspired tenets of altruism and service. No demonstrable renaissance ensued, however.[15]

Charlotte faced her fading popularity squarely. In 1920, she vowed to "'cease to repine,' pitch in, [and] do at once the work that will set me going at best pitch." She aspired by the time she turned sixty-five to "have a solid permanent spreading reputation" and to make at least $25,000 a year, with "enough saved to buy and build in California." The problem could not lie in her message, which, after all, was "so Splendid, so Satisfying, so Simple, so directly leading to all right action." So she blamed her delivery: "I am a dog not to get it across!!"[16]

Relatively infrequent if flattering solicitations still came her way from magazine editors, but more often Charlotte had to drum up work. She told one editor she was tired of being asked to submit something only to have it returned. And she was equally tired of making far less than her other "writing friends, women really less known" because she worked "too cheaply. They get two and three hundred dollars for an article, have done so for years. One editorial friend cheerfully put it—'You can't sell yourself, that's all.'" Throughout her professional life, Charlotte often regretted having more ideas than cents.[17]

In 1920, Charlotte used a check for some Providence property to finally reimburse Houghton for his outstanding, *Forerunner*-related expenses. She and Grace had recently returned to collaborating on plays, a pursuit Charlotte had never fully abandoned. During the *Forerunner* years, she had written two one-act plays and continued to revise a drama entitled *Balsam Fir*.[18]

Figuring optimistically, Charlotte calculated that the two plays she and Grace were planning might net her $50,000 total; she expected to triple that figure if they got made into movies. She also hoped to write five separate film scenarios, which she speculated could bring in as much as $250,000 total. She considered motion pictures the wave of the future, and she wrote one agency that she had a "number of scenarios in mind." Weekly film attendance had doubled, reaching close to 115 million by the end of the twenties.[19] The studios and movie stars were making millions—why not her? But it would be a younger and more consciously literary generation of writers, including F. Scott Fitzgerald and William Faulkner, who would find work as Hollywood screenwriters.

Concerning her own literary career, the signals were mixed. In 1919, both "The Yellow Wall-Paper" and "Similar Cases" were reprinted. The former was solicited by the octogenarian Howells for a 1920 collection of *Great Modern American Stories*; the latter appeared verbatim in the pages of the *New York Times* under a new title and author. Charlotte immediately responded to the plagiarism and demanded an apology from the paper, only to resent the apology's condescending praise of her poem and gentle handling of the plagiarizer.[20] These virtually simultaneous reprintings might be seen as canceling each other out: Charlotte's inclusion among "great" story writers confers canonical status, while the plagiarism suggests her relative obscurity, at least as a poet, since the plagiarist likely assumed he could safely get away with appropriating her once-famous words as his own.

Sales of all of Charlotte's books had fallen off considerably. In 1920, she purchased her dusty inventory from Small, Maynard. She still dreamed of assembling a uniform edition of her collected works, hoping to add a volume each of short stories, articles and essays, allegories, epigrams, and plays, "making a set of twenty-five."

In the 1890s, poetry had started her on her career, and now, in the 1920s, she hoped it would jumpstart it. She planned a second volume of her uncollected poems to be called "Here Also." She also returned to the illustrated volume of "child verse" based on the "Mer-Songs" poems she had composed when Katharine was young. Finally, she envisioned a "book of serious verse, in varied forms, bringing out as has never yet been attempted the historic drama we call 'the woman question,'" by which she meant neither simply suffrage nor that "oscillating confusion we miscall feminism." She completed none of these projects in her lifetime, however. Indeed, only one of them (the collected volume of her verse) ever saw print, and that not until 1996.[21]

In 1922, Charlotte seized the chance to debate Alexander Black in the *Century* over whether women dressed to please men, an issue the two friends had amicably disagreed about in private conversation. Charlotte took the affirmative, recapitulating the argument of her 1915 *Forerunner* serial *The Dress of Women*. Men's clothing was primarily useful, she maintained, whereas women's attire only enhanced sex attraction and sex distinction and (echoing Thorstein Veblen) displayed male "purchasing power." Covering the debate, the *Times* warned any male readers tempted to hash the issue out at home to do so while "protected by a large solid table. . . ."[22]

A proponent of dress reform, Charlotte routinely designed her own clothes and owned several outfits she wore repeatedly until they wore out. She considered herself an astute critic of fashion and was proud of her designs. Their "cheapness" annoyed her friend Grace, however, who felt that Charlotte's refusal to dress better had hurt her career as a public speaker and "lessened her influence."

One of Charlotte's self-designed costumes did cause a stir with her lecture audiences, but for reasons Grace could not have anticipated: "Behold this aged

amazon, stark and grim, covered from neck to wrist and ankle," Charlotte recalled. "Allow also for six layers of covering, the lace, the silk, the 'slip,' and so on
inward. Yet I was told confidentially, for my good, that people had criticized the
costume as indelicate!" (The outline of her bust could be detected, considered
unbecoming in a woman of her advanced years). Charlotte noted the irony of this
prim costume indicting her at a moment when hemlines were rising and necklines
plunging. Given "the 'outlines' now freely shown on our streets and in our parlors,
to say nothing of the limitless exhibition elsewhere," she found it hard to believe
her multilayered costume offended.[23] Indeed, the danger for Charlotte these days
lay in being considered not outré, but passé.

~

> It seems as if, when people say—"The World" they mean their own people. . . .
> *"With Her in Ourland,"* 1916[24]

Charlotte's position on the war in Europe changed along with the nation's. She
initially opposed the war and, indeed, opposed wars in general. She once told
Lester Ward, "I think we overestimate the value of war—that civilization has progressed in spite of it—not because of it. . . ." She authored one of the bibles of the
peace movement, *The Man-Made World.* She also served as a charter member of
the Women's Peace Party (WPP). In a 1915 speech, she maintained that the WPP
wanted "not only to hasten the end of the present war, but to alter humanity so
that there can be no more war on earth."[25]

Throughout the early teens, Charlotte maintained that war epitomized the
"unbridled masculinity" of *The Man-Made World* at its "absurdest extremes."
Peace, by contrast, epitomized the "Human World" she had devoted her career to
realizing. Her faith in both interconnectedness and evolution led her to fear war's
detrimental effects on her dream of "A World Beginning."[26]

At the outset of the Great War, Charlotte participated in forums "Opposed
to Militarism." She also helped to plan an August 1914 "Woman's Peace Parade."
Lillian Wald recalled the event: "Twelve hundred women, sisters in protest against
the horrors of war, walked . . . in Fifth Avenue between walls of silent spectators to
the beat of muffled drums." The marchers wore mourning; Charlotte admitted in
response to a mocking *Times* editorial that "[o]ne black-robed procession" would
not stop the "Pan-European" war, but it might, if repeated, awaken women to
feelings of solidarity that could have worldwide repercussions.[27]

Throughout 1915, Charlotte frequently lectured on peace before "enthusiastic"
crowds. Her prominence in the movement led Henry Ford to invite her to sail on

the *Oscar II*—a ship he had hired to convey pacifists to Europe with the goal of getting soldiers "[o]ut of the trenches by Christmas, never to go back."[28]

The expedition was lampooned by the press, which may explain why Jane Addams, who had signed on to sail before the uproar, "took to her bed" aboard ship. Charlotte defended the mission and expressed "real regret" that prior engagements prevented her from sailing with the delegates. She decried the press treatment of the expedition and predicted that "this courageous effort to bring about peace will go down in history as a white page in a rather dark chapter of national inertia."[29]

As late as 1916, Charlotte remained "a pacifist, of settled conviction." In a September *Forerunner* column she defended the peace movement from its detractors. And in November, she rehearsed her opposition to war's aggressive "masculism" at a "Get Together Meeting" of pacifists in Union Park.[30] She believed America had a part to play in the war in Europe, but only as a mediator: our role was not "to make war" but to "make peace."

Her final 1916 *Forerunner* treatise, *Growth and Combat*, declared war "a peculiar social disease," peculiar because we were supposed to have cured ourselves of it long ago. "In our intricate, mutually dependent modern life," she argued, "when every force of civilization is tending to knit us into ever closer relation, a war is like an earthquake in an art museum. It is an anachronism, an absurdity, a walking nightmare."[31] Belligerence was a primitive throwback; growth, not combat, represented the essence of modern life.

But Charlotte was a pacifist, not a passivist, and she found the passivity of her fellow peace activists exasperating. Moreover, like many Americans, she grew to hate the Kaiser and to detest all things German. Anti-German prejudice crescendoed during the war years: "In the month before the United States entered the war," one historian attests, "tales poured into the War and Justice Departments, often from highly responsible people, about secret organizations which were planning an earthquake of explosions under the direction of the German General Staff once hostilities commenced. Army commanders, especially in the Middle West, braced themselves to suppress insurrections that never materialized." Americans of German descent were suspected of hiding glass in bandages and in food delivered to soldiers, of poisoning wells and spreading the flu, of starting false rumors and of spying. The German language was dropped from school curriculums, sauerkraut was renamed "liberty cabbage," and "many towns, firms, and individuals with German names changed them."[32]

Now eager to "swat the Hun" herself, Charlotte declared Germany "a very Frankenstein among the nations." She considered it an "ultra-masculine culture" that needed to be checked, with violence if necessary. War might cause regression in the short term, but it would ultimately advance civilization, she now surmised, if it could crush a primitive nation-state like Germany. This belief helped persuade her to embrace the necessity of war in 1917.

Charlotte considered Germany a social experiment with "hideous results." The Germans had too hastily transformed the national character in the space of two decades, doing their work too rapidly and doing it "by force, neglecting to study the lines of natural growth." Proud of their transformation, Germans had become haughty and superior, provoking enmity in their neighbors, which the now "insane nation" had fostered into "delusions of prosecution."[33]

Immediately after the United States entered the war, Charlotte created a new lecture series organized around the idea of "Deuchtum" as a "moral disease." Punning on the name, she compared Germany to a deadly germ. Over the course of six lectures, she argued that "the German nation has auto-inoculated itself with its own 'kultur'; developing a virus of terrible intensity, with which it has originated a new crime—the conscious infection of other nations." She accused the country of seeking to "interpenetrate" friendly, free, and peace-loving Christian nations and of "Germanizing them." The world needed to be vaccinated against this virus immediately. If this meant destroying the German people, then so much the better. "Evolution is bigger than a dozen Germanys," she told Grace's brother Harold. "They will become extinct like the Saurians [dinosaurs, i.e.] of old."[34]

With other converts, Charlotte believed President Wilson when he argued that America must enter the war both to "make the world safe for democracy" and to have a say in the peace. In 1917, she explained her decision to disassociate herself from the peace movement: "While still profoundly interested in the establishment and maintenance of Peace," she observed, "my judgment is that the immediate steps toward it require a successful prosecution of the war we have undertaken. . . ."[35]

Suffragists counted among those who "went with a great surge into the arms of the government" during wartime. Their motives were numerous, but many may have hoped that their wartime contributions would lead a grateful government to grant women the vote. Reformers of all stripes considered the war an ideal means, in John Dewey's words, of bucking "the individualistic tradition" and of prioritizing "the supremacy of public need over private possessions."

Ideally, wartime rationing and patriotic zeal would elicit the public-mindedness and self-denial members of the reform community valued. Charlotte shared these values, which may help to explain her facility at finding the good among war's ills. She doubtless felt encouraged by the mobilization process, which another of her contemporaries described as "a story of the conversion of a hundred million combatively individualistic people into a vast cooperative effort in which the good of the unit was sacrificed to the good of the whole. . . ."[36]

Charlotte may have complained of the war costing her work, but she would have lost even more had she not adopted the majority position in a country overwhelmingly supportive of U.S. involvement. The ensuing crackdown on dissent may also help to explain the haste with which activists like Charlotte embraced the government's position. Reformers who had hitherto been viewed as virtuous and respectable were recast as radicals and traitors for challenging conventional wisdom, doubting authority, and proposing new ideas. Congress swiftly passed a series of laws outlawing espionage, sedition, and anarchy, designed to catch anyone expressing disloyalty to the flag, the government, or the armed services. The first amendment notwithstanding, any person who spoke or wrote against the war or the draft now faced arrest.

Fueled by fears of an American version of the recent Bolshevik Revolution, these new laws enabled the Attorney General A. Mitchell Palmer—assisted by the up-and-comer J. Edgar Hoover—to investigate and harass suspected communists and socialists. During the Red Scare, which peaked the winter of 1919–20 and peaked again between 1924 and 1928, more than 1,500 people in the States were fined and arrested, including the Socialist Party presidential candidate Eugene Debs. Some 250 were deported to Russia, among them the anarchists and lovers Emma Goldman and Alexander Berkman. Dissenters and suspected radicals caught up in the dragnet were sent to Ellis Island on the "Red Special," and many were forced to take passage from there for the Soviet Union aboard the *Buford*, nicknamed the "Soviet Ark."[37]

The reformer Frederic Howe, husband of the suffragist Marie Jenney Howe, recalled the effects of the Scare:

> Few people know of the state of terror that prevailed during those years, few would believe the extent to which private hates and prejudices were permitted to usurp government powers. It was quite apparent that the alleged offenses for which people were being persecuted were not the real offenses. . . . [A]ll felt a sentence suspended over their enthusiasms, their beliefs, their innermost thoughts. They had stood for variety, for individuality, for freedom. They discovered a political state that seemed to hate these things; it wanted a servile society, a society that accepted authority . . . without protest.[38]

Howe served as the commissioner of immigration for the Port of New York during the "Great Unrest." With other progressive New Yorkers, he felt especially aggrieved by the repressions in his own city. The mayor divided his constituents into "Americans" and "traitors," and he designated a Committee on National Defense (whose spin-off, the Committee on Women's Defense Work, was chaired by the inveterate suffragist Anna Howard Shaw) to administer loyalty oaths to all city workers, including teachers. The city's Socialist Party periodicals were destroyed and the party's officials rounded up and arrested.[39]

In 1918, the editors of the New York-based socialist magazine the *Masses* were tried and eventually imprisoned for violating the Espionage Act. Although duly elected, the five socialist members of the state legislature were swiftly expelled. This same state legislature produced a four-volume, 10,000-page tome known as the Lusk Report, which one contemporary called "an ammunition dump for persons attacking liberals." The editor of the *New York Evening Post*, the pacifist Oswald Garrison Villard, was even asked to resign his position as president of the Philharmonic Society because "pacifism and music would not mix in wartime."[40]

As a former pacifist and a confessed socialist, Charlotte had cause to be nervous. The Federal Bureau of Investigation kept a file on her in the early 1920s, based primarily on her association with the Intercollegiate Socialist Society. FBI agents identified the society as part of "the Youth Movement in America," which, they claimed, aspired "to undermine and sink, or overthrow, the Government of the United States, and to set up in this country a soviet form of government, such as Russia now boasts." They named Charlotte among those "persons of eminence" who "lent themselves to the occasion" and as "a Socialist and the author of several Communistic songs as well as a lot of socialistic articles and books." The FBI noted her activities twice more but apparently ended its surveillance there.[41]

In truth, Charlotte distrusted communism: she "never joined the party," one contemporary asserted, "wholly disagreeing with their political methods and the Marxian theories of 'class struggle' and 'economic determinism.'" The *Times* might brand her a proselytizer of "the extremist kind of socialism," but in the new century, Charlotte's socialism came closer to lukewarm (or, in the parlance of the day, yellow) than red hot. She supported socialism but not "the action of the Socialist Party—so far," she told a friend soon after the century turned. She consistently favored a peaceful, gradual, and organic definition of social change and therefore remained an evolutionary socialist even in more revolutionary days.[42]

Charlotte's socialist fervor came in waves, peaking in the early 1890s at the outset of her professional career and again in the first decade of the twentieth century, when she vowed she would devote her remaining time to "help establish socialism." In the early 1900s, she routinely offered talks supporting socialism, including one at Upton Sinclair's experimental cooperative community in New Jersey. She also advocated socialist causes, such as better housing for the poor. Toward the end of the decade, she recorded an explicitly socialist resolution in her diary: "The most urgent measure for the Welfare of the human race is the arousing of class consciousness in the working class!"[43]

But this impassioned rhetoric proved the exception to her cooler rule. In the teens, she continued to support local labor strikes and encouraged Houghton to resign from his regiment because it "was used to put down strikes!" She wrote poems supporting labor, spoke at socialist Woman's Days, and argued for the construction of model tenements. Pointedly distinguishing between "legitimate poverty and illegitimate poverty," she nonetheless identified poverty as a "social product" rather than an individual problem.[44]

Many socialists opposed suffrage and put workers' rights before women's rights, but Charlotte was prominent among those who pointed out how many of those workers were women. Through her efforts to encourage and enable women to become self-sufficient, she endeavored to reconcile feminism and socialism at a time when the two movements were often pitted against each other.

Charlotte never disavowed socialism during the Red Scare even while some of her fellow travelers backpedaled. But nor did she go so far as Harriot Stanton Blatch and Alice Stone Blackwell, both of whom stepped up their involvement in the Socialist Party in 1920. Believing socialism had simply been misconstrued, Charlotte endeavored to correct prevalent distortions. She gently chided "[t]hose who fear the violence, the hatred, the sudden demands of the popularly misunderstood versions of Socialism."[45]

She took some risks: for instance, she signed her name at the height of wartime paranoia to a letter protesting the imprisonment of Eugene Debs (a man she claimed to hold in low esteem); Debs was running for president from his jail cell despite sedition charges. She also wrote a personal letter appealing the 1918 conviction of the socialist agitator Rose Pastor Stokes, whose ten-year sentence for violating the Espionage Act—for giving a speech defending the "people" against the "profiteers"—Charlotte considered unjustly extreme.[46]

Stokes was Jewish, and Charlotte denounced Judaism as a misogynistic, ultra-masculine, and illogical "tribal religion." German Jews in particular struck her as an "atrocious combination." But she knew Rose personally from a number of causes and clubs, including the Intercollegiate Socialist Society. Rose and her then-husband, the radical millionaire James Graham Phelps Stokes, had left the Socialist Party with the outbreak of war, but Rose rejoined after the Bolshevik Revolution.[47]

By contrast, Charlotte detested "the Jewish-Russian nightmare, Bolshevism" for eclipsing socialism in the public mind. She especially resented this eclipse because she saw Bolshevism as a setback and a "defilement" of socialist aims. Her

position on the "Russian Experiment" in its early days was more equivocal, however. The Bolsheviks' attempt at popular government may be failing, she opined in
1919, enough so that she felt it might teach the rest of the world "what not to do"
in pursuing change. But she still believed in the necessity of the changes sought.
The revolution, she argued, had shown "the world two things: That if existing
society does not do justice to the wage earners they will show that, in numbers at
least, they are society. And that when it comes to administration of the necessary
affairs of national existence, the mere fact that a man is poor and ignorant does
not guarantee him either intelligence or any other virtue."[48]

Charlotte's decision in her autobiography to tint her radicalism in hues other
than red should be understood within the context of slander and suppression that
defined the mid-twenties, the period during which she produced the first draft of
The Living. Tapping into Bolshevik hysteria, various conservative and patriotic
groups denounced activists in the peace, woman's, and temperance movements
and censured organizations such as the Young Women's Christian Association, the
League of Women Voters, and the American Association of University Women.

The government's Chemical Warfare Department generated one particularly
pernicious document in this smear campaign: in 1923, the department compiled
a "spider-web chart" identifying fifteen suspicious organizations and indicting
twenty-nine radicals, including Jane Addams, Florence Kelley, Inez Haynes Irwin,
and Zona Gale. The chart circulated fairly widely, thanks largely to the efforts of
Henry Ford, a former peace advocate turned reactionary. Ford published it in his
Dearborn Independent; it also appeared in the National Association Opposed to
Woman Suffrage's *Woman Patriot.* "One Spider-Web spawned another (perhaps
many others)," the historian Nancy Cott has observed. Charlotte's name eventually appeared on at least one of these spin-offs, widely circulated, and as widely
protested, in 1928.[49]

A central irony of Charlotte's career after the Great War is that conservatives
denounced her as a radical at a time when she was moving toward conservative
positions, especially concerning immigration. In her anti-immigrant diatribes,
Charlotte tapped into the spirit of "the tribal twenties." During this period, a
fresh wave of postwar immigration coincided with a postwar recession, provoking
nativists to brand immigrants "invaders" and to insist on "quality" over quantity.
Newspapers accentuated, in fear-mongering commentary, the perceived effect
of this influx of immigrants on the country's growing unemployment rate. For
many, the immigrant came to seem "a phobic embodiment of all imagined threats
to elite superiority, from cultural mongrelization and racial dilution to political
anarchism and class war."[50]

Charlotte still devoted most of her time to critiquing women's subjugation and promoting their advancement. But during the postwar period, she also jumped on the nativist bandwagon. She decried the prospect of the "greatest, wealthiest and most powerful nation in the world, overthrown by foreigners, trampled to the dust." Lecturing on the West Coast, where anti-Asian sentiment was particularly intense, she warned 5,000 Pasadena residents in 1922 that, unless significant restrictions were placed on immigration immediately, "this great nation would awake some day and find the government in the hands of foreigners." She claimed that recent immigrants had come to the States not to pursue the beautiful ideals of democracy and independence but instead to obtain the kind of freedom associated with "a free lunch." The idea of "stir[ring] all of the nations together"—the kind of unifying image that in her younger days would have inspired Charlotte to idealistic dreams of world service—now turned her stomach. She compared such unions to breeding mutts: "No fine thoroughbred dogs are made in this manner."[51]

Charlotte's take on immigration bears the stamp of her sociologist friend E. A. Ross, who viewed the country as suffering "for the benefit of pent-up millions in the backward lands" and who concluded that "the blood now being injected into the veins of our people is 'sub-common.'" Echoing Ross, Charlotte acknowledged that the country may have been founded by immigrants, but she maintained that it now faced "sheer importation" as a "flood of low-grade humanity" invaded its shores. The United States had been too hospitable in the past, she declared. It now needed to practice a little nation-saving rudeness to rid itself of these unwelcome guests and to avoid the deleterious influence of these "backward" cultures on its own superior one. If these new immigrants wanted equality, they should seek it in their own lands, not in ours. Charlotte, who had formerly celebrated American diversity, now held with Ross and other xenophobes, including Grace Channing Stetson, that only "a few closely connected races" (Anglos, Saxons, Teutons, Scandinavians, Celts, and Gaels) made up "the American blend."[52]

Charlotte's friends lamented her shifting views, especially her seemingly abrupt reversal on pacifism and world unity. The playwright George Middleton and his wife, the activist (and daughter of the politician Robert La Follette) Fola La Follette, regretted that Charlotte showed "little tolerance for those who opposed our entrance into" the war. The author Zona Gale struggled to comprehend what seemed an "utter contradiction of thought" when Charlotte now insisted, "Race and color make all the difference in the world." She had thus apparently abandoned her longstanding faith in "the unity of man and the need for human growth." Gale wondered how the foremost preacher of this unifying doctrine could now accept and promote division among the world's peoples. As late as 1921, Charlotte could still maintain, "There is no subject which appeals to me at present so much as this obvious and pressing matter of world union." Yet, as Gale noted, her rhetoric during the postwar period seemed designed to foster disunity.[53]

Unable to reconcile the world war with her beliefs in unity and progress, Charlotte changed her beliefs. In the process, she reduced history to recurrent cycles of violence and regeneration. Even before she switched sides on the war, she insisted that it provided "glaring" proof "that what we thought was civilization *won't do*. . . . We have simply got to revise our notions of life and begin again."

Once she accepted this "world conflagration" as inevitable, she predicted that it would produce "a crippled world, a starved and diseased world, a world in ruins." But she also conjectured that a new world would emerge phoenix-like from the ashes, with new houses, clothes, tools, machines, jobs, ideas, and, most important, "new people." She believed "The War to End All Wars" would operate like Noah's flood to wipe the dirty world clean. "The most glorious and hopeful era ever known is before us," she wrote, basing her prediction no longer on the laws of evolution but on the concept of cataclysmic change.[54]

The First World War thus accelerated Charlotte's ideological shift from an idealist position, in which she held that "above all races is humanity," to a more jaded, partisan nationalism in keeping with her emergent belief in "the deep, wide, lasting vital difference between races." Acknowledging the change, she explained that her "general love of humanity remain[ed], with the continuing desire to help it onward." But she credited personal experience, urban living, sociology, and the war with teaching her "the need of varying treatment according to race and nation."

Charlotte considered the shift in her thinking abrupt: "I was forced to see that the 'next steps' in social progress in England, America, or France, were not those most needed in Uganda and Tibet." Yet the record indicates its gradual nature. She blamed her New York years in particular for casting the shadow of "race-prejudice or preference" over her formerly "large, undiscriminating love of Humanity." But evidence from Providence, the Bay Area, and points in between suggests that this shadow had been cast long ago and had merely grown more pronounced during her two-plus decades in the city.[55]

In the war's aftermath, Charlotte finally disavowed even the abstract ideal of the human race as an overarching entity uniting individual races, although "she tolerantly allow[ed]" her followers to retain "their present faith in her own former conviction." After the war, many disheartened public intellectuals likewise relinquished the faith in progress and a brighter future that had served as the dominant ethos of the previous decades. Charlotte's skepticism, however, emerged less because she doubted the universal "laws" of progress than because she doubted whether certain ethnic groups would ever contribute to national reform.[56]

After the Allies' victory, Charlotte joined Carrie Chapman Catt and others who worked diligently "to build support for the League of Nations and further the interests of democratic women." President Wilson's project met strong opposition in the States, however, not only from powerful senatorial foes like Henry Cabot Lodge but from pacifists who feared its defense provisions presaged yet another or multiple wars. When Congress rejected the treaty, Charlotte could scarcely contain her outrage. She mocked the United States for playing the "Piker"—that is, for refusing, despite the support of forty-three other countries, to think of the "common need," forgo greed, and join the League. She deplored the fact that this refusal placed the States in what she took to be the unattractive company of the defeated, despised Axis powers along with the despicable sole other hold-out, Honduras.[57] Charlotte wove her prejudicial assumptions about Central Americans into a whip to castigate her fellow citizens.

Given her shifting beliefs, Charlotte's despair over the defeat of Wilson's plan stemmed less from an abiding faith in the ideal of world unity than from her conviction about the "special place and power" of the United States among nations. Having long cast her notions of progress in an American mold, she believed she was finally witnessing her icon's self-destructive demolition and, with it, the remnants of her beleaguered faith in American exceptionalism. The defeat of the League put the seal on her disillusionment. She subsequently anticipated "the rapidly descending extinction of our nation, superseded by other nations who will soon completely outnumber us. This, with the majority rule of a democracy, means that our grandchildren will belong to a minority of dwindling Americans, ruled over by a majority of conglomerate races quite dissimilar."

Charlotte absolves herself of any responsibility for this dystopian outcome in the penultimate chapter of *The Living*. She again paraphrases E. A Ross, who proffers two similar warnings in his 1914 anti-immigration diatribe *The Old World in the New*: first, "'[t]he Roman world was laughing when it died'" and second, "[a] people that has no more respect for its ancestors and no more pride of race than this deserves the extinction that surely awaits it." Charlotte likewise observes that other nations had risen and fallen over the course of history and adds, "we should perhaps contentedly admit our failure and welcome our superseders. Perhaps they will do better than we."[58] The elitism evinced at the beginning of her autobiography—where she traces her genealogy back to American and British royalty—is as evident at its close, where her pronoun "we" positions herself and her readers in opposition to an imagined, superseding "them."

Charlotte's despair over the League and the nation should not, however, be construed as simply the shallow and reactionary judgment of an increasingly shallow and reactionary thinker. More was at stake than her prejudices. Most historians consider 1920 the end of the progressive era, although progressive ideas lingered on. Indeed, Robin Muncy has convincingly shown that members of a middle-class female reform community continued to work for policy change throughout the 1920s, even as many of their compatriots accelerated their pursuit of pleasure. The rejection of the Treaty of Versailles and America's refusal to participate in the League of Nations, historians have argued, signified a rejection of progressive politics and particularly its "demand for sacrifice and self-control and altruism."

Wilson's dream of an international alliance represented the last gasps of this ethos; its defeat signaled the displacement of progressivism by individualism, the ideal of "civic participation" by "widespread apathy," and "the call for sacrifice" by "hedonism."[59] If Charlotte grew bitter after the war, it was largely because she believed she was witnessing the devastating collapse not just of the known world but also of her long-cherished, service-oriented ethos.

~

> Hard to say what "achievement" I can boast. . . . A promiscuous social philosopher—a general Energizer and spreader of thought, a jack-of-all trade in verse prose and oratory—and one strongly in opposition to the prevailing thought of the whole world. . . .
>
> Letter to Edward A. Ross, 21 June 1932[60]

During the *Forerunner* years, Charlotte had actively promoted woman's suffrage, and she continued to do so during her final years in New York. The movement's doldrums had ended in 1910 after Washington State passed a suffrage referendum; when California came on board the following year, it began to seem as if suffrage's day had finally dawned. In 1915, suffrage referendums were voted down in New York, Pennsylvania, Massachusetts, and New Jersey, but that was the last year the cause suffered defeat.[61]

Charlotte participated in that final California campaign, sleeping with Alice Park in two basement rooms in San Francisco and speaking in a "hall crowded to the doors." That same year, Alice Paul returned to America from England and brought with her tactics learned from the militant British suffragettes. With Lucy Burns, Paul helped to found the Congressional Union; it later merged with

Harriot Stanton Blatch's Women's Political Union to become the National Woman's Party (NWP).

Dedicated to fighting for a federal amendment, the NWP correctly guessed that suffrage would succeed nationally sooner than locally. President Wilson had come around to supporting the right of individual states to decide the suffrage issue but declined to support a federal amendment; the NWP thus opposed his candidacy in 1916. Charlotte—who served on the NWP's advisory council alongside Blatch, Helen Keller, Florence Kelley, and Phoebe Hearst, among others—continued to prefer Wilson over the Republican Charles Evans Hughes, however.[62]

Charlotte's involvement with the relatively youthful NWP suggests she had not yet earned dinosaur status. Still, she sought to defuse the party's radicalism by associating it with "normal" women. By "normal" she meant women who cared for husbands and families; her distinction was more class-based than anything else, intended to chastise the upper-class female "parasites" for whom she reserved most of her venom. The organization's leadership, by contrast, strategically rejected normalcy. Credited with practically inventing the publicity stunt, the NWP sought to modernize a cause led (Paul and others believed misled) by the larger but considerably more staid NAWSA.[63]

Carrie Chapman Catt helped to shake things up a bit when she took over as NAWSA president in 1915. She brought with her skills she had honed orchestrating the 1915 New York State campaign, aided by stalwart foot soldiers, including Charlotte. New York was considered "the cradle of the movement," and local activists in both the 1915 and 1917 suffrage campaigns decided that the time had come for that cradle to be rocked.[64]

Accordingly, they staged open-air meetings with automobiles decked in yellow and parades with marchers dressed in red, carrying placards bearing signatures of over a "million New York women [who] want to vote." On Independence Day, they held a ceremony at the foot of the Statue of Liberty and participated in a nationwide reading of a Woman's Declaration of Independence. Bonfire-lit gatherings, "torchlight processions . . . street dances . . . outdoor concerts . . . open air religious services . . . flying squadrons of speakers": if you could dream it the suffragists did it. Catt recalled,

> Bottles containing suffrage messages were consigned to the waves from boats and wharves with appropriate speeches. Sandwich girls advertised meetings and sold papers. Sixty playhouses had theatre nights, many with speeches between acts. There were innumerable movie nights with speeches and suffrage slides; "flying canvass wedges," "hikes" and automobile tours. The entire State was stirred by the

activities. . . ."What rot!" said some. "What ingenuity!" said others. "Surely the women have gone stark mad," said others.[65]

But their madness had method in it: defeated in 1915, the state referendum passed the legislature in 1917. A year later, on the very day the British House of Lords also accepted the inevitable, the U.S. House of Representatives passed the Nineteenth Amendment by the precise two-thirds required. In 1920, Tennessee became the final state needed to ratify the amendment when a young legislator broke a tie and abandoned his anti-suffrage position, bowing to his mother's wishes. More than seventy years after a small band of intrepid reformers had gathered in Seneca Falls, American women had finally become full citizens.

Charlotte played an active role in both the local and national suffrage campaigns. In 1915, for instance, she engaged in a debate with the founder of the National Association Opposed to Woman Suffrage, Mrs. Arthur M. Dodge. She acquitted herself so favorably that the *Times*—which had staged the debate after Charlotte accused the paper of jaded and unfavorable coverage—applauded her "brilliant" response. The paper cited it as proof that a woman could be "as restrained and able in argument as a man, eschewing personalities and confining herself to principles. . . ."[66] In praising this eschewal, the *Times* for once agreed with Charlotte about how a woman should acquit herself in public.

Charlotte also served as one of the best-known poets of the American suffrage movement. During the *Forerunner* years, she had penned a collection of *Suffrage Songs and Verses* set to popular tunes, and she continued to produce similar ditties for campaigns and competitions. Two earlier poems, "She Walketh Veiled and Sleeping" and "She Who Is to Come," became beloved anthems of the cause and were routinely read whenever suffragists convened.

Charlotte celebrated the national victory with yet another poem, dedicated to "The Women of 1920." The poem encourages women to avoid party politics and to place "World safety, Peace and honor" before factional interests. Charlotte made the same argument at a meeting of the NWP two weeks after ratification. She spoke for many present when she urged women to unite as a mass voting bloc on the model of the Nonpartisan League. Although she expressed ambivalence about a separate woman's party or platform elsewhere, at this meeting she warned that participating in men's corrupt parties would taint the newly enfranchised.[67]

Charlotte's side prevailed, leading to the establishment of the nonpartisan National League of Women Voters, whose mission was to make "every woman a voter." But as it turned out, most women were *not* voters. The 1920 election and subsequent ones confirmed Charlotte's worst fears about the dangers of making suffrage "the *summum bonum*" of the woman's rights movement. The Antis may have warned of "the array of terrible things [that] were going to follow if the ballot was given to women!" But the suffragists ultimately had more cause for concern in victory's aftermath. With other suffragists, Charlotte had hoped that women as a voting bloc would support progressive measures, but the support was as little evident as the bloc. Younger women in particular seemed to greet their enfranchisement with a shrug.[68]

Initially, Charlotte had sought to align herself with more youthful feminists, as her involvement with Heterodoxy illustrates. Heterodoxy was a women's social club formed by the redoubtable suffragist and minister Marie Jenney Howe; as a young woman, Howe had written Charlotte a letter expressing her gratitude for *Women and Economics*. Howe's unorthodox club drew together "unorthodox women," including Inez Haynes Irwin, Crystal Eastman, Elizabeth Gurley Flynn, Zona Gale, Fola La Follette, Elsie Clews Parsons, and Rose Pastor Stokes. In the words of one radical New Yorker, Heterodites were "women who did things and did them openly." Every other Saturday beginning in 1912, the twenty-five inaugural members met in Greenwich Village for luncheon discussions. The club had grown to some eighty members by 1920 and survived until at least 1940, longer than many of its founders.[69]

Charlotte had broken with the club well before then. She stopped attending meetings in 1917, though she remained on friendly terms with many club members, many of whom continued to admire her work. Older and less educated than most of the Heterodites, she would still have been attracted to Howe's founding vision: "We intend simply to be ourselves, not just our little female selves, but our whole big human selves." But the members' simultaneous vision of the group as "the most unruly and individualistic females you ever fell among" likely contributed to Charlotte's disillusionment with Heterodoxy. Asked once by the club to deliver a "'background talk' on her life," Charlotte presented her story as one of "inherited rebelliousness." That rebelliousness surfaced when she left Heterodoxy once "the heresies seemed to center on sex psychology and pacifism," she later reflected.[70]

Not all heretics were offered membership: Margaret Sanger never got beyond an opportunity to speak to the Heterodites. Sanger's biographer Ellen Chesler has speculated that the members may have felt "perhaps reluctant to associate with her avowed radicalism in politics and social behavior, perhaps skeptical of her lack of education and her erratic emotional behavior." Sanger in turn expressed little love for the Heterodites; she regretted having "struck no responsive chord" with any of the members and found it

> unbelievable that they could be serious in occupying themselves with what I regarded as trivialities when mothers within a stone's throw of their meetings were dying

shocking deaths. Who cared whether a woman kept her Christian name . . . [or] wore her wedding ring? Who cared about her demand for the right to work? Hundreds of thousands of laundresses, cloakmakers, scrub women, servants, telephone girls, shop workers would gladly have changed places with the Feminists in return for the right to have leisure, to be lazy a little now and then.

Elsewhere, Sanger criticized Charlotte specifically for being "a conservative and a reactionary, who had lost courage by obtaining too much publicity."[71]

Charlotte voiced no reciprocal reservations about Sanger herself. In 1916, Sanger was tried for circulating birth control pamphlets through the mails—thereby violating the Comstock law prohibiting postal delivery or transportation of material deemed "obscene, lewd or lascivious." Her reservations about the cause notwithstanding, Charlotte attended the National Birth Control League dinner at the Hotel Brevoort arranged by Sanger's supporters.

By the late 1920s, Charlotte had overcome her initial objections and come around to supporting the birth control cause; by that point, she agreed with Sanger that there could be no "Healthy Race Without Birth Control." After the war especially, both women worried about population growth, particularly within certain races and nations. Although Sanger differed from Charlotte in finding ethnic prejudice offensive, like Charlotte, she expressed alarm over Americans' "breeding, breeding, breeding, excess numbers—for what? For another condition like that of Europe in 1914, with its dingy overcrowded communities that sought in blood-shed an outlet and a relief from the tragedy of existence?" Similarly, in a 1920 speech, Sanger argued that "Birth Control will save the world from another and more devastating holocaust such as the great war which has left a continent in one vast stretch of want and misery." Both women feared that unless checked by birth control, the "pressure of population" in overcrowded Japan and Germany would ultimately result in another, deadlier war: about a second war, at least, both were right.[72]

All the same, Charlotte retained her ambivalence about the cause throughout the early 1920s. Birth control flourished as a movement during that decade, the historian Ellen Chesler has argued, "because it wed new personal and sexual interests to the larger set of public concerns that had motivated women in the past." Sanger approved of this wedding, but Charlotte objected. She wanted what birth control would curb (the reproduction of undesirable peoples) and not what it would enable (the free play of desire). Sanger believed in fundamental differences between the sexes, embraced women's sexual nature, considered individual freedom a boon, and promoted "such abstract goals as the development of the 'intuitive forward urge within.'" Her beliefs distinguished her from more orthodox feminists like Charlotte and aligned her with such figures as Ellen Key, Sigmund Freud, and another associate of Key's and Freud's, the sexologist and Sanger's onetime lover Havelock Ellis.[73]

Charlotte worried that the potentially "evil" effects of overindulgence would damage both the race and the individual. She expressed her concerns in her 1922 essay "Back of Birth Control":

> In our day the after-effects of the war, and the morbid doctrines of Freud as to the bad results of "suppressed desires" have accentuated what was always an evil, and made this human disorder ["unbridled indulgence"] not only more common but offensively conspicuous. It is oddly amusing to see people who have flatly repudiated their old religious faith, instantly give the same blind acceptance to any new theory they happen to pick up. Has no one had the mental agility to try the test of comparison on this suppressed-desire bugaboo? How about the people who never suppress their desires? Are they so much better off? The plantation negroes, and their savage prototypes do very little suppressing. . . . The world has but slowly and partially learned the basic lesson of civilization, self-control, and now comes this German psycho-pathologist to tell us it is better to be as unconsciously self-expressive and self-indulgent as the beasts we came from.

Behind Charlotte's objections to birth control lay her objections to Freud, Germans, and all those she associated with the primitive. Behind them as well lay her investment in self-denial, which bucked the postwar, post-Freudian trend toward self-expression and self-indulgence. Indeed, Charlotte appears to have felt it her relatively lonely task to defend the Puritan spirit of her ancestors—a spirit she associated with anti-individualism and service—from its tarnished reputation, during the Freudian era, as sanctimoniously censorious and comically prudish.[74]

By the teens, Freud had achieved celebrity status in America, a country he disliked. By then, one historian contends, "psychoanalysis had eclipsed all other psychotherapies in the nation's magazines. . . . Psychoanalysis received three-fifths as much attention as birth control, more attention than divorce, and nearly four times more than mental hygiene between 1915 and 1918." Psychoanalysis was popularized—and simplified—in such magazines as *McClure's* and *Everybody's Magazine*; *Masses* editor Max Eastman, for instance, used the latter venue to offer up his apostolic creed in hopes of converting new followers to Freud.[75]

Freud's fans and foes mostly responded to these reductions, "filtered through the successive minds of interpreters and popularizers and guileless readers and people who had heard guileless readers talk about it." By the teens, Freud had become the talk of the town in New York, which served as the American epicenter of the Freudian storm. Playwright Susan Glaspell recalled that one "could not go out to buy a bun without hearing of some one's complex."

Another New Yorker and playwright, Floyd Dell of the *Masses*, shared Glaspell's recollection of the Freudian zeal: "Everyone at that time who knew about psychoanalysis was a sort of missionary on the subject, and nobody could be around Greenwich Village without learning a lot about it." Dell considered himself liberated by psychoanalysis and defended its insights in the pages of *Vanity Fair*. Other New York enthusiasts included Mabel Dodge Luhan, who published a detailed account of her therapy in the Hearst papers, and Emma Goldman, who had attended Freud's first and only American lecture series at Clark University in 1909 and remained a loyal disciple.[76]

Articles on Freud peaked in the mid- to late twenties, tilting more toward critique than approbation. The journal *Current Opinion* published many of the critical essays. Charlotte's California admirer Eugene Hough indicted Freud in its pages for obsessing "the world with sex" and for suggesting that "all feelings of satisfaction have a sexual basis." Jane Addams elsewhere offered her own rebuke: "the Freudian theories as to dangers of repression were seized upon by agencies of publicity, by half-baked lecturers and by writers on the new psychology and finally interpreted by tackless youth as a warning against self-control." Wellesley professor Vida Scudder also chimed in, blaming Freud for the current "over-emphasis on sex" and wondering why people had to "pay so much attention to one type of experience in this marvelous, this varied, this exciting world."[77]

The Viennese analyst responded to the backlash, appropriately, by analyzing his attackers. He accused them of Victorian prudery, anti-Semitism, and neuroticism brought on by fear of his theories. Charlotte confessed to none of these motives. Instead, she explicitly linked her loathing for psychoanalysis to its reductive nature. Attributing all human conduct to sex (she accepted the popularization at face value) was comparable to linking Columbus's voyage to a desire for a Caribbean bride or Lindbergh's flight to a pressing date in Paris.[78]

During the Freudian frenzy, Charlotte offered lectures on "The Falsity of Freud" and "The Freudian Fallacy." She vocally denounced the id in the pages of the *Pictorial Review*. She elsewhere ranked "Our Absurd Sexolatry—Exit Sigmund Freud" third among the "Great Issues of Today," right above "Our Brains and What Ails Them" and right below "Races, Nations and Our World: Evaluating Races: Peace—What For?" She made an aborted effort to read and annotate (with numerous exclamation points) parts of Freud's *General Introduction to Psychoanalysis*. She concluded that Freud's theories represented a dangerous regression, "a belated revival of phallic worship."[79]

Charlotte faulted Freud for his monomaniacal emphasis on the formative role of sexuality, for "the lowering of standards in sex relations," and for promoting "as 'natural' a degree of indulgence utterly without parallel in nature." She believed his "sex mania" was "now widely poisoning the world." She argued that it was not "'suppressed desire,' but indulged desire, that writes the foulest chapter in human history."[80] Reducing humanity to sexual urges or drives, she believed, represented a regression to primitivism that countered her program for human progress.

Charlotte insisted that more was at stake in her rejection of Freud than what happened in her bedroom. She felt psychoanalysis had undermined any progress in the relationship between the sexes by constructing a slippery slope that started with "an indecent conversation with a decent woman" and descended from there into "promiscuity" and "free union." Indeed, this old warrior against the double standard worried that Freud's theories represented "the last effort on the part of man to maintain his misuse of the female," an ingenious strategy for getting the supply of sex to keep up with demand. The free-lovers had taken Freud and run with him, "pleased," as Charlotte saw it, "to find a theory which justifies them in doing as they like." Maintaining that there was more to love than "Eros," she enumerated at least six additional and equally satisfying kinds of love.[81]

More to the point, Freud's emphases on inherent contradiction, hidden motives, and submerged meaning reoriented the gaze from the exterior world to the interior psyche. This reorientation fundamentally challenged Charlotte's theory of the self's relationship to the body and the world. Freud's insistence on self-exploration countermanded her message of self-forgetfulness. His inward- and backward-looking therapeutics reversed her outward- and forward-looking methodology. Freud maintained that self-knowledge and recovery derived from prolonged psychic exploration, whereas Charlotte considered a "self abandoning enthusiasm" profoundly remedial. She believed Freud taught that "whatever you wish to do—invent, discover, decorate, sing, dance, act, paint, manufacture, teach—the power that urges you is called sex energy." She insisted instead that service, not sex, constituted the "life force."[82]

Moreover, Charlotte's take on "Our Brains and What Ails Them" was not Freud's. She defined the brain as a "Social Organ" that had to be put to "Social Use." Individual brains must be trained to grasp "this common consciousness . . . which is the recognition of Social Unity." She understood psychology as resembling history or sociology: it explained collective life, not "personal life." Psychology, according to Charlotte, was "ours; it is among and between us, and it changes with the succeeding and improving generations."[83] In lieu of an unconscious, isolated, repressed, and accessible only to the trained psychoanalyst, she proposed a collective consciousness, overt and accessible to all.

Charlotte's theoretical objections to Freud were backed by personal experiences. A rationalist decrying the irrational, she took people at their word and judged them by their stated intentions. She confessed to a longstanding aversion for "[a]nything occult—Psychic—metaphysical," which she identified (even before hearing Freud's name) as "one of the most sharply defined instincts" she possessed. She traced this aversion back to her adolescence and to her mother's friend (the woman she retroactively described as having "a pre-Freudian mind") who had urged Mary to curtail her daughter's rich fantasy life. Charlotte's aversion likely strengthened after she repudiated Dr. Weir Mitchell's etiology. And it doubtless strengthened again after she refused, following her disastrous marriage to Walter and her breakup with Delle, to make the "Love-god" her "ruling deity," as she accused the Freudians and weaker-willed women of doing.[84]

Finally, her antipathy for the "perverted sex philosophy of Freud and his followers" may stem from psychoanalytic interpretations of same-sex bonds as themselves "perverted," signifying "arrested development." Experiences that psychoanalysts branded abnormal and regressive Charlotte knew to be among her most intimate and sustaining while they lasted. She was a woman who had loved other women "that way," living at a time when some 50 percent of unmarried and 30 percent of married women "admitted to intense emotional relationships with other women"; for half of each group, these relationships involved sexual contact.[85] These deeply satisfying encounters were now being scrutinized by psychoanalysts as pathological manifestations of personal desire.

Charlotte loathed the very idea of psychoanalysis. Indeed, when one of these "mind-meddlers" audaciously mailed her an unsolicited analysis, she instructed Houghton to burn the pages unread. It amazed her that "apparently intelligent persons" would permit these mental intruders to rifle through "their thoughts and feelings, and extract confessions of the last intimacy."[86] The motives animating her campaign against psychoanalysis were many and varied, concrete and theoretical, political and impersonal as well as personal. To connect her antipathy for psychoanalysis only to psychic traumas would be to afford Freud the victory she strenuously sought to deny him.

For a time, Charlotte tried to see "this period of fragmentary sexolatry, with its childish exhibitionism" as a fad. She hoped it would soon "be followed by a real recognition of the possibilities of this 'life force' when its whole range was understood." She struggled to position herself as "a sane and wholesome feminist" vis-à-vis the radical feminists and free lovers who had apparently seized the day. In many ways, Charlotte anticipated the second wave of feminism of the 1960s and 70s, with her eagerness to make the personal political and her attention to the politics of gender relations, of housework, and of childcare (which helps to explain her recovery as a major figure during the second wave). Yet she nonetheless found much to dislike in feminist ideology in its early incarnation. She continued to defend feminism against the attacks of misogynists, but whenever the feminist label intimated that she associated with followers of Key and Freud, she shuddered.[87]

By the end of the decade, her antipathy for this branch of the movement was so intense that she recoiled even from flattering attempts to label her "America's leading feminist," for fear of the adverse connotations. A feminism whose proponents proudly promoted "sex rights on the part of women" and proclaimed "the body" its "Magna Carta" did not strike her as a valuable contribution. It doubtless especially troubled her to hear in this new generation's protest against "the sexual slavery of women in loveless marriages as 'legalized prostitution'" a distorted echo of her famous argument in *Women and Economics*.[88]

Charlotte feared the pendulum had swung too far: women seeking their independence had rightly revolted against their mothers' "utter surrender of personality" only to wrongly arrive at "a deification of personality." Instead of committing themselves to fulfilling "social service," they had pursued only "shallow self-indulgence."[89] Their flight from traditional restrictions had led them to "rush from the frying pan and into the fire" of self-expression and self-fulfillment. Their embrace of the personal and the feminine had led them to erroneously repudiate the collective and the human, which Charlotte insisted could never be reduced to the personal.

With others of her generation, she believed that these so-called liberated women hearkened mostly to inner drives and urges. In the words of one of her contemporaries, these younger women demonstrated an "utter lack of response to the battle cries that used to get women into action."[90] The hurly-burly, the dance crazes, the parties, and the automobile tours that defined the popular image of the Roaring Twenties looked from the perspective of reformers of Charlotte's era like inertia masquerading as movement, ennui masked by frenzy, a kind of moving in place (or even backward) utterly alien to the notion of motion Charlotte had long cherished as a form of agency.

Charlotte disdained these "painted, powdered, high-heeled, cigaret smoking idiots" for living only for the self and in the moment. "Young people are, or should be, 'the push' of the world," she argued; they are "the ones that set the pace and provide the motive for world improvement." And yet this generation of pleasure-seekers appeared to be dragging its high heels with malicious glee. She felt especially dismayed that they seemed to be prioritizing themselves over "the future Self—the next generation."[91]

Believing themselves "trail-breakers," they also overlooked the trailblazers who preceded them and made the new freedoms possible. "A wisely ambitious egg," she scolded, "should escape the nest by hatching, not smashing." In a poem she particularly liked called "Twigs," Charlotte employs an extended metaphor to mock "[t]he topmost twigs of a growing tree" who deride the larger trunk and the branches below as "Old Stuff!" These twigs brag that they alone represent "Youth!" "Life!" "The World!" The poem concludes with a smirk: "The tree minds not the little dears— / It has had twigs in previous years."[92]

Yet these twigs proved stronger than she supposed. Many members of the younger generation dismissed Charlotte as a reactionary and their judgment seemed to carry the day. The *Times* promoted Charlotte to the ranks of the aged cranks who "wagged their staffs and beards and lamented the degeneracy of the age." How could a woman, the paper reprovingly inquired, who had long maintained that the world was advancing now simply shake her head and suggest that "everything and everybody are getting worse"?[93]

Charlotte denied the caricature of herself as one of the "disillusioned, dull-eyed critics" who, convinced "of human incompetency and selfishness, . . . point out the all-too prominent failure of humanity. . . ." She defined the stereotypical old woman as an appendage "to the younger generation" and as someone who had "no interests or occupations" of her own, and she defied anyone to say she fit that bill. But she also remained bitterly aware that, in general, "the old and plain *made no impression*—as far as the mental record goes they do not exist."[94] At times, she must have felt that the only way for her to attract sustained attention was to complain.

In her more optimistic moments, Charlotte insisted that "the pleasure of being alive, the pride of being human, the immense and increasing advantages of our interesting world, will convince almost any one of the large and rapid progress of humanity." She had several reasons to celebrate: among them, women remained an increasing presence in the workforce during the postwar period; this remained true even after the soldiers returned from the front and the women who had taken their jobs were sent home. Charlotte did worry, however, that these women might be working for money alone without recognizing that "[l]abor is a social process" benefiting humanity more than the individual. She also feared that these "bachelor" working girls might resist nature's call and bypass marriage and children altogether.[95]

Additionally, Charlotte rejoiced in seeing her once-heretical demand for professional child study become conventional wisdom. In the twenties, universities began offering courses in child development, and both magazines and national organizations devoted to parenting emerged. At a 1919 conference, women doctors pronounced her concept of professional daycare for professional mothers "too radical a doctrine for all present." Yet in California, where Charlotte had been roundly pilloried for her childrearing views and practices, the Oakland *Examiner* belatedly credited her "common sense," noted that one local community was implementing her theories, and added that her transformation from anathema to guru served as "evidence that the world moves perceptibly ahead." Charlotte clipped this column and saved it in her scrapbook. It made her "chuckle," she remarked, "to see the most conscientious mamas proudly doing to their children what I was called 'an unnatural mother' for doing to mine."[96]

The passage of the prohibition amendment in 1917 and its ratification by the states in 1919 ushered in another reform Charlotte sanctioned. Temperance workers had predicted that prohibition "would reduce poverty, nearly wipe out prostitution and crime, improve labor organization, and 'substantially increase our national resources by setting free vast suppressed human potentialities.'" But the supposed Dry Decade became famous for its speakeasies and for bootlegging, and the amendment was repealed in 1933. Charlotte had long been a "total abstainer," though if the punch contained claret she did not object. She regarded both smoking and drinking as men's unnecessary addictions: "one daily drug to stir him up / And one to soothe him down." Yet while she wore her white ribbon to support temperance, she never felt "at all at home in that atmosphere of orthodox religion and strong emotion."[97]

As the twenties progressed, this feeling of not being "at home" also increasingly defined Charlotte's tenure in the city she had lived in longer than any other. Living in New York City kept her in the public eye, but for Charlotte this now represented virtually its only, and a dubious, benefit.

~

> Twenty-two years in New York. Twenty-two years in that unnatural city where every one is an exile, none more so than the American.
> *The Living of Charlotte Perkins Gilman*, 1935[98]

According to the 1920 census, the U.S. population had for the first time become more urban than rural, and the greater metropolitan New York area "grew faster than twenty-eight states combined." Charlotte considered this growth malignant.

Her distaste for the city permeates a poem she wrote about it entitled "The City of Death":

> . . . A city whose own thick mephitic air
> Insidiously destroys its citizens;
> Whose buildings rob us of the blessed sun,
> The cleaning wind, the very breath of life;
> Whose weltering rush of swarming human forms,
> Forced hurtling through foul subterranean tubes
> Kills more than bodies, coarsens mind and soul.
> Destroys all grace and kindly courtesy,
> And steadily degrades our humanness
> To slavish acquiescence in its shame.[99]

In her autobiography, Charlotte attributed her disaffection primarily to the city's foreigners and aesthetes, but loneliness played a part as well. Even while pleading "a nervous sensitiveness, which makes what women call 'society' a painful exhaustion," she craved companionship in New York and mourned a general lack of "friendship and neighborliness" there. She remarked

> Few indeed are the people in New York who will go to see a friend unless they are fed. It is not lack of friendliness, it is lack of time; and also that ridiculous ability to step outside of their villages. Some few dear friends we had, friends I love and am proud to know. Yet even these I saw but little of. My husband and I, not being afraid of distance, went a-calling from time to time, but seldom indeed did people reach 135th Street and climb five flights of stairs to see us.

For a period, Charlotte sought to draw visitors up those stairs by holding a weekly salon or evening. Shades of her Oakland days, she gathered the city's reform-minded denizens, including on occasion Mary Austin and Emma Goldman.

But her smaller, short-term experiment never drew the crowds gravitating toward the famous Fifth Avenue salon of Mabel Dodge Luhan. Luhan was a devotee of Gertrude Stein, an anti-suffragist, and a devout Freudian—three strikes against her in Charlotte's book. At Luhan's salon "Socialists, Trade-Unionists, Anarchists, Suffragists, Poets, Relations, Lawyers, Murderers, Old Friends, Psychoanalysts, I. W. W.'s, Single Taxers, Birth Controlists, Newspapermen, Artists, Modern-Artists, Clubwomen, Women's place-is-in the home Women, Clergymen" and additional, disparate enthusiasts gathered to converse and swap ideas. Whether convened on posh Fifth Avenue or in bohemian neighborhoods, these enclaves proved to Charlotte the city's insularity: "People of similar tastes huddle in little local groups, narrower than villages, as in the vaunted pseudo-artistic settlement, Greenwich Village."[100]

Charlotte's feelings of isolation intensified as old friends passed or moved away. After Lester Ward died in 1913, she eulogized him in a black-bordered obituary in the *Forerunner*. The letters she used to direct to Ward now landed in his nephew-in-law E. A. Ross's mailbox. Like Charlotte, Ross saw no apparent contradiction in simultaneously espousing progressivism and nativism. Charlotte and Ross bonded over their anti-immigrant, anti-Semitic, and pro-eugenics views as well as their mutual prioritizing of "the collective welfare" over "the ravages of egoism." Ross considered Charlotte "the most brilliant woman I have known," he said. He claimed she "had the most beautiful woman's head I ever laid eyes on."[101] Charlotte usually stayed with the Ross family whenever she lectured in Wisconsin, where Ross now taught after being fired from Stanford. She enjoyed visiting the 6 foot 5 sociologist, his 5 foot 1 wife, and the couple's "wonderful boys." The family also enjoyed her "good old-fashioned visits," although they were few and far between.[102]

Charlotte's loneliness increased when Katharine switched coasts. Katharine had been married since 1918 to Frank Tolles Chamberlin, a sculptor eleven years her senior whom she had first met in Rome and then again at the MacDowell Colony in New Hampshire. The couple had settled in Pasadena by 1919. Two children, Dorothy and Walter, arrived in rapid succession while the family struggled to scrape by on meager earnings. Charlotte urged her daughter to consider her regular checks a form of payback: "There has been so much, so very much, that I I [*sic*] failed in giving you, dear child. It is a joy to my heart to be of some use now. And I beg you not to feel it as a debt—it is not even a gift—it is mother's due, long over due!"

Charlotte's desire to make amends for maternal failures sheds light on a curious incident she recorded in her diary around this time. In the fall of 1921, in her sixty-first year, she visited a children's home to "[l]ook for [a] little girl about four."[103] Nothing came of her inquiry, but it testifies to the unsatisfied longings that punctuated her final years in the city.

Well into her sixties, Charlotte continued to be plagued by recurring bouts of "contemptible below par-ness." In the spring of 1922, shortly after arriving home from her first visit to the Chamberlins, she sprained her wrist in a fall and soon found herself physically and mentally incapacitated. She declared her final spring in New York a "flat time" and compared herself to "a vacuous barren shell."[104]

In late March 1922, Houghton's father William passed away, leaving his eldest son $6,000. Several months later, Houghton's Aunt Louise Gilman Lane died, bequeathing a small inheritance and a large house to the two Gilman brothers. The bequest led to "[m]uch excitement & 'figgering'" among the beneficiaries. Charlotte informed Katharine optimistically that, with the two legacies, she and

Houghton "shall total enough," she predicted, "to have a large easy feeling for the rest of our lives!" She added that, since they had not renewed their apartment lease, and since the Aunts' house was now half theirs, she and Houghton were "seriously thinking of going there to live!!!"[105]

Charlotte would miss a few close friends, the movies, and the shops, but she otherwise longed to flee New York. The patrician New Yorker Madison Grant had predicted in 1916 that Americans of the "old stock" would be "literally driven off the streets of New York City by the swarms of Polish Jews," and Charlotte's reflections on her exodus suggest Grant's bigotry matched his foresight.[106] She confessed herself pleased to "escape, forever, the hideous city—and its Jews," not to mention the "nerve wearing noise—the dirt—the ugliness, the steaming masses in the subway." And she delighted to "have the loveliness of New England at its best to live in."

"Leaving New York with measureless relief," Charlotte wrote in *The Living*, "I came in 1922 to this old Connecticut settlement, Norwich Town. . . . After New York it is like heaven."[107] Of course, even earthly paradises could disappoint, as experience should have taught her. The vestiges of her idealism are revealed in her belief that this new "heaven" would be any different.

Norwich

13   "A Returned Exile"
(1922–1934)

> . . . No matter if long years behind
> Show failure deep and dead—
> You have to live your splendid best
> In the short years ahead.
>
>   "You Have To," 1912[1]

Charlotte shed many of her possessions in the course of escaping the "City of Dreadful-all-the-time." She shipped twelve cases, two crates, one box, and three barrels off to Katharine's little Pasadena cottage. But she could not leave everything behind. Some of the problems she faced in Norwich were familiar but less pronounced. Money and work remained scarce, immigrants less so: the proportion of foreigners in the town threatened to surpass New York's (Charlotte estimated that two-thirds of Norwich's population was foreign-born). By the 1920s, the historian John Seelye has observed, New England no longer remained "the bastion of white, Anglo-Saxon, and Protestant purity" it had resembled in Lyman Beecher's day. In an effort to resist this demographic shift, Connecticut in 1896 became the first state in the nation "to regulate marriage for breeding purposes." The state's concern with breeding and its bucolic beauty attracted eager émigrés from the polyglot, polluted city next door. Fed up with New York's "swarms of jostling aliens," Charlotte found it easier in Connecticut to appreciate her surroundings and to associate almost exclusively with "native stock."[2]

The unanticipated problems proved the most vexing. Charlotte may have devoted the majority of her sixty-two years to transcending the personal, but during her dozen years in Norwich she faced personal problems ranging from family feuds to illness and loss. Indeed, she had essentially come full circle and found herself once again ensnared in battles that had defined her childhood and adolescence. The names had changed, but Charlotte was again forced to share a home with a capricious, "unreasonable" woman and a self-absorbed, irascible child-man.[3] Only now, no urgent, compensatory summons from a world seemingly full of promise and opportunity beckoned her to make it an alternative home.[4] Instead, Charlotte faced a future with little left to do and fewer places she wanted to go. After twelve volatile years, she departed Norwich as eagerly as she had arrived.

~

> I find it hard to accept personal ease and settled comfort—it seems somehow demoralizing!
>
>> Letter to Harriet Park Kobold,
>> December 29, 1928[5]

When Charlotte and Houghton were courting, she declared Norwich "the last place I would choose" to live or, she added candidly, "that would choose me!" By the fall of 1922, however, Charlotte settled in the town "with the delight of a returned exile." The Connecticut-born Charlotte found her new environs from the first comfortingly familiar. The town's rich history and reverence for ancestry suited her nicely: the "sweet singer of Hartford," the poet Lydia Sigourney, had been born in the Gilman's house, and Benedict Arnold had apprenticed across the street. Offering a pleasing "similarity in people and in tastes and habits," Norwich provided "more of the home feeling than such a nomad as I had ever hoped for," she contentedly remarked.[6]

Until May 1923, Houghton retained a room in New York and only weekended in Norwich, after which Charlotte sought to "absorb him for keeps." She had been the more enthusiastic proponent of the move: Norwich aggravated Houghton's hay fever and required the surrender of his New York practice. His wife lamented his tendency to hang "on like grim death to old habits" and resisted any talk of returning to New York City. She maintained "that if Houghton builds up a small business here, he will soon be 'at the head of the bar' in his old home, and enjoy it; really enjoy it, and the friends so long known, and the old home." Prying

Francis and Emily Gilman. Francis was Houghton's brother and Charlotte's first cousin. The two couples shared the house in Norwich. Courtesy of Walter Stetson Chamberlin.

Houghton from New York to retire in Norwich constituted an important first step toward her desired final destination: Pasadena.[7]

Meanwhile, Charlotte resolved to make Houghton happy and to remain cheerful, healthy, and pleasant to Houghton's brother Francis and his wife Emily. The original plan called for Emily to run the "expensive old house" and the two couples to share the living quarters and expenses. Initially, Charlotte managed to "get on very nicely indeed with this Brother & Sister. She has splendid qualities—he is a 'dear.'"[8]

With so much going her way, Charlotte declared that she had "not been so gay and hopeful for years." She basked in her beautiful and restful surroundings, savoring the town's "heavenly quiet" (with the exception of the trolley car that regularly clanged past their house). She admired the town's tree-lined streets and majestic homes with "pillared porches, fanlights over rich doorways, wide sweeps of lawn under majestic elms," which, she observed, created "a succession of noble pictures." The rustic beauty of Norwich provided a sharp contrast to congested New York, and Charlotte reveled in the difference: "To step out of doors into beauty and peace—to see the moon as a moon should be seen—just sky & tree tops—and the long sweeping shadow, of great elms across the meadows!" she exulted to Grace. "The quiet—the fragrance, the still loveliness—it delights me daily—& nightly."[9]

The Gilman homestead on Washington Street was called Lowthorpe (the original owners, ancestors to the Gilmans, were named Lathrop). It was built in 1650 in the early settlement known as Norwich Town, north of the growing city of Norwich, in "a narrow strip between wooded hills and the Yantic River." Situated on an acre of land, the house was surrounded on two sides by "a pleasant park, Lowthorpe Meadows, once the 'mowin' lot' of the family."

It was "a roomy old frame house, painted that particular shade of dark red which seems to have been a favorite with many New Englanders of by-gone days." The ceilings were low and supported by white beams. A composite of original structure and new wing, the architecture became even more convoluted after the two couples divided up the house between them, making it necessary "to go 'up-stairs and downstairs' if one wishes to arrive anywhere—through odd passages and halls, around surprising corners." Charlotte's own bedroom-cum-office was situated above the "new" library and measured roughly 22 by 18 feet, "so large that the big roll-topped desk in the corner is almost inconspicuous." Atop the desk sat a bust of her granddaughter Dorothy sculpted by Frank Chamberlin, and decorating the walls were examples of Katharine's artwork, a photograph of Katharine, and an oil painting of Charlotte's mother as a young "belle."[10]

During her years in this historic town, Charlotte wrote, walked, played cro-
quet, socialized with neighbors, and gardened. In February and March, she routinely visited Katharine's family in Pasadena. She offered talks en route on such
favorite targets as Freud and immigration. The idea, she wrote Katharine of her
lecture-funded trips, was to have "all that fun for nothing." Typically, Charlotte
traveled through the South in the winter and returned through the North in the
spring in order to avoid having to pack a winter wardrobe.[11] Houghton accompanied her on the 1927 trek, losing "his heart" to the grandchildren he had never
before seen. This was Houghton's only trip to Pasadena and Charlotte's last before
moving there in 1934. She could never again secure enough engagements to pay
her way, leading her to conclude grimly that she had "no 'pull' any more."[12]

While she could still finance these cross-country treks, her physical feats attracted as much attention as her verbal ones. On a 1925 stopover in Dallas, for
instance, Charlotte visited the local YWCA and "astonished the few beholders
by doing the travelling rings . . . three and back," even though she would turn
"sixtyfive this summer!" She enjoyed showing off her agility elsewhere on this
trip, shocking porters by vaulting onto the upper bunks in sleeper cars and by
climbing down again without the aid of the ladder. Home again in Norwich, she
similarly impressed a visitor by climbing a flight of steps in her garden with "the
light, flying step of a girl." She remained so nimble that well into her sixties she
could walk the mile-and-a-half to the town center and back twice a day without
complaint. Once, for a group of marveling women around her age, she performed
parlor tricks, including jumping over chairs and running up "the stairs two steps
at a time!"[13]

Charlotte credited gardening with keeping her spry. In 1918, she had protested
that she could not "do strenuous out of door work" because, she explained, "it
spoils my machinery!" But she was doing plenty in Norwich and doing just fine.
The balance and harmony she formerly sought in a world she once called "a great
garden full of lovely wonderworking laws" she now sought in her own backyard.
Indeed, cultivating her own garden led her to dream of doing some "'landscape
gardening' of the world," with a global task list including "conquest of vermin,
conservation of resources, endless improvements."[14]

Shortly after arriving in Norwich, Charlotte and a more reluctant Houghton
turned 9,000 square feet of their acre lot into a working garden, the "two elderly
amateurs doing everything except the plowing." Clad in her usual costume of
sweater, knee breeches, and "gaiters to the knee," Charlotte routinely devoted
four hours each day in spring and summer to her garden, "all May the planning
and planting, all June the weed-weed-weeding." Norwich was celebrated as "The

Rose of New England," but the Gilman's flower garden comprised a wide variety of blooms—irises, johnny jump-ups, and yellow alyssum, among others. Their garden encompassed "a lovely arrangement of beds and grass paths, with a glazed earthenware pedestal in soft shades of green, blue and red as a centerpiece. . . ."[15]

The adjacent vegetable garden with its thirty varieties took precedence; it helped to sustain the couple when money grew scarce. Charlotte was especially hard up. She began 1923, for instance, with only the seventy-five dollars Houghton had deposited in her account. Her paeans to women's economic independence notwithstanding, Charlotte resigned herself in Norwich to being "taken care of by Houghton" financially. The garden allowed her to feel she was still working—even if by seeding and weeding instead of publishing and lecturing.

Her one attempt to combine both labors, an essay she wrote on "Gardening and the Baser Passions," was rejected for publication. So Charlotte channeled the passions she formerly brought to her reform career into her garden. By her own estimate, the pastime required "aspiration," "hope," "patience," "faith," "perseverance," "fortitude," and "endurance"—all attributes she had cultivated during the arduous years she had devoted to supporting herself and changing the world. Now she refocused these traits on roughly a fifth of an acre in her own backyard.[16]

Charlotte (left), Houghton, and Katharine Seymour Day in the Gilman's garden, 1932. Photo by Miss Chinn. Courtesy of the Schlesinger Library, Radcliffe Institute for Advanced Study, Harvard University.

A visitor to the Gilman's garden described it as "dear—dear to its owners and makers; so that into it there has come an air of peace and seclusion, the feeling of the soil and the sense of two people working together in companionable silence and harmony to make a place of beauty and a refuge from the clamor of the world." The garden provided Charlotte especially with a sanctuary from a cacophonous world and an increasingly fractious household. She called it her "sanitarium"—a term she had used some twenty years previously to describe Houghton's arms.[17]

Additional refuges could be found in the homes of their friendly neighbors, whom Charlotte described as "well-educated, well-read, well-intentioned." The Gilmans quickly made up in Connecticut for their loneliness in New York. Their set included Norwich residents such as the minister Alexander Abbott and his wife Alice, the lawyer Edwin Higgins, and their neighbor Elizabeth Huntington. It also included more far-flung couples, among them Martha and Robert Bruère and Alexander and Elizabeth Black.

Charlotte continued to write and visit Grace, who lived penuriously in a New York City sixth-floor flat. Grace occasionally grumbled about Charlotte's "incurable good intentions" and "her equally incurable inability to know what will be a favour and what will not, to the person she desires to be useful to." Charlotte's friendships in Norwich proved less complicated and offered the kind of easy companionship she had not experienced since her Providence days.[18]

Not all of Norwich fell at her feet, however. One local woman who encountered her on the street complained afterward, "Mrs. Gilman talked to me like a public meeting!" Charlotte acknowledged this propensity: "I'm *not* a nice person to be close to," she once told Houghton. "I do very well at long range." Even when offstage, she had difficulty shaking her public persona and meeting and treating people as individuals; she tended to be sociological rather than sociable.[19]

Charlotte experienced her greatest difficulties with "the other half of the family," whom she called the "large fly" in the "ointment" that was Norwich. Before moving to town, Charlotte had prophetically observed that people "annoy, exhaust, enrage" us the closer our contact with them. Before long, the two Mrs. Gilmans were barely speaking. Each believed the other was behaving "abominably." Emily grew so vindictive that at one point she attempted to turn their neighbors and servants against Charlotte, an unsuccessful plan that Charlotte claimed only proved "what a stupid person" Emily was.[20]

Houghton with his "angelic" nature usually managed to stay above the fray, but the rest of the household lacked his restraint. In 1925, Charlotte "chloroformed [her] darling pussy cat" (likely the same tortoise shell kitten Francis had given her the previous spring) because she could no longer bear the "suffering, humiliation and anger" she experienced when Emily complained about her feeding the cat at mealtimes and from the icebox at night. The couples soon resorted to dining separately, which meant that six separate meals had to be prepared and served each day. Charlotte deemed these arrangements "comic-grotesque," lacking in both dignity and intelligence, but still preferable to "the hideous atmosphere in which we used to sit at table together."[21]

Charlotte's arguments with "these people" (or "these," as Charlotte and Houghton's sympathetic servant Mary succinctly dubbed them), occurred over matters so trivial they must have especially aggravated a person who preferred to dwell in impersonal realms. One particularly heated battle began as a disagreement over dessert. In June 1930, according to Charlotte's later blow-by-blow, Emily changed her mind and refused to eat the pie she had requested and that Charlotte had ordered for her the previous day; she wanted Charlotte's pineapple instead. Charlotte hid the pineapple and sent in the custard pie, making Francis so mad he threatened to crack Charlotte between his "fingers like a lobster!"[22]

By her own admission, Charlotte had a quick temper and an expression that revealed her every mood. While living at Lowthorpe, she increasingly resented her in-laws' ingratitude and freeloading. Her objections to economic dependence led her to resent Houghton's paying most of the bills while Francis and this "unesteemed sister-in-law" continued to act "as if it was their house and we an unwelcome addition," she complained. Her eugenicist beliefs exacerbated her antipathy: "Francis is sub-normal," Charlotte reported, and the couple "a wretched pair! Poor Emily a cripple & F. [Francis] almost a dwarf and moron."[23] If Charlotte's animus for the personal intensified during this period, then Francis and Emily deserve most of the credit.

~

> I'm convinced that one of our main starvations is lack of contact with people who "belong." I think we "empower" one another when properly related. And most of us have to do with mere "neighbors". . . .
>
> Letter to Grace Channing Stetson,
> February 28, 1932[24]

Houghton and Charlotte remained "quite happy together," especially when apart from the other Gilmans. She called him "Ho" and he called her "Chopkins," the nickname he had bestowed upon his cousin when he was twelve years old. Charlotte had a notoriously poor memory for dates and often forgot birthdays and anniversaries, so Houghton took to reminding her of special occasions with the

Charlotte and Houghton clowning on the steps of their Norwich, Connecticut, home, ca. 1923. Courtesy of the Schlesinger Library, Radcliffe Institute for Advanced Study, Harvard University.

help of "some extra kisses." She did remember their silver wedding anniversary in June 1925: she gave Houghton a monogrammed silver spoon "for strawberry jam bottles," he gave her a silver wristwatch, and in the evening they walked downtown together to catch the silent film *The Last Laugh*.

Even when stretched financially, the couple often sprang for a movie or a play. At home, they enjoyed listening to records on Houghton's beloved Orthophonic Victrola. Francis often simultaneously played his radio, the brothers' different listening preferences providing yet another source of family tension.[25]

For their last Christmas together, Charlotte presented Houghton with a poetic token of their abiding love:

Thirty three years to remember.
From the June I took your name.
And in this remote December
I love you just the same.
Courteous kind and tender,
Patient, loving, and gay;
You scattered a gentle splendor

On every step of the way.
We've been happy together
For all our pleasant past,
And we're going to have pleasant weather
And love to the very last.

Houghton's unassuming, gentle nature helped to buffer Charlotte's more mercurial temperament and provided her with "a safe resting place."[26]

As cousins, they had more in common than most couples after the initial passion cooled. Advice manuals from this era often recommended separate beds for married couples, and the Gilmans shared neither a bed nor a room. On the few occasions when the couple did sleep together—for example, when her nephew Basil and his family descended upon them—neither slept much. But once restored to her own room, Charlotte "revived quickly," or so she informed Katharine; "none of that melancholy—I am stronger than I used to be." By the time she turned seventy, Charlotte believed she had finally dodged "that dreadful *tiredness*, that below zero exhaustion," enabling her to read at last the heavy books that had confounded her in the past.[27]

Her in-laws notwithstanding, Charlotte felt "piggishly happy" in Norwich with Houghton, her garden, her books and food, her view and surroundings, and her "few pleasant friends." She would be pleased, she told Katharine in 1931, to "end my days in such a lovely place, with a comfortable house and an 'inkum.' An inadequate income to be sure . . . but still . . . we are comfortable and happy and better off than 9/10 of the people."[28]

Her fraction included her own daughter. Katharine had recently traded art for genealogy; Charlotte found this new pursuit odd, perhaps because of its persistent backward glance or perhaps because she knew genealogy to be no more in demand than art during the Great Depression. Even in the more affluent 1920s, the Chamberlins eked out a precarious living. For as long as they could afford it, Charlotte and Houghton helped both Katharine's and Thomas's families financially and sent any spare change Basil's or Grace's way. Before the Stock Market crashed, they were especially generous. In 1923, Houghton assumed Katharine and Frank's roughly $3,500 mortgage; that same year, while Charlotte was visiting the West Coast, she found a house for her brother Thomas in Pasadena and signed his lease. In 1924, she estimated that her total annual outlay for Thomas and his family amounted to $1,500.[29]

Thomas had made an unfortunate marriage—his new wife struck Charlotte as both "practically crazy" and "hopeless . . . unreliable—Irish." Thomas apparently shared his sister's penchant for chasing "various 'rainbows'" while seldom attaining even her intermittent successes. Katharine considered her uncle a self-absorbed windbag for whom "nothing exists but his own interests—his talk is entirely *T.A.P.*—not a glimmer of interest in us—our affairs—our children. . . ."[30]

The additional burdens strained Houghton's finances. Since her own earning power had diminished, Charlotte vowed to consume less and prided herself on keeping her expenses to a minimum. As the country began its economic meltdown, the couple remained initially unscathed. Charlotte assured Katharine that she and Houghton could still rely on the "living from the estate. We lost nothing in that panic—we weren't forced to sell at a loss," she explained; ". . . the dividend comes in just the same."[31]

Several years later, however, their outlook had grown bleak. Charlotte confessed to feeling poor for the first time in 1932, though she insisted idealistically, "[s]o long as one has no desires one is not poor." Only the real and pressing desires of her loved ones stirred her to a "grinding need of things, albeit for other people."

By February 1932, the Gilmans could no longer afford to send any money to Katharine; a year later, they possessed only seventeen dollars between them. Charlotte wrung her empty hands in a series of plaintive missives to Katharine: "We've done what we could, where we could, and now that we can't, I just shut my heart up and try not to think about it! It isn't that I don't care—it's that I do care—abominably, and it is a mortifying agony not to be able to do anything."[32]

Her anguish extended beyond Katharine's plight to the general one: the prevalence of so many talented, serviceable, yet unemployed people during the Depression struck Charlotte as a clear sign of disease in "our blundering world." The era's rampant unemployment exposed the limits of her sanguine understanding of work as a formula requiring simply desire on the worker's part and need on the world's part. By 1930, 4.5 million Americans were unemployed; the following year, that number nearly doubled, reaching 8 million. By 1933, the figure stood at 13 million, representing roughly "a quarter of the work force."[33] Desire and need were superabundant: what was lacking were jobs, as well as the infrastructure necessary to generate and sustain them.

During the 1930s, numerous women who could find work did, and married and single women's employment measurably increased. A national debate ensued over whether these women were costing men scarce and necessary work. Over the opposition of women's organizations, state and federal governments attempted to impose sanctions on married women workers. Self-proclaimed former feminists wrote articles renouncing their careers now that they had rediscovered the joys of home and hearth.[34]

Charlotte never publicly intervened in this debate. During the Depression, she remained essentially silent on the issues that had made her fame and that proved pivotal to this period of economic and gender instability. According to Mary Beard, a pioneering historian of women and an admirer of Charlotte, the Depression triggered "a reconsideration of women's role in the world," a reconsideration that in a prior incarnation Charlotte would have welcomed and endeavored to steer.

Instead of focusing on economic reform and women's rights, however, she addressed immigrants' wrongs. Just three months after the October 29 Stock Market crash, for instance, Charlotte journeyed to the city where it occurred to participate on a panel on "Racial Prejudices." The multi-ethnic audience peppered her with "hostile questions" after she defended "the right of the American people who made this country what it is to keep it for themselves."[35]

Charlotte's relative obliviousness to more immediate and concrete concerns surfaces as well in her letters to Katharine, whom she now offered advice instead of funds. She counseled her heavily indebted daughter to practice metaphorical stretching for the pain personality inflicted: "Deliberately let yourself spread along the ages, backward & forward; and sideways among the millions." While the method would not help Katharine make ends meet, Charlotte herself had often discovered that it helped "rest" one's consciousness from "the grinding pressure of personal distress."[36] During these Norwich years, however, she found more to distress her than mere personal matters.

~

Get your work done, to remember!
Nothing can take it away!
So shall the sun of December
Shine brighter than earliest May!

Poem included in a letter to Edward A. Ross,
June 21, 1932[37]

While living in Norwich, Charlotte experienced "ten years of almost unbroken repeated failure" professionally, which dampened her enthusiasm for additional projects. She had gotten off to a strong start initially. Even before she left New York, she had planned the book that became her 1923 *His Religion and Hers*. She told Katharine in 1921 that the *Century* might publish her religion book, perhaps in conjunction with a standard edition of her works.

Charlotte believed her ideas on religion and contemporary mores could "make a real stir, and facilitate the chance of publication." In preparation, she offered several new lectures on religion, composed an outline and a preface, and wrote two articles as drafts for the book's first two chapters. Soon after relocating to Norwich, she felt she had begun to "*see* the book, and to feel that it will be a powerful useful illuminating thing. Religion and feminism are surely popular topics—The time is roaring ripe for such a book," she wrote Grace. "I have Hopes!"[38]

Charlotte had formulated many of her religious principles as early as her sixteenth year, but she had never written them out at book length. *His Religion and Hers* makes her strongest case for a religion that rejects egoism for altruism and trades concerns about an afterlife for concerns about the present life. Her friend Alexander Black observed that Charlotte saw "heaven not as a place but as a race condition," by which he meant that she located heaven within the realm of human possibility rather than in the skies. "Seeing God as within us, to be expressed, instead of above us, to be worshipped," Charlotte argues in the book, "is enough to change heaven and earth in our minds, and gradually to bring heaven on earth by our actions." Defining God as an impersonal force expressed through the human will to progress, she holds "that there is possible to humanity, as soon as we choose, a degree of joy and noble growth" that traditional religions assume can only be attained in heaven.[39]

In lieu of traditional man-made religions, which understood life on earth as "only a necessary evil," Charlotte sought to establish a woman-made faith that rejected the notion of inherent evil and instead saw evil conditions as "quite unnecessary and easy to outgrow." This more feminine religion would be grounded in virtues traditionally associated with the sex, including love, care, and service. Men, she writes in the book's poetic epigraph, have "Filled the world with dark religions / Built on Death. / Death, and the Fate of the Soul;— / The Soul, from the body dissevered," whereas women would base a religion on "Birth, and the Growth of the Soul;— / The Soul, in the body established."

Charlotte thus rejected her Great-Grandfather Lyman's Puritanism for the more compassionate faith embraced by her Great-Uncle Henry and Great-Aunt Harriet. At the same time, she took their softening efforts a step farther by sharply gendering the distinction between a retributive and merciful deity, explicitly casting the deity as maternal rather than paternal in the process. Yet even while reinforcing gender dichotomies, she sought to hasten the approach of a world at once "more human and less sexual," in both senses of the latter word.[40]

Charlotte believed *His Religion and Hers* to be a "useful and timely" book, but she feared its outspoken contempt for psychoanalysis and its "views on the sex question" would be denigrated in a culture with "a Freudian complex" and a sex obsession. She also feared readers' indifference toward "a presentation of religion as a help in our tremendous work of improving this world—what they want is hope of another world, with no work in it." While the book received largely sympathetic reviews, her sociologist friend E. A. Ross cautioned privately that this "imaginative *tour de force*" lacked scientific rigor. He particularly criticized her over-reliance on "Dr. Ward's doctrine of the priority and superiority of the female sex," a doctrine now widely considered dated and flawed.[41]

Charlotte waited two years before responding to Ross, only to immediately pick up the thread of the interrupted argument. She defended Ward loyally in a 1925 letter, while simultaneously signaling that she had moved on by mentioning her "feeble" attempts at starting her autobiography. That same year, she told Katharine that she hoped to make $10,000 from its sales, but, she conceded, "it does not interest me as it ought to. My real interest is in ideas, as you know."[42]

After drafting the initial five chapters of *The Living*, she took a long break, lured by the "irresistible" distraction of her garden. She completed "the 'running string' or story" of the autobiography by the end of 1925, intending subsequently to "take up the sections and write them breezily for serial publication."[43] She revised the autobiography throughout 1926 after unearthing her diaries and a cache of photos. By November of that year, she sent an editor a "dreadful copy" of *The Living*, sans poems and pictures. The editor apparently confirmed her verdict: nearly a decade would pass before the book found a publisher.[44]

The Living of Charlotte Perkins Gilman omits important persons and events and lingers over episodes of chronic ill health, misunderstanding, and disillusionment, thereby inverting the traditional optimistic trajectory associated with the autobiography since at least Benjamin Franklin's day. The literary critic Julianne Fleenor has suggested that Charlotte modeled her life story on the Gothic novel, citing as evidence the genre's requisite brush with madness, its flight from homes that seemed like havens, and the suicide ending. Charlotte did participate in the Gothic's critique of domesticity, and she also hoped that the book would generate the profits usually associated with such popular forms. Still, *The Living* fails to achieve the breathless pace of Gothic page-turners. By Charlotte's own estimate, the opening chapters are "good" and "alive," but the story deteriorates after she describes her mental and physical deterioration, whereas in the Gothic, this would be where the story would start to get interesting.[45]

Although an autobiography typically provides a detailed blueprint of a personality, in Charlotte's case, her personality obstructed both its completion and its flow. To draft *The Living*, she had to overcome her resistance to both retrospection and introspection. She also had to contend with her impression that most of her life had "been a vague unhappy blank." Perhaps most difficult to surmount was her fundamental objection to that most "hateful" of tasks: writing "about one's self!"

As with living itself, *The Living* possessed a primarily functional value for Charlotte: she wrote it mainly to regain public attention the better to disseminate her message of public service. Around the time she returned to the autobiography in the 1930s, she noted in her journal:

> This is splendidly worth doing
> Nobody else can do it!!!
> Poor though it is its [*sic*] the best offering: ought to stir some women.
> One Girl.————————
> One girl reads this, and takes fire!
> Her life is changed. She becomes
> a power————a Mover of others————
> I write for her.[46]

Although autobiographies traditionally focus on the self, Charlotte could motivate herself to write hers only by framing it as a selfless task.

The first draft of *The Living* concludes with the words "*Here's hoping!*" appended to a wish for a decade's more "good work." Charlotte got that decade, but even she increasingly doubted the quality of her work. Her efforts during her last years in Norwich were devoted primarily to *Social Ethics,* her 1914 *Forerunner* serial, a revision of *Human Work* that she was again revising under the snazzier title *Pernicious Adam.* She felt sure its case for an ethics grounded in social interest would preempt existing and erroneous standards. By definitively establishing work as the organic basis of social progress, she hoped to enable society to finally "boil forward!" She believed this updated treatise had the potential to be important, timely, and hugely popular; her supportive agent had assured her *Pernicious Adam* would sell. She would, she vowed, be "cheerfully willing to die when I can get that book properly re-introduced."[47]

Charlotte claimed to enjoy the revision process for the way it set her "brain to coruscating!" But she "sort of 'slumped'" upon finishing. She feared that she had crafted "a very large dull AXE" with dubious appeal to "the 'average mind.'" She tried to place *Pernicious Adam* with five different publishers before giving up, discouraged. She confessed her disappointment over her string of failures to Katharine: "It is not agreeable to have the . . . postponed hopes & plans of a lifetime come up against a blank wall."[48]

Seeking a sympathetic ear in which to pour her professional woes, Charlotte increasingly turned to her younger cousin Lyman Beecher Stowe, in whose luxurious New York City apartment she customarily stayed on her infrequent trips into town. The grandson of Harriet Beecher Stowe, Lyman was active in New York literary circles as both an author and editor. Charlotte made him her literary executor, but she could not persuade him to become her biographer. She told him in 1928 that her "antediluvian reputation" probably explained the disinterest in her work, adding that she was not yet "ready to accept total unworthiness as a reason. . . ."[49]

By 1930, all of Charlotte's books had gone out of print. That same year, the Century Company offered to sell her the plates for *His Religion and Hers* for fifty dollars. Charlotte suspected that the publishing industry considered her "a dottering old lady writing verbose vagaries. . . ." She kept on writing but felt increasingly hampered by the prospect of her work being automatically stamped "old stuff."[50]

~

... it is important for me to keep in touch with other friends—to be seen and met— not be extinct in N.Y.!

Letter to Katharine Stetson Chamberlin,
April 15, 1934[51]

Charlotte did not intend her departure from New York to signal her retirement from public life, but others took it that way. In 1928, a "juvenile" editor rejected one of her manuscripts with the comment, "Mrs. Gilman is not as well known as she was ten years ago." In 1930, Carrie Chapman Catt wrote to inquire about Charlotte's health. She expressed concern that the popular press no longer mentioned Charlotte's "literary contributions to the public," and she included a gift of $100 in her letter. Charlotte subsequently confessed to Catt her "keen distress" over her limited opportunities to address important causes, despite her "real power to stir and convince." On one of the infrequent occasions in the late 1920s when Charlotte did get some attention from the press, readers were asked, "Do you remember her?"[52]

This was not a silly question. A 1925 tally of the "Most interesting women in America" garnered Charlotte eight votes to Jane Addams's ninety-six and Catt's forty-nine, landing her in fifteenth place. Two years earlier, another poll had produced similar results: when the National League of Women Voters (NLWV) asked the public to list the twelve greatest living American women, Charlotte did not make the cut. Catt, who had placed first, promptly objected and suggested a new ranking with Charlotte on top, "because there was a period in the woman's movement when she brought out first one book and then another . . . which were scientifically done and widely read by all classes of people. And I credit those books with utterly revolutionizing the attitude of mind of the entire country, indeed of other countries, as to woman's place."[53] Yet even Catt refers to Charlotte's career in the past tense.

The NLWV slight was remedied somewhat when the organization issued a book in 1930 commemorating the tenth anniversary of the passage of the suffrage amendment. Charlotte was featured first among the four major thinkers covered therein. But a specially published book is not a nationally generated list. Perhaps the most stunning slap came from yet another women's organization: in 1933, the International Congress of Women, in which Charlotte had played so active a role, assembled a list of the 100 best books written by American women during the last century. None of Charlotte's numerous and formative books made the list.[54]

Charlotte attributed oversights like these to the pacesetting younger generation's impatience with anyone whose career peaked "befoh de wah!" She also cited her resistance to classification: the plethora of ill-fitting labels attached to her had never done her justice, she insisted, and the one label that did suit her, "social philosopher," was not a widely recognized or honored profession. Publicly, she interpreted her relative obscurity as the hallmark of success. She and other "Pre-War Radicals" had done what they set out to do, she explained. Now that their once-radical ideas had become mainstream, they could contentedly resign themselves to obsolescence.[55]

Charlotte's diary entries from this period, however, reveal her resistance to being put out to pasture. Throughout her Norwich years, she repeatedly reproached herself for slacking off. She vowed to retrain herself in the habit of working and to sit at her desk three hours each day so that she could accomplish "*something.*" At sixty-five, she dedicated herself to another ten years' work, reminded herself of her many accomplishments thus far, and sketched out a slew of potential projects.[56]

In the past, Charlotte had relied on lecturing to help sustain herself and her fame. In the 1930s, however, the self-identified "glossopod"—a traveler by tongue—rarely traveled or spoke publicly. "I greatly miss my audience," she wrote Alice Blackwell in 1930, "no lectures wanted anymore, and books not taken."[57] She offered free lectures to both the Connecticut League of Women Voters and the Connecticut College of Women, but all she got for her efforts was "one engagement in a neighboring town, audience of ten." Her final "Gilman Week" was staged in Hartford in mid-January 1933, thanks to the organizing efforts of supportive cousins. She had a delightful time but afterward sank into a "sudden 'flatness' as of a deflated balloon."[58]

Twice during the 1930s, Charlotte spoke on behalf of birth control. In 1932, she testified before the U.S. House (where she was accused of slurring Catholicism by Massachusetts Representative John McCormack, the future Speaker of the House). In January 1934, Charlotte joined nearly a thousand supporters attending the Birth Control and National Recovery conference in Washington. The conference was organized by Margaret Sanger and timed to coincide with Capitol Hill hearings. Charlotte spoke on "The World's Mother" at the closing dinner, where she sat on the dais alongside the female "Lindy," Amelia Earhart. Afterward, Sanger praised Charlotte for her inspirational talk delivered with her "usual clarity & force."[59] Several subsequent engagements in New York churches and other small venues—she took what she could get—as well as a handful of talks in Pasadena during her final year of life brought Charlotte's lecturing career to a close.[60]

The farthest afield Charlotte journeyed from Norwich to lecture during the Depression was to Chicago in 1933. She traveled there on Houghton's dime and "on a shoestring, and a very short shoestring at that" for a single engagement at the World Fellowship of Faiths Convention. She felt amply compensated by the enthusiastic reception she received; her talk made "such an impression that they asked for more after I sat down," she reported gleefully, "and I was the last speaker of the evening." Instead of reading her address on "The Social Body & Soul," she "laid it on the desk and 'talked' the same thing." One attendee assured her that she had "not lost in anyway—voice—delivery—fire—anything."[61] No, she might have replied, she had only lost her regular audience.

Charlotte continued to write articles in Norwich, but her annual publication rate numbered no more than five and often came closer to one or two. She welcomed "*any* call" for her "special views" in an era debased by "falsehood and grossness." She even proved willing to bend her principles for the sake of publication. She expressed outrage in 1925 when the *Century* changed the title of a forthcoming essay from "Service, Social and Domestic" to the catchier "Wash-Tubs and Woman's Duty." But she neither pulled the publication nor refused the chance to publish in the magazine again later that year. And in 1929, she "disgracefully held [her] tongue" and submitted a piece to *Good Housekeeping*, despite her ban on Hearst papers, so "desperate" was she "to have something printed."[62]

Charlotte's hopes were raised temporarily in 1928 when the *Forum* solicited additional work. The journal had recently published what its editor described as her "sassy" and "delightful" "Thrills, Common and Uncommon," an essay recapitulating her impersonal philosophy of social service. Yet her subsequent submissions were rejected without comment. (Her next and last publication in the *Forum* would appear posthumously.) Every success sent her spirits soaring, every rejection left her "utterly discouraged," uncertain whether she would ever "write any more—or ever did."[63]

During the thirties, Charlotte was invited to contribute three chapters, one a reprint, to three different books on contemporary life. The last of these chapters appeared in a 1931 collection overseen by V. F. Calverton and Samuel D. Schmalhausen, an editorial pair the *New Republic* dubbed the "sex boys." Charlotte informed Schmalhausen that he should consider her essay on "Parasitism and Civilized Vice" as ballast against the many pieces that would "magnify" sex; when the book, *Woman's Coming of Age*, appeared, she dismissed it as big and "horrid."[64]

Charlotte told Katharine that she expected no profit from these chapters other than a moral one. Through all the disappointments, she kept on writing; she believed, after all, that "to be busy at one's real work is to be happy." But the "discouragements piled up." The more she needed money, the less she felt inclined to work. "Necessity is no incentive to me," she once acknowledged ruefully, "at least a very poor one. . . ."[65]

Ironically, Charlotte's fame waned during a propitious decade for its waxing. The rhetoric of the New Deal resurrected many progressive aims, and the Depression's fundamental challenge to unchecked capitalism led to a resurgence of interest in nineteenth-century reform works. Bellamy's *Looking Backward*, for example, was reclaimed by Depression-era liberals and radicals as "one of the most important expressions of the democratic spirit in American thought."[66]

Even before the Bellamy revival, Charlotte had returned to fiction. She found the work "[h]ard sledding," but the market was larger for literature than for sociology, and she hoped to corner some of it. She still got some mileage out of "The Yellow Wall-Paper," republished by Golden Book in 1933, though she never managed to get it staged as a dramatic monologue in her lifetime.[67]

Her chief hope for a commercial success in the literary realm rested on her murder mystery, *Unpunished*, completed in 1929. Charlotte and Houghton were both avid readers of mysteries; Houghton especially had read countless detective stories, but he declared he had "never seen one like" his wife's. Charlotte identified *Unpunished* as a story that "has murder enough to satisfy the most demanding . . . [and] crime enough for our present day taste," with enough twists and humor to keep readers reading.

Unpunished is a revenge tale that anticipates Agatha Christie's *Murder on the Orient Express* (1934). Both mysteries include multiple killers and attempt to justify rather than merely solve their respective murders. The murdered man in Charlotte's novel, Wade Vaughn, is an unsympathetic, power-hungry blackmailer who enjoys his reign of terror. He is attacked by six of his victims, three of them servants, two the principal and sympathetic love interests. The tragic heroine, Jacqueline ("Jack"), causes the fatal heart attack that kills Vaughn before anyone else can get to him. She seeks to rid his evil presence from her house and revenge her sister's suicide, for which she blames him. Murdering an in-law who made a woman's home feel like a "trap" and who "fretted her constantly in petty ways"—Charlotte's fantasies had become the stuff of fiction.[68] As a genre, detective fiction taps into readers' desires for life to make sense, for questions to have answers, for crimes to be punished, and for persons to be held accountable, all longings the rational Charlotte would have been inclined to indulge, her faltering idealism notwithstanding.

Unpunished contains repeated "dago" slurs of a piece with its author's prejudices and the virulently anti-Italian and anti-Catholic 1920s. Anti-papist sentiment was exacerbated by Sacco and Vanzetti's execution in 1927 and Al Smith's presidential run in 1928. Both Charlotte and Houghton followed the 1928 election closely: Charlotte supported Hoover, but she hoped that if Smith won (he was trounced), it might "startle" the nation into recognizing the Catholic "threat."[69]

While drafting *Unpunished*, Charlotte confessed to "castle-building" again. She dreamed of producing a bestseller that would afford her the immediate pleasure of chicken and the ultimate pleasure of Pasadena winters. She tried to sell the manuscript to various presses, including Putnam's, McCall's, and MacMillan, before abandoning the project, disheartened. The book had seemed her "last hope so to speak," she gloomily informed Katharine. "If that don't go I don't know how I can earn money any more!"[70]

~

> . . . steady good health is the most valuable possession. It means achievement, it
> means happiness, it means money.
>   "We Don't Care to Be Well," 1919[71]

In addition to gardening, Charlotte attributed her continued good health to tonics and especially to Eskay's Neuro-Phosphates. She could have written a *Forerunner* testimonial to its virtues. "It means better appetite, better digestion, better sleep," she informed Grace, "and—best of all *better work!!!*" When she felt the need to fatten up, she took Kepler's Malt & Cod Liver Oil. She also kept "taking my extract of sheep," she told Katharine. "Why not, as well as mutton chops? The result is a steady improvement in cheerfulness and working power." The pills produced no adverse side effects and made her brain feel as if it was "quite sprouting again."[72]

At a checkup in her sixty-first year, Charlotte had learned her posture, formerly considered "perfect for age," was now "slightly drooping." She also learned that her "superior" feet had developed "Corns!" She confessed her chagrin, especially since she had long protested the fashion of pinching and deforming women's footwear. "I have striven all my life to stand erect and high-chested," she wrote her doctor after the appointment, "and to keep my feet free and healthy."

As the years passed, she registered additional signs of aging: she suffered from neuritis, grew thick-waisted, required glasses, and saw in the wrinkled face in the mirror "visibly an old lady." "How hidjus it is when one's machine gives out in spots," she commiserated with Grace.[73]

Yet Charlotte insisted her looks mattered little. Perhaps she would have been considered beautiful if she had only been "sex-conscious and dressed the part"; she also believed that she made "a better-looking old lady than [she] did a young one." Still, she declared, "one does not call a philosophic steam-engine beautiful." Beneath the surface, she still felt as fit as ever, and feeling so made "it so hard not to be *used*—not to have 'a pulpit.'"[74] According to her formula, she could still perform ably and thus should still be useful to society, but instead she felt increasingly like a form without a function.

In her twenties, Charlotte had been wont to overemphasize her symptoms, but in her seventies she tended to make light of them. She had successfully dodged the influenza bullet in 1918, but during the winter of 1931 she came down with pneumonia. Save for scarlet fever in 1874, this was her "first Bed-and-Doctor Illness!" At first, she figured she had caught a bad cold. Houghton was suffering from the grippe, so she relied upon "Dr. Diet, Dr. Quiet & Dr. Merryman" to see her through. Moving very slowly, she managed to perform most of the gardening herself. Soon she developed a continuous, hacking cough that kept her up at night and left her looking so "grey and awful" that she frightened Houghton. Charlotte finally relented and allowed him to call a doctor, but only after "the crisis was past."

Writing from her sick bed, she informed Katharine that "the pneumonia death rate is next to tuberculosis; and that after [age] 65 it is over 80%!" She, however, had in her "pigheaded" fashion gotten "past the danger point." She described the episode to a friend as "a lovely time, lying in bed and *resting* [thrice underlined]. The loveliest feeling! To [be] able to be quite still and not be 'on edge' to do things.'"[75] Her comments reveal the extent of her ongoing transformation: she now craved rest as much as she formerly craved motion.

By the end of 1931, Charlotte tipped the scales at 123 pounds. Since she had never weighed more than 115 in her life, she considered this "corpulence" and consulted her physician about her weight gain in the new year. She told Katharine subsequently that he found "nothing wrong," but it may have been at this visit—she found out early in 1932—that Charlotte learned she had developed inoperable breast cancer.[76]

For a week in 1921, the Gilmans had hosted a breast cancer patient whose doctors were keeping the news of her terminal condition from her. At the time,

Charlotte protested the "farce" of trying "to 'jolly along' a person with so short a shrift." Her mother's prolonged death from the disease had led her to vow not to prolong her own end should she receive a similar diagnosis. Her doctors had given Charlotte about a year to live, and in the end she more than tripled their estimate, but she knew that when the pain became intolerable, she would "step off" quietly and without regret.[77]

In the past, Charlotte's organicism had led her to invoke cancer as a metaphor for social ills. She might, then, have interpreted her diagnosis as a sign of her own inutility. But she opted instead for a more impersonal response and took the news "like a lamb—or a clam," to her doctor's astonishment. As she later explained to Alice Park, "I—consistent humanitarian that I am—why not me!" In making sense of her own disease, Charlotte's anti-individualism outweighed any strict functionalism. "Personally we're getting on, you and I," she observed to Alice Stone Blackwell, "but Personality is such a *little* part of life!"[78]

Even after receiving her diagnosis, Charlotte managed to enjoy pleasant summers and delight in the "dear earth." Illness rarely clouded her days the way financial and familial stressors did. By 1933, the Gilmans were feeling the "squeeze." They were particulary concerned about the cost of heating the drafty old house over the winter. Francis no longer contributed a cent toward the household expenses, leaving Houghton "to carry it all" on the basis of a meager legal practice. According to Charlotte, Francis—who owned a quarter of the house to Houghton's three-quarters—offered two responses to their quandaries: "I haven't got any money" and "let George do it."[79]

Some relief came that year when Houghton was appointed a deputy judge in the Norwich city court at an annual salary of $900. The couple figured that they needed at least twice that much to get by, however. During the Depression, an annual income of $500 or less was considered poverty; $1,000 represented the subsistence level; and $1,500 was deemed the minimum necessary for "minimum comfort."[80]

Hard times only exacerbated household tensions. Charlotte told Grace that even "Houghton, slow to anger, is simmering toward some reaction" against the other Gilmans' cold, ungrateful, and insolent behavior. Francis and Emily threatened a partition suit, and Charlotte and Houghton contemplated selling the place, as Houghton could no longer afford to "'carry' two families."

By January 1934, Charlotte and Houghton had moved into the nearby Wauregan Hotel for the winter in order to avoid wearisome tussles with their housemates and to save on expenses. A chief attraction of the Wauregan was its "Community Dinner Service," which delivered hot meals prepared by "an expert Chef" and "packed in INSULATED SERVITOR CONTAINERS" comparable to those

Charlotte had envisioned in *What Diantha Did* and her other writings on domestic reform. As a hotel resident, she delighted in saving money while "living
in warmth, ease and luxury at our principal hotel, two rooms and a bath, our
victrola, get our own breakfast & our lunch, a fine 'counter dinner' for *50 cts* in the
restaurant," she remarked approvingly.[81]

Their "good, comfortable winter" at the Wauregan only strengthened Charlotte's determination "to *get out of it altogether*"—"it" being their volatile domestic
situation. Grace wrote Katharine that her mother seemed in every way better for
her break from the domestic squabbles. Once Houghton's term as judge expired in
the summer of 1935, the couple planned to hasten to Pasadena. Charlotte seemed
especially anxious to alleviate Houghton's burdens and to provide him with an
"easy old age" in that sunny locale.[82]

In her final years, Charlotte participated in several tributes to other venerable women. In 1932, she played her Great-Aunt Harriet Stowe in a pageant in
Hartford. In 1934, she attended a memorial service for Marie Jenney Howe, where
she joined Floyd Dell, James Weldon Johnson, Senator Robert La Follette, Carrie
Chapman Catt, Harriot Stanton Blatch, and others in eulogizing the Heterodoxy
founder. These remembrances of people passed made it easier for Charlotte to
prepare for her own departure: "What a pleasant provision of nature it is," she
mused to her old friend Alice Blackwell, "that as we grow older our old friends
diminish in number, new ones do not hold as closely, the young workers do not
need us, and it becomes easier and easier to step out!"[83]

But it was not Charlotte's turn to "step out" next. During the Norwich years,
Houghton had "aged under care and worry, shame and disappointment as to
Francis and so on." Charlotte had seven years on her husband and so typically assumed that she would die first, an assumption that strengthened after she received
her cancer diagnosis. But if Houghton did predecease her, she hoped it would
"come quick—a sudden blow."[84]

She got her wish. At 10:44 p.m. on Friday, May 4, 1934, Houghton was returning from a game of bridge, crossing Broadway near Union Square in downtown
Norwich, when he suddenly collapsed. Passers-by rushed to his aid, but he had
apparently died instantly from a massive cerebral hemorrhage. Charlotte had been
at home reading, awaiting his return, when she received a telephone call saying
her husband had fallen "unconscious" in the street. She "'stood at attention' as I
always do in sudden danger," she said, "went down town calmly to a little office
opening on the street,—he lay on the floor at my feet, dead." It was "a very good
way to go," Charlotte wrote her daughter the following day, by which she meant
that it was swift and seemingly painless.[85]

Two weeks after Houghton's death, Charlotte claimed to be "holding out very well." She informed Katharine, "You see there's no one to be sorry for but me—and I'm not going to make much of that? All my Human life is untouched; only the personal life is injured; and I live mostly outside personality." Houghton's death had hurt her personally, but it comforted her to think that his loss made little difference to the living that went on without him. His death thus helped to prove her theory about the self's insignificance in the larger scheme of things.

Moreover, living without Houghton was just another "going without," Charlotte observed, and with "most people" during the Depression she had "had lots of practice in that." Since, in the end, all happily married couples had to face this irrevocable separation, at least she numbered among the few survivors who "can look back on so much unbroken happiness." And at least Houghton had been spared having to see her "wither and die—and he be left alone."[86]

A month out, Charlotte had convinced herself that "it was a beautiful way to die." She told Katharine, "Except for me he was not a happy man." What with financial strains, family tensions, and bad investments, "he would have been glad to go, save for leaving me," she reflected. "So, I have nothing to be sorry for by myself—and that is not a large part of my life." She conceded that she had been grievously hurt—she was struggling to cope with "The Goneness . . . a blank *lack*." But she mattered little overall, and the damage Houghton's death had inflicted would make it that much easier for her to let go of life when her own time came.[87]

Charlotte soon decided to move to Pasadena to be near Katharine and her family. She told her young grandson to expect only "half a Grandmother" when she arrived because, she explained, it "really seems as if half of me was gone." In her youth, bitter experience had taught Charlotte to treat grief as a reminder "to crush all personal sorrow and drop the whole ground of self-interest forever."[88] In her final, grief-stricken year, Charlotte had nothing left to lose but her self.

Pasadena

14   "The Stepping Off Place"
(1934–1935)

We can bear pain, immeasurable, long;
    We can, we must, we evidently do;
Some day, together, we, grown wise and strong,
    Shall end our self-made misery untrue,—
Self-crippled, self-imprisoned, blindly wrong,—
    And, safe at last, shoot upward, glad and free.
                        "To One Who Suffers," 1916[1]

Charlotte's last fifteen months proved as dramatic as any preceding. The grieving widow dismantled her house of twelve years and flew across country to her beloved Pasadena, where she spent her final days near her daughter's family taking any work she could get, preparing her papers, and, as the pain from cancer grew unbearable, plotting her suicide.

For Charlotte, the highlight was relocating to Pasadena, which she had chosen long ago as the best place to live and to die. Since she did not believe in heaven, it was the closest to paradise she ever expected to get. All she needed to "end my days" in peace, she informed Katharine, was a "little house somewhere" in Pasadena, "with a long view if possible—a fig tree—grapes—flowers forever— oranges—grapes—fruit—wow!"[2]

Yet realizing this dream brought with it accompanying worries. By moving to California to die, she feared she might burden Katharine the way her own mother had burdened her. She swore it would be otherwise and took several preemptive steps. First, she vowed not to live with Katharine but instead to secure a room nearby. This would spare Katharine round-the-clock care of her, spare herself care of a house, and afford her more opportunities of "being foot-loose and going here and there."[3] Second, she maintained that she would help more than hurt by contributing to Katharine's financial well-being. Finally, she intended, once the pain for everyone involved outweighed the gain, to orchestrate a quick, painless, and efficient death, the antithesis of her mother's protracted one. On every count, she proved true to her word.

~

> Being Human is so big that a member of Society can bear a personal pain.
> Letter to Alice Park, May 26, 1934[4]

From May to early August 1934, Charlotte bid a prolonged adieu to Norwich. Grace, who had been "stupefied" to only learn of Houghton's death when Lyman Beecher Stowe called for news several days afterward, arrived in Norwich on May 9. She found Charlotte "pathetically bewildered," still reeling from the effects of grief and a lingering cold.

Everywhere Charlotte went in the house and on the grounds brought sorrowful reminders—what she called "an incessant haunting." Outside was the garden, now in Charlotte's words "orphaned," and inside and "hardest of all to face" was the Victrola that had been Houghton's "greatest pleasure" (it would be one of the few items she bothered to crate and ship to the West Coast). She tried to be thankful for "every little convenience" she had afforded her unassuming spouse, but mostly she felt remorseful over what she had not done but might have.[5]

Houghton's death could have wrought a reconciliation between Charlotte and the other Gilmans, but instead Francis and Emily were "behaving like the devil." After declaring himself "'the head of the house,'" Francis had taken over the dining room during Charlotte's accustomed hours, and he proceeded to appropriate the jointly owned furnishings as he saw fit. Charlotte blamed her in-laws for adding to Houghton's burdens and hastening his death.

Francis in turn accused Charlotte of allowing Houghton's pajama-clad body to lie "in a dirty dark room near a cast iron sink, on the hottest week-end of the season!" He was especially incensed by Charlotte's presumptuous decision to cremate his brother (Charlotte, who never owned an automobile, had relied on friends to drive her to the closest crematorium in Springfield, Massachusetts).

Francis resented that Charlotte got "her way" in this matter with no input from the surviving brother. He fired off an irate letter to Houghton and Charlotte's close friend, the Reverend Alexander Abbott, insisting that cremation was not so much Houghton's wish as

> the repercussion of the constant hammering and yammering by a genius, of a reli-
> gion—whether it is His Religion and Hers or not (and you recall what a tremendous
> sensation that book did not make and how universally the world has gone over to her
> ideas); semi-colon, colon, full-stop. A religion I say that she invented, I am surprised
> and dismayed and appalled that an alleged minister, a so called Man of God . . . could
> not induce Charlotte to show Houghton proper respect. . . . [6]

Intense while it lasted, the storm blew over before a week had passed. In the aftermath, Francis meekly approached Charlotte, "patted her on the shoulder, [and] said he 'had no hard feelings.'" "Poor Francis," Grace sighed, "I guess he can't help what he is." Charlotte concurred, referring to her brother-in-law as a "[p]oor little thing."[7]

Sympathetic and affectionate friends were "fairly swarming about." They offered meals and company and made it easier for Charlotte finally to let her faithful servant Mary go. Houghton's closest friend, their lawyer Edwin H. Higgins, handled the estate—or, rather, he spent long hours trying to shore some fragments against its ruins. His revelations about the dismal state of the couple's finances led the survivors to wonder whether bearing his burdens silently had induced Houghton's stroke.

At first, it seemed Charlotte would be left destitute: the $10,000 Houghton had loaned a law partner on borrowed funds remained unpaid, his risky investment in a local race track with Francis had swallowed large and needed sums, and the cost of supporting his own and Charlotte's relatives had depleted any reserves. But in the end, the law partner paid back $6,000 of the loan; a cousin, Elizabeth Gilman, purchased Charlotte's share of the house for a little over a thousand dollars; and the estate proved surprisingly solvent. Charlotte wound up with $700 in cash, 300 shares in various companies, and some $2,400 in dividends; the latter ensured Charlotte two years of $200 monthly allotments.[8] The always frugal Charlotte considered this stipend sufficient, especially since she expected to die within the year. In spite of the initial worry, Charlotte had landed on shaky feet, financially speaking.

She was even shakier emotionally. "So brave and so energetic," Grace declared her, "but really frail, under it all, and at times so terribly, nervously irritable." According to Grace, Charlotte now showed little interest in the outside world, read no papers, and occupied her time increasingly with the "mental diversion" of word games, picture puzzles, and solitaire. At her best, she seemed "so alert and active," but bouts of mental confusion could leave her fearing, "in a dark moment, that she did not think her head would hold out through what she must do." In even darker moments, she declared herself ready to die: "It's little I care," she told Grace. ". . . You see I'm no good to K—, There's nobody to miss me but you—and my brother—and that's not for long." If she found work in California, she would "hang on as long" as she could. Otherwise, however, she would hasten the inevitable, unwilling to grow "much older, with no work and no income!"[9]

Resuming a role she had played nearly fifty years previously, Grace again found herself helping Charlotte to break up house after her marriage had ended. Understandably, she judged Charlotte more fragile and distraught this time around, as she related to Katharine in a July 1934 letter:

> At times she is irritable (an intensification of her old impatience). . . . It is no use to argue with her—about anything. . . . But at times she is her old merry self, and we get a good many laughs. I am *so glad* she does not want to be with you, for it would kill you all. But she has a great craving to feel *near* you, and a real fear that the children may not care for her. "Dorothy won't like the way I look," etc. etc. I laugh at her and tell her you will all have lots of fun together yet. I think you will find that, after the first, she will be very independent and go about a good deal among friends. . . . *At first*, it will mean everything to her to be warmly received, shown affection, made to feel she "belongs."—but I don't think she will be at all dependent, afterwards. . . . She is sensitive,—but a little appreciation goes a long way with her. . . . [I]f you both [Katharine and Frank] can realize the actual frailty, under her apparent energy, you will not be tired by things which once might have tired you. . . .
>
> (She has just come up to lie down a little,—tired out by the noise of opening the boxes. Later I'll go down and list the contents with her.) I asked her for a message and she said "Tell her I've not given out yet—*once*."—which is measurably true.[10]

It is as characteristic of Grace to offer a part-fond, part-exasperated account of Charlotte's volatility as it is of Charlotte to boast of her brave public face.

Charlotte was so anxious to leave the haunting house that she stayed up all night packing at least once and frequently worked into the wee hours. In the end, she shipped sixteen boxes, containing mostly books, manuscripts, pictures, puzzles, clothes, the Victrola, and records. Although frail and fatigued, with dark-circled eyes, Charlotte refused her friend's numerous offers of assistance to the point where Grace felt driven to complain, "Ah no: she must do it all. . . . It is a mania. . . . And she has been undisputed ruler here: Houghton just accepted it. It's useless to worry her, and hopeless to change her—but I don't think anyone else could live with her long, without nervous exhaustion! Yet she's so dear and fine and splendid: one wants to make her as happy as possible."[11]

Grace encouraged the Chamberlins to write frequent notes assuring the for-lorn widow of their love and admiration. Charlotte had not wanted to add to Katharine's worries and so had not yet told her daughter she had cancer, although she had confided in Grace. Grace kept her friend's secret but assured Katharine her mother's life would not last much longer, adding, "Who can wish it? Unless she finds unexpected happiness in some new work." After all, Grace observed, Char-lotte was now in her seventy-fifth year and already "had done great work, lived a full life, and I don't think she cares to live forever!"[12] For Grace as for Charlotte, the value of a life lay in the value of the work and the viability of the worker.

The prospect of returning to Pasadena after so many years kept Charlotte going. Just leaving Norwich wrought a change for the better. By the time she reached New York—after pampering visits with the Stowes in the Berkshires and with Martha and Robert Bruère in the Palisades—she struck Grace as "amazingly refreshed and so some ten years younger than before." Already, for Charlotte, "Norwich and all its complications" were "rapidly receding" (yet another testa-ment to her "vast capacity for forgetting"). She now looked "forward eagerly to my pleasantly limited and peaceful life in Pasadena," she said.[13]

Instead of a train trip of four to five days, Charlotte had opted to fly from New York to California aboard the Lindbergh Line (TWA). She initially objected to the cost, since she hated to waste money better spent on Katharine's family. But her flight turned out to be only slightly more expensive than train travel, and she ultimately decided that she could not forgo the "stimulating experience, even if tiring." It would, she figured, be her "last 'fling.'"[14]

In those early days of commercial aviation, a plane ride was an event in itself. Charlotte's fifteen-hour flight took off at four o'clock in the afternoon on Friday, August 31, and, after a slight delay, arrived early on the morning of Saturday, Sep-tember 1. On the first of two legs, Charlotte received a boxed meal of "3 tiny half-sandwiches, one small cake, two olives, a little carton of canned fruit—mixed, a few grapes, and a cup of coffee" and "ate every scrap." On the second leg, from Kansas City, she made repeated visits to the lavatories due to air sickness. Yet she never regretted her decision. Mist had obstructed her view during the waning daylight hours, but the skies cleared by dark, and she declared "Chicago by night seen from above . . . worth the trip."[15]

In 1907, Charlotte had written an essay speculating about what might happen "When We Fly." Her abiding faith in the positive effects of locomotion made her optimistic about the outcome once people began to move vertically. She pre-dicted profound cultural and moral consequences, including a true international-ism resulting from constant intercourse across national boundaries. She believed international travel would heighten our sense of mutual obligation and hasten the "humanizing" of "mankind more rapidly than ever before." She also anticipated individual consequences and joyfully envisioned a person, "winged and engined, buzzing off, like a huge cockchafer, to soar and circle, dip and rise as he will!" Each of these now "aerial" creatures, she concluded, would have to be afforded "the whole whirring circle of his wings."[16]

A self-described "bird-without-legs," Charlotte had no need to fly literally in order to indulge in metaphorical flights. In 1895, she had written a poem called "Wings," which describes in rapturous terms the sensation of flight from a bird's perspective; she had also earned the nickname "Wings" from one of her admirers— the writer and illustrator Rose O'Neill Wilson. When she finally got the chance to test her hypotheses about the effects of flying, they failed fully to measure up to her flights of fancy. Still, she loved to move and longed to soar, and she now rejoiced at her ability to declare, in all honesty, "I have flown and I have lit!"[17]

~

> Personally I am *very* comfortable, as near happy as I have any right to expect. But "personality" is so *little* compared to all you people I love—and can't help!
> Letter to Grace Channing Stetson,
> September 1934[18]

Charlotte arrived at the Glendale airport around 7:45 a.m. She appeared sleep-deprived, "a little sick and very tired" after the long flight. Katharine had not seen her mother for seven years and was startled to greet a "thin," "weazened" figure who struck her as rather "green" around the gills, "and so vague, rattled and roundshouldered." For her part, Charlotte found her daughter "a good deal older—and worn."

From the airport, they proceeded to Pasadena's Hotel Constance, where Charlotte took a room and where her brother Thomas and his son and namesake soon joined them for breakfast. At least a decade had passed since Charlotte had last seen her brother: she declared him "dreadfull" looking, "a shadowy wreck."[19] Hard times had taken their toll on her family, and the careworn faces of her daughter and brother revealed that Pasadena was no cure-all.

Charlotte intended to stay only temporarily at her hotel. She hoped soon to secure "a 'dignified base'" in Pasadena for lectures and "for the business of living 365 days in the year. . . ." She quickly found a roomy, private, third-floor apartment (formerly the servants' quarters), divided from the only other top-floor flat by both a partition wall and the stairs. The flat was located in a quiet, established boarding house on North Madison Avenue, owned by a Mrs. Harris and managed by "a very nice little Swedish woman." Once a private home, it was "now a species of Old Ladies Home"; of the nine old women rooming there, Charlotte reckoned herself "the spryest!"

Situated on a street lined by elegant older homes, tall palms, and camphor laurels, the house was near both the library and the shops and about a mile in different directions from the Chamberlins and from her brother. Overall, Charlotte felt pleased with her rooms; she claimed to be "oldmaidish by nature and like[d] to have all her fixings just so."[20]

The apartment was equipped with both a kitchenette and a water closet, but it lacked a sink, so Charlotte brushed her teeth while perched on the tub and dumped her coffee grounds down the toilet. Her triple casement window provided a panoramic mountainous backdrop, and from her fire escape she could savor the lovely gardens below. Charlotte referred to this fire escape as her "balcony" and considered it the room's best feature. She often brought her rocker outside and sat with her solitaire board on her lap, with the suitcase she used as a writing desk resting on a chair before her. She enjoyed the sunshine and "that sky-garden of mine," she said; she could peer down from her aerie onto treetops, poinsettias, marguerite daisies, oranges, roses, and other colorful plants. She continued to feel grateful that she had escaped the suffocating atmosphere of Lowthorpe and that she could now pass her days "in sunlight and moonlight too."[21]

On a typical day during that fall of 1934, Charlotte would lie in bed sometimes as late as 8:30 a.m., make her own ten-cent breakfast of bread and butter, fruit, and coffee, and then write for a while. In the afternoons she usually ate lunch out, stopped at the library, and took a walk (often she would ride the cars to the end of a line and walk home, or vice versa). At dusk she visited either Katharine's or Thomas's family until around nine in the evening. The difficulties she had experienced in the state forty years previously might have darkened her return, but she declared otherwise: "I love California," she wrote a friend once she had settled, "and this dear little city is more like home to me than any place on earth."[22] After years of restless roaming, she now felt both at home and at peace.

Soon after arriving, Charlotte sketched out a provisional year of life. She planned to finish her autobiography, write her long poem on women as well as at least six articles, and deliver sixteen lectures. "My!" she exclaimed, "That would be a good finish." She tackled the last task first, conducting a Bible class at Pasadena's First Congregational Church; the minister, a Harvard man named Phelps, drove her to and fro. She also offered a class at a neighbor's and gave the occasional talk; for example, she addressed both "the Girl's Friendly Society" and "a club of colored young people!"—the latter invitation extended on the basis of her relation to Harriet Beecher Stowe. Katharine told Grace that her mother was "either a most marvelous bluffer—or [she] is getting a good deal of pleasure out of her talks, her room and all her fixings—she looks and seems very much better than when she arrived."[23]

In October, Charlotte declared herself "Very comfortably situated, very" and resolved to "do some work." But when she asked herself, "What have I to offer?" she made no reply. She experienced no necessary "'push' to write" and felt discouraged by the possibility that "the scrappy, imperfect, desperately honest work" she had already done was now essentially forgotten.

She did compose a few poems in her final months, including one entitled "This Lovely Earth":

> When you are young and all the world is new,
> When you are old and it is home to you,
> And all through life, in pleasure, hope and pain,
> Laughing in sunlight, resting under rain,
> Taking all weathers at their welcome worth,
> To love and love and love this lovely earth![24]

As the days passed, Charlotte grew increasingly content to simply relax and "love this lovely earth." By December, the mornings she had set aside for writing were typically usurped by leisure activities. She routinely read detective stories ("They are the easiest reading," she told a friend's daughter; "That's why tired people like em"), played solitaire (she referred to the game as "her pipe"), and conducted errands.

Occasionally, she indulged in a fit of "figgering" in an attempt to "'keep accounts,' with small success." During her Pasadena months, Charlotte imposed a strict budget: she spent no more than thirty dollars a month total divided up among rent (twelve dollars), food (ten to twelve dollars), and laundry (two to three dollars), with movies, carfare, and candy consuming the remainder.[25]

Katharine's dear friend Anna Waller had bought the house at 239 South Catalina, next but one to the Chamberlins, and now offered Charlotte its use. Charlotte remained at Mrs. Harris's while the house was being updated. In the interim, she paid frequent visits and took frequent meals with the Chamberlins, concerned by what she found there. Frank suffered from depression and passed most nights in his studio out back, brooding over his disappointments. Charlotte disdained men's economic dependence even more than she did women's. She resented Katharine's having "the whole care on her shoulders," and she was horrified to find her daughter had "largely supported them for some years by borrowing money!"[26] Charlotte had accumulated considerable debt herself when she last lived in California, but borrowing was not the way she had envisioned Katharine following in her footsteps.

Her daughter's housekeeping also troubled her. On Charlotte's last trip to Pasadena in 1927, Katharine had surprised her mother surreptitiously scrubbing the kitchen floor on her hands and knees. In 1934, Charlotte still could not fathom how the Chamberlins "have lived so indifferently in *dirt*—real dirt." She may have made her feelings known; Katharine complained to Grace that her mother liked to "expound . . . she can't just talk. . . ."

Charlotte did expound to Dorothy, Katharine's eldest child, in an attempt to nudge her into doing more of the household chores. Charlotte's habitual forgetfulness apparently extended to her own aversion to housework at Dorothy's age. Charlotte lamented to Grace that Katharine had not "trained" the children "to service"— had not, in other words, heeded Charlotte's advice "concerning children."[27]

Charlotte did manage to enjoy herself with the Chamberlins. She wrote verse with her granddaughter and did puzzles and played games with the family. Whenever possible, she also went to the movies. While in Pasadena, she saw *The Count of Monte Cristo*, *The House of Rothschild*, *Be Mine Tonight*, *Krakatoa*, *Treasure Island*, *The Big Bad Wolf*, and *Three Little Pigs*, among other films. In a corner of Katharine's house, she had established a "memorial" to Houghton, consisting of the Victrola, stacks of records, and a relief of Houghton perched on a bookcase; the family often gathered there in the evenings to listen to music.[28]

Charlotte initially helped out with the children in the late afternoons as well as on Thursday nights. According to her grandson Walter, she rarely scolded either him or his sister. Once, though, what Charlotte identified as a "hyperthesia of the ear, so that loud music or any loud or harsh noise is a distress," led her to speak sharply to the children while they were fashioning homemade footwarmers by wrapping crackling newspapers around soapstone. More than anything, Charlotte helped out financially, writing regular checks to Katharine. By April 1935, she had cleaned out her Pasadena bank account.[29]

Despite the hard times, the Chamberlins managed to make Charlotte's first several months in Pasadena festive. In October, Katharine and a neighbor hosted a tea for Charlotte, to which they invited the actress Katharine Hepburn, among other guests. Charlotte knew Hepburn's mother from the Connecticut League of Women Voters and was a fan of the actress. Hepburn's busy schedule forced her to decline the invitation, but some thirty-five people ultimately attended, including several local actresses and celebrities.

In November, the Chamberlins hosted a lavish Thanksgiving dinner consisting of turkey, crushed cranberry sauce, creamed celery, sweet and white potatoes, squash and mince pies, as well as fruits, nuts, and raisins. The family felt especially thankful for the outcome of a recent high-stakes and closely-watched election: Charlotte's one-time ally, Upton Sinclair, had moved to Pasadena in 1915; after several election defeats, he had switched party affiliation from Socialist to Democrat in order to run for governor in 1934. Charlotte's increasing conservatism led her to hope he would lose, and he did.[30]

More typically, Charlotte blithely ignored events outside her family circle, which she drew ever tighter around her as the months passed. For Christmas, Charlotte provided "quantities of little things for every one"—most scavenged from her bureau drawers, the rest purchased at Woolworths. She presented each child as well as Katharine with ten "white & red packages" and received from the Chamberlins five picture puzzles.[31]

As the year wound down, Charlotte counted leisure time as her chief blessing. She wrote Grace, "I am beginning to understand how women spend their lives, contentedly, without doing anything! It is incredible to my once violently active conscience that I can sit here in comfort and peace and luxury—you see it is luxury to me, my tastes being so limited—to do so little." She was not in great pain and ended the year feeling so invigorated that she defiantly declared, "If I did not know of this lurking enemy, I should say I was perfectly well!"[32]

~

Death is the smallest of crosses
To the worker whose harvest is in.
                              "Get Your Work Done," 1909[33]

How it does improve life to have an end to it!
                              Letter to George Houghton Gilman,
                              December 1899[34]

Charlotte had once read an article on cancer that outlined its progress: ". . . the thing is at first harmless and slow of growth; but something starts it into unholy zeal, it proliferates madly, grows so fast that it is turned in upon itself, and . . . it is the crushed inner parts which generate the poisons from which the victim dies." Her disease followed this course to the letter, with one notable exception: she determined not to die from cancer's poison. "I had not the least objection to dying," she maintained. "But I did not propose to die of this, so I promptly bought sufficient chloroform as a substitute."[35]

Since her diagnosis, Charlotte had stepped up her periodic visits to pharmacies, where she requested enough chloroform to "kill a cat." She knew the approximate dose, having used it to euthanize pets since a young girl. She had also experimented with the drug herself. The ether administered on her frequent trips to the dentist had afforded her "the only complete rest I have ever known," she said. And once as a small child, she had pilfered some of the chloroform her mother used for "sick-headaches" and, liking the smell, poured more and more on her handkerchief until she "dropped off before any real harm was done." With the help of a "little black whip," a terrified Mary brought her groggy daughter back to consciousness, at which point Charlotte lay on the bed and laughed in her mother's face.[36]

Charlotte thought ether "great fun" but willingly postponed the inevitable until it caught up with her. She preferred her Pasadena doctors to her Norwich ones and paid them a reduced rate for several courses of radiation, or "Deep Therapy," as it was then called. She found it helped to cure the swollen arm, due to a weakened lymphatic system, that had accompanied her across country. She suffered from intermittent bouts of nausea and malaise but in the main was "not fussing."[37]

The decline, once it started, was steep. In February 1935, Katharine noticed that her mother was more "fatigued . . . not quite as spry as a while back." Several weeks later, Charlotte told Grace that she felt as good as dead and that "the grasshopper"—one of her many metaphors for cancer—was "getting to be a burden." In early March, she learned her lungs were involved, which explained her hacking cough. As her appetite decreased, her nausea increased. The more difficulty she had tending to her own needs, the more she felt she had reached "the sticking place."[38]

The time had come finally for Charlotte to tell her "pale and frail and overburdened" daughter that she had cancer. Charlotte recognized that her death would deal a devastating financial blow to the family. Frank's "earnings have been about at the vanishing point," Katharine acknowledged to Grace. "Without Mama I guess we all would have vanished," she added.

Katharine's desperate straits kept Charlotte hanging "on just as long as she can stand it to help out," a decision Katharine backed since her mother still derived "a good deal of pleasure out of things." Upon her death, the $200 monthly payments from Houghton's estate would stop altogether, so Charlotte postponed her suicide to give Katharine at least one more check.[39] Charlotte may have devoted her career to teaching the benefits of economic independence, especially for women, but in her own life her daughter's financial dependence made her feel needed and valued until the end.

Charlotte made her final public appearance at the end of March 1935, when the extended Beecher clan gathered at the Mission Inn for a family reunion. Charlotte "was given the place of particular honor at the luncheon." "Alert and keen-eyed . . . the merriest guest present," she told the assembly it pleased her to see her "good stock" doing "*their work*—and that keeps." Life was more ephemeral, however, and to her mind rightly so.

That same March, she penned her "valedictory," an essay supporting euthanasia. She asked Lyman (who had attended the reunion) to try to persuade the *Forum* to publish it posthumously. For some time, Charlotte had contemplated writing "a convincing article on the complete justifiability of suicide under some circumstances." That time had come: her doctors gave her six months, but, she told Lyman, "I say probably less!"[40]

Charlotte now appeared to be "going down hill with alarming rapidity." A slight reprieve came in April when she moved to Anna Waller's house on South Catalina. She enjoyed the quiet street and beautiful gardens. She also felt "very happy about the new conveniences and fixings," especially after she decided to have her bedroom repapered in a soothing blue pattern. She passed most of her days "sitting under the orange tree with petals falling over her" as she reclined in the chaise lounge her former landlady Mrs. Harris had brought over.[41]

Her spirits received an additional boost that same April when the activist and writer Zona Gale responded encouragingly to her plea for help with *The Living*. Gale tactfully dodged pressure to start "du novo," but she did agree to write a lengthy introductory essay and to help find the existing draft a publisher. Gale strongly recommended the book to Appleton's and promised her editorial support, which did the trick: Charlotte secured her first book contract in a dozen years.[42]

The acceptance of *The Living* inspired Charlotte to take a "fresh interest in life." She indulged in one final round of "castle-building" in hopes of ushering her other languishing book projects into print and triggering a Gilman revival thereby. She spent her last weeks revising her autobiography and choosing photographs. She also wrote the brief final chapter, giving short shrift to the near-decade that had passed since completing the earlier draft, but "it did not seem that she had an ounce more strength to expend," Grace later explained to the publisher. Charlotte dedicated the book to Katharine, who owned the copyright and would receive the royalties, and to her grandchildren. In an "Author's Note," she thanked Grace, the Stowes, Zona, Amy Wellington, Edwin Higgins, and other friends who had stood by her during her widowhood and "long illness."[43]

Now neighbors, mother and daughter soon established a pattern to their days. Upon waking, Charlotte phoned Katharine, who brought her mother breakfast in bed consisting of coffee, juice, and toast or biscuit. Afterward, she set Charlotte up outside with water, Digitalis, books, and puzzles to rest and enjoy the morning. Charlotte took lunch at Katharine's and then subsequently returned to her chaise until it was time for a light supper, also at the Chamberlins. After a few word games with Katharine, Charlotte retired to her cottage and to bed. Occasional drives, picnics in the arroyo, and trips up in the mountains rarely lasted longer than two hours, Charlotte's outer limit before exhaustion set in.[44]

Rather than objecting to "being nursed and tended," Charlotte surprised even herself with her "amiable and cheerful submission." Her insistence on making the best of bad situations—combined with her sense of herself as having been deprived, since childhood, of nurturing—led her to relish her "new position of Distinguished Invalid!" She continued to marvel over how much she enjoyed her unhurried days, her work ethic notwithstanding: "It's astonishing how *nothing* I do!" she wrote Grace.[45]

Charlotte now did nothing because she could do no more. Mornings right after waking were her best times, but once she began "walking around and trying to do things," she had to face "how weak she is." Her hearing had been failing for some time, and talking triggered her cough. If she had to communicate, she would "scribble" something. In April, Charlotte began writing "p.p.c." (paid parting call) letters informing distant friends and family of her disease and of her decision to go "peacefully asleep when I get ready," she said.[46]

Nearly all recipients joined her brother in approving her plan wholeheartedly. In a sense, these early notifications enabled Charlotte to attend her own memorial service—a ceremony she intended to forgo as too much fuss—one speaker at a time. Friends responded with tributes to her personal courage and her public service. Alice Stone Blackwell reported Jane Addams's recent death from cancer and added, "now we are to lose you, and the world will seem poorer and more lonesome." Carrie Chapman Catt claimed that all of Charlotte's books sat on her shelves and that she routinely gave them "a little pat of appreciation and think what the world might have been had those books never been written."[47]

Many echoed her cousin Lyman in affirming the difficulty of reconciling Charlotte's description of herself as "old and ill" with their indelible image of her as "a vibrant, radiant, unconquerable and deathless spirit." Her nephew Basil, the boy Charlotte had considered adopting for one wildly desirous moment during her years "at large," thanked her for her "generosity to [him] as a small boy" and for providing him with "an optimistic philosophy that has made life seem very much worth while."[48]

Fortunately, Charlotte wrote her departure letters early. By May, the cancer had spread to her abdomen and liver, both now so enlarged she could scarcely bend forward. She still experienced "days of ups and downs," but mostly she had "so little reserve that any upset takes a lot out of her." The worst came when the "funny 'prickles'" in her neck developed into shingles that traveled from her neck "up to her jaw on the left side (cancer side) and down the spine . . . and on top of the shoulder." She kept from screaming but asked Katharine not to mind if she repeatedly moaned "Ah" and "Oh Dear" as this seemed to help. Her temperature flared and her pulse raced, she lost weight, barely slept, stopped bothering to dress, and could no longer manage to feed herself or play solitaire. She had reached the point where she no longer felt like "herself."[49]

Her physical suffering tested her endurance and her idealism, bringing home the materiality of existence and its consequences to a woman who routinely discounted the body's significance. Charlotte valued her physical body primarily for its use, and her cancer-ridden frame no longer seemed useful. The aging process had helped to lessen her investment, as her poem "Body of Mine" indicates:

> . . . Body of mine that now grows old—
>   Thin, dry, and old—
>   . . . the living world is the frame of me—
> Heart and soul are not found in thee—
>   Body of mine![50]

Charlotte remained enough of an idealist to consider the body confining rather than defining, and the more it confined her, the more she longed to escape.

By June 5, the worst was over, but the disease had reduced her, by her own estimate, to "just bones and drapery!" According to Katharine, "nothing but her desire to get more money out of the estate keeps her going—she sees no point in being so miserable, with nothing to look forward to." After much beseeching and financial assistance from family and friends, Grace had finally agreed to come to Pasadena. Her long-postponed visit was eagerly anticipated by Charlotte, Katharine, the children, and old friends including Augusta ("Gussie") Senter, the woman who had slapped Charlotte for being "an unnatural mother" and whom Katharine regarded as a third mother; by Charlotte's reckoning, Gussie was also on her "last legs."[51]

Now "old, heavily disabled, [and] poor" herself, Grace arrived on June 11, the two widows' shared wedding anniversary. She took the cottage's two front rooms, and Charlotte occupied the two middle ones, with the kitchen and bath shared between them. Charlotte could no longer speak, and Grace could no longer hear, but they managed to play word and letter games together and sit holding hands in companionable silence. Charlotte anticipated "a lot of unpleasantness about 'the order of my going,'" she said presciently, so she was pleased that Grace would be there to help Katharine weather the ordeal.

Katharine and Grace comprised part of the small party thrown to celebrate

Charlotte's seventy-fifth birthday on July 3. With Lyman's monetary gift, Katharine purchased for her mother a bottle each of whiskey and apricot cordial, drinks Charlotte increasingly relied on "when too tired to eat." The scale she received as another present proved her frailty: she now weighed 100 pounds.[52]

"As soon as I'm too weak to totter to the bathroom—off I go," Charlotte told Zona Gale in early August. "I know what it means to be 'tired to death.' And O my dear! *What* a comfort it will be to go to sleep!" Death was no stranger to Charlotte nor to her generation, which doubtless helped to lessen its sting. The list of those she had seen either die or dead included her infant sister, her grandmother and great-grandmother, friends such as May Diman and Conway Brown, not to mention her mother and second husband. Charlotte's close contact with death and her rational outlook helped her to face her own end calmly and squarely.

From early days, the prevalence of death and disease had convinced many mourning Americans—among them, several of her Beecher relatives—of a connection to the spirit world. During Charlotte's adulthood, inventions such as the telegraph, the telephone, and the harnessing of electricity, which relied on invisible conduits, persuaded even such scientifically minded explorers as William James to take spiritualism seriously. Charlotte mocked the concept of embodied ghosts, replete with "ruffles and embroidery" ("who was their laundress?" she wondered). She had nonetheless experimented on occasion with Planchette, insisting that she felt the board move with her fingers lightly placed upon it. She also maintained that her mother had communicated with her shortly after dying, which proved that there was "some common back alley, open to all our minds. . . ."[53]

Charlotte showed little interest in exploring that alley, however. She expressed her beliefs about death and the afterlife to Alice Stone Blackwell in the spring of 1934:

> Have you any belief in personal immortality? I have not, not any *interest* in it. It seems to me a petty idea. But I have a profound confidence in God, the kind of God I see; and am absolutely contented to accept the order of nature.
>
> The immortality I believe in is for the race, for our continuing ascending humanity. To that progress you and I and the others have contributed, in it we live.
>
> Do you remember Whitman—?—
>
> "No words can say how utterly at peace I am about God and about death."[54]

Whitman, whom Charlotte had treasured since first discovering him and who held that "the smallest sprout shows there really is no death," proved as influential on her dying as he had been on her living.

Charlotte's organic philosophy helped to dispel any lingering fear. If dying was a necessary part of living—after all, she observed, "[l]ife without death would be life without growth"—then why should we "fuss" about so fundamental a necessity? If life meant motion and death represented a mere "stepping off," then what could be easier than taking that step once the pace of the individual life had slowed to a crawl? And if collective human life mattered far more than the individual, then why should we object to dying, secure in the knowledge that life would continue undaunted?

For so long, Charlotte had been fueled by a desire to leave off "being me," a desire she could now finally, literally realize. Her indifference to self and self-preservation ran so deep that the dissolution of identity enacted at the moment of death—or "the soul's release / From this small binding entity, / This transient limitation me"—tantalized her with a "sort of 'School's Out!' feeling." She faced her own death complacently because she knew she would be the one ringing the bell for dismissal. All the uncertainties had vanished: she knew the how, the when, and the why, and, just as important, she knew her death would be "peaceful."[55]

Like eugenics, euthanasia seemed to Charlotte a "necessary operation on the social body" in order to eliminate "diseased parts." Neither heartbreak nor financial ruin counted as sufficient motives to self-euthanize; if one could still work, she insisted, one should still live. She deemed suicide permissible only when it entailed the "shortening of unnecessary torture," and she deemed the "last human right" exercising one's option "to cut short unbearable and useless pain." "It is those no longer useful and under sentence of death anyhow who have the right to choose a quicker, easier end," she instructed her despondent son-in-law, neglecting to mention that she herself had been intermittently tempted by suicide since at least her twenties.[56] By 1912, Charlotte had selected her preferred method, which she described in an essay on "Good and Bad Taste in Suicide":

> The neatest suicide I ever heard of was that of a well-bred New England woman, who, for reasons of her own, wished to "discontinue." She waited till Saturday evening. . . . Everything in the house was in order and as clean as a new pin. She took a bath, arranged herself in a clean, fresh nightie, and calmly went to bed. In a large newspaper cone she placed a crumpled towel, poured in a bottle of chloroform, and inverted the cone over her face. Washed and straightened, hands folded on her breast, she was found there, no trouble to anyone.[57]

Charlotte liked this plan so much that when the time came she made it her own.

On August 12, she informed Alice Park that she was experiencing "an ebb-tide feeling there is no dodging." Three days later, she told E. A. Ross that "'[c]omplications' have set in, nephritis and dropsy, and a fairly laughable weakness; so I'm going to go peaceably [sic] to sleep with my beloved chloroform. I'm getting 'fed up' with sheer weakness." At last, she had reached "the stepping off place."[58]

On the evening of Saturday, August 17, after visits from loved ones, Charlotte retired to her bedroom and covered her mouth with a screen filled with chloroform. By the time the Chamberlins and Grace returned from a very late supper, she was, according to Katharine, "peacefully asleep her thin little hands firmly holding the rubber she had placed over the home made cone she had devised—She was already growing cold. . . . [T]here was an air of peaceful triumph in her quiet figure—she had carried out her plan in all details as she had wished." Katharine tucked some sprays of lavender that Alice Park had sent into her mother's hands and then summoned Charlotte's doctor, Hal Beiler, who arrived around 11:30 p.m. Beiler studied art with Frank (his daughter Sally would become Walter Chamberlin's wife), and, at the family's request, he made Charlotte's death mask.[59]

Never having handled a suicide before and thus unfamiliar with the protocol, Beiler neglected to notify the police. Nor did the family contact an undertaker: Katharine was trying to fulfill the requirements of her mother's will, which stipulated no services or intermediaries, just cremation and disposal of the ashes by her family.[60] Because the crematories were closed on Sundays, Katharine did not consult an undertaker until Monday, and the first one she approached refused Charlotte's request of a plain pine box.

Charlotte's body was thus still lying in the cottage on Monday afternoon when the police arrived to investigate the death; the investigators took Charlotte's suicide note away with them. They also informed Katharine that she must choose an undertaker immediately in order for the coroner to be duly notified. The press seized on the story and "made it sound as if Mama had lain neglected from Saturday night till Monday noon and as if I was forced by the coroner" to contact the undertaker, Katharine informed Lyman indignantly. Eventually, an ambulance took Charlotte to the mortuary. On Tuesday, August 20, the coroner permitted the body to be cremated without an inquest. The Chamberlins witnessed the cremation and subsequently scattered Charlotte's ashes in the west fork region of the San Gabriel Mountains. Charlotte had asked in an earlier will that her ashes be spread where they "will do some good," and, in the end, she became the mountains she loved.[61]

Compared to the expense and rot associated with graves, Charlotte considered cremation "[s]uch a clean sweet natural redistribution of things!" Cremation was gaining currency by the thirties as a more sanitary means of disposing of the dead. A theory circulating at the time suggested that many human afflictions could be attributed to dead bodies decomposing underground. Charlotte's concerns, however, were more philosophical than ecological. It perplexed her that people would

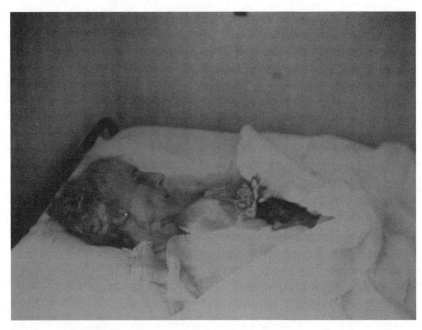

Postmortem photo of Charlotte, August 1935. Courtesy of the Schlesinger Library, Radcliffe Institute for Advanced Study, Harvard University.

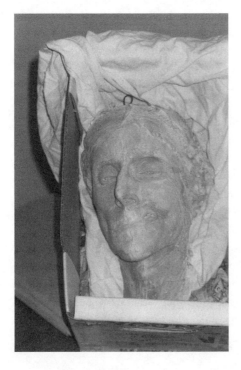

Death mask of Charlotte, 1935. Photo by the author. Charlotte Perkins Gilman's death mask, Charlotte Perkins Gilman papers, permission granted by the Schlesinger Library, Radcliffe Institute for Advanced Study, Harvard University.

want "to preserve physical identity" via graves or other markers "when in the very act of death it ceases. . . ."[62]

Charlotte endeavored to make cremation the default choice at a time when it remained unconventional. Several people she knew and many she admired had set early precedents, including Lucy Stone, her mother Mary (both in 1893), and her two husbands. The list also included her mentor Edward Bellamy, who like Charlotte had requested "no burial place, no tombstone, no record of identity." Instead, he asked that his ashes be scattered from the top of a mountain "on a bright windy day" so that they would be strewn far and wide.[63] For both of these apostles of altruism, the dispersal of that foremost signpost of individual identity, the body, was an end devoutly to be wished.

Charlotte's desire for personal immortality extended only to her words. To ensure this outcome, she left behind a provocative suicide note (published in the papers verbatim and later included in the final chapter of her autobiography). She sought not to excuse her actions so much as to persuade others of their logic. In its entirety, the typewritten, signed note, titled "A Last Duty," reads:

> Human life consists in mutual service. No grief, pain, misfortune or "broken heart" is excuse for cutting off one's life while any power of service remains. But when all usefulness is over, when one is assured of unavoidable and imminent death, it is the simplest of human rights to choose a quick and easy death in place of a slow and horrible one.
>
> Public opinion is changing on this subject. The time is approaching when we shall consider it abhorrent to our civilization to allow a human being to die in prolonged agony which we should mercifully end in any other creature. Believing this open choice to be of social service in promoting wiser views on this question, I have preferred chloroform to cancer.[64]

With her dying words, Charlotte succinctly summarized her philosophy and strove to make her death a beginning rather than an ending. Her personal suffering only mattered because it enabled her to make a public contribution. In the end, then, Charlotte had not simply "preferred chloroform to cancer"; she had preferred living to life.

Postmortem

All we know about death is just dying, and dying is no
proper antithesis to living, because living is continuous,
and dying a mere incident.

"Birth and Death," 1912[1]

Since Charlotte believed life continues after the individual life ends, it seems appropriate to continue her story beyond her death, especially because that death
was widely perceived not as the end of her story but as a story in itself. Even the
obituaries focused more on how she *died* than on how she had *lived*. Of course,
Charlotte had intended her suicide to cause a stir, "promote discussion and help
change an already changing opinion." The time seemed ripe for this discussion:
the editor of an essay collection on euthanasia had solicited a piece from Charlotte
shortly before she died; England's Parliament was debating euthanasia legislation;
other prominent figures, including the photography entrepreneur George Eastman, had taken their own lives; and the Euthanasia Society of America was established only three years after her death.[2] Ironically, then, euthanasia proved one of
the few issues Charlotte supported in her final years that positioned her on the
cutting edge.

Her posthumously published essay on "mercy slaying" appeared in the No-vember 1935 issue of the *Forum*. "The Right to Die" reiterates her belief that life possesses no inherent sanctity other than that accrued by use. Once our usefulness ends, our lives may as well, too. Those who continued to find euthanasia objec-tionable had only their "outdated sense of individuality," their "failure to recog-nize social responsibility" to blame.[3] In dying as in living, Charlotte prioritized the social over the individual, and she encouraged others to do the same.

Charlotte intended her words and deed to justify euthanasia and to establish this "principle for the good of humanity." She thus hoped to perform a service in dying comparable to any she had performed while living. By making her death a matter of public service, she had not simply "lived her philosophy of life to the very end," as one obituary claimed; she had provided it with an afterlife. Indeed, by continuing to make a difference beyond the grave, she seemed to be proving her fundamental tenets about the limits of the self and the limitless repercussions of selfless effort. Or, as her cousin Lyman put it in his condolence note, "her personal" work may have ended, but "her impersonal and infinitely greater work" had "hardly begun."[4]

The *Forum*'s examination of euthanasia extended into the subsequent issue, where two respected physicians weighed in at the journal's invitation. The debate also played out over the airwaves in mid-November, when Charlotte appeared (via an actress reading her part) on the radio interview show *The March of Time*, the first in its series of programs devoted to "mercy slaying." For several months after her suicide, various commentators discussed what one called "the age-old question of self-destruction." Those unfamiliar with her philosophy failed to comprehend how she could have defied "the deepest instinct of humanity, self-preservation," an instinct that had never been Charlotte's strong suit.[5]

Many of the numerous condolence notes Katharine received sought to justify her mother's choice. Harriot Stanton Blatch, Lillian Wald, and Martha Luther Lane numbered among those who approved of Charlotte's actions and admired her "fearlessness." Leading African American intellectuals took up the debate: af-ter Francis Grimké preached a sermon criticizing Charlotte for her lack of Chris-tian forbearance, Dr. Anna Julia Cooper reminded the reverend that Charlotte's life had been triumphant even if her death had been tragic.

The novelist Fannie Hurst and the activist Carrie Chapman Catt also publicly defended their "friend's moral right to take her own life." Catt told reporters that she normally disapproved of suicide except in the case of incurable illnesses like Charlotte's and argued that Charlotte had not taken her life so much as abbrevi-ated it. In the opposing corner stood the Reverend John Hayes Holmes, at whose church Charlotte had delivered one of her last New York talks; Holmes held that only God could decide when life ends. Charlotte's antagonist Ida Tarbell also objected: she said she wished she had been afforded the opportunity to remind Charlotte of the serviceability of the bedridden and of the wisdom of Milton's lines, "They also serve who only stand and wait." These attempts to justify or discredit Charlotte's suicide ironically share a reliance on discourses of individual and privacy rights that Charlotte would have excoriated.[6]

A similar slant informed reaction to her posthumously published autobiography, which one reviewer pronounced to be the story of "an individualist of the great tradition."[7] The genre's formal constraints, which stipulate focusing on the individual life and which made Charlotte wary of writing an autobiography in the first place, shaped reader response despite her repeated insistence throughout *The Living* that both her identity and her story were larger than her self alone. Perhaps these reviewers recognized, as Charlotte had not, the extent and the implications of her lone wolf status.

The publication of *The Living* in early October amid the buzz surrounding her suicide helped to keep Charlotte's name in circulation for the remainder of 1935 and into 1936. The page proofs had arrived in Pasadena on August 19, two days after Charlotte died, so it fell to Katharine to correct them and prepare an index. In general, the autobiography received warm reviews and was hailed as an "amazing record of human will, a necessary addition to Americana." The title had given the publisher pause, but the *New York Times* applauded the choice. Its reviewer deemed the gerund appropriate "for the life story of a personality of such vital quality and dynamic energy as Mrs. Gilman." Charlotte would have smiled to read in the pages of that adversarial paper a testimonial to her undeniable "greatness," but she would have frowned on the reviewer's emphasizing her personality at the expense of her service.[8]

Charlotte had hoped her life story would finally force people to grasp "what all my uproar is about," she said. The lengthiest review of *The Living*, however, treats her as a relic of a bygone era, "a period when hopes were high, when one could joyfully believe, as she did, and act upon the conviction that all great truths were simple." The reviewer, Clara Gruening Stillman, blamed Charlotte's current obscurity on her "sharp limitations," among them her identification with residual traditions, including Puritanism and perfectionism. "Though she thought of herself as a forerunner," Stillman concluded, "she was perhaps a peak rather than a beginning." Far from understanding the "uproar," Stillman wondered why there had ever been a ruckus.[9]

The autobiography sold 808 copies in the first few months, but sales tapered off sharply thereafter. *The Living* turned out to be Charlotte's only book publication during the decades immediately following her death. Projects including *Unpunished*, a second volume of poetry, and the treatise on "Ethics" languished, despite both Charlotte's "castle-building" and the individual and combined efforts of her poetry editor Amy Wellington, her agent Willis Kingsley Wing, and her literary executor Lyman Beecher Stowe.[10]

Meanwhile, Charlotte's personal papers continued to mildew in storage. The historian Mary Beard had thought to house them at a World Center for Women's Archives, writing Charlotte of her plans in a letter dated the day before Charlotte died. The center never materialized despite Beard's unstinting efforts, however, as Katharine discovered when she tried to unload her mother's effects in 1940. (Katharine did finally manage to deposit the bulk of the papers at Radcliffe's Schlesinger library in the early 1970s.)

After swiftly depleting Charlotte's small estate, Katharine made repeated attempts over the course of her long life to raise needed funds via her mother's works. She fared best with "The Yellow Wall-Paper" and with some poems that were also occasionally reprinted over the years. Since Katharine could not afford to purchase them from the publisher, the plates of *The Living* were melted down in 1942 for the war effort, an apt outcome given Charlotte's organicism were it not so blazing a symbol of her obsolescence at mid-century.[11]

Charlotte's aging admirers did their part to keep her memory alive. Several offered tributes to her as, in the words of Alexander Black, "the greatest prophet of the collective this country has produced." At her most prophetic, Charlotte had predicted that her great-great-granddaughters would "have long outgrown our besotted idea that self-interest . . . is man's chief 'incentive'" and would have finally and fully embraced the ethos of altruistic service. Instead, society has grown increasingly atomized, and critics have continued to question Charlotte's absolute antithesis between collectivism and individualism in an effort to reclaim the "individual rights" Charlotte discounted.[12]

In the late 1930s, Harriet Howe wrote a series of articles memorializing Charlotte as "an extraordinary personality" and a woman "200 years ahead of her time." Yet Howe stood with the minority. Settlement and social worker Florence Cross Kitchelt, for instance, who had read Charlotte "with bated breath" in her youth, reflected in the mid-1940s that she seemed "barely modern today."[13] The 1940s and 1950s represent Charlotte's fullest eclipse: virtually nothing was published by or on her during these decades.

The first stirrings of a renaissance came in the late 1950s and 1960s, when historians such as Carl Degler and William Doyle began recovering her pioneering work. In the 1970s, the second wave of feminism brought renewed and almost exclusively favorable attention to the author of "The Yellow Wall-Paper." Elaine Hedges and other influential critics helped to introduce the story and its author to the classroom and, eventually, to the canon. Today, numerous editions of many of Charlotte's works are in print, making a sizable portion of her oeuvre available for closer scrutiny. Charlotte has finally earned an afterlife, although probably not the one she anticipated.

The initial jubilation over a recovered feminist foremother became muted as more of Charlotte's works and views came to light. The 1990s saw the formation of the Charlotte Perkins Gilman Society as well as Charlotte's induction into the National Women's Hall of Fame in Seneca Falls. But by this point the pendulum had already begun to swing toward critique, especially as scholars attended more closely to her views on race, ethnicity, class, and sexuality. In 1989, Susan Lanser published a seminal analysis of the "yellow" in "The Yellow Wall-Paper" in light of Charlotte's anti-Asian prejudice. Since then, numerous essays have elucidated what Catherine J. Golden and Joanna S. Zangrando have called Charlotte's "mixed legacy."[14]

Recent analyses have alleged and simultaneously probed her ethnocentrism, racism, and xenophobia, her nationalism and nativism, her faulty scientific models, her aversion to the political realities and the concrete details of problems she treated as moral abstractions, her romanticization of natural states and of work, her sentimental take on the public sphere, her fairly complacent acceptance of capitalism, her ignorance of business practices, her class-blind and class-biased economic theorizing, her belief in the state and in both education and moral persuasion as forces of change, her blind faith in progress no matter the cost, her elitism, her perfectionism, her sweeping generalizations, her often condescending didacticism, her tendency to minimize women's sexual needs and their actual agency, her homophobia and heterosexism, her surprising reluctance to encourage men to share in the housework, and her overly broad and at times ahistorical conception of woman's subjugation—and this is a condensed list.[15]

Of course, not every take on her life and legacy in the past few decades has been critical, nor are the bulk of these critical examinations dismissive. Charlotte remains as relevant today for her theories about the importance of work for women, managing domestic and familial responsibilities, and living a meaningful life as she does for her views on evolution, ethnicity, and immigration. On all these issues, she helped to set the terms of public debate, for better or for worse, and she merits our attention accordingly.

The best of the recent analyses acknowledge her continued relevance and attend to her ameliorative along with her objectionable arguments. They remind us that Charlotte rose to prominence in her own day due in part to views we find dated today and in part to views that remain pertinent. Thus, when we chastise or dismiss her for her prejudices, we risk discounting not only her larger contributions but also, and more specifically, the cultural power of the ideas and material forces that informed those prejudices then and that continue to inform them, to an extent, even now. Applying today's standards permits us to judge her but may ultimately preclude a fuller understanding of her life and work as well as her lasting and multi-valued impact.[16]

Charlotte would have been the first to admit to "repeated failure[s]" and flaws, but she faulted her self rather than her beliefs. She was quick to criticize her personal defects, in other words, but she rarely bothered to subject the ideas she lived and died by to close scrutiny. Indeed, in her final weeks, she chose to conclude her autobiography by insisting on the longevity and utility of her worldview: "The religion, the philosophy, set up so early, have seen me through," she wrote in the book's last sentence. It pleased her to think that she had developed early on a set of enabling beliefs she continued to find sustaining as her life drew to a close.

Much as Charlotte would have liked others to follow her lead and appreciate her example, she ultimately cared more for understanding than for appreciation.[17] This is an easier desire for a biographer to satisfy, and, in the end, perhaps the best any biographer can offer. At this point, you are holding as close to a full-color, three-dimensional portrait as I could render in black ink on a white page. It is not complete, but then Charlotte may not have minded that, and not just because she objected to biographical projects on principle. For as she once wrote, and as I would like to think pertains to her life as both lived and read, "There is no end to anybody's story, until they are dead, and some people think that is only the beginning."[18]

Abbreviations

MW	Marian Whitney
MWP	Mary Westcott Perkins
RSS	Rebecca Steere Stetson
SBC	Sarah B. Cooper
SWM	Silas Weir Mitchell
TAP	Thomas A. Perkins
WDH	William Dean Howells
WSC	Walter Stetson Chamberlin

BOOK AND MANUSCRIPT SOURCES

Bancroft	Bancroft Library, University of California, Berkeley
Barnard	Barnard College Archives, Barnard College
Brown	Lester Frank Ward Collection, Brown University Library
Butler Library	Columbia University
CC	Charlotte Perkins Gilman, *Concerning Children* (Boston: Small, Maynard & Co., 1900)
Colby	Colby College Special Collections, Colby College
Columbia	Rare Book and Manuscript Library, Columbia University
Cornell	Sarah Brown Ingersoll Cooper Papers, #6543; courtesy of Division of Rare and Manuscript Collections, Cornell University Library
DKD I and II	Denise D. Knight, ed., *The Diaries of Charlotte Perkins Gilman*, 2 vols.
DKJT	Denise D. Knight and Jennifer S. Tuttle, eds., *The Selected Letters of Charlotte Perkins Gilman* (forthcoming, University of Alabama Press)
E	*Endure! The Diaries of Charles Walter Stetson*
EBSA!	Edward Bellamy, *Edward Bellamy Speaks Again!*
FR	Charlotte Perkins Gilman, *Forerunner*, November 1909–December 1916
Fruitlands	Fruitlands Museum, Prospect Hill, Harvard, MA
GECSP	Grace Ellery Channing Stetson Papers, 83-M201, Arthur and Elizabeth Schlesinger Library on the History of Women in America, Radcliffe Institute for Advanced Study, Harvard University
HBSC	Harriet Beecher Stowe Center, Hartford, CT
Hingham PL	Hingham Public Library, Hingham, MA
Houghton	By permission of the Houghton Library, Harvard University
Horrmann	Horrmann Library, Wagner College
Huntington	Huntington Library, San Marino, CA
HR&H	Charlotte Perkins Gilman, *His Religion and Hers: A Study of the Faith of Our Fathers and the Work of Our Mothers* (New York: Century, 1923)
HW	Charlotte Perkins Gilman, *Human Work* (New York: McClure, Phillips, & Co., 1904)
ITOW	Charlotte Perkins Stetson, *In This Our World* (except where otherwise noted, 3rd ed.) (Boston: Small, Maynard & Co., 1898)

L	Charlotte Perkins Gilman, *The Living of Charlotte Perkins Gilman: An Autobiography* (New York: Appleton-Century, 1935)
LOC	Manuscript Division, Library of Congress
LP	Denise D. Knight, ed., *The Later Poetry of Charlotte Perkins Gilman*
NAW	*Notable American Women*, 3 vols.
RIHS	Charlotte Perkins Gilman Papers, MSS 437, Rhode Island Historical Society, Providence
Rochester	Department of Rare Books & Special Collections, University of Rochester Library, University of Rochester
SL	Arthur and Elizabeth Schlesinger Library on the History of Women in America, Radcliffe Institute for Advanced Study, Harvard University (All items are from the main Gilman collection [177/mf-1] unless otherwise noted.)
Smith	Sophia Smith Collection, Smith College
SSB	Lyman Beecher Stowe, *Saints, Sinners, and Beechers*
UVM	Bailey-Howe Library, University of Vermont, Burlington
Vassar	Special Collections, Vassar College Libraries, Vassar College
W&E	Charlotte Perkins Stetson, *Women and Economics: A Study in the Economic Relation Between Men and Women as a Factor in Social Evolution* (Boston: Small, Maynard, & Co., 1898)
Wisconsin	E. A. Ross Papers, Wisconsin Historical Society, Madison
WHMEC	Alice Park Papers, Women's History Museum and Educational Center, San Diego
WJ	*Woman's Journal*
WSCC	Walter Stetson Chamberlin, private collection

Notes

INTRODUCTION

1. "I Am Human," *WJ* (16 July 1904): 226.

2. *L*, 284.

3. In private correspondence, Judith A. Allen has suggested that this decision to use "Charlotte" implies not only a condescending familiarity, it also lacks the deference extended to figures like Ward (I do not call him "Lester," in other words). Ward, however, only went by one surname his whole life as opposed to Charlotte's three; nor do I have any need in these pages to distinguish Ward from his first and second spouses. So while I take Allen's point, I still feel "Charlotte" is the least confusing way to refer to her throughout.

4. Howells, qtd. in CPS to GECS, 9 July 1892, GECSP, SL; West, qtd. in CPG to GECS, 26 May 1924, mf-6, SL; Wells, qtd. in Black, "The Woman," 39; Catt, *New York Times* (20 August 1935): 44. Thanks to Shelley Fisher Fishkin for helping me to refine my thoughts about the anomalous status of "The Yellow Wall-Paper."

5. CPS to KSC, 2 May 1933, folder 10, SL; CPS to KSC, 29 June 1929, folder 100, SL.

6. *L*, 335.

7. "The Commonplace," *Time and the Hour* (26 February 1898): 10–11; *ITOW*, 4–7.

8. CPG, "In the Near Future," *FR* 3 (January 1912): 18; *L*, 73.

9. See my "Introduction," and DK's "Gilman's Breakdown"; the "theorist" is Steele, 122.

10. She calls "life" a verb in *HW*, 203, and she reiterates this point elsewhere: "Our human-ness," she argues in *The Man-Made World*, " . . . is in what we do and how we do it, rather than in what we are" (*FR* 1 [November 1909]: 21). She repeats this mantra again

in her final published treatise, *HR&H*, when she maintains that "[w]e should not say 'life' as a noun but 'living' as an active verb" (98); she also uses the gerund both in the title of her autobiography and in its pages (see, e.g., *L*, 181); beginning with "*well used*," the quotations are from "The New Immortality," *FR* 3 (February 1912): 64.

11. "The Vision and the Program," *FR* 6 (May 1915): 119.

12. Calhoun, 10. In claiming that she redefines, rather than jettisons, the self, I differ from Mari Jo Buhle, who holds that Charlotte "rejects the whole business of selfhood" (Buhle, *Feminism*, 48).

13. *L*, 181.

14. CPG to KSC, 19 May 1934, folder 105, SL; on personality as a "limitation," see "Personality and God," *FR* 2 (August 1911): 204–05; CPS to GHG, 16 September 1898, folder 55, SL.

15. DKD II, 27 July 1893, 545; "social hunger" from Black, "The Woman," 34–35; *Moving the Mountain, FR* 2 (November 1911): 304–05; on the value of the personal realm, see "Thoughts & Figgerings," 26 March 1894, folder 16, SL.

16. On her being a "wreck" and her desire to "leave off being me," see CPS to GHG, 12 October 1897, folder 46, SL; "Little Cell," *ITOW*, 25; CPS to GHG, 17 March 1899, folder 67, SL.

17. On her use of these terms interchangeably, see her "The Influence of Women on Public Life," *Public: A Journal of Democracy* 22 (1919): 571–72; "useful . . . goodfornothing" assessment from CPS to GHG, 16 March 1899, folder 67, SL.

18. CPS to GHG, 16 September 1898, folder 55, SL; CPS to GHG, 14 March 1899, folder 66, SL.

19. *HW*, 134. Charlotte borrowed the term *omniism* from her fellow activist, the radical millionaire J. Graham Phelps Stokes; she cites Stokes's March 1903 *Wiltshire Magazine* article in *HW*. For more on Stokes's influence, see Polly Wynn Allen, 123. See also "I Am Human," *WJ* 16 (July 1904): 226, and "World Rousers," *FR* 6 (May 1915): 132, where she writes, "We! That is the main idea—We!"

20. *Humanness, FR* 4 (December 1913): 334.

21. For general histories of this period, see works by Ballard C. Campbell, Ekirch, George, Ginger, Herreshoff, and Hofstadter. Hofstadter's *Age* discusses Spencer's dualism. See also Wiebe, 198ff, for a discussion of Washington Gladden.

22. See Menand, x–xii. Thanks to Thomas J. Brown for encouraging me to clarify Charlotte's significance vis-à-vis the Beechers and the pragmatists; he also helped me refine my argument about the mixed results of Charlotte's desired synthesis and the "tension between aspiration and reality."

23. "Our Most Valuable Livestock," *Pacific Rural Press* (17 October 1891), oversize folder 1, SL.

24. CPS to GHG, 20 March 1899, enclosure, folder 67, SL; "Eternal Me" was published in *Cosmopolitan* (27 September 1899): 477.

25. I would like to thank the second, anonymous reader for Stanford University Press for helping me to formulate this point as well as the earlier one about the duration of Charlotte's fame.

26. "Hyenas," folder 147, SL. See also "A 'Psalm of Lives,'" *Saturday Review of Literature* 26 (November 1927): 358; "thick description" is Geertz's term.

27. T. S. Eliot, "Choruses from the Rock" (1934), *The Complete*, 96. Eliot asks, "Where is the Life we have lost in living?"

CHAPTER ONE

1. "Heroism," *ITOW*, 14–15; the chapter title is taken from the title of the second chapter of *L*.

2. "A Forerunner and Prophet," typescript, folder 243, SL; "Pioneers," typescript, folder 183, SL.

3. CPG to Mrs. Roantree, 1920, folder 153, SL; *SSB*, 353.

4. "Mrs. Stetson Tries Matrimony Again," *San Francisco Chronicle* (19 June 1900), 80-M112, folder 41, SL; Gale, foreword to *L*, xxix; Bruère, 204.

5. Qtd. in *L*, 325.

6. Lewis Gannett, "Books and Things," clipping, WSCC; LBS, *SSB*, 46; Rugoff, 70–71.

7. Lyman Beecher, qtd. in *SSB*, 28; Catharine Beecher, qtd. in Sklar, *Catharine*, 7.

8. Roxana's letter excerpted in, *SSB*, 39–40; "A Biographical Sketch of Charlotte Perkins Gilman," folder 243, SL.

9. The Beecher biographer referred to in the preceding paragraph is Rugoff, 33–34; Catharine, qtd. in Sklar, *Catharine*, 22; Harriet, qtd. in Rugoff, 35; Caskey, 11–12.

10. Harriet Porter Beecher, qtd. in Rugoff, 36.

11. Theodore Parker, qtd. in "Foreword," *SSB*, n.p.; *SSB*, 391–92; Applegate, 12.

12. Caskey, 381; Applegate, 104; Rugoff, 597–98; Caskey, 363.

13. Mary, qtd. in Rugoff, 550. General information on Lyman's children comes from Rugoff, Caskey, Sklar (*Catharine*), Hedrick, and Applegate.

14. The information on the scandals covered in these two paragraphs comes from Goldsmith, 5–6, 314–16, 349–51, and 353–59.

15. On the human ear, see Nye, xi; on the Byron scandal, see Hedrick, 366–69.

16. Mary, qtd. in Boydston et al., 7–8, and see 357; on the siblings' perception of Mary, see, e.g., Isabella to John Hooker, 30 August 1839, HBSC; see Barbara Welter's classic essay, "The Cult of True Womanhood."

17. *SSB*, 152–53; Hedrick, 27, 51–52.

18. CPS to SWM, 19 April 1887, AG 487C, SL. For more information on Mary Beecher's shaky health, see Catharine Beecher to Louisa Wait, January 1822, folder 14, and Lyman Beecher to Catharine Beecher, 3 December 1823, folder 2, Beecher-Stowe papers, SL; Hedrick, 113–14.

19. Charlotte's take on her relatives in these two paragraphs comes from CPS to SWM, 19 April 1887, AG 487C, SL; the information on William's forgery and its consequences is from Hedrick, 113, 338; CPS to GHG, 11 September 1897, folder 45, SL.

20. CPS to GHG, 17 April 1900, folder 82, SL; Hedrick, 151, 380, 396; on James, see *SSB*, 389; Isabella B. Hooker to John Hooker, 3–7 June 1857, HBSC.

21. Caskey, 112–13; Isabella, qtd. in Caskey, 106; Goldsmith, 197.

22. Isabella, qtd. in Applegate, 28; Wellington, 116; Harriet, qtd. in Rugoff, 543; CPG, "Social Darwinism," *American Journal of Sociology* 12 (March 1907): 713–14.

23. Lyman on "sin," qtd. in Sklar, *Catharine*, 12, and see 245; on Edward, see Caskey, 352–53, 358.

24. Henry published his most sustained attempt to reconcile Darwinism and evangelical religion in his book *Evolution and Religion*, coming to terms with the two conflicting genesis stories by distinguishing between theology and religion and associating theology with science and religion with art. See Hofstadter, *Social*, 29, 38, and see also Kirkpatrick, 137; Applegate, 355, 461; Rugoff, 510–11; Caskey, 246–47; "the whole physical creation" qtd. in Rugoff, 512. Henry's brothers Edward and Charles objected to Darwinism for depleting religion's moral force, for contradicting biblical explanations, and for emphasizing man's rise rather than his sin and fall; for Henry on the latter point, see Rugoff, 511; Caskey, 378.

25. After reading Darwin, Henry modified his Spencerian investment in laissez-faire policies, recognizing that the progress of one group could depend on the destruction of another, a destruction the unfortunate group had a right to resist, even as that resistance unnerved him. "God has intended" qtd. in Dombrowski, 5; Applegate, 461–62; on the "Cleveland letter," see, e.g., Goldsmith, 119; for Henry's abolitionist views and actions, see Rugoff, 318, 373–75, 381–85, 257–58, 271–75, and Goldsmith, 118–19.

26. For Lyman's views, see Caskey, 378–79, and Applegate, 104.

27. CPS to KSC, 31 May 1924, folder 95, SL; the description of the Perkins family comes from Helen Campbell, "Charlotte," folder 266, SL.

28. CPS to SWM, 19 April 1887, AG 487C, SL.

29. CPG to GECS, 26 May 1924, mf-6, SL.

30. "My Ancestors," *FR* 4 (March 1913): 75; "Let Sleeping Forefathers Lie," *FR* 6 (October 1915): 261–63; "Opposing Currents," *WJ* (12 March 1904): 82; untitled poem, *FR* 1 (January 1910): 1.

31. "My Ancestors," *FR* 4 (March 1913): 73, 75.

32. Rugoff, 599.

33. CPS to GHG, 3 November 1897, folder 47, SL. See also CPS to GHG, 12 June 1899, where she writes: "You know things are not just immediate with me—they are antecedent and precedent—all the past and future piled up together. . . ."

34. *L*, 8.

35. Isabella B. Hooker to John Hooker, 3–7 June 1857, HBSC.

36. On Mary and English ivy, see Austin, 293; *L*, 7.

37. *L*, 6; CPS to SWM, 19 April 1887, AG 487C, SL; Walter's locks are held by the Schlesinger Library.

38. The "thwarted" quotation is from *L*, 8; *W&E*, 262–63.

39. CPS to MLL, 8 August 1881, RIHS; "urge . . . " and "Beecher wit . . ." from *L*, 6; CPS to SWM, 19 April 1887, AG 487C, SL; CPS to GHG, 16 September 1898, folder 55, SL.

40. Hedrick, 283; obituary, *San Francisco Chronicle* (4 February 1899), clipping, vol. 7, SL.

41. http://sfpl.lib.ca.us/news/wall1016draft.htm, consulted 28 December 2003; the

rough-handling incident is described in a clipping, folder 296, SL; obituary, clipping, vol. 7, SL.

42. "The Compensation Office," *Devil Puzzlers*, 176; *L*, 4; Warner, qtd. in *Hartford Courant*, obituary, clipping, vol. 7, SL.

43. "Childhood—A Study," *Devil Puzzlers*, 129; CPS to SWM, 19 April 1887, AG 487C, SL.

44. Self-description from "Childhood—A Study," *Devil Puzzlers*, 142; his speech before the teachers is *The Station and Duty*, 2; *Devil Puzzlers*, 168.

45. *L*, 8.

46. "Our Loneliness," *ITOW*, 60.

47. Recollections about her great-aunt's visit and the president's assassination are from Autobiography, "an earlier attempt," folder 234, SL and *L*, 12; FBP, *The Picture and the Men*, copy in WSCC.

48. CPS to SWM, 19 April 1887, AG 487C, SL; *L*, 5; Autobiography, "an earlier attempt," folder 234, SL.

49. "My Forenoon with Baby," *Devil Puzzlers*, 191.

50. *L*, 5–6; undated correspondence between CAP and FBP [ca. 1872], folder 37, SL; FBP to CAP, n.d., folder 26, SL.

51. CPS to GHG, 1 February 1899, folder 64, SL.

52. "The Nurse and the Snake" (poem), folder 197, SL; *Benigna Machiavelli*, *FR* 5 (January 1914): 11; Isabella B. Hooker to Harriet Beecher Stowe, 16 March 1871, qtd. in Goldsmith, 270.

53. *Devil Puzzlers*, 107; Charlotte's recollections of the moves are from *L*, 8, 16, and Autobiography, "an earlier attempt," folder 234, SL.

54. On Aunt C., see Hill, *Making*, 59, and Gernes, 233; *L*, 80.

55. Autobiography, "an earlier attempt," folder 234, SL; on the New York boarding house, see Alden, 554–56, Wegener, "Charlotte," 156n9, and *L*, 15–16.

56. Charlotte's recollections of her youth are recorded in her Autobiography, "an earlier attempt," folder 234, SL, and in "A Forerunner and a Prophet," 1904 biographical sketch, folder 243, SL; TAP to CPG, 19 October 1926, folder 36, SL; her disdain for diarists is expressed in "Art for Art's Sake," lecture ms., folder 171, SL.

57. TAP to CPG, 19 October 1926, folder 36, SL; CAP to TAP, 13 May 1883, in DKD II, appendix B, 888.

58. TAP to CPG, 19 October 1926, folder 36, SL.

59. Autobiography, "an earlier attempt," folder 234, SL.

60. "January 14th: 1880. Autobiography of C. A. Perkins," typescript, folder 233, SL.

61. *L* 9; the school statistics are from Lipow, 34, and Bederman, 268; *L*, 27; Harriet R. Chace to CAP, 12 March 1875, folder 160, SL.

62. KSC to Carl Degler, 24 July 1960, folder 156, SL; *L*, 60.

63. *L*, 30; DKD I, 31 March 1880, 19.

64. *L*, 9; CPG to Ellen Day Hale, 22 January 1934, Vassar; *L*, 10–11; for a fictional version, see, e.g., *Won Over*, *FR* 4 (January 1913): 10–11; Autobiography, "an earlier attempt," folder 234, SL.

65. "A Forerunner and a Prophet," 1904 biographical sketch, folder 243, SL; early writings, folder 159, SL; poem, folder 25, 80-M112, SL.

66. *L,* 10.

67. Autobiography, "an earlier attempt," folder 234, SL; *L,* 23; "make a world" from *L,* 20.

68. On the Rehobeth Christmas, see folder 160, SL; For her practice of doling out fantasies, see CPS to SWM, 19 April 1887, AG 487C, SL; dream described by Hill in Rudd and Gough, 16–18.

69. CPS to SWM, 19 April 1887, AG 487C, SL; Black, "The Woman," 36.

70. "no one stopped it" from CPS to SWM, 19 April 1887, AG 487C, SL; the confrontation and Charlotte's reaction to it are described in *L,* 23–24; on Victorian prudence, see Sicherman, 896.

71. CPS to SWM, 19 April 1887, AG 487C, SL; quote from "Rest and Power," *FR* 6 (October 1915): 271.

72. Autobiography, "an earlier attempt," folder 234, SL; CPS to GHG, 18 September 1897, folder 45, SL.

73. The friend is Black, "The Woman," 36; *L,* 21; the Tweed story is related in "A Biographical Sketch of Charlotte Perkins Gilman," folder 243, SL; *L,* 76.

74. Transcribed poem in juvenile diaries, vol. 12, folder 336, SL.

75. O'Neill, *Divorce,* 20, 24, 25, 62–63; McGerr, 11.

76. *L,* 9; *W&E,* 259–60.

77. Gilkeson, 7, 137; KSC, "Autobiography," WSCC.

78. *L,* 25; CPS to KSC, 22 March 1931, folder 102, SL.

79. *Home,* 41, 217; CPS to GHG, 3 April 1900, folder 82, SL.

80. "utterly incongenial" from CPS to SWM, 19 April 1887, AG 487C, SL; *Benigna Machiavelli, FR* 5 (January 1914): 13; CPS to GHG, 19 September 1898, folder 55, SL; "principal personal ambition" from CPS to GHG, 18 September 1897, folder 45, SL.

81. On vastation, see Edel, 6ff.

82. Hayden, *Grand,* 68; Livermore, 396.

83. *What Diantha Did, FR* 1 (May 1910): 15.

84. Gernes, 235; *L,* 33–34.

85. "Birth," *ITOW,* 1–2; *L,* 36; she discusses duty in CPS to GHG, 4 December 1899, folder 78, SL; juvenile diary, 7 February 1876, vol. 26, SL.

86. Undated correspondence between CAP and FBP [ca. 1874 or 1875], folder 37, SL.

87. Autobiography, "an earlier attempt," folder 234, SL.

88. "*remarkable*" from Margo Culley, qtd. in DKD I, 8; "desperately serious" from *L,* 44; CPG to Miss Hill, 4 December 1921, folder 143, SL; *L,* 39.

89. Hofstadter, *Social,* 41–44.

90. *L,* 39–41; "Charlotte Perkins Gilman's Dynamic Social Philosophy," *Current Literature* 51 (July 1911): 67–70; she discusses the human responsibility to advance evolution in *L,* 42; "As to God," *FR* 5 (January 1914): 6.

91. *HR&H,* 292; CPS to GHG, 1 January 1899, folder 62, SL; *L,* 182; the discussion

beginning with "Living God" is from "A Woman's Utopia," *Times Magazine* I (February 1907): 372.

92. CPG to Miss Hill, 4 December 1921, folder 143, SL.

CHAPTER TWO

1. Chapter title from CAP to ML, 29 July 1881, RIHS; CPG, "To Isadora Duncan," *LP*, 141.

2. *L*, 56; *Won Over*, *FR* 4 (February 1913): 38.

3. *Home*, 257; *L*, 45.

4. *L*, 76; *ITOW*, 33.

5. "An Obstacle," *ITOW*, 103; juvenile diary, March 1877, qtd. in DKD I, 4; Lears, 5.

6. *The Crux*, *FR* 2 (February 1911): 45.

7. Autobiography, "an earlier attempt," folder 234, SL.

8. Autobiography, "an earlier attempt," folder 234, SL; on Providence "folks" thinking her "queer," see CPS to GHG, 8 September 1897, folder 45, SL; resolution to "enjoy myself" recorded in *L*, 44; "utterly charming" from *L*, 49, and "leap" described in *L*, 50.

9. She reflects on her girlhood acquaintances in CPS to GHG, 11 September 1897, folder 45, SL, and in *L*, 48–50; "There's a deal" from CAP to Sam Simmons, 14 November 1881, 80-M112, folder 18, SL; "Caroline Hazard," *NAW* (vol. 2), 169; on Hazard's kindnesses, see DKD I, 387n4; on Channing, see Rugoff, 36–39.

10. *L*, 31; on her Aunt Emily, see CPS to GHG, 18 and 11 September 1897, folder 45, SL; Autobiography, "an earlier attempt," folder 234, SL.

11. On the Gilmans, see DKD I, 17 November and 2 December 1879, 16, and see also letters from CAP to GHG, folder 38, SL.

12. Conley and Campbell, 113; MLL to CPG, 30 April 1935, folder 147, SL; DKD I, 8 January 1879, 6.

13. *Home*, 11; her confession about invalids is from DKD I, 24 February 1881, 41; she calls her mother "illogical" in CPS to SWM, 19 April 1887, AG 487C, SL; the *Hamlet* incident is discussed in *L*, 51; DKD I, 6 March 1879, 10.

14. DKD I, 28 April 1881, 52; *L*, 68–69; DKD I, 28 and 27 April 1881, 51–52.

15. Note penned at bottom of poem "My Home" (1881–1882), and poem itself, folder 198, SL.

16. Charlotte wonders about Thomas in her juvenile diary, 23 November 1878, qtd. in Hill, *Making*, 51; on Hale's help, see MWP to Isabella Beecher Hooker, 11 November 1879, HBSC; KSC to SL, 22 June 1972, folder 156a, SL.

17. On Charlotte's club activities, see DKD I, 8 and 25 January 1879, 6, 7; DKD I, 22 February 1879, 9; DKD I, 22 January and 22 April 1881, 33, 50; on the women's club's free lectures, see Blair, 165; on Phelps, see Carol Farley Kessler, exhibition guide, "Gilman Reads Phelps," prepared for the Fourth International Charlotte Perkins Gilman Conference in Maine, June 2006; on her father and uncle's lectures, see DKD I, 14 March 1880, 19; DKD I, 21 August 1881, 74; on the libraries, see Gilkeson, 89, and DKD I, 3 May 1879, 12.

18. *L*, 56–57, 59.

19. Autobiography, "an earlier attempt," folder 234, SL; her speculation about her "numbness" is from CPS to GHG, 18 May 1898, folder 51, SL.

20. On her first poem, see DKD I, 22 May 1880, 20; the poem itself is reprinted in DKD II, appendix B, 859; FBP to CAP, 15 October 1878, folder 26, SL; for her thoughts on her father's influence, see Autobiography, "an earlier attempt," folder 234, SL; the historian Gail Bederman has argued that Frederic's reading list not only introduced Charlotte to Darwinian anthropology but also shaped her religious belief in the "millennial importance of advancing the white race toward the highest possible civilization" (Bederman, 126–27).

21. Faderman, 179; address by Miss M. Carey Thomas, NAWSA, Baltimore, 8 February 1906, 30 (see also Antler, 24).

22. Note, folder 336, vol. 14, SL; Frazier, n.p.

23. On her various jobs, see Knight, introduction to DKD I, 4–5, and WSC, "Charlotte Perkins Gilman: Her Influence on Four Generations," 11, provided by the author at the Second International Charlotte Perkins Gilman Conference, Skidmore College, 1997.

24. 1880 census; on Soapine, see DK, "An 'Amusing,'" 10, and Mac Donnell; as Knight and Tuttle note, Brown's estate when he died totaled a half of a million dollars; he left small bequests to both Charlotte and Katharine (see DKJT).

25. CAP to ML, 23 August 1881, RIHS; *L*, 37.

26. CPS to GHG, 6 November 1898, folder 58, SL; *Home*, 261.

27. "Personal Problems," *FR* 1 (November 1909): 27. The column recommends her Uncle Hale's *How to Do It*.

28. Hale, *How to*, 30; CPS to SWM, 19 April 1887, AG 487C, SL.

29. Studley, 122ff, 119, 24–25.

30. DKD I, 1 January 1879, 6; *L*, 67.

31. CPS to TAP, 13 May 1883, in DKD II, appendix B, 888; Catharine Beecher, *Physiology*, iii. See also Catharine Beecher, *Letters*, 8.

32. *L*, 64; DKD I, 16 September 1879, 15; Green identifies Blaikie as the "dean" in *Fit*, 204; Blaikie, 72–73.

33. Blaikie, 66, 276ff; see DKD I, 16 September 1879, 15 and juvenile diary, 27 October 1879, qtd. in Hill, *Making*, 66.

34. See, e.g., Lears, 30; Charlotte describes her vision of the gym in CAP to ML, 1 August 1881, RIHS; *L*, 66; for a discussion of Charlotte and the gymnasium, see Lancaster, 40–41.

35. "Making a Change," *FR* 2 (December 1911): 311–15 (thanks to Catherine J. Golden for pointing out this story's relevance); CPS to GHG, 11 October 1899, folder 74, SL.

36. On her tumble and cut, see the following four sources: DKD I, 18 March 1882, 113; poem to Miss Hill, folder 153, SL; CAP to Charlotte A. Hedge, 26 March 1882, folder 153, SL; and CPS to GHG, 19 May 1897, folder 41, SL; CAP to ML, 13 August 1881, RIHS; "The Providence Ladies Gymnasium," *Providence Journal* (23 May 1883) sec. 8: 2.

37. CAP to ML, 4 July 1881, RIHS.

38. *L*, 71, 79–80.

39. Autobiography, "an earlier attempt," folder 234, SL; DKD I, 30 October 1879, 16; MLL to KSC, 25 August 1935, WSCC.

40. CAP to ML, 14 September 1881, RIHS.

41. CAP to ML, 24 July 1881, RIHS; CAP to ML, 8 August 1881, RIHS; CAP to ML, 30 July 1881, RIHS; poem in DKD I, appendix B, 858.

42. CPG to KSC, 2 November 1924, folder 95, SL; Gernes, 271–72.

43. CWS in *E*, 28 September 1882, 106; MLL, "Memories" (1935) and *Journal, 1881–1886*. Bicentennial Microfilm Collection, Hingham PL; Charlotte describes her visit to Hingham in CPS to GHG, 16 October 1898, folder 56, SL. Although she denied feeling depressed prior to her marriage, Charlotte often confessed feelings of depression to Martha. See, for example, CAP to ML, 10 September 1881, RIHS, where Charlotte informed Martha, "I have struck bottom at last. Am all down in a heap—'like lead.'"

44. *L*, 18, 26, 78, 80; CAP to ML, 30 July 1881, RIHS.

45. Faderman, 298, 160; Smith-Rosenberg, "The Female World" in *Disorderly*; on "Smashes," see Sahli, 105 (see also Foucault, who argues in *History of Sexuality* that sex was generally understood prior to the twentieth century as an activity and not yet as an identity); Vicinus, xix.

46. DKD I, 14 May 1881, 58; CAP to ML, 15 August 1881, RIHS.

47. "Lost Women," *FR* 3 (November 1912): 281; "A Cleared Path," *FR* 3 (October 1912): 257; *W&E*, 305.

48. CAP to ML, 22 July 1881, RIHS; CPS to GHG, 12 March 1899, folder 67, SL.

49. CAP to ML, 24 July 1881, RIHS; Erikson, 262; DKD I, 21 and 23 January 1881, 33, 34.

50. CAP to ML, 23 August 1881, RIHS.

51. CAP to ML, 6 August 1881, RIHS; CAP to ML, 8 August 1881, RIHS.

52. All quotations in these two paragraphs are from CAP to ML, 29 July 1881, RIHS.

53. "An Obstacle," *ITOW*, 103.

54. CAP to ML, 30 July 1881, RIHS.

55. DKD I, 5 November 1881, 88; on Charlotte's attempts to salvage the relationship and her ultimate resignation to Martha's engagement, see DKD I, 24 September 1881, 82; 11 and 29 October 1881, 85, 87; and 2 November 1881, 88.

56. On her reliance on other friends, see DKD I, 14, 15, and 16 November 1881, 90; for her reliance on Sam in particular, see DKD I, 16 December 1881, 94; CAP to Sam Simmons, 4 November 1881, 80-M112, folder 18, SL; CAP to Sam Simmons, 31 October 1881, folder 153, SL.

57. DKD II, appendix B, 862–63.

58. "Answer to a Letter from Charles Walter Stetson. Feb. 10th–12th. 1882" (poem), DKD II, appendix B, 867–68; see also DK, "But O My Heart," 276. I have been unable to locate Burleigh's portrait.

59. *L*, 80.

60. DKD I, 25, 30, and 31 December 1881, 96, 97–98.

61. Autobiography, "an earlier attempt," folder 234, SL.

CHAPTER THREE

1. "Heroism," *ITOW*, 16.

2. CAP to MLL, 6 September 1883, RIHS.

3. *Home*, 75.

4. "All the World to Her," *Independent* 55 (2 July 1903): 1613–17; CAP to GEC, 28 February 1884, mf-6, SL.

5. Studley, 200–01.

6. CAP to CWS, 20 February 1883, folder 39, SL.

7. DKD I, 11 January 1882, 103; *E*, 26 January 1882, 25–26.

8. *E*, 29 January 1882, 35, and 26 January 1882, 26; Autobiography, "an earlier attempt," folder 234, SL.

9. *E*, 15 November 1881, 13; KSC, "Autobiography," in WSCC; *E*, 21 April 1883, 169.

10. Information on CWS's biography is derived from GECS, "Catalog of the Memorial Exhibition," 5–6; obituary of Joshua Stetson and interview with KSC, both transcribed in journal by David Goodale, vol. 4, 93-M76, SL; see also KSC, "Autobiography," WSCC; CWS's thoughts on his father are recorded in *E*, 13 May 1882, 73.

11. Background on Stetson's career as an artist comes from GECS, "Catalog," 8, and Hill, introduction to *E*, xxi–xxiii.

12. *E*, 26 January 1882, 27; CAP, qtd. in *E*, 29 January 1882, 33; CAP to Charlotte Hedge, 26 March 1882, folder 153, SL.

13. CAP, qtd. in *E*, 26 January 1882, 28–30.

14. CAP to CWS, 13 and 14 February 1882, folder 39, SL; *E*, 12 April 1882, 66.

15. *E*, August 1883, 12; DKD I, 29 January 1882, 106.

16. Qtd. in *E*, 29 January 1882, 32; her exact words read, "I cannot marry, although I am fitted to enjoy all that marriage can give to the utmost. Were I to marry, my thoughts, my acts, my whole life would be centered in husband and children. To do the work that I have planned I must be free" (CAP to CWS, 29 January 1882, transcribed in *E*, 1 February 1882, 36, 3).

17. "An Anchor to Windward," 31 January 1882, DKD II, appendix B, 866–67.

18. *Home*, 270; "The Refusal to Marry," *WJ* (17 September 1904): 298.

19. "To Choose," *FR* 2 (October 1911): 273; CAP to CWS, 20 February 1882, folder 39, SL.

20. Schreiner, "Life's Gifts," 115–16; "between living and loving" from *Three Women*, *FR* 2 (May 1911): 119; CAP to CWS, 20 and 21 February 1882, folder 39, SL.

21. *E*, 11 March 1882, 57; CAP, qtd. in *E*, 22 March 1882, 62–63.

22. CAP, qtd. in *E*, 6 December 1882, 121; CAP, qtd. in *E*, 2 April 1883, 153; CPS to GHG, 16 and 15 March 1899, folders 66 and 65, SL.

23. Qtd. in *E*, 8 February 1882, 44.

24. Undated verse between CAP and CWS, folder 39, SL; *L*, 78.

25. CWS, "To Charlotte" (poem), DKD II, appendix B, 870; CWS, "Still Loved" (poem), 23 April 1883, DKD II, appendix B, 886; "self imposed exile" from CAP letter, transcribed in *E*, 17 April 1883, 166.

26. Untitled poem, 1 April 1883, DKD II, appendix B, 882.

27. On her wish that Walter were a "girl," see *E*, 8 February 1882, 44; *E*, 21 February 1882, 49–50.

28. *E*, 2 March 1882, 54; "Now Mrs. Perkins" from *E*, 24 April 1882, 68; *E*, 14 August 1882, 88; "little fits" and "she needs" from *E*, 7 October 1882, 107.

29. CAP to FBP, 10 June 1882, folder 37, SL; "dammed up" from *E*, 1 July 1882, 79; *E*, 14 August 1882, 88; misgivings recorded in *E*, 21 March 1882, 60.

30. 83-M201, folder 5, SL, and see DKD II, 1 January 1883, 880; untitled poem, 1 March 1883, DKD II, appendix B, 879, 881–82.

31. *E*, 23 June 1883, 201; CPS to GHG, 8 March 1899, folder 67, SL; on Whitman's organicism, see, e.g., *HW*, 102.

32. *E*, 17 February 1882, 48; *E*, 19 November 1883, 245; *E*, 3 March 1882, 56; "My heart" from *E*, 2 March 1882, 54–55; *E*, 20 May 1882, 74.

33. CAP, qtd. in *E*, 20 May 1882, 74; CAP is qtd. on supporting herself in *E*, 1 May 1882, 69; *E*, 13 May 1882, 72–73 (Walter regretted his harshness when he later read over these entries); CAP, qtd. in *E*, 27 August 1883, 224.

34. *Home*, 268.

35. *E*, 10 August 1882, 82; CWS, "The Painting of *The Portrait*" (poem), DKD II, appendix B, 876; Walter transcribes the same poem in *E*, 25 September 1882, 104–05; it begins, "These many days I've tried to fix the face / Of her I love on canvas. . . ."

36. On the marriage plans and finances, see *E*, 16 September 1882, 100–02, and *E*, 28 September 1882, 106; "dough" from *E*, 9 October 1882, 107; on Charlotte's love, passion, and self-abnegation, see *E*, 1 January 1883, 127–28, *E*, 12 and 19 January 1883, 129–30, and *E*, 16 March 1883, 140.

37. Her confusion is described in *E*, 18 October 1882, 110; oath dated 22 October 1882, DKD II, appendix B, 878; *E*, 21 June 1883, 200.

38. DKD I, 11 February 1883, 175.

39. *E*, 22 March 1883, 144; "In Two Houses," *FR* 2 (July 1911): 171–77.

40. *E*, 19 March 1883, 143; *E*, 22 March 1883, 144–45; *E*, 31 March 1883, 149.

41. E, 27 March 1883, 147; *E*, 31 March 1883, 149; her "Power for Good" resolution, dated 15 February 1883, was inscribed in the back of her 1883 journal, DKD II, appendix B, 881; letter transcribed in *E*, 28 April 1883, 178; "it makes no difference" from letter transcribed in *E*, 24 April 1883, 171.

42. Sermon, 6 January 1883, folder 162, SL (In his *Life Thoughts*, Henry Ward Beecher uses the term "right living" as the definition of piety; he argues that we must please God with our good behavior in the same way children seek to please their parents.); CAP to TAP, 13 May 1883, DKD II, appendix B, 888.

43. *E*, 21 July 1883, 213; CWS, "In Pain" (poem), 14 April 1883, DKD II, appendix B, 883; *E*, 2 April 1883, 154.

44. *E*, 19 May 1883, 187; the details about De Kay's assessment and its effect on CWS are provided by Grace Channing Stetson, his second wife, qtd. in *E*, 19 May 1883, 188n; *E*, 15 May 1883, 185.

45. *The Crux*, *FR* 2 (September 1911): 235; CAP describes painting the "lugubrious picture" in DKD I, 9 November 1883, 233; *E*, 12 November 1883, 244.

46. DKD I, "1883–1884," 246.

47. CAP to MLL, 6 September 1883, RIHS; on leaving the Jacksons, see DKD I, 2 October 1883, 223.

48. DKD I, 27 July 1883, 211; *E*, 2 October 1883, 232.

49. Letter transcribed in *E*, 28 July 1883, 215; for CWS's thoughts on her "relapse," see *E*, 26 November 1883, 246; "turns of affectional paralysis" from DKD I, 25 November 1883, 236; "A Word to Myself," 3 November 1883, DKD II, appendix A, 841–43.

50. DKD I, 31 December 1883, 245–46.

51. DKD I, 1 January 1883, 247; CAP to CWS, 1 January 1884, WSCC. Not long before, Sydney Putnam, the friend who had introduced her to Walter, had drowned under suspicious circumstances, contributing to Charlotte's "mental misery."

52. *E*, 15 January 1884, 253; CAP comments on the show and sales in DKD I, 4 and 5 March 1884, 262; DKD I, 10 March 1884, 264; Eldredge, 33.

53. DKD I, 4 January 1884, 248; "old force" from DKD I, 2 January 1884, 247; DKD I, 11 January 1883, 250; "talk" from DKD I, 26 January 1883, 253.

54. DKD I, 24 February 1884, 260; Mill, *Subjection*, 146; for elucidations of Mill, see Pateman, 293, and Degler, *At Odds*, 392.

55. DKD I, 10 February 1884, 257; CAP to GEC, 28 February 1884, mf-6, SL.

56. She describes her mood in DKD I, 9 March 1884, 263, and 11 March 1884, 264; *E*, 13 March 1884, 256; sermon, 23 March 1884, folder 162, SL.

57. KSC, "Autobiography," WSCC; *E*, 18 August 1884, 259; DKD I, 2 May 1884, 278.

CHAPTER FOUR

1. CPG, "To the Young Wife," *ITOW*, 129–31.

2. CPS to GHG, 12 March 1899, folder 66, SL; *W&E*, 83; CPS to GHG, 10 March 1899, folder 67, SL.

3. *What Diantha Did*, *FR* 1 (February 1910): 15–16.

4. Autobiography, "an earlier attempt," folder 234, SL; *L*, 87; DKD I, 9 May 1884, 280.

5. Catharine Beecher, Letter Eighteenth, *Letters to the People*, 121; see the study by Collier, 15; Elisabeth Marbury qtd. on the "caress" in Comstock, 157.

6. DKD I, 15 June 1884, 286; DKD I, 25 and 26 June 1884, 288; CPS to GHG, 14 October 1899, folder 56, SL.

7. DKD I, 5 August 1884, 295; DKD I, 7 August 1884, 296.

8. *E*, 31 October 1884, 268; untitled poem, *E*, 18 August 1884, 261.

9. Untitled poem, DKD I, 31 December 1884, appendix B, 893–94; DKD I, 4 September 1884, 301; "dreamed of life" from E, 15 September 1884, 264; DKD I, 10 October 1884, 307.

10. Gallery co-owner qtd. in Lillian Whiting, "The Daily Graphic," review, typescript, WSCC; Eldredge, 33; review, *Art Amateur*, September 1884, qtd. in *E*, 265n; *E*, 17 November 1884, 270.

11. *E*, 15 September 1884, 264; CPS talks about reading her "comforter, Walter's journal," in DKD I, 2 February 1885, 315; Walter complains about housework interfering with his art in *E*, 18 January 1885, 272, and *E*, 25 January 1885, 276.

12. Poem ms. in WSCC.

13. DKD I, 11 January 1885, 308; "The Sin of Sickness," *Buffalo Christian Advocate* (5 February 1885): 4.

14. CPS describes her hysteria in DKD I, 17 and 19 February 1884, 318. (Charlotte would meet the nurse again when Pease attended one of Charlotte's lectures in 1923 [CPG to KSC, 2 March 1923, folder 94, SL]); CPS describes the baby's activities in DKD I, 12 March 1885, 322; CPS to SWM, 19 April 1887, AG 487C, SL.

15. DKD I, 23 March 1885, 326; *E*, 28 January 1885, 277; CPS uses the term "the darkness" to describe her melancholy in DKD I, 1883–1884, 247.

16. *L*, 90.

17. *L*, 89; she describes her swift breakdown in CPS to SWM, 19 April 1887, AG 487C, SL, and Walter confirms her version in *E*, 24 August 1885, 278–89; DKD I, 9 and 10 May 1885, 328.

18. DKD I, 14 September 1885, 334; *L*, 154; "The 'Nervous Breakdown' of Women," *FR* 7 (August 1916): 203. See also "One Cause of Nervous Prostration," *Impress* (20 October 1894): 8, and see CPS to SWM, 19 April 1187, AG 487C, SL, where she associates "this agony of mind" with "the child's coming" and claims, "I nursed her in slow tears."

19. Green, *Fit*, 137–38; Lears, 50; for an example of a doctor who followed the theory of the body as a closed energy system, see Clarke, *Sex in Education*; *Home*, 223.

20. On American nervousness, see Lutz, Sicherman, "Paradox of Prudence," 893, Green, *Fit*, 138–40, and Bederman, 132; *Home*, 74.

21. *E*, 2 May 1885, 277; DKD I, 2 May 1885, 327; Autobiography, "an earlier attempt," folder 234, SL.

22. DKD I, 5 August 1885, 329; DKD I, 28 August 1885, 331; *E*, 24 August 1885, 279.

23. *E*, 24 August 1885, 280; DKD I, 30 August 1885, 332; *E*, 24 August 1885, 279.

24. *Three Women*, *FR* 2 (May 1911): 115–23; "Mrs. Power's Duty," *FR* 4 (October 1913): 256; "duties" from "A Word to Myself," 3 November 1883, DKD II, appendix A, 841.

25. *L*, 201; "A Brood Mare," *ITOW*, 161–64, quote from 163.

26. *E*, 12 September 1885, 290; on her periods, see, e.g., CPS to GHG, 20 June 1898, folder 58, SL, and CPS to GHG, 19 December 1898, folder 61, SL; *E*, 24 August 1885, 279–80.

27. *E*, 5 May 1886, 304; *E*, 25 September 1885, 292–93.

28. *E*, 27 August 1885, 282; *E*, 11 September 1885, 290.

29. "The Artist," *FR* 7 (July 1916): 169–73, quote from 170.

30. On Mellin's Food, see DKD I, 5 August 1885, 329, and DKD I, 1 October 1885, 337; the ad is reprinted in Green, *Light*, 41; DKD I, 8 October 1885, 338.

31. *E*, 9 October 1885, 297; *E*, 11 October 1885, 298; *E*, 19 and 23 October 1885, 298–99.

32. *L*, 92–93.

33. Charlotte describes the city as paradise in *L*, 94; McWilliams, 113; "tall men . . ." from "The Superior Northerner," *Land of Sunshine* 3 (October 1895): 211; the doctor's views of the West qtd. in Gosling, 133.

34. Alice Moore McComas, "Pasadena Shakespeare Club," *Impress* (15 December 1894): 7;

the local enthusiast is Charles Frederick Holder, qtd. in Starr, 100; CPG, "Out of Doors," *LP*, 146–47; CPS to MLL, 4 January 1886, RIHS.

35. Starr, 99; the "cranks" are described by Mrs. Charles Stewart Dagget, qtd. in McWilliams, 249.

36. Scheid, 54; Dumke, 89; "Pasadena Alphabet" (poem), folder 198, SL.

37. KSC, "Autobiography," WSCC; "Neighbors in '80s," newspaper clipping, WSCC; GEC celebrates the lush climate in poems including "Southern California" (55–56) and "California of the South" (57–59) in *Sea Drift*. A "normal school" trains high school graduates to be teachers.

38. *L*, 94; poem, folder 205, SL; *E*, 347–48n.

39. CPS to MLL, 4 January 1886, and 13 March 1886, RIHS.

40. On Julia Perkins see DKD I, 21 September 1886, 345, DKD II, 3 October 1886, 347, and DKD I, 11 October 1886, 349; *E*, 27 and 30 April 1886, 302–03.

41. *E*, 27 April 1886, 300; DKD I, 1–3 April 1886, 339; CWS describes his despair in *E*, 27 April 1886, 301; Dr. Keller's visit described in *E*, 17 August 1886, 310; *E*, 28 April 1886, 302.

42. *E*, 30 April 1886, 303.

43. *L*, 95; *E*, 24 November 1886, 322; DKD I, 31 December 1886, 364.

44. DKD I, 1 November 1886, 355; DKD I, 17 December 1886, 361; CWS praises the poem in *E*, 17 August 1886, 311; "The Answer," *ITOW*, 2–4, quote from 4.

45. "On Advertising for Marriage," *Alpha* (1 September 1885): 22; *E*, 15 September 1885, 291.

46. DKD I, 9 October 1886, 349 (Charlotte confessed her regret afterward; as an adult, Katharine claimed her father "must have been furious as well as hurt," though Walter never mentions the incident in his diaries. For KSC's reflections, see vol. 2, David Goodale transcript, CWS papers, 93-M76, SL); CPS's contempt for Brown is expressed in DKD I, 22 October 1886, 351; "A Transparency," *Alpha* (1 December 1886): 6–7, quote from 7.

47. "Why Women Do Not Reform Their Dress," *WJ* (23 October 1886): 338 (Charlotte remained interested enough in dress reform that fall to call on Dr. Mary Walker, but the famous doctor failed to convince Charlotte to adopt reform dress as fully as the doctor had done: Charlotte objected to Walker's aversion to "beauty in costume" [DKD I, 2 November 1886, 355]); on her library trips, see DKD I, 1 January 1887, 367, and DKD I, 6 October 1886, 348; on Walter's moratorium, see *E*, 9 February 1887, 331, and DKD I, 5 February 1887, 373.

48. "The Right to Earn Money," *WJ* (8 January 1887): 12; "Pungent Paragraphs," *WJ* (12 March 1887): 88.

49. "Record of My Daughter Katharine Stetson," WSCC; DKD I, 28 October 1886, 352.

50. DKD I, 14 and 15 February 1887, 374; "What We Are Doing," *Impress* (13 October 1894): 1.

51. "The Woman's Column," *Providence People* (5 March 1887) sec. 1: 3; "Woman," *Providence People* (16 April 1887) sec. 5: 5.

52. DKD I, 20 February 1887, 375; on her cold, see, e.g., CPS to SWM, 19 April 1887,

AG 487C, SL; DKD I, 24 February 1887, 376, and DKD I, 6 March 1887, 377; on the other mothers, see DKD I, 22 February 1887, 375–76.

53. DKD I, 20 March 1887, 380; *E,* 28 April 1887, 335; DKD I, 18 April 1887, 384–85.

54. "Why I Wrote 'The Yellow Wallpaper'?" *FR* 4 (October 1913): 271.

55. CPS to SWM, 19 April 1887, AG 487C, SL. Thanks to Denise Knight for counting Charlotte's diary entries on fatigue. In another passage in her letter to Mitchell, Charlotte directly links her depression to childbirth: "This agony of mind set in with the child's coming. I nursed her in slow tears."

56. Georgiana's end was tragic (see Hedrick, 396). Charlotte claims Mitchell told her disdainfully, "'I've had two women of your blood here already'"(*L,* 95), but I have been unable to determine who the other Beecher patient was, if there was one. Walter's account suggests that Mitchell told Charlotte "he never had but *one* other such case, and that of a lady with the same blood in her veins" (*E,* 7 May 1887, 337, emphasis added); Charlotte discusses Mitchell's deflating rejoinder in *L,* 329; she discusses her work on the article in DKD I, 28 August 1885, 332.

57. Gosling, 37; Rein, 1, 19.

58. SWM, *Lectures on Diseases,* 227; SWM, *Fat and Blood,* 58–59.

59. Poirier, 15; qtd. in Rose, 75.

60. The doctor cultivated friendships with women he considered his intellectual equals; he approved of physical activity for women, disapproved of gender distinctions in physical training before children reached adolescence, and acknowledged the right of certain remarkable individual women to pursue higher education. On Mitchell, see Morantz, 240, Earnest, 230, and Sicherman, 898, as well as Mitchell himself: *Wear and Tear,* 32–36, and *Doctor and Patient,* 83–84.

61. SWM, *Lectures on Diseases,* 276, 38.

62. *L,* 95; Poirier helps clarify the hysteria diagnosis, 17; SWM, *Lectures on Diseases,* 21.

63. *E,* 30 April 1887, 337; *E,* 7 May 1887, 337–38.

64. Lunbeck, 210–11; Smith-Rosenberg, 207–08.

65. See, e.g., SWM, *Doctor and Patient,* 48ff; "Rest and Power," *FR* 6 (October 1915): 271.

66. "Giving," *FR* 2 (December 1911): 316–17.

67. "Their Dressmaker," *WJ* (25 June 1904): 202; *L,* 96; "Why I Wrote 'The Yellow Wallpaper'?" *FR* 4 (October 1913): 271.

68. *L,* 95; William F. Channing to SWM, 1887, qtd. in Tuttle, "Rewriting," 111; SWM, *Lectures on Diseases,* 233.

69. CPG, "'The Yellow Wall Paper'—Its History & Reception," folder 221, SL; "The Yellow Wall-Paper," ms., folder 221, SL; for theories about wallpaper's deleterious effects, see Robin W. Edis, "Internal Decoration," *Our Homes* (London, 1883), qtd. in Green, *Fit,* 118–21. See Heather K. Thomas and Lanser for different interpretations of the paper's yellowness. For readings of the ending as some form of victory, see, e.g., Gilbert and Gubar, *Madwoman,* 89–92, and more ambivalently, Treichler, 191–210. My own reading of "The Yellow Wall-Paper" has been adapted from my *Bodily and Narrative Forms,* © 2000 by the Board of Trustees of the Leland Stanford Jr. University Press, by permission of the publisher.

70. *L,* 118–19; CPS to SWM, 19 April 1887, AG 487C, SL; DKD I, 5 August 1885, 329.

71. *E*, 23 March 1883, 144–45; *E*, 28 March 1883, 148.

72. Anonymous, "New Books and Those Who Make Them," *Boston Daily Advertiser* (10 June 1899): 8, in Golden, *Yellow Wall-Paper: Sourcebook*, 83; *Time and the Hour* (17 June 1899), clipping, folder 301, SL.

73. "pure propaganda" from CPG to WDH, 17 October 1919, bMS Am 1784 (178), Houghton; her accounts of its reception and purpose are from *L*, 121, and "Why I Wrote," 271. Charlotte told her friend Alexander Black that she wrote "The Yellow Wall-Paper" "to preach—if it's literature that just happened" (Black, *Time*, 283). She described the story to her friend Martha as "highly unpleasant" and claimed Walter had "read it *four* times, and thinks it the most ghastly tale he ever read" (CPS to ML, 27 July 1890, RIHS); on the publication and reception history of the story, see Dock.

74. She discusses Mitchell's views on heroism in "Nature of Humanity," *Chautauqua Assembly Herald* (24 August 1904), oversize folder 2, SL.

75. "A New Basis for the Servant Question," *Worthington's Illustrated* 3 (March 1894): 304–09; quote from 306.

76. *E*, 21 June 1887, 341; *E*, 30 June 1887, 342; *L*, 96.

77. *E*, 18 July 1887, 343; *E*, 13 October 1887, 354.

78. See DK, "Charlotte Perkins Gilman's Lost Book," 27.

79. *E*, 6 August 1887, 347–48.

80. CPS to GEC, 21 November 1887, mf-6, SL.

81. *E*, 39 January 1888, 355; "fine old-fashioned" from GEC to WFC, 7 June 1888, GECSP, SL; Charlotte praises Grace in CPS to MLL, 20 January 1890, RIHS. (A lengthier discussion of their "romantic summer" can be found in my "The Two Mrs. Stetsons.")

82. GEC to MTC, 21 and 12 June 1888, GECSP, SL; CPS to GEC, 21 November 1887, mf-6, SL; GEC to MTC, 12 June 1888, GECSP, SL.

83. For Grace's descriptions of the play, see GEC to MTC, 4 July, 12 June, and 13 July 1888, GECSP, SL; "Noblesse Oblige" (poem), *American Fabian* 4 (March 1898): 3.

84. Letter transcribed in *E*, 15 June 1888, 363–64; "hysterics"-from GEC to MTC, 9 July 1888, GECSP, SL; Walter describes his lasting love for Charlotte to Grace's mother at a time when he and Grace were essentially engaged: CWS to MTC, 10 May 1892, GECSP, SL; shortly after he married Grace and took custody of Katharine, he wrote Charlotte complaining of his new bride's faults and confided, "truly, dear, I do not see how I can let her [Katharine] ever leave me again. I wish I need not: rather, I wish we could have her together." CWS to CPS, 9 July 1894, GECSP, SL; for more on this interchange, see my "The Two Mrs. Stetsons."

85. "things are hard" from GEC to MTC, 21 June 1888, GECSP, SL; GEC to MTC, 22 June 1888, GECSP, SL; GEC to MTC, on Walter's lovability, see 9 and 7 July 1888, GECSP, SL; Grace discusses Walter's views of her in undated correspondence between GEC and Dr. Knight, qtd. by Hill in *E*, 196n.

86. GEC to MTC, 8 June 1888, GECSP, SL; GEC to MTC, 7 July 1888, GECSP, SL.

87. Charlotte discusses the oddness of writing comedy in CPS to MLL, 13 March 1886, RIHS; CPS to GEC, 21 November 1887, mf-6, SL; GEC to MTC, 20 June 1888, GECSP, SL; CPS to GEC, 21 November 1887, mf-6, SL.

88. *L*, 105; *E*, 18 October 1888, 366.

89. Autobiography, "an earlier attempt," folder 234, SL; Grace discusses the logistics of their train trip in GEC to MTC, 17 September 1888, GECSP, SL; Walter's vow is in the CWS papers, 93 M76, SL; GEC to family, 9 October 1888, GECSP, SL; "hope and health and joy" from CPG to GEC, 22 September 1888, mf-6, SL; see Tuttle, "West Cure," 106–07.

CHAPTER FIVE

1. "Finding," *ITOW*, 56–57. The chapter title is taken from DKD II, appendix B, "Thoughts & Figgerings," 9 May 1894, 845.

2. "Thanksgiving Hymn for California" (poem), *Pacific Monthly* 1 (November 1889): 49; CPS to RSS, 30 October 1888, BANC MSS 72/218, CWS letters, Bancroft.

3. CPS to Charles Lummis, 15 April 1898, Southwest Museum (thanks to Jennifer Tuttle for providing me with a copy of this letter); "Resolve," *ITOW*, 121.

4. "Pain," 1892 sermon, ms., folder 167, SL.

5. On her Pasadena plans and house, see GEC to MTC, 26 June 1888, GECSP, SL; *L*, 107; Susan Carrier, "Residents Shape Up Triangle," *Los Angeles Times* (19 March 1995): K1, K6; and DKD II, 5 February 1891, 437.

6. CPS to RSS, 30 October 1888, BANC MSS 72/218, CWS letters, Bancroft; CPS to MW, 30 May 1890, Vassar; KSC autobiography, WSCC; *L*, 161.

7. Charlotte's description of the incubus and the subsequent boarder, as well as her comments on the climate, her hammock, and her "drowned" metaphor are from *L*, 107–08; she mentions the flies in "An Honest Woman," *FR* 2 (March 1911): 59–65; she describes her convalescence in CPS to MW, 30 May 1890, Vassar; she discusses the cocaine in Autobiography, "an earlier attempt," folder 234, SL.

8. Walter's rapturous sentiments are appended to the 9 October 1888 entry of CWS diary, CWS papers, 93 M76, SL; he discusses his "call" in CWS diary, 27 August 1888, CWS papers, 93 M76, SL; CWS's trip to the West is described in Eldredge, 46–49; "blossoming" from CWS to RSS, 28 December 1888, BANC MSS 72/218, CWS letters, Bancroft; Eldredge, 52.

9. CPS to MLL, 22 October 1889, RIHS; Walter describes Charlotte's activities and the plans for the new journal in CWS to RSS, 21 July, 3 April, and 12 August 1889, BANC MSS 72/218, CWS letters, Bancroft; see also CPS to Mrs. Severance, 3 November 1889, Huntington Library, and "*The Californian*," flyer, folder 237, SL; CPS to MLL, 16 March 1889, RIHS.

10. Howe, "Charlotte—As I Knew Her," 211–12; CPS to MW, 28 September 1890, Vassar; CPS to MW, 30 May 1890, Vassar.

11. Walter describes the diversions in CWS to RSS, 8 and 20 January and 21 July 1889, BANC MSS 72/218, CWS letters, Bancroft; the Opera House commission is discussed in *L*, 112 and in KSC's autobiography, WSCC, where KSC also describes the fire.

12. CPS to MW, 28 September 1890, Vassar; CPS to MLL, 15 April 1890, RIHS; *A Pretty Idiot*, folder 214, SL.

13. CPS to MLL, 16 March 1889, RIHS; CWS to RSS, 5 May 1889, BANC MSS 72/218, CWS letters, Bancroft; Eldredge, 59.

14. CPS to MW, 30 May 1890, Vassar; Divorce #9078, Charles Walter Stetson vs. Charlotte Perkins Stetson, filed 27 October 1892, Providence Supreme Court; CWS to RSS, 9 July 1889, BANC MSS 72/218, CWS letters, Bancroft.

15. CWS to RSS, 12 and 21 July 1889, BANC MSS 72/218, CWS letters, Bancroft; CPS qtd. in CWS to RSS, 7 June 1889, BANC MSS 72/218, CWS letters, Bancroft.

16. CWS to RSS, 3 November and 30 October 1889, BANC MSS 72/218, CWS letters, Bancroft; "Too Much" (poem), *ITOW*, 57–58; CPS to MLL, 15 August 1889, RIHS.

17. "My Fellow Traveller," *Pacific Monthly* 3 (June–July 1891): 237–41; *L*, 110; CPS to MLL, 27 July 1890, RIHS.

18. "Divorce and Birth Control," *Outlook* (25 October 1928): 130, 131, 153; *L*, 109; on the "whereabouts of Mr. Stetson," see clipping, 25 April 1891, folder 285, SL.

19. "daily, bravely" from CPS to GEC, 3 December 1890, mf-6, SL; CWS to MTC, 29 July 1891, GECSP, SL; CPS to MLL, 20 January 1890, RIHS.

20. The full title of this second of two poems inserted in the 1892 diary reads, "C.P.S. Dec. 30th '91–Dec. 31st 1891. Near 12," DKD II, appendix B, 900.

21. *L*, 114, 115; she records her diagnosis in DKD II, 20 November 1890, 425, and discusses her theories about its origins in CPS to GEC, 3 December 1890, mf-6, SL; on the gap between her public image and private "wretchedness," see *L*, 238, 98.

22. CPS to MW, 28 September 1890, Vassar.

23. On the California literary renaissance, see Wertheimer, 255–56, Walker, *Literary History of California*, 4, 118, and Gertrude Atherton, "Literary Development of California," *Cosmopolitan* (10 January 1891): 272. Atherton's biographer Leider suggests (249n6) that Charlotte was the "EMINENT FEMINIST." Atherton rebuked her in 1932 *Adventures of a Novelist* for neglecting her child on behalf of work and for behaving in a boorish fashion. But Atherton refers to the feminist's child as "a freckled-faced grimy little boy," not a daughter (*Adventures*, 211).

24. On California as a microcosm, see Mowry, 90; for Charlotte's nationalism, see *L*, 131; for an early articulation of the views she expresses in *W&E*, see "Dame Nature Interviewed on the Woman Question as It Looks to Her," *Kate Field's Washington* (27 August 1890): 138–40, especially 139; and for her support of women's causes, see, e.g., "Two Races in One," *Kate Field's Washington* (5 November 1890): 69.

25. "The Ceaseless Struggle of Sex: A Dramatic View," *Kate Field's Washington* (9 April 1890): 239–40.

26. On the "Bellamy craze," see Foner, vol. 2, 44, John Thomas, 262, and Kipnis, 44; Twain, qtd. in Spann, 189. 27; Morris, qtd. in John Thomas, 272; Gronlund, qtd. in Spann, 180; George, qtd. in Schiffman, introduction, *Edward Bellamy: Selected Writings on Religion and Society*, xli.

28. "Why I Wrote 'Looking Backward'," *Nationalist* (May 1890), in *EBSA!*, 199; Lipow, 174; Bellamy espouses gradualism in EB, "Nationalism—Principles, Purposes" address, 19 December 1889, in *EBSA!*, 68; letter to William Dean Howells, qtd. in Lipow, 22.

29. For background on nationalism, see Dombrowski, 101; Bellamy connects na-

tionalism to Christianity in EB, "The Progress," in *EBSA!*, 139, and to evolution in EB, "'Looking Backward' Again," *North American Review* (March 1890), in *EBSA!*, 184; John Thomas, 270.

30. On nationalist clubs, see Kipnis, 44; EB, "The Progress," in *EBSA!*, 137–38.

31. Lipow discusses the percentage of clubs in California, 127; the local observer is Reda Davis, 59; Buhle discusses the proportion of women involved in nationalism in *Women*, 77; see Dombrowski on the sympathy between nationalism and women's concerns, 92–95; EB, "To a Woman's Rights Advocate," in *Talks on Nationalism*, 79–85, quote from 85; on Hale, see Spann, 194.

32. *L*, 122; Vernon is the author of the 1891 sketch, quote from 5; *L*, 122; Howe, "Charlotte—As I Knew Her," 211.

33. EB, "Some Misconceptions of Nationalism," *Christian Union* (13 November 1890), in *EBSA!*, 122; on Charlotte's attraction to nationalism, see her "The Labor Movement," folder 268, SL; Bellamy's plans for women are elaborated in EB, *Looking Backward*, 184–90, and analyzed by Hayden, *Grand*, *148*–49; EB, "To a Disciple of Malthus" in *Talks on Nationalism*, 122; "race purification" is from EB, *Looking Backward*, 191.

34. EB, *Looking Backward*, 185–86; EB, "To a Woman's Rights Advocate," in *Talks on Nationalism*, 82–83.

35. CPS to GHG, 8 September 1897, folder 45, SL; "Book Reviews," *Impress* 1 (September 1894): 6; "forecasting" is from CPS to GHG, 11 May 1897, folder 41, SL (see also CPS to GHG, 29 August 1897, folder 44, SL); CPS to MLL, 15 April 1890, RIHS.

36. See Lipow on Bellamy's debt to positivism and theosophy, 175–76, 227; "entire renunciation" from Blavatsky, 19; see also regarding Comte, EB, "Positive Romance," *Century* (August 1889): 9–20.

37. EB, "The Religion of Solidarity," 4, 14, 17–18; EB, comments added to the manuscript in 1887, "Religion of Solidarity," 26. For additional elucidations of Bellamy's "religion," see Lipow, 44; John Thomas, 86–87; Dombrowski, 86.

38. The fatal blow may have been dealt by the conservative evolutionist William Graham Sumner, whose *Forum* essay "The Absurd Effort to Make the World Over" aimed to expose the "absurdity" of his fellow contributor, Bellamy. Sumner deployed cold, hard scientific facts to deflate Bellamy's idealistic movement at a time when it could scarcely breathe on its own. On nationalism's demise, see Lipow, 31–32, Spann, 202, CPS, "Waste," *New Nation* (6 January 1894): 4, and EB to CPS, 14 January 1894, folder 137, SL; Beard, *Woman as Force*, 26.

39. Geddes and Thompson, 312; DKD II, 2 May 1891, 453.

40. *Kate Field's Washington* (26 August 1891): 90–91.

41. *L*, 110, 115; she credits her Beecher blood in CPG to KSC, 1 April 1932, folder 103, SL; *L*, 138; she talks about her captive audience in "A Biographical Sketch of Charlotte Perkins Gilman," folder 243, SL; "Personality and God," *FR* 2 (August 1911): 204–05.

42. DKD II, 16 January 1892, 492; on the colloquial nature of her talks, see "Things as They Are: Charlotte Perkins Stetson Discusses Them," *Minneapolis Sunday Times* (19 November 1899), folder 286, SL; the reference to "It" appears in CPG to KSC, 1 April 1932, folder 103, SL; "The New Hope," folder 172, SL.

43. DKD II, 27 March 1893, 523, and 1 February 1894, 571; "The Ethics of Woman's Work," folder 171, SL. Thanks to Lawrence Glickman for making this connection to the Brandeis brief.

44. Clipping, *Woman's World*, folder 266, SL; the admirer is Howe, "Charlotte—As I Knew Her," 211; lecture flyers, folder 10, SL; "Heaven Underfoot," folder 169, SL.

45. Clipping, folder 285, SL; "Things as They Are: Charlotte Perkins Stetson Discusses Them," *Minneapolis Sunday Times* (19 November 1899), folder 286, SL; on Schreiner see Howe, "Charlotte—As I Knew Her," 212; on her reading her poetry, see "Woman's Wit," clipping, folder 285, SL, and "An Interesting Lecture," clipping, folder 286, SL.

46. On the fly, see *L*, 195; the reporter's article is entitled "Art and Dress: Mrs. Stetson's Bright Lecture in Irving Hall," folder 286, SL; Howe, "Charlotte—As I Knew Her," 211; DKD II, 27 July 1893, 545.

47. DKD II, 8 April 1894, appendix A, 845.

48. Bellamy, *New Nation* (24 June 1893): 315, and see Scharnhorst, "Making Her Fame," 199; the 1891 essay is by Atherton, 272; for Hale's praise see DKD II, 21 February 1891, 440, and Edward Everett Hale to CPS, 15 July 1890, folder 36, SL; WDH to CPS, 9 June 1890, folder 120, SL. Charlotte responded by informing Howells, "Among all the pleasant things I had hoped for in my work this particular gratification was never imagined. And the best part of it is that there is not a man in America whose praise in literature I would rather win!" (CPS to WDH, 16 June 1890, WDH papers, bMS Am 1784 [178], Houghton).

49. "Similar Cases," *ITOW*, 95–100; on quotability, see "CPS: A Daring Humorist of Reform," *American Fabian* 3 (January 1897): 2; on Wilson, see Beard, *Woman as Force*, 27–28; LFW, *Glimpses of the Cosmos*, 337–40.

50. *LP*, 169–70; she first sent the story to Howells (whose own daughter had recently died under Mitchell's care), who then passed it on to Horace Scudder, the current editor of the *Atlantic Monthly*. Scudder rejected the tale, however, claiming "I could not forgive myself if I made others as miserable as I have made myself" (Horace E. Scudder to CPS, 18 October 1890, folder 126, SL). Howells maintains that he then helped to arrange for its 1892 publication in *New England Magazine*. See WDH, introduction to *Great Modern American Stories*.

51. *L*, 168; DKD II, 18 November 1893, 563.

52. Howe, "Charlotte—As I Knew Her," 214–15; CPS to Mother (Jeanne C. Smith Carr), 18 November 1893, Huntington.

53. The two poems appear in *ITOW*, 34–35 and 62–63; Traubel's review of *ITOW* appeared in *Conservator* 9 (September 1898): 109. See also DK, "'With the first'."

54. On the hasty composition of her purposeful poems, see CPS to GHG, 16 June 1897, folder 42, SL, and CPS to GHG, 23 October 1898, folder 57, SL. See also *L*, 121, where she declares it "a pretty poor thing to write, to talk, without a purpose"; "Apropos of Literature," *Pacific Monthly* 2 (July 1890): 123; "The Love Story," *Pacific Monthly* 2 (September 1890): 176–77; on her poems being read in church, see CPG to LBS, 11 September 1928, Beecher-Stowe papers, folder 416, SL; her conversation with Markham is reported in "A Biographical Sketch of Charlotte Perkins Gilman," anonymous typescript [1920s], folder 243, SL. Though an early subscriber, Hattie Howe also disparaged the

poems as "not poetry in the true meaning." See Howe, "Charlotte—As I Knew Her," 214–15; "nails" from "Stetson Reception," *Topeka State Journal* (13 June 1896): 6.

55. *Bookman* (June 1895): 33.

56. WDH to CPS, 11 July 1894, folder 120, SL; EB to CPS, 14 January 1894, folder 137, SL; qtd. in *Impress* 2 (17 November 1894): 10.

57. *L*, 54; Wellington, 123; DK, "But O My Heart," 270.

58. "Thoughts & Figgerings," 26 March 1894, folder 16, SL.

59. Charlotte both records the talk and she notes that she was chosen to be the last speaker because "people will wait for *her!*" in DKD II, 17 February 1891, 439; speech qtd. in Millicent Bell, "Pioneer," *New York Review of Books* (17 April 1980), 10–14, quote from 10–11; she relates the stick incident in CPS to MW, 30 May 1890, Vassar.

60. The first meeting between her father and Katharine is recorded in DKD II, 19 March 1891, 445; a subsequent meeting is described in DKD II, 16 April 1891, 449; on Katharine's school, see CPS to MW, 28 September 1890, Vassar; DKD II, 24 February 1891, 440.

61. *L*, 155, 158, 161.

62. *ITOW*, 174.

63. *CC*, 194, 199; this was a point she reiterated in treatises including *CC* and *Home*, in stories including "Martha's Mother," "What Occupation?," "My Poor Aunt," and "Joan's Defender," and in poems including "Motherhood," "To Mothers," "Only Mine," "The Burden of Mothers," and "Full Motherhood." "Martha's Mother," *FR* 1 (April 1910): 1–6; "What Occupation?" *FR* 2 (August 1911): 199–204; "My Poor Aunt," *FR* 4 (December 1913): 309–12; "Joan's Defender," *FR* 7 (June 1916): 141–45; "The Mother's Charge" *ITOW*, 167–68; "To Mothers," *ITOW*, 66–69; "Only Mine," *FR* 1 (October 1910): i; "Full Motherhood," *FR* 6 (October 1915): 272.

64. *CC*, 197; see also *On Child Study*, the Booklover's Library, folder 179, ("3 articles n.d. 1890s,") SL; "Our Overworked Instincts," *FR* 1 (December 1910): 12–13; see also "The Permanent Child," *FR* 1 (December 1910): 16–17.

65. *Home*, 40; on Walter and Grace taking "Kate," see CPS to GEC, 3 December 1890, mf-6, SL, CWS to the Channings, 29 July 1891, GECSP, SL, and CPS to GEC, 22 January 1893, mf-6, SL. As an old woman, Katharine maintained that she hated her childhood nickname "Kate," so I have referred to her throughout as Katharine.

66. CPS to MLL, 4 September 1890, RIHS (See also her reflections on Grace's departure and her "year of great growth and pain" in DKD II, 31 December 1890, 428); "inseparable" from CPS to MW, 30 May 1890, Vassar; her lengthy lament is recorded in CPS to GEC, 3 December 1890, mf-6, SL; on her wish for Walter, see CPS to GHG, 11 September 1897, folder 45, SL.

67. For her "rule" about people and her bathing suit metaphor, see CPS to MW, 28 September 1890, Vassar; on the PCWPA, see J. June Croly, 253; on Delle, see DKD II, 12 and 21 May 1891, 454, 455; on the divorce, see DKD II, 11 June 1891, 460.

68. "my girl" from DKD II, 14 July 1891, 466; "lonesome for delight" from DKD II, 25 August 1891, 472; poem, folder 205, SL; "To Me at Last (To A. E. K.)" (poem), DKD II, appendix B 899.

69. DKD II, 13 August 1891, 470n2, and see DK, "But O My Heart," 281; *L*, 78; CPS to GHG, 7 March 1899, folder 66, SL.

70. Katherine Bement Davis, qtd. in Fitzpatrick, 202–03. Lane has deflected a homoerotic reading of Charlotte and Delle's relationship by erroneously attributing the words of sociologist E. A. Ross—"I am altogether heterosexual and cannot do my best work unless in love and loved" (EAR, *Seventy Years of It*, 20)—to Charlotte herself. Lane further maintains that this assertion is "confirmed by her life's work" and by her two marriages (349). Charlotte would probably have agreed with Ross that she needed love to "do her best work," but she would have had less cause or need to insist on heterosexuality.

71. *L*, 143; KSC, "Autobiography," WSCC; on her friends' approval, see GEC to MTC, 5 July 1892, KSC transcript, WSCC, and CWS to MTC, 29 July 1891, GECSP, SL.

72. "sad" from DKD II, 28 July 1891, 468; GEC to MTC, KSC transcript, WSCC.

73. Biographical information on Delle comes from Knapp, *This Then Is Upland Pastures*, title page; "Adeline Knapp," *New York Times* (26 June 1909): BR 402 (thanks to Elizabeth Judd for this source).

74. Filler, 77; Charles Edwin Markham to the editor of *Scribner's Magazine*, 20 January 1895, Horrmann; on Delle's generosity, see *L*, 143; CPS to GHG, 27 October 1899, folder 75, SL.

75. Biographical information derived from *Who Was Who in America* (vol. 1), 685. See also Hinkel and McCann (*Biographies of California Authors*), 122, and Wallace (*Dictionary of North American Authors*), 253, and *San Francisco Examiner* (7 June 1909): 4.

76. On anti-Chinese agitation, see Sandmeyer; on Delle's prejudice, see Scharnhorst, "Plain Language," 396–98.

77. Qtd. in Reda Davis, 78, and see also Delle and Charlotte's mutual interest in "What Working Women Want" (DKD II, 25 January 1894, 570).

78. Knapp, *An Open Letter*, 8; Knapp, "Do Working Women Need the Ballot?" 3, 5; "traitors" from "The Anti-Suffragists," *ITOW*, 152–54, quote from 154.

79. 18 September 1891 ms., qtd. in *L*, 133.

CHAPTER SIX

1. CPS, "The Duty Farthest," *Impress* (17 November 1894): 5.

2. "An Extinct Angel," *Kate Field's Washington* (23 September 1891): 199–200.

3. "Our Domestic Duties," folder 166, SL.

4. DKD II, 27 July 1893, 545.

5. First two quoted phrases from CPG to AP, 11 August 1930, WHMEC; on personality as "the limit of our moral sense," see "Nursery-Mindedness," *FR* 1 (April 1910): 9; "Seeking" and "Finding" (poems), *ITOW*, 55–57.

6. "Mother to Child," *ITOW*, 140–42. See also her poem "Only Mine," *FR* 1 (October 1910): 1.

7. "Living from Day to Day," *Christian Register* (1 January 1891): 4, oversize folder 1, SL.

8. Delle's offer is described in CWS to the Channings, 29 July 1891, GECSP, SL; the possible transfer is discussed in CWS to GEC, 29 July 1891, GECSP, SL; Oakland background from Doyle, 60.

9. "An Interesting Lecture," clipping, folder 286, SL; KSC, "Autobiography," WSCC.

10. "California Literary Genius" from clipping, folder 266, SL; on Bierce's changing views on women, see Walker, *San Francisco's*, 237 and 254; on Hearst, see Brasch, 29, and DK, "Charlotte Perkins Gilman, William Randolph Hearst, and the Practice of Ethical Journalism"; Walker, *San Francisco's*, 241–42.

11. Bierce, "Prattle," *San Francisco Examiner* (4 February 1894) and (20 September 1891); see also Bierce's mocking treatment of Charlotte's poem, "She Who Is to Come." On the Bierce–Stetson relationship and Charlotte's plea to Brander Matthews to stop Bierce's mischief, see Oliver and Scharnhorst. As one of Charlotte's sympathizers complained, Bierce "knew little or nothing of the merits or demerits of the woman whom he nevertheless hooted and jeered and pelted with that variety of mud which is the ammunition in his cannon" (clipping, folder 298, SL). As late as 1929, Charlotte was still referring to Bierce as "the Public Executioner and Tormentor" (CPG to Mr. Williams, 3 April 1929, in DKJT).

12. "Charlotte P. Stetson," *San Francisco Call* (28 May 1893): 6; on Mary's transfer from Thomas to Charlotte, see *L*, 132; DKD II, 18 September 891, 474–75.

13. Howe, "Charlotte—As I Knew Her," 212; for references to illnesses, see DKD II, 24 January 1892, 493, and DKD II, 1 February 1892, 494, and see also Wegener, "'What a Comfort'"; on Mary, see DKD II, 6 and 29 February 1892, 495, 497.

14. DKD II, 16 September 1892, 503; Howe, "Charlotte—As I Knew Her," 212; KSC, "Autobiography," WSCC.

15. On Hough's visits, see, e.g., DKD II, 16 and 24 September 1893, 553, 555, and DKD II, 6 March 1894, 576. As Denise D. Knight has clarified, Mary Hill erroneously infers that Charlotte referred to Markham in her diaries as "Darling," when in fact Charlotte was referring to a "Mrs. Darling" (DKD II, 23 September 1893, 555n4); on Miller, see Walker, *San Francisco's*, 82, 342ff, and CPG to KSC, 6 January 1934, folder 343, SL; on Coolbrith, see *NAW* (vol. 1), 379; on Hough, see, e.g., DKD II, 9 February 1892, 495, DKD II, 12 February 1893, 517, DKD II, 15 March 1893, 521; DKD II, 7 March 1894, 576; DKD II, 8 July 1894, 591; Howe, "Charlotte—As I Knew Her," 213. Howe speculates that this party happened in 1892, but given Charlotte's contention that her father avoided her mother before she died, it seems more likely that it occurred in 1893.

16. Howe, "Charlotte—As I Knew Her," 213; CPS to MW, 19 March 1894, Vassar; Charlotte complains in DKD II, 31 December 1892, 507, and in DKD II, 26 December 1891, 487.

17. For her premise about living with women, see DKD II, 12 January 1892, 491; "The Giant Wisteria," *New England Magazine*, NS 4 (June 1891): 480–85; for an analysis of "Through This," see DK, "The Reincarnation of Jane," 287–302; Charlotte records writing the story in DKD II, 23 January 1893, 514.

18. Howe, "Charlotte—As I Knew Her," 212; on her "creative instinct" and the "strain" see DKD II, 25 October 1892, 504; *L*, 133; on her productivity, see, e.g., DKD II, 25 July 1891, 467, and see also Charlotte's Record of Mss., vol. 23, SL; DKD II, 31 January 1893, 515.

19. J. June Croly, x. "Jennie June" Croly, as Scharnhorst mentioned in private correspondence, was the mother of Herbert Croly, the progressive author of *The Promise of*

American Democracy, "The Spirit of the Times in Art," folder 172, SL; for examples of Charlotte's thoughts on the club movement, see *L*, 257; *W&E*, 164.

20. On the motives of club women, see Gere, 45, and Blair, 67; on the local clubs she participated in, see, e.g., DKD II, 14 November 1891, 481; 25 and 23 March 1891, 445; and *L*, 166; Charlotte's invitation to the fair is mentioned in DKD II, 10 February 1893, 517; "moves the world" from Ellen Henrotin, qtd. in Sklar, *Florence*, 243; Henrotin spoke for many present in Chicago and voiced Charlotte's sentiments exactly when she declared that "[t]he value of one person's mind or one person's work is steadily diminishing; it is the associate mind, the many hearts beating as one, that now moves the world"; on world citizenship, see also Gere, 158–59.

21. DKD II, 1 March 1893, 519.

22. State of Rhode Island and Providence, Petition for Divorce to the Supreme Court, folder 1, SL; the reporter's comments are from "No Corsets on Her," *Minneapolis Journal* (21 December 1892), folder 282, SL; exhibits 1 and 2, CPS to CWS, June 16 and 4 July 1891, Divorce #9078, Charles Walter Stetson vs. Charlotte Perkins Stetson, filed 27 October 1892, Providence Supreme Court; for a press account that cites but misdates one of these letters and contains some minor inaccuracies, see "Stetson Objects to Reform," *San Francisco Examiner* (morning edition) (20 December 1892): 3–4. On file at the Providence Supreme Court are transcripts of Charlotte's supposed letters; the originals were withdrawn by decree of the presiding judge.

23. CWS to MTC, 20 December 1892, GECSP, folder 147, SL; CWS to GEC, 23 December 1892, GECSP, folder 148, SL.

24. CWS to MTC, 22 December 1892, GECSP, folder 147, SL.

25. *L*, 143; clipping, folder 247, SL.

26. "The Wife and the Writer: Should Literary Women Be Addicted to the Marriage Habit?" *San Francisco Examiner* (morning edition) (19 December 1892): 18, folder 247, SL.

27. On her "foolish" denials, see "Newspaper 'Pogroms,'" *FR* 6 (February 1915): 33–34, quote from 33; "The Wife and the Writer," *San Francisco Examiner*, folder 247, SL.

28. "Stetson Objects to Reform," *San Francisco Examiner* (morning edition) (20 December 1892): 3–4; on her disdain for the press, see "A Contemptible Trick," *FR* 6 (March 1915): 84; "Newspapers and Democracy," *FR* 7 (December 1916): 314, and "The Yellow Reporter," *LP*, 46–48.

29. For divorce rates and statistics, see Degler, *At Odds*, 166, O'Neill, *Divorce*, 29, 97, 207–08, and Elaine T. May, *Great Expectations*; Allen Thorndike Rice, ed., "Are Women to Blame?" *North American Review* (January–June 1889): 622–42; Lavinia Hart, "The Divorce Germ," *Cosmopolitan* 37 (1904): 201–06; on *The Nation* essay, see O'Neill, *Divorce*, 21.

30. On suffrage and divorce, see Kraditor, *Ideas*, 115–16; Anna B. Rogers denounces "the latter-day cult," qtd. in McGerr, 85–86.

31. "A Sociological Study," *Los Angeles Times* (22 December 1892), folder 282, SL; nationalist qtd. in Scharnhorst, "Making Her Fame," 199; examples of others' sympathy are recorded in DKD II, 19, 20, and 23 December 1892, 506.

32. Bierce, "Prattle," *San Francisco Examiner* (25 December 1892) sec. 6: 5–6; see also Oliver and Scharnhorst, 32–45.

33. "Women of Brains as Wives," *San Francisco Examiner* (25 December 1892): 2–3. The paper did not relinquish a story easily: in late February 1893, Charlotte observed "The Examiner sent a man . . . to interview me on my views on the Marriage Question—the decrease of marriage." Although the reporter refused to take no for an answer—"He begs, he tries to fool me into conversation, he argues, he offers to pay me, he threatens covertly"—she succeeded "in getting rid of him. Am exhausted by the contest, however" (DKD II, 23 February 1893, 518).

34. "Thoughts and Figgerings," 26 March 1894, folder 16, SL.

35. *L*, 150; DKD II, 17 September 1893, 554; "The Poor Ye Have Always with You," *New Nation* (4 June 1892): 356.

36. "The Wolf at the Door" (poem), *ITOW*, 177; DKD II, 24 December 1892, 506, recounts the "destitute" rumor; on her parents' loans, see also DKD II, 3 October 1892, 503; DKD II, 2 February 1893, 516; DKD II, 3 July 1893, 540. For an analysis of the conflict between Gilman's message of economic independence for women and her often dire financial straits, see Karpinski, "Economic," 38.

37. On hired help, see DKD II, 9–12 December 1892, 505; "lovely" from DKD II, 31 March 1894, 580; on difficulties with Katharine, see, e.g., DKD II, 25 and 26 January 1894, 570.

38. KSC, "Autobiography," WSCC; Katharine comments on her mother's lack of influence in KSC to Carl Degler, draft 1, WSCC; for a lengthy interview with the adult Katharine, see Lane, 310ff.

39. DKD II, 31 December 1891, 487; on daughterly obligation, see *CC*, 163–64; CPS to GEC, 22 January 93, mf-6, SL.

40. Howe, "Charlotte—As I Knew Her," 216; CWS to MTC, 10 May 1892, folder 147, GECSP, SL.

41. DKD II, 13 September 1892, 502; DKD II, 21 December 1892, 506.

42. DKD II, 31 December 1892, 507 (the diary manuscript for this entry is torn in places); see also *L*, 141.

43. *L*, 143–44; "perfect obliteration" from "Our Most Valuable Livestock," *Pacific Rural Press* (17 October 1891), oversize folder 1, SL.

44. Howe, "Charlotte—As I Knew Her," 212–13.

45. *L*, 143; Knapp, *One Thousand.*

46. DKD II, 21 January 1893, 514; "Mother sinking," DKD II, 3 and 6 March 1893, 519, 520.

47. *L*, 9.

48. "To Me at Last" (poem), DKD II, appendix B, 899; for references to good days, see DKD II, 2 and 8 January 1893, 510, 511; on their "fusses," see DKD II, 13, 16, 17, and 19 January 1893, 512, 513; On Wetmore, see, e.g., DKD II, 12 July 1893, 541; on ill health, see DKD II, 16 June 1893, 513; DKD II, 30 January 1894, 571; DKD II, 28 February 1894, 574.

49. AEK to CPS, 16 May 1893, folder 137, SL; see also DKD II, 4 July 1893, 545 (Charlotte refused to return this note when Delle asked for it back); her weary acknowledgment occurs in DKD II, 14 May 1893, 531; DKD II, 15 July 1893, 542; on the debt, see AEK to CPS, 10 March 1894, folder 137, SL; CPG to KSC, 10 May 1929, folder 100, SL;

CPG also discusses her thinking about debt during her "hardest times" in a letter to KSC, 19 July 1930, folder 101, SL.

50. DKD II, 5 February 1893, 516; "Pain," sermon, folder 167, SL (Charlotte records writing this sermon in DKD II, 26 December 1891, 487); "How Our Work Affects Us," folder 166, SL. Charlotte's language here calls to mind Dr. William Ellery Channing, Grace's grandfather, whose unpublished manuscripts Grace assembled for publication in 1887. Dr. Channing argued therein that "Force of purpose—concentrating the mind on a noble work—sacrifices to this—have we not here the elements of greatness?"(37).

51. "How Our Surroundings Affect Us," folder 166, SL.

52. DKD II, appendix A, 843.

53. "Mother to Child" (poem), *ITOW*, 140–42.

54. "Thoughts & Figgerings," DKD II, appendix A, 843; "Waste" (poem), *New Nation* (6 January 1894): 4.

55. "Mrs. Stetson Tries Matrimony Again," *San Francisco Chronicle* (19 June 1900), addenda to CPG papers, 80-M112, folder 41, SL; in late March, she had consulted a divorce lawyer but "to no great purpose" (DKD II, 21 March 1893, 522; CWS to MTC, 10 March 1893, folder 147, GECSP, SL).

56. On Grace's visit, see DKD II, 7 February, 11 February, and 16 February 1894, 572–73; "failure to provide" from "A Cook Stove Throne," *San Francisco Examiner* (2 March 1894); CPG, "Alimony," *FR* 3 (March 1912): 82; and see also her "Shameful Money," ca. 1915, typescript, folder 176, SL.

57. *L*, 167; for Charlotte's acknowledgment of the press attention, see DKD II, 1, 4, and 5 March 1894, 574, 575; "A Cook Stove Throne," *San Francisco Examiner* (2 March 1894); "She Gives Him to Another," *San Francisco Examiner* (4 March 1894) sec. 12: 1–2, in clippings in re. 1894 divorce, addenda to CPG papers, 80-M112, folder 40, SL.

58. Divorce decree, folder 1, SL; DKD II, 18 April 1894, 583; CPS to GECS, 4 July 1895, mf-6, SL; *L*, 167.

59. "Thoughts & Figgerings," "Wed. May 9th, 1894," folder 16, SL; *L*, 163–64; reference to borrowing money and "darling" from CPS to Mary D. (Robbins) Phelon, 18 June 1894, qtd. in DKJT.

60. "An Unnatural Mother," *Impress* (16 February 1895), 4–5.

61. "Oh a thousand things fill me with perturbation and my heart at the mere thought beats like a school girls when she desires, but half dreads, to meet her lover in the lane," Walter wrote Grace; additional details of his attempts to delay Katharine's arrival are provided in CWS to GECS, ca. May 1894, [letter fragment], carton 5, folder 150, GECSP, SL; CWS to KBS, 9 April 1894, WSCC; for Grace's complaint, see GECS to KSC, 10 April 1934 and 8 May 1934, GECSP, SL.

62. Howe, "Charlotte—As I Knew Her," 215; *L*, 163 (see also Charlotte's 1897 letter to Katharine, in which she promised that, when the two met again, Katharine would find her mother "a different person . . . from the sick feeble mother you had then, poor and shabby and struggling to keep the roof overhead and the table well covered" [CPS to KBS, 14 March 1897, folder 89, SL]); CPS to Mary D. (Robbins) Phelon, 18 June 1894, qtd. in DKJT.

63. *L*, 163; on her pain during the separation, see CPS to GHG, 1 October 1897, folder 46, SL; KSC to Carl Degler, drafts 1–4, WSCC; KSC, "Autobiography," WSCC; Hill, *Making*, 234–35.

64. See CPS to GECS, 9 January 1895, mf-6, SL, for references to Katharine flourishing; CPS to GECS, 26 June 1895, mf-6, SL; her reflections on the visit are recorded in CPS to GECS, 4 July 1895, mf-6, SL; *Benigna Machiavelli*, *FR* 5 (April 1914): 98.

65. Howe, "Charlotte—As I Knew Her," 215; *L*, 180; the unpublished sketch is titled "A Forerunner and a Prophet," 1904, folder 243, SL; on Winifred Black, see *L*, 145, and *NAW* (vol. 1), 154–56. See also "Notable Woman Visiting Utah," *Deseret Evening News* (27 November 1899), in which Charlotte mentions Black's review and concludes that Black either never read her book or "maliciously misrepresented and perverted its contents and meaning" (folder 266, SL). For more on the scandal over Charlotte as an "unnatural mother," see Henry Bigelow, "Literary Wives," *San Francisco Wave* (n.d.), WSCC.

66. Austin, 293; Lummis, 350. Thanks to Jennifer Tuttle for helping me to find this defense and sharing a copy with me. As Knight and Tuttle note, Walter Stetson wrote Lummis and thanked him for defending Charlotte, if only for their daughter's sake (see DKJT); according to Austin, 293, and Bingham, 42, 235, Lummis's "unusual" house, El Alisal, in the Arroyo Seco, served as "a western version of the European Salon," and his monthly illustrated magazine promoted the southern California literary renaissance.

67. CPG qtd. by Gale, foreword to *L*, xxvi.

68. *Home*, 233–34; *W&E*, 290; on quality mattering, see "Mothers and Mothers," *FR* 7 (January 1916): 24–25, and "Personal Problems," *FR* 1 (December 1909): 29; on social homemaking, see Golden, "'Light of the Home,'" 138.

69. "Mrs. Gilman Seeks Wider Motherhood," *New York Times* (19 March 1914) sec. 8: 8.

70. "The Woman of Fifty," *FR* 2 (April 1911): 98; cf. EB, "How I Wrote 'Looking Backward'," in *EBSA!* 217ff; on the remarriages of both her father and Walter, see DKD II, 11 and 18 June 1894, 587, 588.

71. On her "chapters," see "Thoughts & Figgerings," Wednesday May 9th, 1894, folder 16, SL; "Good Will," *LP*, 125; "Work and Sleep" (poem), folder 198, SL, note on ms.

72. CPS to GHG, 16 May 1898, folder 51, SL.

73. CPS to GECS, 9 January 1895, mf-6, SL. See also her confession that with the work she planned to accomplish, she was "glad to have Kate gone for a while in spite of the hole in [her] heart" (CPS to "Cousin Mary," 18 June 1894, in DKJT); on her hunt for funds, see DKD II, 13 July 1894, 592.

74. *Impress* (July 1894): 2; DKD II, 22 September 1893, 554; DKD II, 9 October 1893, 557.

75. Howe, "Charlotte—As I Knew Her," 215; *L*, 171.

76. *Impress* (May 1894): 1; Howe, "Charlotte—As I Knew Her," 215; on the success leading to a second year, see Reda Davis, 89; the 1894 congress opened to the public during Charlotte's last weeks with Katharine, and she promptly put her daughter to work. Katharine remembered having "a beautiful time licking stamps and envelopes" prior to the congress; during the event itself she "was appointed page. This gave me a feeling of

great importance as I went here and there delivering messages. Afterwards I received a formal letter of thanks from the secretary" (KSC, "Autobiography," WSCC).

77. "Report of Recording Secretary," *Impress* (May 1894): 5; *L*, 172.

78. "The Reception of Mrs. Campbell," *Impress* (3 November 1894): 6; biographical information on Campbell from "Helen Stuart Campbell," *NAW* (vol. 1), 280–81; Helen Campbell, "Charlotte," folder 266, SL.

79. For her thoughts on Campbell, see CPS to GHG, 18 May 1897, folder 41, SL; on Tyner, see CPS to GECS, 9 January 1895, mf-6, SL, and *L*, 171; "the bravest . . ." from CPS to GHG, 3 and 15 November 1899, folder 76, SL.

80. *Impress* (May 1894): 4; *Impress* (6 October 1894): 7.

81. On her triumph, see DKD II, 6 September 1984, 599; on financing the *Impress*, see DKD II, 26 and 27 February 1894, 574; 21 September 1894, 600; see also Karpinski, "Economic," 38, and Baldwin, 175; "Report of Editor of *The Impress* for year beginning Oct. 1893 to Sept. '94, inclusive," folder 238, SL.

82. *Impress* (6 October 1894): 1–4; *L*, 173; "idiomatic voice" from Baldwin, 176, 179–80; CPS to GHG, 22 July 1897, folder 43, SL.

83. "Model Menus," *Impress* (8 December 1894): 9; on the manager's resignation, see DKD II, 2 August 1894, 595; "arduous task" from CPS to MW, 19 March 1894, Vassar; DKD II, 24 August 1894, 598.

84. DKD II, 30 November 1894, appendix A, 845; CPS to GECS, 9 January 1895, mf-6, SL.

85. "Bright, Brave, and Independent," *Impress* (3 November 1894): 2; "As Others See Us," *Impress* (22 December 1894): 16; *Impress* (20 October 1894): 3.

86. On Delle, see DKD II, 7 June 1894, 585, and DKD II, 13 July 1894, 592; "suppress my rampant personality" from "Report of Editor of *The Impress* for year beginning Oct. 1893 to Sept. '94, inclusive," folder 238, SL.

87. Howe, "Charlotte—As I Knew Her," 215; *L*, 173; KSC wrote a note about Walter's illustrations that accompanies the 22 December 1894 issue of *Impress*, vol. 2, SL.

88. "The Women Writers," folder 312, SL; "Prattle," *San Francisco Examiner* (10 March 1895) sec. 6: 4.

89. "The Pig and the Pearl," *ITOW*, 109–10; DKD II, 28 July 1894, 595.

90. On her hopes for recovery, see DKD II, 15 June 1894, 588; CPG to KSC, 21 July 1931, folder 102, SL.

91. Annie Laurie, "All the Comforts of a Home," *San Francisco Examiner* (22 May 1895), oversize folder 1, SL. Susan B. Anthony and Anna Howard Shaw again attended, Jane Stanford of the railroad and university Stanfords having paid their way. The congress was not billed as a suffrage event, but the attendees unanimously passed a resolution supporting the franchise, reflecting their esteem for the two stalwart suffrage leaders. Anthony received an especially warm welcome (Shaw called her "the belle of the ball"), reigning over the meetings from "a big chair decorated with yellow marguerites" (Reda Davis, 90; Anthony et al.).

92. "The American Wife," *San Francisco Examiner* (22 May 1895), oversize folder 1, SL; "In Childhoods [*sic*] Realm," *San Francisco Call* (26 May 1895) sec. 25: 3. Charlotte

objected at the time to the *Call*'s coverage of the congress in general but remained silent about their singling her out ("Mrs. Charlotte Stetson Perkins; Regarding Women's Congress," Letter to the Editor, *San Francisco Call* [22 May 1895]). The reversal in her name in the header may be either an unintentional slip or another insult.

93. "antagonized. . . ." from the preceding paragraph is from Helen Campbell, "Charlotte," folder 266, SL; CPS to GECS, 4 July 1895, mf-6, SL.

CHAPTER SEVEN

1. "Two Callings," *Home*, vii–xi.

2. "A Woman-at-Large," *Impress* (29 December 1894): 3; *L*, 294.

3. *L*, 176, 181.

4. Frances Willard, qtd. in McGerr, 53; on "the flag of domesticity," see McGerr, 83; CPS to GHG, 8 August 1897, folder 44, SL.

5. On the safety of a wandering life, see CPS to GHG, 14 October 1898, folder 56, SL; *L*, 181–83.

6. *Benigna Machiavelli*, *FR* 5 (April 1914): 100; CPS to GECS, 25 February 1896, mf-6, SL.

7. "Closed Doors" (poem), 1898, reprinted in *LP*, 168–69; " . . . Reformer" from CPS to MW, 11 January 1897, Vassar; "tree" metaphor from CPS to GHG, 19 September 1898, folder 55, SL; CPS to GHG, 19 September 1898, folder 55, SL.

8. DKD II, appendix B, 904; Knight renders these lines in verse, as did Charlotte on the flyleaf of her 1899 diary, but see also *L*, 251, where Charlotte presents the same lines in prose.

9. *L*, 176–77.

10. CPS to GECS, 15 June 1895, mf-6, SL.

11. She mentions her father's offer in CPS to GECS, 15 June 1895, mf-6, SL; CPS to GECS, 26 June 1895, mf-6, SL.

12. McGerr, 53; CPS, "The College Settlement," *Impress* (February 1894): 2.

13. *L*, 179–80. As Scharnhorst observed in private correspondence, "Cooper was the proofreader who very nearly killed Bret Harte's 'The Luck of Roaring Camp' prior to its publication in 1868—she was a pioneer in the kindergarten movement in the US and a cousin of Robert Ingersoll."

14. John Townsend Trowbridge, "Reminiscences of Walt Whitman," *Atlantic Monthly* (February 1902): 166; CPS to GECS, 25 February 1896, mf-6, SL; CPS to GHG, 21 September 1898, folder 55, SL.

15. On sociology, see Dorothy Ross, 85ff; on Charlotte's sociological bent, see *L*, 182–83, and Scharnhorst, *Charlotte*, 43–44; "How on earth" from CPS to GHG, 20 December 1899, folder 78, SL; "We need" from "The Sociologist and the Reformer," *FR* 6 (September 1915): 243–44.

16. Sklar, "Hull House," 658–77; on Chicago, see Hofstadter, *Age*, 174, and Fitzpatrick, 34; Scharnhorst, (*Charlotte*, 74, 82) notes that Sinclair cites Charlotte in ch. 30 of *The Jungle* (1906) and that her *Home* anticipates Sinclair's critique of adulterated food.

17. On the death rate, see Feffer, 108; on labor unrest, see Fitzpatrick, 35; Rosenberg, 1.

18. "humanistic . . ." from Allen F. Davis, xiii; Feffer, 110.

19. For background on Addams and the settlement, see Allen F. Davis, 12, 112; Sklar, *Florence*, 376n73; "call" quotation from Carson, 8.

20. Hofstadter, *Age*, 163; McGerr, xiv; Ceplair, 43; Hofstadter, *Age*, 212.

21. Allen F. Davis, 31, 33–34.

22. Hayden, *Grand*, 171.

23. Webb, qtd. in Conway, "Women Reformers," 174; Allen F. Davis, 31.

24. Hayden, *Grand*, 164; Ginger, 89; Carson, 61.

25. Allen F. Davis, 31. Davis also notes that this "clubbish" atmosphere and Starr's emphasis on aesthetic education drew some criticism: Thorstein Veblen praised the settlement movement but suspected its underlying motive was to incubate, "by precept and example, . . . certain punctilios of upper-class propriety in manners and customs." Sinclair Lewis would condemn settlements more caustically as "cultural comfort stations . . . upholding a standard of tight-smiling prissiness" (both qtd. in Allen F. Davis, 17).

26. Allen F. Davis, 106; by the time Charlotte arrived in mid-summer of 1895, Addams could confidently conclude, "the ward is really cleaner" (Addams, qtd. in Allen F. Davis, 154); on Kelley, see Sklar, "Hull House," 664.

27. Kelley, qtd. in Sklar, *Florence*, 172; CPS to KBS, 15 September 1895, folder 89, SL.

28. CPS to GECS, 3 May 1896, mf-6, SL; on staying until the following summer, see CPS to GECS, 16 September 1895, mf-6, SL.

29. CPS to GECS, 16 September 1895, mf-6, SL; Bedell, 162; *L*, 185.

30. Rosenberg, 33.

31. *L*, 184; "refuge" from CPS to GHG, 26 May 1900, folder 84, SL; "Saint Jane" from *Impress* 1 (February 1894): 1; "mixed living," from CPS to GECS, 16 September 1895, mf-6, SL.

32. "crazy quilt" from Feffer, 93–94; "Such a flux . . . tires me much" from CPS to GHG, 15 May 1900, folder 83, SL; "vortex" from CPS to GHG, 2 December 1898, folder 60, SL. As the years passed, Charlotte's distaste grew: see, e.g., her poem "The Melting Pot" (*LP*, 52–53):

> A melting pot has to be made
> With particular care,
> And carefully sampled and weighed
> As to nature, proportion and grade
> Are the ores mingled there. . . .
> But if all these ingredients here
> Should comingle at will,
> Neither cake nor yet soup will appear,
> There's one name for a mixture so queer—
> That is swill.

Hull House's recipe for progress—a combination of democratic ideals and practical interventions that left the settlement workers, in one historian's words, "[m]ore concerned for the immigrants themselves than with debates over assimilation and deterioration of Anglo-Saxon stock" (Allen F. Davis, 93)—increasingly struck Charlotte as a recipe for disaster.

33. "Wonderful Miss Addams" from CPS to GHG, 15 May 1900, folder 83, SL; CPS to GECS, 16 September 1895, mf-6, SL; on Addams and association, see McGerr, 66. Addams defined *association* more concretely than did Charlotte, using the term to refer to efforts to unite diverse socioeconomic and ethnic groups by encouraging all to identify with "the common lot"; the resident is Leonora O'Reilly, qtd. in Allen F. Davis, 19.

34. Addams, "The Subjective Necessity," 2, 6; on settlement workers' bridging divides, see McGerr, 67.

35. For Addams' take on "high ideals," see Louise W. Knight, 4; on "'practical' things," see CPS to GECS, 25 February 1896, mf-6, SL, and see also Beer and Joslin, 9; she mocks this practicality in CPS to GECS, 16 September 1895, mf-6, SL; *Won Over*, *FR* 4 (May 1913): 126.

36. "at bottom" from CPS to GHG, 21 September 1898, folder 55, SL; *L*, 182.

37. She still defined living as "doing," (see *HR&H*, 98–99), but increasingly doing meant diagnosing; Higham, "Reorientation," 94.

38. CPS to KBS, 15 September 1895, folder 89, SL; CPS to KBS, 14 October 1895, folder 89, SL. See also CPG to KBSC, 20 August 1895, folder 89, SL, for Charlotte's comments on the poor neighborhood and numerous immigrants.

39. On her distant relationship with Addams, see CPS to GHG, 9 December 1898, folder 60, SL; for Addams's impression, see Jane Addams to Mary Smith, cited in Anne Firor Scott, "'New-Model Woman',", 442–53; on her poor "mixing" skills and her similarity to a "watchtower," see Black, *Time*, 285; Charlotte's assessments of her interpersonal skills are offered in CPS to GHG, 25 May 1897 and 27 April 1900, folders 41 and 82, SL.

40. Black, "The Woman," 34; for her effect on crowds, see CPS to GHG, 4 May 1897, folder 41, SL; both her complaint about Hull House and her "small fish" assessment are voiced in CPS to GECS, 16 September 1895, mf-6, SL.

41. "Gone to Live at Hull House," *San Francisco Chronicle* (25 July 1895): 25; on Addams's inner circle, see Muncy, 15, 14; CPS to SBC, 10 November 1895, Cornell.

42. CPS to KBS, 15 September 1895, folder 89, SL; Dewey qtd. in Carson, 89; on Hull House as a domestic, feminine space, see Muncy, 9, and see also Sklar, who writes, "Jane Addams asserted her female identity by decorating Hull House as if it were her family home," *Florence*, 187.

43. CPS to GECS, 8 June 1896, mf-6, SL.

44. CPS to KBS, 14 October 1895, Folder 89, SL; on her experience at Little Hell, see *L*, 184–85; on her feelings for Virtue, see DKD II, 14 April 1896, 616; CPS to GHG, 8 September 1898, folder 55, SL.

45. CPS to SBC, 10 November 1895, Cornell.

46. *L*, 185–86, 279; CPS to SBC, 10 November 1895, Cornell.

47. "Thoughts & Figgerings," folder 16, SL.

48. Susan B. Anthony to Jane Addams, folder 155, SL.

49. CPS to LFW, 1 January 1896, Brown.

50. *Pure Sociology*, 20. Both Samuel Chugerman and Clifford Scott provide helpful background information on Ward's evolutionary views; see also Stocking, 242, 255; Bannister, 126–27; Page, 29–32; Pittenger, 78; and Hofstadter, *Social*, 69–83 and 137, as well as

LFW, *Pure Sociology*, especially 296, 313, 325, and 338ff; on Ward's reform Darwinism in particular, see Bannister, 4, 11; Dorothy Ross, 91, 141–42.

51. Daniels, 75, discusses Ward's neo-Lamarckian views; CPS to GHG, 7 October 1899, folder 74, SL.

52. On her secondhand knowledge, see Bannister, 59; her father had also introduced her to the widely circulating *Popular Science Monthly*, edited by Spencer's zealous American proponent, Edward L. Youmans; for her understanding of evolution as growth, see, e.g., "Fighting, Growing and Making," *FR* 4 (January 1913): 18, *W&E*, 34, and *HR&H*, 241–42. Charlotte read Geddes and Thompson's 1895 *Evolution of Sex* in November 1897. Ward cites their theory of gendered metabolism somewhat favorably yet adds that their work is "pervaded with the androcentric spirit" (LFW, *Pure Sociology*, 315–16n6). Charlotte may have learned about Edward Bellamy's comparable take on evolution through, e.g., his "Talks on Nationalism—To an Evolutionist," 178–79, 181, 182. For an overview of Charlotte's evolutionary theories, see Doskow, "Charlotte," 9–22.

53. "Having Faith in Evolution," *FR* 6 (November 1915): 299; "Social Darwinism," *American Journal of Sociology* 12 (March 1907): 713–14.

54. CPG to LFW, 20 January 1904, Brown; LFW, "Our Better Halves," 266–75: Ward's woman–trunk analogy from 275; LFW, "The Past and Future of the Sexes," 542; "Our Better Halves," 272, 275.

55. Mason, 147; for Mason's influence on Jane Addams, see Deegan, 226–27; for Mason's influence on CPS, see CPG to George T. Cooke, 21 December 1909, Fruitlands; on Stanton see Kraditor, *Ideas*, 101.

56. Walsh, 158.

57. On reading Ward at the conference, see CPS to LFW, 24 January 1896, Brown; Ward had "long known and admired" Helen Campbell (LFW to CPS, 17 January 1896, folder 124, SL). Charlotte may have learned of Ward's theories from Campbell or perhaps from Ward's nephew-in-law, the Stanford sociologist E. A. Ross, whom she met while in California; Charlotte's praise for gynæcocentrism is expressed in "Apropos of Prof. Ward's Theory," *WJ* (16 April 1904): 122; CPS to LFW, 24 January 1896, Brown, and *Moving the Mountain*, *FR* 2 (May 1911): 136; see also *With Her in Ourland*, where a fictional sociologist insists, "Of course, there is no getting around Lester Ward. . . . No one can study biology and sociology much and not see that on the first physiological lines the female is the whole show. . . ." (*FR* 7 [November 1916]: 28). At least one scholar (Doyle, 161) has argued that Charlotte essentially derived her pro-woman arguments from Ward.

58. Her references to her originality and to "The Brood Mare" appear in CPS to GHG, 22 July 1897, folder 43, SL; CPG to LFW, 4 August 1904, Brown. For a more detailed analysis of Charlotte's relationship with Ward, see my "His and Herland."

59. CPS to SBC, 1 February 1896, Cornell.

60. Bly, 2; *WJ* qtd. in Anthony et al., 256.

61. On her thrilling speech, see CPS to SBC, 1 February 1896, Cornell; on the mumps, see DKD II, 27 January and 2 February 1896, 607; "Hearing of the National American Woman Suffrage Association. Committee on [*sic*] the Judiciary, House of Representatives, Washington, D.C., January 28, 1896," *Votes for Women: Selections from*

the National American Woman Suffrage Association Collection, 1848–1921, http://memory. loc.gov/cgi-bin/query/r?ammem/naw:"afield+(SOURCE+"band(rbnawsa+n990 (accessed September 21, 2001).

62. Stanton, 214, 215; CPS to GECS, 25 February 1896, mf-6, SL; Anthony et al., 263–64.

63. CPS to SBC, 1 February 1896, Cornell; CPS to GECS, 25 February 1896, mf-6, SL; on her many lectures, see *L*, 190, and "Trips and Lectures," folder 96, SL.

64. CPS to GECS, 3 May 1896, mf-6, SL; DKD II, appendix A, "Thoughts & Figgerings," 7 March 1896, 846; on Campbell and the McCrackens, see DKD II, 14–15 March 1896, 613, and *L*, 190; *Mag-Marjorie, FR* 3 (October 1912): 265, and *FR* 3 (June 1912): 154.

65. DKD II, 16 March 1896, 613; *L*, 190.

66. CPS to GHG, 14 September 1898, folder 55, SL.

67. CPS to SBC, 1 February 1896, Cornell; on the Chicago Household Economics Society, see Hayden, *Grand*, 186–87; CPS to GECS, 3 May 1896, mf-6, SL; on the benefits of travel and many friends, see CPS to GHG, 14 October 1898, folder 56, SL; CPS to GHG, 20 November 1899, folder 77, SL; on her periods, see CPS to GHG, 7 and 8 October 1898, folder 56, SL and CPS to GHG, 25 October 1898, folder 57, SL.

68. *The Crux, FR* 2 (April 1911): 101.

69. On her homelessness, see CPS to GHG, 19 September 1898, folder 55, SL; on the inconveniences of travel, see "Psychic Jujitsu," *FR* 7 (April 1916): 90–92, quote from 90; see also "Wanted, A Railroad Cafeteria," *FR* 7 (February 1916): 33–34, and "Social Attentions," *FR* 6 (November 1915): 295–99.

70. *L*, 102; on the kindness of strangers, see "Social Attentions," 295; on loneliness, see CPS to GECS, 25 February 1895, mf-6, SL; CPS to GHG, 10 July 1897, folder 43, SL.

71. Charlotte praises her stepfamily in CPS to CWS, 23 April 1896, folder 2, SL; she speaks of dropping them in CPS to GHG, 16 May 1898, folder 51, SL; on her "thin" recovery, see CPS to GECS, 3 May 1896, mf-6, SL.

72. "trot" from CPS to CWS, 23 April 1896, folder 2, SL; on her trip to Providence, see CPS to GECS, 3 May 1896, mf-6, SL; she uses the same "broad grin" phrase when she describes her trip to Providence to Walter: CPS to CWS, 23 April 1896, mf-6, SL.

73. "wonderful" from CPS to GECS, 8 June 1896, mf-6, SL; Kansas Equal Suffrage Association Resolution, folder 137, SL; on not journeying to California, see CPS to SBC, 1 February 1896, Cornell; on the California suffrage campaign, see Buhle, *Women and American Socialism*, 215, and Reda Davis, 102.

74. For her plans to attend the conference in London, see CPG to CWS, 23 April 1896, folder 7, SL; on the cattle, see *L*, 199; "A Sea Voyage," *FR* 5 (June 1914): 149–50.

75. On representing herself as a socialist, see *L*, 198, and see also CPS to GECS, 8 June 1896, mf-6, SL; for her views on Marx, see *L*, 187, and Pittenger, 73–74; "kid glove Socialist" from CPS to GHG, 11 January 1899, folder 62, SL.

76. See "A Socialist Prayer," *FR* 2 (May 1911): 124; "the sinking . . . " from *W&E*, 107; on socialism as the antithesis of individualism, see "When Socialism Began," *American Fabian* 3 (November 1897): 1–2; she describes the "wildest dreams" in CPS to GHG, 28 October 1899, folder 75, SL. Alexander Black claimed of Charlotte that to "the religion

of socialistic effort she was warmly responsive; to the theology of socialism she was cold" (Black, "The Woman," 35).

77. She boasts of speaking in the rain in DKD II, 26 July 1896, 631; she describes the visit in DKD II, 2 and 3 August 1896, 633, 632, and see Kirkland for an account of CPS's stay with the Webbs and her encounter with Shaw.

78. On Fabianism, see Pittenger, 75–76, Weintraub, 10–11, and Ceplair, 43n; see also M. Cole, 84ff; "cuckoo" from Dell, 54; Shaw qtd. in Lippmann, 280. Alexander Black erroneously claimed of Charlotte that "a capital S could not be attached to her. She could speak before the Fabians in England, beside Bernard Shaw and his compatriots, but they could not make a Fabian out of her" ("The Woman," 35).

79. Jenkin, 113–23; Hough, 3.

80. On her feeling "small," see CPS to LFW, 10 December 1896, Brown; *L*, 209–10; "heavy sledding" from DKD II, 18 November 1896, 645.

81. CPS to Charles Lummis, 14 [19?] September 1896, Southwest Museum. Thanks to Jennifer Tuttle for sharing this letter with me; on her Pasadena plan, see CPS to GECS, 8 June 1896, mf-6, SL.

82. CPS to GHG, 29 May 1900, folder 84, SL.

83. She describes her "up stairs room" in DKD II, 20 November 1896, 647, and in a letter to Katharine notes that she has been "installed in the funniest little room! It is only 5 ft. 6 in. wide! About 12 or 13 long, and seven high. . . ." (undated correspondence between CPS and KSC, folder 89, SL); the end of the "golden days" are described by John L. Thomas, 334; "The Room at the Top" qtd. in *L*, 189.

84. DKD II, 31 December 1896, 653; DKD II, "Thoughts & Figgerings," 1 January 1896, 846.

85. CPS to GECS, 11 January 1897, mf-6, SL; CPS to MW, 11 January 1897, Vassar.

86. Susan B. Anthony to CPS, 17 January 1897, folder 137, SL; description of Cleveland from CPS to GECS, 21 March 1897, mf-6, SL; "1897," itinerary, folder 10, SL.

87. "A Woman and Her Pet Ambition," *Rochester Democrat* (14 March 1897), oversize folder 1, SL.

88. *L*, 219.

CHAPTER EIGHT

1. DKD II, appendix A, "Thoughts & Figgerings," 5 April 1897, 847. An abbreviated version of this chapter appears as my "Love and Economics."

2. "Women," *Chicago Journal* (29 December 1898), clipping, folder 266, SL; CPS to GHG, 17 May 1900, folder 84, SL.

3. For an early elaboration of her theories, see "Woman," *Providence People* (16 April 1887): 5; on devising them in California, see CPG to AP, 11 August 1930, WHMEC (thanks to Jennifer Tuttle for providing me with a copy of this letter); also see *L*, 235.

4. Rosika Schwimmer, "The Feminist Bible," clipping, folder 299, SL; "book of the age" from Muzzey, 268; Carrie Chapman Catt, qtd. in "Charlotte Gilman Dies to Avoid Pain," *New York Times* (20 August 1935): 2.

5. *W&E*, 300; CPS to GHG, 10 March 1898, folder 49, SL.

6. "Is Cupid a Convention?" *Independent* (15 August 1907): 373–75.

7. *W&E*, 25; CPS to GHG, 17 May 1900, folder 84, SL.

8. CPS to GHG, 19 September 1898, folder 55, SL.

9. DKD II, 8 and 10 March 1897, 663; Mary Frances Beecher to KSC, 27 August 1935, folder 238, GECSP, SL (May [Mary Frances] and her twin sister Margaret were the adopted daughters of James and "Frankie" Beecher; after Frankie married Charlotte's father Frederic, Charlotte considered the two girls her stepsisters); "*Delightful time*" from DKD II, 28 March 1897, 667.

10. DKD II, 20 March 1897, 666; WDH qtd. in Beard, *Woman as Force*, 26; Charlotte repeats WDH's praise of her profile and brains in CPS to GECS, 9 July 1929, mf-6, SL.

11. WDH, introduction; on his "kind hand" see CPS to GHG, 20 October 1898, folder 57, SL. In a letter to Charlotte dated 30 June 1897, WDH encouraged her to quote him to publishers "as cordially in favor [of the new edition of *In This Our World*] as your self respect will allow"; CPS criticizes Howellsian realism but refers to the author's "authority" in CPS to MLL, 27 July 1890, RIHS; she also discusses WDH's attending her lecture and his approval in CPS to GECS, 21 March 1897, mf-6, SL.

12. *L*, 222; CPS to GHG, 4 May 1897, folder 41, SL; CPS to CWS, 23 April 1897, folder 7, SL.

13. The "mother" comparisons are from CPS to GHG, 18 May 1897, folder 41, SL, and see also CPS to GHG, 4 June 1897, folder 52, SL; "huckleberry" analogy from undated correspondence between CPS and GHG [ca. April 1897], folder 40, SL; "the deer sweet joy . . ." from DKD II, appendix A, 18 January 1898, 848; CPS to GHG, 2 April 1898, folder 49, SL; "love and freedom" from CPS to GHG, 14 November 1899, folder 76, SL.

14. Background on Houghton derived from CPG to WSC, 29 January 1931, WSCC, and from KSC to Carl Degler, 24 July 1960, folder 156, SL; CPS to GHG, 21 April 1898, folder 49, SL.

15. "Queer People," *Cosmopolitan* 27 (June 1899): 172; CPS to GHG, 11 May 1898, folder 50, SL.

16. CPS to GHG, 12 May 1898, folder 50, SL; on falling short of her "ideal," see CPS to GHG, 18 May 1897, folder 41, SL; CPS to GHG, 21 May 1898, folder 51, SL; "He don't get it" from DKD II, 2 March 1898, 717; CPS to GHG, undated note, 1897, folder 40, SL; "not literary" from CPS to GHG, 9 February 1899, folder 64, SL.

17. CPS to GHG, 21 February 1899, folder 65, SL; "supernaturally nice" from CPS to GHG, 6 September 1897, folder 45, SL; CPS to GHG, 25 July 1899, folder 71, SL.

18. CAP to GHG, 23 November 1879, and see all CAP to GHG, 1879–80 letters, folder 28, SL; "aunt Charlotte" from CAP to GHG, card, folder 153, SL; CPS to GHG, 11 May 1897, folder 41, SL.

19. CPS to GHG, 25 April 1897, folder 40, SL, and see also "A Sestina," "Pantomime," "Triolet—To My Cousin's Politeness" in this same folder; CPS to GHG, 11 September 1897, folder 45, SL.

20. CPS to GECS, 1 May 1897, mf-6, SL; she describes the Kansas offer in CPS to GHG, 28 April 1897, folder 40, SL; "simply bursting . . . winter in New York" from CPS to GHG, 18 May 1897, folder 41, SL.

21. "A Sestina," 1 May 1897, folder 41, SL; "Houghton habit" from CPS to GHG, 8 June 1897, folder 42, SL; CPS to GHG, 25 April 1897, folder 40, SL.

22. On Martha, see CPS to GHG, 2 September 1897 and 27 October 1898, folders 45 and 57, SL; "the very *charmingest*" from an undated note [ca. April 1897], folder 40, SL; CPS to GHG, 19 May 1897, folder 41, SL.

23. CPS to GHG, 27 July 1897, folder 43, SL; on wooing him first, see CPS to GHG, 25 January 1899, folder 61, SL; CPS to GHG, 12 October 1897, folder 46, SL; "fell all over you" from CPS to GHG, 11 July 1897, folder 43, SL; CPS to GHG, 4 June 1897, folder 42, SL.

24. CPS to GHG, 23 August 1897, folder 44, SL; "all summer . . ." from CPS to GHG, 8 August 1897, folder 44, SL; CPS to GHG, 11 May 1897, folder 41, SL; on her "promiscuous lonesomeness," see DKD II, 22 July 1897, 685. By "n. g." Charlotte probably meant "no good"; the initials did not signify "non-gainful" until the new century, when the U.S. census introduced the abbreviation—to Charlotte's disgust—to designate housewives' status. Of course, for Charlotte, "non-gainful" amounted to essentially the same thing as "no good." For her use of "N. G." in the sense of "not gainful," see, e.g., the coverage of her 1909 debate with Anna Howard Shaw: "Husbands Do Not Support Their Wives: Wives Themselves Decide Question," (7 January 1909), clipping, folder 287, SL. And see her "N. G.," *FR* 2 (June 1911), 168. Charlotte routinely destroyed Houghton's letters to her.

25. CPS to GHG, August 9 1897, folder 44, SL; on the visit with Katharine and the Stetson's trip, see CPS to GHG, 3 August 1897, folder 44, SL; DKD II, 15, 16, and 17 August 1897, 688, and Eldredge, 81; "very mixed up and tired" from DKD II, 14 August 1897, 688; "Rules . . . " from *L*, 231; DKD II, 14 August 1897, 688.

26. CPS to GHG, 12 April 1900, folder 82, SL; CPS to GHG, 12 November 1898, folder 59, SL.

27. CPS to GHG, 10 March 1899, folder 66, SL.

28. On her new insights, see DKD II, 1 July 1897, 682, and CPS to GHG, 10 July 1897, folder 43, SL; on her inspiration, see DKD II, 4 March 1893, 519; on the book's composition, see CPG to Mrs. Fenyes, 20 September 1905, in DKJT; DKD II, 31 August 1897, 690; CPS to Mr. Garrison (incomplete letter), 5 January 1898, Smith; *L*, 237; and DKD II, 8 October 1897, 695; *L*, 235–40: her run is described on 235.

29. CPS to GHG, 10 July 1897, folder 43, SL; *W&E*, 5, 33; on "sexuo-economic," see, e.g., *W&E*, 23, 121, 261, and 339.

30. *W&E*, 220; Pittenger, 79; "miserable failure" from "Women and Men," *London Daily Chronicle* (26 June 1899), folder 299, SL; on social housekeeping, see works by Douglas, Kelley, Matthews, and Muncy.

31. "hen . . . " from "Talks with Club Women—Charlotte Perkins Stetson Back in Chicago—English Women as Smokers," *Times-Herald* (12 November 1899), clipping, folder 266, SL; Charlotte claimed the book had been translated into "German, Dutch, Italian, Russian, Hungarian and Japanese" in an advertisement in *FR* 6 (December 1915): n.p.; Howe, "Charlotte—As I Knew Her," 216; on her ideas receiving "a world hearing" and reaching "recognized leaders of thought in foreign countries," see CPS to GHG, 5 and 13 October 1898, folder 56, SL; on Walter's reaction see CPS to GHG, 30 June 1898, folder 52, SL.

32. Review of *Women and Economics*, *Boston Evening Transcript*, clipping, folder 299, SL.

See also Charlotte Perkins Stetson," *Current Literature* 25 (February 1899), folder 299, SL, where the reviewer especially admires "[t]he really absorbing interest of its argument even to the least scientific reader" and proclaims it "a book hard to lay down"; *Minneapolis Journal* (17 November 1899), vol. 7, SL; "Charlotte Perkins Stetson," *Current Literature,* 115.

33. Lummis, *Land of Sunshine* (11 July 1899), folder 299, SL; Jane Addams to CPS, 19 July 1898, folder 137, SL; Florence Kelley to CPS, 26 July 1898, folder 137, SL; Charlotte mentions discussing her theories with Addams while writing the book in CPS to GHG, 20 July 1897, folder 43, SL.

34. Qtd. in Buhle, *Women,* 59. See also Harriot Stanton Blatch, who declared at an 1898 congressional hearing that "the growing recognition of the economic value of the work of women" represented "[t]he most convincing argument upon which our future claims must rest" (Blatch, qtd. in Ellen DuBois, *Woman Suffrage,* 187–88); "The Woman Question," *Cosmopolitan* (October 1899): 664; ASB, "Mediaeval Prof. Peck," *WJ* (17 June 1899): 196.

35. Peck, "The Cook-Stove in Poetry," *Bookman* (8 September 1898): 50–53, quote from 51 (see also folder 126, SL); for her thoughts on Peck, see CPS to GHG, 2 April 1899, folder 68, SL, and CPS to GHG, 30 March 1899, folder 67, SL; "A Conservative," *ITOW,* 100–01.

36. For her fears about "excessive individualism," see Wellington, 125–26; on her personality and fame, see, e.g., CPS to GHG, 27 June 1898, folder 52, SL, and CPS to GHG, 20 and 21 December 1898, folder 61, SL.

37. CPS to GHG, 3 April 1900, folder 82, SL.

38. CPG to EAR, 28 November 1900, Wisconsin, and see also *L,* 259; on Thomas, see Rosenberg, 40. Charlotte knew of Thomas's work in general and thought highly of his Ward-inspired reform Darwinism.

39. She first met Veblen and read his *Theory of the Leisure Class* (1899) in 1900; see Scharnhorst, *Charlotte,* 46, where he maintains that Charlotte's "The Social Service Bureau" draws on Veblen; for Charlotte on Veblen, see CPS to EAR, 1 February 1900, and CPG to EAR, 28 November 1900, Wisconsin.

40. "the progress . . . " from Buhle, *Women,* 26–27; CPS to GHG, 22 and 10 July 1897, folder 43, SL.

41. EB, "Talks on Nationalism—To a Woman's Rights Advocate," in *Talks on Nationalism,* 80; "loveless . . . " from EB, "Why a New Nation?" (1894) in *EBSA!,* 25–26 (Van Wienen also discusses the overlap between *Looking Backward* and *Women and Economics*); Stanton, qtd. in Goldsmith, 135.

42. CPS to GHG, 8 August 1897, folder 44, SL; on Charlotte's keeping this book close by, see her "Comment and Review" in *FR* 2 (July 1911): 197–98; for similarities between the two women's theories, see Winkler, 1, and Schreiner, *Woman,* 3–5, 8–11. Both Charlotte and Schreiner rely on the term *parasitism,* perhaps borrowed from sociologists including Ross and Ward (see, e.g., EAR to LFW, 22 February 1892, Wisconsin). The concept itself had been around since at least Catharine Beecher's day (*Physiology,* 147), and was defended by Teddy Roosevelt in 1917 (Theodore Roosevelt, "The Parasite Woman: The Only Indispensable Citizen," *The Foes of Our Own Household* [1917] in *Theodore Roosevelt,* 323–27); on the racial/ethnic implications of the term *parasitism,* see Bower.

43. She comments on the paper in CPS to GHG, 3 November 1899, folder 76, SL. Schreiner's own sociological meditation on the condition of women, *Woman and Labor* (the "Bible of the British Women's Movement") was published in 1911, although a first volume was completed and bound as early as 1888. Schreiner published excerpts from the work in *Cosmopolitan* in 1899; the book manuscript was destroyed that same year when Schreiner's house burned down during the Boer War. Charlotte deemed her own book the "superior" to *Women and Labor* but wondered if Schreiner's original manuscript would have outstripped her own effort. (See CPG to KSC, 1 April 1932, folder 103, SL); the second-hand report of Schreiner's praise is from CPS to GHG, 9 January 1900, folder 79, SL.

44. Helen Campbell, *Household*, 141, 235; CPS to GHG, 19 May 1897, folder 41, SL.

45. She denies influences in CPS to GHG, 10 July 1897, folder 43, SL; CPS to GHG, 11 May 1897, folder 41, SL.

46. CPS to GHG, 10 July 1897, folder 43, SL; on Houghton's assistance, see DKD II, 2 January 1898, 708; DKD II, 22 and 23 February 1898, 715; and CPS to GHG, 22 September 1898, folder 55, SL.

47. CPS to GHG, 30 December 1897, folder 48, SL; on waiting until "37," see CPS to GHG, 2 February 1899, folder 64, SL; for her pun on *W.E.*, see CPS to GHG, 16 February 1899, folder 65, SL; CPS to GHG, 22 September 1898, folder 55, SL.

48. CPS to GHG, 6 March 1899, folder 66, SL.

49. The descriptions of her life, her "Treason," and her hopes and prayers are from CPS to GHG, 8 May 1898, folder 50, SL; "undertake . . . demanded by the world" from CPS to GHG, 5 March 1899, folder 66, SL; CPS to GHG, 26 July 1899, folder 71, SL.

50. CPS to GHG, 20 June 1898, folder 52, SL; CPS to GHG, 31 May 1897, folder 41, SL; "cold end of the swing" from CPS to GHG, 3 November 1897, folder 47, SL; CPS to GHG, 16 March 1899, folder 67, SL.

50. CPS to GHG, 16 September 1898, folder 55, SL.

51. On her dependence on Houghton, see CPS to GHG, 12 October 1897, folder 46, SL, and CPS to GHG, 20 December 1899, folder 78, SL (the latter contains her jest). See also the letter in which she writes, with tongue in cheek, "'Every true woman wishes to be supported by the man she loves!!!'" (CPS to GHG, 12 December 1899, folder 78, SL); CPS to GHG, 4 November 1897, folder 47, SL; CPS to GHG, 29 July 1899, folder 71, SL.

52. *W&E*, 280; CPS to GHG, 10 November 1897, folder 47, SL.

53. CPS to GHG, 30 August 1898, folder 54, SL.

54. CPS to GHG, 20 February 1898, folder 49, SL.

55. Charlotte records the outbreak of war in DKD II, 21 April 1898, 724; information on the war and protest from Faulkner, 253–55; "Socialism and Patriotism," *American Fabian* 4 (May 1898): 5–6, quote from 6; she complicates this position in "War as a Socializer," *American Fabian* 4 (June 1898): 5–6.

56. CPS to GHG, 27 May 1898, folder 51, SL; "a woman . . ." from CPS to GHG, 13 May 1898, folder 50, SL; on masculinity and the martial ideology, see Lears; Higham, "Reorientation" 78–79; CPS to GHG, 13 May 1898, folder 50, SL.

57. On spreading herself "in drawers," see CPS to GHG, 12 April 1900, folder 82, SL; CPS to GHG, 20 December 1899, folder 61, SL; CPS to GHG, 6 March 1899, folder 66,

SL; "certain ideal of home" and "plan of living" from CPS to GHG, 16 September 1898, folder 55, SL; on the importance of motion see, for instance, her joy that with Houghton her "freedom of motion" was guaranteed (CPS to GHG, 22 May 1898, folder 51, SL), as well as the poem she wrote around this time, "We All Like Motion," folder 199, SL; "the world . . ." from CPS to GHG, 6 May 1898, folder 50, SL.

58. In CPS to GHG, 18 May 1898, folder 51, SL, for example, Charlotte tells Houghton she could afford him only "the part that stays home"; her joke about "man's duty" is from CPS to GHG, 7 November 1898, folder 58, SL; on their "paradox," see CPS to GHG, 11 May 1898, folder 50, SL, and see also CPS to GHG, 22 May 1898, folder 51, SL; trousers reference from CPS to GHG, 7 March 1900, folder 81, SL.

59. DKD II, 23 August 1890, 417; on Lyman, see Applegate, 25; qtd. in Scharnhorst, "Making Her Fame," 196.

60. "Toward Monogamy," *Nation* (11 June 1924), reprinted in *Our Changing Morality*, ed. Freda Kichwey (New York: Albert and Charles Boni, 1930), 53–66, quote from 58–59; she discusses birds and beasts in *L*, 323, and see also *HR&H*, 87, 124–25; she calls celibacy foolish in "Toward Monogamy," 65, and describes sex as "good" in *HR&H*, 166; *W&E*, 40. Charlotte also used "oversexed" to refer to excessive masculinity.

61. CPS to GHG, 18 December 1898, folder 61, SL; "cold queer . . . " from CPS to GHG, 18 December 1898, folder 61, SL; CPS to GHG, 11 May 1898, folder 50, SL.

62. She mentions Houghton's puns in CPS to GHG, 23 October 1898, folder 57, SL; on her wants, see CPS to GHG, 2 December 1898, folder 60, SL; CPS to GHG, 30 August 1898, folder 54, SL; "a full . . . " from CPS to GHG, 20 March 1899, folder 67, SL.

63. CPS to GHG, 28 October 1899, folder 75, SL.

64. CPS to GHG, 12 June 1898, folder 52, SL; CPS to GECS, 11 January 1897, mf-6, SL.

65. CPS to GHG, 20 and 22 June 1898, folder 52, SL; on the need to "come out forever from the feelings of shame and regret," see "Thoughts & Figgerings," 18 January 1898, folder 16, SL; CPS to GHG, 22 June 1898, folder 52, SL. For her renewed doubts about marriage, motherhood, and work (including housework) in the wake of her realizing that her depression was chronic, see CPS to GHG, 14 July 1898, folder 53, SL.

66. Her assessment of her "innards" and "brain" is from CPS to GHG, 27 October 1898, folder 57, SL; on menopause as the cure, see CPS to GHG, 14 September 1898, folder 55, SL; and see CPS to GHG, 26, 27, 29, and 31 July 1899, folder 71, SL.

67. "hopelessly crippled" from CPS to GHG, 16 September 1898, folder 55, SL; "drop me . . . " from CPS to GHG, 27 June 1898, folder 52, SL; CPS to GHG, 21 January 1899, folder 63, SL, and see also CPS to GHG, 14 September 1898, folder 55, SL.

68. CPS to GHG, 14 September 1898, folder 58, SL; CPS to GHG, 14 October 1898, folder 56, SL. See also CPS to GHG, 3 October 1897, where she attributes her foul mood to "a personal feeling—the wanting of something for oneself," folder 47, SL.

69. On whether to have children, see CPS to GHG, 10 February 1898, folder 49, SL, and CPS to GHG, 20 May 1898, folder 51, SL; her epistolary mothering is described in CPS to GHG, 8 November 1897, folder 47, SL; on conscious mothering and the "nightmare-y state" see CPS to GHG, 29 May 1898, folder 51, SL.

70. DKD II, 17 April 1898, 723; on the arrangements and landlady, see DKD II, 23 June 1898, 731–32, and DK, *Study of the Short Fiction,* 51–53; CPS to GHG, 17 June 1898, folder 52, SL; the bedtime routine is described in CPS to GHG, 23 June 1898, folder 52, SL.

71. On the weather, see DKD II, 17 August 1898, 737; CPS to GHG, 22 September 1898, folder 55, SL; " . . . smothering. . . ." from CPS to GHG, 29 July 1898, folder 53, SL; CPS to GHG, 7 August 1898, folder 54, SL; DKD II, 20 August 1898, 738.

72. CPS to GHG, 21 June 98, folder 52, SL; "two live people" from CPS to GHG, 14 June 1898, folder 52, SL; CPS to GHG, 12 March 1899, folder 66, SL. See also the letter in which she writes Houghton that her "foreground is quite empty. You are at present the only figure in it. Katharine even is not in the foreground in the sense I mean—of intimacy and interrelation" (CPS to GHG, 1 October 1897, folder 46, SL).

73. CPS to GHG, 22 June 1898, folder 52, SL; "cuddle. . . ." from CPS to GHG, 16 June 1898, folder 52, SL; CPS to GHG, 23 June 1898, folder 52, SL.

74. *L,* 248; she discusses the Stetsons' disapproval in CPS to GHG, 20 October 1898, folder 57, SL; CPS to GECS, 13 October 1898, mf-6, SL.

75. CPS to GHG, 15 January 1900, folder 79, SL; GECS, "The Children of the Barren," *Harper's Monthly* (March 1907): 512–19, quote from 518. The story is revealingly titled, since Grace experienced at least one miscarriage while married to Walter.

76. "good of the world" and "personal goal" are from CPS to GHG, 16 September 1898, folder 55, SL; "Up and Down," *Arena* (20 October 1898): 478–79; she describes the poem in *L,* 246. Her friend and editor Amy Wellington concurred, praising its "true grandeur" (Amy Wellington to CPG, 5 August 1935, folder 125, SL).

77. "*Moving the Mountain,*" *FR* 2 (November 1911): 304.

78. CPS to GHG, 14 September 1898, folder 55, SL; "last lap" from CPS to GHG, 7 November 1898, folder 55, SL.

79. See CPS to GHG, 22 November 1898, folder 59, SL, which mentions Russell's objections to the idea of the female lead being a doctor and also refers to Charlotte's intent of turning the play into a novel; on her renewed dramatic aspirations, see DKD II, 707; DKD II, 5 February 1898, 713; CPS to GHG, 3 November 1898, folder 58, SL.

80. On her father's death, see *L,* 215, CPS to GHG, 1 January 1899, folder 62, SL, and CPS to GHG, 9 February 1899, folder 64, SL; on Frederic's difficulty "earning much—if anything," see *L,* 191.

81. *L,* 215; CPS to GHG, 4 June 1899, folder 70, SL.

82. On Ruskin, see Bliss and Binder, 1079, and Eltweed Pomeroy, "A Sketch of the Socialist Colony in Tennessee," *American Fabian* 3 (April 1897): 4. By the time of Charlotte's 1899 visit, Wayland had left the colony, which subsequently relocated "to a better site" in the same region; for Charlotte's impression of her visit, including her conclusions about colony life, see CPS to GHG, 1 and 4 February 1899, folder 64, SL. Later in life— at the height of the Red Scare, admittedly—she was even more dismissive, referring to the Ruskin Colony as "another one of those sublimely planned, devotedly joined, and invariably deserted Socialist Colonies. Only ignorance of the real nature of social relation can account for these high-minded idiocies" (*L,* 252); "Sodom" reference from CPS to GHG, 15 February 1899, folder 65, SL.

83. DKD II, 21 February 1899, 764; southern fan qtd. in *L*, 254; "An Evening with Kipling," *Goldsboro Daily Argus* (14 March 1899): 4; for her itinerary, see "Trips and Lectures," 1899, folder 10, SL.

84. DKD II, 10 March 1899, 766; "German Jewesses" from DKD II, 4 May 1899, 779; DKD II, 5 and 6 May 1899, 775.

85. *L*, 257; "Golden Rule . . . " from "International Council of Women," *Encyclopedia of Social Reform*, 644; "Great houses . . . " from *L*, 257; Mrs. Arthur Scaife, "The Entertainment of the Congress," Report of Transactions of the Second Quinquennial Congress," 1899, 286, folder 261, SL; she describes the duchess in *L*, 261.

86. Description of the closing ceremony from folder 6, SL; *L*, 264; "Queen Victoria and Women," letter to the editor, *New York Times* (25 July 1899). Charlotte pleaded fatigue and did not accompany the many attendees, the aged Anthony included, who lined up midweek to take tea with Queen Victoria. The entourage waited two long hours in the courtyard of Windsor Castle, only to stand idly by while only two people were introduced to the queen: one representative conference delegate and the one titled delegate (Lady Aberdeen). It is this visit to Windsor Castle that Blackwell refers to in her commentary.

87. *L*, 258; *Women in Industrial Life*, 198–202; Charlotte records that her talk was met "with cordial approval" in DKD II, 27 June 1899, 783; Aberdeen, *Women in Education*, 12; *New York Times* (2 July 1899).

88. "Anglo-Saxon" from "An American Writer: Mrs. Stetson at the Sesame Club," *London Chronicle* (16 May 1899), clipping, folder 288, SL; the council's goals are stipulated in *Women in a Changing World*, 3.

89. Charlotte's impressions are recorded in her article on "The Woman's Congress of 1899," *Arena* 22 (September 1899): 342–50, quote from 345; the negative assessments are from Vivaria, 145–64. Vivaria raises an eyebrow at "The lady who spoke of '*the unpaid services of the housewife*'" [161]; *New York Times* (2 July 1899); Low, 199.

90. CPS to GHG, 20 June 1899, folder 70, SL; "An American Writer. Mrs. Stetson at the Sesame Club," *London Chronicle* (16 May 1899), folder 288, SL; "lion" from *L*, 260, and see also CPS to GHG, 5 July 1899, folder 71, SL, where she concludes she had "made a ten strike just as I hoped."

91. CPS to GHG, 25 July 1899, folder 71, SL; "I've got . . . shameful," from CPS to GHG, 26 July 1899, folder 71, SL; CPS to GHG, 28 July 1899, folder 71, SL.

92. "usual dreary twilight" from *L*, 261; quotations describing her longings for her restful "husband" from CPS to GHG, 8 June 1899, folder 70, SL; "sanitarium," CPS to GHG, 16 May 1899, folder 69, SL; CPS to GHG, 18 October 1898, folder 57, SL; daisy incident described in DKD II, 30 May 1899, 779.

93. On the "maddening" trip, see CPS to GHG, 14 July 1899, folder 71, SL; on the voyage home and events upon her return, see *L*, 269–70; on her plans for another book, see DKD II, 26 September 1899, 794.

94. On Pond's desire, see CPS to GHG, 19 August 1899, folder 72, SL; information on Pond's career derived from "Death of Major J. B. Pond," *Daily Northwestern* (Oshkosh, WI: Monday evening)(22 June 1903), and Pond, "Introduction: First Question Answered,"

Eccentricities of Genius (New York: G. W. Dillingham Company, 1900), http://www.wlhn .org/james_pond/ (accessed July 1, 2004).

95. Charlotte describes Gates in *L*, 273–74. Like Charlotte, Gates made an unhappy first marriage but a happy second one. Unlike Charlotte, Gates had thirteen children, two from her first marriage, eleven from her second; only four of the latter survived into adulthood (one young son inadvertently shot and killed his sister). Charlotte would declare Gates, who wrote and spoke on behalf of a variety of causes, "the greatest child of her great father" (CPG to AP, 28 February 1932, WHMEC); Susa Young Gates, "Charlotte Perkins Gilman," *Deseret News* (30 April 1927), vol. 7, SL.

96. On her lecture agents, see *L*, 272; CPS to GHG, 24 December 1899, folder 78, SL; CPS to KBS, 16 September 1899, folder 8, SL; and CPS to GHG, 31 October 1899, folder 75, SL; "tyranny" quote from CPS to GHG, 24 November, 1899, folder 77, SL.

97. She laments her bragging in CPS to GHG, 21 November 1899, folder 77, SL; the reporter's question appeared in the *Chicago Times Herald* (12 November 1899), clipping, folder 266, SL.

98. On Campbell, see CPS to GHG, 3 November 1899, folder 76, SL; CPS to GHG, 24 November 1899, folder 77, SL; and CPS to GHG, 9 May 1900, folder 83, SL.

99. Praise of her speaking skills from DKD II, 24 April 1897, 671; "Mrs. Stetson's Views," *Toledo Blade* (23 October 1899), folder 266, SL, and "Notable Woman Visiting Utah," *Deseret Evening News* (27 November 1899), folder 266, SL; she relates the Christ comparison in CPS to GHG, 17 February 1899, folder 65, SL; "a healthy . . ." from "Authority on the Law of Economics," *Denver Daily News* (23 November 1899), vol. 7, SL.

100. CPS to GHG, 10 November 1899, folder 76, SL; her assessment of her mothering skills is from CPS to GHG, 23 August 1899, folder 72, SL; on Basil Perkins, see CPS to GHG, 4 December 1899, folder 78, SL, and CPS to GHG, 16 January 1900, folder 79, SL.

101. CPS to GHG, 26 and 23 October 1899, folder 75, SL; CPS to GHG, 10 December 1899, folder 78, SL.

102. On paying off her debts; see *L*, 274–75, CPS to GHG, 10 December 1899, folder 78, SL (from which the phrase "financial picnic" comes), and DKD II, 16 December 1899, 805. For an itemized list of her debts, including those to Knapp and Paul Tyner, see CPS to GHG, 1 January 1900, folder 79, SL.

103. "Remarkable Literary Success of Mrs. Charlotte Perkins Stetson," *Oakland Enquirer*, folder 266, SL; the "hulking young professor" and Charlotte first met at Stanford in March 1894. The *Impress* covered the sociologist's lecture on "The Social Plaint" *Impress* (24 November 1894): 2; for her impressions of Ross and his family, see *L*, 259, CPS to GHG, 20 December 1899, folder 78, SL, and CPS to GHG, 15 June 1899, folder 70, SL; DKD II, 16 March 1894, 577.

104. For Lummis's welcome, see *Land of Sunshine* 12 (March 1900): 302, and Charles Lummis to "Winner" (CPS), 29 December 1899, Huntington; Harriet Howe to CPS, 25 November 1899, enclosed with CPS to GHG, 1 December 1899, folder 78, SL.

105. Her impression of Walter is recorded in CPS to GHG, 24 December 1899, folder 78, SL; KSC, "Autobiography," WSCC; Charlotte's recollections are from DKD II, 1 January 1900, 813, and CPS to GHG, 5 January 1900, folder 79, SL.

106. She describes the slap in CPS to GHG, 25–26 December 1899, folder 78, SL, and see also DKD II, 25 December 1899, 806; "unnatural mother" from CPS to GHG, 25 December 1899, folder 78, SL.

107. On the Stetsons' regarding her as selfish, see CPS to GHG, 25 December, 1899, folder 78, SL, and CPS to GHG, 20 January 1900, folder 79, SL.

108. On her desire to counter their European emphasis with an American one, see CPS to GHG, 5 and 6 January 1900, folder 79, SL; "overweighted" from CPG to KBS, 23 September 1911, WSCC; CPS to GHG, 5 January 1900, folder 79, SL.

109. CPS to GHG, 21 January 1900, folder 79, SL.

110. CPS to GHG, 1 January 1900, folder 79, SL; for her dubious earning projections, see CPS to GHG, 5 October 1898, folder 56, SL; "very meager" from *L*, 270; total royalties mentioned in CPS to GHG, 21 March 1900, folder 81, SL; CPS to GHG, 21 and 22 March 1900, folder 81, SL.

111. "Dr. Clair's Place," *FR* 6 (June 1915): 141–45, and see also, e.g., CPS to GHG, 16 and 8 February 1900, folder 80, SL; "Mrs. Charlotte Perkins Stetson," *Denver Daily News* (23 November 1899), vol. 7, SL. She later changed the title to *Human Work* to avoid confusion with Louisa May Alcott's novel *Work*.

112. Folder 16, SL; she reports Walter's reaction in CPS to GHG, 11 April 1900, folder 82, SL; CPS to GHG, 23 October 1898, folder 57, SL; ". . . heart . . . head" from CPS to GHG, 23 May 1900, folder 84, SL.

113. TAP to CPS, 3 April 1900, folder 28, SL; Charlotte laments the cousin's responses in CPS to GHG, 18 February 1900, folder 80, SL; the responses include Margaret Whitney to GHG, 15 April 1900, folder 110, SL (Whitney's letter also contains the reference to Charlotte's being "clever and aspiring"); Julia [GHG's cousin] to GHG, 14 May 1900, folder 110, SL; and Emily Gilman to GHG, Tuesday Evening, folder 110, SL.

114. CPS to GHG, ca. 7 May 1900, qtd. in Hill, "Journey," 363; she grapples with her doubts in "Thoughts & Figgerings," 9 May 1900, folder 16, SL; "Her Housekeeper," *FR* 1 (January 1910): 6.

115. On her relationship with doctors, see Wegener, "'What a Comfort'," and see also DKD II, 30 April 1900, 814; on having children, see CPS to GHG, 16 May 1900, folder 84, SL.

116. On their changing plans for the ceremony, see DKD II, 27 May 1900, 814, and CPS to KSC, 11 October 1926, SL; CPS to GHG, 7 June 1900, folder 85, SL.

117. Wedding announcements, folder 1, SL; "obey . . . " from CPS to GHG, 10 April 1900, folder 82, SL; see clippings, folder 283, SL; "very nice" from DKD II, 11 June 1900, 814.

118. *L*, 284. See also "Names—Especially Women's," *FR* 2 (October 1911): 261–63, where she enumerates the many problems with women not retaining their given names.

119. On her efforts to prevent an "exhibition," see CPS to GHG, 7 March 1900, folder 81, SL; "Among the Women's Clubs," *Boston Sunday Herald* (15 July 1900), folder 266, SL.

120. "Mrs. Stetson Tries Matrimony Again," *San Francisco Chronicle* (19 June 1900), 80-M112, folder 41, SL; "A Second Chance in the Lottery," *San Francisco Examiner* (June 1900), folder 283, SL.

121. For "the happy ending," see *L*, 281, and see also CPS to GHG, 12 May 1898, folder 50, SL, where she refers to their "happily ever after"; long quotation from CPS to GHG, 11 October 1899, folder 74, SL; on their home as a model, see CPS to GHG, 4 October 1899, folder 74, SL; CPS to GHG, 26 July 1899, folder 71, SL.

CHAPTER NINE

1. "Human Work," *FR* 2 (November 1911): 291. The chapter title derives from Charlotte's 1912 short story, "A Cleared Path," in which the heroine convinces her future husband that "A woman may love a man as well as any woman ever did, yet not be willing to give up her work when it is not necessary—if she holds it a higher duty" (*FR* 3 [October 1912]: 253–58).

2. "End of the Century," *Impress* (6 October 1894): 2; "remain feminine" from "Woman, the Discovery of the Century," *Success* (January 1901): 554–55, oversize folder 1, SL; "of a growing . . ." from CPS to GHG, 21 September 1898, folder 55, SL; CPS to GHG, 21 April 1900, folder 82, SL.

3. Seitler, 7; see also Hill's decision to end her efforts in 1896, in part because, she told me in private correspondence, she considered the twentieth-century record sparse.

4. CPS to GHG, 9 October 1898, folder 56, SL; "Talks with Clubwomen," *Chicago Times Herald* (12 November 1899), folder 266, SL.

5. "What have I to give the world?" "Thoughts & Figgerings," n.d. (possible second page of 12 April 1901 entry on opposing page), folder 16, SL; "Come now . . ." from CPS to GHG, 16 September 1898, folder 55, SL; CPS to GHG, 11 April 1900, folder 82, SL.

6. DKD II, 811.

7. Charlotte discusses the Cold Spring arrangements in CPS to GHG, 27 January 1900, folder 79, SL; see DKD II, 16 and 19 July 1900, 815, for examples of her recurring depression; "queer species" from CPS to GHG, 9 May 1900, folder 83, SL; on needing Houghton's help, see CPS to GHG, 11 May 1900, folder 83, SL; she describes her new project in CPS to LFW, 15 January 1901, Brown.

8. Isabella Beecher Hooker, *Womanhood: Its Sanctities and Fidelities* (Boston, 1873), qtd. in *SSB*, 350; Isabella Beecher Hooker to Olympia Brown, 25 April 1901, Olympia Brown Collection, SL.

9. She insists on her "line of study" in "An American Writer. Mrs. Stetson at the Sesame Club," *London Chronicle* (16 May 1899), folder 388, SL; "mothers . . . homelife" from CPS to GHG, 26 July 1899, folder 71, SL; CPS to GHG, 5 November 1899, folder 77, SL.

10. Dedication, *CC*, n.p.; *CC*, 193–95, "a too self-sacrificing mother" from 195.

11. *L*, 232–33; *CC*, 277.

12. On kindergartens, see Reda Davis, 14–15, and see also the review essay in *Impress* (24 November 1894): 104; on children's poverty, treatment, and rights, see Jacob Riis, *Children of the Poor*, Charles Loring Brace, *The Dangerous Classes of New York*, and Sklar, *Florence*, 158ff.

13. CPG to LBS, 11 September 1928, Beecher-Stowe papers, folder 416, SL; "gloves" reference from review of *CC*, clipping, folder 302, SL; "as a person . . ." from "Charlotte Perkins Gilman: An Appreciation and a Criticism," *New Age* (2 March 1905): 138; *CC*, 123; on the professionalization of childcare, see Koven and Michel, who cite CPG's "The New

Mothers of a New World" as their epigraph and discuss efforts to translate the private responsibility of mothers into "*public* policy" (2); see also Muncy.

14. First line from "Moving" (poem), *FR* 3 (September 1912): 236–37.

15. AP to Harriet Park, 23 August 1935, WHMEC (thanks to Jennifer Tuttle for sharing this letter with me); "Life back . . ." from CPS to GHG, 10 May 1900, folder 83, SL; DKD II, 31 December 1900, 816.

16. Charlotte's thoughts on parenting are from CPS to GHG, 6 December 1899, folder 78, SL, and "Thoughts & Figgerings," 13 September 1900, DKD II, appendix A, 849; outings are described in KSC, "Autobiography," WSCC; KSC, qtd. in Lane, 327; "make city life attractive" from KSC, "Autobiography," WSCC.

17. "Thoughts & Figgerings," 9 May 1900, folder 16, SL; on her trips, see *L*, 287–88; "Our Uneasy Consciences," *Saturday Evening Post* (16 June 1900): 1182; "Better than Santa Claus," *Christian Register* (12 December 1907): 1402–03; their celebration is described in *L*, 290.

18. On New York, see Faulkner, 34, and *New York*, 251; "see out . . . " from *L*, 317.

19. On the Avondale flat, see *L*, 282, and KSC, "Autobiography," WSCC (the first month was free); on the Barthelmess family, see KSC, "Autobiography," WSCC, and *L*, 283; their domestic arrangements are discussed in CPS to GHG, 18 and 17 March 1900, folder 81, SL.

20. "The Beauty of a Block," *Independent* (14 July 1904): 67–72, and "The Passing of the Home in Great American Cities," *Cosmopolitan* 38 (December 1904): 137–47.

21. For their typical day, see KSC, "Autobiography," WSCC, and *L*, 287; for her two-hour ideal, see *Moving the Mountain*, *FR* 2 (March 1911): 82, and see also *Humanness*, *FR* 4 (April 1913): 110; on her finances, see *L*, 290.

22. On her projections, see: "Marrying and Money," *WJ* (26 March 1904): 98; CPS to GHG, 27 September 1899, folder 73, SL, where she predicts she will be living on her "income soon"; and CPS to GHG, 10 November 1899, folder 76, SL, where she optimistically projects an annual income of $4,000; on Houghton's income, see CPS to GHG, 21 November 1899, folder 77, SL; she dismisses his prejudice and discusses compensation in CPS to GHG, 15 and 19 November 1899, folders 76 and 77, SL.

23. CPS to GHG, 20 December 1898, folder 61, SL.

24. Bliss and Binder, "New York City," *Encyclopedia of Social Reform*, 827ff; Brasch, 45.

25. On McClure's reluctance, see, e.g., DKD II, 17 January 1903, 830; on Charlotte's journalism, see Fishkin, 234–48.

26. "Newspaper Sins," 1906, ms. fragment, folder 183, SL; on Hearst and Gilman, see DK, "Charlotte," 46–58, and see also Charlotte's poems "Hyenas" and "The Yellow Reporter" in *LP*, 46, as well as "The Daily Squid," *FR* 6 (August 1915): 206; on Hearst's move to New York City and his journalism, see CPS to Brander Matthews, 19 October 1892, Butler Library, and EAR, *Old World*, 233.

27. On the Hearst–Pulitzer war, see Bliss and Binder, "New York City," *Encyclopedia*, 827, see also the entry on "William Randolph Hearst," 569, and see Higham, *Strangers*, 127ff; on Charlotte's opposition to Hearst's candidacy for president, see "Not a Woman's Candidate," *WJ* (20 February 1904): 58.

28. Rauchway, 3–4; Brasch, 29–31; Bliss and Binder, "William Randolph Hearst," *The Encyclopedia of Social Reform*, 569; for Charlotte on McKinley, see DKD II, 2, 6, 14, and 19 September 1901, 818.

29. See Gere, 139.

30. "Malthusianism and Race Suicide," *WJ* (3 September 1904): 282; on motherhood, see her "Woman and Duty," *New York Tribune* (26 February 1903) sec. 7: 1.

31. Catt and Shuler, 282; *L*, 294.

32. CPS to GHG, 7 October 1899, folder 74, SL.

33. On their illnesses, see *L*, 290; "brain cells" from CPS to GHG, 10 May 1898, folder 50, SL; on what to blame and her vanished hopes for a "permanent recovery," see CPS to GHG, 22 September 1898, folder 55, SL; "tightrope" reference from CPS to GHG, 18 May 1897, folder 41, SL.

34. See Martin and Martin, 91–92.

35. Descriptions of Summer Brook come from *L*, 230; KSC, "Autobiography," WSCC; and, for the sibling references and division of labor, W. P. D. Bliss, qtd. in Mastrianni, 37; Charlotte describes Prestonia in CPS to GHG, 11 May 1897, folder 41, SL; she describes her "*fine*" time in CPS to GHG, 3 August 1897, folder 44, SL; see also "The Joys of Summerbrook" and KSC's explanatory note, both folder 205, SL, and see Mastrianni, 36–41.

36. "If I were a Girl Again: Advice from a Thinker," *Success* (1903): 5372, and see Lutz, 229.

37. She records her first call on the doctor in DKD II, 10 December 1901, 819; for Jacobi's course of treatment, see Sicherman, 891n4, and DKD II, 17 December 1901, 820; for Charlotte's description of the treatment and the chart she produced, see *L*, 291, and DKD II, 14 January 1902, 821; for Jacobi on women's diseases, see Jacobi, *Question of Rest*, 205.

38. On CPG's faith in female doctors, see Wegener, "'What a Comfort'," 45–73; biographical information from "Jacobi, Mary Corinna Putnam," *NAW* (vol. 2), 263–65; on the differences between Jacobi and Gilman, see Sicherman, 896–97, 893; CPG, "The Passing of the Home in Great American Cities," *Cosmopolitan* 38 (December 1904): 137–47, "*steered*" quote from 144.

39. She says she is feeling better in CPG to LFW, 30 June 1903, Brown; on basketball, see *L*, 292, and DKD II, 25 and 28 January 1902, 821; on bicycle statistics, see Higham, "Reorientation," 80; "vehicle" quote from Green, *Fit*, 229; on the bicycling craze and ensuing sales, see Green, *Fit*, 228–32; for her discomfort with biking, see CPS to GHG, 18 May 1897, folder 41, SL, and see also DKD II, 27 October 1901, 818.

40. See "Ill Fed Humans," *New York Tribune* (7 April 1903) sec. 7: 4; mother and daughter collaborated on works including "Love and Friendship" and "A Romance of El Paso," folder 224, SL.

41. A doctor acquaintance of Grace's also happened to be journeying on the *S.S. Princess Irene* and kept an eye on Katharine during the voyage.

42. CPG to KSC, 10 September 1931, folder 102, SL; "bird . . ." from CPS to GHG, 3 April 1900, folder 82, SL; "resting place" from "Work and Ethics," 19 February 190[?] (ms. faded and torn), "Thoughts & Figgerings," folder 16, SL; on her marital bliss, see CPG to Mrs. Severance, 25 January 1904, Huntington; on the fun and games, see

DKD II, 13 January 1901 and 24 March 1901, 817; on finishing *HW*, see DKD II, 31 December 1902, 829.

43. "To Houghton: Thanksgiving 1902," folder 205, SL.

44. "Thoughts & Figgerings," 9 October 1905, folder 16, SL.

45. See *New York Times* (12 March 1903) sec. 7: 1 for lecture description; see also the *New York Tribune* of that same date, both of which covered Charlotte's lectures at the Civitas Club; these and other clippings from this period are contained in vol. 24, folder 7, SL; "sympathetic chronicler's" quote is from "Charlotte Perkins Stetson Gilman: A Forerunner and a Prophet," folder 243, SL.

46. "Get Thee to a Nunnery, Go?" *Truth* 21 (May 1902): 107; "Baby Gardens for Tots under Kindergarten Age," *Brooklyn Daily Eagle*, clipping, vol. 24, folder 7, SL.

47. On her personality not coming through in print, see *Brooklyn Daily Eagle* (27 February 1903), folder 287, SL; the praise is drawn from Howe, "The Personality," 211–16; Wellington, 115–131; Frank R. Stockton, "Men, Women and Events," *Cosmopolitan* 27 (August 1899): 453–55; *Brooklyn Daily Eagle*, vol. 24, folder 7, SL; "scintillating" from "Talks with Clubwomen," *Times-Herald* (12 November 1899), folder 266, SL.

48. "Addressed to Success," typescript, folder 133, SL; for "Over the Top" and Bryan dinner, see *L*, 256–57; the series is described in the letter from *Booklovers* (July 1901), folder 126, SL (and see the course she offered: "Ideals of Child Culture: A Talk by CPG," pamphlet, folder 220, SL); for the translation of her poem, see letter dated 22 January 1901, folder 155, SL; CPG to Mr. Page, 6 January 1904, Barnard.

49. *Brooklyn Daily Eagle* (27 February 1903), folder 287, SL, see also the August 1904 *Chautauqua Herald* articles, oversize folder 2, SL, and Hayden, *Grand*, 124; "Womanest" from CPG to Mrs. Sweet, 22 September 1903, Rochester; "most heretical" from *L*, 286; "good. . . . blasphemous" from "Home and the World," *Chautauqua Assembly Herald* (27 August 1904), oversize folder 2, SL.

50. Poem qtd. in *L*, 286; "hurling . . ." from CPS to GHG, 17 October 1898, folder 57, SL; *Home*, 57; see also 94, 100.

51. On the myths and costs of domesticity, see *Home*, 276, 176, 181; for an analysis of Gilman's sentimental take on the public sphere, see my "'The World Was Home for Me'"; "cradle" references from *Home*, 183; "a surgical . . . " from *The Critic*, folder 309, SL; pruning metaphor from *Home*, 13.

52. "ancient coop" from *Home*, 226; her pledge is recorded in CPS to GHG, 16 September 1898, folder 55, SL; she describes her mother in *L*, 8.

53. On the Mass. Bureau, see Kessler-Harris, 110; "The Home," *Los Angeles Express* (12 December 1903), folder 303, SL; "The Influence of the Home," *Boston Transcript* (11 November 1903), folder 303, SL.

54. "The Ideal Home," *New York Times* (26 December 1903), folder 303, SL; see also the review of *The Home* in the *Toledo Times* (20 December 1904), which declared Charlotte's solutions to infant mortality and childrearing "so rank, radical and unconvincing that it is hard to believe she is even serious in her views. She would save the children by taking them away from their mothers!" Finally, see Irene Gardner, who asked irately in her piece for the same paper, "Why doesn't Mrs. Gilman go about with an ax and smash

the homes?" (17 November 1904), folder 303, SL; "*The Home,*" *Los Angeles Herald* (15 November 1903), folder 303, SL; additional insinuations surface in "Evolution of the Home," *San Francisco Call,* folder 303, SL, and "*The Home,*" *Saturday Evening Post* (20 February 1904), folder 303, SL.

55. The review that asks this question is "*The Home,*" 1907, clipping, folder 303, SL; see also the 23 January 1904 review of *The Home* for the *Chicago Chronicle*, which presents a definition of the "sacred" antithetical to Charlotte's: ". . . be sure that in the throwing away of domestic work you do not throw away with it the sacred individuality which is the first essential of the home" (folder 295, SL); on whether her heart is in her home, see "Home Life" (1904), clipping, folder 295, SL.

56. CPS to GHG, 3 February 1898, folder 49, SL.

57. For an exemplary critique of her unconvincing reforms, see "*The Home,*" *The Ethical Record* (1907), folder 303, SL; on keeping reforms within "woman's sphere," see Muncy, 36–37; "What Work Is," *Cosmopolitan* 27 (October 1899): 678–82, quotes from 678; on work as an essential right/duty, see "Comment and Review," *FR* 2 (December 1911): 338.

58. Studley, 166; CPS to SWM, 19 April 1887, AG 487C, SL; for a California lecture, see, e.g., "Our Place Today," lecture ms., 21 January 1891, folder 164, SL; review of "Women in the Business World," *Impress* (19 January 1895): 10.

59. *Humanness,* *FR* 4 (April 1913): 110; on altruism and evolution, see *CC,* 152, and see *W&E,* 279; *HW,* 185.

60. *HW,* 13; *HW,* 188; *HW,* 121; on "human" versus "ego" nature, see *HW,* 153.

61. On the mother as ideal, unselfish worker, see *HW,* 151, 211; *HW,* 214.

62. *HW,* 389.

63. Her assessment is made in *L,* 275; for her revisions, see *Our Brains and What Ails Them, FR* 3 (1912); *Humanness, FR* 4 (1913), and *Social Ethics, FR* 5 (1914); see also CPG to KSC, 2 August 1932, e.g., and CPG to KSC, 18 August 1932, folder 103, SL. Charlotte found her revisions of *Human Work* even more "unsatisfactory" than the original version, but she continued to revise the book up until her final days in hopes of making it the cornerstone of her "social service." See "Introductory," *Humanness, FR* 4 (January 1913): 20; *L,* 332; CPG to KSC, 1 November 1932 and 3 May 1934, folders 103 and 105, SL; and CPG to GECS, 5 November 1933, mf-6, SL.

64. She acknowledges the book's faults in *L,* 275, and see *Humanness, FR* 4 (January 1913): 20; see, e.g., the negative reviews in the *Brooklyn Eagle* and *Boston Transcript* (20 July 1904), folder 303, SL; Lummis, "That Which Is Written," *Out West* (September 1904): 299–301, folder 309, SL.

65. For her praise and continued reliance on Ward, see CPG, "Woman's Place," *Chautauqua Assembly Herald* (25 August 1904): 1, 6, 8; CPG to LFW, 20 January 1904, Brown; LFW to CPG, 10 April 1904, qtd. in Gale, foreword to *L,* xvi; on the new research, see especially Rosenberg, 69ff and 103–04; for Weismann's challenge of Lamarck, see Stocking, 239, 253–54, and Hofstadter, *Social,* 98; "biological friends" from CPG to LFW, 15 March 1906, Brown.

66. Lippmann, 222. The *American Journal of Sociology* also accused her of elitism for

arguing that working women were automatically liberated by their work; she talks about taking a break in CPS to Mrs. Severance, 25 January 1904, Huntington.

67. *HW*, 59, 151, 372–73; the negative comments on *HW* are from *New York City Commercial Advertiser* (16 June 1904), folder 310, SL, and "Befuddled with Housework," *New York Tribune* (6 October 1904), folder 310, SL.

68. The reporter who asked her the question wrote "Should Wives Work?" *Success* (September 1902): 501–02; on her overly illuminated public life, see "Woman's Interests: Charlotte Perkins Gilman," *New Age* (2 March 1905): 138.

69. *HW*, 362–63.

70. "The Woman's Congress of 1899," *Arena* 22 (September 1899): 342–50, quote from 349.

CHAPTER TEN

1. "Missing the Way," *WJ* (26 March 1904): 98.

2. First stanza of "For This New Year" (poem), *WJ* (9 January 1904): 2; her thoughts on "now" from "From Now On," *WJ* (2 January 1904): 2; "A New Year's Letter," *WJ* (2 January 1904): 2.

3. Her thoughts on the uses of suffrage are recorded in "Comment and Review," *FR* 7 (December 1916): 335, and "Suffrage," *FR* 1 (May 1910): 24.

4. EB, "Talks on Nationalism: To a Woman's Rights Advocate," in *Talks on Nationalism*, 80; her critique of its individualism and pedestrianism is from "Suffrage Work," *WJ* (5 March 1904): 74; CPS to GHG, 25 August 1897, folder 44, SL. See also CPS to MLL, 27 July 1890, RIHS, where she writes, "I'm glad you have seen the sense in equal suffrage. I never was a very ardent suffragist, it has long seemed such a foregone conclusion that I can't get all excited over it. But it is vitally essential." And see Zona Gale, who said of Charlotte, "she never thought of suffrage for women as anything more than one iron in that fire. Useful, expectable, inevitable. That, of course. Then more, more!" (Gale, foreword to *L*, xxiii); finally, see *L*, 131, where she writes that "the basic need of economic independence seemed to me of far more important than the ballot . . ."; "help and service . . . progress" from "Vital Issues," *WJ* (2 January 1904): 2.

5. See her speech on "The Duties of Today" at the National American Convention of 1903, *History of Woman Suffrage* (vol. 5), 71; "At the Convention," *WJ* (20 February 1904): 58; "Vital Issues," *WJ* (2 January 1904): 2; "What Is Practical?" *WJ* (23 April 1904): 130; her complaint is expressed in "An Advancing Cause," *Current Literature* 36 (April 1904): 388–89.

6. "Private Morality vs. Public Immorality," *FR* 1 (January 1910): 11.

7. "A Forerunner and a Prophet," 1904 biographical sketch, folder 243, SL.

8. Information on the journal, the family, and Stone's death from Blackwell, *Lucy Stone*, 282, and "Alice Stone Blackwell," *NAW* (vol. 1), 156–58, and see also my "The Woman's Journal;" "serving . . ." from CPS to GHG, 4 October 1899, folder 74, SL.

9. ASB, *Lucy Stone*, 236–43, Catt qtd. on 243; "Comment and Review," *FR* 3 (April 1912): 111.

10. "52 . . ." from CPG to Caroline Severance, 25 January 1904, Huntington; "The World's Mother," *WJ* (2 January 1904): 2.

11. On working gratis and the profit share, see "A New Department," *WJ* (26 December 1903): 1, and CPG to Caroline Severance, 25 January 1904, Huntington; for the editorial prediction, see "Concerning Women," *WJ* (2 January 1904): 1; "Human Betterment" from "What Are Vital Issues?" *WJ* (26 March 1904): 98; for the increasing controversy over CPG's views, see, e.g., L. N., "Housework Defended," *WJ* (26 March 1904): 98; CPG, "Why This Insistence?" *WJ* (24 September 1904): 308; and ASB, "Mrs. Gilman on Strawberry Jam," *WJ* (24 September 1904): 308.

12. ASB, "The Thirst for Fame," *WJ* (24 December 1904): 412. In one of her final columns, Charlotte discusses the journal's own failures, linking its financial difficulties to suffragists' failure to rally around the journal and boost its total subscriptions: "To My Readers in Especial," *WJ* (3 December 1904): 386; see also Finnegan, 145–46.

13. "This 'Craving for Notoriety'," *WJ* (17 December 1904): 402.

14. ASB, "The Thirst for Fame," *WJ* (24 December 1904): 412.

15. "Is the Woman's Movement Slow?" *WJ* (30 July 1904): 242.

16. "An Advancing Cause," *Current Literature* 36 (April 1904): 388–89; on expediency, see Buhle, *Women*, 93, Kraditor, *Ideas*, 44–45, and Cott, 239.

17. On "crackpots," see Flexner, 209; CPG, "The 'Anti' and the Fly," *FR* 1 (January 1910): 22; on the forum, see Kraditor, *Ideas*, 41; NAWSA pamphlet, 1913, and see "Arguments of Anti-Suffragists Are Answered by Mrs. Charlotte Perkins Gilman, Editor and Writer," *Cincinnati Enquirer* (3 November 1913), folder 287, SL.

18. On Blatch, see Flexner, 243, "Harriot Stanton Blatch," *NAW* (vol. 1), 172–74, and Blatch and Lutz, 92; information on the "Equality League" comes from Ellen DuBois, "Working," 190–92, Buhle, *Women*, 224, Blatch and Lutz, 91ff and 110–17, and Flexner, 244; on the WPU's tactics, see Ellen DuBois, "Working," 197, 200–01; Flexner, 244.

19. For CPG's suffrage activities, see CPG to GECS, 26 June 1914, and August 1914, mf-6, SL; CPG, "Is Feminism So Dreadful?" *Delineator* 85 (August 1914): 6; *History of Woman Suffrage*, 243ff and 264–65; CPG to Caroline Severance, 4 June 1909, Huntington; on the Vassar visit, see Blatch and Lutz, 107–08.

20. "A Suggestion on the Negro Problem," *American Journal of Sociology* 14 (July 1908): 78–85.

21. Anne Firor Scott, *Natural*, 169.

22. On the "voteless citizens" montage, see Reda Davis, 89; for discussions of suffragists' views of immigrants and illiterates, see Robert Allen, 161; Buhle and Buhle, 29–30; see also Kraditor, *Ideas*, 125, for a speech by Catt on the "great danger" of "the ignorant foreign vote"; on Addams, etc., see Kraditor, *Ideas*, 137–39, and Flexner, 211.

23. Charlotte mentions the Douglass visit in DKD II, 3 June 1898, 729, and see also Aptheker, 8; On Cooper, see Washington, 3–15 (thanks to Mary Moynihan for bringing the articles on Cooper and DuBois to my attention); for examples of racist comments, see DKD I, 27 April 1881, 52; CPG to KSC, 22 March 1923, folder 94, SL; CPG to KSC, 31 March 1923, folder 94, SL; and CPG to KSC, 14 March [1925], folder 96, SL.

24. For an example of her use of stereotypes, see *W&E*, 141, e.g., and see also *CC*, 134, where she seeks to prove that we do not treat our babies well by citing the example of the South, where parents entrust the care of their babes to "the distinctly lower races" they

enslaved; see Bederman, 122, 125, and Bower for analyses of how gender inflects CPG's understandings of race and ethnicity, and vice versa.

25. Michaels traces this tendency to blame culture in *Our America*; on the East Indian gentleman, see *Impress* (20 October 1894): 1, and see Newman, 134; for her references to slavery as an "awful mistake" see *With Her in Ourland*, *FR* 7 (June 1916): 154; and on whites who "cheated," see "Race Pride," *FR* 4 (April 1913): 90.

26. See Anthony et al., 78, Kraditor, *Ideas*, 136 ff, and Mary Gray Peck, 130; "improve the human stock" comes from *Report*, Hearing before the Committee on Woman Suffrage of the U.S. Senate, 16 February 1904.

27. On Louisiana as relatively benighted when it came to woman suffrage, see "A 'Women's Rights' Map of the United States, 1910," in Dorr, 101; on the paper and the letter, see Robert Allen, 161–62; Mary Gray Peck, 130.

28. "National American Convention of 1905," *History of Woman Suffrage*, 149; Grover Cleveland, "Would Woman Suffrage Be Unwise?" *Ladies' Home Journal* 12 (October 1905): 7–8; see also Gere, 31, for a description of Cleveland's argument.

29. Clipping, unidentified Chicago area paper, 16 August 1906, folder 310, SL.

30. EB, "An Echo of Antietam," *Century* (July 1884), and see also John Thomas, 244–45; Lipow, 285; EB, *Equality*, 364–65 (in private correspondence, Scharnhorst notes the resonance of Bellamy's concept of an "industrial army" here); "biologically . . ." from Pittenger, 85–86.

31. See EAR, *Social*, 387, and John S. Haller, 151–52; McGerr, 182–84: Baker qtd. in McGerr, 191.

32. On Dixon, *Birth of a Nation*, and the Klan, see Fitzpatrick, 140; on Hoffman, see Bannister, 190–91 and 193; on paternalism versus laissez-faire policies, see John S. Haller, 206–07, Pittenger, 85, and Bannister, 191.

33. Ginger, 238; Walling in particular was a vocal advocate of the NAACP and of democracy as well as a critic of social Darwinism (he faulted Charlotte for her dogmatism and elitism in this regard) and of lynching and racial violence; Walling, 365, and see also Bannister, 200; on both Walling and Baker, see Brasch, 116–17.

34. "To Make the Negro Work," *Literary Digest* 37 (10 October 1908): 499–500; CWS to KBS, 19 December 1908, vol. 3, 80-M112, SL.

35. "A Suggestion on the Negro Problem," *American Journal of Sociology* 14 (July 1908): 78–85, quotation from 81.

36. "Hope," *FR* 2 (January 1911): 8.

37. CPG to Ida Hursted Harper, 7 March 1904, Huntington; Carrie Chapman Catt to CPG, 28 May 1935, in DKJT, and see also Van Voris, 232.

38. Details on the conference from *L*, 298, and see CPG's dispatches and accounts: "From Germany," *WJ* (25 June 1904): 202, "At the Convention," *WJ* (20 February 1904): 58, "An Advancing Cause," *Current Literature* 36 (April 1904): 388–89, and "The Growing Power of Women: Impressions of the Congress in Berlin," *Booklovers* 4 (September 1904): 385–90.

39. LFW to CPG, 10 April 1904, qtd. in Gale foreword to *L*, xvi; Carrie Chapman Catt comments on Charlotte's "army of admirers" in a letter quoted in *WJ* (3 September

1904): 281; International Congress of Women, Berlin, folder 7, SL; *L*, 298. Alexander Black said of this Berlin sojourn, "This lithe American woman, who, when she kindled, seemed to be all eyes, who could blaze without heat, and who had a way of looking like a militant Madonna, may well have puzzled those who had theories of an American type" ("The Woman," 39).

40. *L*, 187; CPG to LFW, 20 January 1904, Brown; Harper qtd. in Van Voris, 62.

41. On her return trip, see *L*, 301. In *Atlantic Crossings*, Daniel T. Rodgers discusses progressivism as a transatlantic phenomenon, and while she made for an uncomfortable progressive, Charlotte's transatlantic tours help to illustrate his point; "thunder" reference from "The Servant Difficulty; How to End It; Interview with Mrs. Perkins Gilman," *London Daily News* (21 February 1905), folder 289, SL; for an account of the lecture and the men's exit, see *New York Evening Post* (9 March 1905), folder 287, SL; for more on her views on male versus female beauty, see *Home*, 210–11.

42. "The Servant Difficulty; How to End It; Interview with Mrs. Perkins Gilman," *London Daily News* (21 February 1905), folder 289, SL.

43. "At the Convention," *WJ* (20 February 1904): 58; "The Growing Power of Woman: Impressions of the Congress in Berlin," *Booklovers* (September 1904): 385–90; on the trip to Rome, see *L*, 300.

44. "Thoughts & Figgerings," 9 October 1905, folder 16, SL.

45. KBS to Anna Waller, 10 January 1905 and 27 April 1905, both transcribed by David Goodale, vol. 2, CWS papers, 93 M76, SL.

46. On the new house, see *L*, 295, and KSC, "Autobiography," WSCC; on the "Servant Problem," see her "A New Basis for the Servant Question," *Worthington's Illustrated Magazine and Literary Treasury* (March 1894): 304–09, quote from 308, and Katzman, 223.

47. On boarding, see Degler, *At Odds*, 393–94, and Hayden, *Grand*, 21; for Charlotte's views on boarding, see *L*, 295, and CPS to GHG, 1 April 1900, folder 82, SL, the latter of which contains the "prate gloomily" reference. For positive portrayals of women running boarding houses, see *Benigna Machiavelli*, "Martha's Mother," "Mrs. Beazley's Deeds," and "The Jumping-off Place"; "Without 'Bo(a)rders'" spoofs Mary Austin's style, folder 125, SL.

48. CWS to KBS, 19 March 1908, David Goodale's transcript of letter and KSC's response, vol. 3, CWS papers, 93 M76, SL.

49. for her reflections on her husband, see "Thoughts & Figgerings," 9 October 1905, folder 16, SL, and see also "Thoughts & Figgerings," 18 September 1900, 16; *Women and Social Service*, address before the Boston Equal Suffrage Association, 4 November 1907; "Five Kinds of Love," *Harper's Bazaar* 42 (January 1908): 63–65.

50. *L*, 303; "good for nothing" from CPG to EAR, 15 March 1906, Wisconsin; "Thoughts & Figgerings," 2 July 1906, folder 16, SL.

51. Dreiser, 57.

52. "Climbing," *FR* 2 (December 1911): 317.

53. On magazine coverage, see Green, *Fit*, 246ff, and Lutz; on "brain fatigue" as a myth, see Nathan Hale, 141.

54. "Human Pain," *WJ* (27 August 1904): 274; on the delusion of individual happiness,

see "The New Immortality," *FR* 3 (March 1912): 63; CPG, "In What Fields Do Women Excel?" *Boston Sunday Globe* (24 November 1907) sec. 36: 3–4.

55. "A Woman's Utopia," *Times Magazine* 1 (January 1907): 216; (February 1907): 373; (March 1907): 499; and (January 1907): 215; see also Kessler, *Charlotte*, 48–49, and Scharnhorst, *Charlotte*, 80–83 (a fourth installment exists in page proofs, folder 260, SL).

56. "Gilman in Praise of Beautiful Man," *New York Evening Sun* (9 March 1905), folder 287, SL; "Light on Socialism" *New York Times* (23 January 1909) sec. 8: 1; "Famous Woman to Lecture," *San Francisco Bulletin* (17 July 1905), folder 287, SL.

57. The debate on "The Future of the Home" appeared in the *Independent* (4 October 1906): 788–98, with Charlotte weighing in on "Home Worship," Mrs. L. H. Harris deeming Charlotte's views "Monstrous Altruism," and Charlotte responding to Harris by asking "Why 'Monstrous?'" In a subsequent issue, the *Independent* offered "A Father's View of the Home" (18 October 1906): 911–14, from which the "rubber gloves" quotation comes. The debate was also covered in the *New York Tribune*, the *Boston Herald*, and *Harper's Weekly* 50 (27 October 1906): 1522–23, from which the quoted assessment derives; the friend is Black, "The Woman," 34.

58. Charlotte calls Shaw "formidable" in CPG to SBC, 1 February 1896, Cornell; for an earlier debate, see CPG "Should Wives Work?" *Success* 5 (September 1902): 501–02, and Effie S. Black, "Should Wives Work?" *Success* 5 (November 1902): 686–87; for coverage of the 1909 debate, see Nixola Greeley-Smith, "Husbands Do Not Support Wives: Wives Themselves Decide Question," (7 January 1909), clipping, folder 286, SL; "Woman Is Man's Horse, Declares Mrs. Gilman," clipping, folder 286, SL; Ellen DuBois, *Woman Suffrage*, 194; Cott, 189; and Kraditor, *Ideas*, 120–21.

59. CPG to LFW, 2 January 1907, Brown.

60. "The Woman of Fifty," *Success* (October 1908): 622–23.

61. Her projections for the next twenty-five years are from "Thoughts & Figgerings," 7 November 1908, folder 16, SL; "Lifters" from "Thoughts & Figgerings," January 1908, folder 16, SL; CPG to KSC, 22 September 1930, SL.

CHAPTER ELEVEN

1. "There Are Those Who Can See," *LP*, 107–08.

2. Pamphlet, Mary Ware Dennet papers, MC 392/M-138, SL; "Does a Man Support His Wife?" *FR* 2 (September 1911): 240–46. Charlotte and Houghton's publishing company, Charlton, did publish a pamphlet version of the 1911 debate with both sides represented.

3. "longing to . . ." from Seitler, 82; see also Kessler, *Daring to Dream*.

4. Gale, foreword to *L*, xxxii, and see Conlin, vol. 2, 433; "How to Argue," [ca. 1915], folder 15, SL; "Our Place Today," lecture, 21 January 1891, folder 164, SL.

5. "Comment and Review," *FR* 1 (February 1910): 24.

6. CPS to GHG, 2 April 1899, folder 68, SL.

7. Folder 16, SL, and see Kessler, *Daring to Dream*, 34.

8. CPG to Mabel Hay Barrow, 23 March 1909, Barrow family papers, bMS Am 1807.2 (195), Houghton; CPG to Caroline Severance, 6 April 1909, Huntington.

9. CWS to KBS, 16 September 1909, WSCC; "entirely . . ." from *L*, 304; full-page advertisement, *FR* 7 (February 1916): back cover.

10. "The Illustrator and the Story," *Denver Republican*, clipping, folder 313, SL; the fan quoted is Middleton, 128; "From Letters to Subscribers," *FR* 1 (September 1910): 27–29.

11. *L*, 304–05.

12. *L*, 304; "Thoughts & Figgerings," 28 June 1908, folder 16, SL.

13. On Dreiser, see *L*, 304, and Theodore Dreiser to CPG, 17 October 1908, folder 126, SL (Dreiser offered her $40 for an article); "in the public eye" from "Literature as an Expression of Man's Views," 1909, folder 287, SL; see correspondence with publishers, folder 126, SL.

14. "As to Purpose," *FR* 1 (November 1909): 32; *Daily Palo Alto Times* (2 December 1909), clipping, folder 313, SL; *Lounger* (February 1913), clipping, folder 313, SL.

15. " . . . heaven forefend . . . " from (Chicago) *Unity* (11 November 1909), clipping, folder 313, SL; on the *Masses* and the *Liberator*, see O'Neill, *Divorce*, 200–01, and Sochen, *The New*, 73; on the other women's magazines, see Doyle, 140ff. The weekly *Woman's Journal* was also still valiantly afloat despite Blackwell's failing health, criticism from its board, and "very little help & no pay" (ASB to CPG, 12 April 1912, folder 141); by 1917, it had joined with two other journals to form the *Woman Citizen*.

16. "Comment and Review," *FR* 3 (January 1912): 27; Spacks, 216.

17. *L*, 305; "to beat. . . . the band!" from CPG to Isabel Chapin Barrow, 10 January 1910, Barrow family papers, bMS Am 1807.1 (208), Houghton; for her advertising strategies, see *FR* 1 (January 1910): 32, and back cover.

18. *L*, 305, and see "Our Distributing Centres: THE FORERUNNER," *FR* 7 (June 1916): inside back cover.

19. AP identifies CPG as the inventor of the *FR* in her letter to *Daily Palo Alto Times*, clipping, folder 313, SL; on her incentives, see "The Editor's Problem," *FR* 1 (September 1910): 26, "Our Standing Offers," *FR* 6 (October 1915): back cover, and advertisements, *FR* 6 (October 1915): n.p.; snippets from "To Those Specially Interested in This Magazine, or Specially Interested in Fifty Dollars," *FR* 1 (October 1910): 29.

20. "From Letters to Subscribers," *FR* 1 (September 1910): 27–29.

21. "Some of the Reasons Why I Publish the Forerunner," *FR* 5 (December 1914): 28.

22. "Educated Bodies," *WJ* (4 June 1904): 178; reprinted in *FR* 5 (April 1914): 94–95.

23. "To Those Specially Interested in This Magazine, or Specially Interested in Fifty Dollars," *FR* 1 (November 1910): 29.

24. "Then This," *FR* 1 (November 1909): 1.

25. "As to Purpose," *FR* 1 (November 1909): 32; on women's magazines, see "Coming Changes in Literature," *FR* 6 (September 1915): 235; see also Cane, 95, and Cranny-Francis, 174ff.

26. "For 1911," *FR* 1 (January 1910): 28; "A Small God and a Large Goddess," *FR* 1 (November 1909): 1–4.

27. Clipping from *Social Progress*, 24 October, WSCC, and on the congress, see CPG's "The Woman Suffrage Congress in Budapest," *FR* 4 (August 1913): 204–06; invitation to the International Woman Suffrage Alliance in Budapest, 20 July 1912, folder 152, SL.

28. "A Sea Voyage," *FR* 5 (June 1914): 149–50; folder 8, SL; "immense favorite" from Joseph O'Brien, "The Woman's Congress," *Colliers National Weekly* (1913): 7–9, oversize folder 3, SL; her comments on the similarity of people are from "The Woman Suffrage Congress in Buda-Pest," *FR* 4 (August 1913): 205; "Comment and Review," *FR* 4 (June 1913): 165.

29. Praise for homogeneity from "From Letters of Subscribers," *FR* 1 (November 1910): 28; Austin, 326; in "Baulked; or, Ways a Little Harder," *FR* 3 (June 1912): 141–45, Charlotte subtly offers this defense by claiming that the story "does not bear a suspicious resemblance to anything, unless to those previously appearing in this magazine" (141).

30. Charles Lummis to Mrs. Charlotte Perkins Stetson Gilman, 27 November 1910, Southwest Museum (thanks to Jennifer Tuttle for the copy of this letter); Black, *Time*, 283.

31. On Austin, see *L*, 285, and see also Graulich; the parody is "Without Bo(a)rders" ("Joke, for a Husband, Jan. 8, 1922"), folder 125, SL; Charlotte recorded Austin's assessment in DKD II, 21 August 1921, 836; Black, *Time*, 283.

32. On Browning's influence, see Heilman, 176; "Charlotte P. Stetson," *San Francisco Call* (28 May 1893) sec. 7: 6; *Minneapolis Journal* (17 November 1899), scrapbook, oversize vol. 7, SL.

33. "Summary of Purpose," *FR* 7 (November 1916): 286–90; "The World and Three Artists," *FR* 1 (October 1910): 8–9.

34. On the Armory Show, see Wertheim; "morasses . . . intimacy" from "Artist, Illustrator and Cartoonist," *FR* 7 (October 1916): 272; Eliot, "Tradition and the Individual Talent," *Sacred Wood* (1920), 192.

35. On artists' "social service," see *HW*, 263, 266; "that the Great Service . . ." from "Comment and Review," *FR* 4 (April 1913): 111–12; for more on her aversion to modernist tenets, see DKD II, 17 April 1894, 583, and Heilman, 176–77.

36. "A Mischievous Rudiment," *FR* 3 (January 1912): 1–5; on Allen's plea, see Higham, "Reorientation," 82–83; "Our Androcentric Culture," *FR* 1 (March 1910): 22; see also "Literature an Expression of Man's Views," 1909 clipping from New Jersey paper, folder 287, SL.

37. "Say It Again," *FR* 5 (February 1914): 44.

38. Advertisement, *FR* 6 (December 1915): n.p.; "originality . . ." from Pond lecture flyer; *New York Times* (26 February 1911), folder 305, SL; for additional praise, see also *Independent* (13 April 1911): 793, and "Things Worth While in the Realm of Books," (14 May 1911), clipping, folder 309, SL.

39. For men's share of the blame, see MMW and "Charlotte Perkins Gilman Puts Man on the Grill," *New York Times* (15 January 1911) sec. 14: 1; the 1916 *FR* treatise *Growth and Combat* also rehearses this male–female division, and as early as 1907, in "Is Cupid a Convention?" Charlotte argues, "The men fought and made love; the women were things to be fought for and made love to" ("Is Cupid a Convention?" *Independent* [15 August 1907]: 374); finally, see also CPG to LFW, 26 January 1908, Brown, and T. D. A. Cockerell, review of *The Man-Made World, or Our Andocentric Culture, Dial* (16 June 1911): 471–72, which acknowledges her debt to Ward.

40. *Our Androcentric Culture, FR* (1 November 1909): 22; *FR* 1 (December 1909): 22; and *FR* 1 (December 1910): 24.

41. *Los Angeles Herald* (14 May 1911), folder 309, SL; Beer, introduction to *Kate*, 19; for Charlotte's views on her own literary output see *L*, 306 and 98.

42. Advertisement, *FR* 1 (October 1910): back cover.

43. *What Diantha Did*, *FR* 1 (November 1909–December 1910), and see Rambo, 152; Charlotte first mentioned her desire to write "good villain" stories in a letter to Houghton (10 November 1899, folder 76, SL). Mrs. Benigna Macavelly (the spelling evolved over time) appears in "A Coincidence," *FR* 1 (July 1910) and surfaces again in three 1912 *Forerunner* stories, "Mrs. Elder's Idea," "An Innocent Girl," and "Maidstone Comfort." She also plays the meddling neighbor in the 1913 *FR* novel *Won Over*; "a happier life . . . " from *What Diantha Did* (New York: Charlton, 1910), 2; for the definitive treatment of Charlotte's utopianism, see Kessler, *Charlotte*. As Kessler speculates (73), *Won Over* may be based on Charlotte's 1909 unpublished play, *Interrupted*, just as *Mag-Marjorie* appears to be based on her unpublished 1910 play, *The Balsam Fir*.

44. Nietzsche, 4–5; Wilson, 271–92.

45. On her "evolutionary paradigm," see Hausman, 492; "The Rabbit, the Rhinoceros & I," *FR* 3 (March 1912): 83; see also her debate with the fatalist, described in *L*, 137, and see *Home*, 59.

46. Wilcox's "Will" is cited in Howe, "Charlotte—As I Knew Her," 214; Black, *Time*, 285.

47. The proponent is Charles Davenport, qtd. in Mark Haller, 3; Charlotte's discomfort is expressed in "Prize Children," *FR* 1 (May 1910): 10, and see also "Killing the Failures," *Buffalo Evening News* (13 June 1919) sec. 7: 1–4. As early as 1904, however, a reviewer proclaimed that the "'New Science' of Eugenics Has an Apostle in Mrs. Charlotte Perkins Gilman" and called *Human Work* "A Plea for the Elevation of the Race en Masse—The Already Elevated Should Not Wait, but Should Assume the Lifting Power of the Social Spirit." "News of the Book World" (review of *HW*, Minneapolis paper 28 July 1904, clipping, folder 304, SL); "Race Improvement," *Independent* 66 (25 March 1909): 629–32.

48. "The Sanctity of Human Life," *FR* 7 (May 1916): 128–29.

49. Black, *Time*, 284; on politics and eugenicists' faith in science, see Mark Haller, 17, 61–63, and Hofstadter, *Social*, 161–62.

50. On Mendel and Galton, see Mark Haller, 58–60, and Higham, *Strangers*, 150–52; Wells quoted in Jim Holt, "Measure for Measure: The Strange Science of Francis Galton," *New Yorker* (24 and 31 January 2005): 84–90, quote from 90.

51. On Indiana, see McGerr, 214; on the first office and the colleges, see Mark Haller, 58, 72; on nativism, see Painter, 309; on Strong, e.g., see Gere, 57.

52. On the magazines, see Chesler, 519n19; on the *Literary Digest*, see Higham, *Strangers*, 198; on state measures, see Hofstadter, *Social*, 162; Mark Haller, 58; on eugenics as a fad, see Hofstadter, *Social*, 161.

53. On supporters and dissenters, see Hofstadter, *Social*, 166, Bannister, 165, Rosenberg, 129, and Mark Haller, 144–45, and for Wald's views, see her *Windows*; on the broad tent, see Mark Haller, 85; "great slums . . . " from Hofstadter, *Social*, 162. For a detailed analysis of Charlotte's critique of prostitution and her efforts to eradicate it, see Judith A. Allen, "Reconfiguring Vice."

54. On female reformers, see Chesler, 122; Hofstadter, *Social*, 167, 169; "What May We Expect of Eugenics," *Physical Culture* 31 (March 1914): 219.

55. "a new ethic . . . " from Mark Haller, 10; "What May We Expect of Eugenics," *Physical Culture* 31 (March 1914): 221.

56. Advertisement for *The Crux*, *FR* 6 (December 1915): back cover; on women going West, see her "The Duty of Surplus Women," *Independent* 59 (19 January 1905): 126, 129; for readings of *The Crux* along these lines, see Seitler, and Tuttle's "Gilman's *The Crux*."

57. *Man-Made World*, 69.

58. *The Crux*, *FR* 2 (September 1911): 239; on reading Ibsen, see DKD II, 18 March 1893, 521, and for CPG's library, see Scharnhorst and Knight, 197.

59. *The Crux*, FR 2 (September 1911): 238–39; on the social purity movement, see Nathan Hale, 252, and Connelly, who contends that 60 percent of all adult American males contracted either of these diseases at some point in their lives (201–02). Charlotte cites the statistic as well in a cautionary letter to her daughter: CPG to KSC, 16 November 1923, folder 94, SL.

60. "international . . . stock" from Judith A. Allen, "Reconfiguring Vice," 191; for her applause, see "Comment and Review," *FR* 1 (April 1910): 22–23, and see "Comment and Review," *FR* 2 (January 1911): 25–27 for her favorable comments on Morrow's *Social Diseases and Marriage*; on the movement, see Simmons, 160.

61. *FR* 6 (December 915): back cover; on the "medical secret," see Connelly, 202; the October 1916 issue of the *Forerunner* is exemplary in this respect for containing both "The Vintage" and a promotion for the American Social Hygiene Association (*FR* 7 [October 1916]: 253ff); *The Crux*, *FR* 2 (October 1911): 268.

62. *Moving the Mountain*, *FR* 2 (June 1911): 165; for "Baby Utopia," see *FR* 6 (October 1915): n.p., and see as well "A Baby Utopia," *New York Times* (4 February 1912) sec. 52: 3, which also contains the "a short-distance . . . grow" quotation; "women woke . . ." from *Moving the Mountain*, *FR* 2 (April 1911): 109; *Moving the Mountain*, *FR* 2 (November 1911): 304.

63. *Moving the Mountain*, *FR* 2 (July 1911): 194; "A Baby Utopia," *New York Times* (4 February 1912) sec. 52: 3; on New York's population, see Menand, 381.

64. On Tennyson, see CAP to ML, 13 August 1881, RIHS, and see Gilbert and Gubar, *No Man's*, 72; on searching for her "Sullivan," see CPG to Witter Bynner, 10 May 1911, Witter Bynner papers, bMS Am 1891.28 (188), Houghton; "think marks" from "From Letters of Subscribers," *FR* 1 (September 1910): 29.

65. *Herland*, *FR* 6 (January 1915): 12; *Herland*, *FR* 6 (July 1915): 185; "Comment and Review: As to Parthenogenesis and Humanity," *FR* 7 (March 1916): 83.

66. On Bierce, see Oliver and Scharnhorst, 58; on Weismann, see Pittenger, 83–84; *Herland*, *FR* 5 (May 1915): 128; *Herland*, *FR* 6 (August 1915): 209.

67. *Herland*, *FR* 6 (June 1915), 153–55, and see *Herland*, *FR* 6 (July 1915): 184.

68. "Bisexual" here means neither our present-day understanding of someone who is attracted to both males and females, nor the sense George Chauncey identifies as prevalent in turn-of-the-century New York of a person considered simultaneously "both male and female," an intermediate sex. Instead, Charlotte means a world consisting of both

men and women, as opposed to a land of only Hers. See Chauncey, 49; "Crown . . ." and "*unmotherliness*" from *With Her in Ourland, FR* 7 (May 1916): 126; Ellador vows to die childless in *With Her in Ourland, FR* 7 (December 1916): 319, 321.

69. On the racial politics of *With Her in Ourland*, see Weinbaum, 295, and see also Long, 171–93; *With Her in Ourland, FR* 7 (July 1916): 184.

70. CPS to GHG, 5 February 1899, folder 64, SL.

71. "Personal Problems," *FR* 1 (June 1910): 25, and *FR* 1 (September 1910): 25.

72. *L*, 74; see also "The Woman of Fifty," *FR* 2 (April 1911): 97.

73. "Thoughts & Figgerings," January 1908, folder 16, SL; "Two Rooms and a Bath," ca. 1915, folder 15, SL.

74. On her forsaken vacation, see CPG to Mabel Hay Barrow, 23 March 1909, Barrow family papers, bMS Am 1807.2 (195), Houghton; her visit to Katharine is described in KSC, "Autobiography," WSCC; on Duncan, see "To Isadora Duncan," typescript, folder 186, SL; "The Dancing of Isadora Duncan," *FR* 6 (April 1915): 100; and on Gilman and Duncan, see Scharnhorst, "Reconstructing *Here Also*," 261–62; KSC discusses the frieze in an undated note in WSCC.

75. "a sulky" from CPG to Isabel Chapin Barrow, 10 January 1910, Barrow family papers, bMS Am 1807.1 (208), Houghton; CPG to KBS, 5 August 1913, folder 9, addenda to CPG papers, 83-M201, SL; on their isolation, see DKD II, January 1916, 834, and DKD II, "Notes: To Do This Year" [1914], 833.

76. "Good Cheer" and other poems in the series "River Windows" are in *LP*, 142–44; CPG to KSC, 23 September 1911, WSCC.

77. On Walter's death, see *L*, 295–96, KSC, "Autobiography," WSCC, and Eldredge, 103; CPG to GECS, 21 July 1911, mf-6, SL; CPG to KSC, 23 September 1911, WSCC; GECS to Dr. E. B. Knight, 6 May 1912, qtd. in *E*, xli.

78. *L*, 296.

79. CPG to Mary Austin, 28 December 1914, Huntington; DKD II, "Notes: To Do This Year" [1914], 833; on the legacy, see two letters from Tillinghast & Collins, Edward P. Jastram, 28 July and 11 August 1915, folder 115, SL.

80. CPG to Isabel Chapin Barrow, 10 January 1910, Barrow family papers, bMS Am 1807.1 (208), Houghton; "these lecture . . ." from CPG to EAR, 6 April 1915, Wisconsin; CPG to Mrs. Peet, October 1911, Huntington.

81. Praise from *Reedy's Magazine* (14 September 1913), folder 266, SL, and complaint from "A Suffragist," letter to CPG, 4 August 1914, folder 141, SL; Franklin in Sydney (Australia) *Stock-Station Journal* (6 December 1912), folder 266, SL; "Noted Lecturer Is Exponent of Wider Feminist Movement," *Oregon Sunday Journal* (28 March 1915), vol. 7, SL.

82. Ceplair, 192; on the emergence of the term *feminism*, see Cott, 3–5.

83. "Mrs. Gilman's Scorn Strikes 'Masculism'," *New York Times* (2 April 1914) sec. 11: 1; see also the paper's coverage of the series from 14 February through 9 April 1914; on her manager and revenue, see William B. Feakins to CPG, 4 June and 15 October 1914, folder 140, SL.

84. Middleton, 128; "As to Home Cooking: Mr. Finck Takes Mrs. Gilman to Task for her Aspersions," *New York Times* (16 March 1914) sec. 8: 4; Clara (Savage) Littledale

papers, diary entries for 4 March 1914 and 1 and 8 April 1914, 1903–56, A-157, SL. Clara Savage married Harold Aylmer Littledale in 1920 and took his surname. She became the first editor of *Parents' Magazine*.

85. Middleton, 128; for an example of the antagonistic dialogue between the paper and Charlotte, see the *New York Times* editorial (7 February 1915), to which CPG responded twice with letters to the editor; "Mrs. Gilman Asks Evidence" (VIII 1: 7) and "Mrs. Gilman Speaks Again" (VIII 5: 8), both in *New York Times* (14 February 1915); for the paper's anti-suffrage argument, see "General Defenses of Woman Suffrage" in Kraditor, *Up*, 218; "Most Famous . . . " from "What Is 'Feminism'," *Boston Sunday Herald* (3 September 1916), oversize folder 1, SL.

86. For the spoof of fast women, see "Proofs for the Suffragists," *New York Times* (27 March 1914) sec. 10: 3, and see Charlotte's response, "Mrs. Gilman Calls Science to Witness," *New York Times* (9 April 1914) sec. 10: 8.

87. "End of Romance" from "Even Barbers Rebel at Shearing Women," *New York Times* (16 March 1916) sec. 13: 3; on Rodman see Hayden, *Grand*, 200–01 and 333n47, and also Sochen, *The New*, 50–52. A schoolteacher herself, Rodman was deeply embroiled in the mid-teens in the controversy over allowing mothers to teach in New York City schools, a controversy Charlotte followed closely; "monstrous . . . " from *New York Times* (24 Jan 1915) sec. 5: 9.

88. On Sedgwick see *New York Times* (15 February 1914); see also Bederman, 160–62, and CPG, "Biological Anti-Feminism," *FR* 5 (March 1914): 64–67; on Sargent, see *New York Times* (28 November 1910), clipping, WSCC, and see CPG, "A Modern Woman on the Modern Girl," *Pictorial Review* (October 1911): 10, oversize folder 1, SL; on Wright, see her "Comment and Review: The Unexpurgated Case of Sir Almoth Wright," *FR* 4 (November 1913): 303–08, and her "Sir Almoth Wright's Diagnosis" and "Ultra-Male" (poems), *FR* 3 (June 1912): 153; ironically, Charlotte had used Sargent's models of male and female bodies, displayed at the 1893 Chicago World's Fair, to illustrate her own points about the warping effects of domesticity on the domesticated.

89. Tarbell's critique of Gilman (whom she identifies only as "one of the popular leaders in the Woman's movement") appears in *The Business*, 222ff (both Tarbell quotes from 222); CPG, "Making a Man of Herself," *The Woman Voter* 3 (June 1912): 8–9. Several responses to Tarbell are included in this issue of *The Woman Voter* under the heading "Ida Tarbell Answered."

90. "Comment and Review," *FR* 3 (March 1912): 84; see also "Miss Tarbell's 'Uneasy Woman'," *FR* 3 (February 1912): 37–39 and "Comment and Review," *FR* 1 (August 1910): 24–25; the dialogue between Conger-Kaneko and CPG is covered by Conger-Kaneko in her "The Progressive Woman Off the Track," *Progressive Woman* (1912): 11–12, folder 313, SL.

91. When Charlotte was in Europe in 1904 and 1905, she "was told that Ellen Key considered my work as in strong antithesis to hers." "On Ellen Key and the Woman Movement," *FR* 4 (February 1913): 35; Walling, 325, and see also "Charlotte Gilman's Reply to Ellen Key," *Current Opinion* 54 (March 1913): 220–21.

92. For Key's views, see her *Century*, 93, 88f, 201, 233–34, and her *Renaissance*, 115, and see also Cott, 48–49.

93. Key, *Century*, 58; Key, "Education," 50; also see Buhle, *Feminism*, 39.

94. For CPG's distinction between the two feminisms, see "On Ellen Key and the Woman Movement," *FR* 4 (February 1913): 36, and "Social Ethics," *FR* 5 (March 1914): 76–82; see also "Ellen Key's Attack on 'Amaternal' Feminism," *Current Opinion* 54 (February 1913): 138–39, and "The Conflict Between 'Human' and 'Female' Feminism," *Current Opinion* (April 1914): 56; CPG reviews *The Century* in "The New Motherhood," *FR* 1 (December 1910): 18; she reviews *Love and Marriage* in "Comment and Review," *FR* 2 (October 1911): 280–82.

95. "On Ellen Key and the Woman Movement," *FR* 4 (February 1913): 35; CPG offers her critique of Key's individualism in "Comment and Review: *The New Motherhood*," *FR* 1 (December 1910): 17–18, and "Comment and Review," *FR* 2 (October 1911): 282; Key, *Century*, 63, 75–76, 88.

96. "On Ellen Key and the Woman Movement," *FR* 4 (February 1913): 35–38, quote from 37; on reading Key versus Gilman, see Rheta Childe Dorr, qtd. in Cott, 46; "Talmud" from Dell, 83; Key cites Nietzsche in, e.g., *Renaissance*, 111; and on Key's status in the States, see Buhle, *Feminism*, 41–42.

97. Gleason, 40; the Croly quote is the title of his 1909 book; Lippmann, 222–23.

98. "Our Humanness," *FR* 4 (January 1913): 24; for Charlotte's view of European decadence, see Judith A. Allen, "Debating," 7; CPG's parting comments are from "A Summary of Purpose," *FR* 7 (November 1916): 287; on (im)moral feminism, see also her "Feminism," (typescript of essay for Bliss and Binder's *Encyclopedia of Social Reform*), folder 175, SL.

99. "Giving," *FR* 2 (December 1911): 317.

100. *L*, 308, 310.

101. "To My Real Readers," *FR* 7 (December 1916): 326; *L*, 307.

102. "Announcement," *FR* 7 (June 1916): n.p.

103. "A Summary of Purpose," *FR* 7 (November 1916): 287.

104. Letters from readers, folder 142, SL; "The Forerunner: The End of a Great Paper," *Sydney Stock-Station Journal* (16 March 1917), folder 313, SL; she discusses her publishing plans in "To My Real Readers," *FR* 7 (December 1916): 326; "Gilman's Works," *FR* 7 (February 1916): back cover.

105. "A Summary of Purpose," *FR* 7 (November 1916): 290; on pain and social consciousness, see *HW*, 130–31, 187.

CHAPTER TWELVE

1. "Begin Again," *FR* 4 (January 1913): 27. She also uses the phrase "begin again" in her essay "A World Beginning," *FR* 6 (January 1915): 26, vis-à-vis her changing stance on the war and the world.

2. "monogamous" from CPG to Mr. Vance (of the *Pictorial Review*), 19 March 1919, folder 132, SL; "Sex O'Clock in America," *Current Opinion* (55 August 1913): 113–15; on the emergence of the new bohemianism, see Stansell; on primitivism and "middle class formulations of male dominance," see Bederman, 160–61, 168, 169; Harry Thurston Peck, 405.

3. *L*, 318–19.

4. "age of sheer . . . " from 1914 social Gospel announcement, qtd. in McGerr, 224; Daniel Bell, 134; the reformer is Shailer Mathews, qtd. in O'Neill, *The Woman Movement*, 260; Addams, *Second Twenty*, 192.

5. For the various monikers, see Muncy, xi–xv, Brown, 1, Weinberg, 163–64, and Higham, *Strangers*, 268ff; "marked retreat . . . " from Hofstadter, *Age*, 286.

6. CPG to Harold Channing, 28 December 1916, folder 12, addenda to CPG papers, 83-M201, SL, and on the importance of playing versus winning the game, see also *Humanness*, *FR* 4 (December 1913): 330; "The Socialist and the Suffragist" (poem), *FR* 1 (October 1910): 25.

7. "Killing the Failures," *Buffalo Evening News* (13 June 1919) sec. 7: 1, 4. The quote continues: "The better fitted a person is to serve society . . . the less fit he usually is to struggle with other people and get ahead of them."

8. "more complex" from "The Passing of the Home in Great American Cities," *Cosmopolitan* 38 (December 1904): 137–47, quote from 146–47; "no fool" from "Vanguard, Rear-Guard, and Mud-Guard," *Century* (July 1922): 350.

9. DKD II, appendix A, "Thoughts & Figgerings," 3 July 1920, "Sixty years old," 851.

10. "Thoughts & Figgerings," 23 July 1917, folder 16, SL.

11. CPG to Anne Martin, 14 May 1918, BANC MSS P-G 282, Anne Henrietta Martin papers, Bancroft.

12. "better than nothing" from CPG to EAR, 10 June 1918, Wisconsin; "war work" from CPG to Anne Martin, 5 August 1919, BANC MSS P-G 282, Anne Henrietta Martin papers, Bancroft; her fraction comes from CPG to Anne Martin, 29 March 1918, BANC MSS P-G 282, Anne Henrietta Martin papers, Bancroft; "obliterated" from CPG to KSC, 20 April 1921, folder 92, SL; blurbs quoted in CPG to Mrs. Roantree, 15 September 1920, folder 152, SL.

13. CPG transcribes the *Evening Mail* quotation in her letter to Mrs. Roantree, 15 September 1920, folder 152, SL; she tells Katharine about the *Tribune's* and other tributes in her letter to KSC, 5 July 1922, folder 93, SL; she describes the tour and Revue in *L*, 310–11.

14. CPG to Anne Martin, 22 March 1919, BANC MSS P-G 282, Anne Henrietta Martin papers, Bancroft; CPG to Mr. Vance, 19 March 1919, folder 132, SL; *L*, 310.

15. Reporter qtd. in CPG to Mrs. Roantree, 15 September 1920, folder 152, SL; Charlotte considered Alexander Black's "The Woman Who Saw It First" a "lovely" tribute, done "beautifully," and called Amy Wellington's book chapter on her (in *Women Have Told*, 115–31) a "rounded" portrait "illuminated by the light of hero worship" (qtd. in *New York Times Book Review* [23 March 1930], clipping, WSCC). The frail Wellington, a poet and an editor at *Current Opinion*, had demonstrated her "pure love and discipleship" to Charlotte ever since the *W&E* days. On Wellington's health, see DKD II, 9, 15, 17, 19, 20, and 22 July 1922, 837; on her status as Charlotte's "little adorer," see CPS to GHG, 29 September and 1, 3, and 12 October 1899, folders 73 and 74, SL.

16. "Thoughts & Figgerings," 3 July 1920, "Sixty years old," folder 17, SL; "have . . . across!!" from "Thoughts & Figgerings," 2 April 1920, folder 17, SL.

17. See DKD II, 21 July 1921, 835; she promised one editor (CPG to Mr. Holt, 15 May

1921, folder 152, SL) that if he "really want[ed her] stuff there is plenty of it, easily ready"; she complains about her lower rate and inability to sell herself in CPG to Mr. Vance, 19 March 1919, folder 132, SL; for an example of her financial self-reprimands, see "Thoughts & Figgerings," 23 July 1917, folder 16, SL.

18. On the check and paying off her debt, see CPG to KSC, 23 February 1920, SL, and see "Thoughts & Figgerings," 3 July 1920, 60th Birthday, folder 17, SL; on playwriting, see CPG to GECS, 11 August 1920, mf-6, SL, and see CPG to KSC, 9 May 1921, folder 92, SL.

19. For her optimistic financial projections, see "Thoughts & Figgerings," 3 July 1920, 60th birthday, folder 17, SL, and see CPG to GECS, 11 August 1920, mf-6, SL; "number of scenarios" from CPG to Jason Joy, 30 September 1925, folder 144, SL, and see also CPG to Mr. Frederic Palmer, 22 January 1921, folder 143, SL; for her thoughts on films, see her "The Beauty of the Earth," *Buffalo Evening News* (29 August 1919) sec. 7: 2–4, and "Movies and the Mind," *Buffalo Evening News* (14 August 1919) sec. 7: 1–3; for movie attendance figures, see Cott, 147.

20. See WDH to CPG, 7 October 1919, folder 120, SL; CPG to WDH, 17 October 1919, WDH papers, bMS Am 1784 (178), Houghton; *New York Times* editorial on A. L. Priest's rewriting "Similar Cases" as a poem he called "Ancient History," (9 October 1919), folder 153, SL; clippings of poem and her letter to *New York Times* (8 October 1919), folder 310, SL.

21. "making a set" from CPG to Marshall, Jones & Co., 1 December 1920, folder 152, SL; on her plans for the two volumes of verse, see "In stock," typescript, folder 20, SL; the posthumous volume is *LP*.

22. "Do Women Dress to Please Men?" *Century* 103 (March 1922): 651–55; see also *The Dress of Women, FR* 6 (January 1915): 20. Charlotte received $150 for the article, which she discusses in CPG to KSC, 15 October 1921, folder 92, SL; review, *New York Times Book Review* (26 February 1922) sec. 3: 9.

23. GECS to KSC, 6 March 1929, folder 129, GECSP, SL; she recounts the objections in *L*, 319; for her views on women's fashion, e.g., see her *The Dress of Women, FR* 6 (January 1915): 20, and "Fashion Beauty and Brains," *Outlook and Independent* 7 (August 1929): 578–79.

24. *With Her in Ourland, FR* 7 (March 1916): 69.

25. CPG to LFW, 1 June 1908, Brown; for her status in the peace movement, see Degen, 25; CPG's speech and *New York Times* coverage (5 February 1915) both qtd. in Walsh, 363–64.

26. "unbridled masculinity" from "Masculism at Its Worst," *FR* 5 (October 1914): 257–58; "its absurdist extremes" from *Our Androcentric Culture, FR* 1 (October 1910): 21; "A World Beginning," *FR* 6 (January 1915): 26; see also Conway, "The Woman's Peace Party," and Hobbs.

27. "Opposed to Militarism," *New York Times* (18 December 1914) sec. 15: 1; Lillian Wald quotes the *New York Herald* (30 August 1914) coverage of the parade in *Windows*, 286; "Good for the Women," letter to editor dated 26 August 1914, *New York Times* (28 August 1914) sec. 8: 5.

28. For her lectures, see "Advocates a 'World City,'" *New York Times* (6 January 1915)

sec. 15: 5, "Split on War and Votes," *New York Times* (20 February 1915) sec. 7: 3, and "Women Ridicule Security League," *New York Times* (16 June 1915) sec. 4: 6; on her invitation, see DKD II, 27 November 1915, 834; Ford, qtd. in Degen, 134.

29. On the ridicule and Addams, see Carson, 155, and O'Neill, *Everyone*, 169; "Comment and Review: The Ford Peace Expedition," *FR* 7 (January 1916): 26–27, and see also "The Ford Party and the Newspapers," *FR* 7 (March 1916): 73–76.

30. "a pacifist . . . " from "A Word with the Pacifists on How to End This War," *Philadelphia Public Ledger* (18 July 1916) sec. 10: 6–7; "The World Conference We Need," *FR* 7 (September 1916): 232–34; on the November meeting, see Maida Herman Solomon papers, folders 296 and 299, MC 418, SL.

31. On America's role, see "A Question of the Government?" *FR* 7 (January 1916): 4–5; and see "Why? To the United States of America 1915–1916," *FR* 7 (January 1916): 4–5; *Growth and Combat*, *FR* 7 (November 1916): 305.

32. On hating the Kaiser, see Buhle, *Women*, 312; Higham, *Strangers*, 208.

33. "swat . . . culture" from "Studies in Social Pathology," *FR* 7 (May 1916): 120; "Comment and Review," *FR* 6 (August 1915): 223.

34. "Constructive Patriotism," lecture flyer attached to CPG to EAR, 10 June 1918, Wisconsin; CPG to Harold Channing, 28 December 1916, folder 12, 83-M201, SL.

35. On the rationale for America's entrance, see O'Neill, *Everyone*, 183–84; for CPG's view that war might be necessary to peace, see "Comment and Review," *FR* 2 (September 1911): 253; CPG to Mrs. Karsten, 28 August 1917, in DKJT.

36. On suffragists, see Tax, 199, and Cott, 93–94; Dewey qtd. in McGerr, 282; Grosvenor Clarkson qtd. in McGerr, 299.

37. On the war's effect on her career, see CPG to Mrs. McIntyre, 20 November 1917, Colby; McGerr, 308; information on the suppression of dissent and the Red Scare is derived from Brown, 5 and 19, Painter, 379, and Cott, 63.

38. *The Confessions of a Reformer*, 278–79.

39. On New York, see Painter, 379, O'Neill, *The Woman Movement*, 186, and Daniel Bell, 104–05; on the Socialist Party, see Buhle, *Women*, 312.

40. On the *Masses*, see Leach, 27–47; on the Lusk Report, see Van Voris, 190; on Villard, see Sochen, *The New*, 113.

41. 21 and 23 December 1923 entries in Federal Bureau of Investigation file, Charlotte Gilman. Obtained under the Freedom of Information Act. In this same file, she also shows up on a list of members of "The National Council of the Peoples Legislative Service," an otherwise classified (i.e., all information redacted) and undated report that also contains the names of Zona Gale and Jane Addams, among others; finally, her name appears on a report dated March 3, 1923 in association with the New Youth movement.

42. "A Biographical Sketch of Charlotte Perkins Gilman," folder 243, SL; "Light on Socialism," *New York Times* (23 January 1909) sec. 8: 1–2; on yellow as the color of lukewarm socialists, see Leach, 27; CPG to Mrs. Severance, 25 January 1904, Huntington; she told William English Walling that her brand of socialism (like Bellamy's) proposed "the orderly and gradual socialization of industry in the interest of all classes" (CPG to William English Walling, 28 July 1925, Huntington).

43. DKD II, appendix A, "Thoughts & Figgerings," 9 October 1905, 850; on her socialist activities, see "Housing for the Poor," *New York Evening Post* (18 November 1905): 4, CPG to Mr. Spargo, 23 September 1908, University of Vermont, and "Women's Day in Philadelphia," *Progressive Woman* (April 1911): 16; on CPG and Upton Sinclair, see Goodman, 160ff, and Polly Wynn Allen, 47; DKD II, 27 May 1909, 833.

44. On Houghton's resignation, see KSC to Jeanette Cheek, 8 April 1973, qtd. in Lane, 327; for her socialist contributions, see the two poems, "We as Women" and "To Labor," she contributed to a collection called "The Voices of Labor," pamphlet (Chicago: National Woman's Trade Union League of America, 1919), see also "Three Great Poems," (*Appeal to Reason*, 2nd ed.[Girard, KS], 1922), which includes "To Labor," and, finally, see Ganobcsik-Williams, 33; CPG offers her pointed distinction in "Poverty and Woman," National Conference on Social Welfare—Social Welfare Forum, proceedings, 1917, 10–15.

45. See Blatch and Lutz, 316–17; "Alice Stone Blackwell," *NAW* (vol. 1), 158; "CPG and Her Dreadful 'Views'," *Springfield Homestead* (9 May 1917), folder 294, SL.

46. "Debs and the Poets," by Ruth Le Prade, introduction by Upton Sinclair, flyer enclosed in Ruth Le Prade to CPG, n.d., folder 142, SL; on her feelings for Debs, see CPS to GHG, 24 March 1899, folder 67, SL; the letter she wrote on behalf of Stokes is CPG to the Honorable Thomas W. Gregory, U.S. Attorney General, 9 June 1918, folder 153, SL. The decision in Stokes's case was ultimately reversed in 1920 by an appeals court and the case was dismissed late in 1921.

47. On her anti-Semitism, see, e.g., "Growth and Combat," *FR* 7 (April 1916), 108; on her aversion to German Jews, see her letter to KSC, 14 June 1920, folder 91, SL; on Stokes, see "Historical/Biographical Note," Guide to the Rose Pastor Stokes papers, processed by Dorothy Swanson, (2003 Tamiment Library/Robert F. Wagner Labor Archives. All rights reserved, New York University Libraries, Publisher); CPG still liked Rose's estranged husband James Graham Phelps Stokes; she informed him after her departure from New York that he was "one of the few" she "hated to leave in leaving the dreadful city" (11 January 1923, James Graham Phelps Stokes Collection, Columbia).

48. "the Jewish-Russian" from *L*, 320; "defilement" from CPG to English Walling, 28 July 1925, Huntington; "The 'Russian Experiment,'" *Buffalo Evening News* (9 April 1919) sec. 12: 4–5.

49. See Cott, 247–50, "One Spider-Web" from 250; Lemons, 209–25; O'Neill, *Everyone*, 228–29; Van Voris, 195.

50. For examples of anti-immigrant polemics, see Warne, and see also E. A. Ross and Roy E. Barber, "Slow Suicide Among Our Native Stock," *Century* 107 (February 1924): 504; "tribal twenties" from Higham, *Strangers*, 267; "a phobic . . . " from Brodhead, 134.

51. Her anti-immigrant views are expressed in "U.S. Rushing Toward Ruin Unless Immigration Tide Is Checked, Says Mrs. Gilman," *Morning Sun*, "Lecture 1921" [probably 1922], folder 294, SL, and "What Good Is Freedom," *Buffalo Evening News* (17 May 1919) sec. 7: 6–7; see also "Immigration, Importation, and Our Fathers," *FR* 5 (May 1914): 118–19.

52. EAR, preface to *Old World*, n.p. and 285; "Is America Too Hospitable?" *Forum*

(October 1923): 1983–89; on Grace's involvement in the movement to "Keep Our Country Ours," see GEC[S] "New England," (15 April 1916), clipping, WSCC.

53. Middleton, 128; "Race and color . . ." from *With Her in Ourland*, *FR* 7 (April 1916): 94; Gale, foreword to *L*, xxxi; CPG to Mr. Holt, 16 [15?] May 1921, folder 152, SL.

54. "A World Beginning," *FR* 1 (January 1915): 26; "world conflagration" from *L*, 329; "a crippled . . . before us" from "Constructive Patriotism," lecture flyer enclosed with CPG to EAR, 10 June 1918, Wisconsin, and see also "Worrying about the World," *Buffalo Evening News* (1 August 1919) sec. 5: 3–4.

55. *L*, 329, 317, 284.

56. "she tolerantly . . ." from Gale, foreword to *L*, xxxi; on the postwar shift, see Seelye, 578–79.

57. "to build . . . " from O'Neill, *Everyone*, 225, and see Cott, 250–51, 244–46; "Pikers," *New York Times* (31 October 1920), reprinted in *LP*, 57–58; "We and Honduras," *LP*, 56.

58. "special place . . . " from "Constructive Patriotism," lecture flyer enclosed with CPG to EAR, 10 June 1918, Wisconsin; EAR, *Old World*, 304; "we should . . . " from *L*, 324.

59. On the afterlife of progressivism, see Muncy and see also McGerr, 313; "demand . . ." from Hofstadter, *Age*, 281–82, and see McGerr, 309.

60. CPG to EAR, 21 June 1932, Wisconsin.

61. See Becker, 3; Catt and Shuler, 288–93.

62. Alice Paul to CPG, 2 August 1927, WSCC; on the NWP, see Flexner, 259, Lunardini, 53, Lunardini and Knock, 655–71, and "The National Woman's Party," *FR* 7 (August 1916): 214–15; CPG expresses her support for Wilson over his Republican opponent, Charles Evan Hughes, in "Comment and Review: Some Women Voters," *FR* 7 (December 1916): 334; see also her "Comment and Review," *FR* 7 (December 1916): 336.

63. "The Woman's Party," *FR* 2 (November 1911): 290; on its modernizing strategies, see Lemons, 153, Irwin, 357, and Cott, 53–54.

64. Blatch kept her distance, distrusting Catt's methods and leadership. Blatch, 230ff and 244ff; see "Harriot Stanton Blatch," *NAW* (vol. 1), 172, and see also Van Voris, 117–30; "the cradle" from Mary Gray Peck, 233.

65. On the staged suffrage events, see Ellen DuBois, "Working," 197, Buhle, *Feminism*, 233–34, Flexner, 251–2, and Blatch and Lutz, 190ff and 245ff; Emily H. Bright to KSC, 20 August 1935, WSCC; "million . . . " from Catt and Shuler, 295; Catt's recollections of Independence Day and the block quote are from Catt and Shuler, 287, 288–89.

66. See "Mrs. Gilman Speaks Again," *New York Times* (14 February 1915) sec. 8: 5; "A Rational Position on Suffrage," *New York Times* (7 March 1915) sec. 14: 1; and "Topics of the Times," *New York Times* (9 March 1915) sec. 8: 4.

67. *Suffrage Songs and Verses* (New York: Charlton, 1911); examples of additional songs include "Another Star" and "Let Us Go Free," both in folder 204, SL; "Woman of 1920," *LP*, 58–59; on the post-victory future of the National Woman's Party (NWP), see O'Neill, *Everyone*, 275–78 (the *New York Call*'s July 9, 1920 coverage of Charlotte's speech qtd. on 275), Lemons, 183–84, and Lunardini, 153; Cott, 66–68, 244–45, and Degen, 25; on her ambivalence, see "Do We Want a Political Party for Women?" *FR* 6 (November

1915): 285–86. In 1921, Charlotte resigned from the NWP, objecting to its decision to pursue an equal rights amendment. See also "Woman's Achievements Since the Franchise," *Current History* (October 1927): 7–14, where Charlotte identifies potential adverse consequences of the amendment and maintains "that kind of equality is not desired by all women" (8); Charlotte also opposed the NWP's endorsement of a disarmament resolution and the establishment of a Woman's Committee on World Disarmament, this even though she had originally embraced the disarmament cause as her own.

68. "*summum bonum*" from *L*, 318; on the League and the disappointing 1920 and 1924 elections, see Lemons, 50–51, and see Cott, 86. 97, 102, and 107–08; "the array . . ." from "Mrs. Demos," *Buffalo Evening News* (13 August 1919) sec. 7: 1–3; on Charlotte's hopes for the younger generation, see "A Woman's Party," *Suffragist* 8 (February 1920): 8–9, and on their indifference, see Lunardini, 153.

69. See Howe letter reprinted in Gale, foreword to *L*, xx–xxii; descriptions of Heterodoxy from Schwarz, 9, 17–18, 98.

70. Both "we intend . . . " and "the most . . . " in Cott, 39, and see also Schwarz, 104; Howe on Charlotte's talk, qtd. in Schwarz, 20; "the heresies . . ." from *L*, 313, and see Buhle, *Feminism*, 26, 48, and Buhle, *Women*, 291, 296.

71. Chesler, 97–98; long quotation from Sanger, 108–09; "Call Woman's Paper Obscene," *Evening Mail* (4 April 1914), folder 295, SL.

72. Chesler, 51, 139–40, 209; Margaret Sanger, "No Healthy Race Without Birth Control," *Physical Culture* (March 1921), 147–50; Sanger, "Hotel Commodore Speech," LOC, Margaret Sanger papers, 8 December, 1920, LCMSP 129, 593–95, http://www.nyu.edu/projects/sanger/hotelc.htm. Transcribed by the Margaret Sanger Papers Project, 1999 (accessed July 7, 2003); Charlotte similarly worried about the effects of overpopulation in countries like Germany, Japan, and China and agreed that "This 'pressure of population'" helped to explain "the wholesale brigandage of war" ("Back of Birth Control," *Birth Control Review* [6 March 1922]: 31–33). Both women also opposed abortion.

73. Chesler, 209; on Sanger's sexuality and her views on sexuality, see Kennedy, 134.

74. "Back of Birth Control," *Birth Control Review* (6 March 1922): 31–33, quotation from 31. Subsequent issues contained responses to, and rebuttals of, Charlotte's argument; on the Puritan spirit falling out of favor by the 1920s, see Seelye, 568–70.

75. Nathan Hale, 397–98; Max Eastman, "Exploring the Soul and Healing the Body," *Everybody's Magazine* 32 (June 1915): 741–50; Max Eastman, "Mr.-er-er—Oh! What's his name?" *Everybody's Magazine* 33 (July 1915): 95–103.

76. "filtered . . . " from Doyle, 210; Glaspell's *Road to the Temple* from 1927, qtd. in Buhle, *Feminism*, 6; Dell qtd. in Burnham, 120, and see Buhle, *Feminism*, 8; on New York(ers) and Freud, see Nathan Hale, 399, Buhle, *Feminism*, 26–28, and Gifford, 128–45.

77. On the tilt, see Nathan Hale, 477; Hough, "How Psycho-Analysis Has Obsessed the World with Sex," *Current Opinion* 56 (1914): 441–42. Psychoanalysis was elsewhere ridiculed in *Current Opinion* for being unscientific and fantastic (see Nathan Hale, 405–08). Charlotte's friend and admirer Amy Wellington was associated with *Current Opinion*; see "A Biographical Sketch of Charlotte Perkins Gilman," typescript, folder 243, SL; see Addams, *Second Twenty*, 296–97; Scudder, qtd. in Faderman, 251.

78. On Freud's response, see Decker, 2; for an analysis of Charlotte's objections, see Doyle, 210–11 and 238.

79. "What the 'Threat of Man' Really Means," *Pictorial Review* 16 (June 1915): 2; "Great Issues of Today," folder 10, SL; see "Extracts from Freud's *General Introduction to Psychoanalysis*," and "Our Transient Sexolatry," both in folder 19, SL, and see undated reading list, folder 22, SL; "a belated . . . " from *HR&H*, 170.

80. She faults Freud in "This 'Life Force'" (undated article, likely post-1922), folder 181, SL, as well as in *L*, 323; "now widely poisoning" from "The New Generation of Women," *Current History* (8 August 1923): 731–37, quotation from 736; "not 'suppressed' . . ." from "Vanguard, Rear-Guard, and Mud-Guard," *Century* (July 1922): 351.

81. On the slippery slope, see *HR&H*, 164–65; on the free-lovers, see "Is Progress a Delusion?" *Buffalo Evening News* (18 August 1919) sec. 7: 4–6; "Six and Eros," *FR* 3 (February 1912): 54.

82. On self-forgetfulness as a virtue, see, e.g., "Toward Monogamy," *Nation* (11 June 1924): 673; on looking inward as an "unnatural attitude," see, e.g., *Our Brains and What Ails Them*, *FR* 3 (March 1912): 82; on Freud's therapy, see Gosling, 169; on CPG's "self abandoning enthusiasm," see DKD I, 31 December 1886, 364; "whatever . . . " from *HR&H*, 166.

83. *Our Brains and What Ails Them*, *FR* 3 (March 1912): 77, and *FR* 3 (December 1912): 334; on psychology being "ours. . . ," see *Herland*, *FR* 6 (November 1915): 242.

84. CPS to GHG, 24 August 1897, folder 44, SL; "pre-Freudian" from *L*, 23; "Love-god" from "Is Cupid a Convention?" *Independent* (15 August 1907): 373–75.

85. "perverted . . . " from *HR&H*, 164, and on Freud and homosexuality, see Faderman, 314–15; Katharine Bement Davis, 1918 study, cited in Rosenberg, 197–20. See also Faderman (325) for gynecologist Robert Latou Dickinson's data. Dickinson's statistics were lower: he deduced that 28 women out of the 350 whose sexual histories he compiled had been involved in genital relationships with other women.

86. *L*, 314.

87. On her hopes that Freudianism was a fad, see "This 'Life Force,'" ms., folder 181, SL; she positions herself as "sane" in Mary Hutcheson Page to Mrs. Parker, 10 March 1917, Woman's Rights Collection, folder 76, SL. Thanks to Lawrence Glickman for helping me to draw parallels between Charlotte's views and those embraced during the second wave of feminism.

88. She gripes about her status as the leading feminist in CPG to GECS, 21 August 1929, Mf-6, SL; "sex rights . . . " is Inez Milholland's claim, qtd. in Cott, 42; Dell proclaims the body a "Magna Carta" in *Women as World Builders*, 44–45; "the sexual slavery . . . " from Trimberger, 104.

89. "Are We Pendulums?" *FR* 6 (June 1915): 174; "social . . . indulgence" from "Vanguard, Rear-Guard, and Mud-Guard," *Century* (July 1922): 349–50.

90. CPG, "The Problem of the Unhappy Woman," *Beautiful Womanhood*, folder 253, SL; the contemporary is Margaret Culkin Banning, "The Lazy Thirties," *Harper's Monthly Magazine* 154 (February 1927): 357–65; see also Margaret Deland ("The Change in the Feminine Ideal," *Atlantic Monthly* [March 1910]: 292), who also holds that the

younger generation pursued individualism as a way of repudiating their mother's ideal of "selflessness."

91. "painted . . ." from CPG to KSC, 19 December 1931, folder 102, SL; "What Young People Are For," *Buffalo Evening News* (12 July 1919) sec. 13: 3–5; "the future Self" from "This 'Self-Development'," *FR* 7 (June 1916): 157–58.

92. "Vanguard, Rear-Guard, and Mud-Guard," *Century* (July 1922): 348–53, "trail-breakers" from 352, and "A wisely ambitious" from 349; "Twigs," *Life* (21 February 1924): 4 (CPG also sent a copy of "Twigs" to EAR).

93. For the younger generation's take, see "A Biographical Sketch of Charlotte Perkins Gilman," 1920s, folder 243, SL, and see also Gale, foreword to *L*, xxv; "Deboshed Young Folks," *New York Times* (9 July 1922) sec. 4: 4; also see Charlotte's letter to the editor accusing the paper of "animus more than judgement" (CPG to Editor of *New York Times* [12 July 1922], folder 152, SL).

94. "Is Progress a Delusion?" *Buffalo Evening News* (18 August 1919) sec. 7: 4–6; on the stereotypical old woman, see "Comment and Review: Where Are the Old Ladies?" *FR* 3 (December 1912): 335–36; on the invisibility of older women, see "The Woman of Fifty," *FR* 2 (April 1911): 96.

95. "the pleasure . . ." from "Is Progress a Delusion?" *Buffalo Evening News* (18 August 1919) sec. 7: 4–6; on women in the workforce, see Kessler-Harris, 227ff; on social versus financial motives for working, see "His Own Labor," *Buffalo Evening News* (16 August 1919) sec. 6: 7–8; "These Bachelor Girls," *Buffalo Evening News* (16 September 1919) sec. 9: 5–7.

96. On child development, see Cott, 91; on the women doctors, see "Mrs. Gilman Urges Hired Mother Idea," *New York Times* (23 September 1919) sec. 1: 36, and see also Wegener, "'What a Comfort'," 56–57; "Comment," [in Charlotte's hand, "Oakland Examiner"], clipping, folder 302, SL; "chuckle" from *L*, 320.

97. On temperance goals, see Robert Woods, qtd. in Allen F. Davis, 226; she discusses abstaining except for doctored punch in *L*, 86; "His Crutches" (poem), *FR* 1 (December 1909): 18; on her discomfort within the temperance movement, see *L*, 61.

98. *L*, 316.

99. Census figures qtd. in Cott, 145; "The City of Death" (poem), *FR* 4 (April 1913): 104. See also "Making Towns Fit to Live In," *Century* 102 (July 1921): 362, 363, where she compares unhealthy urban sprawl to a cancer.

100. *L*, 317; on her "evening," see CPG to Mary Austin, 28 December 1914, Huntington (thanks to Denise Knight for providing me with a copy of this note); the description of Luhan's salon is qtd. in Wertheim, 63, and see also Buhle, *Feminism*, 1; *L*, 317.

101. EAR, *Social Control*, 293, and on Ross's nativism see Higham, *Strangers* 117, and Page, 232; Ross pays his compliments to CPG in *Seventy Years of It*, 60.

102. On the visits and the Ross family, see CPS to GHG, 21 December 1899, folder 61, SL; CPG to EAR, 9 July 1918, Wisconsin; EAR to CPG, 9 October 1918, and see also EAR to CPG, 19 July 1918, Wisconsin. Ross was fired from Stanford in 1900, either because of his anti-immigration, anti-Asian comments or because of his support of public ownership of industry at an institution founded by a railroad baron (perhaps both). The incident would lead to the formation of both the American Association of University

Professors and the tenure system. On his firing, see CPG to EAR, 28 November 1900, Wisconsin.

103. CPG to KSC, 28 April 1921, folder 92, SL; DKD II, October 1921, 836.

104. "contemptible" from CPG to KSC, 10 May and see also 17 May 1922, folder 93, SL; on her final spring, see CPG to KSC, 10 May 1922 and 25 April 1922, folder 93, SL.

105. On the death and legacy, see CPG to KSC, 3 April and 9 August 1922, folder 93, SL, and see DKD II, 10[?] August 1922, 837; on moving to Norwichtown, see CPG to KSC, 5 August 1922, folder 93, SL, and see also CPG to KSC, 7 September 1922, folder 93, SL.

106. Grant, qtd. in Mark Haller, 149. Rudyard Kipling—a writer Charlotte both admired and parodied—once called New York City "[a] despotism of the alien, by the alien, for the alien, tempered with occasional insurrections of decent folk" (Thomas Bailey Aldrich quoting Kipling, qtd. in Hofstadter, *Age*, 178).

107. "escape . . . live in" from CPG to KSC, 5 August 1922, folder 93, SL; *L*, 324.

CHAPTER THIRTEEN

1. "You Have To," *FR* 3 (November 1912): 300.

2. "City of Dreadful . . . " from CPG to EAR, 12 April 1925, Wisconsin; details on the move and shipment from KSC to CPG, 1 November 1922, folder 10, 80-M112, SL, and from autobiographical attempt, folder 233, SL; Seelye, 629; "to regulate . . ." from Mark Haller, 47; "swarms . . . " from CPG to ASB, 19 January 1923, LOC; CPG's estimate concerning Norwich's foreign-born population and her reference to "native stock" are from *L*, 324. Charlotte was asked to get involved with the Norwich Americanization Project to help deal with the town's 20,000 foreign citizens ("Semi-Annual Report of the Norwich Americanization Institute, June to December, 1922," typescript, folder 143, SL).

3. CPG to KSC, 30 January 1929, folder 100, SL.

4. "Two Callings," *LP*, 75–78.

5. CPG to Harriet Park Kobold (secretary-treasurer of the Woman's Party of America and daughter of the suffragist Alice Park), 29 December 1928, Harriet Park Kobold papers, G487a, SL.

6. CPS to GHG, 29 December 1898, folder 61, SL; "with the delight . . . " from *L*, 326; CPG to ASB, 19 January 1923, LOC; *L*, 324.

7. CPG to GECS, 27 October 1922, folder 11, GECSP, SL; "on like grim death" from CPG to KSC, 10 October 1923, folder 94, SL; "that if Houghton . . . " from CPG to GECS, 2 August 1923, folder 12, GECSP, SL; she discusses the Norwich move as a step toward Pasadena in CPG to KSC, 5 August 1922, folder 93, SL.

8. DKD II, appendix A, "Thoughts & Figgerings," 23 July 1925, 853; "expensive . . ." from CPG to KSC, 4 September 1922, folder 93, SL; "get on. . . ." from CPG to GECS, 27 October 1922, folder 11, GECSP, SL.

9. "not been so gay . . ." from CPG to GECS, 27 October 1922, folder 11, GECSP, SL; reference to the trolley's noise from Delia Van Deusen, "Gardening for Harmony," unpublished sketch, folder 243, SL; *L*, 325–26; "To step out . . ." from CPG to GECS, 8 August 1923, folder 12, GECSP, SL.

10. Thanks to Sydna A. Byrne for securing information about the house and its own-ers for me; *L*, 325–36; for Lowthorpe, see, e.g., "Charlotte Perkins Gilman has Left for California," *Morning Bulletin* (8 September 1934), clipping, folder 266, SL; description of red exterior and interior rooms of house from Delia Van Deusen, "Gardening for Har-mony," unpublished sketch, folder 243, SL.

11. For examples of her cross-country lecturing, see "Immigration Scorned in Lecture: Mrs. Charlotte Perkins Gilman Has Warning for This Country, Predicts Ruin If Not Stopped," *Pasadena Star News* (10 March 1926), folder 294, SL, and "Fiction of America Being Melting Pot Unmasked by Charlotte Perkins Gilman," *Dallas Morning News* (15 February 1926) sec. 7–8: 9, 15; "all that fun" from CPG to KSC, 27 March 1922, folder 93, SL; on her itinerary and wardrobe, see CPG to Miss Strong, 2 April 1925, folder 233, SL, and "Noted Lecturer Surprises with Athletic Agility," *Dallas Dispatch* (11 February 1925), folder 294, SL.

12. "his heart" from CPG to GECS, 2 September 1927, mf-6, SL; "A Biographical Sketch of Charlotte Perkins Gilman," folder 243, SL; "no pull" from CPG to KSC, 11 March 1934, folder 105, SL.

13. CPG to Miss Strong, 2 April 1925, folder 233, SL; see also "Noted Lecturer Sur-prises with Athletic Agility," *Dallas Dispatch* (11 February 1925), folder 294, SL; "the light, flying . . ." from Delia Van Deusen, "Gardening for Harmony," unpublished biographical sketch, folder 243, SL; she describes her parlor tricks in CPG to AP, 5 September 1928 and 1 April 1932, WHMEC.

14. See CPG to Anne Martin, 14 May 1918, BANC MSS P-G 282, Anne Henrietta Martin papers, Bancroft; "a great garden" from CPS TO GHG, 7 November 1898, folder 58, SL; DKD II, appendix A, "Thoughts & Figgerings," 11 August 1930, 854.

15. *L*, 326–37; "gaiters" from CPG to WSC, 1 April 1932, WSCC; "all May . . ." from CPG to AP, 29 June 1928, WHMEC; "two elderly amateurs" and the description of their flowers and centerpiece from Delia Van Deusen, "Gardening for Harmony," unpublished biographical sketch, folder 243, SL.

16. On the garden as sustaining, see *L*, 327, and see also CPG to Harold Channing, 28 July 1931, in which she claims she raised twenty-eight edible veggies (and expresses her distaste for carrots and turnips), folder 12, 80-M112, SL; "$75" from DKD II, "Notes," [1923], 837; "taken care of" from DKD II, appendix A, "Thoughts & Figgerings," 7 May 1924, 852; "Gardening and the Baser Passions," 18 April 1930, ms., folder 129, SL.

17. Delia Van Deusen, "Gardening for Harmony," unpublished biographical sketch, folder 243, SL; "sanitarium" from CPG to KSC, 13 March 1929, folder 100, SL.

18. On her Norwich friends, see CPG to the Mills, 28 December 1923, Women's Rights Collection, Smith, and *L*, 325; Grace complains in GECS to KSC, 7 December 1929, folder 130, GECSP, SL; on her "beloved" friends, see *L*, 333, and CPG to ASB, 19 January 1923, LOC.

19. The neighbor's remark is recorded in Black, *Time*, 285; CPS to GHG, 12 October 1897, folder 46, SL; on her difficulty with individuals, see Black, "The Woman," 35.

20. "large fly" from CPG to Harriet Park Kobold, 31 December 1929, Harriet Park Kobold papers, G487a, SL; "annoy . . ." from "Some Advantages of 'Visiting'," *Buffalo*

Evening News (21 May 1919) sec. 6: 3–4; CPG to AP, 18 July 1930, WHMEC; CPG to KSC, 16 April 1930, folder 101, SL.

21. On the cat, see CPG to GECS, 26 May 1924, mf-6, SL, and DKD II, 29 July 1925, 838–39; on their separate arrangements, see CPG to AP, 8 July 1930, WHMEC, CPG to GECS, 24 April 1930, mf-6, SL, and CPG to AP, 28 February 1932, WHMEC.

22. DKD II, appendix A, "Thoughts & Figgerings," 25 June 1930, 853–54; for more on the fallout, see CPG to KSC, 14 February 1930, folder 101, SL.

23. On Charlotte's "horrid temper," see CPG to KSC, 28 August 1927, folder 98, and 19 August 1931, folder 102, SL; "un-esteemed" from CPG to GECS, 24 April 1930, mf-6, SL; "as if . . . " from CPG to AP, 18 July 1930, WHMEC; descriptions of Francis and Emily from CPG to GECS, 3 May 1934, mf-6, SL.

24. CPG to GECS, 28 February 1932, folder 11, 80-M112, SL.

25. "quite happy together" from CPG to AP, 18 July 1930, WHMEC; on their anniversaries, see CPG to KSC, 13 June 1921, folder 92, SL, and 17 June 1925, folder 96, SL; on their movie habit, see CPG to KSC, 27 February 1933, folder 104, SL; on listening preferences, see CPG to WSC, 16 August 1930, WSCC.

26. CPG to GHG, "Xmas 1933" (poem), folder 110, SL; "resting place" from "Work and Ethics," "Thoughts & Figgerings," 19 February 19[??], folder 16, SL.

27. On sleeping customs, see Green, *Fit*, 267; CPG to KSC, 3 November 1933, folder 104, SL; "that dreadful" from CPG to KSC, 11 February 1931, folder 102, SL.

28. "piggishly" from CPG to KSC, 19 June 1931, folder 102, SL; "few pleasant" from CPG to AP, 18 July 1930, WHMEC; "end my days . . ." from CPG to KSC, 19 August 1931, folder 102, SL.

29. On genealogy, see CPG to GECS, 18 April 1932, mf-6, SL; on supporting her family, see, e.g, DKD II, 26 June and 27 July 1924, 838 (by the end of June in 1920, for instance, Charlotte had sent Katharine $2,500); see CPG to KSC, 26 June 1920, folder 91, SL; see GHG to Frank Chamberlin, 29 March 1923, folder 10, SL; on Thomas's family's move from Hailey, Idaho, to Pasadena, see CPG to KSC, 17 January 1923, folder 94, SL, as well as CPG's note on a copy of "If You Are Queer," folder 253, SL; for a while, Grace's brother Harold Channing stayed with Thomas; her 1924 expense estimate is recorded in DKD II, appendix A, "Thoughts & Figgerings," 7 May 1924, 852.

30. For Charlotte and Katharine's impressions of Thomas's wife and Thomas himself, see CPG to KSC, 5 and 10 September 1923, folder 94, SL; KSC to CPG, 4 September 1923, folder 23, 80-M112, SL.

31. On their finances and her consumption, see CPG to KSC, 7 January 1930, 11 August 1930, and 27 February 1933, folders 101 and 104, SL; "living . . . same" from CPG to KSC, 12 January 1930, folder 101, SL.

32. "So long as" from CPG to GECS, 18 April 1932, mf-6, SL; CPG to GECS, 13 March 1933, mf-6, SL; "We've done . . . " from CPG to KSC, 25 November 1932, folder 103, SL.

33. CPG to KSC, 3 December 1930, folder 101, SL; unemployment figures from Kessler-Harris, 250–51.

34. See Cott, 266, on numbers and sanctions, and see Kessler-Harris, 254, 257, 376n2, and 276n26; on renouncing feminists, see Kessler-Harris, 253; Jane Allen, "You May

Have My Job: A Feminist Discovers Her Home," *Forum* (April 1932): 228–31, and see also Irwin, 422–23.

35. Beard, *America*, 4; on the panel, see CPG to ASB, 30 December 1929, LOC, and "Immigration Law Hit at Ford Hall," ([ca. 17 January] 1930), clipping, folder 294, SL. In 1927, Charlotte described herself as "now most interested in the specific qualities of different races, and the effect of promiscuous interbreeding among them, as it applies to our immediate national problems"; she ranked the decline in morals among the younger generation as her second most pressing concern (CPG to L. L. Bernard, 26 September 1927, in DKJT).

36. CPG to KSC, 2 May 1933, folder 103, SL.

37. Cited in CPG to EAR, 21 June 1932, Wisconsin.

38. "ten years . . . " from CPG to KSC, 2 May 1933, folder 103, SL; she discusses *HR&H* with Katharine in CPG to KSC, 28 July 1921 and 26 October 1922, folders 92 and 93, SL; "*see* . . . " from CPG to GECS, 27 October 1922, mf-6, SL; for her lecture on "A Lopsided Religion," see CPG to ASB, 19 December 1923, LOC; see also CPG, "Religion Being Re-Moulded by the Influence of Women," *Reconstruction* (May 1919): 148–49.

39. *HR&H*, 283; 46; Black, "The Woman," 41; "Seeing" from *HR&H*, 292; "there is possible . . . " from "Old Religion and New Hopes," *FR* 6 (February 1915): 35.

40. "only a necessary evil" from *HR&H*, 194; "evil . . . ," "essential and permanent," and "quite unnecessary . . . " from "Old Religion and New Hopes," *FR* 6 (February 1915): 35; "Two" (prefatory poem), *HR&H*, n.p.; "more human . . . " from *HR&H*, 278. The book revisits themes Charlotte had touched on before: for instance, both *HR&H* and *W&E* include chapters called "The Natural Beginning of an Unnatural Relation," devoted to explaining how women became dependent on men and their subsequent over-development of feminine traits at the expense of human traits; see *HR&H*, 172ff.

41. *L*, 327; EAR to CPG, 25 December 1923, reprinted in Gale, foreword to *L*, xvii; the sympathetic reviews Charlotte clipped are collected in folder 307, SL.

42. CPG to EAR, 6 July 1925, Wisconsin; Charlotte elsewhere sought to defend Ward's theories from the challenge posed by German biologist August Weismann: see *CC*, 9–12, e.g.; for her optimistic sales projection, see CPG to KSC, 9 October 1925, folder 96, SL.

43. She talks about the distraction of her garden in both CPG to KSC, 4 May 1925, folder 96, SL, and CPG to Miss Strong, 2 April 1925, folder 233, SL; "'running string' . . . publication" from CPG to KSC, 23 November 1925, folder 96, SL.

44. On unearthing her diaries, see CPG to KSC, 19 November 1926, folder 97, SL; "dreadful copy" from CPG to Mr. Vance, 22 November 1926, folder 152, SL (in 1923, Vance credited Charlotte with the success of his magazine, *The Pictorial Review*. See his letter in folder 123, SL). There were other publishers who expressed interest, but none wanted to close the deal (see, on publishers' interest, CPG to KSC, 9 October 1925, folder 96, SL). Charlotte continued to work on the ms. sporadically but fruitlessly: she wrote the daughter of a friend in late 1928 that "the Autobiography does not 'go'" (CPG to Harriet Park Kobold, 29 December 1928, Harriet Park Kobold papers, G487a, SL).

45. On its omissions and inversions, see Beer, "Charlotte," 56; Fleenor, 117; CPG to Zona Gale, 14 December 1934, 152, SL, and see also CPG to LBS, 27 May 1935, folder 416, Beecher-Stowe papers, SL, for Charlotte's sense that she wrote best when describing "the

living years—before my collapse" and in which she calls the "latter part of the autobiography" "so poor."

46. CPG to Zona Gale, 14 December 1934, folder 152, SL; "hateful . . . self!" from CPG to Miss Smith, 24 May 1922, folder 152, SL; see Weinbaum, 275, for a similar point about her resistance; DKD II, appendix A, 26 December [1932?], 855.

47. *L*, 331; "boil forward" and "cheerfully willing . . . " from CPG to LBS, 29 June 1932, folder 416, Beecher-Stowe papers, SL; she says her "nice agent thinks it's a sure seller!" in CPG to KSC, 4 October 1927, folder 98, SL, and see also on its potential timeliness and popularity, e.g., CPG to LBS, 11 September 1928, folder 416, Beecher-Stowe papers, SL; CPG to EAR, 11 September 1928, Wisconsin, identifies her agents as "Brandt & Brandt—as good agents as any in New York."

48. "brain to coruscating" from CPG to ASB, 7 January 1928, LOC; "very large dull AXE" from CPG to EAR, 11 September 1928, Wisconsin; for an example of a letter to a publisher, see CPG to Benjamin Huebsch, 1 March 1932, LOC (Mary Jo Deegan and Michael Hill later published an edition of *Pernicious Adam* [Praeger, 2004]); CPG to KSC, 19 August 1931, folder 102, SL.

49. "Lyman Beecher Stowe: Author-Editor-Lecturer," flyer, WSCC; on trying to persuade LBS to write her biography, see CPG to KSC, 15 April 1934, folder 105, SL; CPG to LBS, 16 July 1928, folder 416, Beecher-Stowe papers, SL.

50. On the Century's offer, see CPG to Charles C. Albertson, 8 March 1930, Columbia; "dottering . . . " CPG to LBS, 26 April 1933, folder 416, Beecher-Stowe papers, SL; proof she still planned to write from DKD II, appendix A, "Thoughts & Figgerings," 31 July 1933, 855; "old stuff" from CPG to KSC, 2 May 1933, folder 104, SL.

51. CPG to KSC, 15 April 1934, folder 105, SL.

52. Charlotte quotes the editor in CPG to LBS, 6 July 1928, folder 416, Beecher-Stowe papers, SL; Carrie Chapman Catt to CPG, 6 November 1930, Catt papers, LOC (Catt was dividing up a prize she received among fellow suffragists when she sent Charlotte $100); CPG to Carrie Chapman Catt, 1 November 1933, folder 152, SL; "Do you remember her?" from "Gossip: Mind Stretching," *Country Life and Stock and Station Journal* (5 February 1926), folder 310, SL.

53. Result of "Most interesting Women in America" survey, (28 November 1925), oversize folder 2, SL, and see also "How the Vote Stood," (28 November 1925), oversize folder 2. SL; "Mrs. Catt Selects 12 Greatest Women," (May 1923), clipping, folder 295, SL, and see also both "Twelve Great Women Will be Feted," *Pasadena Star News* (7 February 1924), folder 296, SL, and CPG to Carrie Chapman Catt, 22 November 1930, Catt papers, LOC.

54. On the NLWV book, see Lane, 7–8; on the 100 books, see Rosika Schwimmer's letter to the editor of the *New York Times Book Review* (3 September 1933) sec. 13: 5. That same year, the author and feminist Zona Gale ranked Charlotte first on her personal list of "nine immortals," but only in response to yet another oversight, as Charlotte had been left off a Columbia University historian's list of figures likely to appear prominently in histories fifty years hence (see CPG to "Kind Cousin Mine," 22 February 1933, HBSC, and see also unnamed cousin to LBS, 18 February 1933, folder 112, SL).

55. "befoh de wah" from CPG to AP, 11 August 1930, WHMEC, and see also CPG to ASB, 29 October 1930, LOC, where Charlotte writes, "These very young readers editors & critics have no use for minds over thirty!"; "social philosopher" from CPG to Carrie Chapman Catt, 22 November 1930, Carrie Chapman Catt papers, LOC, and see also CPG to LBS, 11 September 1928, folder 416, Beecher-Stowe papers, SL, where she claims, "I've been so be-labelled with the various 'causes' I conscientiously worked for, that few have recognized the real value of the contribution to social understanding"; "Where are the Pre-War Radicals?" *The Survey* (1 February 1926): 564, and on the symposium staged in that issue of *The Survey*, to which twenty-five "Pre-War Radicals" contributed (the only two women were Gilman and Tarbell), see Hofstadter, *Age*, 286–87, and Ceplair, 301n.

56. DKD II, appendix A, "Thoughts & Figgerings," 25 August 1924, 852; DKD II, appendix A, "Thoughts & Figgerings," 23 July 1925, 853.

57. On the importance of lecturing, see biographical sketch, 1920s, folder 243, SL; "I'm a 'glossopod' you remember—I travel on my tongue!" from CPG to the Mills, 28 December 1923, Women's Rights Collection, Smith, and see also the two limericks from Houghton that refer to Charlotte as a "Glossopod" (also as "Mrs. God"), "Thanksgiving," 1924, folder 144, SL; CPG to ASB, 29 December 1930, LOC.

58. *L*, 332–33, and see also CPG to ASB, 28 July 1931, LOC, where she discusses lecturing for the Connecticut League and enjoying it "hugely"; on the Gilman Week, see CPG to Katharine Seymour Day, 25 November 1932, 1 January and 22 February 1933, HBSC, and a handful of 1933 letters thanking her hosts and friends in folder 152, SL; "sudden 'flatness'" from CPG to Katharine Seymour Day, 22 February 1933, HBSC.

59. On her testimony and participation in the birth control movement, see Kennedy, 234, Ceplair, 274, and CPG to Margaret Sanger, 26 May 1932, Florence Rose papers, Smith (thanks to Thomas J. Brown for providing me with the biographical information about McCormack); on the 1934 conference, see Margaret Sanger to CPG, 4 February 1934, Margaret Sanger papers, Smith; Chesler, 344, 345, and 566n12, and see also CPG to Margaret Sanger, 31 January 1934, Florence Rose papers, Smith.

60. These engagements included a talk in New York at John Haynes Holmes Community Forum and a couple for the League of Nations association; Charlotte also gave several more informal talks after she moved to Pasadena. On her lecture opportunities, see CPG to AP, 13 February 1934, WHMEC; Chesler (345) erroneously identifies the 1934 birth control conference as Charlotte's final appearance.

61. "shoestring" from CPG to EAR, 16 August 1933, Wisconsin; "such an impression" from CPG to LBS, 26 September 1933, folder 416, Beecher-Stowe papers, SL; handwritten comment about her talking the paper on "The Social Body and Soul" typescript, folder 173, SL; attendee's praise recorded in CPG to KSC, 21 September 1933, folder 104, SL.

62. "*any* . . . grossness" from CPG to AP, 18 July 1930, WHMEC; on the title change, see CPG to KSC, 22 July 1925, folder 96, SL and "Wash-Tubs and Woman's Duty," *Century* 110 (June 1925): 152–59; on violating her Hearst boycott, see CPG to GECS, 28 May 1929 and 6 July 1929, mf-6, SL. Between 1906 and 1909, Charlotte also published several pieces in two Hearst publications, *Harper's Bazaar* and *Cosmopolitan*. Hearst had taken

these publications over fairly recently; perhaps she did not know they were under his control. *Good Housekeeping* never published her 1929 piece.

63. On the *Forum* and her discouragement, see CPG to GECS, 30 June 1928, mf-6, SL; her final *Forum* publication was "The Right to Die—I," *Forum* XCIV (November 1935): 297–300.

64. "sex boys" from Buhle, *Feminism*, 94; CPG to Mr. Schmalhausen, 28 July 1930, folder 122, SL; "horrid" from CPG to AP, 11 August 1930, WHMEC.

65. "to be busy" from CPG to ASB, 7 January 1928, LOC; CPG to KSC, 11 October 1930, folder 101, SL; "Necessity" from CPS to GHG, 6 July 1898, folder 53, SL.

66. Lipow, 3.

67. "Hard sledding" from CPG to GECS, 6 July 1929, mf-6, SL; on "The Yellow Wall-Paper," see, e.g., CPG to LBS, 26 September and 1 December 1933, folder 416, Beecher-Stowe papers, SL.

68. On mystery reading, see CPG to KSC, 8 March 1929, folder 100, SL; "never seen" from CPG to KSC, 20 April 1929, folder 100, SL, and see Golden and Knight, afterword to *Unpunished*, 221; Charlotte's description comes from the epigraph, Golden and Knight, n.p.; "trap. . . . ways" from Golden and Knight, 70, 86, and see 238n23.

69. Hofstadter, *Age*, 300–01; CPG to GECS, 30 June 1928, mf-6, SL. Houghton, who typically voted Democratic, thought "well of Smith" and voted for him in 1928, nullifying his wife's vote for Hoover; he had voted for La Follette in 1924 (see CPG to KSC, 25 July 1928 and 11 November 1928, folder 99, SL, and CPG to KSC, 7 December 1924, folder 95, SL).

70. "castle-building" from CPG to KSC, 30 January 1929, folder 100, SL; on her publishing attempts, see letters in folder 129, SL, and see CPG to KSC, 10 May 1929, folder 100, SL; CPG to KSC, 8 March 1929, folder 100, SL.

71. "We Don't Care to Be Well," *Buffalo Evening News* (30 August 1919) sec. 14: 7–8.

72. She praises her tonic in CPG to GECS, 27 October 1922, folder 11, GECSP, SL; "Kepler's" from DKD II, "Notes," [1922], 836; CPG to KSC, 6 September 1920, folder 91, SL. In a July 12, 1920 letter to Katharine, Charlotte identifies the sheep pills as "thyroid tablets—made from sheep's thyroid gland," prescribed by a female doctor in improve Charlotte's "general health and mental power" (folder 91, SL).

73. CPG to Dr. Dunn[ing], 3 October 1921, folder 152, SL; on her "30 inch waist," see CPG to Katharine Seymour Day, 7 June 1932, HBSC; "visibly" from CPG to KSC, 26 August 1933, folder 104, SL; CPG to GECS, 14 July 1933, mf-6, SL.

74. *L*, 71, 223; "it so hard" from CPG to ASB, 1 April 1932, LOC.

75. CPG to KSC, 6 April 1931, GECSP, SL; on Charlotte's dodging the earlier influenza epidemic, see GHG to Anne Martin, 13 November 1918, Huntington; "a lovely time" from CPG to ASB, 1 April 1932, LOC, and see also CPG to GECS, 25 March 1931, mf-6, SL.

76. "corpulence" from CPG to Harriet Park Kobold, 28 December 1931, Harriet Park Kobold papers, G487a, SL; CPG to KSC, 5 February 1932, folder 103, SL; on the diagnosis, see DKD II, "Memoranda," [1934], 840, and *L*, 333.

77. On the houseguest with cancer, see CPG to KSC, 13 June 1921, folder 92, SL; Harriet Howe relates that Charlotte vowed, while watching her mother die, "If this

should come to me, in future years, I will *not* go through with it. It is needless"; "step off" from CPG to KSC, 18 Jun 1930, folder 101, SL.

78. For her use of cancer as metaphor, see, e.g., *Home*, 197; CPG to AP, 22 February 1935, WHMEC; CPG to ASB, 9 June 1925, LOC.

79. "dear earth" from CPG to GECS, 12 October 1932, Mf-6, SL; on their financial constraints, see CPG to AP, 21 September 1933, WHMEC; on Francis's responses, see CPG to GECS, 13 March 1933, mf-6, SL.

80. On Houghton's judgeship, see CPG to KSC, 14 April 1933, folder 104, SL; income figures from Beard, *America*, 506.

81. "Houghton, slow to anger" from CPG to GECS, 13 March 1933, mf-6, SL; "'carry'" from CPG to LBS, 16 December 1932, folder 416, Beecher-Stowe papers, SL; CPG to KSC, 6 January 1934, folder 105, SL; "Advertisement for the Wauregan," clipping, "Jan. 10," WSCC; Charlotte expresses her delight in CPG to AP, 13 February 1934, WHMEC.

82. GECS to KSC, 10 April 1934, folder 138, GECSP, SL; on the planned move to Pasadena, see CPG to LBS, 16 December 1932, folder 416, SL, and CPG to KSC, 6 January 1934, folder 105, SL; "easy old age" from CPG to KSC, 3 November 1933, folder 104, SL.

83. On the Hartford pageant, see CPG to KSC, 22 May 1932, folder 103, SL, GHG to Katharine Seymour Day, 20 May 1932, HBSC, and CPG to Katharine Seymour Day, 1 and 7 June 1932, HBSC; on the Howe memorial service, see Schwarz, 102; CPG to ASB, 15 April 1934, LOC.

84. "aged under care" from CPG to KSC, 3 November 1933, folder 104, SL; on her assumption that she would be the first to die, see CPG to KSC, 21 November 1930, folder 101, SL, and see also CPG to KSC, 2 August[?] 1932, folder 103, SL. In another letter to Katharine, Charlotte contemplates what she would do if Houghton died first: either move to Pasadena and become "an old nuisance" to her daughter's family "or just step off. That's always the open door, thank goodness" (CPG to KSC, 18 June 1930, folder 101, SL). After Houghton died, Katharine wrote to Grace, "Mama has always had a feeling that Houghton might go first—apparently based only on the dread of losing him" (KSC to GECS, 10 May 1934, folder 218, GECSP, SL); "come quick" from CPS to GHG, 16 November 1898, folder 59, SL.

85. Descriptions of Houghton's death from CPG to Zona Gale, 14 December 1934, folder 152, SL, and obituary (5 May 1934), folder 285, SL; "a very" from CPG to KSC, 5 May 1934, folder 105, SL.

86. "no one to be sorry" from CPG to KSC, 19 May 1934, folder 105, SL; on "going without," see CPG to KSC, 15 June 1934, folder 105, SL; "can look back" from CPG to Anna Waller, 26 May 1934, Barnard; "wither and die" from *L*, 334.

87. "it was a beautiful . . . not a large part of my life" from CPG to KSC, 4 June 1934, folder 105, SL; "Goneness" from CPG to GECS, 10 January 1935, mf-6, SL.

88. CPG to WSC, n.d., WSCC; her reminder is recorded in *L*, 80.

CHAPTER FOURTEEN

1. "To One Who Suffers," *FR* 7 (February 1916): 44.

2. CPG to KSC, 3 November 1933, folder 104, SL.

3. She swears otherwise in CPG to KSC, 19 May 1934, folder 105, SL; "being foot-loose" from GECS to KSC, 20 May 1934, folder 138, GECSP, SL.

4. CPG to AP, 26 May 1934, WHMEC.

5. GECS to KSC, 8 May 1934, folder 138, GECSP, SL; "pathetically" from GECS to KSC, 10 May 1934, folder 138, GECSP, SL; "incessant haunting," "orphaned," and "every little convenience" from CPG to GECS, 12 June 1934, mf-6, SL; the remaining quotations are from GECS to KSC, 10, 12, and 20 May 1934, folder 138, GECSP, SL.

6. Descriptions of Francis's behavior from GECS to KSC, 10 May and 5 July 1934, folder 138, GECSP, SL; on friends driving her to the cremation, see CPG to KSC, 5 May 1934, folder 105, SL; Francis Gilman to Alexander Abbott, 9 May 1934, folder 114, SL.

7. GECS to KSC, 12 May 1934, folder 138, GECSP, SL; CPG to KSC, 15 June 1934, folder 105, SL.

8. On the friends and Mary, see GECS to KSC, 12 May 1934, folder 138, GECSP, SL; on Houghton's finances, see GECS to KSC, 25 May 1934, folder 138, GECSP, SL; for Charlotte's legacy, see Edwin W. Higgins to CPG, 15 August 1934, folder 119, SL.

9. "So brave . . . irritable" from GECS to KSC, 20 May 1934, folder 138, GECSP, SL; descriptions of Charlotte's mental state from GECS to KSC, 9 and 12 July 1934, folder 138, GECSP, SL; her thoughts on her future are from CPG to GECS, 22 May and 4 June 1934, mf-6, SL.

10. GECS to KSC, 9 July 1934, folder 138, GECSP, SL.

11. On Charlotte's packing, see GECS to KSC, n.d.[late July] 1934, folder 139, GECSP, SL; for her shipment, see CPG to KSC, 1 August 1934, folder 105, SL; Grace complains in GECS to KSC, 25 July 1934, folder 138, GECSP, SL.

12. She encourages the Chamberlins in GECS to KSC, 20 and 25 May 1934, folder 138, GECSP, SL; she speculates about Charlotte's short future in GECS to KSC, 20 July 1934, folder 138, GECSP, SL.

13. GECS to KSC, 23 August 1934, folder 139, GECSP, SL; CPG to KSC, 13 August 1934, folder 105, SL.

14. On her decision to fly, see GECS to KSC, 23 August 1934, folder 139, GECSP, SL; "stimulating experience" from CPG to KSC, 13 August 1934, folder 105, SL; "last 'fling'" from CPG to AP, 7 August 1934, WHMEC, and see also GECS to KSC, 23 August 1934, folder 139, GECSP, SL.

15. Her description of the flight and meal, as well as her praise of the view, comes from CPG to GECS, 1 September 1934, mf-6, SL; see also CPG to KSC, 11 August 1934, folder 105, SL.

16. "When We Fly," *Harper's Weekly* (9 November 1907): 1650, 1664.

17. "Wings," *ITOW*, 64–66; Rose O'Neill Wilson to CPG, 9 November 1913, folder 121, SL. The poem reads in part:
A sense of wings—
  Soft downy wings and fair—
Great wings that whistle as they sweep
Along the still gulfs—empty, deep—
  Of thin blue air. . . .

Such mighty plumes—strong-ribbed, strong-
    webbed—strong-knit to go
        From earth to heaven!
        Hear the air flow back
        In their wide track!
    Feel the sweet wind these wings displace
        Beat on your face!
See the great arc of light like rising rockets trail
        They leave in leaving—
        They avail—
        These wings—for flight!

"I have flown" from undated correspondence between CPG and the Bruères (ca. September 1934), folder 117, SL.

18. Undated correspondence between CPG and GECS (ca. 14 September 1934), mf-6, SL.

19. "a little sick" from WSC, "Experiences with Charlotte Perkins Gilman," paper presented at Second International Charlotte Perkins Gilman Conference, Skidmore College, 1997; Katharine's impressions of her mother are conveyed in KSC to GECS, 10 September 1934, WSCC; "a good deal older" from CPG to GECS, 10 September 1934, mf-6, SL; on Thomas, see CPG to GECS, 1 September 1934, mf-6, SL.

20. "dignified . . . year . . . " from CPG to KSC, 17 July 1934, folder 105, SL; her description of her room and the other tenants comes from CPG to Harriet Park Kobold, 10 January 1935, Harriet Park Kobold papers, G487a, SL, and see also CPG to LBS, 6 January 1935, folder 416, Beecher-Stowe papers, SL; she describes its location to CPG to GECS, 5 September 1934, mf-6, SL; "oldmaidish" from KSC to GECS, 30 November 1934, WSCC.

21. She describes her room, routine, balcony, and delight out-of-doors in CPG to GECS, 5 September, 4 November, 7 and 21 December 1934, mf-6, SL, and see CPG's letters in the Harriet Park Kobold papers, G487a, SL; see also CPG to LBS, 6 January 1935, folder 416, Beecher-Stowe papers, SL.

22. Information on her typical day is culled from KSC to GECS, 30 November 1934, WSCC, CPG to AP, 15 September 1934, WHMEC, and CPG to GECS, 7 December 1934, mf-6, SL; "I love California" from CPG to ASB, 11 January 1935, LOC. Yet in another letter written shortly before she died, Charlotte passionately refused the title "California woman" and described herself as "sitting up in bed . . . raging over this old grievance," i.e., her unfair treatment during her previous tenure in the state (CPG to Mrs. Coats, 21 June 1935, in DKJT).

23. She plans her year in "Thoughts & Figgerings," September 1934, folder 17, SL; on her classes, see CPG to GECS, 4 November and 7 December 1934, mf-6, SL. Charlotte was also once again invited to attend the annual birth control conference in DC, but she sent a poem in her stead (Florence J. Harriman to CPG, 29 January 1935, folder 147, SL); "For Birth Control" (poem), enclosed with CPG to Margaret Sanger, 7 February 1935, Margaret Sanger papers, http://www.nyu.edu/projects/sanger/gilman.htm [accessed June 4, 2003]); KSC to GECS, 9 December 1934, WSCC.

24. "Thoughts & Figgerings," 28 October 1934, folder 17, SL; "'push'" from CPG to GECS, 7 December 1934, mf-6, SL; "scrappy, imperfect" from CPG to Zona Gale, 14 December 1934, folder 153, SL; CPG to LBS, 12 April 1935, folder 416, Beecher-Stowe papers, SL. In this same letter she mentions also recently writing her poem "Happiness." According to her grandson, she also wrote "The Grapevine" in her final days; "This Lovely Earth," *LP*, 107.

25. "easiest reading" from CPG to Harriet Park Kobold, 10 January 1935, Harriet Park Kobold papers, G487a, SL; "pipe" from KSC to Carl Degler, 24 July 1960, folder 156, SL; "'keep accounts'" from CPG to GECS, 7 December 1934, mf-6, SL; on her allowance, see "Thoughts & Figgerings," 7 November 1934, folder 17, SL, CPG to GECS, 5 September 1934, mf-6, SL, and KSC to GECS, 10 September 1934, WSCC, and see also CPG to LBS, 6 January 1935, folder 416, Beecher-Stowe papers, SL.

26. On Anna's house, see WSC, "Experiences with Charlotte Perkins Gilman," paper presented at Second International Charlotte Perkins Gilman Conference, Skidmore College, 1997, and see CPG to LBS, 29 March 1935, folder 416, Beecher-Stowe papers, SL; on Frank's depression and the Chamberlins' debts, see CPG to GECS, 20 February 1935, 4 November 1934, and 3 March 1935, mf-6, SL; see also KSC to readers of folders 89–106, folder 88, SL.

27. Katharine describes finding her mother cleaning in KSC to GECS, 23 July 1934, WSCC; "*dirt*" from CPG to GECS, 21 December 1934, mf-6, SL; on Charlotte's expounding, see KSC to GECS, 27 December 1934, WSCC; on Dorothy, see KSC to GECS, 15 July 1934, WSCC; for her attempts to get the children to help out, see CPG to GECS, 7 and 21 December 1934, mf-6, SL.

28. The list of movies is culled from KSC to GECS, 30 November, 26 September, and 12 November 1934, WSCC; CPG to GECS, 23 September 1934, mf-6, SL; and KSC to GECS, 16 December 1934, WSCC; on the "memorial," see KSC to GECS, 10 September 1934, WSCC.

29. "hyperthesia" from Autobiography, "an earlier attempt," folder 234, SL; WSC, "Experiences with Charlotte Perkins Gilman," paper presented at Second International Charlotte Perkins Gilman Conference, Skidmore College, 1997; bank book, WSCC.

30. KSC to GECS, 16 and 23 October 1934, and Katharine Hepburn to KSC, 28 October 1934, WSCC; in the latter, the actress expresses a desire "to see Mrs. Gilman again." Charlotte had recently seen Hepburn in *Bill of Divorcement* and *Little Women*; she wrote Grace, "It is a delight to have someone like that to count on" (CPG to GECS, 14 December 1933, mf-6, SL); Thanksgiving description from KSC to GECS, 31 November 1934, WSCC, and undated correspondence between CPG and GECS (ca. 1934), mf-6, SL; on Sinclair's run, see McWilliams, 296–99; clippings, folder 280, SL.

31. On presents, see, e.g., CPG to LBS, 6 January 1935, folder 416, Beecher-Stowe papers, SL.

32. Quotes in this paragraph are from CPG to GECS, 7 December 1934, mf-6, SL; see also CPG to Katharine Seymour Day, 22 May 1935, in DKJT, where she tells her cousin, "cancer [is] not at all dreadful, so far."

33. "Get Your Work Done," (poem), *FR* 1 (December 1909): 29.

34. CPS to GHG, 23 December 1899, folder 61, SL.

35. Description of cancer from "Making Towns Fit to Live in," *Century* 102 (July 1923): 363–64; *L*, 333.

36. "kill a cat" from WSC, qtd. in DK, "The Dying," 156; "complete rest" from *L*, 278; for more on her use of chloroform, see DKD I, 393n26, DKD I, 11 May 1883, 191, and DKD II, 1 October 1902, 825; CPG to GHG, 17 April 1900, folder 82, SL; the incident that frightened her mother is described in Autobiography, "an earlier attempt," folder 234, SL.

37. Details of her Pasadena treatment are from CPG to GECS, 5 September and 4 November 1934, mf-6, SL.

38. KSC to GECS, 4 February 1935, WSCC; "grasshopper" from CPG to GECS, 20 February 1935, mf-6, SL. Her "grasshopper" metaphor may be a reference to the Bible and in particular to Ecclesiastes 12:5: " . . . the almond tree shall flourish, and the grasshopper shall be a burden, and desire shall fail: because man goeth to his long home, and the mourners go about the streets"; her worsening symptoms are described in Dr. Edmund P. Shelby to CPG, 9 March 1934, folder 123, SL, and for "sticking place," see CPG to GECS, 3 March 1935, mf-6, SL; see also Edwin W. Higgins to CPG, 1 March 1935, folder 119, SL.

39. "pale and frail" form CPG to GECS, 3 March 1935, mf-6, SL; KSC to GECS, 11 May 1935, WSCC; on her estate and reasons for hanging on, see "Charlotte Perkins Gilman, Pasadena, June 30, 1935," AP's recollection, WHMEC, and Edwin W. Higgins to CPG, 1 March 1935, folder 119, SL.

40. "Notable Family Reunion at Inn," Riverside California newspaper clipping (26 March 1935), folder 285, SL; CPG to LBS, 29 March 1935, folder 416, Beecher-Stowe papers, SL; "a convincing article" from CPG to GECS, 21 July 1932, folder 280, GECSP, SL; "I say" from CPG to LBS, 29 March 1935, folder 416, Beecher-Stowe papers, SL.

41. Descriptions of her alarming decline and of Anna Waller's house and Charlotte's reaction to it are from KSC to GECS, 21 April 1935, WSCC, and WSC to GECS, 14 April 1935, WSCC.

42. On Gale and the autobiography, see CPG to Zona Gale, 14 December 1934, folder 153, SL, Zona Gale to CPG, 31 May 1935, folder 419, Beecher-Stowe papers, SL, and materials in folder 118, SL; the latter also includes a copy of Gale's letter to Mr. John L. B. Williams of Appleton-Century; see LBS to CPG, 31 May 1935, and CPG to LBS, 29 March 1935, folder 416, Beecher-Stowe papers, SL; finally, see CPG to GECS, 20 March 1935, mf-6, SL; on Appleton's and the contract, see LBS to CPG, 26 June and 4 July 1935, folder 35, Beecher-Stowe papers, SL. Charlotte's friends and family felt the "tonic" of publication might "work wonders" and postpone her demise: see GECS to LBS, 21 June 1935, folder 420, Beecher-Stowe papers, SL, and AP to KSC, 23 August 1935, SL (AP calls the publication of *L* "almost a miracle").

43. Undated correspondence between GECS and Appleton's, qtd. in Lane, 359; "Author's Note," *L*, n.p.

44. Descriptions of the daily routine are from KSC to GECS, 21 April and 11 May 1935, WSCC; descriptions of outings from KSC to GECS, 21 April 1935, WSCC.

45. CPG to GECS, 17 April 1935, mf-6, SL; "new position" from CPG to AP, 22 April 1935, WHMEC; CPG to GECS, 20 March 1935, mf-6, SL.

46. "how weak" from KSC to GECS, 21 April 1935, WSCC; on her hearing, voice, and scribbling, see CPG to GECS, 25 April 1935, mf-6, SL; and see KSC to GECS, 21 April 1935, WSCC; "peacefully asleep" from CPG to AP, 22 April 1935, WHMEC. Thanks to Denise D. Knight for tracking down the meaning of the "p.p.c." abbreviation with the help of an able researcher. To quote Knight,

"p.p.c." is French for pour prendre congé, "to take leave" or "I am leaving." We are indebted to Cindy J. Hall for providing both the translation and interpretation of this abbreviation. Hall notes that in his *Dictionary of Phrase and Fable* (1898), English editor E. Cobham Brewer (1810–1897) remarks that "p.p.c."—or "paid parting call" in English—was "sometimes written on the address cards of persons . . . when they pay their farewell visits." Hall further notes that "Pour Prendre Congé" is the title of a poem by American writer Dorothy Parker (1893–1967), which appeared in the July 1927 issue of *The New Yorker* (DKJT).

47. On how people responded to the news, see CPG to GECS, 20 February 1935, mf-6, SL; for personal tributes, see, e.g., Mrs. Harry P. [Elizabeth] Wilcox to CPG, 22 April 1935, folder 47, SL; ASB to CPG, 23 May 1935, folder 47, SL; Carrie Chapman Catt to CPG, 28 May 1935, folder 47, SL.

48. LBS to CPG, 19 May 1935, folder 35, SL; Basil Perkins to CPG, 1 May 1935, folder 31, SL.

49. On CPG's ups and downs and reserve, see KSC to GECS, 9 and 29 May 1935, folder 219, GECSP, SL; descriptions of the shingles derived from KSC to GECS, 1 and 2 June 1935, folder 219, GECSP, SL, and KSC to LBS, 10 June 1935, folder 416, Beecher-Stowe papers, SL.

50. "Body of Mine," *LP*, 119–20.

51. "just bones" from CPG to "My dear old friend" [EAR], 11 July 1935, Wisconsin; "nothing but her desire" from KSC to GECS, 1 June 1935, folder 219, GECSP, SL, and see also 2 June 1935, folder 219, GECSP, SL; "last legs" from CPG to LBS, 23 April 1935, folder 416, Beecher-Stowe papers, SL. Charlotte noticed Katharine's delight in seeing Grace again and mused, Grace "has been more of a mother to her than I have, in many ways; has influenced her character more, I think. . . ." (CPG to LBS, 27 May 1935, folder 416, Beecher-Stowe papers, SL).

52. "'order of my going'" from CPG to LBS, 23 April 1935, and for details of their arrangements in sharing the house, see CPG to LBS, 27 May 1935, folder 416, Beecher-Stowe papers, SL; see also GECS to LBS, 25 June 1935, Folder 420, Beecher-Stowe papers, SL; on the birthday celebration, see CPG to LBS, 10 July 1935, Folder 416, Beecher-Stowe papers, SL.

53. CPG to Zona Gale, 5 August 1935, AG 487C, SL; on spiritualism and the Beechers, see Caskey, ch. 10; "These Too, Too Solid Ghosts," *Forum* 75 (February 1926): 238–44.

54. CPG to ASB, 15 April 1934, LOC; the last line of this quotation, as Scharnhorst, *Charlotte*, notes (117), paraphrases Whitman. See DK, "'With the first'," and see also untitled typescript [article fragment], 14 March 1933, folder 183, SL. The reference is to section 48 of Whitman's *Leaves of Grass*.

55. On the unreasonable fear of death, see "Happiness," *FR* 5 (September 1914): 232–33,

and *HW*, 300–02; on life without death, see Autobiography, "an earlier attempt," folder 234, SL, and *L*, 40; "Eternal Me," in "Communication: Transient Limitation," scrapbook, folder 49, 80-M112, SL; "Schools Out!" from CPG to KSC, 25 November 1932, folder 103, SL; "peaceful" from CPG to GECS, 17 April 1935, mf-6, SL.

56. "on euthanasia," see "Right to Die—I," *Forum* XCIV (November 1935): 299; "shortening" from "Self Control," *FR* 2 (February 1911): 36; "last human . . . useless pain" from "Dr. Clare's Place," *FR* 6 (June 1915): 144; she reports her remarks to Frank in CPG to GECS, 20 March 1935, mf-6, SL; on the issue of her own attraction to suicide, see, e.g., CPS to GHG, 7 November 1897, folder 47, SL as well as her more morose correspondence with CWS in the early 1880s.

57. "Good and Bad Taste in Suicide," *FR* 3 (May 1912): 130.

58. CPG to AP, 12 August 1935, and see AP's transcription, "copy of letter August 23, 35," WHMEC; CPG to EAR, 15 August 1935, Wisconsin; "stepping off place" from CPG to Zona Gale, 5 August 1935, AG 487C, SL.

59. KSC to LBS, 20 August 1935, folder 416, Beecher-Stowe papers, SL; KSC to AP, 20 August 1935, WHMEC. Katharine later made a plaster cast from the mask that now resides at SL. See WSC, "Charlotte Perkins Gilman's Last Visit with me," conference presentation.

60. KSC to LBS, 20 August 1935, folder 416, Beecher-Stowe papers, SL. See also "Charlotte Gilman Dies to Avoid Pain," *New York Times* (20 August 1935), folder 284, SL.

61. On not having a service, see CPG's will, 12 May 1934, folder 284, SL; details of the disposal of her body from KSC to LBS, 20 August 1935, folder 416, Beecher-Stowe papers, SL, and see "Charlotte Gilman Dies to Avoid Pain," *New York Times* (20 August 1935), folder 284, SL; for the location of her ashes, see David Goodale's journal, folder 115, CWS papers, 93-M76, SL; "do some good" from an earlier will, dated 14 November 1924, folder 1, SL.

62. "Such a clean" from CPG to GECS, 11 January 1897, mf-6, SL. See also "Beauty from Ashes," *FR* 6 (November 1915): 300–01; on cremation as more sanitary, see "Cremation," in Bliss and Binder, *Encyclopedia of Social Reform*, 331–32; "to preserve . . . it ceases" from "Why Graves," *WJ* (27 August 1904): 274; see also "The Last Grave," *Buffalo Evening News* (15 April 1919) sec. 25: 4–5.

63. Bellamy, qtd. in Dombrowski, 86–87.

64. *L*, 333–34; for similar points made some twenty years previously, see "Euthanasia Again," *FR* 3 (October 1912): 262–63.

POSTMORTEM

1. "Birth and Death," *FR* 3 (November 1912): 299.

2. "promote discussion" from CPG to GECS, 17 April 1935, mf-6, SL; on the increased interest in euthanasia, see Pauline Wolinski to CPG, 12 May 1935, in DKJT, and "The Right to Die," *The Survey* (September 1935): 274; see also DK, "The Dying."

3. "The Right to Die—I," *Forum* XCIV (November 1935): 297–300.

4. "this principle" from CPG to GECS, 17 April 1935, mf-6, SL; "lived her philosophy" from *Pasadena Star News* (19 August 1935), clipping, folder 284, SL; on "serviceable lives," see "A Justifiable Exit," ms., folder 226, SL; LBS to KSC, 20 August 1935, WSCC.

5. Editor's note, "The Right to Die—I," *Forum* XCIV (November 1935): 300; on the radio program, see KSC to LBS, 15 November 1935, folder 416, Beecher-Stowe papers, SL; "the age-old" from Uncle Dudley, "Communication: Transient Limitation," (1935), scrapbook, folder 49, 80-M112, SL; "the deepest instinct" from John Barry, "Ways of the World: Ending a Life of Service," *San Francisco News* (27 August 1935), clipping, WSCC.

6. Lillian Wald to KSC, 21 August 1935, Harriot Stanton Blatch to KSC, 22 August 1935, and MLL to KSC, 26 August 1935, all in WSCC; on the response of African American intellectuals, see Mary Helen Washington, "Anna Julia Cooper: The Black Feminist Voice of the 1890s," *Legacy* 4 (1987): 10; Catt, Hurst, Holmes, and Tarbell, all qtd. in "Mrs. Catt Defends Friend's Moral Right to Take Her Own Life," *New York World-Telegram* (20 August 1935), folder 284, SL; on the final point, see Hurst's comments in the article on Charlotte's private decision. Thanks to Carol Farley Kessler for identifying the line from Milton's Sonnet 16, "On His Blindness"; Tarbell does not provide an attribution.

7. "Business Women's Bookshelf," *Independent Woman* 14 (November 1935): 381–82; see also Clara Gruening Stillman, "Dynamic Woman in the Years of High Hopes," *New York Herald Tribune* (review of *The Living*), (20 October 1935), scrapbook, folder 49, 80-M112, SL, where Stillman calls Gilman "the fine flower of the American individualist tradition."

8. On the posthumous preparations and publication of *L*, see John L. B. Williams (D. Appleton-Century Company) to KSC, 12 and 26 August 1935, folder 127, SL, and KSC to LBS, 20 August 1935, Beecher-Stowe papers, folder 416, SL; "amazing record" from "A Woman with a Will," *Los Angeles Times* (10 November 1935), scrapbook, folder 49, 80-M112, SL; Florence Finch Kelly, "Charlotte Gilman," *New York Times Book Review* (28 June 1936) sec. 6: 15.

9. "my uproar" from CPG to Katharine Seymour Day, 5 December 1932, HBSC; Clara Gruening Stillman, "Dynamic Woman in the Years of High Hopes," *New York Herald Tribune Books* (review of *The Living*), (20 October 1935), scrapbook, folder 49, 80-M112, SL.

10. Sales figures in Lane, 361; on publishing her other works, see, e.g., Amy Wellington to CPG, 3 July [1935], folder 125, SL, and see Willis Kingsley Wing to CPG, 12 June 1935, in DKJT. In 2004, Michael R. Hill and Mary Jo Deegan edited and published Gilman's "Ethics" as *Social Ethics: Sociology and the Future of Society* (Westport, CT: Greenwood Publishing Group, 2004).

11. On the Women's Archives, see Ellen DuBois, *Woman Suffrage*, 229–30, and Mary Beard to CPG, 16 August 1935, WSCC; LBS forwarded Beard's typed letter and the accompanying description of "An International Feminist-Pacifist Archive" to Katharine (LBS to KSC, 2 September 1935, WSCC); on her attempts to keep her mother's works in circulation, see KSC to Mr. Doyle, 24 July 1960, folder 156, SL; D. Appleton-Century Company to Mrs. Catherine [*sic*] B. S. Chamberlain [*sic*], 14 December 1942, folder 127, SL (the publishing company invoked "General Conservation Order NO. M-99 from the Printing and Publishing Division of the W.P. B. [, which] provides that all book plates not having an assured future be turned into the country's metal pool in connection with our

war effort. . . ."); in 1996, Denise D. Knight edited and published a volume containing CPG's "later poetry."

12. Black, *Time*, 285; for her prophecy, see "Her Visioning of Growth: Due Salutations to Our Great-Great-Grandchildren," undated, folder 255, SL; on the rejection of the antithesis and the reassertion of individual rights, see Polly Wynn Allen, 123, 125.

13. Howe, "The Personality," 118; Florence L. Cross Kitchelt to Frances Maule [*Independent Woman* editor], 1 August 1947, Florence L. Cross Kitchelt papers, folder 146, SL.

14. See Degler, "Charlotte," and Doyle; for the initial work of recovery and redemption, see, e.g., the work of Elaine Hedges, Annette Kolodny, and collections edited by Catherine Golden, Joanne Karpinski, and Sheryl L. Meyering; Lanser, 415–41.

15. For examples of these critiques, see Polly Wynn Allen, 78–79, 116–17, 123, 127, 130, 140–41; Judith A. Allen, "Reconfiguring Vice," 177; Degler, "Charlotte," n27; Dombrowski, 28; Hayden, *Grand*, 183, 196–97, 301; Ganobcsik-Williams, 18; Karpinski, "Economic"; Levitas, 82–83; Newman, 147; Pittenger, 87–88; Rosenberg, 206; Carter-Sanborn; Weinbaum, 177; Zauderer, 153.

16. For examples of these nuanced approaches, see Judith A. Allen, "Reconfiguring Vice," 194, and see also Ganobscik-Williams.

17. "repeated failure" from *L*, 102; "The religion, the philosophy" from *L*, 335. On her desire for recognition, see *Won Over, FR* 4 (February 1913): 38, where she writes: "It is not approval only that young people desire, though that is balm to their souls, but recognition—to be known for what they are. . . ." She made much the same point in an 1897 letter to Houghton, where she noted how much even "the most assured person apparently may secretly long for the deep full force of *recognition*. Not approval—but recognition. To be seen, truly, and appreciated for what one *is*" (CPS to GHG, 11 September 1897, folder 45, SL).

18. *Benigna Machiavelli, FR* 5 (December 1914): 314.

Select Bibliography

PRIMARY SOURCES
Manuscript Collections
Bailey-Howe Library, University of Vermont, Burlington
Bancroft Library, University of California, Berkeley
Barnard College Archives, Barnard College
Brown University Library
Bryn Mawr College Library
Butler Library, Rare Book and Manuscript Library, Columbia University
Colby College Library
Cornell University Library, Division of Rare and Manuscript Collections
Fruitlands Museum, Prospect Hill, Harvard, MA
Harriet Beecher Stowe Center, Hartford, CT
Hingham Public Library, Hingham, MA
Horrmann Library, Wagner College
Houghton Library, Harvard University
Henry E. Huntington Library, San Marino, CA
Library of Congress
Rhode Island Historical Society Library, Providence
University of Rochester Library
Arthur and Elizabeth Schlesinger Library on the History of Women in America,
    Radcliffe Institute for Advanced Study, Harvard University

Sophia Smith Collection, Smith College
Vassar College Libraries, Vassar College
Wisconsin Historical Society, Madison
Women's History Museum and Educational Center, San Diego

Full citations of all sources by Charlotte Perkins Gilman, as well as all consulted manuscripts and library and private holdings, are provided in the Notes.

ADDITIONAL WORKS CITED

Aberdeen, Countess of, ed. *International Council of Women: Report of Transactions of the Second Quinquennial Meeting Held in London July 1899.* London: T. Unwin Fisher, 1900.

———. *Women in Education, the International Congress of Women of 1899* (vol. 2). London: T. Unwin Fisher, 1900.

———. *Women in Industrial Life, the International Congress of Women of 1899* (vol. 6). London: T. Unwin Fisher, 1900.

Addams, Jane. *Second Twenty Years at Hull House, September 1909 to September 1929, with a Record of a Growing World Consciousness.* New York: Macmillan, 1930.

———. "The Subjective Necessity for Social Settlements." *Philanthropy and Social Progress; Seven Essays Delivered Before the School of Applied Ethics at Plymouth, Mass., During the Session of 1892.* New York: Crowell, 1893.

———. *Twenty Years at Hull House, with Autobiographical Notes.* New York: Macmillan, 1910.

Alden, W. L. "Some Phases of Literary New York in the Sixties." *Putnam's Monthly* 3 (February 1908): 554–56.

Allen, Jane. "You May Have My Job: A Feminist Discovers her Home." *Forum* (April 1932): 228–31.

Allen, Judith A. "Debating Gilman's 'Feminism.'" Paper presented at the Third International Charlotte Perkins Gilman Conference, Columbia, SC, March 2001.

———. "Reconfiguring Vice: Charlotte Perkins Gilman, Prostitution, and Frontier Sexual Contracts." In Jill Rudd and Val Gough, eds., *Charlotte Perkins Gilman: Optimist Reformer (173–99).* Iowa City: University of Iowa Press, 1999.

Allen, Polly Wynn. *Building Domestic Liberty: Charlotte Perkins Gilman's Architectural Feminism.* Amherst: University of Massachusetts Press, 1988.

Allen, Robert, with Pamela P. Allen. *Reluctant Reformers: Racism and Social Reform Movements in the United States.* Washington, DC: Howard University Press, 1983.

Anthony, Susan B., et al. *History of Woman Suffrage* (6 vols.). National American Woman Suffrage Association, 1881–1922.

Antler, Joyce. *The Educated Woman and Professionalization: The Struggle for a New Feminine Identity, 1890–1920.* New York: Garland, 1987.

Applegate, Debby. *The Most Famous Man in America: The Biography of Henry Ward Beecher.* New York: Doubleday, 2006.

Aptheker, Bettina. "W. E. B. DuBois and the Struggle for Women's Rights, 1910–1920." *San Jose Studies* 1 (May 1975): 7–16.

Atherton, Gertrude. *Adventures of a Novelist* (reprint). New York: Arno, 1980.

———. "The Literary Development of California." *Cosmopolitan* (10 January 1891): 272.

Austin, Mary. *Earth Horizon, Autobiography.* Boston: Houghton Mifflin, 1932.

Baldwin, Kenneth Huntress. Untitled. In Denise D. Knight, *Charlotte Perkins Gilman: A Study of the Short Fiction* (175–84). New York: Twayne, 1997.

Banning, Margaret Culkin. "The Lazy Thirties." *Harper's Monthly Magazine* 154 (February 1927): 357–65.

Bannister, Robert C. *Social Darwinism: Science and Myth in Anglo-American Social Thought.* Philadelphia: Temple University Press, 1979.

Beard, Mary R. *America Through Women's Eyes.* New York: Macmillan, 1933.

———. *Woman as Force in History: A Study in Traditions and Realities.* New York: MacMillan, 1947.

———. *Women's Work in Municipalities* (orig. 1915). New York: Arno, 1972.

Becker, Susan D. *The Origins of the Equal Rights Amendment: American Feminism Between the Wars.* Westport, CT: Greenwood, 1981.

Bedell, Leila G. "A Chicago Toynbee Hall." *Woman's Journal* 20 (1889): 163.

Bederman, Gail. *Manliness and Civilization: A Cultural History of Gender and Race in the United States, 1880–1917.* Chicago: University of Chicago Press, 1996.

Beecher, Catharine E. *Letters to the People on Health and Happiness* (orig. 1855). New York: Arno, 1972.

———. *Physiology and Calisthenics for Schools and Families.* New York: Harper & Brothers, 1856.

Beer, Janet. "Charlotte Perkins Gilman and Woman's Health: 'The Long Limitation'." In Val Gough and Jill Rudd, eds., *A Very Different Story: Studies on the Fiction of Charlotte Perkins Gilman* (54–67). Liverpool: Liverpool University Press, 1998.

———. *Kate Chopin, Edith Wharton, and Charlotte Perkins Gilman: Studies in Short Fiction.* New York: St. Martin's, 1997.

———, and Katherine Joslin. "Diseases of the Body Politic: White Slavery in Jane Addams 'A New Conscience and an Ancient Evil' and Selected Short Stories by Charlotte Perkins Gilman." *Journal of American Studies* 33 (1999): 1–18.

Bell, Daniel. *Marxian Socialism in the United States.* Princeton, NJ: Princeton University Press, 1952.

Bell, Millicent. "Pioneer." *New York Review of Books* (17 April 1980): 10–14.

Bell, Susan Groag, and Karen M. Offen, eds., *Women, the Family, and Freedom: The Debate in Documents* (2 vols.). Stanford, CA: Stanford University Press, 1983.

Bellamy, Edward. *Edward Bellamy Speaks Again! Articles—Public Addresses—Letters.* Chicago: Peerage, 1938.

———. *Equality.* New York: D. Appleton & Company, 1897.

———. *Looking Backward.* Boston: Ticknor & Co., 1888.

———. "Positive Romance." *Century* 38 (August 1889): 625–30.

———. "Religion of Solidarity." In Joseph Schiffman, ed., Edward Bellamy: *Selected Writings on Religion and Society* (orig. 1955). Westport, CT: Greenwood, 1974.

———. *Talks on Nationalism.* Chicago: Peerage, 1938.

Berkin, Carol R. "Private Woman, Public Woman: The Contradictions of Charlotte Perkins Gilman." In Carol Ruth Berkin and Mary Beth Norton, eds., *Women of America: A History* (150–73). Boston: Houghton Mifflin, 1979.

Bingham, Edwin. *Charles F. Lummis: Editor of the Southwest.* San Marino, CA: Huntington Library, 1955.

Black, Alexander. *Time and Chance: Adventures with People and Print.* New York: Farrar & Rinehart, 1937.

———. "The Woman Who Saw It First." *Century* 107 (November 1923): 33–42.

Blackwell, Alice Stone. *Lucy Stone: Pioneer Woman Suffragist.* Alice Stone Blackwell Committee, 1930.

Blaikie, William. *How to Get Strong and How to Stay So.* New York: Harper & Brothers, 1879.

Blair, Karen. *The Clubwoman as Feminist: True Womanhood Redefined, 1868–1914.* New York: Holmes and Meier, 1980.

Blatch, Harriot Stanton, and Alma Lutz. *Challenging Years: The Memoirs of Harriot Stanton Blatch.* New York: G. P. Putnam's Sons, 1940.

Blavatsky, Helena Petrovna. *Key to Theosophy.* London: Theosophical Publishing Society, 1889.

Bliss, William D. P., and Rudolph M. Binder. *Encyclopedia of Social Reform: Including All Social-Reform Movements and Activities, and the Economic, Industrial, and Sociological Facts and Statistics of All Countries and All Social Subjects* (3rd ed.). New York: Funk & Wagnalls, 1908.

Bly, Nellie. "Nellie Bly with the Female Suffragists." *New York World* 4 (26 January 1876): 2–3.

Bower, Stephanie. "'I am the Squaw': Parasitism and Race in Charlotte Perkins Gilman's Writings." Paper presented at the Third International Charlotte Perkins Gilman Conference, Columbia, SC, May 2001.

Boydston, Jeanne, Mary Kelley, and Anne Margolis, eds. *The Limits of Sisterhood: The Beecher Sisters on Women's Rights and Woman's Sphere.* Chapel Hill: University of North Carolina Press, 1988.

Brace, Charles Loring. *The Dangerous Classes of New York.* New York: Wynkoop & Hallenbeck, 1872.

Brasch, Walter M. *Forerunners of Revolution: Muckrakers and the American Social Conscience.* Lanham, MD: University Press of America, 1990.

Brodhead, Richard R. *Cultures of Letters: Scenes of Reading and Writing in Nineteenth-Century America.* Chicago: University of Chicago Press, 1993.

Brown, Dorothy M. *Setting a Course: American Women in the 1920s.* Boston: Twayne, 1987.

Bruère, Martha S., and Mary R. Beard. *Laughing Their Way: Women's Humor in America.* New York: Macmillan, 1934.

Buhle, Mari Jo. *Feminism and Its Discontents: A Century of Struggle with Psychoanalysis.* Cambridge, MA: Harvard University Press, 1998.

———. *Women and American Socialism, 1870–1920.* Urbana: University of Illinois Press, 1981.

————, and Paul Buhle, eds. *The Concise History of Woman Suffrage.* Urbana: University of Illinois Press, 1979.

Burnham, John C. "The Influence of Psychoanalysis upon American Culture." In Jacques M. Quen and Eric T. Carlson, eds., *American Psychoanalysis, Origins and Development: The Adolf Meyer Seminars* (52–69). New York: Brunner/Mazel, 1978.

Calhoun, Craig, ed. *Habermas and the Public Sphere.* Cambridge, MA: MIT Press, 1992.

Campbell, Ballard C., ed. *Human Tradition in the Gilded Age and Progressive Era.* Wilmington, DE: SR Books, 2000.

Campbell, Helen (Stuart). "Charlotte Perkins Stetson—A Sketch." *Time and the Hour* (16 April 1898): 7–8; excerpted in *Bookman* 12 (November 1900): 204–06.

————. *Household Economics; A Course of Lectures in the School of Economics of the University of Wisconsin.* New York: G. P. Putnam's Sons, 1896.

Cane, Aleta F. "The Heroine of Her Own Story: Subversion of Traditional Periodical Marriage Tropes in the Short Fiction of Charlotte Perkins Gilman's Forerunner." In Aleta F. Cane and Susan Alves, eds., *"The Only Efficient Instrument": American Women Writers and the Periodical, 1837–1916* (95–112). Des Moines: Iowa University Press, 2001.

Carrier, Susan. "Residents Shape University Press Triangle." *Los Angeles Times* (19 March 1995): K1, K6.

Carson, Mina J. *Settlement Folk: Social Thought and the American Settlement Movement, 1885–1930.* Chicago: University of Chicago Press, 1990.

Carter-Sanborn, Kristin. "The Imperialist Anti-Violence of Charlotte Perkins Gilman." *Arizona Quarterly: A Journal of American Literature, Culture, and Theory* 56 (Summer 2000): 1–36.

Caskey, Marie. *Chariot of Fire: Religion and the Beecher Family.* New Haven, CT: Yale University Press, 1978.

Catt, Carrie Chapman, and Nettie Rogers Shuler. *Woman Suffrage and Politics: The Inner Story of the Suffrage Movement.* Buffalo, NY: Hein Publishing, 2004.

Ceplair, Larry, ed. *Charlotte Perkins Gilman: A Nonfiction Reader.* New York: Columbia University Press, 1991.

Channing [Stetson], Grace Ellery. "The Children of the Barren." *Harper's Monthly* (March 1907): 511–19.

————, ed. *Dr. Channing's Notebook; Passages from the Unpublished Manuscripts of William Ellery Channing, Selected by His Granddaughter.* Boston: Houghton Mifflin, 1887.

————. *Sea Drift: Poems.* Boston: Small, Maynard & Company, 1899.

"Charlotte Perkins Stetson." *Current Literature* 25 (February 1899): 115–16.

"Charlotte Perkins Stetson: A Daring Humorist of Reform." *American Fabian* 3 (January 1897): 1–3.

"Charlotte Perkins Stetson as a Social Philosopher and Poet." *Poet Lore* 11 (March 1899): 124–28.

Chauncey, George Jr. *Gay New York: Gender, Urban Culture, and the Making of the Gay Male World, 1890–1940.* New York: Basic Books, 1994.

Chesler, Ellen. *Woman of Valor: Margaret Sanger and the Birth Control Movement in America.* New York: Doubleday, 1992.

Chugerman, Samuel. *Lester F. Ward, the American Aristotle: A Summary and Interpretation of His Sociology* (orig. 1939). New York: Octagon, 1965.

Clarke, Edward H. *Sex in Education; or, A Fair Chance for Girls* (orig. 1873). Boston: Houghton Mifflin, 1892.

Cole, Margaret. *The Story of Fabian Socialism* (rev. ed.). New York: John Wiley & Sons, 1961.

Collier, Virginia MacMakin. *Marriage and Careers: A Study of One Hundred Women Who Are Wives, Mothers, Homemakers, and Professional Workers, for the Bureau of Vocational Information.* New York: Channel Bookshop, 1926.

Comstock, S. "Marriage or Career?" *Good Housekeeping* 94 (June 1932): 32–33, 159–62.

Conley, Patrick R., and Paul R. Campbell. *Providence: A Pictorial History.* Norfolk, VA: Donning Co., 1982.

Conlin, Joseph R., ed. *The American Radical Press, 1880–1960* (2 vols.). Westport, CT: Greenwood, 1974.

Connelly, Mark Thomas. "Prostitution, Venereal Disease, and American Medicine." In Judith Walzer Leavitt, ed., *Women and Health in America: Historical Readings* (196–221). Madison: University of Wisconsin Press, 1984.

Conway, Jill. "The Woman's Peace Party and the First World War." In J. L Granatstein and R. D. Cuff, eds., *War and Society in North America: Papers Presented at the Canadian Association for American Studies Meeting, Fall 1970* (52–65). Toronto: T. Nelson, 1971.

———. "Women Reformers and American Culture, 1870–1930." *Journal of Social History* 5 (Winter 1971–72): 164–77.

Cott, Nancy. *The Grounding of Modern Feminism.* New Haven, CT: Yale University Press, 1987.

Cranny-Francis, Anne. "Spinner of Dreams, Weaver of Realities." In Val Gough and Jill Rudd, eds., *A Very Different Story: Studies on the Fiction of Charlotte Perkins Gilman* (161–78). Liverpool: Liverpool University Press, 1998.

Croly, Herbert. *The Promise of American Life.* New York: Macmillan, 1909.

Croly, J. June. *History of the Woman's Club Movement in America.* New York: H. G. Allen & Co., 1898.

Dancis, Bruce. "Socialism and Women in the United States, 1900–1917." *Socialist Revolution* 6 (January–March 1976): 81–144.

Daniels, George, ed. *Darwinism Comes to America.* Waltham, MA: Blaisdell, 1968.

Davis, Allen F. *Spearheads for Reform: The Social Settlements and the Progressive Movement, 1890–1914.* New York: Oxford University Press, 1967.

Davis, Cynthia J. *Bodily and Narrative Forms: The Influence of Medicine on American Literature.* Stanford, CA: Stanford University Press, 2000.

———. "'Concerning Children': Charlotte Perkins Gilman, Mothering, and Biography." *Victorian Review* (special issue on the cultural work of biography) (2001): 102–15.

———. "His and Herland: Charlotte Perkins Gilman 'Re-presents' Lester F. Ward." In Claire Roche and Lois Cuddy, eds., *Evolution and Eugenics in American Literature.* Lewisburg, PA: Bucknell University Press, 2003.

———. "Introduction." In Cynthia J. Davis and Denise D. Knight, eds., *Charlotte*

Perkins Gilman and Her Contemporaries (ix–xvii). Tuscaloosa: University of Alabama Press, 2004.

———. "Love and Economics: Charlotte Perkins Gilman on 'The Woman Question.'" *ATQ: 19th C. American Literature and Culture* 19 (special issue on "The Woman Question")(December 2005): 243–58.

———. "The Two Mrs. Stetsons and the 'Romantic Summer'." In Cynthia J. Davis and Denise D. Knight, eds., *Charlotte Perkins Gilman and Her Contemporaries* (1–16). Tuscaloosa: University of Alabama Press, 2004.

———. "The Woman's Journal." In Gary Scharnhorst and Tom Quirk, eds., *American Literature in Historical Context, 1870–1920*. New York: Twayne, 2006.

———. "'The World Was Home for Me'": Charlotte Perkins Gilman and the Sentimental Public Sphere." *Arizona Quarterly* (forthcoming 2010).

———, and Denise D. Knight, eds. *Charlotte Perkins Gilman and Her Contemporaries.* Tuscaloosa: University of Alabama Press, 2004.

Davis, Reda. *California Women: A Guide to Their Politics, 1885–1911.* San Francisco: California Scene, 1968.

"Death Takes Noted Poet." *Pasadena Star-News* (19 August 1935): ?.

Decker, Hannah S. "Psychoanalysis and the Europeans." In Jacques M. Quen and Eric T. Carlson, eds., *American Psychoanalysis: Origins and Development. The Adolf Meyer Seminars* (1–19). New York: Brunner/Mazel, 1978.

Deegan, Mary Jo. *Jane Addams and the Men of the Chicago School.* New Brunswick, NJ: Transaction Books, 1988.

Degen, Mary Louise. *The History of the Woman's Peace Party.* Baltimore: Johns Hopkins University Press, 1939.

Degler, Carl. *At Odds: Women and the Family in America from the Revolution to the Present.* New York: Oxford University Press, 1980.

———. "Charlotte Perkins Gilman on the Theory and Practice of Feminism." *American Quarterly* 8 (Spring 1956): 21–39.

Deland, Margaret. "The Change in the Feminine Ideal." *Atlantic Monthly* CV (March 1910): 289–302.

Dell, Floyd. *Women as World Builders: Studies in Modern Feminism.* Chicago: Forbes, 1913.

Dock, Julia Bates, comp. and ed. *Charlotte Perkins Gilman's "The Yellow Wall-paper" and the History of Its Publication and Reception: A Critical Edition and Documentary Casebook.* University Park: University of Pennsylvania Press, 1998.

Dombrowski, James. *The Early Days of Christian Socialism in America.* New York: Columbia University Press, 1936.

Dorr, Rheta Child. *What Eight Million Women Want.* Boston: Small, Maynard & Company, 1910.

Doskow, Minna. "Charlotte Perkins Gilman: The Female Face of Social Darwinism." *Weber Studies* 14 (Fall 1997): 9–22.

———. *Charlotte Perkins Gilman's Utopian Novels.* Cranbury, NJ: Associated University Press, 1992.

Douglas, Ann. *The Feminization of American Culture.* New York: Knopf, 1978.

Doyle, William T. "Charlotte Perkins Gilman and the Cycle of Feminist Reform." PhD dissertation, University of California, 1960.

Dreiser, Theodore. *Sister Carrie.* New York: Norton, 1970.

DuBois, Ellen. *Woman Suffrage and Women's Rights.* New York: New York University Press, 1998.

———. "Working Women, Class Relations, and Suffrage Militance: Harriot Stanton Blatch and the New York Woman Suffrage Movement, 1894–1909." *Journal of American History* 74 (June 1987): 34–58.

DuBois, W. E. B. *Darkwater: Voices from Within the Veil.* New York: Harcourt, Brace, and Howe, 1920.

Dumke, Glenn S. *The Boom of the Eighties in Southern California.* San Marino, CA: Huntington Library, 1944.

Earnest, Ernest P. *S. Weir Mitchell, Novelist and Physician.* Philadelphia: University of Pennsylvania Press, 1950.

Eastman, Max. "Exploring the Soul and Healing the Body." *Everybody's Magazine* 32 (1915): 741–50.

———. "Mr. Er-er-er-Oh! What's His Name?" *Everybody's Magazine* 33 (1915): 95–103.

Edel, Leon. *Henry James: A Life.* New York: Harper & Row, 1985.

Ekirch, Arthur A., Jr. *Progressivism in America: A Study of the Era from Theodore Roosevelt to Woodrow Wilson.* New York: New Viewpoints, 1974.

Eldredge, Charles C. *Charles Walter Stetson: Color and Fantasy.* Lawrence: Spencer Museum of Art, University of Kansas Press, 1982.

Eliot, Charles W. *The Conflict Between Individualism and Collectivism in a Democracy.* New York: Charles Scribner's Sons, 1912.

Eliot, T. S. "Choruses from the Rock." In *The Complete Poems and Plays of T. S. Eliot.* London: Faber and Faber, 1969.

———. *The Sacred Wood: Essays on Poetry and Criticism.* London: Methune, 1920.

Erikson, Erik. *Childhood and Society.* New York: Norton, 1950.

Faderman, Lillian. *Surpassing the Love of Men: Romantic Friendship and Love Between Women from the Renaissance to the Present.* New York: William Morrow, 1981.

Faulkner, Harold. *Politics, Reform, and Expansion, 1890–1900.* New York: Harper, 1959.

Feffer, Andrew. *The Chicago Pragmatists and American Progressivism.* Ithaca, NY: Cornell University Press, 1993.

Filler, Louis. *The Unknown Edwin Markham: His Mystery and Its Significance.* Yellow Springs, OH: Antioch Press, 1966.

Fishkin, Shelley Fisher. "'Making a Change': Strategies of Subversion in Gilman's Journalism and Short Fiction." In Joanne B. Karpinski, ed., *Critical Essays on Charlotte Perkins Gilman* (234–48). New York: G. K. Hall, 1992.

Fitzpatrick, Ellen. *Endless Crusade: Women Social Scientists and Progressive Reform.* New York: Oxford University Press, 1990.

Fleenor, Julianne E. "The Gothic Prism: Charlotte Perkins Gilman's Gothic Stories and Her Autobiography." In Sheryl L. Meyering, ed., *Charlotte Perkins Gilman: The Woman and Her Work* (117–31). Ann Arbor: UMI Research Press, 1989. Originally published in *The Female Gothic* (227–41), Julianne E. Fleenor, ed., Montreal: Eden, 1983.

Flexner, Eleanor. *Century of Struggle: The Women's Rights Movement in the United States.* Cambridge, MA: Belknap Press/Harvard University Press, 1959.

Foner, Philip S. *History of the Labor Movement in the United States* (2nd ed.). New York: International Publishers, 1975.

Foucault, Michel. *History of Sexuality* (vol. 1). New York: Vintage, 1980.

Frank, Gill. "'I told you I loved her that way': Charlotte Perkins Gilman's Same-Sex Sexual Relationships and the Meanings of Sexual Variance in the 19th Century." Paper presented at the Fourth International Charlotte Perkins Gilman Conference, Portland, Maine, June 2006.

Frazier, John R. *A History of Rhode Island School of Design.* Providence, RI: RISD, 1961.

Gale, Zona. Foreword to *The Living of Charlotte Perkins Gilman* (xiii–xxxviii). New York: D. Appleton-Century, 1935. Excerpted in *The Nation* CXLI (25 September 1935): 350–57.

Ganobcsik-Williams, Lisa. "The Intellectualism of Charlotte Perkins Gilman: Evolutionary Perspectives on Race, Ethnicity, and Class." In Jill Rudd and Val Gough, eds., *Charlotte Perkins Gilman: Optimist Reformer* (16–41). Iowa City: University of Iowa Press, 1999.

Geddes, Patrick, and J. Arthur Thompson. *The Evolution of Sex.* London: W. Scott, 1889.

Geertz, Clifford. *The Interpretation of Cultures: Selected Essays.* New York: Basic Books, 1973.

George, Henry. *Progress and Poverty: An Inquiry into the Cause of Industrial Depressions, and of Increase of Want with Increase of Wealth. The Remedy.* New York: D. Appleton & Company, 1881.

Gere, Anne Ruggles. *Intimate Practices: Literacy and Cultural Work in U.S. Women's Clubs, 1880–1920.* Urbana: University of Illinois Press, 1997.

Gernes, Todd. "Houp La! Charlotte Perkins Gilman, Martha Luther Lane, and Young Women's Literary Culture in Nineteenth-Century Providence." In his "Recasting the Culture of Ephemera: Young Women's Literary Culture in Nineteenth-Century America." PhD dissertation, Brown University, 1992.

Gifford, Sanford. "The American Reception of Psychoanalysis, 1908–22." In Adele Heller and Lois Rudnick, eds., *1915, The Cultural Moment: The New Politics, the New Woman, the New Psychology, the New Art, and the New Theatre in America* (128–45). New Brunswick, NJ: Rutgers University Press, 1991.

Gilbert, Sandra M., and Susan Gubar. *The Madwoman in the Attic: The Woman Writer and the Nineteenth Century Literary Imagination.* New Haven, CT: Yale, 1979.

———. *No Man's Land: Sexchanges* (vol. 2). New Haven, CT: Yale University Press, 1989.

Gilkeson, John S., Jr. *Middle-Class Providence, 1820–1940.* Princeton, NJ: Princeton University Press, 1986.

Ginger, Ray. *Age of Excess: The United States from 1877 to 1914.* New York: Macmillan, 1965.

Gleason, William. "'Find Their Place and Fall in Line': The Revisioning of Women's Work in *Herland* and *Emma McChesney & Co.*" *Prospects: An Annual of American Cultural Studies* 21 (1996): 39–87.

Golden, Catherine, ed. *The Captive Imagination: A Casebook on The Yellow Wallpaper.* New York: Feminist Press, 1992.

———. "'Light of the Home,' Light of the World: The Presentation of Motherhood in Gilman's Short Fiction." *Modern Language Studies* 26 (Spring 1996): 135–47.

———, ed. *The Yellow Wall-Paper: A Sourcebook and Critical Edition.* New York: Routledge, 2004.

———, and Denise D. Knight, eds. *Unpunished: A Mystery.* New York: Feminist Press, 1997.

———, and Joanna Schneider Zangrando, eds. *The Mixed Legacy of Charlotte Perkins Gilman.* Newark: University of Delaware Press, 2000.

Goldsmith, Barbara. *Other Powers: The Age of Suffrage, Spiritualism, and the Scandalous Victoria Woodhull.* New York: Knopf, 1998.

Goodman, Charlotte Margolis. "Paper Mates: The Sisterhood of Charlotte Perkins Gilman and Edith Summers Kelley." In Catherine Golden and Joanna Schneider Zangrando, eds., *The Mixed Legacy of Charlotte Perkins Gilman* (160–71). Newark: University of Delaware Press, 2000.

Gosling, F. G. *Before Freud: Neurasthenia and the American Medical Community, 1870–1910.* Champaign: University of Illinois Press, 1987.

Gough, Val, and Jill Rudd, eds. *A Very Different Story: Studies on the Fiction of Charlotte Perkins Gilman.* Liverpool: Liverpool University Press, 1998.

Graulich, Melody. "'I Thought at First She Was Talking About Herself': Mary Austin on Charlotte Perkins Gilman." *Jack London Journal* 1 (1994): 148–58.

Green, Harvey. *Fit for America: Health, Fitness, Sport, and American Society.* New York: Pantheon, 1986.

———. *The Light of the Home: An Intimate View of the Lives of Women in Victorian America.* New York: Pantheon, 1983.

Hale, Edward Everett. *How to Do It.* Project Gutenberg e-book. http://www.gutenberg.org/dirs/etext05/8hdit10h.html/ (accessed February 17, 2003).

Hale, Nathan G., Jr. *Freud in America Vol. 1, Freud and the Americans: The Beginnings of Psychoanalysis in the United States, 1876–1917.* New York: Oxford University Press, 1971.

Haller, John S. *Outcasts from Evolution: Scientific Attitudes of Racial Inferiority, 1859–1900.* Urbana: University of Illinois Press, 1971.

Haller, Mark. *Eugenics: Hereditarian Attitudes in American Thought.* New Brunswick, NJ: Rutgers University Press, 1963.

Hart, Lavinia. "The Divorce Germ." *Cosmopolitan* 37 (1904): 201–06.

Hausman, Bernice L. "Sex Before Gender: Charlotte Perkins Gilman and the Evolutionary Paradigm of Utopia." *Feminist Studies* 24 (Fall 1998): 489–510.

Hayden, Dolores. "Charlotte Perkins Gilman and the Kitchenless House." *Radical History Review* 21 (Fall 1979): 225–47.

———. *A Grand Domestic Revolution: Feminists' Revolt Against the American Home, 1884–1931.* Cambridge, MA: MIT Press, 1980.

"Hearing of the National American Woman Suffrage Association. Committee on [*sic*] the Judiciary, House of Representatives, Washington, D.C., January 28, 1896." *Votes for*

Women: Selections from the National American Woman Suffrage Association Collection, 1848–1921. http://memory.loc.gov/cgi-bin/query/r?ammem/naw:"afield+(SOURCE+" band(rbnawsa+n990/ (accessed September 21, 2001).

Hedges, Elaine R. "Afterword." *The Yellow Wallpaper* (37–63). New York: Feminist Press, 1973.

———. "'Out at Last'? 'The Yellow Wallpaper' After Two Decades of Feminist Criticism." In Catherine Golden, ed. *The Captive Imagination: A Casebook on The Yellow Wallpaper* (319–33). New York: Feminist Press, 1992.

Hedrick, Joan. *Harriet Beecher Stowe: A Life.* New York: Oxford University Press, 1994.

Heilman, Ann. "Overwriting Decadence: Charlotte Perkins Gilman, Oscar Wilde, and the Feminization of Art in 'The Yellow Wall-Paper.'" In Catherine Golden and Joanna Schneider Zangrando, eds., *The Mixed Legacy of Charlotte Perkins Gilman (175–88).* Newark: University of Delaware Press, 2000.

Heller, Adele, and Lois Rudnick, eds. *1915, The Cultural Moment: The New Politics, the New Woman, the New Psychology, the New Art, and the New Theatre in America.* New Brunswick, NJ: Rutgers University Press, 1991.

Herreshoff, David. *American Disciples of Marx: From the Age of Jackson to the Progressive Era.* Detroit: Wayne State University Press, 1967.

Higham, John. *Strangers in the Land: Patterns of American Nativism, 1860–1925.* New Brunswick, NJ: Rutgers University Press, 1955.

———. "The Reorientation of American Culture in the 1890's." *Writing American History: Essays on Modern Scholarship* (73–102). Bloomington: Indiana University Press, 1970.

Hill, Mary A. "Charlotte Perkins Gilman: A Feminist Struggle with Womanhood." *Massachusetts Review* 21 (Fall 1980): 503–26.

———. "Charlotte Perkins Gilman and the Journey from Within." In Val Gough and Jill Rudd, eds., *A Very Different Story: Studies on the Fiction of Charlotte Perkins Gilman* (8–23). Liverpool: Liverpool University Press, 1998.

———. *Charlotte Perkins Gilman: The Making of a Radical Feminist, 1860–1896.* Philadelphia: Temple University Press, 1980.

———, ed. *Endure: The Diaries of Charles Walter Stetson.* Philadelphia: Temple University Press, 1985.

———, ed. *A Journey from Within: The Love Letters of Charlotte Perkins Gilman, 1897–1900.* Lewisburg, PA: Bucknell University Press, 1995.

Hinkel, Edgar J., and William E. McCann, eds. *Biographies of California Authors and Indexes of California Literature.* Oakland: Alameda County Library, 1942.

Hobbs, Margaret. "The Perils of 'Unbridled Masculinity': Pacifist Elements in the Feminist and Socialist Thought of Charlotte Perkins Gilman." In Ruth Roach Peirson, ed., *Women and Peace: Theoretical, Historical, and Practical Perspectives* (149–69). London: Croom Helm, 1987.

Hofstadter, Richard. *The Age of Reform: From Bryan to F.D.R.* New York: Knopf, 1955.

———. *Social Darwinism in American Thought* (orig. 1944). Boston: Beacon, 1964.

Hough, Eugene. "How Psycho-Analysis Has Obsessed the World with Sex." *Current Opinion* 46 (1914): 441–42.

————. *The Confessions of a Reformer.* New York: Charles Scribner's Sons, 1925.

————. "The Work and Influence of Charlotte Perkins Stetson in the Labor Movement." *American Fabian* 3 (January 1897): 12.

Howe, Harriet. "Charlotte Perkins Gilman—As I Knew Her." *Equal Rights* (5 September 1936): 211–16.

————. "The Personality of Charlotte Perkins Gilman." *Equal Rights* 25 (October 1939): 118.

Howells, William Dean, ed. *The Great Modern American Stories* (orig. 1920). New York: Garrett Press, 1969.

"Ida Tarbell Answered." *The Woman Voter* 3 (June 1912): 7–13.

International Council of Women. *Women in a Changing World: The Dynamic Story of the International Council of Women since 1888.* London: Routledge & Kegan Paul, 1966.

Irwin, Inez Haynes. *Angels and Amazons: A Hundred Years of American Women.* Garden City, NY: Doubleday, 1933.

Jacobi, Mary Putnam. *"Common Sense" Applied to Woman Suffrage: A Statement of Reasons Which Justify the Demand to Extend the Suffrage to Women, with Consideration of the Arguments Against Such Enfranchisement, and with Special Reference to the Issues Presented to the New York State Convention of 1894.* New York: G. P. Putnam's Sons, 1894.

————. *The Question of Rest for Women During Menstruation.* New York: G. P. Putnam's Sons, 1877.

James, Edward T., Janet Wilson James, and Paul S. Boyer, eds. *Notable American Women: A Biographical Dictionary* (3 vols.). Cambridge, MA: Belknap Press/Harvard University Press, 1971.

James, William. *Principles of Psychology* (2 vols.). New York: Henry Holt, 1890.

Jeffreys, Sheila. *The Spinster and Her Enemies: Feminism and Sexuality, 1880–1930.* Boston: Pandora, 1985.

Jenkin, Thomas P. "The American Fabian Movement." *Western Political Quarterly* 1 (June 1948): 113–23.

Karpinski, Joanne B., ed. *Critical Essays on Charlotte Perkins Gilman.* New York: G. K. Hall, 1992.

————. "The Economic Conundrum in the Life Writing of Charlotte Perkins Gilman." In Catherine Golden and Joanna Schneider Zangrando, eds., *The Mixed Legacy of Charlotte Perkins Gilman* (35–46). Newark: University of Delaware Press, 2000.

————. "When the Marriage of True Minds Admits Impediments: Charlotte Perkins Gilman and William Dean Howells." In Cynthia J. Davis and Denise D. Knight, eds., *Charlotte Perkins Gilman and Her Contemporaries* (17–31). Tuscaloosa: University of Alabama Press, 2004. Originally published in Shirley Marchalonis, ed., *Patrons and Protégées: Gender, Friendship, and Writing in Nineteenth-Century America* (212–34). New Brunswick, NJ: Rutgers University Press, 1994.

Katzman, David. *Seven Days a Week: Women and Domestic Service in Industrializing America.* New York: Oxford University Press, 1978.

Kelley, Mary. *Private Woman, Public Stage: Literary Domesticity in Nineteenth-Century America.* New York: Oxford University Press, 1984.

Kennedy, David M. *Birth Control in America: The Career of Margaret Sanger.* New Haven: Yale University Press, 1970.

Kessler, Carol Farley. *Charlotte Perkins Gilman: Her Progress Toward Utopia with Selected Writings.* NY: Syracuse University Press, 1995.

———, ed. *Daring to Dream: Utopian Stories by United States Women: 1836–1919.* Boston: Pandora Press, 1984.

Kessler-Harris, Alice. *Out to Work: A History of Wage-Earning Women in the United States.* New York: Oxford University Press, 1982.

Key, Ellen. *Century of the Child.* New York: G.P. Putnam's Sons, 1909.

———. "Education for Motherhood." *Atlantic* 112 (July 1913): 49–50.

———. *Renaissance of Motherhood.* Trans. Anna E. B. Fries. New York: G.P. Putnam's Sons, 1914.

Kipnis, Ira. *The American Socialist Movement: 1897–1912.* New York: Columbia University Press, 1952.

Kirchwey, Freda, ed. *Our Changing Morality: A Symposium.* New York, Albert & Charles Boni, 1930.

Kirkland, Janice. "Mrs. Stetson and Mr. Shaw in Suffolk: Animadversions and Obstacles." In Cynthia J. Davis and Denise D. Knight, eds., *Charlotte Perkins Gilman and Her Contemporaries* (87–102). Tuscaloosa: University of Alabama Press, 2004.

Kirkpatrick, Frank G. "'Begin Again!': The Cutting Social Edge of Charlotte Perkins Gilman's Gentle Religious Optimism." In Joanne B. Karpinski, ed. *Critical Essays on Charlotte Perkins Gilman* (129–43). New York: G. K. Hall, 1992.

Knapp, Adeline. "Do Working Women Need the Ballot?" An Address to the Senate and Assembly Judiciary of the New York Legislature. New York: New York State Association Opposed to Woman Suffrage, 1908.

———. *One Thousand Dollars a Day: Studies in Practical Economics.* Boston: Arena Publishing Co., 1894.

———. *An Open Letter to Mrs. Carrie Chapman Catt.* New York: New York State Association Opposed to the Extension of Suffrage to Women, 1899.

———. *This Then Is Upland Pastures.* East Aurora, NY: Roycroft Printing, 1897.

Knight, Denise D. "An 'Amusing Source of Income': Charlotte Perkins Gilman and the Soapine Connection." *Advertising Trade Quarterly* (Summer 2001): 8–12.

———. "'But O My Heart!': The Private Poetry of Charlotte Perkins Gilman." In Jill Rudd and Val Gough, eds., *Charlotte Perkins Gilman: Optimist Reformer* (266–84). Iowa City: University of Iowa Press, 1999.

———. *Charlotte Perkins Gilman: A Study of the Short Fiction.* New York: Twayne, 1997.

———. "Charlotte Perkins Gilman's Lost Book: A Biographical Gap." *ANQ* 14 (Winter 2001): 26–31.

———. "Charlotte Perkins Gilman, William Randolph Hearst, and the Practice of Ethical Journalism." In Cynthia J. Davis and Denise D. Knight, eds., *Charlotte Perkins Gilman and Her Contemporaries* (46–58). Tuscaloosa: University of Alabama Press, 2004. Originally published in *American Journalism* 2 (Fall 1994): 336–47.

————, ed. *The Diaries of Charlotte Perkins Gilman* (2 vols.). Charlottesville: University of Virginia Press, 1994.

————. "The Dying of Charlotte Perkins Gilman." *American Transcendental Quarterly* 13 (1999): 137–59.

————. "Gilman's Breakdown and the Art of Autobiographical Omission." Paper presented at the Association of Writers and Writing Programs Conference, SUNY-Albany, April 1999.

————, ed. *The Later Poetry of Charlotte Perkins Gilman*. Newark: University of Delaware Press, 1996.

————. "The Reincarnation of Jane: 'Through This': Gilman's Companion to 'The Yellow Wallpaper'." *Women's Studies: An Interdisciplinary Journal* 20 (1992): 287–302.

————. "'With the first grass-blade': Whitman's Influence on the Poetry of Charlotte Perkins Gilman." *Walt Whitman Quarterly Review* (Summer 1993): 18–29.

————, and Jennifer S. Tuttle, eds. *Selected Letters of Charlotte Perkins Gilman* (forthcoming).

Knight, Louise W. *Citizen: Jane Addams and the Struggle for Democracy*. Chicago: University of Chicago Press, 2004.

Kolodny, Annette. "A Map for Rereading: Or, Gender and the Interpretation of Literary Texts." *New Literary History* (1980): 451–67.

Koven, Seth, and Sonya Michel, eds. *Mothers of a New World: Maternalist Politics and the Origins of Welfare States*. New York: Routledge, 1993.

Kraditor, Aileen S. *The Ideas of the Woman Suffrage Movement, 1890–1920*. New York: Columbia University Press, 1965.

————, ed. *Up from the Pedestal: Selected Writings in the History of American Feminism*. Chicago: Quadrangle, 1968.

Lancaster, Jane. "'I could easily have been an acrobat': Charlotte Perkins Gilman and the Providence Ladies' Sanitary Gymnasium 1881–1884." *ATQ* 8 (March 1994): 33–52.

Lane, Ann J. *To Herland and Beyond: The Life and Work of Charlotte Perkins Gilman*. Charlottesville: University Press of Virginia, 1990.

Lanser, Susan. "Feminist Criticism, 'The Yellow Wallpaper,' and the Politics of Color in America." *Feminist Studies* 15 (Fall 1989): 415–41.

Leach, Eugene E. "The Radicals of *The Masses*." In Adele Heller and Lois Rudnick, eds., *1915, The Cultural Moment: The New Politics, the New Woman, the New Psychology, the New Art, and the New Theatre in America* (27–47). New Brunswick, NJ: Rutgers University Press, 1991.

Lears, T. J. Jackson. *No Place of Grace: Antimodernism and the Transformation of American Culture, 1880–1920*. New York: Pantheon, 1981.

Leider, Emily Wortis. *California's Daughter: Gertrude Atherton and Her Times*. Palo Alto: Stanford Uniersity Press, 1991.

Lemons, J. Stanley. *The Woman Citizen: Social Feminism in the 1920's*. Urbana: University of Illinois Press, 1973.

Levitas, Ruth. "Utopian Fictions and Political Theories: Domestic Labour in the Work of Edward Bellamy, Charlotte Perkins Gilman and William Morris." In Val Gough and

Jill Rudd, eds., *A Very Different Story: Studies on the Fiction of Charlotte Perkins Gilman* (81–99). Liverpool: Liverpool University Press, 1998.

Lipow, Arthur. *Authoritarian Socialism in America: Edward Bellamy and the Nationalist Movement.* Berkeley: University of California Press, 1982.

Lippmann, Walter. *Drift and Mastery: An Attempt to Diagnose the Current Unrest.* New York: Kennerley, 1914.

Livermore, Mary. "Cooperative Housekeeping." *The Chautauquan* 6 (April 1886): 396–99.

Long, Lisa A. "Charlotte Perkins Gilman's *With Her in Ourland*: Herland Meets Heterodoxy." In Cynthia J. Davis and Denise D. Knight, eds., *Charlotte Perkins Gilman and Her Contemporaries* (171–93). Tuscaloosa: University of Alabama Press, 2004.

Low, Frances H. "A Woman's Criticism of the Women's Congress." *The Nineteenth Century* 46 (August 1899): 192–202.

Lummis, Charles. "Western Letters." *Land of Sunshine* (May 1900): 350.

Lunardini, Christine A. *From Equal Suffrage to Equal Rights: Alice Paul and the National Woman's Party, 1910–1928.* New York: New York University Press, 1986.

———, and Thomas J. Knock. "Woodrow Wilson and Woman Suffrage: A New Look." *Political Science Quarterly* 95 (Winter 1980–1981): 655–71.

Lunbeck, Elizabeth. *The Psychiatric Persuasion: Knowledge, Gender, and Power in Modern America.* Princeton, NJ: Princeton University Press, 1994.

Lutz, Tom. *American Nervousness, 1903: An Anecdotal History.* Ithaca, NY: Cornell University Press, 1991.

Mac Donnell, Kevin. "Trade Cards by Charlotte Perkins Gilman: The Young Artist's Soapine and non-Soapine Designs." *American Trade Card Quarterly* (Fall 2001): 18–28.

Mason, Otis T. *Woman's Share in Primitive Culture.* New York: D. Appleton & Company, 1894.

Martin, Prestonia Mann, and John Martin. *Feminism, Its Fallacies and Follies.* New York: Dodd, Mead, 1916.

Mastrianni, Enid. "Summer Brook: Prestonia Mann Martin's Mountain Utopia." *Adirondack Life* (July/August 2000): 36–41.

Matthews, Glenna. *The Rise of Public Woman: Woman's Power and Woman's Place in the United States, 1630–1970.* New York: Oxford University Press, 1992.

May, Elaine Tyler. *Great Expectations: Marriage and Divorce in Post-Victorian America.* Chicago: University of Chicago Press, 1980.

McGerr, Michael. *A Fierce Discontent: The Rise and Fall of the Progressive Movement in America, 1870–1920.* New York: Free Press, 2003.

McWilliams, Carey. *Southern California Country: An Island on the Land.* New York: Duell, Sloan and Pearce, 1946.

Menand, Louis. *The Metaphysical Club.* New York: Farrar, Straus and Giroux, 2001.

Meyering, Sheryl L., ed. *Charlotte Perkins Gilman: The Woman and Her Work.* Ann Arbor: UMI Research Press, 1989.

Michaels, Walter Benn. *Our America: Nativism, Modernism, and Pluralism.* Durham, NC: Duke University Press, 1995.

Middleton, George. *These Things Are Mine: The Autobiography of a Journeyman Play-wright*. New York: Macmillan, 1947.

Mill, John Stuart. *The Subjection of Women*. New York: D. Appleton & Company, 1870.

Mitchell, S. Weir. *Doctor and Patient* (orig. 1888). New York: Arno, 1972.

———. *Fat and Blood: An Essay on the Treatment of Certain Forms of Neurasthenia and Hysteria*. Philadelphia: J. B. Lippincott, 1884.

———. *Lecture on Diseases of the Nervous System, Especially in Women*. Philadelphia: Henry C. Lea, 1881.

———. *Wear and Tear, or Hints for the Overworked* (5th ed.). Philadelphia: J. P. Lippincott, 1891.

Morantz, Reginal Markell. "The Perils of Feminist History." In Judith Walker Leavitt, ed., *Women and Health in America: Historical Readings* (239–45). Madison: University of Wisconsin Press, 1984.

Mowry, George. *The California Progressives*. Berkeley: University of California Press, 1951.

"Mrs. Catt Defends Mrs. Gilman's Suicide." *New York Times* 21 (21 August 1935): 7.

"Mrs. Charlotte Perkins Gilman." *Current Literature* 36 (May 1904): 511.

"Mrs. Charlotte Gilman, Poet, Ends Her Life." *Chicago Tribune* 1 (20 August 1935): 5–6.

Muncy, Robin. *Creating a Female Dominion in American Reform, 1890–1935*. New York: Oxford University Press, 1991.

Muzzey, Annie L. "The Hour and the Woman." *Arena* (August 1899): 263–72.

"Neighbors in '80s Helped Mold Pasadena." *Pasadena Star-News* (11 March 1956).

Newman, Louise. *White Women's Rights: The Racial Origins of Feminism in the United States*. New York: Oxford University Press, 1999.

New York: A Guide to the Empire State. Compiled by the Writer's Program of the WPA. New York: Oxford University Press, 1940.

Nietzsche, Friedrich. *Thus Spoke Zarathustra*. Walter Kaufmann, trans. New York: Penguin, 1976.

Nordau, Max. *Degeneration* (2nd German ed.). New York: D. Appleton & Company, 1895.

Nye, Russel B. "Introduction." *Uncle Tom's Cabin*. New York: Washington Square Press, 1965.

Oliver, Lawrence J., and Gary Scharnhorst. "Charlotte Perkins Gilman vs. Ambrose Bierce: The Literary Politics of Gender in Fin-de-Siècle California." In Cynthia J. Davis and Denise D. Knight, eds., *Charlotte Perkins Gilman and Her Contemporaries* (32–45). Tuscaloosa: University of Alabama Press, 2004. Originally published in *Journal of the West* (July 1993): 52–60.

O'Neill, William. *Divorce in the Progressive Era*. New Haven, CT: Yale University Press, 1967.

———. *Everyone Was Brave: The Rise and Fall of Feminism in America*. New York: Quadrangle, 1969.

———, ed. *The Woman Movement: Feminism in the United States and England* (orig. 1969). Chicago: Quadrangle, 1971.

Page, Charles H. *Class and American Sociology: From Ward to Ross*. New York: Dial, 1940.

Painter, Nell I. *The Progressive Era*. New York: Random House, 1985.

Pateman, Carole. "Feminist Critiques of the Public/Private Dichotomy." In S. J. Benn and G. F. Gaus, eds., *Public and Private in Social Life* (281–303). Kent: Croom Helm, 1983.

Peck, Harry Thurston. "Twenty Years of the Republic." *Bookman* 23 (June 1906): 404–05.

Peck, Mary Gray. *Carrie Chapman Catt: A Biography.* New York: H. W. Wilson, 1944.

Peirce, Melusina Fay. "Cooperative Housekeeping." Series of five articles. *Atlantic Monthly* (November 1868–March 1869).

———. "Cooperative Housekeeping." *The Woman's Journal* (29 March 1884): 102.

Perkins, Frederic Beecher. *Devil Puzzlers: And Other Studies.* New York: G. P. Putnam's Sons, 1877.

———. *The Picture and the Men: Being Biographical Sketches of President Lincoln and His Cabinet.* New York, A. J. Johnson: 1867.

———. *The Station and Duty of American Teachers as Citizens, in View of the Materialism of the Age.* Hartford: Association of the Alumni of Connecticut State Normal School, October 7, 1857.

Pittenger, Mark. *American Socialists and Evolutionary Thought, 1870–1920.* Madison: University of Wisconsin Press, 1993.

Poirier, Suzanne. "The Weir Mitchell Rest Cure: Doctor and Patients." *Women's Studies* 10 (1983): 15–40.

Rambo, Sharon M. "*What Diantha Did*: The Authority of Experience." In Sheryl L. Meyering, ed., *Charlotte Perkins Gilman: The Woman and Her Work* (151–71). Ann Arbor: UMI Research Press, 1989.

Rauchway, Eric. *Murdering McKinley: The Making of Theodore Roosevelt's America.* New York: Hill and Wang, 2003.

Rein, David. *S. Weir Mitchell as a Psychiatric Novelist.* New York: International Universities Press, 1952.

Rice, Allen Thorndike, ed. "Are Women to Blame?" *North American Review* (January–June 1889): 622–42.

Riis, Jacob. *Children of the Poor.* New York: Charles Scribner, 1892.

Rodgers, Daniel T. *Atlantic Crossings: Social Politics in a Progressive Age.* Cambridge, MA: Harvard University Press, 1998.

Roosevelt, Theodore. *Theodore Roosevelt: An American Mind.* Mario R. Dinunzio, ed. New York: St. Martin's, 1994.

Rose, Jane Atteridge. "Images of Self: The Example of Rebecca Harding Davis and Charlotte Perkins Gilman." *English Language Notes* (June 1992): 70–78.

Rosenberg, Rosalind. *Beyond Separate Spheres: Intellectual Roots of Modern Feminism.* New Haven, CT: Yale University Press, 1982.

Ross, Dorothy. *The Origins of American Social Science.* New York: Cambridge University Press, 1991.

Ross, Edward Alsworth. *The Old World in the New: The Significance of Past and Present Immigration to the American People.* New York: Century, 1914.

———. *Seventy Years of It: An Autobiography of Edward Alsworth Ross* (orig. 1936). New York: Arno, 1977.

———. *Social Control: A Survey of the Foundations of Order.* New York: Macmillan, 1901.

Rudd, Jill, and Val Gough, eds. *Charlotte Perkins Gilman: Optimist Reformer.* Iowa City: University of Iowa Press, 1999.

Rugoff, Milton. *The Beechers: An American Family in the Nineteenth Century.* New York: Harper & Row, 1981.

Sahli, Nancy. "Smashing: Women's Relationships Before the Fall." *Chrysalis* 8 (Summer 1979): 17–27.

Sandmeyer, Elmer Clarence. *The Anti-Chinese Movement in California.* Urbana: University of Illinois Press, 1939.

Sanger, Margaret. *Margaret Sanger: An Autobiography.* New York: Norton, 1938.

Scharnhorst, Gary. *Charlotte Perkins Gilman.* Boston: Twayne, 1985.

———. "Making Her Fame: Charlotte Perkins Gilman in California." *California History* 64: (Summer 1985): 192–201.

———. "Reconstructing *Here Also*: On the Later Poetry of Charlotte Perkins Gilman." In Joanne B. Karpinski, ed., *Critical Essays on Charlotte Perkins Gilman* (249–68). New York: G. K. Hall, 1992.

———. "'Ways That Are Dark': Appropriations of Bret Harte's 'Plain Language from Truthful James.'" *Nineteenth Century Literature* 51 (December 1996): 377–99.

———, and Denise D. Knight. "Charlotte Perkins Gilman's Library: A Reconstruction." *Resources for American Literary Study* 23 (1997): 181–219.

Scheid, Ann. *Pasadena: Crown of the Valley: An Illustrated History.* Northridge, CA: Windsor Publications, 1986.

Schreiner, Olive. *Dreams.* Boston: Roberts Brothers, 1892.

———. *Woman and Labor* (4th ed.). New York: Stokes, 1911.

Schwarz, Judith. *Radical Feminists of Heterodoxy: Greenwich Village: 1912–1940.* Lebanon, NH: New Victoria, 1982.

Scott, Anne Firor. *Natural Allies: Women's Associations in American History.* Urbana: University of Illinois Press, 1991.

———. "'A New-Model Woman.' Review of *Charlotte Perkins Gilman: The Making of a Radical Feminist, 1860–1896*, by Mary A. Hill." *Reviews in American History* 8 (December 1980): 442–47.

Scott, Clifford. *Lester Frank Ward.* Boston: Twayne, 1976.

Seelye, John. *Memory's Nation: The Place of Plymouth Rock.* Chapel Hill: University of North Carolina Press, 1998.

Seitler, Dana. "Introduction." *The Crux.* Durham, NC: Duke University Press, 2003.

———. "Mothers, Eugenic Feminism, and Charlotte Perkins Gilman's Regeneration Narratives." *American Quarterly* 55 (March 2003): 61–88.

"Sex O'Clock in America." *Current Opinion* 55 (August 1913): 113–14.

Sicherman, Barbara. "The Paradox of Prudence: Mental Health in the Gilded Age." *Journal of American History* 62 (1976): 890–912.

Simmons, Christina. "Modern Sexuality and the Myth of Victorian Repression." In Kathy Peiss and Christina Simmons, eds., *Passion and Power: Sexuality in History* (157–77). Philadelphia: Temple University Press, 1989.

Sinclair, Upton. *The Jungle* (orig. 1906). New York: Penguin, 2006.

Sklar, Kathryn Kish. *Catharine Beecher: A Study in American Domesticity*. New Haven, CT: Yale University Press, 1973.

———. *Florence Kelley and the Nation's Work: The Rise of Women's Political Culture, 1830–1900*. New Haven, CT: Yale University Press, 1995.

———. "Hull House in the 1890s: A Community of Women Reformers." *Signs* 10 (1985): 658–77.

Smith-Rosenberg, Carroll. *Disorderly Conduct: Visions of Gender in Victorian America*. New York: Knopf, 1985.

Sochen, June. *Movers and Shakers: American Women Thinkers and Activists, 1900–1970*. New York: Quadrangle, 1973.

———. *The New Woman: Feminism in Greenwich Village, 1910–1920*. New York: Quadrangle, 1972.

Spacks, Patricia Meyer. *The Female Imagination*. New York: Knopf, 1975.

Spann, Edward K. *Brotherly Tomorrows: Movements for a Cooperative Society in America, 1820–1920*. New York: Columbia University Press, 1989.

Stansell, Christine. *American Moderns: Bohemian New York and the Creation of a New Century*. New York: Metropolitan, 2000.

Stanton, Elizabeth Cady. *The Woman's Bible* (orig. 1895–1898). New York: Arno, 1972.

Starr, Kevin. *Inventing the Dream: California Through the Progressive Era*. New York: Oxford University Press, 1985.

Steele, Meile. *Theorizing Textual Subjects: Agency and Oppression*. Cambridge: Cambridge University Press, 1997.

Stetson, Charles Walter. *Endure: The Diaries of Charles Walter Stetson*. Mary Armfield Hill, ed. Philadelphia: Temple University Press, 1985.

Stocking, George W. *Race, Culture, and Evolution: Essays in the History of Anthropology*. New York: Free Press, 1968.

Stowe, Lyman Beecher. *Saints, Sinners, and Beechers*. New York: Blue Ribbon Books, 1934.

Studley, Dr. Mary. *What Our Girls Ought to Know*. New York: Funk & Wagnalls, 1882.

Sumner, William Graham. "The Absurd Effort to Make the World Over." *Forum* 17 (1894): 92–102.

Tarbell, Ida. *The Business of Being a Woman*. New York: Macmillan, 1912.

Tax, Meredith. *The Rising of the Women: Feminist Solidarity and Class Conflict, 1880–1917*. New York and London: Monthly Review, 1980.

Thomas, Heather Kirk. "'[A] kind of debased Romanesque' with '*delirium tremens*': Late-Victorian Wall Coverings and Charlotte Perkins Gilman's 'The Yellow Wall-Paper.'" In Catherine Golden and Joanna Schneider Zangrando, eds., *The Mixed Legacy of Charlotte Perkins Gilman* (189–206). Newark: University of Delaware Press, 2000.

Thomas, John L. *Alternative America: Henry George, Edward Bellamy, Henry Demarest Lloyd, and the Adversary Tradition*. Cambridge, MA: Belknap Press/Harvard University Press, 1983.

Thomas, W. I. "On a Difference in the Metabolism of the Sexes." *American Journal of Sociology* 3 (July 1897): 31–63.

Treichler, Paula. "Escaping the Sentence: Diagnosis and Discourse in 'The Yellow Wall-paper.'" In Catherine Golden, ed., *The Captive Imagination: A Casebook on The Yellow Wallpaper* (191–210). New York: Feminist Press, 1992.

Trimberger, Ellen Kay. 'The New Woman and the New Sexuality: Conflict and Contradiction in the Writings and Lives of Mabel Dodge and Neith Boyce." In Adele Heller and Lois Rudnick, eds., *1915, The Cultural Moment: The New Politics, the New Woman, the New Psychology, the New Art, and the New Theatre in America* (98–115). New Brunswick, NJ: Rutgers University Press, 1991.

Tuttle, Jennifer S. "Gilman's *The Crux* and Owen Wister's *The Virginian*: Intertextuality and 'Woman's Manifest Destiny'." In Cynthia J. Davis and Denise D. Knight, eds., *Charlotte Perkins Gilman and Her Contemporaries* (127–38). Tuscaloosa: University of Alabama Press, 2004.

———. "Rewriting the West Cure: Charlotte Perkins Gilman, Owen Wister, and the Sexual Politics of Neurasthenia." In Catherine Golden and Joanna Schneider Zangrando, eds., *The Mixed Legacy of Charlotte Perkins Gilman* (103–21). Newark: University of Delaware Press, 2000.

Van Voris, Jacqueline. *Carrie Chapman Catt: A Public Life.* New York: Feminist Press, 1987.

Van Wienen, Mark W. "A Rose by Any other Name: Charlotte Perkins Stetson (Gilman) and the Case for American Reform Socialism." *American Quarterly* 55 (2003): 603–34.

Veblen, Thorstein. "The Economic Theory of Women's Dress." *Popular Science Monthly* 56 (November 1894): 198–205.

———. *Theory of the Leisure Class* (orig. 1899). New York: Modern Library, 2001.

Vernon, Di. "Charlotte Perkins Stetson." *San Francisco News Letter* (28 March 1891): 5.

Vicinus, Martha. *Intimate Friends: Women Who Loved Women, 1778–1928.* Chicago: University of Chicago Press, 2004.

Vivaria, Kassandra. "On the International Congress of Women." *North American Review* 159 (August 1899): 145–64.

Wald, Lillian. *Windows on Henry Street.* Boston: Little, Brown, 1934.

Walker, Franklin D. *The Literary History of Southern California.* Berkeley: University of California Press, 1950.

———. *San Francisco's Literary Frontier.* New York: Knopf, 1939.

Wallace, William Stewart. *Dictionary of North American Authors Deceased Before 1950.* Toronto: Ryeson, 1951.

Walling, William English. *Larger Aspects of Socialism.* New York: Macmillan, 1913.

Walsh, Correa. *Feminism.* New York: Sturgis & Walton Co., 1917.

Ward, Lester F. *Glimpses of the Cosmos* (Vols. 4 and 5, Emily Palmer Cape and Sarah E. Simons, eds.). New York: G. P. Putnam's Sons, 1913–1918.

———. "Our Better Halves." *Forum* 6 (1888): 266–75.

———. *Pure Sociology: A Treatise on the Origin and Spontaneous Development of Society.* New York: MacMillan, 1903.

———. "The Past and Future of the Sexes." *Independent* (8 March 1906): 541–45.

Warne, Frank Julian. *The Immigrant Invasion.* New York: Dodd, Mead, and Co., 1913.

Washington, Mary Helen. "Anna Julia Cooper: The Black Feminist Voice of the 1890s." *Legacy* 4 (1987): 3–15.

Wegener, Frederick. "Charlotte Perkins Gilman, Edith Wharton, and the Divided Heritage of American Literary Feminism." In Catherine Golden and Joanna Schneider Zangrando, eds., *The Mixed Legacy of Charlotte Perkins Gilman* (135–59). Newark: University of Delaware Press, 2000.

———. "'What a Comfort a Woman Doctor is!': Medical Women in the Life and Writing of Charlotte Perkins Gilman." In Jill Rudd and Val Gough, eds., *Charlotte Perkins Gilman: Optimist Reformer* (45–73). Iowa City: University of Iowa Press, 1999.

Weinbaum, Alys Eve. "Writing Feminist Genealogy: Charlotte Perkins Gilman and the Reproduction of Maternalist Feminism." *Feminist Studies* 27 (Summer 2001): 271–302.

Weinberg, Julius. *Edward Alsworth Ross and the Sociology of Progressivism.* Madison: State Historical Society of Wisconsin, 1972.

Weintraub, Rochelle, ed. *Fabian Feminism: Bernard Shaw and Woman.* University Park: Penn State University Press, 1977.

Wellington, Amy. *Women Have Told: Studies in the Feminist Tradition.* Boston: Little, Brown, and Co., 1930.

Welter, Barbara. "The Cult of True Womanhood, 1820–1860." *American Quarterly* 18 (1966): 151–74.

Wertheim, Arthur. *The New York Little Renaissance: Iconoclasm, Modernism, and Nationalism in American Culture, 1908–1917.* New York: New York University Press, 1976.

Wertheimer, Barbara Mayer. *We Were There: The Story of Working Women in America.* New York: Pantheon, 1976.

Who Was Who in America. Vol 1. Chicago: Marquis, 1981.

Wiebe, Robert H. *The Search for Order, 1877–1920.* New York: Hill and Wang, 1967.

Wilson, Christopher. "Charlotte Perkins Gilman's Steady Burghers: The Terrain of Herland." *Women's Studies* 12 (1986): 271–92.

Winkler, Barbara Scott. *Victorian Daughters: The Lives and Feminism of Charlotte Perkins Gilman and Olive Schreiner.* Occasional Paper in Women's Studies, no. 13, American Culture Program. Ann Arbor: Women's Studies Program, University of Michigan Press, 1980.

Zauderer, Naomi B. "Consumption, Production, and Reproduction in the Work of Charlotte Perkins Gilman." In Jill Rudd and Val Gough, eds., *Charlotte Perkins Gilman: Optimist Reformer* (151–72). Iowa City: University of Iowa Press, 1999.

Index